**WITHDRAWN**
UTSA LIBRARIES

# LIFE OF
# JEHUDI ASHMUN

Painted by N.Jocelyn.  Eng.d by S.S.Jocelyn.

JEHUDI ASHMUN.

# LIFE OF
# JEHUDI ASHMUN,
## LATE COLONIAL AGENT IN LIBERIA

By
RALPH RANDOLPH GURLEY

*The Black Heritage Library Collection*

 BOOKS FOR LIBRARIES PRESS
FREEPORT, NEW YORK
1971

First Published 1835
Reprinted 1971

Reprinted from a copy in the
Fisk University Library Negro Collection

INTERNATIONAL STANDARD BOOK NUMBER:
0-8369-8749-7

LIBRARY OF CONGRESS CATALOG CARD NUMBER:
73-149867

PRINTED IN THE UNITED STATES OF AMERICA

# LIFE

OF

# JEHUDI ASHMUN,

LATE

COLONIAL AGENT IN LIBERIA.

WITH

## AN APPENDIX,

CONTAINING

EXTRACTS FROM HIS JOURNAL AND OTHER WRITINGS; WITH A BRIEF SKETCH OF THE LIFE OF THE REV. LOTT CARY.

BY RALPH RANDOLPH GURLEY.

SECOND EDITION.

NEW-YORK:
ROBINSON & FRANKLIN,
SUCCESSORS TO LEAVITT, LORD & CO:

1839.

THE copy-right of this Work is secured to the Author by an entry made in the Office of the District Court of the District of Columbia, on the 18th day of February, 1835.

# CONTENTS.

### CHAPTER I.

Birth and childhood of Ashmun—Studious habits—Early resolution—Religious impressions—Collegiate course—Visit to Connecticut—Removal from Middlebury to Burlington—Conclusion of his studies at college.

### CHAPTER II.

Early character—First attachment—Sympathy for the heathen—Removal to Maine—License to preach—Efforts to found a theological seminary in Maine—Marriage—Distrust and alienation of friends—Imprudence—Reliance on his integrity.

### CHAPTER III.

Embarks for the South—Extracts from his Journal—Touches at New-York—Reflections on his own follies and the uncharitableness of others—Sketch of an erring vagrant—Arrival at Baltimore—Sad thoughts—Seeks Divine Direction.

### CHAPTER IV.

Bold and Independent Character—Unbroken by Misfortune—Commences a Religious Paper—It fails—Views of the Maryland Episcopal Convention—Granville Sharp's Agency in founding Episcopacy in America—Influence of this Agency on the African Cause—Ashmun's removal to Washington and connection with the Theological Repertory—Reviews the Colonization Society's Report—Attempts the Publication of the African Intelligencer—Connects himself with the Episcopal Church—Doubts about a Profession—Letter from Bishop Moore—Application for Orders—Fluctuation of purposes—Embarrassed State of the Repertory.

## CHAPTER V.

Writes the Life of the Rev. Samuel Bacon—Facts in the History of the Colonization Society, connected with this Work—Report of Messrs. Mills and Burgess—Law concerning recaptured Africans—Departure of the Elizabeth—Outline of the Life and Death of Mr. Bacon—Circumstances and manner in which this Memoir was composed—Differences touching the Repertory—Secret Griefs—High and holy Purposes of Ashmun.

## CHAPTER VI.

Salutary lessons of Providence—Slavery—Origin—Slave Trade—Slavery in the United States—Federal Constitution and views of its Framers—Favorable to the general influence of Liberty—Spirit of the Reformation—Growth of the spirit of humanity towards the colored race—Foremost stand of the Quakers in the African cause—Origin of African Colonization—Of the American Colonization Society—Views of its Founders—Early Proceedings—First Agents and Expedition—Purchase of Territory by Captain Stockton and Dr. Ayres at Cape Montserado—Removal of Colonists thither.

## CHAPTER VII.

Mr. Ashmun sails for Africa—Causes and Measures which led to it, including Rev. William Meade's visit to Georgia—Recaptured Africans to be sent from there—Personal Embarrassments—Attends to the outfit of the Strong—Joined at Baltimore by Mrs. Ashmun—Incidents of the Voyage—System of operations commenced on his arrival at the Colony—Perilous condition of the Strong before landing of her passengers—Conference with some of the Principal Chiefs—Lurking enmity of the Natives—Preparations for Defence—War—Noble courage and conduct—Successful repulse of the banded forces of the Natives—Arrival of the British Colonial Schooner Prince Regent—Generous aid of her Commander and Major Laing—Peace—Tribute to Ashmun.

## CHAPTER VIII.

Sickness—Noble devotion of Midshipman Gordon and his associates—Illness of Ashmun—Aid rendered by a Colombian Schooner—Want of Supplies—Restoration of Captive Children—Visit of the Cyanne—Efforts of Capt. Spence and crew—Dr. Dix, Mr. Richard Seaton—Visit of Mr. Ashmun to Settra Kroo—Arrival of Dr. Ayres—Mr. Ashmun's earnest request for Teachers—Incident—His Thoughts on Trade—Drafts from Fayal—Stands not well in the Public Confidence—Receives little countenance from the Government or Society—His manly Fortitude—Confidence in

CONTENTS. v

Truth—Terms on which he will remain in Africa sent to the Board—State and Prospects of the Colony.

## CHAPTER IX.

Perplexity and uncertainty of his affairs—Rules of Conduct—Private Journal—Industry and Energy in his Studies—Religious Character—Extracts touching this Subject—Sense of Injustice done him—Still neglected—Return of Dr. Ayres—Proposition to the Board—Discontent of the Settlers—Mutiny—Firmness and Decision of Ashmun—Arrival of the Cyrus—Spirit of Revolt—Want of Supplies—Address of Mr. Ashmun to the Colonists—Their continued Indolence and Disaffection—Writes to the Board—Feeble Health—Determines to visit the Cape De Verds—Hemórrhage when about to embark—Expects to die—Declaration of Integrity.

## CHAPTER X.

Lowest Point of his Depression—Gradual Recovery of Strength—Journal at Bissao and the Cape De Verds—Remonstrance of the Colonists to the Board—Appropriation for the Benefit of Ashmun—The Board Address the Colonists—Charges sent from the Colony against Ashmun—Distrust of his Character—Uncertain Affairs—Special Agent sent to the Colony.

## CHAPTER XI.

Writer's Interview with Mr. Ashmun at the Cape De Verds—Impressions of his Character—He resolves to return to the Colony—Passage—Investigations into charges against him at the Colony—All false—Causes of the Moral and Political Disorders there—Organization of the Government—Adoption of it by the Settlers—Restoration of order and mutual confidence—Mr. Ashmun is empowered as Agent until report is made to the Government and Society.

## CHAPTER XII.

Reluctance of men to abandon old, even if erroneous, opinions—Report of the Special Agent unfavorably received—Mr. Ashmun permitted to try the New Form of Government as an experiment—Despatches showing its utility—Negotiations with the Bassa Chiefs—Ability exhibited by Mr. Ashmun in his communications to the Managers—Favorable Report of a Committee on his Despatches—His Situation—His Conduct—*first*, in respect to himself, *second*, to the Colony, and *third*, to the Board of Managers—Arrival of the Hunter—Negotiations for the St. Paul's Territory—His remarks touching his connexion with the Repertory—Proceedings of the Board in relation to the New Form of Government and Mr. Ashmun's Character—Adoption of the former—Vindication of the latter—Mr. Ashmun's position.

## CHAPTER XIII.

His circumstances in the Colony—Influence upon the settlers—Anticipation of an early death—His principles—Purposes—Talents for business—Attention to the poor and afflicted—Sickness among the Hunter's emigrants—Requests a physician—Survey of the St. Paul's purchase—Thinks of visiting the U. States—Fourth of July celebration—Slave trade—Examination of the coast from Cape Mount to Trade Town—Piracy—Destruction of slave factories—Condition of the Colony at the close of 1825—Mr. Ashmun's opinion of the importance of aid from the national government—The writer's thoughts on this subject.

## CHAPTER XIV.

The doctrine of Divine Providence—Mr. Ashmun's belief in it—Effect of his trials on his character—Activity and industry—Brief extracts from his private Journal—His humility and its effects upon his opinion of himself.

## CHAPTER XV.

Managers of Charitable Institutions—Of the Colonization Society—Mr. Ashmun at the head of a prosperous Colony—His desire for more emigrants—For regular commercial intercourse with America—His opinion of assistants—Of a Board of Agents—Expedition by the Vine—By the Norfolk—Dr. Peaco's arrival—Baptist Mission—Rev. Horace Sessions—Rev. Calvin Holton—Settlements on the St. Paul's and Stockton Creek—Agency House at Caldwell struck by lightning—Expedition against Trade Town—Effect in suppressing the Slave Trade—Letter to Dr. Blumhardt—Indisposition of Mr. Ashmun—Absence of Dr. Peaco—Cape Mount Trade—Leases of Land—Tax for support of schools—Piracy—Necessity for a Sloop of War—Line of Packets—Want of Schools—Annual Election and firmness of Ashmun—Panic among the Settlers—Robbery of Bassa People—Negotiations with Cape Mount Chiefs—Acquisition of Territory—Extract from last Letter of Mr. Ashmun in 1826.

## CHAPTER XVI.

Mr. Ashmun's last entire year of labor—Reputation—Growth of the Society—Visit of the Shark—Capt. Norris—Arrival of the Doris—Of the Norfolk—Disappointed purpose of Mr. Ashmun to visit the United States—Preparations for Emigrants—Necessity of throwing Emigrants upon their efforts—Injury to the Colonial Schooner—Illness of Mr. Ashmun—Visit to Sierra Leone and the Pongas—Description of that River and Country—Correspondence with Sir Neil Campbell—Treaty of Peace with Trade Town—War between the Chief of Sesters and his neighbor of Trade Town—Peace—Infirmary of Invalids—Schools—Method of subsisting Emigrants in Africa—Views in regard to the United States' Agency for recaptured Africans—Visit of the Ontario—Captain Nicolson—Swiss Missionaries—Government of the Colony—Condition of the People—Accessions of Territory—Plan of Mr. Ashmun for extending Colonization among the Natives—Policy towards them—Religious state of the Colony—Address of Colonists—Ashmun's ardour in pursuit of intellectual and moral improvement—Melancholy thoughts—Religious feelings and hopes.

## CHAPTER XVII.

Arrival at Liberia of the Doris, Randolph, and Nautilus—Visit of Mr. Ashmun to the Colonial Factories—His excessive labors, Sickness, Embarkation for the United States—Arrival at St. Bartholemews—Compelled to stop there—Visits St. Christophers—Letter to his Parents—Arrival at New Haven—Decline—Death—Funeral—Conclusion.

## APPENDIX.

No. 1. Extracts from the Early Diary of Mr. Ashmun.
No. 2. Resolutions of the Maine Society School.
No. 3. Papers touching the importance of Missionary Efforts in Africa.
No. 4. Notes on Trade.
No. 5. Supposed Error.
No. 6. Subjects reported on by the Special Agent—Extracts from the Colonial Journal—Remarks on the most economical mode of subsisting the Colony—On Temperance.
No. 7. Liberia Farmer.
No. 8. Letter to Rev. Dr. Blumhardt.
No. 9. Ashmun's Vindication of his conduct in destroying the Slave Factories.
No. 10. Letters of Chief Justice Marshall and Ex-President Madison, on African Colonization.
No. 11. Miscellaneous Papers of Ashmun, including—What rules are to be observed to improve the gift of prayer—Advantages of Devotion—Divine Providence—The Prophecy of Malachi—The Social Affections—Punishment of Murder by Death—Religious Principles—Dreams—History of one's self—Qualifications of an Agent for Liberia—Notes on Africa—Visit to Peter Bromley's—Colonial Notices—Sketches of Character—Letter to the Church in Champlain—Letter to his Younger Brothers—

ALSO,

SKETCH *of the Life* of the Rev. LOTT CARY.

# LIFE OF ASHMUN.

## CHAPTER I.

In an age, like this, when men are remarkably occupied with schemes of private enterprise, and large plans for human improvement, the Biography of an individual will be well nigh unnoticed, unless it exhibit in the subject of it, evidences of extraordinary intellect or illustrious virtue. Nor is it to be expected or desired that public attention should be directed to ordinary merit, while there are great and shining examples upon which it may be fixed. Life is too short to be wasted upon trifles; and while the active spirit of the times is unfavourable to the calm and steady contemplation of individual character, the more important it is, that such character, if held up for imitation, should possess rare worth and brightness.

The following pages are submitted to the public without an apology, because the individual to whom they relate, not in the writer's opinion only, but in the judgment of the Christian community, at least, both of this and other countries, deserves an extended memorial. The Author, however, cannot enter upon his work, without humbly invoking the aid of that Divine Being, who, while He sometimes kindles in human souls the pure flame of His own spirit, that they may bless and guide mankind, can alone preserve and extend the influence and light of their example to the remotest generations of the world.

JEHUDI ASHMUN was born in the town of Champlain, New York, on the 21st of April, 1794. He was the second son, and third child in a family of ten children. His father, Samuel Ashmun, Esq. married early in life, and soon after, settled in Champlain, then a wilderness; and though exposed to numerous inconveniences and hardships, his industry and enterprise soon placed him in circumstances of independence, while his intelligence and moral worth secured for him the confidence of his fellow-citizens, among whom, for many years, he sustained the office of a Justice of the Peace. The childhood of young Ashmun was distinguished by a thoughtful and reserved manner, intense application to books, reliance upon his own powers, and ambition to excel in all his studies.* Every leisure hour was improved; he early accustomed himself to keep a Journal, and would sometimes omit to take his meals, that he might have opportunity to record in it, such thoughts or events as he deemed worthy of remembrance. The father of Ashmun, considering the number of his family and his moderate means, designed to grant to his children those literary advantages only, which were afforded by the common schools of the country, in expectation that their lives would be devoted

* The following anecdote is related of him: While a schoolboy, a premium was offered by his instructer, for the best composition which should be furnished in the school. Many of the pupils were older than himself, and the time allowed to prepare the pieces was short. So confident was he, however, of success, that he promised his mother, to bring to her a certificate of his triumph. When his elder brother was announced as entitled to the reward, Jehudi exclaimed, "you mean me, master!" And instead of being disturbed by the smiles of his fellow-pupils, he still insisted that his opinion was correct, and wrote a certificate for himself, and carried it home to his mother.

to agricultural pursuits; but the love of knowledge cherished by the subject of this Memoir, and his importunities that he might be allowed to gratify it, finally induced his parents to consent that he should seek a liberal education, provided reliance was placed mainly upon his own exertions to defray the expense. This condition was cheerfully accepted, and at the age of 14, he commenced his studies, in preparation for College, under the tuition of the Rev. Amos Pettingill, the worthy Minister of his native place, with whom he made rapid progress, and strengthened the confidence of his friends in his final success.

At this time he appears to have had no fixed religious principles, and occasionally to have indulged doubts of the truth of Christianity. The example of pious parents, and particularly the tender admonitions of his mother, had deeply affected him at the early age of six years, and the impressions then made were never entirely effaced; yet it was not until his 17th year, that Divine Truth exerted, in his own judgment, a regenerating influence on his mind. The date of this event is recorded in his Journal, the 26th of June, 1810. Having been absent from home, during most of the preceding winter, and in the society of irreligious persons, his chief desire and purpose had been, as he expressed them, "to secure the es-'teem of his fellow-beings and feed on earthly pleasures."—The effect of cherished imaginations of future distinction and happiness in the world, during this brief period, contributed more in his opinion, to harden his heart against God, than two years of previous impenitence. The most solemn truths, the kindest parental exhortations had lost their power to move him. While he was thus insensible to the claims of the Almighty upon his affections and his services, the attention of the people of his native village was particularly turned to religion, and a youth of his acquaintance had been led to devote himself to the cause of the Redeemer. A remark of this youth, at a social prayer-meeting, expressive of his own happiness has a child of God, appears first to ave arrested the attention, and excited strongly the feelings of Ashmun. An awful darkness enveloped him, and he was overwhelmed in guilt and misery. But after a short season he was enabled, as he ever afterwards believed, to trust in the Saviour, and to consecrate himself wholly and forever to His service.

At the commencement of his studies in the spring of 1810, a consciousness that he was morally unqualified for the Clerical profession, and doubts of obtaining an education sufficiently extensive for that of the Law, had strongly inclined him to a Medical course; but the radical change now experienced in his character, determined him to direct all his efforts to a preparation for the Christian Ministry. In July of this year, he became a member of the church in Champlain, and for several months after, so vivid were his impressions of religious truth, that he was impelled to exhibit them to others, imagining that they must even feel, as he felt, their importance; and so emboldened was he in his zeal, as not only to expostulate with the impenitent, and dispute with those of opposite sentiments, but even to remonstrate with his Pastor upon the necessity of a more earnest and active discharge of the duties of his office. Thus early was manifested that resolute enthusiasm which continued through life to be one of the most striking traits of his character. In a Journal penned by Mr. Ashmun in 1823, we find the following allusion to the change which occurred in his purposes at this period of his life: "My views (when I commenced study) were, from the ' narrowness of my circumstances, moderate enough. But I ' was assiduous and always preferred my books to my sports; ' and found as I proceeded, my ambition kindle and my in-
' tentions enlarge. An event which followed in a few months, ' changed entirely the direction of my studies, and served to ' fix for many years,. every vacillating purpose. My atten-
' tion was, in June, 1810, wholly turned to the interests of ' futurity. The rewards of fame, and conscious superiority ' of any intellectual or personal endowments, which I might

' come to possess, were too light in the balance, to weigh
' down, in my estimation, the everlasting well-being of myself
' or others. Thus predisposed to the profession of Divinity,
' I adopted, with little hesitancy, the advice of my friends to
' make it the object of my pursuit."

This revolution in his moral character, instead of diminishing, increased the energy of his exertions to acquire knowledge, and prepare himself for public usefulness. He became the more anxious to obtain all the advantages of a collegiate education. He distinguished himself as a punctual and active member of a Debating Society, and referred in after life, to the exercises and discipline of this Institution, as having contributed greatly to his success and influence in College.

"In 1811, (he observes in the Journal from which we have
' already quoted) I rejected an offer to facilitate my prepara-
' tion for the Bar, which I had reason to believe was advan-
' tageous. This was in Troy; and I believe that, at that
' time, no offer of emolument, or of earthly distinction, would
' have seduced me from my purpose." The following letter, addressed to a gentleman of Castleton, Vermont, illustrates his well-combined humility, self-reliance, and good judgment at this early period of his life:—

Troy, July 22, 1811.

' Dear Sir:—On the 4th of July, after having written to
' you from Carver's, I was carried to Paulet, where I stayed
' until the next day, and arrived here on Saturday. A stran-
' ger, unrecommended to any person, and unacquainted with
' every person in town, with but a few shillings in my pock-
' et, and unpossessed of any lucrative trade or other faculty,
' I began to feel the force of poverty; yet was persuaded, that
' if I trusted in Him in whom I ought to trust, I should be
' disposed of in the best manner with all my spiritual and
' temporal concerns. Should I fail to obtain employment or
' be reduced to abject circumstances, I knew I ought to pos-

'sess faith to be made better, and turn my affections to
' another world. But I found it much easier to commend the
' patience of others in circumstances of necessity, and imagine
' a temper of mind which they should possess, than to support
' these in my own case. However, after sustaining repeated
' negatives, every one increasing my anxiety, I providentially
' applied at the place where I have since resided, which is the
' only place in Troy or Albany, where, to my present know-
' ledge, I could have found a support in any decent employ-
' ment. The gentleman with whom I am, is an Attorney,
' the principal Justice of the village; was educated at Middle-
' bury; has a very small family, a growing fortune, and treats
' me with the greatest respect. A small part of my time is em-
' ployed in assisting him among his papers, the rest I devote
' to study and reading. He finds me every thing, clothing
' excepted. He appears well satisfied with me, and offers to
' instruct me in study and maintain me on the present terms
' for three years, provided I will turn my views to the Law,
' which without opposing my whole inclination and violating
' what I deem to be duty, I cannot assent to. Weak and un-
' worthy as I am, I feel, or trust I wish to feel, a desire to be
' made instrumental in promoting the best, the greatest, and
' final good of my fellow-beings, and to devote my life wholly
' to the immediate service of God. This I judge myself not
' sufficiently qualified to do, (besides moral defects, which fre-
' quently hold me in suspense,) without considerable and un-
' interrupted study. To obtain opportunity for this, is my
' main concern of a worldly nature. Earthly honours, plea-
' sures, and wealth, for some reason, appear vain when put in
' competition with evangelical utility, and I have not an in-
' ducement to pursue them. But how to act, I know not; I
' feel unwilling to take any ground from which I shall hereaf-
' ter be obliged to recede, because the shortness of life and
' the value of youthful days render inexpedient, measures lia-
' ble to variation and change. One of these two measures I

' would willingly resort to, either to obtain a loan of money to
' be repaid after my College life, with or without interest, or to
' engage and constantly do some business, the avails of which,
' at the end of three or more years, would assist me in acqui-
' ring an education. Perhaps neither of these is practicable,
' and should one or both be so, I know not the means of in-
' troducing myself to them. I want advice. I have none
' present to give it. You must do it, Sir, and take the only
' recompense I can bestow, my gratitude. It is not poverty
' that causes me to shrink from abandoning literary pursuits;
' nor is it, I trust, wordly disrespect—but the certainty of being
' less capable of extensive usefulness. I hope you will by no
' means fail of giving this an answer immediately, and thus
' confer lasting obligations on
  ' Your respectful and
   ' Obedient Servant,
        ' J. Ashmun."

Of the result of this application, we are ignorant; yet, he appears not to have entered Middlebury College until September, 1812, more than a year after the date of this letter.— During his residence at Middlebury, his habits were those of unwearied diligence in study, and ardent and elevated devotion in the duties of religion. He regularly attended numerous religious meetings; assisted in conducting them; and though but seventeen years of age, was regarded by the pious and able men of that town, as a useful and efficient coadjutor. To secure the means of support, he was obliged to instruct a school during the vacations, and even prolong his exertions as teacher beyond these periods, so that severe and unremitted application to study was indispensable to enable him to maintain an honourable scholastic reputation. "When I look back ' upon him," says one of his most intimate friends, "as unri-
' valled for talents (as it was conceded he was, by the officers
' and his companions in our College); when I look upon him

'as improving on the models of Schwartz, Van Der Kemp, and
'Brainerd, and see him copying our Lord and Redeemer with
'such holy diligence and constant spirituality, I feel that the
'History of his Life will be an inestimable accession to the
'treasures of American Biography. If your life of him should
'exhibit him such as he is to my mind's eye, I should feel that
'the distribution of the work to every reader of such things in
'the United States, was an object not unworthy of the efforts
'of my life.'*

His health soon became so impaired, by his mental efforts, as to compel him to desist from them, and to resort for the restoration of his strength, to the exercise, and varied scenes and incidents of a tour through a delightful part of New England. He travelled slowly as far as Hartford, Connecticut, and though at times so reduced as almost to despair of ever returning to his friends, his exertions, in several towns where existed extraordinary attention to religion, were frequent and great; and

* Under date of April 13, 1813, Mr. Ashmun expresses grief that he had been led to engage in political debates to his own unutterable sorrow and the injury of the Saviour's cause. O! my Saviour, God, he exclaims, sooner may I perish from the earth, than bring another stain upon thine immaculate cause. It will be recollected that this was during the last war, and the frontier settlements were exposed to the enemy. Mr. Ashmun had just before this visited his native place, Champlain, and witnessed its desolations. "Well, he observes, might she adopt the strain of the lamenting Prophet, almost literally fulfilled upon her." "And He hath violently taken away His tabernacle, as if it were of a garden: He hath destroyed His places of the assembly. The Lord hath caused the solemn feasts and the Sabbaths to be forgotten in Zion, and hath despised in the indignation of His anger, both the King and the Priest." "For three months the churches had not once been assembled, and their Minister had been removed. The movements of war had rolled a deluging torrent of vice in upon them; sickness had carried off some from the church, and many from the people; Sabbaths were neglected; and finally, to verify the literal sense of the above passage, the house of Divine worship had been burned with fire." Probably this was the time, when, as we have been told, young Ashmun organized and took command of a military corps, and showed the elements of those powers which were so signally developed in his defence of the African Colony.

his Journal\* at this time, affords evidence of his disposition not only to improve every opportunity of usefulness, but to derive instruction from every observation of nature or mankind, and from all the various daily occurrences of life. The writer can never forget the description of Ashmun, as he then appeared, by an eminent Christian of Wethersfield, Connecticut, at whose hospitable mansion he remained during his stay there, and whose virtues are alluded to with much sensibility in his Journal. His youthful figure, tall but spare, had an air of striking dignity; and his pale and emaciated countenance, expressed the feelings of one who habitually communed with God, and viewed every object in the light of the eternal world. All his thoughts and affections seemed occupied with religion; this was the chief subject of his conversation; and its truths were uttered by him with a manner and in a tone of such earnestness, as convinced all in his presence, that to his mind they were of unspeakable importance, and that he was most benevolently anxious to extend their dominion over the minds of others. In his public addresses, great maturity of thought, combined with the glow of a vigorous imagination, and the feelings of a sublime devotion, gave him powerful influence over his audience. Hundreds felt his appeals, as those of a dying man, who had caught the spirit of the Apostles, and who, ready to depart, yet lingered near the end of his course, to admonish and exhort those who would soon see his face no more.

In this tour, and other shorter excursions to various parts of Vermont, Mr. Ashmun spent most of the summer of 1814, and found himself in the autumn, greatly improved in health; and prepared again to renew his studies at College. He remained at Middlebury until the autumn of 1815, when with the view of relieving himself from some pecuniary embarrassments, he became a student at the Vermont University, Bur-

\*Appendix 1.

lington. He expressed also an earnest desire of promoting the cause of religion in that Institution, which he thought had been less firmly sustained, than in that with which he stood connected. He concluded his studies at College in the summer of next year, and was distinguished among those who received, at the commencement, literary honours. Among his papers, are two orations prepared for this occasion,—one in English, the other in Latin; (the former marked rejected)— but both exhibiting a bold and aspiring spirit, and a maturity of knowledge and judgment seldom attained at so early a period of life.

## CHAPTER II.

The elements of intellectual strength are generally mingled in the human character with ardent feelings and powerful passions. The talents which render men capable of great and noble actions may, if perverted, cover them with all the disgrace and infamy of crime. Ashmun was naturally self-confident, proud, ambitious. His imagination was warm, his passions ardent, his sensibility extreme. He became a Christian; but his religious sentiments, at this time, were deeply tinged with a romantic enthusiasm which pervaded the constitution of his youth. In allusion to this period, he some years after observed: "My genius and habits much of the time ' were decidedly of the ascetick cast. I determined not only to ' forsake the gay, but even the civilized world; and spend my ' life among distant savages. And from long dwelling on this ' prospect, and naturally directing my inquiries and reading ' by it, I came to acquire a passion for the sacrifice."

An attachment formed in 1815, to the lady whom he afterwards married, exerted a powerful influence on the course of his future life. Wholly engaged in preparing himself for Missionary labors among the Heathen, his own reflections, and the advice of friends, convinced him of the propriety of seeking a connexion with some lady who would cheerfully forsake her country and kindred, to co-operate in his benevolent design of imparting the knowledge and hopes of Christianity to Barbarians. A sublime devotion, a burning zeal to forsake all the delights of home, and all the enjoyments of civilized society, for the cause of the Redeemer, and the benefit of the miserable Pagans, were to him most admirable and attractive in the female character. Towards a lady, in whom he thought he perceived an "almost perfect similarity to his own, of views, feelings, solicitude, and sentiments," he professed to cherish a deep and tender affection. "I praise," said he to her, " the glorious Giver of all our blessings, for what He has conferred upon me, and I trust upon the Pagan nations (whose cause I must always plead), in disposing you to regard them with so much tenderness, and even me in the favourable light you do." But he spoke this in much ignorance of the character of her whom he addressed, and in more perhaps of his own. Happy for both, had the delicate, nicely proportioned, and naturally allied qualities of the mind and heart, contributed equally with the harmony of their religious principles and purposes, to preserve the constancy of their mutual love.

From some cause, not well explained, the course of this affection was, in January, 1816, suddenly chilled and interrupted; and for nearly two years after, the question of his marriage to this lady, appears to have been regarded by both as unsettled. They were soon widely separated from each other—*he* having accepted the situation of Principal in the Maine Charity School, established at Hampden in that State, and *she* having become a Teacher in the family of a respectable Clergyman in North Carolina.

Mr. Ashmun now occupied a station well adapted to develope his enterprise and energy of character. In 1810, an association of gentlemen had been formed in Portland, Maine, under the denomination of the "Society for Theological Education," with the design of aiding indigent young men to prepare for the Christian Ministry. Some hundreds of congregations in that State and the contiguous parts of New Hampshire, were destitute of any regular religious instruction, and vigorous measures to increase the number of educated ministers, seemed indispensable to relieve the moral wants of the community.—In February, 1812, this association obtained a charter, and a year afterwards, a Committee of the same, were incorporated with the title of the Trustees of the Maine Charity School. Their number was restricted to fifteen, and they were invested with all necessary powers for laying the foundations of a Theological Seminary. In October, 1816, these Trustees resolved, with the small amount of funds at their command, to open a Charity School at Hampden, and direct their efforts towards securing to it such patronage as might finally elevate it to a level with most of the Literary and Theological Institutions of our country.

In entering upon the discharge of his duties as Principal of this school, Mr. Ashmun was far from abandoning his long cherished purpose of devoting himself to the cause of Foreign Missions. The motives which governed him, are clearly revealed in a letter addressed in April, 1818, to a friend who proposed to accept, for a short time, a commission of agency to promote the interests and resources of the infant Seminary:—
"With this, he observes, you will probably receive credentials
' from the Secretary of the Board of Trustees of this Institution,
' appointing you their Agent. I am grateful to you, but far
' more to God, for your offer. I ought to have no motive for
' tarrying, connected as I am with the Seminary, but to glorify
' the God of Missions, by assisting in *the establishment* of the
' Institution, expecting to quit it the month it can dispense with
' my services, and shall have acquired strength and *cohesion*

'*of parts* enough to bear a transfer, safely, to other hands.
' Do not, dear brother, hence imagine, that I regard myself the
' principal or benefactor of the ' Maine Charity School.' Pro-
' cul talis cogitatio esto. But I offered my services in the ca-
' pacity in which I act, at a crisis which, between the want of
' funds and encouragement on the part of its original projec-
' tors and the number and influence of its decided opposers in
' Maine and Massachusetts proper, it would not otherwise have
' been able to survive. I was willing to risk more than any
' other person, who could have been procured to supply my
' place—*if there can be* any *risk in* DUTY ; darkness rested
' on the Institution's prospects ; it had no Professor of Divi-
' nity—its want of funds prevented any suitable candidate for
' that important post from hazarding a connexion with the
' Seminary. I took my ground, and assured the Trustees and
' public, that I would not abandon my post till I saw the School
' established. When it was seen that it had an actual exist-
' ence, it obtained patronage. Professor W. offered at the
' same time to share his part of the hazard, on condition that
' I renewed my engagement to persist in my connexion until
' the condition of the Seminary should authorize my resig-
' nation. Thanks be to God,* His smiles begin to brighten up
' our sky. Every cent obtained, you see, is so much to shor-
' ten the period of my confinement. Come, dear Brother,
' and help me off ; help me to fulfil my engagements to the
' School, and thus obtain my release. But I am shocked !!—
' Perhaps the consideration just named, ought to be no motive
' for you to stir an inch. The salvation of 150,000 souls in
' Maine, however, MAY. There is another. How many
' ages will elapse before all the Andovers and Princetons
' which ever will exist in America, will not only supply our
' present, but all our increase of population with Ministers
' from the *Academician Groves ?* Institutions on the foun-
' dation on which the ' Maine Charity School ' is built, have
' for ages flourished in Great Britain. It is well known what

' names brighten the catalogue of their graduates, and have
' kindled an inextinguishable radiance on the dissenting com-
' munion of that Island. Why may not these Seminaries, if
' God has made such an honourable and extensive use of
' them in England and Scotland, be serviceable in America?
' *Serviceable?* But, dear Brother, if we would not witness the
' alternative of the perdition and lasting Paganism of the peo-
' ple of half our immense territory, are not Institutions on this
' plan indispensable? Astonishing! that the attempt to erect
' Seminaries of this description has been so long delayed.—
' Can we rationally doubt that our example will be followed
' as soon as the beneficial operation of the Seminary shall
' have been seen? I almost see an Institution rise in the
' centre of the State of New York—in the western parts of
' Pennsylvania and 'in Virginia—in Maryland—the Caroli-
' nas, and before the lapse of many years, in the whole range
' of the Mississippi States. Whoever undertakes the patron-
' age of a truly valuable enterprise, must expect delays, oppo-
' sition, and discouragements of every description. Let us
' both set our shoulders to the wheel, and make the establish-
' ment of the ' Maine Charity School,' our great and principal
' domestic work, before we go to serve Christ abroad."

When Mr. Ashmun took charge of this School in October,
1816, there were but six students, dependent upon him alone,
for instruction. The village of Hampden had no settled Minister and no organized Church. He saw that every thing was
to be done for the Seminary, and much for the religious interests of the community in which it was founded. Though
he had but just completed his studies at College, and had
never enjoyed the usual advantages of a theological education, yet the doctrines of religion had long been subjects of
his habitual reflection, and his course of reading such as to
render him familiar with the methods of illustrating them,
and the arguments mainly relied on for their defence. He
believed that a license to preach the gospel would give him

a more powerful and extended influence, and therefore sought and obtained one in November or December of this year.

Though feeble in health, his exertions both as an instructer of youth, and as a preacher during the winter and spring of 1816-17, were earnest and uninterrupted, and remarkably blessed of God. Never can the writer forget with what sensibility Mr. Ashmun, at a time when darkness covered all his prospects, and the tossings of the ocean beneath him, seemed tranquillity compared with his fortunes, alluded to the effects of his labours at Hampden, and soothed his troubled spirit by the thought, that He who had once so graciously smiled upon his efforts, would never utterly withdraw from him the light of His love.* In a masterly Essay, found among his papers, designed to show the importance of the Seminary rising under his care, he observes: "The Holy Ghost, in less than six 'months after the establishment of it, converted the desert 'spot upon which it had been seated, into a spiritual Eden; 'and in less than a year, from the stones of the wilderness, 'reared up a living Church of more than thirty members, in-'to which the members of the School were immediately incor-'porated."

It was obvious to Mr. Ashmun, that efficient measures must be adopted to place the Maine Charity School upon a broad and durable foundation, or it must utterly fail to supply a number of ministers adequate to the demands of the large and rapidly increasing population by which it was surrounded.— He saw the necessity of elevating it at once to the rank of a

* We may judge something of Mr. Ashmun's labours, at this time, from the following extract of a letter dated March 10th, 1817, addressed to him by a venerable Clergyman, one of the Trustees of the School: "You have preached 25 times in two months; that is, 15 times more than you ought to have preached. You do right to tell me your faults, and I shall do right in reproving you. *Hear me, then.* If you will persist in preaching at such a rate, your race will be short. You ought to begin as you can hold out. Preach only when duty calls, and attend more to a regular course of studies. Count me not your enemy, because I thus write. It is not the language of hatred, but of love."

Theological Institution, endowed with Professorships for its various departments. While, therefore, he preached frequently; attended, weekly, numerous religious meetings, and instructed the students under his direction, in every branch of their literary, scientific, and theological studies; the energy of his thoughts was principally directed to the great object of so exhibiting to the public, the importance of the Seminary, and so recommending it to their regard, as to secure for it general and liberal patronage. He presented to the Trustees such a view of the immense benefits to be expected from it, as inflamed their zeal and elevated their hopes. The manuscript Essay now before us, affords evidence that he had considered the remote and less obvious, as well as the nearer and more palpable advantages, which it, well-founded and sustained, would confer, not on the people in its immediate vicinity only, but on our country and the world. It proves how comprehensively he was accustomed to survey, at this early age, human nature and human affairs.

In April, 1817, he accepted the appointment of Missionary, for the period of two months, under the authority of the Trustees of the Maine Missionary Society; and subsequently, during his residence at Hampden, as his circumstances would permit, engaged in the service of that association.

Through his efforts, mainly, it is believed, the Trustees of the Maine Charity School were enabled, in November, 1817, to appoint a Professor of Theology, a Professor of Classical Literature, and a Tutor to superintend the Academical studies in the Institution; to state to the public, that they were ready to provide for an additional number of students; that the plan of their Seminary combined the principal features of the Hoxton Academy in England; and that it was their intention to render its advantages equal to those of the best English Seminaries. They published an exposition (probably from the pen of Ashmun), comprising a brief history of the origin and progress of the Seminary; a view of its design, plan of

Government, course of studies ; enumerating the advantages expected from it, and concluding with an impressive appeal to the whole Christian community, urging them to sustain it, as involving interests of universal concern. Mr. Ashmun was elected the Professor of Classical Literature.

His studies at this period were various; and he sought knowledge from every scene and character he observed. His Journals and other writings of this date, show that no means of information were neglected, and not an hour lost. He grasped at every thing which he thought might contribute to render him a wiser or a better man.* His zeal for the cause of Missions continued intense ; and he sought the counsel of distinguished Clergymen, as to the propriety of forthwith placing himself under the direction of some Missionary Society.

The embers of a former affection were now re-kindled; and with confession that he had wrongfully attempted to extinguish them, Ashmun sought to renew correspondence with her who had long held the first place in his esteem. To one or two letters addressed to her early in 1818, kind answers were received ; but such as left unrevealed her precise sentiments towards him. His former tenderness towards her, however, revived ; he declared that he had never found such a friend as he had lost by the forfeiture of her confidence and affection ; and that he seldom thought of her but with tears.

While in this state of suspense, a vision of singular brightness rose upon his sight, and an image, to him, of unrivalled loveliness became enshrined in his heart. He felt the captivating effect of charms surpassing what he had imagined of beauty or excellence in woman. The chain that had been worn uneasily, was exchanged for the golden links of enchant-

---

*Among his compositions of this day, are Sermons, Theological Essays, Lectures on Biblical History and Chronology, a Journal of a Visit to Boston and Andover, full of remarks on the country, men, and things, remarks on his own religious character, &c.

ment; but alas! Honor and Religion soon bade him sever the bond which he wished to be eternal.

He had declared his purpose of again offering himself to the acceptance of the lady who had first shared his love—had promised to meet her in the autumn in New York; and yet in ignorance of her views, had rashly given his heart to another.*

"Into what," he exclaimed in August, 1828, "an ocean 'of perplexities and sorrow have I precipitated myself and 'friends, by taking a few steps in 1816, without asking coun- 'sel of the Lord, or depending on His guidance. I wish to 'forget myself, and to have my C. forget me also."

From Boston, in September, he wrote: "I sometimes al- 'most wish that I might sink out of existence, and vanish 'from the memory of all my friends and the world at once 'and forever. 'Tis presumptuous! But what can I do? If 'I live, I fear I shall only widen the breach I have already 'occasioned in the happiness of my friends, and sully the 'character of my God's Religion.—I know not with what 'emotions I shall meet you—or what will be the result of 'that meeting—there is a bottom to this tempestuous ocean, 'where we so often sink below our depth; and God knows, 'though we may not, where that bottom is. Before me all is 'dark as the abysses of night, except when faith catches a 'gleam from the throne of Him who spake the promises."

He recognized the sacredness of his early professions, and determined, whatever might be the consequence, to vindicate their sincerity, their truth, and their honour.

His marriage to Miss C. D. Gray, took place in New York, on the 7th of October, 1818.

Having spent a short time in New York, and visited Philadelphia to solicit funds for the Maine Seminary, it was concluded that Mrs. Ashmun should occupy, for a few months,

---

*———"for love is a flattering mischief, that hath denied aged and wise men a foresight of those evils that too often prove to be the children of that blind father,—a passion that carries us to commit errors with as much ease as whirl· winds remove feathers"——— IZAAK WALTON's *Life of Donne.*

her former situation in North Carolina, while he discharged the duties of his Professorship at Hampden. But vague and injurious rumors preceded him on his return, and the event of his marriage was found to have alienated his friends and irritated many who stood ready to take up weapons against him. Slander was busy, suspicion was afloat, and his conduct the common topic for remark and censure throughout a large portion of the country. "I have lost my influence, he ' observed, and blotted my character as a Christian in public ' opinion, throughout all the Eastern States." The students of the Seminary sought to be excused from attending his Lectures ; the confidence of the Trustees in his character,* was, to some extent, weakened, and all his prospects of usefulness blighted. " The Foreign Missionary Society," he remarks, " I am certain, would not at present, admit me into ' their service, should I apply to it. No Society which I ' know, would at present, employ me to preach." Thus cast out from the good opinion of a community so deeply indebted to his labours, he resigned his situation April 7th, 1819, and embarked for the South with no treasure but a lofty mind— no guide but Him who often leads his servants through dark and unknown ways to the honours of His kingdom.

We attempt not to justify, or even excuse Ashmun, for conduct which injured both himself and others, and which excited in his own mind repentance not less painful than sincere. But his sin was rather against prudence than integrity. It sprang from morbid sensibility and an undisciplined judgment, not from the calculations of a hypocritical, or the baseness of a selfish and malicious soul. Young, rash, self-confident, enthusiastic, a passionate admirer of the graces of the female character, he forgot the precepts of wisdom, and while plunging darkly into a perilous abyss, trusted for safety rather to some remarkable interposition, than to the usual and settled order of Providence.

* See Appendix 2.

## CHAPTER III.

On the 5th of April, 1819, Mr. Ashmun was engaged in preparations for his final departure from Maine. His Journal of this date, shows how deeply and painfully he realized the circumstances connected with this event. He describes himself as "unusually depressed; as undecided and irresolute; ' as without any earthly friend near him; as having no defi- ' nite scheme of future labours or settled prospect before him, ' to fix his attention and direct his efforts; finally, as weak in ' faith and disinclined to the duty of prayer, and as having, ' by the neglect of this duty, greatly multiplied, and foolishly ' retained his burdens."

In the afternoon of the 5th he left Hampden; and on the 6th of April, arrived at Bucksport; from which place, on the 9th, he took passage for New York. The following extracts from his Journal, of the 6th, 7th, and 8th of that month, develope his thoughts and feelings at this time:—

"*April 6th.*—Reading Mather to-day, I was deeply impres- ' sed with the subject of the first chapter, which is the import-

' ance of living like dying men continually. The next, re-
' kindled in my breast a desire to make God's glory my su-
' preme pursuit in life. I saw and felt the importance of im-
' mediately reforming in relation to two besetting sins. I am
' sorely borne down occasionally, but derive some support from
' the Throne of God. In reading Colonel Gardiner's Life
' lately, I found good desires and good resolutions considerably
' strengthened in my mind."

*April 7th.*—This evening I was invited out to tea with
' Mr. and Mrs. B. and a few of the villagers. I found my pa-
' tience and humility severely tried by the coolness and pointed
' neglect or dislike with which I was treated. May I submit
' myself under the mighty hand of God, and be silent. Why
' should a living man complain—a man for the punishment
' of his sins? I know I deserve it from God, and if all my
' guilt were known, should also from my fellow-men."

"*April 8th.*—I spent the day very agreeably and profitably
' with the Rev. Mr. B. Reading Witsius on Election, Effec-
' tual Calling and Faith—Poole on Revelation—Recorder—
' several articles in Jeremy Taylor's Casuistry—and Dr. Lynn
' and Colonel Dunham's Eulogies of Washington; I sadly
' neglected to cultivate intercourse and communion with God,
' and wanted the comforts of His spirit."

The weather during the earliest days of the voyage, was rough; yet, Mr. Ashmun, while amid winds and waves which at one time threatened the destruction of the vessel, and much afflicted with sea-sickness found time for reflection, and to record the following observations:—

"I know not that I have gained much as a Theologian, or
' a Christian. 'Tis wrong to live so unprofitably. I am re-
' lieved that I have left my connexions in Maine; almost every
' object there, brings a painful association. Still I feel con-
' cerned at the uncertainty of my future condition in life. I
' go forth, I hardly know where, or to what work, with a des-
' ponding mind, and a bleeding character. I fear, I shall for

' the first reason, be unable to act to much effect ; and for the
' second, be unfit for usefulness in the Church of God. Still
' I have not ceased to hope in the arm of the Lord of hosts."

Alluding to the severe sickness, which confined him for one whole day to his birth, he exclaims : "Ah ! what was
' life to me now ! I found for some reason which I have not
' yet scrutinized, that during my sickness, my conscience
' wrought more powerfully than is customary, and my whole
' past life seemed in duration a dream—and the world a mere
' show-box of vanities. I was in agony, that amidst so many
' enormous sins, I had done so little in obedience to God, or
' in the service of the Redeemer. O ! how unprepared to die!
' I greatly needed supports which I did not possess. That
' greatest of all temporal afflictions, beset me during my suf-
' ferings with overpowering severity. I ought to have learnt,
' that if we watch not, to keep the word of our Saviour's pa-
' tience in seasons of health and exemption from trials, He
' will leave us to burne alone in the midst of the furnace.—
' Though not in despair, perhaps on account of my presump-
' tion and stupidity; yet, during months past, I have been
' much in doubt of my good estate, and am now far from the
' possession of a comfortable evidence. And did I ever need
' it more ?

"*To what am I to attribute so serious a calamity, as a state
' of uncertainty, relative to my eternal well-being ?*

"First, and chiefly. To my neglect of prayer, meditation,
' self-examination, and the reading of the Scriptures. Under
' the generel term *neglect*, I include *remissness* in the above
' named duties.

"Secondly. *To my unsteady mode of life, which has in
' part, caused those neglects since September last.*

"Thirdly. *To the slight attention bestowed on other and
' relative duties.*

"Fourthly. *To the commission of sins of uncommon, if
' not of unprecedented heinousness.*

"And lastly. *To the want of humiliation on account of* ' *them.*"

The remarkable talent of Mr. Ashmun for observation, and the acquisition of knowledge, in all circumstances, is strongly illustrated by the Journal from which the preceding sentences are quoted. We find not only a record of his religious views, but of the books read by him, with his opinions of them; as also notes of the courses of the wind and vessel, as well as accounts of the Capes, Islands, Light-Houses, and principal Towns passed by; their distances from each other, with every interesting fact that could be ascertained in regard to their condition and history.

No affliction rendered Mr. Ashmun, when in health, incapable of exertion; and neither his regret for the past, nor his apprehensions for the future, ever caused him to neglect the advantages and duties of the present moment. His faith in Providence was deep and settled; and though the waves might dash over his bark, nor sun nor star for many days appear, he still firmly grasped the helm, with eyes raised toward Him whom he knew both the winds and seas obey. The activity and versatility of his mind, as well as his religious sensibilities during this voyage, will be very clearly exhibited in select passages, which we here copy, from his Journal.

*April* 13*th*, 1819.

"*Saurin's Sermons.*—These Sermons are fascinating.— ' The vivacity of sentiment and expression, with which they ' sparkle, kindling at times into a chastened and affecting ' glow of eloquence, certainly present a model of sermonizing ' highly worthy of imitation. But Saurin, though often just, ' and seldom *dangerously* erroneous in his expositions of ' Scripture, is very general in his views of all doctrinal sub- ' jects. I can easily conceive, that under such a Pastor, error ' might creep into a flock undetected, and produce considera- ' ble ravages, before the evil would create alarm.

"The style of Saurin's preaching marks, I have supposed,

'the declining period of the Flemish Churches. Saurin's
' impassioned eloquence might fan the dying embers of vital
' piety into a temporary blaze; but his sermons could not ad-
' minister that substantial fuel which was necessary to per-
' petuate and increase its warmth.

" I can conceive of Saurin's animated addresses, and urgent
' exhortations, given without due discrimination, as of the
' spirited encouragements of a brave General, which, indeed,
' might quicken the movements of his troops, and apparently
' sharpen the combat, while their manœuvres are regulated by
' no system, their shots directed at random, and their intrench-
' ments, in the ardour and hurry of the fight, quite overleaped.
' We would commend the bravery of the General, and might
' admire the courage and gallantry of his men, but should
' probably see the better disciplined enemy, in the end, master
' of the field."

*April* 14*th.*
" This morning at six, I found on rising, that we had made
' the round shoals of Nantucket, the light bearing about south-
' west, three leagues distant, wind east, light, and weather
' pleasant.

" The Town of Nantucket is situated on the north-western
' part of the Island, and is full in view as we sail down the
' channel. There appeared about thirty small sail, at anchor
' before the Town, which the Captain said are fishermen and
' whalers principally, and owned by the Islanders.

" The soil of this Island is more productive than that of
' Cape Cod, and the face of it about equally uneven, and the
' surface equally elevated.

" Most of the inhabitants are either Quakers, or the descen-
' dants of Quakers—unite fishing with agriculture, and are
' generally industrious, thriving and moral. The distance
' from shore to shore, at Nantucket, is six or eight leagues.—
' From Nantucket light, to that of Holme's Hole, Martha's
' Vineyard, is thirty miles.

"At half past three, passed Holme's Hole. It is built at the
' bottom of a navigable Bay, which extends inland more than
' two miles. On the extremity of the western head, at the en-
' trance of the Bay, is the light. Sailing by H. H. you have
' a fair prospect of Falmouth on the main side, only four miles
' distant from Holme's Hole light. It shows about equal to
' Holme's Hole. Between the main, and a chain of Islands
' called Elizabeth Islands, which make a part of the south-
' eastern side of Buzzard's Bay, you have a prospect through
' from the main channel to the Bay. Small vessels may pass
' through this opening, which is directly west.

"Having stood on a little beyond H. Hole light, westward,
' we bore away south-west, through the middle of the channel,
' between Martha's Vineyard and Elizabeth Islands. On the
' largest of these is a good harbour, called Tarpaulin Cove,
' where is a public house and a light.

"Martha's Vineyard appears a little more elevated, and
' much more productive, than Nantucket.

*April* 15*th.*

"Rocked about until near night, when the wind freshening
' at south-east, we run into Newport Harbour, where I went
' ashore and passed the night.

*April* 16*th.*

"Rose early and walked through the Town. Found one
' principal street running from north to south, a little nearer
' the water than the eastern extremity of the Town, from
' which short streets led off at right angles either way. East
' of this street, there are two, and in some parts of the Town,
' more streets running parallel. West, there is no parallel
' street. There are several very decent, and one elegant
' house for public worship. By a singular mixture of the
' different orders of architecture in the construction of the
' lofty and highly embellished spire of the latter, its beauty
' and effect are much impaired. The houses on the princi-

'pal street, are (less than one half) of brick—the other houses
' and shops of the Town are chiefly of wood.

" The Fort, built on an Island directly opposite the Town,
' three quarters of a mile distant, presents a very beautiful
' appearance, and is thought to be a place of strength.—
' There is, likewise, a strong post, on the point of the Island,
' projecting to the south-west of the Town, and making one
' shore of the narrowest part of the channel leading in.

" Nearly opposite this post, but farther to the west and south,
' on Canonicut Island, is a circular Castle, built of stone, and
' though small, has a commanding elevation, and the appear-
' ance of strength.

" The light at the entrance of Newport Harbour is on Ca-
' nonicut Island, two miles from Town. From Point Judith
' light, to that on Gull Island, is thirty-five miles. This light
' is at the entrance of Long Island Sound, although Montaug
' Point projects eastward several miles beyond it.

" Up the Sound, are Gull Island, New London, Falcon
' Island, New Haven, Huntington and Sandy Point lights.

" NEW YORK, SABBATH, *April* 18*th.*

"Early this morning, our Pilot came aboard, and before
' nine, we were safely moored.

" Attended at Dr. Mason's church, Murray street, in the af-
' ternoon. The services were conducted by a Clergyman who
' appeared to be a man of education and piety, and a Scotch-
' man; forcible in his delivery, energetic and perspicuous in
' his style; he was deficient in nothing necessary for a good
' preacher, except elegance and modesty.

" *April* 20*th.*

" This morning, got under sail for Baltimore. The nar-
' rows, nine miles from New York, are fortified 1st, by a
' strong work on a little Island situated near the Long Island
' shore.

" 2nd. By a battery, not so strong, on the Long Island
' side, nearly level with the water, and perhaps by a battery

' on the height above. But this I could not, from the water,
' discover if there be any.

"3rd. By a powerful battery on Staten Island side, direct-
' ly opposite the works on the east side, and just above high
' water level.

"4th. By a still stronger fortification on the heights, di-
' rectly in the rear of the last mentioned, and overlooking it
' entirely.

" The channel is here, perhaps, three quarters of a mile
' wide ; ship channel, about south-west, six or eight miles,
' after passing the narrows, and thence south, south-east,
' nearly to Sandy Hook light.

" Went ashore at Sandy Hook. Found the whole point of
' the Peninsula to have been formed by the rake of the sea,
' on a sandy bottom. The old man keeping the light, in-
' formed us that since the building of the principal light-
' house, 1762, the whole of the Peninsula north of it, had
' been formed by the action of the sea. This alluvial point,
' is at least half a mile in extent. The sand is very coarse,
' yellow, and, only in the interior of the Hook, mingled with
' a very small portion of vegetable mould. There are three
' lights on this point. The first house, built 1762, is of stone,
' octagonal, eight stories, exclusive of the basement, four feet
' high. Height from the foundation, one hundred and two
' feet. Its light revolves—has eighteen lamps, six ranged on
' each side of a triangular frame, so that thrice every minute
' the light alternately brightens and lessens, and is thus dis-
' tinguished from every other light on the American coast.
' Nine hundred gallons of oil are consumed annually, in
' feeding the lamps in this and the two inferior lights on this
' point.

" The upper story of this light-house has its floor entirely
' coppered, and the sides entirely glazed with iron window
' sashes. The cap is either of sheet iron or copper, and at
' the apex, is the funnel. The lamps consist of a tin pot,

' which contains the oil—a cylinder in which the wick is
' inserted and burns, fed from the tin pot in the rear—a glass
' cylinder in which the blaze is enclosed, and a copper backed
' burnished semi-spherical concave reflector of fifteen inches
' diameter.

" The frame is carried round by a little simple machinery,
' wrought by means of a weight that descends through five
' stories and is raised by means of a crank at top.

MONDAY, *April* 26*th*.

" At half past seven o'clock this morning, went ashore on
' the extremity of the point, (Little Point Comfort) which we
' found indeed to be completely insulated at high water. Lit-
' tle Point Comfort is a barren neck of land, composed almost
' entirely of fine white sand. Its light is sixty feet high, the
' house built of cut stone of considerable size. Compared with
' the light-house at Sandy Hook, the structure of this is very
' slight, consisting of a single layer of stones from bottom to
' top. The steps in the stairway, are each a single stone, rest-
' ing on the one next below, at one end, for support, and in-
' serted into the wall at the other. The light does not re-
' volve—is produced by nine lamps, arranged in two tiers,
' and fixed on a circular frame. The coppered and inside
' burnished reflectors, are of the same construction as those of
' Sandy Hook; and in front of each, through which every ray
' is refracted, is placed a plain convex lens, of eight inches di-
' ameter, consisting of a species of green coloured glass, such
' as is used for sky lights in the quarter decks of vessels.

" The shrubbery of this spot is to me almost entirely new.
' It consisted of live oak, ivy, myrtle, whortle bushes, prickly
' pears, cedar and coarse marsh grass, such as I saw at Sandy
' Hook. The land is a perfect level. The soil loose and san-
' dy, but by no means unproductive. A few apple trees were
' seen in a flourishing state. Peach and cherry trees produce
' the best fruit and yield it plentifully. The planter whom
' we visited, has a small family of six or eight slaves em-

'ployed, males and females, in planting sweet potatoes. Saw
'a small patch of land on which cotton had been raised
'the last year. The plant is eighteen inches high—branches
'forth in long slender twigs in every direction. It is planted
'in rows three feet asunder, and the plants are about eighteen
'inches apart. I should judge that six or eight pods or burs,
'might grow on a single plant. The seeds are lodged in the
'ground in May, and the cotton gathered in September.

"Negroes perform nearly the whole of the labour in this
'part of Virginia. The opinion I have formed of their treat-
'ment here, is favorable to the humanity of their masters.—
'They appear cheerful, hearty, and some of them, even ro-
'bust. The houses provided to shelter them are small, and
'many of them of wretched appearance. I judge they are
'incommoded by the smallness of the apartments into which
'the husbands and wives, parents and children, of numerous
'families are sometimes crowded together.

"Generally no leisure or respite is allowed the slaves, ex-
'cepting on the Sabbath. The value of a man slave is en-
'hanced to his master, when he has on the same plantation,
'a wife to whom he is attached, and diminished when his
'wife belongs to another plantation.

"Every plantation in this part of Virginia, is supposed to
'manufacture the clothing of the negroes that belong to it,
'from the rearing of the raw material to the forming of the
'cloth into garments. The dress of the men and boys, is
''either of white or colored cotton cloth—a mixture of cotton
'and wool or wool alone. Whatever may be the material,
'the fabric is very coarse. Some of the men have shoes and
'all are furnished with hats or caps. The dress of the men
'consists of a short or jacket, coat, shirt, and trowsers; of the
'women, of a frock and petticoat, together with some cover-
'ing for the head, and in the winter, shoes and stockings.—
'The dress of the females, is a strong, double, coarse white
'cloth.

"To clothe a negro a year, costs from twenty to thirty dol-
' lars. His services may be purchased for from fifty to sev-
' enty dollars. A woman's for about half the same. The
' price of an able-bodied negro man, is from five to seven
' hundred dollars.

"The slaves are ignorant, without any principles of reli-
' gion, or commonly of morality, and doubtless as vicious as
' their condition and constant application to labour, will per-
' mit them to be.

"*Digression.*—On Friday last, after our Pilot had stept
' aboard our Schooner from his boat, he asked if we would
' give to a poor fellow a passage to Baltimore? Being an-
' swered in the affirmative, a young man of genteel figure,
' but in a very rusty dress, and of uncleanly appearance, dis-
' covered himself above the companion way of the Pilot boat,
' and without trunk or bundle, sprung aboard. He waved an
' affectionate adieu to those he left behind, and by his pronun-
' ciation, showed himself to be a foreigner. His clothing was
' worth to a person furnished with any other, less than five
' dollars. He soon discovered himself to be profane and dis-
' solute; and to have been reduced from better circumstances
' to his present most pitiable condition.

"During the remainder of the passage, we learned that he
' is a native of the Isle of Man—of reputable parentage and
' whose youth had been spent in the lap of mistaken indul-
' gence. For at least a dozen years, he was attached to the
' British Army and Navy, alternately; in connection with
' which, he had served in different capacities—but never
' held a commission in either. He had served in India, South
' America, the Mediterranean, Spain, British America, and
' the north of Europe. Had received in fourteen different
' engagements, as many different wounds, lost two brothers,
' the one in South America, and the other in Spain. And
' about nine months ago, in order to see the United States,
' left the British service, contrary to the advice of those

'whose counsel should have governed him, and was passing 'on foot, through the forest of New Brunswick, in order to 'gain our eastern settlements, when he was met and attacked 'by a bear, from which he with difficulty escaped with his 'life. As singular as the facts may be, I think his statement 'is corroborated by that which appeared soon after, in the 'public papers, that without any weapon of defence, a man 'had closed with the animal who reared himself for the as-'sault; and while nearly crushed to death in the rude embrace 'of his savage assailant, had the presence of mind to draw a 'knife from his pocket, and actually deliver his own life, by 'destroying that of the bear. He suffered severely, and has 'hardly recovered from the injuries he sustained.

"Having arrived in the United States, he loitered from 'town to town, without engaging in any regular employ-'ment that might gain him an honourable and permanent 'livelihood.

"In Norfolk, where he arrived in a packet from N. York, 'a few days ago, he spent the last of his money, and pawned, 'for less than half their value, every article of clothing with 'which he could dispense, and appear in the streets without 'positive indecency; and thus destitute, undertook to per-'form a journey on foot, from that town to Baltimore, two 'hundred miles. Having travelled to York, not more than 'thirty miles, which he was three days in effecting, he found 'himself entirely pennyless, and too lame to proceed. At no 'great distance from that place, his entreaties prevailed with 'the master of a Pilot boat, to receive him on board, in order 'to obtain for him, if possible, a passage to Baltimore, in some 'vessel bound up the bay. He had now been on board the 'boat about a week. His object in visiting Baltimore, is to 'ask pecuniary assistance of relatives living in that place, or 'to obtain a birth in some South American Privateer; or a 'passage to that country, in order to regain a theatre of war, 'on which alone he appears fitted or able to act a part, that

' will secure him from the most abject indigence, and morti-
' fying sufferings.
 " This affecting case enforces many a salutary and instruc-
' tive lesson.
 " 1st. Reason may be impaired almost to extinction, by
' the habitual indulgence of the appetites. This young man
' would not, and with scarce a figure of speech, it may be
' said, he could not calculate, while spending his last dollar
' in scenes of dissipation and intemperance, on the most obvi-
' ous, direct, and inevitable consequences of his folly. Until
' he actually felt the accumulated distresses which he now
' suffers, his reasoning powers were, from long disuse, unable
' to apprize him of their approach, when even the next step
' was about to give him the plunge.
 " 2nd. It would be absolutely impossible to convince this
' young man, that there are any religious or intellectual plea-
' sures worth the seeking, or even the possession. So entirely
' subdued are all the nobler faculties of the man by the exces-
' sive indulgence of those of the brute, that he is hardly con-
' scious of possessing any other. If we except those plea-
' sures which are purely animal, and those derived through
' the medium of a most voluptuous imagination, he knows
' and can know, in this world, not the shadow of enjoyment.
' I greatly question, whether any habit of acting, or abstinence
' which he can form, to say nothing of the difficulty of en-
' gaging him in a different course—a difficulty which has
' seldom or never been overcome in a similar case—I say
' that no habit he can form, would, without a supernatural
' change of his moral taste and affections, render any other
' than a life of sensual indulgence, tolerable.
 " What is true in *his* case, may be in others ; and sanctions
' this general maxim:—Every repetition of criminal sensual
' indulgence, tends to merge the intellectual in the animal
' part of the man. And when from inveterate habit, the ap-
' petites acquire the ascendancy, the way of reformation is

'effectually barred. Divine grace alone can remove the ob-
'structions, and that only by renewing the heart.

"3rd. Another lesson derived from this case, is, that the
'dissolute man will sacrifice *every* other thing to his degrad-
'ing pleasures—his soul—his friends—his reputation—his
'veracity—none are too valuable to be immolated, if immo-
'lated they must be, or his pleasures relinquished.

"4th. A dissolute life destroys that sensibility which the
'near approach of death awakens in the mind of the reflecting
'and virtuous man. Two causes may be assigned for this
'fact: The one, that such are without a habit of reflection,
'and measure their miseries rather by what deprives them,
'and *what they feel depriving them*, of sensual enjoyments,
'than by what they anticipate. Their principle of estimating
'their circumstances, (if they can be said to form estimates by
'any principle) is depressed towards that which actuates the
'unthinking consciousness (for want of a better word) of
'irrational animals, when such evils of delights as awaken
'their sensations, approach them. It is little more than sen-
'sation.

"Another cause which commonly operates to produce in
'the minds of the dissolute, a profound insensibility to the
'fear of death, is a defective and erroneous view of the na-
'ture of death, as respects its consequences. Whatever may
'have conduced to their profligacy, will itself either cut them
'off from the means of correct religious instruction, or pre-
'vent religious doctrines and all serious ideas from acquiring
'a seat in their mind. The most formidable quality that, in
'the estimation of our profligate, death possesses, is its power
'to end his revels, and remove him from the scene of his
'earthly delight.

"Blessed religion of my Saviour, whose principles fortify
'the soul against the assaults of temptation, from the appe-
'tites! Whose efficacy alone can rescue the enslaved soul

'from their power. O may I bind its doctrines on my heart,
'and carry its spirit into all the details of my conduct."

Several other extracts from this Journal, will be found in the Appendix. How depressed were his spirits, and yet how sustained he was, by considerations becoming his character and profession, will be manifest from the thoughts left on record by him, just before landing at Baltimore.

"*April* 29.

"I am wearied with the profaneness, vulgarity, senseless
'garrulity and levity of the uncultivated crew with which I
'sail. This is now the 21st day of my confinement on board,
'excepting two days spent in New York. I am wearied with
'the frequent disappointments that have occurred in our pro-
'gress. I am wearied with my confinement to a small,
'crowded, filthy cabin; to a still more filthy and lumbered
'steerage; and to a deck loaded with spruce logs, piled more
'than six feet high. There is hardly a lucid spot amid the
'general gloom. If I look for friends, alas! I have not
'one on whose bosom I can repose this head, with per-
'fect complacency, and unqualified confidence! There
'is not a being on earth from whom I have the most distant
'hope of receiving the least aid in preparing for future
'usefulness and happiness in life, or in obtaining an eligible
'situation when prepared. The God of Heaven must
'be my patron or I have none. I am going into the
'midst of strangers. Not the least acquaintance have I with
'an individual I ever expect to see again in the State of Ma-
'ryland or Virginia. I am now twenty-five years of age; al-
'most three from College, have no profession; and my em-
'ployment has been such since I left College, as to form me
'to habits unfavorable to the acquisition of one. I am in-
'volved in debt, possess neither books nor money, and have a
'delicate and beloved wife to provide for. I am wearied
'with the same daily round of dull employment and still
'duller indulgences; of studying in circumstances forbidding

'the exercise of half the strength of my mental powers; of
'sleeping immoderately, because I have nothing to do; or to
'enjoy, sufficiently interesting to keep me awake; of con-
'versing on subjects, and in a style but ill suited to afford me
'much satisfaction in accommodation to the taste and capa-
'cities of my companions, and of eating for amusement while
'the inactive manner of passing my time, scarcely renders
'food necessary.

"I am disgusted with my heart, when I look within. I
'am grieved with my conduct, when I review my life. I am
'dissatisfied with my friends and acquaintance, and they with
'whom I have recently been more intimately associated. The
'past is a blank or a field of strife, or a scene of trials. The
'present is tasteless; all around me, and respecting me is un-
'real and unsatisfactory. The future is a dreary expanse of
'storms and clouds, pervaded, indeed, by a few faint gleams
'of hope. I am broken with disappointments; have been rob-
'bed by the perfidy and ignorance of supposed friends, and
'the malevolence of enemies, of my reputation, worth more
'than life. The frown of Heaven is upon me. My hopes
'for eternity are clouded. My soul is full of carnal desires
'and worldly attachments. And how I support these bur-
'dens is to me unaccountable. But away with these com-
'plaints, and let me repress every needless emotion of con-
'cern. God, who I hope has loved me in his Son, from eter-
'nity, is powerful, and good, and faithful, as in the day of my
'espousals. *Why should a living man complain, a man for*
'*the punishment of his sins? Though the fig tree should*
'*not blossom, &c. Though the mountains should be carried*
'*into the midst of the sea, &c. Let none of these things*
'*trouble me, &c.* Here are promises enough, rich enough,
'large enough, free enough. Have I faith or a hearty de-
'sire, a desire which God sees and approves as sincere, to em-
'brace them?

"*April* 30. Baltimore appears in sight. While I felici-
' tate myself in being so near the end of an unpleasant and
' protracted voyage, the whole distance being about one thou-
' sand miles, I still feel a degree of concern in looking into
' futurity. A new era commences in my life, the moment I
' step ashore. O God, thou hast been my hope and my firm
' support in the past years of my life. Do not forsake me
' now, though my sins render it more suitable that I should
' be abandoned to myself, than ever before ; and more than
' ever, since I first confided in Thee, discourage my hope and
' weaken my confidence in thy mercy. Raise me, O God,
' and hold me up. Go with me and lead me into the midst
' of strangers in a strange place. Suffer me not to be reduced
' to poverty and want, lest I be diverted from my great object.
' I desire not wealth without an increase of grace, lest I be
' lifted up—more fatally attached to the world, and less de-
' voted to the service of the Redeemer. Give me the wisdom
' of a serpent, the gentleness of a dove, the active, persevering
' spirit of thine ancient Apostles, ever to deserve in the esti-
' mation of my fellow-men a fair reputation, and above all, the
' honour to turn many to righteousness, and then, grace to
' ascribe to Thee alone, all honour, thanksgiving and glory,
' forever, through Jesus Christ. Amen."

Who, that is acquainted with human nature, does not see amid the morbid feelings and unsubdued passions of Ashmun, at this crisis, a faith of power, both in the Providence and word of God, working to overcome all that opposed it, and with an energy which nothing could long be able to resist?

## CHAPTER IV

The mind of Ashmun was earnest, bold and independent. It has been remarked by a friend, that his independence increased with his difficulties and embarrassments. His spirit rose unbroken and triumphant from beneath the heaviest weight of misfortune. His errors in judgment at this period related rather to the opinions and dispositions of others, than to his own abilities. They grew out of inexperience and that enthusiasm which too frequently imparts to objects the hues of the imagination, rather than " the colours of reason." He had been more successful, had he expected less from others; not less successful, had he looked for more from himself.

Immediately after his arrival in Baltimore, he sought the acquaintance of several respectable Clergymen, rented a house, and issued proposals for receiving under his instruction, a select class of young ladies, to be educated in the higher branches of literature and science. His views in this respect, were so little encouraged, that he soon turned his thoughts to the establishment of a weekly paper, of a religious

character, and designed especially to give regular abstracts of Missionary and other religious intelligence. Several thousand copies of the first number of this paper, "The Constellation," were printed, and vigorous measures adopted to extend its circulation. To a friend he writes: "You must
'be prepared to learn, that by many, it is neglected—by ma-
'ny suspected—by many disapproved—by many patronized,
'and its appearance hailed as auspicious to Baltimore. All
'this I expected; and if I regret any thing, it is that the two
'first numbers have not a more fixed and prominent evange-
'lical character. I had my motives for sending it out as I
'did; but had I to commence the paper anew, I should draw
'the lineaments of its intended character a little more dis-
'tinctly."

Owing to various causes, principally to want of general information concerning the views and character of the Editor, all hope of succeeding with this paper, soon vanished; and Ashmun found himself involved in debt, among strangers, with no prospect of immediate and profitable employment.

Several members of the Maryland Episcopal Convention, then in session at Baltimore, were desirous of establishing, in the District of Columbia, a periodical publication, which, resembling in evangelical character the Christian Observer, should be a repository for whatever might advance the cause of literature, humanity, or divine truth; and a gentleman* of

---

* The Rev. Dr. Keith, of the Episcopal Theological Seminary, in this District, who has favoured me with the following observations and anecdote, concerning Ashmun:

"He was as remarkable in youth, as in mature years. A most decided, energetic character, determined, if possible, to accomplish something on a large scale, for the benefit of the human race. He was a very good specimen of the old Puritan character, and would have been in his element among the first settlers of New England. He was a first rate scholar, and most determined and devoted Christian. He was a student of the Academy at Middle-

the Convention, a friend of Mr. Ashmun at College, suggested that he should accompany him to Washington, and occupy the situation of instructer, in a respectable family, until arrangements could be made for his permanent connection with the proposed publication.* The suggestion was adopted, and Mr. Ashmun proceeded, the next day, to Washington.

Not unfrequently, in the Divine Wisdom, are the lines of Providence (long concealed from human view, and so far as known by their immediate effects, in their relations and directions distinct,) revealed, converging towards the same point, and finally uniting on one and the same great object of good to mankind. The Episcopal Church in America, before the Revolution, though it embraced in its communion a large portion of the wealth and intelligence of

bury, entered College there, and in his senior year, I think, went to Burlington, where he graduated. After leaving Maine, he came to Baltimore, and commenced the publication of a religious paper called the Constellation. He was without funds, and his paper did not succeed. He published but one number, (it was a weekly,) consisting of 4,000, which he sent round the city, in the hope of getting subscribers; but I believe he did not obtain more than two or three hundred. He was a stranger there, and had no friends or patrons. He had, besides, contracted a debt to the printer, and for his board. Happening to be in Baltimore at this time, to my great surprise, I found him there, which gave me the first intelligence of his having left Maine. * * *
\* \* \* \* \* \* I persuaded him to come on with me. We were to start in the stage together; it was in the month of June. On coming to the stage-office at 5 in the morning, instead of Ashmun, I found a note from him, saying, that his straitened circumstances rendered it proper for him to travel in a cheaper way, and that he would meet me in Georgetown. On the arrival of the stage at Washington, the first person I met, was my expected fellow-traveller; and on inquiry how he arrived there before the stage, which was in by eleven o'clock, was informed that he had walked!! Instead of taking the School, however, he undertook the publication of the Repertory, and became a candidate for orders in the P. E. Church.

* The Theological Repertory.

the southern colonies, was feeble in discipline, deficient in piety, and very inadequately supplied with Ministers of zeal and power. To no individual, perhaps, is this Church more indebted for her establishment on broad and solid foundations, than to Granville Sharp. At the close of the Revolutionary war, there was no Bishop residing in America. After the Declaration of Independence, as no American Clergyman would take an oath of allegiance to the King, Episcopal ordination could not be obtained.

Mr. Sharp was well known in the United States by his writings against the slave trade and slavery, and for his consistent and able defence of the rights of the colonies. Several of his Tracts had been widely circulated by Anthony Benezet and other members of the Society of Friends; and he ever regarded the success of his endeavours for the establishment of Episcopacy in this country, "as one of the extraordinary effects of the zealous exertions of the Quakers, jointly with the Author of those Tracts, in the cause of African freedom; though neither party had the least idea of any such consequence arising from their united labours." These exertions had secured for Mr. Sharp, a high reputation for wisdom and integrity. Great respect was felt for his opinions on any subject; and venerating, as he did, the doctrines and liturgy of the English Church, he deemed it his duty to exert all his influence with the friends of that Church in this country, and her prelates in England, for introducing into America, the order of Bishops; hoping that it might prove, in the language of the English common-law, the strength of the Republic,* and greatly conduce to the progress and triumphs of Christianity.

In a note to the Law of Retribution, published in 1776, and subsequently, in two other Tracts, Mr. Sharp maintained the right of the Clergy, and people of every diocese, to

---

* Ordo Episcoporum est robur reipublicæ.

elect their own Bishop; and while by these writings\* and an active correspondence with Dr. Franklin and other eminent men in this country, he did much to promote the election of Bishops by the American Episcopal Convention; by his efforts with the Archbishop of Canterbury, and other Dignitaries of the same Church, he obtained assurances that the obstacles to ordination should be removed, and that persons selected by the American Convention, and duly qualified for the Episcopal office, should receive consecration at their hands.

On the 4th of February, 1787, Mr. Sharp had the happiness of witnessing the consecration of two Bishops elect, from America, Dr. White of Pennsylvania† and Dr. Prevoost of New York, (and subsequently, in 1790, of Dr. Madison of Virginia,) by the English Primate. While he thus saw accomplished, an object for which he had long laboured in the most zealous and indefatigable manner, he disclaims all idea of merit for his exertions, and devoutly attributes the success of them, entirely to the Providence of God. How would this great Philanthropist rejoice to know, that the Church, for which, during her infancy, he evinced so deep a concern, has risen to manly strength; extended her influence; multiplied her numbers; brought to her ministrations distinguished learning, talent and piety; and especially, that his own benevolent spirit towards the African race, animates the hearts of many of her honored sons, who at all hazards, and any sacrifices, would transplant, from America so blest by his labours, to Africa that so shared in his sympathies, the

---

\* One tract on Congregational Courts, and the other on the Election of Bishops. "This latter, was particularly useful in promoting Episcopacy in America. Even Dr. Franklin (bred a Dissenter) and Dr. Rush declared their approbation of it in letters to the Author; and the two first Bishops that were sent to England for consecration, declared that they should not have been sent, had not the Author's endeavours prompted the business."—*Memoirs of G. Sharp.*

† The present Right Rev. William White of that State.

germs and principles of all human improvement.* Who can estimate the value of the blessings which this Church is capable of conferring upon Africa! And considering the extent and power of her influence in the Southern States, and the energy and liberality with which her most enlightened members in those States have sustained the cause of African Colonization, may we not hope, that the same Providence, which, by the efforts of Granville Sharp for the relief of the distressed Africans, wrought to strengthen her interests and complete her organization, will work in her mightily to regenerate Africa and to build up over that vast continent of superstition and crime, the empire of truth, liberty and holiness?

Nor can the connection of Mr. Ashmun with this Church, and the Theological Repertory devoted to its interests, be deemed an unimportant event, as it tended powerfully to awaken among its members that zeal and effort in behalf of Africa, which are contributing to elevate her wretched children to all the privileges and honours of a Christian people.

Soon after his arrival at Washington, the arrangements for the publication of the Repertory, a monthly Magazine of thirty-two pages, were concluded, and the first number made its appearance in the month of August. The Episcopal Clergy of the District of Columbia, exercised over this work a general superintendence, while the ordinary duties of Editor, and the whole of its pecuniary concerns, were assumed by Mr. Ashmun. No similar work then existed South of New York, and the conductors of the Repertory felt urged by

* The Biographer of Mr. Sharp, may have estimated too highly his influence in promoting the interests of the Episcopal Church in America. From reference to the venerable Bishop White's History of this Church in the U. States, the writer is of opinion, that such is the fact. Bishop White published his own opinions tending to the introduction of the Laity into the Ecclesiastical Counsels, as early as 1783, and various causes contributed to place the Episcopal Church in America on its present foundation; yet Mr. Sharp's agency was important—his efforts early, constant, and persevering.

the peculiar wants and circumstances of the Episcopa. Church, and by the increasing necessities for religious intelligence and enterprise, to inculcate in its pages, not only sound doctrine, but a spirit of enlarged Christian benevolence. They sought to raise the standard of individual piety, to inflame the zeal, enliven the hopes, concentrate the action, and extend and augment the charity of the Church.

All the articles for this work were examined and arranged by Mr. Ashmun; many were from his own pen; and the high respectability of his character, and the extensive patronage which it soon received, are in great measure to be attributed to the activity and resolution with which he devoted himself to its interests. He visited Baltimore, Philadelphia and New York, and engaged in an extensive correspondence to promote its circulation.

A Review of the Second Annual Report of the American Colonization Society, written by Mr. Ashmun, and published in the earliest numbers of the Repertory, shows how carefully, even then, he had investigated the principles and facts on which this Society is founded; how he comprehended its various relations and the vastness of its object; and how thorough was his conviction, that a Colony to accomplish any benevolent purpose, must be pervaded by the spirit and power of Christianity. The introduction to this Review, is in the following words:

"Never, perhaps, in the History of man, has an object af-
' fording equal scope for the exercise of Christian benevo-
' lence, been found capable of engaging in its support such a
' compass and variety of powerful motives, as that of the Ame-
' rican Colonization Society. Though in itself this object is
' simple and definite, and to superficial observation, of limited
' and even questionable utility, the beneficial consequences
' of its success gradually unfold to the mind, on a rational in-
' vestigation of its nature, and may be traced up to the high-
' est pitch of moral magnificence.

"On a comparative survey of the different benevolent enter-
' prises in which religion and humanity have hitherto enga-
' ged the various portions of the American community, we
' state it as our decided conviction, that the Colonization of
' the free blacks of this country in Africa, is an object deserv-
' ing to be ranked among the most rational, practicable and
' beneficial; and has powerful claims on their prompt and
' united support. And among all the anniversary reports to
' which the systematic prosecution of these enterprises has
' given rise, we venture to say, that none has been read with
' more awakened attention, and deeper interest, by the Ameri-
' can Public, than that, the title of which stands at the head
' of this article."

In the conclusion, his views of the qualifications indispensable for the officers of the proposed Colony, and the basis upon which it should rest, are thus strongly stated.

"On a subject so important as that of the character and ca-
' pability of those who are to act as the Instructers and Magis-
' trates, and to administer the affairs of the Colony, there can
' hardly be any discrepancy of opinion. That instructers
' should be men of piety—that magistrates should be upright
' prudent and discerning—that both should exhibit a strictly
' moral and virtuous deportment, none can doubt. And that
' all should be decidedly Christian in profession, principles
' and temper, who will hesitate to decide, that considers the
' nature of the establishment, the durability of all impressions
' made upon its early character—and the influence which
' the example of such as hold conspicuous stations, never
' fails to exert.     *     *     *

"It is an opinion which we believe is built on incontestible
' grounds, that *an African Colony, in order to answer any*
' *benevolent design, must have for its basis the promotion of*
' *the Christian Religion*—first, within the Colony itself,
' and subsequently, by means of the Colony among the
' contiguous tribes. Of these objects, the last is so in-

'volved in the first, that to this alone, our remarks shall be
'confined.

"It is undeniable that a community may be established un-
'der the most refined and excellent system of civil policy—
'that it may cultivate to any extent, the arts, the sciences, the
'literature of civilized society; it may add to its refinement,
'wealth and power—and to these the customary appendages
'of national greatness, and still exhibit in its irreligious and
'heathenish character, the most affecting marks of national
'debasement and moral wretchedness.

"The amount of religious knowledge possessed by the Af-
'rican class of our population, bond or free, is unhappily
'small; and the influence of Christian principles among
'them, feeble indeed. And it hardly need be inquired, what
'after a few years, would be the religious character of a Colo-
'ny of black people, collected even from this Christian coun-
'try, and fixed without the means of Christian improvement
'in the midst of African Paganism. They would speedily
'divest themselves of every vestige of superiority in their re-
'ligious notions or practice to their surrounding neighbours,
'and cease to be distinguishable from them, except by the
'sturdiness and variety of their vices. Their irreligion
'would render them immoral—their immorality factious, con-
'temptible and wretched. * * Will any deed of benevo-
'lence in relation to them, be performed by the simple process
'of their removal from this country? Let the early history
'of Sierra Leone reply. Those Colonists, though not utterly
'without the privileges of religion, yet enjoyed so irregular
'and defective a supply, that, with a few exceptions, they
'wasted away an unprofitable existence, uninfluenced by its
'spirit, and died without its hopes.

"The settlement of Sierra Leone never experienced prospe-
'rity, till through the influence of the Church Missionary So-
'ciety, its form and administration were strictly accommoda-
'ted to the religious improvement of the people. There is

' now not a child in the Colony for which provision is not
' made to afford it a competency of useful learning and reli-
' gious instruction—not an adult for whom a seat is not pre-
' pared in the Sanctuary. Since the propitious era marked
' by the commencement of this state of things, the settlement
' has exhibited an aspect of vigour and health unknown be-
' fore.

"We hesitate not to declare our opinion, that no Colonist
' should be suffered to land in Africa, who with his offspring,
' cannot enjoy in a good extent the advantage of Christian in-
' struction. Infinitely preferable is a state of bondage, in a
' land where they *may* acquire a knowledge of the true God,
' and the great Salvation, than to be abandoned to ignorance
' and vice, on the remote shores of Africa.

"But the Christian Religion is the only basis on which a
' prosperous Colony can be reared; and it is a sure one."*

During his connection with the Repertory, (a period of nearly three years,) not only did Mr. Ashmun continue to send forth through its columns, much intelligence concerning Africa, the slave trade, and the American Colonization Society; but in 1820, with the approbation of the Managers of that Society, he commenced the publication of THE AFRICAN INTELLIGENCER, a monthly Journal, of thirty-two pages, designed to give a complete view of the proceedings of the Colony—of the Board in this country—of the measures of Government for the suppression of the slave trade—as also to illustrate by facts, and enforce by arguments, the claims of the African cause. He had for some time sought diligently, to add to his knowledge of Africa, and of all plans proposed for her benefit; and at Washington had neglected no means of ascertaining fully, the views and purposes of the Managers of the Colonization Society. They respected his talents, had occasionally availed themselves of his services,

* Appendix 3.

and were prepared to expect from his labors, as Editor of the Intelligencer, great and beneficial results. Unfortunately, no general interest was felt in the object of the work, which appeared in a solitary number, and expired.

At this period, Mr. Ashmun was greatly perplexed and agitated on the subject of a profession for life. "Indeed," he remarks, "my mind has been distracted on this subject, since 'the autumn of 1818. So nearly balanced have been the 'reasons for and against entering upon the sacred Ministry of 'the Gospel, as either to hold my mind completely in a state 'of suspense, or to prevent my engaging with vigour in the 'requisite preparations. Several times, certainly not less than 'three, have I been on the point of abandoning all further 'thoughts of the sacred profession, and turning my attention 'to some other pursuit." Though he had been licensed to preach by the Congregational Clergy of Maine, and for two years had successfully proclaimed the Gospel under their sanction, the painful events that occasioned his departure from that State, and the peculiar circumstances in which he found himself at the South, constituted valid reasons, in his judgment, for uniting himself to the communion, and engaging in the service, of the Episcopal Church. After his arrival at Washington, he regularly attended on divine worship in this Church,—on one occasion preached, and at an early day, entered his name as a candidate for ordination in the Diocese of Virginia. His views of religious truth, continued mainly unchanged; while the more he examined and the better he knew the Church, with which he now stood connected, the stronger became his attachment to her worship, discipline and polity.\*

In January, 1821, he considered, seriously, the question,

\* Mr. Ashmun was no high-churchman. He would have concurred fully, I doubt not, in the following remarks of the Rev. Leonard Bacon in his "Manual for Young Church Members," a book which deserves to be read by every Minister and member of the Church: "There is no high-church doctrine in

whether or not, he should enter the Ministry. He had then reached the 27th year of his age. "I can," he observes, "look
'over my last two years, as over the blank leaves of my note
'book; or rather the miserable waste paper, covered with
'blots and unintelligible scrawls, and a thousand useless scraps
'of Latin, poetry, half finished sentences, and a midnight spec-
'ulation on the moon. I have dipped into many studies, but
'mastered none. I doubt, indeed, whether my mind is in so
'well disciplined a state, or is in any degree better furnished,
'than at that time. The Lord forgive me." "O God, my
'Judge," he exclaims, "aid me with thy unerring guidance.
'May I not judge nor decide rashly. May I properly de-
'pend on the intimations of thy Spirit and thy Providence;
'and properly exercise my own reason and judgment; and in
'my final decision, preserve a good conscience, and obtain
'thy blessing; and whatever pursuit I adopt, may I still be
'thy entire and devoted servant; and hold, as I have profess-
'ed before many witnesses, all my powers, and all my influ-
'ence sacredly consecrated to Thee, in Jesus Christ my Lord
'and Redeemer. Amen."

To this question Mr. Ashmun brought all the energies of his mind,—it occupied his thoughts almost exclusively for several days, and he sought direction from the oracles of God. That sense of Religion which enables its professor to discern

the New Testament. I do not mean by a high-churchman, one who holds to this or that particular form of Church order; for, as I understand the word, there are high-churchmen in every sect. By a high-churchman, I mean any man, whether Episcopalian, Presbyterian, or Congregationalist, who believes that his form of church organization has an exclusive divine right, and that every church not formed exactly according to the pattern which he imagines he has seen in the mount, is guilty of schism, of usurpation, and of offering strange fire before God. Such a man finds himself constrained to stand aloof from all Christian intercourse with those who are not of his ecclesiastical household, and to act as if his distinguishing principles of church order were of more importance than all the points of Christian truth which he and the 'dissenters' hold in common. It is in reference to this exclusiveness, where-ver it may be found, that I say, there is no high-church doctrine in the New Testament."

in present actions the seeds of good or evil everlasting, rendered him cautious in forming a decision, in the consequences of which the highest interests of himself and others might be deeply involved.*

That he had early devoted himself to the Ministry, in gratitude to God for his deliverance from condemnation and the power of sin; had professed this to be his only object during his classical studies; had often privately renewed the dedication of himself to this *work;* had already for two years preached the Gospel with success; had since his cessation therefrom, relaxed from the strictness of Christian duty and lost much of religious consolation ; that in the view of the world, his piety and consistency might appear questionable, should he engage in any other pursuit; all these weighty considerations urged him to decide upon the Ministry as a profession: While a consciousness of past imprudences and a belief that these would be magnified by the ungenerous; that the enemies of religion would impute them to his principles, and Christianity suffer thereby; that his motives for leaving the Congregational church would never be so understood by his Congregational and Presbyterian brethren, as to revive towards him, in their minds, perfect confidence; that such confidence could hardly be expected, even from Clergymen of his own Church; that consequently his own zeal and in-

* "But, however satisfactory to his judgment and conscience, this body of evidence may have proved, Mr. Bacon never contemplated the work [of the Ministry] without trembling. The greatness of its responsibilities, and the consequences as they must affect his own eternal state, of a faithful or negligent performance of its duties, presented themselves to his enlightened mind with awful interest. This feeling was enhanced by a survey of the effects which his Ministry must produce on the present and everlasting happiness of a multitude of his fellow-mortals; and on the interests of Christ and the manifestation of the divine glory in the Church and the world! Had his faith been less vigorous, and his love and fear of God less operative, his sensations in the anticipation of this work, would have been proportionably less overwhelming."—*Mr. Ashmun's Life of the Rev. S. Bacon.*

fluence would be checked and reduced; these, with other reasons, and especially that of his enlarging prospects of usefulness as a Layman, finally inclined the scale, and he determined to abandon all thoughts of the sacred office.

In this decision, his understanding, rather than his heart, acquiesced: since we find him almost immediately turning from the study of the Law,* to which, when this decision was formed, he resolved to devote a portion of his time, to that of Theology; and expressing the opinion, that he " was not ' at liberty to engage in any pursuit entirely secular." One of his most valued friends advised strongly, that he should continue his connection with the Repertory; and in a letter to Bishop Moore, dated February 6, 1821, Mr. Ashmun, after alluding to the character and importance of that work, and to the improbability that any one, not better qualified for the Ministry than himself, could be found to conduct it, alleges his own concern for its usefulness and duty to its interests, as reasons which might be deemed sufficient for his declining longer to remain a candidate for Holy orders.†

* Among his notes written while in Africa, we find the following sentences: "In 1821, I undertook to study Medicine. But my time being otherwise engaged, I was obliged, in a few weeks, to throw up the pursuit. A few months afterwards, I entered with great resolution, and under greater embarrassments on the study of Law. I had my daily bread to earn by my daily labour; and the weight of a most losing literary enterprise to sustain."

† We cannot deny ourselves the pleasure of inserting here, the reply of the venerable Bishop of Virginia:

RICHMOND, FEBRUARY 9, 1821.

*Dear Sir:*—I perceive from your communication of the 6th of January, that you still appear very undecided upon the subject of the Ministry, and that you consider the duty you owe the Repertory, as equally imperious with that of clerical engagement. While your mind continues in that state, I would decidedly recommend a continuance in your present pursuit; as it would be impossible for you to esteem yourself called to the Ministry, until duties of a sacerdotal character operate with such power, as to bear down every other consideration.

When the period arrives, in which the Almighty shall make ths appeal to your heart, "What dost thou hear, Jehudi?" all temporal considerations will

In that pathless wilderness of thought, where the spirit of Ashmun seems to have roamed at this period, his hopes alternately rose and fell; his purposes wavered with the varying aspect of Providence; but his will was true to Virtue; and the "countenance of God," "the sun of the human soul,*" threw in light and gladness upon many spots of fearfulness and gloom. There were seasons, when far away from the agitating passions and pursuits of men, the speculations of philosophy and the contests of ambition, he refreshed himself by the cool and transparent fountains fast by the oracles of God, and mingled the voice of his devotion with the songs of the birds among the branches. There were moments when faith had well nigh the power of vision, when mounting up with wings as an eagle, until earth was lost to his

lose their charms in your view; and neither bars nor bolts will prevent you from making your escape, and listening to the voice of the great Shepherd.

Although I do not wish to inculcate the necessity of such a call to the Ministry, as men of sober understanding would style enthusiastic, still I believe, that the impression of ministerial duty, when the summons shall be really given, will be so strong, and the impulse so great, that the mind will rest satisfied with nothing less, than the pursuit of the important object. There will then be no halting between two opinions! your only cry will be, "lead me forth in thy truth, and guide me, thou who art the God of my salvation;" all minor considerations will be swallowed up in the ardent wish to save souls, and reason and religion will both point to the same distinct, clear and soul convincing mark.

The Minister of Religion, unless borne up and impelled by such principles, would sink under the arduous duties of his office; the opposition of those for whom he labors would overwhelm him; but supported by such considerations, considerations resting on eternal objects, he can endure hardships as a good soldier of Jesus Christ; and when the people of his charge are asleep upon their pillows, he will stand as a watchman upon the wall: breast every storm: ward off every blow: and think and pray, and provide for his flock, with due vigilance.

When the Almighty shall be pleased to effect a full impression upon your heart, and you feel anxious to embark in the sacred cause, remember, that should I be spared, you will find in me a friend—a friend disposed to further and promote your views.

\* Young.

sight, he descried the glories of the celestial City, realized that there were the treasures of his heart, and felt that it was happiness enough to find a home forever, in that land of everlasting rest.

From January to July, 1821, he was occupied in conducting the Repertory, and in literary and theological reading and study. The subject of the Prophecies received a portion of his attention; while he occasionally reviewed the classical authors which he had perused with pleasure and profit in his youth.

Still, the inclination of his will, the strong current of his affections, was towards the sacred Ministry; and on the 7th of July, 1821, he addressed the following letter to the Bishop of Virginia:

"*Right Rev. and Dear Sir :*—After much prayer for the
' sure guidance of the great Head of the Church, I am at length
' brought fully to the conviction, that I ought to delay no lon-
' ger an application for orders. It is with much trembling
' and many fears, that I offer myself; but my hope in the
' grace of Him who can support and make me faithful, is
' stronger than my fears; and from my heart, I am willing to
' trust to His promises, and go forward. However useful the
' Repertory may prove, I do not think it right for me to re-
' linquish the Ministry in order to conduct that work; nor
' can I conscientiously suffer my purpose of resuming the sa-
' cred functions of a Christian Minister to continue longer
' unsettled and indefinite (as hitherto) through my own neg-
' lect.

"I hope the Repertory will continue to be published with
' an improving character; and I am disposed to do what I
' can, consistently with other duties, to promote both its per-
' manency and usefulness. Should I receive ordination this
' summer, it might and probably would be deemed advisable
' for me to maintain for several months longer my connexion

'with that publication; nor have I at present, distinctly in
'view, any vacant situation which, in the event of my ordi-
'nation, I might immediately and constantly supply. But
'during my stay in the District, I think that I might be use-
'fully employed in a sort of desultory ministration in the vi-
'cinity.

"My reading for the last two years, as you may well sup-
'pose, has been miscellaneous. I long to be in a condition
'to devote my undivided attention to the appropriate pursuits
'of a theological student, but plainly cannot enjoy the privi-
'lege while my present cares and labours lie upon me. I am
'willing, however, to offer myself for examination in the stu-
'dies prescribed by the canons, as the former grounds of my
'application for orders were set aside. For the examination,
'I submit it to yourself to make the requisite arrangements,
'and beg you to afford me reasonable information.

"You probably will recollect the circumstances in which
'my first application to you was made. Although I am at
'the present time a resident of Alexandria, yet I shall proba-
'bly in a few days, return to the north side of the Potomac.
'In my last conversation with Bishop Kemp, (more than a
'year ago,) he advised me to proceed in my studies until I
'should be ready for ordination; and said, that at that period,
'a proper course could be taken. Am I to understand that it
'is to be a matter of arrangement between Bishop Kemp and
'yourself? You will, Sir, have the goodness to advise me.
'as far as necessary, on this point.
  'I am, Right Rev. and Dear Sir,
    'With sincere respect and esteem,
      Your dutiful servant,
        'J. ASHMUN.
"*Right Rev. R. C. Moore.*"

In reply, Bishop Moore expressed doubts of the propriety of granting ordination to candidates not prepared to devote themselves entirely to the Ministry; but stated that he should be disposed to make an exception in favour of the present applicant, (his connection with the Repertory being limited to a short period,) provided a letter dismissory should be obtained from the Bishop of Maryland. But the object appears never further to have been prosecuted. The purposes of Mr. Ashmun again fluctuated; the embarrassed state of the pecuniary affairs of the Repertory, upon which alone he depended for support, required vigilant attention; and his engagement in the composition of a work which he hoped might prove advantageous to himself and of public utility, rendered his immediate introduction into the Ministry impossible.

There was an invisible Hand guiding the subject of this Memoir through all his uncertainties and perplexities; and which subsequently, when he had attained the height of his destiny, lifted the veil from the past, pointed out the windings of his way, and revealed to him the mysteries of Providence.

## CHAPTER V.

Numerous and various causes now united to prepare Mr. Ashmun for his great work in Africa. That at this time, he should have undertaken to write the Life of the Rev. Samuel Bacon, who had died in the first attempt to found a Colony of free persons of colour from the United States in Africa—that he should have accomplished this task under a painful weight of cares and anxieties, not only with energy, but enthusiasm, is remarkable: since, hardly any literary enterprise would have promised less of distinction or profit to the Author, and none, perhaps, contributed so effectually to qualify him for that station, which by providential and most unexpected events, he was soon to occupy. A Biography will seldom attract immediate and general notice, unless the subject, the author, or both, have excited beforehand, some public interest. Neither the varied and instructive history, the devoted piety, the affecting death of Bacon, nor the talents of Ashmun, could supply the want of celebrity. Mr. Bacon's course in

Africa, by which only he was extensively known, had been sad and brief, while Mr. Ashmun was a young man, just stepping forth alone, and a stranger, upon the open stage of life.

Enthusiastic as it was, he can hardly be believed, that he indulged large expectations of the success of this work. He engaged in it that he might render a just tribute of respect to an early martyr in the cause of African colonization ;* bring out in a clear light, from the retirements of individual experience, those traits of Christian character, which gave him strength in action, and support in adversity and in death; and thus animate American christians, by the power of his example, to prosecute and complete the work of justice and mercy (for which he had counted his life an unworthy sacrifice) towards a land the most suffering and outraged on earth.— In the salutary exercise of his intellectual powers, the prospect of some relief from pecuniary difficulties, and the hope of conferring a substantial benefit on a poor orphan boy, the son of Mr. Bacon, he found additional, though subordinate motives.

The encouraging intelligence communicated in the Report of Messrs. Mills and Burgess, who, under the authority of the American Colonization Society, in the year 1818, visited and explored the African coast, induced the Board of Managers to

* "To his visit to the Metropolis at this time, the writer of this Memoir is indebted, for the only opportunity he enjoyed, of cultivating with Mr. Bacon a personal intercourse. Short as the term of his stay was, it proved amply sufficient to discover to the observation of those with whom he associated, many of the estimable characteristics of his mind. Such was the simplicity of his manners, and the candour of his character, as to show out in the most natural expressions, the genuine qualities of the heart. The impression which these were capable of making on the mind of one, till then a stranger, has constituted his chief motive for engaging in the interesting labour of preparing for the world this humble memorial of his worth. It seeks no higher merit, than that of giving to one of the brightest examples of piety and Christian benevolence, in this age, a just exhibition.—*Life of Bacon, page 237–38.*

adopt early measures for selecting and sending out a company of free men of colour, disposed to become pioneers in the difficult enterprise, of laying upon that shore the foundations of a Christian Colony.

The President of the United States was authorized, by an Act of Congress of the 3d of March, 1819, to restore to their own country, any Africans captured from American or foreign vessels, attempting to introduce them into the United States, in violation of law, and to provide, by the establishment of a suitable agency on the African coast, for their reception, subsistence, and comfort, until they could return to their relatives, or derive support from their own exertions. Happily there existed between the Executive of the United States and the Managers of the Colonization Society, every disposition mutually to aid each other in effecting their objects in Africa, which, though distinct, were alike philanthropic, and to be accomplished far more easily by concerted, than by separate action. "It was determined to make the station of the Gov-
' ernment Agency, on the coast of Africa, the site of the Colo-
' nial Settlement; and to incorporate in the Settlement all the
' blacks delivered over by our ships of war to the American
' Agent, as soon as the requisite preparations should* be com-
' pleted for their accommodation."

In February, 1820, in the ship Elizabeth, chartered by the Government, Mr. Bacon embarked at New York, for Africa, as principal Agent of the United States, accompanied by John P. Bankson assistant, and Dr. Samuel A. Crozer, Agent of the American Colonization Society, and a company of eighty-eight emigrants, who, in consideration of their passage and other aid from Government, agreed to prepare, on such spot as might be selected, by the erection of suitable buildings, and the cultivation of the ground, for the reception of the Africans who might be delivered over to the protection of the Agent.

This expedition proceeded by way of Sierra Leone to the Island of Sherbro: the season of arrival was unhealthy, the emigrants were landed on low, alluvial ground, where, in the course of a few weeks, by exposure and disease, all the Agents and more than twenty of the emigrants perished. Many a heart was touched with sorrow at the event, and the light of many hopes grew dim.

The Life of Bacon is comprised in an octavo volume, of about three hundred pages. Of this, too large a portion, perhaps, relates to his youth, and to incidents and events in his history, unimportant in themselves, but which the Biographer has skillfully exhibited in many striking relations, and used as the connecting thread of his own thoughts and reflections. Interesting facts are stated in regard to the literary and religious Institutions of New England; discriminating observations on human nature enliven the narrative; which abounds every where with useful, and in some parts with original and profound remarks on the doctrines, experience, and practice of Christianity.

We are prompted to introduce select passages from this Memoir, as well from regard to the reputation of the author, and the moral beauty of the character he has portrayed, as that, by a few specimens the Public may be enabled to judge of the general merits of the work.

The Rev. Samuel Bacon was born in Sturbridge, Worcester County, Massachusetts, in 1781. His mother, of whom death deprived him in his early childhood, was a woman of a kind, pious, charitable, humble, and gentle spirit. His father was a man of strong understanding, good judgment, of a bold, enterprising, intrepid character; but of a rough and severe temper. The education of young Bacon, until his twentieth year, was almost wholly neglected; his attendance for a few weeks, at a grammar school, first excited in his mind an earnest desire for knowledge; which he resolved to gratify as soon as he should be released from parental restraint. No sooner had he become of age, than he devoted himself wholly to the pursuit of a liberal education; though he incurred thereby his father's displeasure, and became an exile from the home of his youth. By industry, perseverance, and the most rigid economy, he finally obtained an education at Harvard College. His exertions, privations, and confinement to study, injured his health; and his condition, during the last year of his College life, is thus described:

"It was in vain longer to struggle against his increasing
' and extreme debility, attended with some of the most alarm-
' ing symptoms of a pulmonary consumption. He tore him-
' self away from the scene of literary enchantment; and was
' enabled by the seasonable aid of some generous benefactor,
' to indulge himself for a few weeks, in several short excur-
' sions into the interior of New England. The change of
' objects, society, and air, and especially the release from the
' confinement and studies of College, thus obtained, produced
' a trifling abatement of the most dangerous symptoms of
' his complaint; and he revisited Cambridge in June, to at-
' tend the customary examination of the candidates for the
' first degree. * * He appears to have passed it with repu-
' tation. * * The commencement in September, when
' his class-mates received their degrees, he was not able, from
' his illness, to attend; and continued several months in a
' state of almost hopeless debility. He was entirely sensible
' of the dangerous character of the disorder, and of its almost
' certain termination in his dissolution. For several months
' he expected the event with confidence; but appears to have
' contemplated it with composure, and even indifference.—
' The tremendous prospect scarcely extorted a single cry for
' mercy, or excited a thought for the fate of his soul. This
' alarming destitution of feeling in an accountable and rational
' being, can easier be accounted for, than vindicated. His
' life had been uniformly, and in an uncommon degree, up-
' right, admitting the correctness of the standard of duty
' which he had adopted. He cheerfully recognised his obli-

'gations towards his fellow creatures, as far as their present
'convenience was concerned; and it was his pleasure to ful-
'fil them; but this was the limit of his benevolence, and of
'his most extended notion even of religious duty. His vast
'obligations to God, and the Saviour,—obligations enforced
'by all the goodness concerned in his creation, and preserva-
'tion, and all the grace displayed in his redemption, and
'which are comprehended in the summary injunctions of
'both departments of revelation, 'to love the Lord, with all
'the soul, the mind, and the strength,'—these obligations,
'even in the confident anticipation of an early call into the
'presence of his Creator, were wholly unfelt. Let it be re-
'collected that Mr. Bacon, at no period of his life, certainly
'not at the one now under review, was accustomed to restrain
'his reflections on other subjects, however grave and serious.
'On topics of this kind, from the natural sobriety of his cha-
'racter, and contemplative turn of his mind, his thoughts
'more readily dwelt than on any other. * * His case is a
'common one. Death, to the prosperous man of the world,
'is usually little more than the idea of his ceasing to enjoy
'the pleasures of life; to the tender husband or parent, its
'most appalling idea is that of his widowed and orphan fami-
'ly; to the rich, it is formidable as involving a new disposi-
'tion, or the dissipation of his estate; to the scholar, as the
'termination of his studies; but to the languid and suffering
'victim of a slow decay, it often presents itself as opening an
'obscure and gloomy but not unfriendly asylum, from the
'ravages of disease and pain. There is, indeed, an apparent
'variety in the views with which these different characters
'regard the awful close of their mortal existence. But sup-
'pose them uninfluenced by Christian principles, and they
'agree in more respects than they differ. Death itself, and
'its consequences, as they affect the soul, are regarded as lit-
'tle more than a final sleep, of no importance except as it al-
'ters their relation to the things of the present life. The

'convincing power of the divine Spirit, by discovering to the
'mind the purity and extent of the law of God, by impressing
'on the heart a sense of His holiness and justice, and arousing
'the conscience from its sleep, and false hope from its dreams
'of bliss, can introduce a new and awakening train of reflec-
'tions in the breast not of the dying only, but of the living.—
'Such a man can neither live nor die, without awful forebod-
'ings, and intolerable anguish of spirit, till he has some assu-
'rance that his condemnation is reversed, and his peace es-
'tablished in Heaven. Mr. Bacon was not so convinced, and
'saw the probable approach of the closing scene of his life
'without emotion. But his God was merciful. He had in
'reserve for him, blessings of which he had never even con-
'ceived the value. Towards the close of autumn the most
'formidable of his symptoms disappeared."

Having engaged in the study of the Law, and conducted, for a short season, a weekly newspaper in Worcester, Massachusetts, he was induced, by the flattering representations of a friend, and the hope of benefit, both to his health and spirits, from a milder climate, to visit Philadelphia, and establish a school in that City. His anticipations were not realized, nor did he derive any important assistance from his friend. His Biographer remarks :

"In this country, nothing can be more fallacious than the
'hopes excited in young men by the promises of patronage.
'In whatever department of life the proffered interest is to
'be exerted in their favour, the probable result is the same.
'The very constitution of our society renders the expectation
'of rising under individual patronage most precarious. No
'individual is secure for a day of being able to retain the in-
'fluence over any portion of the community, which he be-
'lieves himself to possess. He may, at any time, be required
'to struggle,—and struggle in vain, perhaps, with the popu-
'lar current, to maintain his own interest. The connexion
'from which a young man may have expected important be-

'nefits, so far from assisting, may thus come to prove the great-
'est detriment to his advancement. These remarks will be
'seen to have a special application to the profession of the
'law. But they must be true as general maxims, so long as
'society is young in America, and probably as long as the re-
'publican principles remains unchanged in the government,
'and so largely pervades all the inferior departments of the
'community. Success in no honorable pursuit can reasona-
'bly be anticipated on any other condition than that of the
'blessing of God, upon diligent, persevering, and upright in-
'dustry."

At this period, "a cheerless infidelity had usurped in his
'mind, the place of a resigned confidence in the guardianship
'of Heaven; and converted any just impressions of the doc-
'trine of a particular providence and agency that might re-
'main, into a source of dread, rather than of relief. But Re-
'ligion, at this time, afforded him about as little annoyance
'as peace. It was not the subject which occupied his atten-
'tion."

After having wandered on foot, in the winter, into the interior of Pennsylvania, and encountered and overcome many obstacles, Mr. Bacon opened a school in Lancaster, acquired reputation as a teacher, and for three years, exerted himself unremittingly, for the benefit of his pupils, (amounting sometimes to one hundred) and made large sacrifices to improve the system and raise the standard of education.

In 1812, he was appointed and accepted the office of a Second Lieutenant in the Marine Corps of the United States. Of a duel in which he was engaged with a brother officer, Mr. Ashmun remarks:

"Destitute of that inward fear of God, and that principle
'of obedience to His authority, which alone can render the
'soul superior to the tyrannical laws of a perverted and spu-
'rious honour; and a stranger to the power of divine grace
'in restraining the inordinate dominion of the passions, he

' was easily seduced by pride and resentment, to engage in a
' duel with an officer in the same corps, on the pretext of ter-
' minating some trivial disagreement. His antagonist in this
' rash and criminal enterprise, had formerly been one of his
' most intimate and confidential friends, to whom he had
' once regarded himself as under very particular obligations!
' Which of the parties was the aggressor, and deserved the
' severest reprehension, in the quarrel which led to this af-
' fair, is no part of the writer's object, and cannot be that of
' the Christian reader, to inquire. Suffice it to say, that Mr.
' Bacon lived to express the deepest abhorrence of the un-
' natural act, and to regard the individual who participated
' with him in the sin and the peril of it, with a feeling of af-
' fection and respect, which all the blood that has ever flowed
' in voluntary assassinations could never inspire. The wretch-
' edness of a common apostacy, and the blood of a univer-
' sal atonement, to the faith of a Christian, cannot fail to
' present such considerations as must bind him with the tie
' of essential brotherhood to every individual of his species.
' On the basis of this sublime view of the mutual relations of
' men, was Mr. Bacon's benevolence for all his fellow-men
' eventually established. Under the influence of this spirit,
· suppose him to receive an injury which should directly af-
' fect his character. Still, it must be a brother who inflicted
' it; and whom, because he *was his brother*, it would be im-
' possible for him to injure in return. Mr. Bacon's subse-
' quent detestation of the practice of duelling, was likewise
' founded on the knowledge which faith had revealed to him
' of the strictness and purity of God's holy laws, and the 'ex-
' ceeding sinfulness of sin.'"

His marriage in 1814, to Miss Anna Mary Barnitz, was productive of much happiness; but her death in 1815, overwhelmed him with unutterable distress. "He saw in the
' stroke, the hand of Omnipotence, and trembled. But he was
' neither humbled under it, nor constrained to withdraw his
' heart nor his confidence from the world."

In the latter part of the year 1816, Mr. Bacon became the subject of powerful religious impressions; and the terrors of conscience acting upon a system enfeebled by disease, led him for a time to expect a sudden death by the visitation of God. "His spirit (says his Biographer,) found no rest; it had re-
' ceived a wound, which every recollection aggravated, and
' all his attempts to heal, were worse than idle. The hand
' of the Almighty had inflicted it, and the remedy was only
' with Himself." In the anguish of his soul, he resorted for advice to a Minister of Christ.

" The Clergyman found it needful to appease the violent
' agitation of his mind; and afterwards imparted to him a
' variety of counsel; the purport of all which seems to have
' fallen much short of Mr. Bacon's expectations; and he re-
' turned disappointed and dejected. Perhaps no pastoral du-
' ty, not even that which the ordinary death-bed calls upon
' a minister to perform, is so awfully momentous, or so diffi-
' cult, as that of directing the mind of a convinced and tho-
' roughly awakened sinner into the narrow path of salvation.
' Advance, he must; and the very next step taken in such a
' crisis, may be decisive of his eternal doom. The skilful
' physician will endeavor to accommodate the advice afford-
' ed in different cases, to their respective circumstances; but
' the example of the primitive ministers of the gospel, and
' the very nature of the sinner's wants, unite in determining
' that counsel to be the safest; and generally far the most be-
' neficial, which shall most magnify the offices of the Saviour,
' and enforce an immediate recourse, by faith, to his cross.—
' The more intelligibly this act of faith can be explained to
' his mind, and the more essential to his salvation, it can be
' made to appear, the more efficacious, as a means of grace,
' the advice will be likely to prove. The inquirer himself,
' it is always to be presumed, is a very incompetent judge of
' the treatment best adapted to his own case. Mr. Bacon's
' disappointment, on this occasion, to whatever it might be
' owing, was probably serviceable to him: as it more effectu-

'ally taught him the fallacy of all expectations of relief not
'founded on the mercy and power of God alone. The peru-
'sal of 'Doddridge's Rise and Progress,' which was put into
'his hands at the time, was an important help; as by pre-
'serving him from absolute despair, it gave him the power of
'concentrating his thoughts without distraction, on the great
'doctrines of salvation.  *  *  *  *

"At what moment the gift of faith was first imparted, and
'his heart brought to bow with entire submission to the yoke
'of Christ, does not plainly appear. But, from the period to
'which this part of the narrative refers, he seems never, even
'for a day, to have remitted the pursuit of his salvation; and
'scarcely to have declined, by a single relapse, from those
'high attainments in faith and holiness, which he was ena-
'bled, through an abundant supply of grace, to make with a
'rapidity seldom exceeded by the most favoured Christian.—
'But it will be seen that the original corruptions of his heart
'were not at once eradicated, nor the current of habit revers-
'ed, by an absolute exertion of divine power. But grace
'eventually accomplished this work by engaging all the pow-
'ers of his mind in a long and arduous course of exertion,
'vigilance and self-denial. His conflicts were often sharp
'and painful: but commonly of momentary continuance.—
'The fervency of his prayers, and the habitual prevalence of
'a vigorous faith, gave him an easy and rapid conquest of
'his spiritual foes. Nearly every struggle against sin proved
'to him the occasion of a new victory over it, till, by a dispen-
'sation as merciful to him, as mournful to the world he left,
'he was early translated to the scene of his everlasting tri-
'umph."

For more than two years, from the period of his conversion to the faith of Christ, Mr. Bacon was almost exclusively
occupied in efforts to promote the cause of Sunday schools.
In July, 1819, it was stated in the Report of the Sunday
School Society in York, Pennsylvania, "That there were

'then thirty-three schools, employing about two hundred and
' twenty teachers, and containing two thousand two hundred
' scholars within the County. These, with a very few excep-
' tions, were all the fruits of Mr. Bacon's personal exertions,
' and owed much of their success, and the interest which they
' held in the public mind, to his efficient superintendence."—
The following extracts from this Biography, exhibit the elevated Christian character of this servant of God :

"Prayer has been significantly styled the natural respira-
' tion of the new-born soul ; and the gently distilling influ-
' ence of the divine Spirit, the etherial element on which it
' habitually feeds. The subject of this memoir has been seen
' in a laborious, but ineffectual struggle with the opposing
' principles of his nature, to hold himself to the stated perform-
' ance of this duty, even after long and frequent intervals of
' its allowed neglect. But now the holy work proceeds al-
' most without constraint, or interruption. Nearly every ex-
' pression of his feelings is blended with a fervent invocation
' to the Author of all spiritual influences, for an increase of
' those very desires which prompt his petitions. Commu-
' nion with God, through his Son, and by the Holy Spirit,[*] is
' now the most delightful, and therefore an uniform exercise
' of the soul. It is the highest end to which it aspires and an
' employment, in which could it be wholly absorbed, it would
' repose its tired energies with inconceivable delight.     *     *

"But the Saviour's benediction and promise, 'blessed are
' they that hunger and thirst after righteousness, for they
' shall be filled,' have their partial accomplishment in the
' present world. To very few could the qualification on
' which this promise depends, be appropriated with more
' manifest propriety, than to Mr. Bacon. The command of
' the Saviour, 'ask that your joy may be full,' was, likewise,
' through grace, in a good degree obeyed by him. He was

[*] Eph. II. 18.

'incessant in his petitions for this very blessing. Why is it,
'that the doctrine of the divine influence on the minds of the
'saints, has fallen in this age, if not into partial discredit, yet
'into so low and restricted a practical use, among those who
'are most interested in it? The orthodox cannot, indeed,
'disbelieve the promises which relate to so great a blessing;
'the doctrine is retained in all our formularies of faith; but
'why is it not more valued? Why are the blessings which it
'implies, so remissly sought,—and so little expected? Next
'to the truth, that our redemption has been effected by the
'blood of the Son of God, none more deeply concerns our
'blind and corrupted race, than that of the purchase and
'mission of the Holy Spirit to purify our hearts, bring down
'a foretaste of Heaven into our souls, and enlighten our un-
'derstandings to comprehend the divine mysteries of the gos-
'pel. No promises are more intelligible and express, than
'those which relate to this inestimable privilege of believ-
'ers. * * Had every professing Christian afforded in his
'own example, the same practical illustration of the nature
'and extent of the operations of the Spirit on the heart, as
'the subject of this memoir, not only would its opposers be
'silenced, but so illustrious a feature of our holy religion
'would impart to the whole system, in the view of the world,
'a glory which it has never exhibited since the age of the
'apostles. * * * * * *

"Mr. Bacon's very theory in religion, may be properly
'termed, practical. He could conceive of nothing that de-
'served the name which did not comprehend love to God,
'faith in the Saviour, and charity to men,—each manifesting
'itself in its appropriate fruits. Hence, the barriers which
'some others choose to throw around themselves, and the
'members of their own particular religious sect, and which
'are sustained chiefly by certain verbal definitions of subor-
'dinate points of faith, were to him unknown; and unless

'interposed by the bigotry of others, in a manner that obliged them to be felt, were wholly disregarded."

In November, 1818, while arguing a cause, Mr. Bacon was insulted by his opponent at the Bar, and charged with falsehood. Having noted this in his Journal, he adds:

"The time was, when I should have instantly seized a 'deadly weapon on such an occasion ; and suffered nothing 'but blood to atone for the indignity:—I acknowledge it 'with remorse and shame. But, thank God, I have no dis- 'position now to injure any man. Several gentlemen of the 'bar have taken advantage of my religion, more than once, 'when I fully believed, and do still believe, that I was stating 'the truth, to call me a liar.' They all know that if I were a 'sinner like themselves, or if I were as once I was, they 'would as soon have eaten coals of fire, as accused me to my 'face of 'lying.' But they know also, that my nature is now 'changed, and that my religion, and my dispositions forbid 'my retaliating evil for evil: I thank God he holds the reins 'of my passions in his own hand, and all this abuse is not 'suffered to make me angry. I receive these things as a part 'of that persecution with which I have laid my account as 'the portion of 'all who will live godly in Christ Jesus.''

We would gladly, did our limits permit, introduce much larger portions of this valuable Memoir. The account of Mr. Bacon's reflections in view of the Ministry, and his ultimate decision to devote himself to this work, is highly interesting. He was ordained a Deacon in the Protestant Episcopal Church by the Rt. Rev. Bishop of Philadelphia, on the 6th of September, 1819. He devoted himself to his work with the zeal of an Apostle. He immediately entered, for a few weeks, into the service of the Philadelphia Bible Society ; and in the brief space of sixty-nine days, passed through twenty-one counties of Pennsylvania, preached seventy-four discourses, and travelled more than one thousand miles.

In January, 1820, he visited Washington, and received his appointment for Africa. He had been long a warm and active friend to the people of colour, and from its origin, to the American Colonization Society.*

Having visited his relatives and friends in Pennsylvania, for the last time, he superintended the embarkation of the emigrants at New York; from which port, he sailed on the 7th of February. After a short but agreeable visit to Sierra Leone, he proceeded with the entire company of emigrants to Sherbro, where they had obtained permission to reside until an eligible site for the proposed Settlement could be purchased on the mainland. It was soon found to be the policy of the native Chiefs to embarrass and postpone any final negotiations for lands, that they might compel the Agent to comply with their exorbitant demands. The fever seized upon all the Agents, with the exception of Mr. Bacon, and became general among the settlers. His situation, at this crisis, is thus described:

"To a person placed in Mr. Bacon's circumstances, at this
' period, and actuated by his disinterested and benevolent
' spirit, it is not to be supposed, that a prudential regard for
' his own health, would occur with sufficient force, to occa-
' sion any relaxations in his attentions to others. The fol-
' lowing enumeration of duties which he undertook at this
' time daily to perform, shows, but too clearly, that he im-
' posed upon himself a task, to which human strength is ut-
' terly unequal. Some of the privations and labours to
' which he submitted, manifestly appear to have been impru-

* Mr. Bacon had for several years, been a useful member of the Abolition Society of Pennsylvania. His benevolence was, however, of too disinterested a character, to suffer him to withhold, from any good cause, the support and patronage which he could afford it. At an early period of the operations of the Colonization Society, he perceived that their measures were inspired by the same philanthropic principle, as those of the Abolition Society; and conceived them to be much more practicable, more systematic, and equally expansive in their final objects.—*Ashmun's Life of Bacon*, p. 154.

'dent and unnecessary. But it would be improper too se-
'verely to censure in him a fault which few besides would be
'liable to commit. 'Who can describe the burden under
'which I am obliged to struggle, in feeding this people,—en-
'during their complaints,—listening to their tales of trouble,
'—inquiring into their sufferings,—administering medicine,
'—labouring with my own hands in building houses for
'them,—and toiling at the oar, and handling casks, in un-
'loading the vessel and landing the goods!—In addition to
'all this, I have the spiritual concerns of the whole company
'to look after. I go without stockings, entirely,—often with-
'out shoes;—scarcely wear a hat, and am generally without
'a coat;—I am up early, and not in bed until ten, or eleven
'o'clock. I eat little, and seldom use any other refreshments
'except hard ship-bread, salt meat and water.' 'I labour
'more,—am more exposed to heat, and wet, and damp, and
'hunger, and thirst, than any one; and yet, blessed be God,
'I continue in health.' 'In addition to all this, I have the
'weight of the whole interest on my mind :—all the care,—
'all the responsibility,—all the anxiety. But God be praised,
'I have peace within.' 'There are eight entire families sick,
'amongst whom there is not one able to dress his own food,
'or wait upon a child. Oh God, who *can* help, but thou.'

"'Is it asked, do I yet say 'colonize Africa?' I reply, yes.
'He that has seen ninety native Africans landed together in
'America, and remarked the effects of the change of climate
'through the first year, has seen them as sickly as these.—
'Every sudden and unnatural transition produces illness.—
'The surprising fertility of the African soil, the mildness of
'the climate, during a great part of the year, the numerous
'commercial advantages, the stores of fish, and herds of ani-
'mals, to be found here, invite her scattered children home.—
'As regards myself, I counted the cost of engaging in this
'service before I left America. I came to these shores *to die;*
'and any thing better than death is better than I expect.'"

In the midst of the general distress, Mr. Bacon felt the approaches of disease.

"He distinctly expressed more concern on account of the
' sufferings of the people, and the darkening prospects of the
' enterprise, than on account of his own illness. In contem-
' plating his own death, he saw little, except a bright and
' boundless expanse of glory piercing with its light the gloom
' which hung over the dying scene. But his heart was wrung
' with the anticipation of the event, as it would affect the
' welfare of the colonists, and the success of the expedition.
' On this theme he had vented his feelings in the most pathetic
' language. But even in this heaviest, and doubtless his last
' trial, he found relief by a vigorous effort of faith in the mer-
' cy of God; and by ultimately confiding in the wisdom and
' righteousness of all his purposes."

At this gloomy period, a Schooner belonging to the Colonial Government of Freetown, touched at Sherbro, and consented, at the request of Mr. Bacon, who was without medical aid, and extremely ill, to receive him on board the next morning, and convey him to Sierra Leone. As the boat containing him approached this vessel at the appointed time, she hoisted her anchor, and put to sea. He attempted to overtake her, but it was impossible. For two days was he exposed, in an open boat, to the burning rays of a tropical sun. On the evening of the 30th of April, he was landed at Cape Shilling, an English settlement, and very hospitably received by Captain William Randle, the superintendent of the station. But no kindness could save him from the stroke of death.—No language can here be more pertinent than that of his Biographer.

"During the next day, he was able to recline for short in-
' tervals on a sofa; and to take a small part in the conversa-
' tion. But his disorder was hastening rapidly to a fatal ter-
' mination. He perceived it, and expressed in the intervals
' of his sensibility, his acquiescence in the sovereign pleasure

' of God. The cause in which he had embarked retained a
' strong interest in his affections to the last. In his last con-
' versation, he feebly asked, ' Dear Brother Randle, do you not
' think we have happiness reserved that will———?' As the
' interrogatory was unfinished, the gentleman to whom it was
' addressed, did not immediately reply ; when Mr. Bacon con-
' tinued, ' What do you say to my question ?' A hope was
' then expressed, that the Saviour would reserve for both, a
' happiness which should abundantly compensate their pres-
' ent sufferings. He replied, and they were some of his last
' words, 'Ah ! that is all I want.'

"This last effort of reason and speech took place about
' eleven o'clock on the night of the 1st of May. The lan-
' guid current of life ebbed gradually away, until half past
' four, on the following morning, when he expired. His re-
' mains were interred on the same day, in the burial ground
' attached to the church in the settlement ; and though depos-
' ited by the hands of strangers, on a foreign and pagan shore,
' they rest under the sure protection of the Christian's Saviour,
' and in 'the certain hope of a glorious resurrection.'

" In his person, Mr. Bacon was tall ; the structure of his
' frame was masculine, and rather indicative of strength,
' than characterized by symmetry of proportion. His features
' were strongly marked; and the expression of his counte-
' nance blended an interesting pensiveness with the lineaments
' of an intelligent and vigorous mind. His attachments were
' ardent ; his passions quick and violent; and his friendships
' affectionate and permanent. He was impatient of opposi-
' tion, rapid in his movements, and determined in his purpo-
' ses. Inflexible integrity, unbounded generosity, and a sin-
' cerity incapable of disguise, run through the entire texture
' of his character.

" His learning was various, and his taste classical ; but the
' first was not profound, nor the last exact. His legal ac-
' quirements were all of the useful kind ; his standing at

'the bar respectable; and his professional reputation in-
'creasing.

"By regeneration, every constitutional excellence was
'heightened, and a foundation laid for those pre-eminent spir-
'itual attainments, in which he had few equals,—perhaps no
'superiors. His zeal has been seen to be ardent; his devotion
'entire; his hopes, elevated to sublimity; and his faith invin-
'cible. The love and fear of God tempered together in just
'proportions, formed the prevalent feeling of his heart; his
'very thoughts were prayer; his habit of obedience to the
'divine laws, prompt and unhesitating; and his 'love of the
'christian brotherhood, unfeigned.' The mystery of 'God
'manifest in the flesh,' and the character, work and offices of
'the Redeemer, formed the theme of his untiring admiration,
'his incessant rejoicing, his increasing gratitude, and his high-
'est praise. In the service of such a Master, enforced by
'such motives, his talents, health, and life, were regarded as
'infinitely too cheap an offering. To him they were all de-
'liberately consecrated: for him, they were all cheerfully re-
'signed. And his memory shall be blessed. The American
'church will long cherish it with affection: and it shall here-
'after freshen in the hearts of millions in another hemis-
'phere, when the work in which he fell shall have its con-
'summation in the civilization of Africa, the return of all her
'exiles, and the subjection of a countless population to the
'dominion of CHRIST."

In the composition of this work, Mr. Ashmun exhibited remarkable diligence and self-control; constantly fortifying himself by the exercise of his intellectual and moral faculties against circumstances well adapted to break his spirit and lay its honours in the dust. He was not indifferent or insensible to present things, but felt their inferiority to those of the future; nor could objects finite, brief, perishing, fill that eye, to which Faith had revealed the infinite and eternal glories of the Spiritual Universe.

A respected friend,* in whose family Mr. Ashmun resided as an inmate for nearly two years, in Washington, has favoured me with the following observations on his character and habits, and particularly as these were evinced in his preparation of the Life of Bacon :

"Mr. Ashmun was naturally of a weakly constitution, and 'predisposed to pulmonary disease : and although the preser-'vation of his health required great caution and prudence 'against undue labor and exposure to the variable climate 'and weather of this City, yet such was the warmth of his 'zeal in the prosecution of any favourite object, and such his 'persevering labours in surmounting all difficulties in his 'way, that the very exertions which he put forth for the ac-'complishment of his purpose, seemed to subserve the dou-'ble purpose of imparting stimulus to his weak system, and 'additional fortitude to sustain him under extraordinary ef-'forts.

" In proportion to the magnitude of the object he proposed 'to effect, he successfully rallied the energies of his mind 'and body, nor relaxed for a moment, until the work was 'done.'

"This determination of purpose was strikingly manifested 'in the manner and circumstances in which he wrote the 'Memoir of the Rev. Samuel Bacon.

"He had been requested, by the brother of the deceased, to 'perform this arduous task ; and being put in possession of 'the necessary documents for that purpose, he entered upon 'the execution of it with all that ardour and unyielding per-'severance so peculiar to his character.

" After he had arranged the materials for the work, he used 'often to shut himself in his room, and for days could be 'seen only at his meals. And more, during the short days 'of winter, rather than be interrupted by a regular atten-

---

* The Rev. William Hawley.

'dance on the meals of the family, he would often direct the 'servant to prepare him a cold collation for the day; and by 'the dawn of the morning, whether there were rain, hail, or 'sunshine, be on his way to his study, on Pennsylvania Ave-'nue, (about half a mile distant) where he would remain un-'til ten at night, unceasingly occupied in the work in which 'he had engaged.

"He had at this time charge of the 'Washington Theologi-'cal Repertory;' in the Editorial department of which, he 'took an active part, and furnished many important and use-'ful papers. As a scholar and author, there was something 'very peculiar in his composition, and preparation for the 'press. He always wrote very fast, and sometimes very con-'fusedly; throwing upon paper, as it were, the first concep-'tions of his mind on the subject; and he then revised and re-'viewed, cut and carved it to suit his taste, often transposing 'whole sentences and paragraphs, and erasing and interlin-'ing to an incredible extent. He erased and corrected more 'than any person I have known.\* The manuscript papers 'of the Memoir, now in my possession, are a great curiosity.

"In his intercourse with the family, he was uniformly kind, 'affectionate, and courteous, and left on the minds of all, an 'impression highly favourable to his general worth and ex-'cellence of character."

Of this Memoir, two thousand copies were published; distinguished Clergymen recommended the work; Mr. Ashmun visited Baltimore, Philadelphia, and New York, and attempted to dispose of it; but the sales were very limited, and the Author found to his regret, that the effort from which he had expected relief, had increased his difficulties. He now felt the pressure of heavy debts on account of the Repertory,

---

\* We think this remark must be limited to his *earlier productions for the press*, since most of his Journals, written in Africa, exhibit few alterations. He was not easily satisfied with his own works, and was constantly disciplining his mind for greater objects than he had yet achieved.

which from its origin he had sought rather to render able and useful, than of advantage to himself.

A misunderstanding between him and the gentlemen, his associates in superintending the publication, relating to its pecuniary management, exposed his conduct to suspicion, and added to the perplexity of his affairs. Reserved both by inclination and habit on matters of private concern, he perhaps sometimes was silent, when he should have made explanation; and while acting in his integrity, forgot what discretion would have dictated, as due to the opinions of others. A failure to meet engagements for the Repertory might, it was thought, injure the entire character of the work, since the separation of the pecuniary and Editorial responsibilities, and their independence of each other, had doubtless escaped generally public attention. The disapprobation of friends, the reproaches of creditors, and worse than either, a conviction that it was impossible for him, in the situation he then occupied, speedily to extricate himself from embarrassment, were bitter ingredients in his daily cup. But he bowed his head to no useless sorrow. He was calm, uncomplaining, and active. He knew that to seek sympathy, is generally to lose in respect, more than is gained in compassion; and that for a wounded spirit, the only remedy is divine. No mortal eye can penetrate those deep and secret places of the heart, where griefs spring up and are nourished from the very fountains of life. Some such were rooted, perhaps, in the soul of Ashmun.* Some barbed thoughts were there, some dark ima-

---

\* On one of the leaves of his Journal, we find the following lines :
>There lives on earth a form, whose name
>Deep in this heart must buried rest;
>Whose lov'd remembrance pours a flame
>Of wasting anguish thro' my breast:
>A strong enchantment wraps the scene,
>Though mem'ry views it with despair;
>Nor floods nor mountains stretch'd between,
>Nor time arrests its visits there.

ginings of perished hope and broken joys, some gentle echoes of a voice now dead, some gleams reflected from a sun now set, but they were buried in his bosom alone, as in the vaults of a sepulchre. He braced his soul for duty; he walked before men, as one who was with them for high purposes; he sought help from God, and confided in his Providence; and like the father of the faithful, called to go out from his country and kindred, he obeyed, and went out, not knowing whither he went.

## CHAPTER V.

As Christians, we cannot doubt that the Almighty, in the permission of great moral evils and the miseries which ensue, not less than in the provision and application of their appropriate remedies, designs to teach His people salutary lessons, and discipline them for their immortal state. In the fury of human passions, the concussions and convulsions of human society, is seen the nature of vice; while in the calm pursuits and meek and united devotions of a happy people, stands in contrast the mighty principle of virtue,—both illustrating by their opposite effects, the benevolence and justice of the Divine Government. History reports the trial of human nature, of all gradations of intellectual advancement, in all countries, circumstances, and times. And by the experience of ages, are we taught to centre in the Christian Religion, all our hopes of the permanent peace, liberty, and happiness of mankind.

Slavery existed among all the nations of antiquity; the

right of the victor to the person or even to the life of the vanquished, universally admitted in ancient times, was its main source; it increased with the growth of nations and the multiplication of wars, until in the Roman Empire, during her most powerful period, one half (sixty millions) of her population, wore the yoke of a cruel and ignominious bondage. In the less civilized nations of Europe, a policy more humane than the Roman, could not be expected; and the institution of slavery every where prevailed among those who finally invaded the Territories, dissolved the Government, and shared among themselves the vast dominions of Rome.

Christianity though designed and adapted to introduce perfect principles of benevolence into universal society; to remedy its moral evils by the gentlest process; to mould its Institutions into the noblest forms, and control them by the best spirit; encountered the pride, selfishness, and obduracy of the human heart; all the combinations of established interest, authority, and power. When we consider that this Religion made her way, not by force, but persuasion; that she sought dominion only over the reason, conscience, and will of man; accepted an imperfect, if a sincere obedience; wrought to improve the whole character and condition of mankind, not by the violence of sudden revolution, but by the regeneration of individual souls; by the insinuation of right principles and the infusion of a pure spirit into the general mass, we cannot be surprised that slavery should have long withstood her power. Yet, from the first, "the humane spirit of this Religion struggled with the maxims and manners of the world, and contributed more than any other circumstance, to introduce the practice of manumission."* The friends of man can never thunder forth too frequently nor too loudly, in the ears of those who would quote Scripture in justification of slavery; that it was Christianity which ameliorated the con-

* Robertson.

dition of slaves under the Roman Government; inclined Constantine to render their manumission much easier than formerly; and which, "in conformity with its principles, claims the merit of having gone farthest towards the abolition of this debasing institution," throughout nearly all Europe. "In
' the opinion of Grotius, it was the great and almost the only
' cause of abolition. The professed and assigned reasons for
' most of the charters of manumissions, from the time of Gre-
' gory the Great, to the thirteenth century, were the religious
' and pious considerations of the fraternity of men, the imita-
' tion of the example of Christ, the love of our Maker, and the
' hope of redemption. Enfranchisement was frequently given
' upon a death-bed, as the most acceptable service that could
' be offered; and when the sacred character of the Priesthood
' came to obtain more universal veneration, to assume its func-
' tions, was the immediate passport to freedom."*

* The following extracts from Ward's Law of Nations, are too interesting to be omitted:

"We have seen in a former chapter, the universal existence of slavery during the earlier ages, and it was shown to be chiefly owing to the efforts of Christianity, that the institution was abolished. In the attempt to effectuate the abolition, and the success which in the end attended it we have a full proof of the *general* influence of this religion upon the mind, since no passage of the New Testament has absolutely *forbidden* the custom; and it is merely, therefore, from the spirit of the system of morality there displayed, that men collected what ought to be their conduct in this respect. Commanded to look upon all mankind as their brethren, it wanted little combination of the reasoning faculties, to discover that it was incompatible with such an injunction, to hold them in chains, exclusive of the benevolent effects upon the heart, which this religion was calculated, *generally* to produce, and which, when produced, did that from analogy, which was not expressly commanded. After this, and what was said in the beginning of this section, it is of little consequence to object that the custom of slavery remained for a great length of time, or that the church itself was possessed of numbers of slaves. We have shown that the custom of enfranchisement, was the effect, chiefly, of pious and Christian motives, and that the example was generally set by the ministers of religion. No law, it must be owned, is to be met with, by which the custom was abolish-

While beneath the light and power of Christianity, the last vestiges of slavery were well nigh effaced from the soil of Christendom; the African slave trade arose, which, whether regarded as productive of crime or misery, stands an evil unparalleled in the annals of the world. That nations which from considerations of humanity and piety, had abolished slavery, should lend their sanction to this atrocious commerce, would be inexplicable, did we not recollect the new World just brought to light by the genius of Columbus, and that the temptations of gain in supplying labourers for her vast and fertile fields, overcame alike the remonstrances of reason and of conscience.

Early in the fifteenth century, the Portuguese under authority from the Pope, explored the African coast, planted colonies, and reduced the Africans to slavery. Their exam-

ed all at once, nor could such a law have ever been justified: I do not mean on account of the claims of the rights of property, (which, if they are incompatible with divine institutions, should never be so much considered as to retard their effect) but on the principles of the very benevolence, which it was meant to consult; for the men who would have been the object of it, being thus thrown suddenly on the world, without protection or the means of support, would have been put in a worse condition than they were in before. It must be owned, also, that avarice, and the love of absolute dominion, might have thrown considerable obstacles in the way of abolition. When *Saurez* marks the difference which he very justly holds, between the law of nature, and the law of nations, he adduces among other proofs, the abolition of slavery as arising from the positive institution of the *Christian* church.

But nothing on this subject can be more forcible than the language of the learned Sir Thomas Smith, speaking of bondage and bondmen:—" Howbeit," says he, since our realme hath received the Christian, which maketh us all in Christ *brethren*, and in respect of God and Christ, *conservos:* men beganne *to have conscience,* to hold in captivitie and such extreme bondage, him whom they must acknowledge to be their brother; and as wee used to terme him *Christian;* that is, who looketh in Christ, and by Christ, to have equal portion with them in the gospel and salvation. Upon this scruple, the holy fathers and friars, in their confessions, and specially in their extreme and deadly sicknesses, burthened the consciences of them whom they had in their hands; so that temporal men, by little and little, by reason of that terror in their conscience, were glad to manumitte all their villanies.' "—*From Ward's Law of Nations.*

ple excited all the maritime powers of Europe to engage in the slave trade, which soon became a source of wealth and a subject for negotiation between nations, and which prosecuted for three centuries, is believed to have consigned more than twenty millions of unfortunate Africans to bondage or death.*

Among the circumstances of this trade, are found whatever is dark in treachery, or odious in cruelty, or horrible in war ; whatever afflicts the body, or degrades and tortures the mind ; in fine, whatever has been feared or imagined of evil in the cup of human life.†

---

\* " The wholesome decrees of five successive Roman Pontiffs granted, conveyed and confirmed to the most faithful King a right to *appropriate* the kingdoms, goods, and possessions of all infidels, wherever to be found, *to reduce their persons to perpetual slavery,* or *destroy* them from the earth, for the declared purpose of bringing the Lord's sheep into one dominical fold, under one universal Pastor. \* \* \* We suppose, then, that eight millions of slaves have been shipped in Africa for the West India Islands and the United States; ten millions for South America, and perhaps two millions have been taken and held in slavery in Africa. Great Britain and the United States have shipped about five millions, France two, Holland and other nations one ; though we undertake not to state the proportion with exactness. The other twelve millions we set to Portugal. Twenty million slaves at £30 sterling each, amount to the commercial value of £600,000,000. *Six hundred times ten hundred thousand pounds sterling traffic in the* SOULS OF MEN.

"By whom hath this commerce been opened, and so long and ardently pursued ? The subjects of their *most Faithful, most Catholic, most Christian, most Protestant* Majesties, *defenders of the faith ;* and by the citizens of the *most republican* States, with the sanction of *St. Peter's* successor."—*Dr. James Dana's Discourse on the African Slave trade,* 1790.

† " Freighted with curses was the Bark that bore
　　The Spoilers of the West to Guinea's shore ;
　　Heavy with groans of anguish blew the gales
　　That swell'd that fatal bark's returning sails."
" Loud and perpetual o'er the Atlantic waves,
　　For guilty ages, roll'd the tide of Slaves ;
　　A tide that knew no fall, no turn, no rest,—
　　Constant as day and night from East to West,
　　Still wid'ning, deep'ning, swelling in its course
　　With boundless ruin and resistless force."—MONTGOMERY.

At an early period, and under the authority of English law, slaves were introduced into the American colonies; in some cases, in utter disregard of remonstrances addressed by the people of those colonies, to the Parliament and the Throne.

Slavery grew with our growth; it soon became interwoven with all the interests and habits of society; and our fathers at the commencement of the Revolutionary contest, found the evil too deep-rooted, extensive and complicated, to admit, in their judgment, at that season of peril to their own liberties, of a remedy. They felt that it was an institution at variance with their whole political creed; that morally wrong in its origin, it could be perpetuated only by the violation of all justice, and in contempt of all charity; but they consoled themselves with the reflection that it had been forced upon them, and that while the removal of it suddenly, in that time of general agitation and distress, was impossible, it might be effected (should their independence be secured) during a calm and prosperous state of the public affairs.

They perceived, however, that even then homage was due to consistency of principle, and to the general opinion of mankind.

"The confederated colonies did not confine themselves to
' the assertion of the broadest theory of political rights; they
' descanted upon the topics of philanthropy and universal jus-
' tice, of Christian charity and humility; and in reproaching
' the mother country with the contrariety between her prac-
' tice and professions, with her insensibility to human suffering
' and degradation, they took credit to themselves for the re-
' verse. It was in alleged pursuance of those high considera-
' tions and pretensions to which I have adverted, that their
' Delegates in Congress, without being specially empowered,
' passed and promulgated several months before the Declara-
' tion of Independence, (6th April, 1776,) a resolution that no
' slaves should be imported into any part of the confederation."*

* Free remarks on the spirit of the Federal Constitution. Philadelphia, 1819.

The ordinance of 1787, prohibiting slavery or involuntary servitude in the North-west Territory; the restriction of the right to recover therefrom fugitive slaves to the *original* States; the exclusion of the word slave from the Constitution; the early enactments for the suppression of the slave trade; the delegation by the Constitution to Congress of the power to regulate the commerce between the States;* and the recorded sentiments of many of the great men who laid the foundations of our National Government, all show a desire to confine slavery within the smallest possible limits; to adapt legislative measures in such manner as to extend the funda-

---

* The Constitution declares "that the migration or importation of such persons as any of the States, *now existing*, shall think proper to admit, shall not be prohibited by the Congress, prior to the year 1808." It is most manifest that the Constitution does contemplate, in the very terms of this clause, that Congress possess the authority to prohibit the migration or importation of slaves; for it limits the exercise of this authority for a specific period of time, leaving it to its full operation ever afterwards. And this power seems necessarily included in the authority which belongs to Congress, "to regulate commerce with foreign nations *and among the several States.*" No person has ever doubted that the prohibition of the foreign slave trade was completely within the authority of Congress, since the year 1808. And why? Certainly only because it is embraced in the regulation of *foreign commerce;* and if so, it may for the like reason be prohibited since that period, between the States.

Commerce in slaves since the year 1808, being as much subject to the regulation of Congress as any other commerce, if it should see fit to enact that no slave should ever be sold from one State to another, it is not perceived how its constitutional right to make such provision could be questioned.—*Memorial (reported by Daniel Webster and others) of the inhabitants of Boston, to Congress,* 1819.

"Mr. Madison stated, in the Virginia Convention, that the restriction upon Congress, in regard to the suppression of the slave trade, was a "restraint on the exercise of a power expressly delegated to Congress, namely, that of regulating commerce with foreign nations." Governor Randolph made the same allegation (p. 428, Virginia Debates). The general act of Congress of 1807, suppressing the slave trade, shows a sense of an entire control over the domestic commerce in slaves, by the regulations which it makes respecting their transportation coastwise. The exception made in favor of internal transportation would have been wholly superfluous, had not a constitutional power been felt to exist."—*Free Remarks, &c.*

mental principles of civil and religious liberty; to express a deep sense of the importance of those principles ; and finally, to lend no sanction, even by a word, to the morality of a system, which long established in some of the States, (free and independent up to the time when the Union was formed,) it was necessary to *recognize*, but not to *approve.*

It is a subject for everlasting regret, that public sentiment in some States (particularly in South Carolina and Georgia)\* at the time of the adoption of the Federal Constitution, was unprepared to accede to the immediate abolition of the slave trade ;† or to measures for the ultimate removal of slavery ; objects then desired by a large portion of the American people, neither at that time, difficult of accomplishment, and which are now known to have been demanded by a wise regard to the public interest, as well as the more solemn considerations of national duty.

The Federal Constitution was the result of a compromise between the North and the South. " The Southern States," said Mr. Madison, " would not have entered into the union of ' America, without the temporary permission of the slave ' trade." When the Constitution was submitted, the great question to be decided was, whether a union on such terms were as satisfactory to the several States concerned, as would

---

\* The two States mentioned in the text, Georgia and South Carolina, were particularly averse to any interference with the slave trade, on the part of the Federal Government. In the convention, most of the States were anxious to insert a provision authorizing the immediate total abolition of the diabolical traffic. This was resisted, peremptorily by the two just mentioned ; and the compromise was at length effected, which is found in the ninth section of the first article of the Constitution.—*Free Remarks, &c.*

†Alluding to the restraint put upon the prohibition of this trade by the Constitution, a Society for the abolition of slavery, in Baltimore, in their address to Congress in 1791, hold the following language:

" Whilst we deem this restraint a temporary sanction to the partial infraction of the rights of man, recognized by the laws of some of the States, and so far a defect in the noble structure of our liberties, yet such is our regard to the original solemn compact of society, that we solicit no deviation from the principles established by it."

produce a preponderating good? The States being all free and independent, no one could, in any sense, be answerable for any injustice in the legal code of another; nor can we perceive that the law of conscience could, independent of circumstances, impose an obligation upon a State, in which there was no legalized injustice to refuse to unite for purposes of general utility, with a State in which the existence of such injustice could not be denied.

At the time the Constitution of the United States was established, the necessities of our country urgently demanded a new form of Government. Unanimity in the adoption of it was justly considered as a matter of the first importance.—Many of those who gave their support to the Constitution, while they saw with regret, that it recognized moral wrong in the laws of some of the States, felt that circumstances were imperious, and did it with the hope and belief, that the National Union would favour the cause of general liberty; and that the system of slavery would be abolished at no distant period, in all the States, either by the sense of duty, the influence of example, the inducement of interest, or by all combined. They could not believe that the eyes of any free and Christian community, especially in this country, could long be closed to that light of truth beginning even then to be widely diffused, which revealed the utter condemnation of slavery as a permanent institution. But they felt, that the main responsibility touching this subject, was with those States who reserved to themselves the sovereign and exclusive right to regulate and control it within their respective limits.

It deserves notice, that in the year 1776, memorable on account of the Declaration of our National Independence, a motion was made in the British House of Commons to this purport,—that the slave trade is contrary to the laws of God and the rights of man. It is remarkable, likewise, that the year 1787 gave establishment both to our Federal Constitu-

tion, and to the Committee in London for the abolition of the slave trade; that during this year the foundations of the Sierra Leone Colony were laid, and that through the efforts of Anthony Benezet and others, it could then first be said, that "not a single slave remained in possession of any acknow-
' ledged Quaker in America."*

The spirit of the reformation was the spirit of freedom.— From the time when the Bible was sent forth in a popular language, this spirit began to revive in Europe; and immediately before our Revolution, the advocates of universal humanity and general liberty, had by their writings made a deep impression upon the public mind in England and America.— Their divinely tempered weapons from the armory of God, threw the brightness of the sun into the dark mazes and defences of political wickedness, and the strong holds of despotic power.

It should be engraven upon our memories, that some of the main principles, relied on by our fathers, to justify their National Independence, were the same relied on (not in vain) to overthrow the slave trade, and which the friends of man have long regarded as of sufficient power, gradually, to subvert and destroy all institutions limiting the intelligence, debasing the character, or darkening the hopes of men.

"If" (said Congress, July 6th, 1775, in setting forth the causes for war against the parent country) "it were possible
' for men who exercise their reason to believe, that the Divine
' Author of our existence intended a part of the human race
' to hold an absolute property in, and unbounded power over
' others, marked out by infinite goodness and wisdom as the
' objects of a legal domination, never rightfully resistable,
' however severe and oppressive, the inhabitants of these colo-
' nies might at least require from the Parliament of Great
' Britain, some evidence that this dreadful authority over
' them, has been granted to that Body.

* Life of Granville Sharp.

"But a reverence for our great Creator, principles of hu-
' manity and the dictates of common sense, must convince
' all those who reflect upon the subject, that Government was
' instituted to promote the welfare of mankind, and ought to
' be administered for the attainment of that end."

The great truth briefly expressed by our Saviour, *that between man and man, in all possible circumstances, there exists the obligation of a reciprocal benevolence—a benevolence not occasional and narrow, but constant and large as self-love*, gleams forth from the discussions of the Revolutionary period as an acknowledged general light and law of humanity exactly adapted to produce all that happiness among men, which can consist with our present physical condition and the arrangements and ordinations of Providence.

Motives of interest and duty conspired to hasten the abolition of slavery in several of the Northern States; and the growing sense of humanity and religion produced numerous manumissions in the States of the South, so that a class of free people of colour arose and greatly increased. Few in numbers compared with the whites; distinguished from them by complexion, but allied thereby, and by habits and recollections to the slaves; poor and uneducated, and frequently exposed to the "contempt of the proud," though *legally* free, they realize the entanglements of a degrading and rigorous bondage. Not only prejudices, but circumstances, and the very state of society are against them. Worthless is all liberty which neither frees the spirit, improves the condition, nor raises the character. It is not by a criminal prejudice alone that the man of colour is here depressed. But were this the sole cause against him, as it derives continuance, if not origin from his condition and character, to improve these is the way to destroy it, and the mode by which the improvement of both, can be rendered most easy, rapid, and extensive, is that prescribed by benevolence to the African race.

Towards this unfortunate race, the spirit of humanity has been increasing since before the American Revolution, in most parts of the civilized world; and the enactment of laws by all Christian nations against the slave trade, proves with what power and success, the advocates of truth and justice, have urged their affecting claims in behalf of Africa and her children upon the view and moral sense of mankind. Already has England blown the trumpet of jubilee for eight hundred thousand slaves, whose shouts of rejoicing have gone up to Heaven, from Islands, where nature, dressed in loveliness, has long seemed to endure with indignant and saddened countenance, the crimes and outrage of oppression.*

No human commendation can be a just tribute of respect to the Society of Friends for their foremost stand against the slave trade, and for those solemn tones in which they have continued annually to speak out, and warn the rulers of Christendom to cease from a policy, beneath which thousands were perishing in despair, while their cries pierced the ear of Heaven and invoked the wrath of the Eternal. The writings of Woolman and Benezet, of Sharp and Wilberforce and Clarkson, with a host of others, through whose serenity and meekness shone a burning zeal and a fearless courage, have awoke sentiments, which will never permit inactivity among the benevolent, while Africa or the world bears the foot-print of a slave. That benevolence towards the people of colour must operate exclusively, or mainly, to secure for them im-

---

* The moral influence of the step just taken by the British nation will be universal and powerful; it is impossible to resist it. It is the greatest achievement ever made in the cause of human liberty—at the same time, that it is the most notable act of humanity—that the world has ever beheld. The purchase of our national independence bears no comparison with it. It is radical; it is a public and solemn concession of right, where there was no power in the sufferer to gain it. It was the struggle—it is the triumph of principle. Every nation—all the world sees it, and will feel it. It is an expression and a demonstration of "the spirit of the age."—*Letter from London, to the Editor of the New York Observer.*

mediately, in this country, the highest political rights, is a recent discovery which seems unauthorized either by Reason, the Word or the Providence of God.

Dr. Fothergill, a member of the Society of Friends in England, first suggested, and Granville Sharp first executed (by founding the Sierra Leone Colony) the project of colonizing free men of colour in Africa. The philanthropic Dr. William Thornton of Washington, proposed in the year 1787, to conduct a company of free coloured emigrants from the United States to Africa, but circumstances beyond his control frustrated his design. The subject was discussed in the Legislature of Virginia early in the present century, and the General Government requested by that Body to aid in the selection and acquisition of Territory adapted to the purposes of the contemplated Colony.

But the establishment of the American Colonization Society resulted less from political motives, than from Christian benevolence. The devoted Mills, singly intent upon doing good in silence and humility, during his journeys of usefulness, sought information in regard to the people of colour: and while his prayers were offered to Heaven in their behalf, his heart was animated by hope, that they would finally return to Africa, and bear with them the principles of a purer and better life, to her barbarous population. The venerated Finley, justly honoured as the founder of the Society, sought his happiness in the relief of the wretched and the service of God, and laboured for the good of the coloured man under the impulse of a disinterested spirit.

Nor ought we to forget, that long before the formation of the Colonization Society, there were generous souls in Virginia, and probably in other parts of the South, touched with a tender and affecting charity towards the people of colour, whose daily and nightly thoughts were fixed upon their dark condition, and who in grief and prayer sought to teach, comfort, and guide those of them who dwelt within the limits of their influence, trusting that the Father of mercies, who had lighted up their hearts with His grace and love, would kindle other hearts also, until the Nation should arise in power for the redemption of Africa.

In a future world the fact may stand revealed, that from the sacred retirements of a few devout ladies in Virginia, who at the Saviour's feet had learnt better lessons than this world's philosophy could teach, emanated a spirit of zeal and charity in behalf of the afflicted Africans, which has widely spread; inspired Ministers and Statesmen with an almost divine eloquence in their cause, and given to this cause an impulse which nothing shall be able to resist.*

The American Colonization Society was founded in Washington City, in December, 1816. The patriotic and pious from various parts of the country, united in its organization.† They could not close their eyes upon the following facts:

1. That the slavery of two millions of coloured persons in the Southern portion of this Union was under the exclusive control and legislation of the slaveholding States—each having the sole right of regulating it within its own limits.

---

\* I have the utmost confidence in the power of maternal fire-side instructions. Many pious parents, especially mothers, in Virginia, at the close of the Revolution, finding themselves at peace in their homes of freedom, felt a sympathy for those around them who had derived little or no benefit from the arduous contest just terminated. They desired to lead their children in the paths of divine wisdom, but they saw them exposed to an evil rising like a mountain barrier in their path. They were enabled, however, daily and faithfully to study the Holy Scriptures, and to instil into the minds of their children, principles which are now silently pervading the hearts of thousands, and working a glorious change in their whole moral state. That law, which the Apostle James styles a royal law, a perfect law of liberty, is of power to remedy the most wide spread, deep, and formidable evils, that have ever deformed the beauty, weakened the strength, or sapped the foundations of any Society. Let all parents study this law, and all ministers explain and enforce it, as the simple, but sublime and everlasting principle of order and happiness on earth and in Heaven.

† Names of the original members of the Society:—H. Clay, E. B. Caldwell,

2. That the two hundred thousand coloured persons scattered throughout the Union and legally free, enjoyed few of the advantages of freedom.

3. That there were powerful causes operating to frustrate all efforts to elevate very considerably men of colour in this country, which could not exist to prevent their elevation in a separate community from the whites.

4. That the voluntary separation of the coloured from the white race, was in reason and the public judgment, so desirable, on general principles of benevolence, that a union of the wise and pious from every State and section of the country in support of measures proposed for the good of the coloured race yet tending to no such a result, could not be expected.

5. That the success of any measures for the good of this race, must depend in a great degree on such union.

6. That Africa was inhabited by fifty to one hundred millions of uncivilized and heathen men, and that to render as far as practicable the elevation of her exiled children, conducive to the deliverance and salvation of her home population, was required alike by philanthropy and piety.

In view of these facts, what humanity and benevolence to the coloured race suggested, was embodied in the Constitution of the American Colonization Society. It was expected that the operations of this Society, would unfetter and invigorate the faculties, improve the circumstances, animate

Tho. Dougherty, Stephen B. Balch, Jno. Chalmers, Jun. Thos. Patterson, John Randolph of Roanoke, Robt. H. Goldsborough, William Thornton, George Clarke, James Laurie, J. I. Stull, Dan'l. Webster, J. C. Herbert, Wm. Simmons, E. Forman, Ferd'no. Fairfax, V. Maxcy, Jno. Loockerman, Jno. Woodside, William Dudley Digges, Thomas Carberry, Samuel J. Mills, Geo. A. Carroll, W. G. D. Worthington, John Lee, Richard Bland Lee, D. Murray, Robert Finley, B. Allison, B. L. Lear, W. Jones, J. Mason, Mord. Booth, J. S. Shaaf, Geo. Peter, John Tayloe, Overton Carr, P. H. Wendover, F. S. Key, Charles Marsh, David M. Forest, John Wiley, Nathan Lufborough, William Meade, William H. Wilmer, George Travers, Edm. I. Lee, John P. Todd, Bushrod Washington.

the hopes and enlarge the usefulness of the free people of colour; that by awakening thought, nullifying objections, presenting motives convincing to the judgment, and persuasive to the humanity of masters, they would encourage emancipation; that in Africa their results would be seen, in civilized and Christian communities; in the substitution of a lawful and beneficial commerce for the abominable slave trade; of peaceful agriculture for a predatory warfare; knowledge for ignorance; the arts that refine for vices that degrade; and for superstitions vile, cruel and bloodstained, the ennobling service and pure worship of the true God. It was believed that the fellowship of the North with the South, in African Colonization, would tend powerfully to produce just opinions on the subject of slavery, and prepare for the removal of the evil without endangering the integrity and peace of the Union. It was clear, that the principles and measures of the Society, interfered not with those who desired to ameliorate the condition of the people of colour, bond or free, who might remain in our country; but in fact, contributed to produce those kind and considerate sentiments towards both, which alone can admit them to all the privileges, possible to them while here, and denied a distinct national existence.*

* My view of the system of slavery, as it exists among us, is briefly this:—Individual masters are morally bound to treat their slaves as their consciences honestly consulted, decide that they themselves would reasonably or rightfully expect to be treated in the same condition and circumstances. And this perfect law of Christianity, should govern political bodies, no less than individuals. Adopting this, the royal law of Christ, as a universal, perfect rule of duty between man and man, in all conditions, circumstances and times, it follows, therefrom:

1st. That any doctrine or practice which would justify or maintain slavery as a perpetual system, is abominable; because reason and conscience in the breast of every man, assert his natural capability for freedom, and of course, that this capability belongs to other men. And as his judgment must decide that it could never be right for others to consign him and his posterity to perpetual and involuntary servitude, so does it equally, that he can never justly contribute to perpetuate a system which consigns others to that condition.

2d. That human liberty should never be weighed in the balances with mo-

But the founders of the Society saw not "by what authority 'we could limit the Almighty and tie down the destiny of 'the coloured people, to a condition so low, (or why they 'should be satisfied with it) compared with the blessings of 'nationality."*

During the year 1818, Messrs. Samuel J. Mills and Ebenezer Burgess, were commissioned by the Society to proceed by the way of England to the English settlements, and other parts of the Western coast of Africa, to acquire information

ney, or estimated by dollars and cents. There is no man who does not regard his own liberty as more precious than property, and in the same light, is he to regard the liberty of others.

3d. All rigorous laws imposed on those subjected to this system, (not necessary for the good of the enslaved, or indispensable to the preservation of the public peace and safety) cannot too soon be abolished. Such, I believe there are; and every humane and Christian man should exert his influence to have them erased from the State codes.

4th. Where the system exists, those who have the political power, are as much bound to proceed *benevolently* in their measures to remedy and remove it, as they are to proceed at all. They must not forget that "civil society is an institution of beneficence; and law itself is (or should be) beneficence, acting by rule." Nor that "restraints on men, as well as their liberties, are to be reckoned (in a sense) among their rights." They ought not to attempt to do that suddenly and by a blow, which they know may be done more safely and beneficially with caution and preparation.

5th. It *may be* the duty of individual masters to liberate their slaves, before the State is morally bound to enact laws for the *entire* and universal abolition of slavery. For particular slaves may be qualified for freedom, and their masters may have ability to place them where such freedom would be to them a benefit, while the great mass of the slave population are unqualified for *perfect* freedom; and the State feels prohibited by motives of enlarged benevolence, from conferring it, instantly, upon them. There is no danger that either States or individuals at the South, will act too soon or too earnestly on the subject. The great object should be, I humbly conceive, to awaken in all minds a sense of justice and benevolence towards our whole coloured population. All should immediately and earnestly unite in preparing them for freedom. When qualified therefor, there should be no hesitation in conferring it upon them. "It is advanced in the eternal constitution of things, that men of intemperate minds, cannot be free. Their passions forge their fetters."

* Dr. Beecher.

and ascertain whether suitable Territory could be purchased for the proposed Colony. They conferred with the friends of Africa in England, from whom they experienced the utmost kindness, and received letters to the Governor of Sierra Leone; visited that Colony, the Gambia and Sherbro, and having fulfilled their arduous duties, embarked for the United States. The death of Mr. Mills while on his return, deprived the world of one of the best of men. From the very interesting and satisfactory reports of these Agents, the Society was encouraged to proceed in its enterprise.

We refer to a former chapter, for some account of the first expedition (in 1820) to Africa, and the sufferings of the emigrants at Sherbro Island, during which the Agent of Government, Mr. Bacon, his assistant Mr. Bankson, and the Society's Agent Mr. Crozer died, from the combined influences of exposure, excessive effort, and the fever of the country.

Early in the year 1821, the brig Nautilus, chartered by the United States' Government, conveyed to Africa, Messrs. J. B. Winn and Ephraim Bacon, Agents of Government; and the Rev. Joseph R. Andrus Principal, and Mr. Christian Wiltberger, Assistant Agent of the Colonization Society, with a small number of emigrants. In obedience to instructions, the Agents on their arrival at Sierra Leone, sought and obtained permission from the Government of that Colony, for the emigrants by the Nautilus, as well as for those in the Sherbro country, to remain at Foura Bay, an extensive and cultivated plantation, in the immediate vicinity of Freetown, until suitable land should be obtained for the site of the intended Colony. Messrs. Bacon and Andrus visited different points on the coast, particularly Grand Bassa; the natives of which district, consented to receive the people from America, but declined making the least concession towards an abandonment of the slave trade. Soon after their return to Sierra Leone, Mr. and Mrs. Bacon, in consequence of severe illness, embarked for the United States; and in the course of a few weeks, Mr. Andrus and Mr. and Mrs. Winn, were removed by death, to their eternal reward.

The duties of chief Agent, were now discharged by Mr. Wiltberger, until the arrival of Dr. Eli Ayres, who had received an appointment to that office, late in the autumn of 1821. Mr. Wiltberger then proceeded to Sherbro, and accompanied such of the people as had remained at that place, with their effects, to Foura Bay. In the month of December, Captain Robert F. Stockton, of the United States' Schooner Alligator, arrived at Sierra Leone, and consented to accompany Dr. Ayres to Cape Montserado, to obtain, if possible, Territory for the Colony. These gentlemen urged negotiations for several days with the chiefs of the country; and finally, by great skill and perseverance, obtained a valuable tract of land, including Cape Montserado, affording, as was believed, an eligible situation for the first settlement.

Dr. Ayres proceeded without delay to Sierra Leone, directed several of the emigrants (mostly single men) to make ready for their departure in one of the Colonial Schooners, and sailing with them, arrived at Cape Montserado on the 7th of January, 1822. Others followed on the sixteenth of February. It was found necessary for Dr. Ayres again to visit Sierra Leone, from which place he returned with all the remaining Colonists, on the 7th of April. He found the settlement in confusion and alarm. Hitherto the Colonists had occupied a small and unhealthy Island, in the mouth of Montserado river. The natives had shown much duplicity, and a determination, if possible, to expel the Colonists from the country. But possession was finally obtained of Cape Montserado. In a slight contest with the natives, the storehouse had taken fire, and most of the provisions and utensils of the Colony been destroyed.

Sickness began to prevail, and the Agents were among the afflicted; the rainy season had just set in; provisions were scanty, and the friendship of the natives furnished no ground for reliance. Under these circumstances, it was proposed, that such as desired, should return to take up a temporary residence at Sierra Leone. Mr. Wiltberger offered to remain with such as should decide on maintaining their position on the Cape, which most of them nobly resolved to do, even at the hazard of their lives.

In July of this year, the little band, having endured great trials and hardships, were enabled entirely to abandon the Island, and place themselves beneath their own humble dwellings, on the Cape. Both Agents before this, judged it necessary to return to the United States, leaving an intelligent and honest emigrant,* General Superintendent of affairs. Few, destitute, and exposed to the treachery of savage foes, far away from the abodes of civilized man, this feeble company found shelter under the wing of Divine Mercy, and patiently awaited those aids and supplies, which their necessities demanded, and which they trusted the Almighty power, that had so long been their safeguard, would in due season afford.

* Elijah Johnson, of New York.

## CHAPTER VII.

Mr. Ashmun embarked for Africa, at Baltimore, in the brig Strong, on the 20th of June, 1822.

Congress, by an Act of the 2d of March, 1807, prohibited, under heavy penalties, the importation of slaves from a foreign country, into any State or Territory of the United States; and yet, left slaves imported in violation of law, subject to any regulations not contravening the provisions of said Act, which the Legislatures of the several States or Territories, might adopt.

The Legislature of Georgia, by a Law passed on the 19th of December, 1817, empowered the Governor to sell for the benefit of the State, any negroes, mulattoes or persons of colour brought into it, in violation of the laws of the U. States; and the proceeds of sales, to a considerable amount, made in pursuance of this Act, were soon after deposited in the Treasury of that State.* By the last section of this Act, however, the Governor was authorized, in case the Colonization So-

---

* The Act of Congress, of the 3d of March, 1819, has forever put it out of the power of a State so to dishonour itself, by disposing of the liberty of oppressed strangers.

ciety should, before the sale of any such persons, undertake to transport them to Africa or elsewhere, at the sole expense of the Society; and also, to defray any expenses which might have been incurred by the State on their account, to promote, as he might deem expedient, the benevolent views of the Society.

On the 7th of April, 1819, the Managers of the American Colonization Society, having been informed that on the 4th of May following, from thirty to forty Africans, unlawfully introduced, were to be sold in the capital of Georgia, authorized the Rev. William Meade\* (who had accepted a brief agency for the Board, and to whose efforts then, and since, the Society is deeply indebted,) to proceed to Milledgeville, and assume all responsibilities necessary to prevent the sale, and secure the restoration of these unfortunate men to their own country. He arrived just in season to rescue these poor Africans from the peril of their situation, and to find in their joy and in that of many sympathizing bosoms, an ample reward for exertions even more laborious than those he had so promptly made for their relief. The case between certain Spanish claimants to these Africans and the State, had not yet been decided; and they were therefore left to await the result, which if favourable (as expected) to their freedom, would, by consent of the Governor of Georgia, place them at the disposal of the American Colonization Society. For ability to indemnify Georgia for any expense she had incurred in their behalf, the Managers relied both upon the liberality of the public, and the justice of the American Government, which by the Act of the 3d of March, 1819, had fully recognized the moral obligation of extending protection to such injured strangers.

Early in the spring of 1822, eighteen of these Africans, declared free by a competent tribunal, arrived in Baltimore,

---

\* The present Assistant Bishop of Virginia.

under arrangement of the President to convey them thence to Africa, in conformity to the law, and at the expense of the United States. In the brig Strong, chartered for their accommodation, the Managers of the Colonization Society obtained passage for thirty-five additional emigrants and various stores; the charge of the entire expedition being entrusted to Mr. Ashmun, with instructions (should he return in the brig) to report the condition and prospects of the Colony; or in case of the sickness or absence of the Agents, to remain in Africa as principal Agent, until some other individual should be appointed to that office.

It is believed Mr. Ashmun was impelled to leave his country, rather by a desire to realize from commercial operations, the means of discharging heavy debts, which should he continue in America, he saw it impossible soon to pay, than by any expectation of occupying the station which Providence destined him to fill with such distinguished honour and success. That he felt for the cause of African Colonization an ardent affection, and hoped essentially to promote it, is certain. But his thoughts were directed to a plan of extensive trade, which he imagined might prove of some advantage to himself, while it contributed to conciliate and civilize the Africans, and to augment the resources and facilitate all the operations of the Society.* The information he would obtain by a visit to the African coast, must, he concluded, enable him to judge of proper measures for effecting his object; and on his return, all the details of the plan might be satisfactorily adjusted, with the various parties concerned. He regarded the scheme probably at the time of his departure, as something of an adventure, since it does not appear that he had submitted it to the consideration of the Managers of the Society.† His re-

---

* In his Journal he remarks: "In 1822, the mercantile mania possessed me for a few weeks."

† See Appendix No. 4.

flections upon it, during the voyage, were communicated to the Board, and it constitutes the principal topic of one of his earliest letters from the Colony.

He was employed for nearly a month at Baltimore, in soliciting donations from the citizens, purchasing supplies, and superintending all transactions preparatory to the departure of the expedition; and his letters to the Society, show both his benevolent concern for the comfort of the emigrants, and his habits of attention, even then, to the minute details of business.

The accidental death of an African boy, who, when first missed, was supposed to have absconded, is thus noticed:

"*May* 8*th*, 1822.

"A melancholy disclosure! The little African boy, men-
' tioned yesterday, was drowned. He was drawn out of the
' dock this morning at 11 o'clock. It seems that he watched
' his opportunity when all others were below, to go upon the
' wharf, and the wind being high, he was precipitated over.
' Poor fellow! He was a fine child—told me the evening be-
' fore, that his mistress in Savannah, taught him morning and
' evening, 'to pray to the Good Man above.' He has had a
' decent burial. His companions are much affected."

It was at first determined, that Mrs. Ashmun should remain, with her friends, in the United States; but her affectionate solicitude to accompany her husband, finally induced him to consent that she should become his companion, in the uncertain and perilous fortunes of the voyage.

On the 15th of May, all the emigrants assembled on the quarter-deck of the vessel—"a laborious, orderly, and plain company," said Mr. Ashmun, "who go out with sober views, and will add real strength to the Colony;" and in the presence of many of the Clergy and citizens of Baltimore, listened to an exhortation from the Bishop of Maryland, who, in conclusion, implored in behalf of the little company, the divine blessing, and commended them to the protection of the Almighty.

Off Annapolis, on the 21st of May, (the day after the Strong left Baltimore) Mr. Ashmun wrote to the Secretary of the Colonization Society:—"We had a short service, Sunday 'evening at 4 o'clock on the quarter-deck; have daily, morn-'ing devotions at six, and evening at seven; the native boys 'are distributed among the other people; our accommodations 'are comfortable—my wife's health improves; and in fine, 'the blessing of God remarkably rests on our external circum-'stances. I pray that His grace may visit and rest upon all 'abundantly."

While detained by contrary winds near the Capes of Virginia, he addressed a letter to the same gentleman, on the subject of the African trade, expressing the belief, that it might be rendered, in an important degree, conducive to the objects of the Colonization Society; that by it, properly conducted, the attention of the natives might be turned from the slave trade, to an honourable commerce, and find it for their interest to remain in peace with the Colonists, who on their part, would derive therefrom, very important advantages.— He judged it desirable, that in the vicinity of Montserado, this trade should be conducted by American merchants; that the productions and capabilities of Africa, might be brought before the eyes of the American people; and that by the frequent and regular passage of ships between the United States and that country, every facility might be given to emigration. He suggested that half the expense incurred by the Society, might be saved, were vessels to sail regularly from Baltimore, with freights for this trade, and return with cargoes from Africa; and finally declared his purpose to do what he could to promote the object with the natives and the settlement, presuming that he should thus meet the wishes of the Society, and subserve the interests of the Colony.

Soon after the Strong left the Capes of Virginia, she encountered a heavy gale for eight days; during which, no attempt was made to proceed; and being a miserably dull sailer, she did not arrive at Fayal, (one of the Azores) before the first of July. From this place, Mr. Ashmun wrote, that the "emigrants had uniformly evinced the most peaceable and 'industrious dispositions; that they had been formed into 'about ten classes—to each of which, was appointed an in-'structer, to act under his superintendence; that these class-'es were assembled twice a day, and instructed from four to 'five hours; that all had sensibly improved; that they had 'seldom been hindered from worship twice on the Sabbath, 'or from morning and evening devotions; that all the people 'were apparently moral; and that the example of such as pro-'fessed religion, had been productive of the most salutary ef-'fects, and gave reason to expect their good conduct and use-'fulness in Africa."

At Fayal, the cargo and ballast which had been displaced by the storm, were overhauled and adjusted; supplies of fresh provisions, water, and vegetables, taken in; and after the detention of a week, the Strong pursued her course, and completed her voyage on the 8th of August—eighty-one days from Baltimore.

On the 9th of August, 1822, Mr. Ashmun stood, for the first time, on Cape Montserado; and having ascertained that both Agents had left the country, assumed, agreeably to instructions, and in fulfilment of his pledge to the Board, the direction as principal Agent of the affairs of the Colony. He summoned all his energies, surveyed rapidly the field of labour, and deferred not an hour, the commencement of his work.—He found a respectable Colonist in charge of the public concerns, but no books or documents defining the limits of the purchased Territory, the state of negotiations with the natives, or throwing light upon the duties of the Agency.

Cape Montserado, elevated from seventy-five to eighty feet above the sea, forms the abrupt termination of a narrow tongue of land, in length thirty-six miles, and from one and a half to three miles in breadth; bounded on the South-west by the ocean, and on the North-east by the rivers Montserado and Junk, running in nearly opposite directions, their head waters being at a short distance from each other; the isthmus between, constituting the junction of the Montserado Peninsula, to the mainland. The site chosen for the original settlement, (now Monrovia) is two miles from the point of the Cape, on the ridge, approaching here to within one hundred and fifty yards of the river, to which, therefrom, there is a steep descent. This site, and a large portion of the Peninsula, was, when ceded to the Society, covered with a lofty and dense forest, entangled with vines and brushwood; the haunts of savage beasts, and through which the Barbarians were accustomed to cut their narrow and winding pathways to the coast.

When Mr. Ashmun arrived, a small spot had been cleared, about thirty houses constructed in native style, with a storehouse entirely too small to receive any supplies in addition to those it then contained. The rainy season was at its height; the public property had been chiefly consumed by fire; some of the settlers already on the ground, were but imperfectly sheltered; and for those just arrived, no preparation had been made; the settlement had no adequate means of defence while the chiefs of the country could no longer conceal their hostile designs. The whole population of the settlement, including the emigrants by the Strong, did not exceed one hundred and thirty; of whom, thirty-five only, were capable of bearing arms.

A comprehensive system of operations was immediately commenced, to relieve the wants and improve the condition of the infant Colony, and afford security against the dangers to which it was exposed.

A Colonial Journal was opened with the design of recording therein, all important transactions and events.*

* "This Journal, I judged fit to open on the day of my landing, and intend

Separate inventories were entered in a book, of the public stores found in the Colony, and of those sent in the Strong, both by the U. States and the Society.

Orders were given for the erection of a store-house; for completing a building just commenced (designed as a market-house) for the recaptured Africans; and that the best accommodations, the case would admit, should be prepared, in the houses already occupied, for the newly arrived emigrants.

On the 9th of August, the Strong was forced from her moorings with the loss of one of her anchors; and on the 10th, her cable again parted, when being near the beach, and the wind blowing directly on shore, she was, with extreme difficulty, saved from destruction. After a vain attempt for forty-eight hours to sail out of the bay formed by the promontories of Cape Montserado and Cape Mount, the small anchor was providentially recovered, and she was again brought to a fixed position, but at the distance of five miles from the settlement. During this perilous season, the Agent, with nearly all the emigrants, were on board.

The people were safely landed on the 13th and 14th, but owing to the great distance of the brig, to the prevalence of boisterous weather, the loss of the principal boat employed in the service, and the sickening of the boatmen, it became a work of great toil and difficulty, to bring her cargo to land. "But after four weeks of incessant exertion, the Agent enjoy-
' ed the satisfaction of seeing the passengers and property all
' safe on shore; the latter secured in an extensive store-house;
' and most of the former in a good measure protected from
' the incessant rains of that inclement season."*

---

that a copy of it shall always remain in the Colony, open for public inspection and use; and a duplicate agreeing with the former, even to the paging, be from time to time, sent home to the Board, as the best and only effectual means of keeping them fully informed of what passes in the settlement."— *Mr. Ashmun's Letter to the Board.*

\* Ashmun's History.

Efforts were made without delay, to ascertain, as far as practicable, the dispositions of the principal chiefs of the country, and by offers of an honest and friendly trade, and by proposals to receive and instruct their sons in the English language, to bind them in the most amicable relations to the Colony. The Journal contains the following account of the Agent's interview with King Peter* and King Long Peter, on the 14th of August:

"The chiefs inquired whether goods had been sent by the
' brig to pay for the lands?

"*Answer.* The Society believed that nearly the whole
' price had been paid to King Peter many moons ago, accord-
' ing to the contract, and had sent out very few goods for
' that purpose.

"*Question.* Had Dr. Ayres arrived in America before the
' Agent left there?

"*Answer.* Certainly not. The Society, therefore, gave
' the present Agent no instructions in relation to the purchase
' of the lands. But the next arrival from America, after
' Dr. Ayres should have reached there, would bring fresh
' instructions on the subject, adapted to the present state of
' things. King Peter might be assured that the Society
' would be governed by the strictest justice, and the truest
' friendship, in all their transactions with him and his head
' men: and that he would never find them to shrink from
' any of their engagements. They would hear with great
' regret of King Peter's refusal of a part of the goods, which
' he agreed by the deed to receive for the lands. But they
' were and would be King Peter's friends. They had sent a
' letter to King Peter and his head men, which the Agent
' would deliver whenever he should express his readiness to
' receive it.

"King Peter then desired to have the letter. The letter

* For his age and influence, regarded as the patriarch of the tribes in the immediate neighbourhood of the Colony.

' was delivered and interpreted to the King, and seemed to
' come very seasonably, and to produce a good effect on his
' feelings. He observed in conclusion:

"Should more goods and fresh instructions in relation to
' the lands arrive from America, he would call a general pala-
' ver of the Kings and head men concerned in the cessions
' of the lands, and be governed by their sentence; that mean
' time he would remain as he had been a friend; that his age
' and rank, he thought, entitled him, according to the custom
' of the country, to some consideration, which he would be
' glad to have the Agent express by a present of whatever he
' might have to spare; but which he could receive only as a
' present."

To this, the Agent replied:

"He was willing, in behalf of the Society, to express his
' respect for King Peter's age and character, by a small pres-
' ent, which he would send to his town, as soon as conve-
' nient, after receiving the goods ashore."

On the 16th of August, the Agent visited King Bristol,[*]
thirteen miles distant; "stated to him his friendly disposition;
' thanked him for his friendship towards the settlers, and de-
' sired the same amicable feelings and intercourse might be
' perpetual. He further offered to open with King Bristol
' and his people, a fair and mutually advantageous trade, to be
' conducted, on the one part, in American and European
' goods; on the other, in the productions of the country."

To this, King Bristol replied in substance, that he was
pleased with the formation of the settlement of American people; that he should continue to feel friendly to the establishment; that different and distinct tribes inhabited the country,
and it would be unjust and ungenerous to adopt an opinion
unfavourable to all, from the misconduct of one or two Kings;
that he was old, and it was time that his character as a King

---

[*] Written sometimes Brister.

and man, was known; that he hoped he and his people should prove worthy of confidence; that he was quite willing to open trade with the settlement, and would engage to protect it; was glad to see the Agent, and intended soon to pay the Colony a friendly visit.

Though there was little reason to question the sincerity of these Chiefs, it was manifest, "that under smooth and friend-
' ly appearances, there lurked in the minds of many of the
' head men, a spirit of determined malignity, which only
' waited for an opportunity to exert itself for the ruin of the
' Colony."

While, therefore, the Agent gave orders that the fifteen recaptured Africans should form a community by themselves, under a judicious superintendent directed to regulate their hours, lead them in family devotion, and instruct them in reading, writing, arithmetic, and the principles of Christianity; that they should be taught agriculture and trained up in habits of cleanliness, order, and industry; that the plan of the town should be extended, and lots assigned to the new emigrants; that a comfortable house should be erected for the Agent; that several natives (mostly the sons of head men) should be admitted as labourers; and for compensation, be assisted to acquire knowledge of the English language; that as far as practicable, the grounds should be cleared, and planted with the most useful vegetables; he deemed it necessary to give prompt and principal attention to works of defence. Still he did not expect the dangers to which the Colony was so soon to be exposed. He did not look for any unity in the counsels, or combination among the forces of the Chiefs; and without these, he felt confident that their hostile endeavours might be frustrated.*

\* September 12th, he wrote to the Board :

"There is not a head man within fifty miles of us, who can arm properly fifty men. They are cowardly in the extreme, and have little control over their men. Besides, there is the same political selfishness existing among them, which seems to check the prosecution of their ambitious schemes among the

In proceeding with a narrative of events connected with the Colony at this crisis, and of the means by which it was sustained against invading and barbarous foes, we must be guided, mainly, by light which he has furnished, who stood amid the scenes described, under God, the guardian genius of a spot upon which Liberty and Religion had just planted their feet, to contend for existence with the powers of darkness.

"So early," says Mr. Ashmun, "as the 18th of August, the
' present Martello tower was planned; a company of labour-
' ers employed by the Agent, in clearing the ground on which
' it stands; and a particular survey taken of the military
' strength and means of the settlers. Of the native Ameri-
' cans, twenty-seven, when not sick, were able to bear arms;
' but they were wholly untrained to their use; and capable in
' their present undisciplined state of making but a very feeble
' defence indeed. There were forty muskets in store, which,
' with repairing, were capable of being rendered serviceable.
' Of five iron guns and one brass attached to the settlement, the
' last only was fit for service, and four of the former required
' carriages. Several of these were nearly buried in the mud,
' on the opposite side of the river. Not a yard of abatis, or
' other fence-work, had been constructed. There was no fix-
' ed ammunition, nor, without great difficulty and delay, was
' it possible to load the only gun which was provided with a
' sufficient carriage.

"It was soon perceived that the means as well as an organ-
' ized system of defence were to be originated, without either
' the materials or the artificers usually considered necessary
' for such purposes. In the organization of the men, thirteen
' African youths attached to the United States' Agency, most

---

different States of Europe. * * * It is morally certain, we shall not be taken by surprise, and with God's blessing, no force they can raise, will much injure us, if prepared for them."—*Sixth Annual Report of the Colonization Society, pages* 40 *and* 41.

' of whom had never loaded a musket, were enrolled in the
' Lieutenant's corps, and daily exercised in the use of arms.—
' The guns were, one after another, with infinite labour,
' transported over the river, conveyed to the height of the
' peninsula, and mounted on rough truck carriages, which in
' the event proved to answer a very good purpose. A mas-
' ter of ordnance was appointed, who, with his assistants, re-
' paired the small arms—made up a quantity of fixed ammu-
' nition, and otherwise aided in arranging the details of the
' service.

"'The little town was closely environed, except on the side
' of the river, with the heavy forest in the bosom of which it
' was situated—thus giving to a savage enemy an important
' advantage of which it became absolutely necessary to de-
' prive him, by enlarging to the utmost, the cleared space
' about the buildings. This labour was immediately under-
' taken, and carried on without any other intermission, than
' that caused by sickness of the people, and the interruption
' of other duties equally connected with the safety of the
' place. But the rains were immoderate and nearly constant.

"In addition to these fatiguing labours, was that of main-
' taining the nightly watch;—which, from the number of
' sentinels necessary for the common safety, shortly became
' more exhausting than all the other burdens of the people.—
' No less than twenty individuals were every night detailed
' for this duty, after the 31st of August."*

* "On this day, the strength of the Colony was thus organized, and the accompanying orders issued:
　1. The settlement is under military law.
　2. E. Johnson is Commissary of Stores.
　3. R. Sampson is Commissary of Ordinance.
　4. L. Carey, Health Officer and Government Inspector.
　5. F. James, Captain of brass mounted field-piece; and has assigned to his command, R. Newport, M. S. Draper, William Meade, and J. Adams.
　6. A. James, Captain of Long 18; and under his command, J. Benson, E. Smith, William Hollinger, D. Hawkins, John and Thomas Spencer.

On the 25th of August, Mr. Ashmun experienced the first attack of fever, and three days afterwards, had the pain to see Mrs. Ashmun seriously affected by the same disease.

Sickness soon commenced among the company of recent emigrants, and prevailed so rapidly, that on the 10th of September, of the whole number, only two remained in health. "The Agent was enabled by a merciful Providence, to main-
' tain a difficult struggle with his disorder, for four weeks; in
' which period, after a night of delirium and suffering, it was
' not an unusual circumstance for him to be able to spend an
' entire morning in laying off and directing the execution of
' the public works."

About the first of September, the intercourse between the settlement and the people of the country, had nearly ceased, and the native youths who had been residing in the Colony, were daily deserting in consequence of recent intelligence conveyed to them by their friends.

"The plan of defence adopted was to station five heavy
' guns at the different angles of a triangle which should cir-

7. J. Shaw, Captain of the Southern Picket Station, mounting two iron guns. To his command are attached S. Campbell, E. Jackson, J. Lawrence, L. Crook, and George Washington.

8. D. George, Captain of Eastern Picket Station, mounting two iron guns; attached are A. Edmondson, Joseph Gardiner, Josh. Webster, and J. Carey.

9. C. Brander, Captain of a Carriage mounting two swivels, to act in concert with the brass piece, and move from station to station, as the occasion may require; attached are T. Tines, and L. Butler.

10. Every man is to have his musket and ammunition with him even when at the large guns.

11. Every Officer is responsible for the conduct of the men placed under him, who are to obey him at their peril.

12. The guns are all to be got ready for action immediately—and every effective man is to be employed on the Pickets.

13. Five stations to be occupied by guards at night, till other orders shall be given.

14. No useless firing permitted.

15. In case of an alarm, every man is to repair instantly to his post and do his duty.

'cumscribe the whole settlement—each of the angles resting
'on a point of ground sufficiently commanding to enfilade
'two sides of the triangle, and sweep a considerable extent of
'ground beyond the lines. The guns at these stations were
'to be covered by musket proof triangular stockades, of which
'any two should be sufficient to contain all the settlers in their
'wings. The brass piece and two swivels mounted on travel-
'ling carriages, were stationed in the centre, ready to support
'the post which might be exposed to the heaviest attack. After
'completing these detached works, it was in the intention of
'the Agent, had the enemy allowed the time, to join all toge-
'ther by a paling to be carried quite around the settlement;—
'and in the event of a yet longer respite, to carry on, as ra-
'pidly as possible, under the protection of the nearest forti-
'fied point, the construction of the Martello tower; which, as
'soon as completed, would nearly supersede all the other
'works; and by presenting an impregnable barrier to the
'success of any native force, probably become the instru-
'ment of a general and permanent pacification. Connected
'with these measures of safety, was the extension to the ut-
'most, of the cleared space about the settlement, still leaving
'the trees and brushwood, after being separated from their
'trunks, to spread the ground with a tangled hedge, through
'which nothing should be able to make its way, except the
'shot from the batteries.

"This plan was fully communicated to the most intelligent
'of the people; which, in the event of the disability or death
'of the Agent, they might, it was hoped, so far carry into ef-
'fect as to ensure the preservation of the settlement."

On the 6th of September, the Agent convened the people, read to them the instructions of the Board, and published such laws, by-laws and regulations as he deemed essential to the public welfare. "Taken together," he remarks, "they 'comprize all the special written laws which exist in the set- 'tlement." In addition to sundry explanations touching the particular laws, he offered on the occasion several remarks, in substance, as follows:

"That the government of the Colony ought to be a govern-
' ment of reason, religion, and law, and not that of a master
' over his refractory servants; that the Agent should comply
' with the instructions of the Society, consult the interest of
' the Colony, and abide strictly by the sense of the Constitu-
' tion as far as he understood them in all the regulations he
' should establish; that he intended to represent the Society
' as if present; that no more nor more rigid laws should be
' passed than were judged *necessary;* and that laws once
' passed, it need not be said must be obeyed, or the penalty
' suffered; that he sincerely devoted himself, while Divine
' Providence should continue him in his present situation, to
' the welfare of the settlement. And his first wish was to
' see it prosperous. He sympathized with not a few present,
' who had encountered and sustained dangers and hardships
' of a trying nature. It was the wish of the Society, it was
' his wish to see them as soon as possible, rewarded for all
' their sufferings, by a home abounding with peace and all the
' comforts of this life, and the best means of preparing for one
' infinitely better. He had the satisfaction to regard himself
' as the personal friend of many present, and hoped these feel-
' ings would be interrupted by no fault or indiscretion on
' either part."

On the 12th of September, the Agent wrote the following sentences in the Colonial Journal:

"Rain falls in floods. The sick all seem better except Mrs.
' Ashmun. She is speechless, and almost without the use
' of her reason. There is no rational hope of her recovery.
' All remedies on which her husband dares to venture, have
' been tried in vain. He now with a burdened heart, resigns
' her up to her God, and scarcely able to support himself,
' painfully watches over what he considers the last hours of
' her mortal existence. When last possessed of the power of

' reflection, she declared herself happy in her God—and to
' possess not a wish which was not absorbed in His holy will.
' The reading of the Scriptures seemed perceptibly to feed and
' revive her faith in the precious Redeemer. She seemed to
' have intercourse with God in prayer. Her husband may
' follow her in a few days, or weeks at most; and he here
' ventures to record it as the first wish of his heart, that the
' will of the Lord may be done."

Mr. Ashmun strove manfully against the power of his disease, and the tide of distressing thoughts which rushed upon him as he beheld his wife, "a female of most delicate consti-
' tution, lying under the influence of a mortal fever, in the
' corner of a miserable hut, (to ventilate which in a proper
' manner was impossible,) on a couch literally dripping with
' water, which a roof of thatch was unable to exclude—cir-
' cumstances rendering recovery impossible, and in which
' even the dying struggle almost brought relief to the agoni-
' zed feelings of surviving friendship."* She expired on Sunday the 15th of September. "Her life," observes he who knew her best, "had been that of uncommon devotion and
' self-denial, inspired by a vigorous and practical faith in the
' Divine Saviour of the world; and her end, according to His
' promise, was ineffable peace." To this, we add, that in the recollections of her friends, are the impressions still vivid of her zeal and charity in behalf of the neglected and ignorant of this, and the wretched heathens of other lands; and how, from early youth, it had been her chief desire, that it might be her work and honour, to guide the untaught children of some uncivilized region, to the God of her hope and salvation.

It was a kind dispensation of Providence, that the Agent was spared to make the most important arrangements for the defence of the settlement, before the hand of disease rendered

---

* Mr. Ashmun's Letter to Captain Spence.

him entirely incapable of exertion. From the middle of September, until the first week of November, he remained in an extremely low and dangerous state, nearly incapable of motion, and conscious of little but suffering. As soon as the force of his disease was somewhat abated, he discovered that much had been effected by the industry of the people; that on the whole Southern quarter of the settlement, the trees had been cleared away and so thrown together, as in a good measure to obstruct the approach of an enemy. Their routine of daily labour and nightly watching, however, had been such as to forbid their completing the preparations; the Western station was still uncovered; and the long gun, intended for its chief defence, unmounted. On the 7th of November, the Agent was able to "recommence entries in the Journal, ' and thereafter daily to take an increasing share in the ope- ' rations of the people."

In the mean time, the Kings and head men of the country, had held secret meetings to discuss and decide upon measures of hostility to the Colony. By the diligence and fidelity of an individual whose name has not been divulged, the Agent "was informed of the sentiments of each, and often furnished with the very arguments used in their debates."— Some diversity of opinion existed in the war-council. Two or three of the Chiefs were opposed to the war, but a large majority, not fewer than nine or ten, resolved to unite their forces and make an early attack upon the settlement. The Agent, through one of their number who was undecided on his course, informed them "that he was perfectly apprized of ' their hostile deliberations, notwithstanding their pains to ' conceal them; and that if they proceeded to bring war upon ' the Americans, without even asking to settle their differences ' in a friendly manner, they would dearly learn what it was ' to fight white men."*

* A phrase by which civilized people of all colours and nations, are distinguished in the dialect of the coast.

"On the 7th of November," says Mr. Ashmun, "intelligence
' was received at the Cape that the last measures had been
' taken preparatory to an assault on the settlement, which
' was ordered within four days. The plan of attack being
' left to the head warriors, whose trade it is to concert and
' conduct it, was not to be learnt.

"The Agent was able, with assistance, to inspect the works,
' and review the little force the same evening. He stated to
' the people the purport of the intelligence just received;
' that 'war was now inevitable; and the preservation of their
' property, their settlement, their families, and their lives, de-
' pended under God, wholly upon their own firmness and
' good conduct; that a most important point in the defence
' of the place, was to secure a perfect uniformity of action,
' which should assure to every post and individual the firm
' support of every other. To this end, they must as punc-
' tiliously obey their officers as if their whole duty were cen-
' tered, as it probably was, in that one point; and every man
' as faithfully exert himself, as if the whole defence depend-
' ed on his single efforts. A coward, it was hoped, did not
' disgrace their ranks; and as the cause was emphatically
' that of God and their country, they might confidently ex-
' pect His blessing and success to attend the faithful dis-
' charge of their duty.'—Every thing was then disposed in
' order of action, and the men marched to their posts. They
' lay on their arms, with matches lighted, through the night.

"On the 8th, the Agent, by an effort which entirely ex-
' hausted his strength, proceeded to examine the obstruction
' thrown in the way of the avenues to the settlement; and
' perceived to his extreme mortification, that the west quarter
' was still capable of being approached by a narrow path-way,
' without difficulty; and that the utmost exertions of the
' workmen had accomplished only the mounting of the re-
' volving nine pounder at the post; by which the path was
' enfiladed; but that the platform was still left entirely ex-

' posed. The eastern quarter was about equally open to the
' approach of the enemy, but the station was protected by a
' stockade, and a steep ledge of rocks made the access difficult.

"Picket guards of four men each were detailed, to be posted
' one hundred yards in advance of each of the stations,
' through the night. No man was allowed to sleep before
' the following day, at sun-rise; and patrols of native Afri-
' cans were dispersed through the woods in every direction.
' An order was given to families occupying the most expos-
' ed houses, to sleep in such as were more centrally situated.*

"Throughout the 9th, the order established on the pre-
' ceding day continued; and some progress made in the la-
' bour of falling trees, and otherwise obstructing every prac-
' ticable access to the settlement.

"Sunday, November 10th. The morning was devoted,
' as usual, to the refreshment of the settlers, none of whom
' had slept for the twenty-four hours preceding. At 1 P. M.
' all were remanded to their fatigue and other duties, till
' sun-set; when the order appointed for the preceding night
' was resumed. The women and children attended divine
' service.

"Intelligence had reached the Agent early in the day, that
' the hostile forces had made a movement, and were crossing
' the Montserado river a few miles above the settlement; but
' the patrols made no discovery through the day.—At sun-
' set, however, the enemy again put themselves in motion,
' and at an early hour of the night, had assembled, as was af-
' terwards learnt, to the number of six to nine hundred men,
' on the peninsula, where, at the distance of less than half a
' mile to the westward of the settlement, they encamped till
' near morning. Their camp, afterwards examined, extend-

* In the multitude of cares devolving on the Agent, who dictated most of his instructions from his bed, the measures necessary to secure the proper observance of this order were unhappily omitted; and the rashness of the misguided individuals who disobeyed it, met with a signal punishment.

'ed half a mile in length, and induces a strong probability
'that the number of warriors assembled on this occasion, has
'been altogether underrated.*

"The most wakeful vigilance on the part of the settlers, was
'kept up through the night.—But, with a fatality which was
'quite of a piece with all the hindrances that had impeded
'the progress of the defences on the western quarter, the
'picket-guard in advance of that post, ventured on a violation
'of their orders, by leaving their station, at the first dawn of
'day; at which it was their duty to remain till sun-rise. The
'native force was already in motion, and followed directly in
'the rear of the picket-guard. The latter had just rejoined
'their gun, about which ten men were now assembled; when
'the enemy suddenly presenting a front of ten yards in width,
'at sixty distant, delivered their fire, and rushed forward
'with their spears to seize the post. Several men were killed
'and disabled by the first fire, and the remainder driven from
'their gun without discharging it. Then, retiring upon the
'centre, (see the arrangement of the guns, p. 131,) threw the
'reserve there stationed, into momentary confusion; and had
'the enemy at this instant, pressed their advantage, it is hard-
'ly conceivable that they should have failed of entire success.
'Their avidity for plunder was their defeat. Four houses
'in that outskirt of the settlement, had fallen into their hands.
'Every man on whose savage rapacity so resistless a tempta-
'tion happened to operate, rushed impetuously upon the pil-
'lage thus thrown in his way. The movement of the main
'body was disordered and impeded; and an opportunity af-
'forded the Agent, assisted principally by the Rev. Lot Cary
'to rally the broken force of the settlers. The two central
'guns, with a part of their own men, and several who had

* The number given above, is deduced from the discordant accounts given by the kings of the country, after the termination of hostilities; some of whom rated it much higher; but all were ignorant of the true number, and all were interested to state it as low as would obtain credit.

' been driven from the western station, were, with a little ex-
' ertion, brought back into action, and formed in the line of
' two slight buildings, thirty yards in advance of the enemy.

"The second discharge of a brass field-piece, double-shot-
' ted with ball and grape, brought the whole body of the ene-
' my to a stand. That gun was well served, and appeared to
' do great execution. The havoc would have been greater,
' had not the fire, from motives of humanity, been so directed
' as to clear the dwellings about which the enemy's force was
' gathered in heavy masses. These houses were known at
' that moment to contain more than twelve helpless women
' and children.

"The eastern and southern posts, were, from their situa-
' tion, precluded from rendering any active assistance on the
' occasion; but the officers and men attached to them, deserve
' the highest praise, of doing their duty by maintaining their
' stations, and thus protecting the flank and rear of the few
' whose lot it was to be brought to action.

"A few musketeers with E. Johnson at their head, by pass-
' ing round upon the enemy's flank, served to increase the
' consternation which was beginning to pervade their un-
' wieldy body. In about twenty minutes after the settlers
' had taken their stand, the front of the enemy began to re-
' coil. But from the numerous obstructions in their rear,
' the entire absence of discipline, and the extreme difficulty
' of giving a reversed motion to so large a body, a small part
' only of which was directly exposed to danger, and the delay
' occasioned by the practice of carrying off all their dead and
' wounded, rendered a retreat for some minutes longer, im-
' possible. The very violence employed by those in the
' front, in their impatience to hasten it, by increasing the con-
' fusion, produced an effect opposite to that intended. The
' Americans perceiving their advantage, now regained pos-
' session of the western post, and instantly brought the long
' nine to rake the whole line of the enemy. Imagination can

'scarcely figure to itself a throng of human beings in a more
'capital state of exposure to the destructive power of the ma-
'chinery of modern warfare! Eight hundred men were here
'pressed shoulder to shoulder, in so compact a form that a
'child might easily walk upon their heads from one end of
'the mass to the other, presenting in their rear a breadth of
'rank equal to twenty or thirty men, and all exposed to a gun
'of great power, raised on a platform, at only thirty to sixty
'yards distance! Every shot literally spent its force in a sol-
'id mass of living human flesh! Their fire suddenly termi-
'nated. A savage yell was raised, which filled the dismal
'forest with a momentary horror. It gradually died away; and
'the whole host disappeared. At eight o'clock the well
'known signal of their dispersion and return to their homes,
'was sounded, and many small parties seen at a distance, di-
'rectly afterwards, moving off in different directions. One
'large canoe employed in reconveying a party across the
'mouth of the Montserado, venturing within the range of the
'long gun, was struck by a shot, and several men killed.

"On the part of the settlers, it was soon discovered that
'considerable injury had been sustained.

"One woman* who had imprudently passed the night in
'the house first beset by the enemy, had received thirteen
'wounds, and been thrown aside as dead. Another,† flying
'from her house with her two infant children, received a
'wound in the head, from a cutlass, and was robbed of both
'her babes; but providentially escaped. A young married
'woman,‡ with the mother of five small children, finding
'the house in which they slept surrounded by savage ene-
'mies, barricadoed the door, in the vain hope of safety. It
'was forced. Each of the women then seizing an axe, held

* Mrs. Ann Hawkins; who after long and incredible sufferings recovered, and is yet living.

† Mrs. Minty Draper,

‡ Mary Tines.

'the irresolute barbarians in check for several minutes lon-
'ger. Having discharged their guns, they seemed desirous
'of gaining the shelter of the house previous to reloading.—
'At length, with the aid of their spears, and by means of a
'general rush, they overcame their heroine adversaries, and
'instantly stabbed the youngest to the heart. The mother,
'instinctively springing for her suckling babe, which recoil-
'ed through fright, and was left behind, rushed through a
'small window on the opposite side of the house, and provi-
'dentially escaped to the lines, unhurt, between two heavy
'fires.

"The Agent had caused a return to be made at 9 o'clock,
'which certainly exhibited a melancholy statement of the
'loss sustained by the little company. But it was animat-
'ing to perceive that none—not even the wounded in their
'severest sufferings, were dispirited, or insensible of the sig-
'nal providence to which they owed the successful issue of
'their struggle.

"It never has been possible to ascertain the number of the
'enemy killed or disabled on this occasion. The only entry
'made on the subject in the Colonial Journal, is dated No-
'vember 15th; and states, 'The following circumstances
'prove the carnage to have been, for the number engaged,
'great. A large canoe, from which the dead and wounded
'could be seen to be taken, on its arriving at the opposite
'side of the Montserado, and which might easily carry
'twelve men, was employed upwards of two hours in ferry-
'ing them over. In this time, not less than ten or twelve
'trips must have been made. It is also known, that many of
'the wounded were conveyed away along the south beach,
'on mats; and that the dead left of necessity in the woods,
'where many fell, are carried off by their friends every night.
'But two days ago, twenty-seven bodies were discovered by
'a party of friendly Condoes employed by the Agent for the
'purpose. On entering the wood, the offensive effluvium
'from putrid bodies, is at this time intolerable.'

"The numerical force of the settlers amounted to thirty-
' five persons, including six native youths not sixteen years of
' age. Of this number, about one half were engaged.

"At 9 o'clock, the Agent, after advising with the most sen-
' sible mechanics, and others of the settlers, issued an order
' for contracting the lines, by excluding about one-fourth part
' of the houses, and surrounding the remainder, including
' the stores, with a musket-proof stockade; at the angles of
' which, all the guns were to be posted. The fence palings
' and building materials of individuals, were taken for this
' palisade, of which, before night, more than eighty yards
' were completed.

"This work was resumed early the next day, and far ad-
' vanced towards a completion, before it was judged safe to
' devote an hour even to the melancholy duty of burying the
' dead; which was performed on the evening of the 12th.—
' By contracting the lines, the number of men necessary to
' guard them, was considerably reduced; and thus a relief for
' the people obtained, which their sickly and feeble state ab-
' solutely called for. As early as the 14th, one-half of their
' number were released from camp duty, after 8 o'clock in
' the morning; but every man remanded to his post through
' the night. An additional gun was mounted and posted on
' the same day: on the 17th, the artillerists were newly or-
' ganized; and every day witnessed either some improve-
' ments in the discipline of the men, or in the means of de-
' fence and annoyance.

"It could not fail, in the state of utter abandonment and
' solitude to which this little company was reduced, to be
' felt as an encouraging circumstance, that Tom Bassa, a
' prince of some distinction, should, at this moment, have
' sent a message to assure the Colony of his friendship; and
' in testimony of his sincerity, to have forwarded a small pre-
' sent of the productions of the country.

"The enclosure was completed on Sunday morning, the

' 17th; when about one-half of the people had the privilege
' of celebrating Divine service—a privilege which many of
' them very highly appreciated.

"It is not to be either concealed, or made the object of a too
' severe censure, that several of the people should have yield-
' ed, as soon as leisure was afforded for reflection, to the dis-
' couraging circumstances of their situation. There were
' not at this time, exclusive of rice, fifteen days' provisions in
' store. Every individual was subjected to an allowance
' which could not sustain animal strength, under the burden
' of so many severe and extraordinary labours. Nothing
' could be obtained from the country. Seven infant children
' were in the hands of an enemy infuriated by his recent loss-
' es. The native forces were certainly not dispersed; but it
' was no longer in the Agent's power either to learn the inten-
' tions of the chiefs, or to convey any message through to
' them. Add to these unpleasant ingredients of their lot, the
' more cruel circumstance, perhaps of all, that the ammuni-
' tion of the Colony was insufficient for a single hour's de-
' fence of the place if hotly attacked, and an apology may sure-
' ly be found for the very alarming despondency which was
' invading the minds of several of the settlers.—It was a hap-
' py providence that, at this critical moment, the Agent's health
' was so far mended, as to put it in his power often to attend
' the men, at their posts and labours, by night and day—to
' animate them by every method which his invention could
' suggest—and when these failed, to draw from their despair
' itself, an argument for a faithful discharge of their duty.—
' In this difficult labour, he was ably and successfully sup-
' ported by several of the most sensible and influential of the
' Colonists."

An earnest, but ineffectual effort was now made to engage
the Kings in a treaty of peace. The state of the settlement,
as well as motives of humanity, urged that no proper means
should be neglected of bringing the war to a termination.

The enemy was assured "that the Americans came with
' friendly intentions; that they had evinced those friendly
' intentions in all their intercourse with the people of the
' country; that they were willing to settle a peace, but were
' also prepared to carry on the war, and render it immensely
' more destructive than it had yet been found to their foes."—
But though messages were daily exchanged with the Chiefs
for a time, and though they professed a pacific disposition, it
was known that they were earnestly engaged in securing allies from all quarters, and the Agent made diligent preparations for a second attack.

"The 23d of November was devoted to humiliation, thanks-
' giving, and prayer, both on account of the recent success,
' and losses, and the actual perilous state of the settlement.
' Two days afterwards, the most pressing wants of the peo-
' ple were relieved by a small purchase from a transient tra-
' der touching at the Cape."

A generous foreigner, Captain H. Brassey of Liverpool, arrived on the 29th, "and nearly exhausted his own stores to
' relieve the distresses of the sick and wounded, and exerted
' an extensive influence, acquired by long acquaintance with
' the Chiefs, to disarm their hostilities." But in vain. "It
' was ascertained to be their purpose to renew that very night,
' with a large reinforcement, their efforts to destroy the set-
' tlement. The presence of Captain Brassey's large ship in
' the harbour, induced them to defer the attack."

In a letter dated November 30, addressed to the Board, Mr. Ashmun writes: "All the tribes around us are combined in war
' against us. Their principal object is plunder. We are
' surrounded only with a slight barricade, and can only raise
' a force of thirty men. Have not time, limits, nor the means
' to erect an effectual and permanent fortification. Nor any
' means except what casually offers of sending to Sierra Le-
' one for aid. We endeavour to make God our trust. I have
' no idea but to wait here for His deliverance—or to lay our

'bones on Cape Montserado." After many suggestions in regard to supplies by future expeditions, he concludes: "Dear ' Sir, pray for us fervently, that if living, God Almighty ' *would* be with us."

Mr. Ashmun thus describes the contest on the morning of the 2d of December:

"The Agent, for the first time, spent the whole night (29th) ' at the different posts; and had the satisfaction to perceive ' every man attentive to his duty, and every thing connected ' with the defence in a state of the most perfect preparation. ' The wood had been cleared for a considerable space about ' the town. The enemy in order to approach within musket ' shot of the works, was obliged to place himself unsheltered, ' in the open field; and could advance upon no point which ' was not exposed to the cross-fire of two or more of the posts. ' The stockade for a distance on each side of all the several ' stations, was rendered impenetrable to musket shot; and in ' every part afforded a shelter, behind which the defenders ' might indulge the confidence of being nearly secure—a ' point of the very first importance to be secured to the un- ' practised soldier.

"November 30th was spent by the people in the order of ac- ' tion, as it was known that the enemy in the neighbourhood ' were in the actual observation of all that passed within the ' lines. No pickets could be safely trusted during the ensu- ' ing night without the enclosure; but the men attached to ' the different stations were ranged along the stockade at ' five yards distance from each other, with orders to repair to ' their guns on the moment the alarm was given. The ' Agent, spent with the fatigue of waking two successive ' nights, had reclined at thirty minutes past four, the 2d inst. ' upon the light arms which he carried, when the onset was ' made. The works were attacked at the same moment on ' nearly opposite sides. The enemy's western division had ' made their way along the muddy margin of the river, un-

'der the protection of the bank, to the north-western angle
'of the palisade; when, on rising the bank so as to become
'visible from the western post, they had opened upon it a
'sudden and brisk fire, which was promptly and very steadi-
'ly returned by the iron gun, supported by the reserve field-
'piece from the centre. The assailants were repulsed with
'considerable loss. Ten minutes afterwards they renewed
'the onset, and forcing their way higher up the bank than
'before, contended with greater obstinacy, and suffered still
'more severely. A third attempt was made to carry this
'post; but with the same ill success.

"On the opposite quarter the assault had commenced at the
'same moment, with still greater vigour. A large body had
'concealed themselves under a precipitous ledge of rocks for-
'ty yards distant; whence they crept nearly concealed from
'view, within the same number of feet of the station; when
'they suddenly rose, delivered their fire, and rushed forward
'with the utmost fury. At this moment, the two-gun battery
'was unmasked, and opened upon them with immediate ef-
'fect. After a very few discharges, the body of the enemy
'having thrown themselves flat upon the earth, disappeared
'behind the rocks. Their marksmen had taken their sta-
'tions behind projecting rocks, fallen trees, and large ant-
'hills, and still kept up a constant and well directed fire; un-
'der the cover of which the main body rallied and returned
'to the attack not less than four times; and were as often re-
'pulsed by the well directed fire of the large guns; which
'was purposely reserved for those occasions.

"The Agent at this moment perceiving the enemy in mo-
'tion towards the right, under cover of a small eminence
'which favoured their design, proceeded to the southern post,
'which had not yet been engaged, and ordered it to open
'upon them the moment their movement brought them with-
'in the range of its guns. The order was punctually obey-
'ed; which exposed a large number of the assailants to a

' galling cannonade both in front and flank, in a situation
' where their own arms could prove of no effectual service to
' them. The assault on the opposite side of the town had
' been already repulsed; and the signal for a general retreat
' immediately followed. This order was obeyed with such
' promptitude, that the most entire silence succeeded, and
' every warrior disappeared almost instantaneously.

"Not the most veteran troops could have behaved with
' more coolness, or shown greater firmness than the settlers,
' on this occasion. Such had been their hardships, and dis-
' tressing suspense for the last twenty days, that the first vol-
' ley of the enemy's fire brought sensible relief to every breast;
' for it gave assurance that the time had arrived which was to
' put a period to their anxieties.

"The final repulse of the assailants on the western quarter
' took place in seventy minutes from the commencement of the
' contest; the attack upon the eastern post, was prolonged
' ninety minutes; and of the two, was much the most obsti-
' nate and bloody. Three of the men serving at the guns of
' that station, Gardiner, Crook, and Tines, were very badly,
' the last mortally, wounded. The Agent received three
' bullets through his clothes, but providentially escaped un-
' hurt. As the natives in close action load their muskets
' (which are of the largest calibre) with copper and iron slugs,
' often to the enormous measure of twelve inches, their fire
' is commonly very destructive. In this conflict of scarcely
' an hour and a half, the quantity of shot lodged in the paling,
' and actually thrown within the lines, is altogether in-
' credible; and that it took effect in so few cases, can only be
' regarded as the effect of the special guardianship of Divine
' Providence.

"The number of assailants has been variously estimated;
' but can never be correctly ascertained. It is known to be
' much greater than of those engaged on the 11th. Their
' loss, although from the quantities of blood with which the

'field was found drenched, certainly considerable, was much 'less than in the former attack.

"The Agent has often said that their plan of assault was 'the very best that they could have devised. It was certainly 'sustained and renewed with a resolution that would not dis- 'grace the best disciplined troops. But they were not fully 'apprised of the power of well served artillery. None of the 'kings of this part of the coast are without cannon. But to 'load a great gun, is with them the business of half an hour; 'and they were seriously disposed to attribute to sorcery the 'art of charging and firing these destructive machines from 'four to six times in the minute."

The result of this action disheartened the foe, and animated for a moment, the hopes of the Colonists. But the situation of the latter, was most distressing. The small number still more reduced—no aid near—provisions scanty, so that for six weeks they had been on an allowance of meat and bread; the sufferings of the wounded, relieved by little surgical knowledge, less skill and no proper instruments, indescribable; and on an equal distribution of the shot among the guns, not three rounds remaining to each! "We cried unto God," says Mr. Ashmun, (in his letter to the Board of the 7th of December,) "to send us aid, or prepare us, and the Society at home, for 'the heaviest earthly calamity we could dread."

On the following night, an officer at one of the stations, alarmed by some movement in the vicinity, discharged several muskets and large guns, and this circumstance was providentially the means of bringing relief to the almost despairing settlement.

The British Colonial Schooner Prince Regent, laden with military stores, and having on board Major Laing, the celebrated African traveller, with a prize crew commanded by Midshipman Gordon, and eleven seamen of his British Majesty's sloop of war Driver, was at this time passing the Cape on her way to Cape Coast Castle, when her officers arrested by the sound of cannon at midnight from the shore, resolved to ascertain the cause of so extraordinary a circumstance.— No sooner did they learn the truth, and behold a little company of brave men contending for their lives against the leagued forces of nearly every barbarous tribe on that part of the coast, than they generously offered all the aid in their power. By the influence of Captain Laing, the Chiefs were bound to a truce, and to refer all matters of difference between them and the Colony, to the judgment of the Governor of Sierra Leone; while Midshipman Gordon, with eleven seamen, voluntarily consented to remain, and see that the agreement was preserved inviolate. As the Chiefs had no just grounds of complaint, the provision for a reference was never afterwards recollected. The Prince Regent left at the Colony a supply of ammunition, and took her departure on the 4th of December. From that hour the foundations of the Colony were laid in a firm and lasting PEACE.

And who was he, that "single white man," on that distant forest-clad shore, unbroken in spirit, though bowed beneath the heavy hand of sorrow and sickness, casting fear to the winds, directing and heading by day and night, a feeble, undisciplined, dejected, unfortified band of thirty-five emigrants, against whom the very elements seemed warring, while a thousand to fifteen hundred armed savages were rushing to destroy them? Who was he, that in reliance on God for wisdom and might, imparted such skill and courage to this little company,—so ordered every plan and guided every movement; that the fierce foe retired panic struck before them, and they stood rescued and redeemed from impending destruction?

Was he a veteran soldier, inured to danger, familiar with suffering, and bred amid scenes of battle and blood? Was he there adorned by badges of military honour, conscious of a reputation won by deeds of "high emprise," and stimulated to valour by hopes of glory and fears of disgrace?

That was no tried, no ambitious soldier. He was a young man, bred to letters, of retired habits, educated for the Ministry of Christ, unknown to fame,—the victim of disappointment, burdened with debt, and touched by undeserved reproach. He had visited Africa in hope of obtaining the means of doing justice to his creditors; and impelled by Humanity and Religion, had consented, without any fixed compensation, to give, should they be required, his services to the Colony. He found it in peril of extinction. He hesitated not. He failed not to redeem his pledge. He gathered strength from difficulty, and motive from danger. No thronging and admiring spectators cheered him; no glorious pomp and circumstance were there to throw a brightness and a beauty even upon the features and terrors of death. He stood strong in duty, covered by the shield of Faith. His frame shaken by disease; the partner of his life struck down by his side; amid the groans of the afflicted and in the shadow of Hope's dim eclipse, he planned and executed, with the ability of the bravest and most experienced General, measures which saved the settlement, and secured for Liberty and Christianity, a perpetual home and heritage in Africa. Raised up and guided by an Almighty, though invisible Hand, to build a city of righteousness on that shore of oppression, before which the makers of idols should be confounded, and those in chains come over* to fall down in worship, and exclaim as they beheld her light, surely God is in Thee, no weapon formed against him could prosper; no wasting destruction by day, or pestilence walking in darkness, had power to defeat the work.

* Isaiah 45th chapter, 14th and 16th verses.

## CHAPTER VIII.

---

The agitations of this sanguinary conflict, were succeeded by the ravages of disease and the gloom of death. Within four weeks from the time of the departure of the Prince Regent, over Midshipman Gordon and eight out of the eleven seamen who remained with him, the graves were closed.—The conduct of these generous Englishmen, deserves to be remembered forever. Hardly had they stepped on the African shore, to assist a few humble, distressed, but brave men, to whom they were bound only by the common ties of humanity, from whom they could expect no reward, and who might have perished almost unobserved, when they fell and were borne in the arms and amid the lamentations of those whom they came to relieve, to the place of the dead.

The funeral of Midshipman Gordon, was attended by nearly all the Colonists, and by the officers of several vessels, (two of them armed cruisers) then lying in the harbour, and his remains were interred, shrouded in the British flag, with the honours of war. "To express," said Mr. Ashmun in announcing the melancholy event to Lieutenant Rotheray of the British Navy, "the regret I feel, that a measure so full of 'benevolence as the leaving this little force with us, should 'have so disastrous an issue, it is superfluous to attempt, as I 'should but wrong my own feelings. We have derived from 'the presence of these unfortunate men, a great benefit: it as- 'sisted in a powerful manner to allay the warlike spirit of the 'natives, inspired a fresh spirit of resolution into our people, 'and relieved them for nearly three weeks from a part of their 'almost insupportable burthens. I shall rest it with the hon- 'our of my Government, to make such an acknowledgment 'of the favours rendered by the officers and other Agents of 'your's employed on this coast, as justice and a proper esti- 'mate of the beneficial influence of international favours 'given and received, plainly dictate."

Mr. Ashmun's health, which had been improving for some time, was now injured by excessive exertion; and on the 16th of December, he relapsed into a slow, but constant fever, that resisted the power of all ordinary remedies, and left him no hope of recovery. "From despair on the one hand, and a 'sense of duty on the other," he received from the hand of a Frenchman, professing some medical knowledge, (and who providentially arrived on a transient visit at this crisis) a potion, one of the ingredients of which was a large spoonful of calomel. A distressing salivation ensued, and the fever left him.

In the mean time important services were rendered by the officers and crew of a Columbian armed schooner, which anchored on the 8th of December, and remained four weeks at the Colony. Her mechanics contributed to place the settlement in a better state of defence, and the wounded derived sensible relief from the kind attentions of her skilful Surgeon.

It was the middle of February before the Agent was able to resume the active duties of his station. He saw that every possible exertion was required to prepare for the approaching season of rains. With the exception of the store-house, there was but one shingled roof and frame house in the settlement. Many of the cabins were without floors, covered with thatch, affording but an imperfect shelter. The war had for months, occupied wholly the attention of the Colonists, and deranged all their habits of industry and private affairs.

"We long," said Mr. Ashmun at this time in a letter to the Board, "for an arrival from home. Our provisions are short; ' but we have some tobacco, and the country abounds in cat-
' tle, goats, fowls, and vegetables, which tobacco will always
' buy in almost any quantities. Our last barrel of salted pro-
' visions is to be opened next Saturday. But we do not
' complain. God has not, and will not fail to be our provi-
' der. I have only to regret, that the war has put back our
' improvements nearly or quite a whole year. But I firmly
' believe the work of fighting is over, and that future emi-
' grants will enjoy without molestation, all the fruits of their
' industry." To the Secretary of the Society, on the 20th of February he wrote:—"Divine Providence has since my last,
' been gradually dispersing the clouds which then overhung
' us. We have opened a trade with a wealthy tribe in the
' interior for bullocks. They cost fifteen bars* each. Our
' people begin to breathe freely. We still keep up a strict
' watch at night, but are able with safety to reduce it, so as
' to make it very little burdensome to the Colonists. Our
' wounded, though unable to labour, are once more moving
' about with their slings and crutches, and we have just be-
' gun to build and repair the houses in which ourselves and
' (if any arrive) the fresh emigrants are to spend the rains.
' Finally, the progress of the Colony is now *forwards*, and
' not as it has been for months past, retrograde.

"My health is nearly restored. I stand a monument of
' God's mercy, and behold the graves of fifteen white persons
' around me; all of whom have died since I landed on the

---

* About eight dollars.

'Cape. Help me to praise the Lord; and pray—fervently
'pray, that I may spend a life thus astonishingly preserved,
'in some humble way of usefulness, to His blessed cause in
'Africa and the world."

On the 5th of March he wrote:—"We have all our cap-
'tives back again. The Kings met and agreed to send them
'without any demand. It was, however, expected we would
'make them a present. This I did. The little things were
'all much uncivilized. Some had forgotten the English lan-
'guage. Some had forgotten their own parents! Others
'had actually gone wild. And to avoid their friends, scud
'like fawns into the bushes.

"By a British vessel, we have the pleasing information that
'the American ship of war, Cyane, is at Sierra Leone. She
'will touch here on her cruise, and I hope bring despatches;
'not a letter having been received in the Colony from Ame-
'rica, since my arrival.

"I have said in several letters, *that I thought myself re-
'covering*. But I am now convinced, that in this climate, it
'is vain to expect to recover the health I enjoyed in Ameri-
'ca: certainly impossible for *me*, in my present situation, to
'be any thing else but a sick man.

"It is not my nature to complain with too much facility.—
'But think you see a young man formed for society, sepa-
'rated almost entirely from the civilized and Christian world;
'his constitution broke with a fever of six months; his only
'earthly comforter snatched away; mingling for months to-
'gether his own groans and sighs with those of the sick,
'wounded, and dying; almost for weeks together pained with
'the sight of the corpses of the whites who had undertaken
'to reside here for our protection; the complaints of the Co-
'lonists, a statement of their wants, their application for a
'thousand things with which it is impossible to supply them,
'constantly presenting themselves; every public work to be
'planned and superintended; the movements of the natives

'to be closely watched, and their hostile designs to be provid-
'ed against; provision made by trade, &c. &c. for the sub-
'sistence of the people; for their shelter against the ap-
'proaching rains; and a ceaseless anxiety to lay the founda-
'tion of the Colony in a way that will not be detrimental to
'its future prosperity; the books to be kept (and they are
'not kept as they should be) and correspondence carried on;
'think, my Dear Sir, of all this falling upon an individual,
'and say, can he recover his wonted health of body or strength
'of mind? I might go on enumerating other causes of my
'feeble and crazy state of health, but it is painful to have said
'what I have. I have done it, in the hope of showing that
'no *one*, and hardly *two* Agents can do the duties required
'here, or attempt it without betraying the interests of the
'cause, or sacrificing himself."*

An account of the suffering state of the settlement, from the pen of Mr. Ashmun, in the Sierra Leone Gazette, with information derived from other sources, induced the commander of the Cyane, Captain Robert Trail Spence, though his health was impaired, and his crew enfeebled by a cruise of twelve months in the West Indies, to adopt efficient measures for the relief and safety of the Colony. He saw the importance of leaving an armed vessel on the coast, and by the most energetic exertion, the hulk of the old schooner Augusta, which had been abandoned by former Agents of the U. States' Government at Sierra Leone, was drawn from the mud, fitted for sea, and bearing six guns, with a crew of twelve men, placed under command of Lieutenant Dashiell, to guard the coast, and render to the Colony every possible aid, in any exigency. Captain Spence deemed it a solemn duty to ensure, if possible, the safety of the establishment,

* This letter was dated "Christopolis," &c. Mr. Ashmun inquires near the close—"Have the Board fixed a name for the Town? I am not satisfied with Christopolis, and seldom use it. I wait the instructions of the Board on this subject."

and having incurred a heavy pecuniary responsibility in the purchase therefor, of lumber, stores, and ammunition at Sierra Leone, directed, ῀on his arrival, a large portion of his crew to assist, for twenty days, the settlers and native labourers, in the construction of a commodious house for the Agent, and a stone fortress which he trusted (to use his own expression) might prove a "tower of strength." In the midst of his benevolent exertions, he saw the Surgeon of his ship, Dr. Dix, seized with the fever, and after a short illness expire—a victim to his generous zeal, for the welfare of the Colony. This lamented man, had watched with interest the progress of the Colony from its earliest existence,—had visited and administered relief to the emigrants when at Sherbro; "and the tears of a grateful people," said Mr. Ashmun, "fell into his grave, which they covered with their own hands over his ashes."

The rapid progress of disease among the seamen on shore, compelled Captain Spence to leave incomplete the works he had commenced; nor could his earnest and sympathizing endeavours prevent, soon after his departure, the loss of nearly forty of his brave men.

The important works undertaken, and greatly advanced during the visit of the Cyane, were planned and superintended by Mr. Ashmun; and the correspondence between him and the commander of that vessel, inserted in the Appendix to the Seventh Report of the Colonization Society, bears testimony alike to the depth and soundness of his judgment, and to the liberality and disinterestedness of that intelligent officer. Mr. Richard Seaton, the first Clerk of the Cyane, consented, with the approbation of Captain Spence, to remain as assistant to Mr. Ashmun, who saw, that alone and with health impaired, it was impossible to fulfil the numerous and arduous duties of the Agency.

On the 21st of April, Mr. Ashmun, "worn down with cares and fatigue," having organized the labouring force, and obtained the consent of Mr. Seaton to superintend the public works, sailed in the Augusta for Settra Kroo, two hundred miles South-eastward, for the purpose of conveying thither forty Kroomen, (who had given three weeks' labour for their passage) and conciliating the regards of the native Chiefs of the country. During his absence of twenty-one days, nothing escaped his observation; he examined the features of the coast, visited and ascertained the dispositions of several tribes, and having engaged twenty-five Kroomen as labourers, and made some purchases of valuable articles from the natives and the English factory at Sesters, he returned to the Cape on the 13th of May.

"One century ago," he remarks,* "a great part of this line
' of coast was populous, cleared of trees, and under cultiva-
' tion. It is now covered with a dense, and almost continu-
' ous forest. This is almost wholly a second growth—com-
' monly distinguished from the original by the profusion of
' brambles and brushwood, which abounds amongst the larger
' trees, and renders the woods entirely impervious, even to
' the natives, until paths are opened by the bill-hook.

"The native towns are numerous, but not large. The peo-
' ple raise their own rice, cassada, and palm oil; and procure
' their guns, powder, clothes, tobacco, knives, cooking uten-
' sils, and luxuries from French slave traders. We saw at
' least three vessels of this description.

"Every tribe visited on this trip, declared by its Prince or
' head man, its intention to preserve with us a good under-
' standing, and to trade freely to the Colony. The particu-
' lars of our late war, especially the result of the two engage-
' ments, have been reported far and near, and given to the
' Colony a character for strength and invincibility, which
' must in different ways contribute greatly to its advan-
' tage."

* Appendix to the Seventh Report of the Colonization Society.

On the return of the Agent, the Colonists were found to have continued their labours, under the direction of one of their own number; while Mr. Seaton had experienced a severe attack of the fever of the climate.

Aware of the dangers of the settlement, the Managers had early in the preceding winter, determined to despatch a reinforcement of emigrants with stores, under the direction of Dr. Ayres, whose improved health now permitted him to resume his duties as principal Agent and Physician in the Colony. This gentleman embarked at Baltimore with sixty-one coloured passengers, on the 16th of April, and arrived at Cape Montserado on the 24th of May. Such an accession to the numbers and resources of the Colony, could not fail to confirm the hopes and resolution of the earlier settlers who had so long borne up against want, and malevolence, and misfortune.

The amiable Seaton having languished nearly two months, resolved as the only means of prolonging life, to return in the Oswego to the United States. "The bloom of youth," says Mr. Ashmun, "had just ripened into the graces of manhood,
' and given to a person naturally prepossessing, the higher or-
' nament of a benevolent and highly accomplished under-
' standing. He perceived his services were needed by a Co-
' lony which had interested his heart; and he gave them.—
' Becoming the voluntary companion and assistant of the so-
' litary Agent, he saw the Cyane sail from the coast with
' composure, on the 21st of April. His conciliating manners,
' aided by a judicious procedure, deepened in the hearts of
' the Colonists, the impression first made by his disinterested-
' ness. Seldom has the longest friendship power to cement
' a more cordial union, than had begun to rivet to this gene-
' rous stranger the heart of the writer; when in the first week
' of May he was assailed by the alarming symptoms of fever.
' The fatal issue of the attack has been already anticipated
' by the reader. He had long maintained the doubtful strug-

' gle—when on the —— of June, five days after embarking
' in the Oswego, he resigned his spirit to God who gave it."

Notwithstanding his many pressing engagements, and the illness which had so severely afflicted him nearly up to this time, Mr. Ashmun had neglected no opportunity of transmitting to the Managers of the Colonization Society, an account of his proceedings, with all such facts and statements, as he thought might aid their deliberations, and light the way to measures best suited to promote the permanent welfare of the Colony.

He was earnest in his requests, that education, not only in letters and science, but in morals and religion, should be esteemed of vital importance.

In a letter forwarded by the Cyane, after enumerating sundry improvements which he designed to make, he observes—
"Our little school is kept in operation, but it is a feeble affair.
' Our poor liberated captives work hard and cheerfully, but
' receive little instruction. My heart often bleeds for them
' and others in similar circumstances. When can you send
' out an accomplished and pious schoolmaster? Permit me
' to say a word about a Minister of the Gospel. We are
' starving for want of the able, regular administration of the
' word and ordinances. Does not *even the Colony* deserve
' the attention of some Missionary Society? Let it be con-
' sidered that a zealous Minister, Catechists, &c. residing in
' the town, may bestow any part of their time and labours on
' the heathen. They may open schools on the opposite side
' of the river, which will immediately be partially filled with
' heathen youth and children. They may form in town a
' Missionary family. The people of this part of the coast have
' no inveterate anti-religious prejudices to prevent their
' attending every Sabbath or oftener, to hear the Divine word.
' Very good interpreters can be procured for a trifling com-
' pensation. I am certain that an able Minister of the Gos-
' pel, clothed with all the authority and prerogatives of a

' commissioned ambassador of the Lord Jesus, is the man
' now wanting. Let Catechists attend him."

"I wish," continues Mr. Ashmun, "to afford the Board a
' full view of our situation, and of the African character. The
' following INCIDENT, I relate not for its singularity, for simi-
' lar events take place, perhaps, every month in the year; but
' it has fallen under my own observation, and I can vouch
' for its authenticity:—King Boatswain, our most powerful
' supporter and steady friend among the natives, (so he has
' uniformly shown himself) received a quantity of goods in
' trade from a French slaver, for which he stipulated to pay
' young slaves. He makes it a point of honour to be punctual
' to his engagements. The time was at hand when he ex-
' pected the return of the slaver. He had not the slaves.—
' Looking round on the peaceable tribes about him, for her
' victims, he singled out the Queahs, a small agricultural and
' trading people, of most inoffensive character. His warriors
' were skilfully distributed to the different hamlets, and
' making a simultaneous assault on the sleeping occupants, in
' the dead of night, accomplished, without difficulty or re-
' sistance, the annihilation (with the exception of a few towns)
' of the whole tribe. Every adult man and woman was mur-
' dered; every hut fired; very young children *generally*
' shared the fate of their parents. The boys and girls alone
' were reserved to pay the Frenchman."

He thus concludes this letter:—"God Almighty has surely
' given us His powerful aid and effectual blessing. I pros-
' trate myself before His holy Throne, and humbly acknow-
' ledge His own right hand made visible for our temporal sal-
' vation. That He would send down upon us spiritual bless-
' ings in great abundance, and on all to whom the Colony
' looks up in America for support and direction, is my earnest
' prayer."

It has been stated already, that from the first, Mr. Ashmun
proposed, as one great object of his voyage, to ascertain the

resources, and make particular observations on the trade of Africa; and to establish under the sanction and auspices of the Colonization Society, regular commercial intercourse between that country and the United States.

His letters to the Secretary of the Society, from the Capes of Virginia, and from Fayal, contain some of his thoughts on the subject. In September, soon after his arrival in Africa, his opinions and plans were more fully developed. He informed the Board of Managers, that he had not over estimated the value of the trade; that the Territory owned, by the Society, abounded with camwood, which in some places extended down to the coast, and formed one-third part of the forest trees; that although it cost labour to obtain it, and the natives were indolent, still an Agent with suitable goods, time at command, and constantly residing at the settlement, might probably collect from two to three hundred tons every three months; that four cargoes might be sent home in a year,* the profits on which, would pay the expense of the ships employed; that with no leisure for any thing of the kind, he had done something to revive the trade; and finally, that if relieved from the direction of the Colony, and appointed (should Dr. Ayres decline) Agent of the United States' Government for the recaptured Africans, he would be able, without taking from the time occupied in duties to his charge, to conduct a trade of considerable extent, tending to civilize the natives, and of much advantage to the Society.

On his way to Africa, at Fayal, he had judged it necessary to purchase a small quantity of supplies, and give in payment drafts on the United States' Government and the Society.— Observing on his arrival the destitution of the Colony, he obtained of the owners of the Strong, goods to the amount of fourteen hundred dollars, for which was taken in payment, an order on the Society, payable at the end of six months. In

---

* This opinion we believe to have been erroneous.

his letter of advice, he suggested that the Society could either pay for these goods, and thus realize all the profits to be derived from them, or should he be appointed Agent for the recaptured Africans, and receive (as other Agents had done) a years' salary in advance—the whole or such portion as the Society should choose, might be applied in payment. He did not, however, conceal his desire, that the obligation should be assumed by the Society, and that his salary (should there be one) might go to the extinction of his debts in the U. States.

Unfortunately he stood not now in the clear light of public confidence. The malign eye of suspicion was upon him.— The Managers of the Society participated in the general distrust. He had left the country without offering apology or explanation to those who were dissatisfied with his management of the Repertory; feeling no obligation to unveil his private affairs, and cherishing too much respect for his own integrity, to volunteer in its defence. Suspicions which were at first, from misapprehension indulged against him, borrowed shape and distinctness from the imagination—grew by time, and at length, gained with many, the weight of certainty and truth.

On the 24th of May, Dr. Ayres had returned to the Colony as principal Agent, both of the Government and Society.— By despatches that came with him, Mr. Ashmun had the mortification to learn, that his drafts, both on the Government and Society, had been dishonoured; that neither had made any appropriation for his benefit; that he had been appointed to no Agency by the Government; that the Society had invested him with no authority; but while it gratefully acknowledged his services, and engaged liberally to reward them, had left the amount of his compensation, for the past, undetermined; and for the future, a matter for negotiation with the principal Agent.

The Roman satirist, amid his kindling conceptions of an extended civil war, seemed to see the whole earth subdued, except the inflexible soul of Cato.* A noble tribute this, to firmness, that grew firmer when the storm raged, and the waves dashed higher and heaving against it. The stoic philosophy might have taught Ashmun, that reason is the proper remedy for grief; that the combat with the dark aspect and reverses of fortune is great—the achievement divine; for empire, for freedom, for prosperity, for tranquillity;† but he had been educated in the school of Christ, and relied mainly for triumph upon the Revelation and Providence of God. He knew that events were ordered by Almighty Wisdom and Goodness; that silence became a sinner under the correction of Heaven; that He who had set him in darkness, could bring him forth to honour; that fruit, sweet and healthful, might be plucked from adversity; and that a meek and resolute acquiescence in the Divine Will, was the best remedy for present evil—the sure preparative and pledge of future and eternal good. He remembered God. He listened to that voice which often speaks, though man perceiveth it not. He considered how the Divine Mercy had shone upon his afflictions; how his pride had been humbled and his heart loosened from the world; how his soul had been kept back from the pit, and his life from perishing by the sword; and cheered by these tokens of Providence, he cried unto God his strength, and took refuge under the shadow of the Almighty.

It appears to have been early a habit with Mr. Ashmun, to be so constantly occupied with his own duties, as to have little time or inclination, to intermeddle with the appropriate duties of others. He knew that officious advice is seldom

* Audire magnos jam videor duces,
Non indecoro pulvere sordidos,
Et cuncta terrarum subacta
Preter atrocem animum Catonis.
Hor. II B. 1st Ode.
† Epictetus, Book II, Chap. 18.

followed, and that faults are often aggravated by censure. As for reputation, he was convinced, that no man ever acquired it, by declaring that it was his by desert, or won it by entreaty; that it was a light emanating from great and virtuous actions, which envy might dim for a time, or ignorance darken, but which the hand of Truth never failed, finally, to hold up pure and unclouded, to the admiration of the world.

By the return of the Oswego, he informed the Board, "that 'by ordinary success in trade on the coast, he could realize 'at least four times the sum he should ever ask or expect, 'either of the Government or Society; that it was his wish, 'however, (unless compelled to resort to some other employ- 'ment) to lend his services to the cause of the Society, as 'long as they should be required; that he felt unworthy of 'the vote of thanks passed by the Board, for endeavouring to 'perform, as well as he could, the arduous and perilous du- 'ties connected with the defence of the Colony; and that to 'know that any part of his conduct merited the approbation 'of the Board, was among the most powerful motives for 'endeavouring, in future, to deserve it."\*

Under date of the 21st of July, having acknowledged the receipt of the letter by which he had been referred to Dr. Ayres for a settlement of the specific conditions on which his services should in future be rendered, he observes: "I have 'freely stated to him, that whatever might be a paramount 'motive with me for consenting to stay in Africa, my most 'decided convictions of duty, forbade me, under present cir- 'cumstances, to indulge the thought, without a definite and

---

\* A small present of clothing had been sent to him by the Oswego, in allusion to which he observes: "The valuable present of clothing which I have received, has proved doubly so from the seasonableness of its arrival. But I need not say that it deserves, in my estimation, a much higher value from the occasion of the donation, and the enlightened source from which it proceeded. The grateful sentiment it has inspired, will long survive the period when the articles themselves shall have ceased to be of any value."

'certain pecuniary remuneration. The amount of salary I
'have, likewise, fixed at *twelve hundred and fifty dollars*
'per annum, besides my subsistence and a passage home to
'the United States, should I live until it might be proper to
'return.

"Less than the above might have been asked with, perhaps,
'a show of disinterestedness. But it would have been mere-
'ly a show—an ostentation of liberality, resulting, as it cer-
'tainly must, in a disregard and sacrifice of the claims of
'justice. *More,* out of a regard to the present state of the
'Society's finances, and from the expectation that the salary
'shall be *certain,* I was willing not to ask."

After stating that there were conclusive objections against accepting any privilege of trade in lieu of a portion of this salary, he adds: "The payment of it in America as it falls due
'—say of a sum not to exceed one half, to drafts made in the
'course of the year, and the balance at the year's end, it is
'judged, will be considered by the Board, as not only the
'simplest, but the most economical mode of compensating
'either their present, or any other Agents, either in Ameri-
'ca or Africa. A stipulation to this effect, leaves the mind at
'rest on a subject to which it must, otherwise, very often, and
'probably with anxiety, recur. The Board have then the
'right to expect, and to claim the unremitting and undivided
'services of their Agents, and will find it comparatively easy
'to proceed, with the most unhesitating decision, in instruct-
'ing, appointing, or removing them.

"I await the Board's ratification or rejection of the forego-
'ing arrangement, which I hope they will find it convenient
'to transmit by the next Packet.\*

---

\* In the month of June, a resolution was adopted by the Board, appointing him assistant Agent; (without, however, fixing his compensation) but as notice thereof, did not probably reach him until late in the autumn, soon after which, all the concerns of the Colony (in consequence of the return of Dr. Ayres) again devolved upon him, if for no other reason, he appears not to have adverted to the fact in any of his letters.

"For compensation to the 24th of May, 1823, I shall, for 'the present, look solely to the Government."

He gave the Board, by the same conveyance, an account of the state and prospects of the Colony. "I have determin-
' ed," he remarks, "to let no opportunity pass without humbly,
' but earnestly, representing to the Board, and every influen-
' tial correspondent I have in America, the spiritual and mo-
' ral necessities of your Colonists. A Missionary and two
' Schoolmasters, with a female Teacher, are needed beyond
' measure.

"Our last accounts from America, filled us with hope in
' relation to the future prospects of the Society at home.—
' There were evident symptoms of a disposition in the Ame-
' rican public to look earnestly at the subject. They will, I
' believe, come on as fast, perhaps, as the good of the Colony
' shall require. It is not desirable at present, that more than
' three or four shipments of sixty persons each, be made in
' the year. But the proportion may increase, and that very
' largely, every year. Let one hundred families be well set-
' tled with a good house and perfectly improved lot to each,
' in town—and a plantation without, well cultivated; let a
' Hospital, Ware-house, and temporary Receptacles for new
' comers be prepared—and the wheels of the machine—its
' schools, courts, &c. get a good momentum on them, in a
' proper direction, and Sir, you may throw in new settlers
' as fast as your funds will probably admit."

To a friend, about the same time, he wrote: "After discou-
' raging delays, and severe trials, the Colony now appears to
' be established on a much more solid footing than it could
' have been without them. I speak of the effects of our afflic-
' tions, as they relate to the establishment *here*, without
' knowing how they have affected the public mind and the
' interests of the cause, at home; but hope and believe they
' will be overruled to advance it even there. The delays and
' dangers encountered in acquiring the secure possession of
' a Territory, will endear it, and greatly enhance its value, to

' the settlers for a long time to come. They have, even the
' most worldly, been *driven* by the extremity of their circum-
' stances, to supplication and prayer. The truly pious among
' us have thus contracted the habit of regarding, and acknow-
' ledging the hand of God in all their ways; and of trusting
' His gracious promises more implicitly, both for soul and bo-
' dy, for this world and the next. Indeed, I think I can say
' of a goodly number, that their chastisements have increased
' in them, visibly, 'the peaceable fruits of righteousness.' I
' beg your prayers that such may prove their blessed effect
' on your unworthy Brother and Servant in the profession of
' the Gospel.

"We are now one hundred and fifty strong, all in health,
' (I speak of the Colonists) have about fifty houses, including
' three store houses, and a heavy substantial stone tower,
' fourteen feet high, mounting six pieces of ordnance. We
' have a good framed house surrounded with a piazza. Dr.
' Ayres has brought out the frame of another of equal dimen-
' sions. Harmony and a good degree of industry, at present
' prevail. Thus you see, that we are prepared to go on and
' fulfil the anxious wishes of the friends of the cause, in rela-
' tion to the cultivation of the lands, and the formation of a
' regular, moral, and happy society."

## CHAPTER IX.

The presence of Dr. Ayres diminished, for a time, the cares and responsibilities* of Mr. Ashmun, who considering how uncertain was the time he might remain in Africa, resolved to add as much as possible to his stock of general knowledge, and prepare himself for any change in his fortunes. Though he perceived that the tide was fast ebbing with him towards an ocean dark and unexplored, he knew that "wisdom is more precious than rubies," and whatever vicissitudes or dangers might await him, of whatever else he might be deprived, he would retain her incomparable treasure.

Amid the perplexity and uncertainty of his affairs,

---

* In a letter to a friend, dated June 5th, he writes: "I am recovered, except swollen ankles and legs, and consequent weakness throughout the system. But Dr. Ayres by assuming a weight of cares which has oppressed me for months, will thus, as Agent, probably promote my perfect recovery much more effectually than he could by medical prescription."

he summoned his intellectual powers to their highest efforts. Probably, during no equal period of his life, did he pursue his studies with more enthusiasm or success, than from the arrival of Dr. Ayres in May, 1823, to his departure in December of the same year. The following rules for conduct, dated September, 1823, indicate the principles which animated, and the spirit that then sustained him:

"*Let all thy ways be established.*"

"1. Never to be guilty of a *meanness* which my most 'virtuous and spirited children (should I be blessed with chil- 'dren possessing these qualities) would blush to see published 'to the world as a part of a parent's Biography.

"2. Never, unless compelled by poverty which fetters the 'freedom of my own Agency, to accept of a situation, or en- 'gage in an occupation contrary to the habits of my educa- 'tion, below that rank in life to which my talents entitle me, 'or which experience or observation have taught me would 'cramp the exercise of abilities, either natural or acquired.

"3. To study and avail myself of a quick sense of pro- 'priety, in all matters, small or great, of morality, judgment, 'manners, dress and business.

"4. To build on my own foundation, and to study none 'but the most perfect examples, living or dead.

"5. To prefer the society of dead authors of eminence, to 'that of living actors, of simple mediocrity.

"6. To regard the contracting of a debt, as a mortgage of 'personal liberty and moral principle. (John Basilworth II, 'of Russia, affixed a brand of infamy on such as contracted 'debts they could not pay, and sent them into banishment.)

"7. To avoid exposing myself to the degradation of es- 'pousing measures, which the situation of a weaker or more 'ignorant man may give him the power to defeat.

"8. Never to assert, without being able to prove to a can-

' did and sensible man, my proposition: never to advise un-
' less sure that the neglecter of my counsel will repent his
' folly.

"9. Never to talk without the undivided attention of all
' to whom I address my discourse.

"10. Always to utter my sentiments with precision and
' propriety—even should it cost me some previous reflection;
' and never begin an expression without bringing it to a
' perfect close.

"11. Let me search after truth, and contract such an af-
' fection for it as to endure in my mind no rival prejudices,
' or opinions, *on any* subject whatever.

"12. To run the risk of being candid, open, sincere; and
' abandon utterly the friendship and confidence of any civi-
' lized man base and depraved enough to attempt to gain an
' undue advantage of these qualities.

"13. Never to commence an enterprise without being
' well assured of its utility; and having undertaken, never to
' abandon it unaccomplished.

"14. To do whatever I undertake in the best possible
' manner,—always allowing for the time and means I can
' employ on the object.

"15. To acquire a style of writing and expression, of con-
' ception and feeling—of manners and deportment, which
' destitute of servility, locality and mannerism, shall pass
' current among the best ranks of people of all professions and
' in all countries.

"16. To become master of the grammatical construction
' and written form of the Italian, (as the key to all the Southern
' European) and perfectly familiar with the French, langua-
' ges; both as written and spoken.

"17. To make the Latin (written) a second vernacular.

"18. To continue my inquiries and reflections on what-
' ever subject may engage them, until either my information
' is perfectly exact, or the means of extending it exhausted.

"19. To eat meat, fish or fowl, but at one meal in twenty-
' four hours, except when fatigue, sickness, exhaustion, or
' some extraordinary occasion requires a departure from the
' rule; and in my meals to observe moderation.

"20. To vitiate no one of the appetites so far as to render
' it necessary to health, to mental vigour, or bodily ease, to
' continue the indulgence.

"21. To be rigorously exact in keeping my pecuniary
' accounts; that I may not appear mean in my disburse-
' ments.

"22. To turn every portion of my time to good account.

"23. To despise all wit but the pure attick.

"24. To have as little connexion as possible with the
' conceited, the overbearing, the pedantic, the blustering;
' and finally, with all who are incapable of measuring and
' esteeming solid acquirements and intellectual superiority,
' even when sheltered from the vulgar stare by a plain and
' unassuming external demeanor.

"25. In my estimation of others, let ignorance, when no
' opportunity has been had to remove it, be treated with kind-
' ness and indulgence; where it co-exists with a wish and ef-
' fort to remove it, let it command my favour and assistance;
' where it is accompanied with the contented complacency of
' the fool whom it debases, let it make me blush for the heart
' of a brute in the form of a human being; but, when with
' swaggering pretensions either to knowledge or respect on
' some other grounds, it merits an equal share of the pro-
' foundest contempt and detestation.

"To conclude,—I fully believe in a particular Providence
' regulating and ordering the conduct and purposes of men;
' so as to leave the voluntary agent accountable. We shall
' be instruments to fulfil the Divine purposes *nolentes volentes*.
' If wickedness succeed for a time, it prospers by the Divine
' decree and can only proceed a given number of links in
' its chain."

His private Journal contains the following notices of his studies during this period. On the 4th of November, after alluding to the "mercantile mania which had possessed him" the preceding year, he observes: "This gave way in the 'early part of 1823, to the ambition of becoming the general 'scholar, acquiring an easy and correct style, and that varie-'ty of knowledge necessary as a qualification to a periodical 'essayist, whose views should embrace, at the same time, 'both popularity and general usefulness.

"But my reflections were too active to suffer me long to 'acquiesce in so precarious a prospect. We must have bread. 'And this pursuit would starve any one in the U. States. 'Besides, what is a man's life worth to him for any present 'happiness it is capable of imparting, without possessing the 'respect of his fellow-men, and some reputable rank in the 'scale of society? Old as I am, I reflected, I have formed 'myself to industrious and studious habits. My mind has 'more strength and vigour, perhaps, than at any previous 'period of my life. Even the most intricate investigations of 'literature, and of any of the sciences except mathematics, 'are a pleasure to me. I am disentangled from many of the 'embarrassments of my private circumstances. I shall, per-'haps, enjoy as much of life, even while studying a profes-'sion as in any other pursuit, or in no pursuit, during the 'same period,—shall stand an equal chance of being esteem-'ed by others, and shall cultivate my mind as much by that 'as any other study. Accordingly, about the middle of Au-'gust, I recommenced the Law.

"While going through the first volume of Blackstone, I 'read Junius, the History of England by Aquetil, Dr. Ro-'bertson's America, a part of Marshall's Life of Washington, '(third volume,) Hamilton's political writings, a part of Ro-'bertson's Scotland, Voltaire's essays, the Pioneers, and Ma-'dame De Stael's Delphine, (volume first,) in French; besides 'a variety of historical and political tracts.—I read with

'great deliberation and accuracy—and did not begin on the
'second volume before the 20th of October.

"I have now nearly completed the volume, reviewing a
'large portion of it as I proceed—and except Burr's Trial,
'and the article Law in Rees' Encyclopedia, have engaged in
'little foreign reading."

On the 28th of the same month, he writes: "Through the
'good Providence of God, I have this evening finished, in the
'midst of countless interruptions, frequent indispositions,
'and sometimes depressing anxieties, Blackstone's Commen-
'taries; and that with occasional reviews and as much applica-
'tion of thought as I was master of. A rule which I have
'generally observed, is to leave no passage without obtaining
'as clear and distinct a conception of the meaning as the
'means in my power admitted. But I have several times
'departed, I confess, from this rule, from mere lassitude and
'weariness; sensations which none but law students in tro-
'pical Africa can fully know the difficulty of conquering.
'I now begin to consider myself a sort of indented appren-
'tice to the Law, and do flatter myself that the most irk-
'some part of the study, consisting in the first rudiments
'and leading technical phrases of the science, are gone
'through with.

"I had the satisfaction to remark, in reading the last book,
'that I recollected the principles of the three first, as they
'were casually alluded to; and very seldom had occasion to
'refer back for the explanation of recurring technical terms
'and phrases. The only notes I have taken, are about a
'score of legal modes of expression—choosing, according to
'Dr. Watts' advice, to make the text itself my common-place
'book.

"The studies which I have occasionally mingled with the
'perusal of the two last volumes, have been, a review of
'French Grammar—Voltaire's critical writings—his History
'of the Religious wars in France, and a part of the Henri-

' ade—Mosheim's Church History, (volume third,) English
' History, and a few unconnected articles in Rees' Encyclo-
' pedia. I have also begun to throw together, in a concise,
' and somewhat of a methodical form, a synopsis of my re-
' ligious faith, for my own use. The proofs being familiar
' to my thoughts, I have commonly neglected to state at
' length. This last, I endeavour to make a serious and pro-
' fitable engagement.

"I have, lastly, with an air I fear of tyro pedantry, written
' out a few very brief and imperfect law theses, of which I
' hope very soon to be heartily ashamed.

"I think I have devoted, of absolute time to the Commen-
' taries, about four hours daily, a little short of three months;
' and as may well be supposed, have suffered considerably
' in health by the effort: for this labour is not a substitute,
' but an addition to all my official services in the Colony.—
' But a person in my circumstances, at the age of twenty-
' nine, *must* use exertion and perseverance in acquiring a
' profession to which he has not yet been bred—or reconcile
' himself to the mortification and meanness of being a smat-
' terer all his days."

It is evident from the Journals and other manuscripts of Mr. Ashmun, that the preceding extracts present but a partial view of the variety and extent of his studies and investigations during the period to which they relate. He rejoiced like a strong man to run the race of improvement, and shook despondency from him in his giant course. In consequence of the protracted illness of Dr. Ayres, his expectations of relief from public duty, were but in a small degree realized. But no moment escaped the use of his industry, and the action of his mind was increased by pressure.

That his religious character had been the subject of a somewhat varied, but decided declension, during the interval between his departure from Maine and a period subsequent to his arrival in Africa, is to be inferred as Mr. Ashmun's opinion, from several passages in his writings. Nor was it to be expected that a mind like his, (considering the nature of the discipline which Providence had selected for his benefit,) should on no occasion have evinced feelings hostile to the dictates of true wisdom, and its own settled principles of duty.

His sins were not concealed from himself, and he sought not to cover them before God. His remarks upon his religious state and experience show, that he cherished habitually a deep reverence for the Word and Providence of God; and that he felt the supreme importance of possessing an interest in the Divine favour. Wounded pride might prompt occasional severity of remark, or impatience be excited by reiterated disappointment; yet soon after his arrival in Africa, his heart appears to have been pervaded with a sense of his sinfulness, to have submitted humbly to afflictions, and sought with earnestness, the benefits which he trusted they were intended to convey to his soul. If misanthropy ever cast her shadow upon him, it was only until he could raise his eyes towards the Heavens, and behold them bright with love to mankind. His circumstances when he penned the Journal from which we present a few extracts, should not be forgotten. That he was not meeker than Moses, and more patient than Job, should not be remembered to his reproach.

*March* 16*th*, 1823.

"This is the third day of my possessing comfortable health
' after lying about six months under a variety of distressing
' and dangerous disorders. I had a public thank-offering
' put up in the morning for my recovery. Heavenly Father,
' make me more thankful; and may gratitude, and obedience,
' and humility, and deadness to the world, take place in me
' of those lusts and vices which ruled my soul and stained
' my life before my affliction.

"Have lately addicted myself to reading the word of God.

"Have had some *religious,* and I believe spiritual comfort
' to-day. May the living Spirit, and enlightening word of
' God my Saviour, lead me condescendingly along, till I shall
' have acquired a little stability, a little strength, and a little
' saving knowledge of Thee, O my precious Redeemer. Be-
' setting sins, passion, pride, and love of the world.

*April* 13.

"The cares and business of the past two weeks, have occu-
' pied nearly all my thoughts. My captious and irritable dis-
' positions, not being well guarded, have prevailed. But God's
' spirit, I believe, is not entirely withdrawn. He still fulfills
' the office of convincing, if not of sanctifying and comforting.
' I feel and lament my want of gratitude to God for temporal
' and spiritual blessings, but more the former than the latter.

"I am burdened with my own sloth and stupidity in my
' Heavenly Master's work. Alas! alas! my insincerity, in
' prayer, in reading God's word, in religious conversation.

"I use my unruly tongue too much; and it is naturally 'full
' of deadly poison.' 'In a multitude of words there wanteth
' not sin;' and so I have found it. O Lord God, help me by
' Thy Grace, to bridle this member, that with it, I may also
' govern the whole body—through Jesus Christ my Lord.

"I am sometimes anxious to exhibit more of the practical
' power of religion to the numerous strangers who are now
' with us. They have seen little in me to demonstrate its in-
' fluence on the character and conduct. I fear that some as-
' sociate its very idea with my infirmities. But I look to
' Thee, O God, for pardon, for wisdom, for sanctification, for
' a right spirit and grace to live a holy life. It is my desire.
' Thou hast inspired it. O Father, increase it; perfect it,
' fulfil it; and be Thine the glory, ages without end. Amen.

SUNDAY, *June 8th.*

"How difficult for a person whose heart is but slightly im-
' bued with sanctifying grace, to persevere in keeping a reli-
' gious diary! What has caused this chasm of nearly two

'months—the omission of eight entries in this? Spiritual
'indifference. But is the nearly extinguished spark rekin-
'dled in my breast, that I now resume it? I dare not say it.
'But *some* more regularity and freedom prevails, in the per-
'formance of private duties, than has lately been usual. I
'have consecrated a little spot for retirement, meditation, and
'prayer, at no great distance from the house. While here
'waiting on God, a spirit of supplication, if I deceive not
'myself, has been afforded; and a divine peace, for short
'seasons, possessed my heart. What treasures of grace have
'I forfeited, by neglecting, more punctually heretofore to
'avail myself of a similar arrangement! I am conscious
'that God delights in the faithful performance of all His
'gracious promises, and of none more than His engagement
'to bless the means of an increase of grace which He has
'Himself ordained.

*July 27th.*

"I suffer great loss from irregularity in my private devo-
'tions. While I had a place to retire to, sacred to prayer and
'reflection, I could perceive, I thought, some signs of a prin-
'ciple of life in my heart. Independent of the answers that
'may have been granted to my formal petitions, the practice
'had a salutary effect on my temper and deportment through
'the day. I felt a joyous, though still imperfect, confidence
'that God was my conductor in all my enterprises and la-
'bours—and that He exercised a special preventive and over-
'ruling Providence in all that regarded me, limiting or con-
'verting to good, the effects of thousands of my heedless
'words and actions.

"The pursuit of gain, has presented attractions which I
'never discovered before. This is the perversion of a pur-
'pose, originally good. I have debts to pay; and money
'must be raised. But once given up to the pursuit, my
'thoughts directly extended themselves to other views of
'personal aggrandizement; and slothful self-indulgence.—

' These sometimes give to the object a chief value. I am
' convinced of the force and truth of the Apostle's declaration,
' That the love of money, &c. That they that will be rich, &c.
' And where money is the main drift of existence, how does
' the vile passion stifle in its birth every noble sentiment
' of the soul! Adieu! sympathy in the joys or sorrows of
' others. Adieu! to every liberal feeling—every beneficènt act.
' Adieu! from that moment, strict integrity of principle and
' practice. Adieu! that openness and candor of character,
' worth to the possessor more than a ton of gold. Adieu! that
' sensibility of social feeling, which is the source of by far
' the most cordial of our earthly enjoyments. Adieu! enjoy-
' ment too. The chase is, in itself, vexatious and wounding,
' beyond any other. Few are more liable to disappoint the
' deluded votary.

SUNDAY, *August* 3*d*.

"Yesterday, I received by the return of the Augusta, from
' Sierra Leone, the tidings of the death of Lieut. Dashiell—a
' shock of corn taken into his Master's granary fully ripe.—
' Often had we mingled our devotions, while cruising the
' African coast; and several times entered into a very par-
' ticular detail of our mutual griefs and temptations. His
' were many; but they were richly mingled with spiritual
' comforts, and overcome by a vigorous faith in the Redeemer.
' The unexpected intelligence of his death, depresses my
' spirits. I have not a hold on Christ strong enough to sus-
' tain Christian equanimity amidst the shifting scenes and
' mixed events of this miserable world. Prosperity elates me
' with inordinate and presumptuous joy. Adversity sinks
' my heart below the humble level at which it ought to rest,
' buoyed up by Christian hope. Like the chameleon, I take the
' colour of contiguous objects. My Redeemer! approach, that
' I may receive and reflect *Thy* image. My mind is habitu-
' ally filled half with hope and half with despair. I know
' not of what spirit I am. I am an egregious trifler, even in

'Religion: O Lord, enlighten, if Thou hast ever chosen me.
'Resolutions falter, and rules fly under almost every change
'of situation and feeling. But it is an endless work that I
'have entered upon. I give over exclaiming all infirmity,
'all corruption, all perverseness about me. In my Re-
'deemer all is perfection, holiness, and grace. Sink where,
'and when I may, millions will rejoice eternally in Him.—
'Lord, restore and save Thy servant in Him.

*August* 24.

"The climate is not unpleasant. I can pursue any piece
'of intellectual labour as assiduously, and succeed as well in
'it, as I ever could in my life. For these benefits thrown
'back upon me after I believed Divine Providence had with-
'drawn them from me forever, I do not, I confess it with
'shame, render to God a reasonable tribute of gratitude.—
'There is my Heavenly Benefactor to whom I am not grate-
'ful! Tell me, conscience, am I, or am I not, this disingen-
'uous wretch? Where's the man that would not resent
'such a requital? Among my best friends, which possesses
'the friendship that would survive it? Lord God, merciful
'and gracious, what reason have I to admire and praise the
'forbearance which it is the property of infinite love to exer-
'cise, if no instance of it but that registered in my own expe-
'rience, had ever come to light?

*August* 31.

"I have meditated to-day on the four remarkable interposi-
'tions of Divine Providence, in the progress of my life, to
'preserve me from courses, which if entered upon, could hard-
'ly have been relinquished before they would have conduct-
'ed me to my ruin.

"Now, the first sentiment which a review of this very small
'portion of God's merciful Providence ought to awaken, is
'gratitude, and the first act which it should dictate, thanks-
'giving. In the next place, may it not authorize some little
'hope, that God has thus restrained my own hands from dis-

' qualifying myself to do any more good in the world, in or-
' der to use me for that very purpose, before He calls me out
' of it? Where there is a foundation for indulging a confi-
' dence of this nature, I say let hope build upon it. We need
' encouragement, as well as our fears, to excite us to duty."

Mr. Ashmun, it is presumed, was at this time, not fully aware of the imputations cast upon his character, by individuals in the United States; yet he saw, and keenly felt, that his services in Africa were undervalued, and that the confidence to which, thereby, he was justly entitled, was withheld. That "chastity of honour which feels a stain like a wound," will not censure harshly, the transient sentiment which dictated the following passages:—

"I am now advancing rapidly to the meridian of my day.
' I am without a profession, without patrimony or friends to
' advance me to a station of usefulness, responsibility and in-
' fluence; and, at present, without country or a sound state
' of bodily health.

" My dear and honoured parents excepted, I am a stranger
' at large in the world, and the world a wilderness to me,
' without a solitary point of attraction. I charge much of
' my unhappiness upon myself, and will not abjure my coun-
' try. But that country has failed to afford me the means,
' and to protect me in the pursuit of happiness, although I
' have spent all the most valuable part of my life in qualify-
' ing and exerting myself for public usefulness. Should Af-
' rica reject me, I should float with equal indifference, to
' whichever of the four quarters of the globe the wind and
' the current might sweep me. Possibly I may find a resting
' place yet, this side of my grave, where affection may again
' strike root, and a little verdant spot again freshen into love-
' liness. Possibly, the decline of life may slide me into some
' vale, where a new circle of friends shall repair the wreck of
' former attachments—where the storms of existence shall
' exhaust their force on the barrier which secures my retreat

' —where new attachments shall create themselves in suc-
' cession, and where I may impart enjoyment to others, and
' come in for a small share of it myself.

"Such is my reverie. It contains some reflections which
' rather tend to harden, than improve the heart, and it ought
' not to be indulged."

On his arrival, Dr. Ayres had done what he could to promote the comfort and health of the emigrants who came with him in the Oswego; but he soon became ill, and was compelled to trust to the representations of the Rev. Lott Cary, (faithful, but without medical education, or then, much experience,) in prescribing for those who were suffering like himself from the disease of the country. The houses of the newly arrived company, were miserably constructed; and by the inclemency of the season, scanty supplies of Hospital stores, and want of adequate medical aid, eight out of their number (sixty) died.

In the course of the autumn, the town lots were laid off and distributed among the settlers; and a Committee of their number appointed to make monthly reports to the Agent, of the agricultural industry and improvements. Some of the earliest and most intelligent Colonists refused to receive their lots, (alleging that they had, under the sanction of the Agent, on a former occasion, drawn the lots already occupied by them,) and resolved to prepare and transmit an appeal to the Board.

The proposition of Mr. Ashmun in regard to the terms on which he would remain in the service of the Society in Africa, was considered by the Managers on the 25th of September, when they decided that, considering the resources of the Institution, they could not make the arrangements and appropriate the salary required; but that they would make him as full and fair a compensation for any services he might be desired by Dr. Ayres to render to the affairs of the Colony, as their funds would enable them to do, and that while residing with Dr. Ayres and employed in assisting him, he should be maintained and provided for at the expense of the Society.* Of this decision, Mr. Ashmun appears to have been informed in December, at the very time when Dr. Ayres had resolved, for the benefit of his shattered health, and in the hope of relieving the necessities and embarrassments of the Colony, to embark for the United States. The Packet (belonging to a trading company of Baltimore) by which came despatches, and in which Dr. Ayres resolved to return home, brought eleven recaptured Africans sent out by Government, who were restored to their friends residing at no great distance from the Colony. She gave discouraging accounts of the resources and prospects of the Society, returned a bill drawn on Government by Mr. Ashmun (for articles of indispensable necessity) protested, and having disposed of nearly all her cargo at the Rio Pongas, left goods not exceeding the value of one hundred dollars at the Cape.

Mr. Ashmun had been more than a year in Africa; with the assistance of God had saved the Colony from extermination; devoted himself in sickness, as well as health, to its interests; and now learned, that neither the Government nor the Society had made any appropriation for his benefit; and that (although to the latter had been submitted a distinct proposition,) neither had determined the amount to which his past or future services should entitle him. Should he abandon the Colony at this crisis, when the principal Agent was leaving it, its ruin seemed inevitable. The most influential Colonists were greatly dissatisfied with the distribution of the town lots; their confidence both in the Board and their Agents was shaken, and a spirit of insubordination had already shown itself, menacing destruction to all law and authority. One in-

* A resolution was adopted by the Board at this time, that in case of the death or absence of the principal Agent, and his failure to designate a successor, the person next in authority, should for the time being, assume and discharge the duties of principal Agent.

dividual declared that he and his associates would not submit to Government twenty-four hours after the departure of the Fidelity; but the energy of Mr. Ashmun, who declared that subordination should be enforced, even at the expense of life, compelled him to revoke the threat, and pledge himself to the maintenance of the laws.

Mr. Ashmun felt that it was a great misery not to know whom to trust, a greater not he trusted;* but the greatest of all a consciousness of being unworthy to be trusted, he could bless God was still with him no matter of experience. The motto of the venerable Archbishop Whitgift, seems to have been his—*"vincit qui patitur"*—he conquers that endures. He resolved to remain at his post, and trust himself to patience, to time, and to truth. He knew that no man's case is desperate, whose conscience has not turned to be his enemy.

On the 5th of December, he wrote to a friend:—"In regard
' to my private affairs, they are as discouragingly perplexed
' as I can well imagine. If exile, and bread and water were
' all, nobody should hear me complain, if I thought duty re-
' quired my submission. But to be compelled to withhold
' justice from my friends and incur their censures, and *lose*
' *their confidence*, requires stoicism indeed, and I am no phi-
' losopher.

"And in yielding to feelings which I am as unwilling as
' unable to repress, I must trouble yourself and the Board with
' the following proposition:—

"*That whenever my services shall close, with the Socie-*
' *ty's approbation, their compensation shall be liquidated*
' *by the payment within two months thereafter, of two hun-*
' *dred dollars—and one hundred and fifty dollars quarterly*
' *afterwards till the whole is discharged with or without in-*
' *terest at their option. This arrangement, however, not to*
' *bar any earlier payments the Board may be pleased to*

* South.

'make, in case they come into possession of sufficient
'funds.

"My claim on the United States has not yet positively been
'rejected. I shall send per the Fidelity, a brief memorial in
'the nature of a bill in equity, to Mr. Monroe, about which
'there shall be nothing official whatever. My Dear Sir, I
'cannot tell you how sorely my natural pride is mortified by
'these humiliating steps. But you who understand my rea-
'sons, will justify them. The Board will feel themselves
'unrestrained by any motives of regard to my private inter-
'est, to revoke my appointment by return of Packet; although
'I have not absolutely decided to resign, if left to me, till
'another arrival or two then future."*

The provisions when Dr. Ayres left the Colony, were sufficient, with strict economy, and such supplies of rice as might
be expected from trade with the natives, to subsist the settlers
for four months. Happily a small schooner of about seven
tons, had been sent out by the Fidelity, to be employed by the
Agent in securing provisions from different points of the
coast. Tobacco, however, then an almost indispensable article in the African trade, was nearly exhausted, and a small

* Far be it from the writer to censure the Managers; but they were like
other men fallible; and that they continued so long to withhold their confidence
from Mr. Ashmun, was, he believes, an error.

The following notice of a communication he had received from a Committee of the Board, shows his determination not to be misapprehended on a matter touching his own rights:

"The gentlemen seem not to have understood a certain point of my request.
I did not ask *consent* to vest money any where, because, if they can advance
me funds, tis for me to vest them either in South sea stock, Bank of Venice
stock, or African trading stock. Having a small interest in the last, is not to
turn me into a Clerk, or African Factor—situations which I will accept, never.
I asked the Society, if it were convenient for them to advance a sufficient
sum, on account of salary, to be good enough to buy stock with it; and receive
in reply, that they *do not object to my buying stock for myself*. I mention this trifle
without the least feeling of disrespect to the Board. But having already, too
many obligations to my fellow-men, I am not willing they should suppose them
multiplied, where *I can feel no new ones myself.*"

supply which it was hoped Dr. Ayres might purchase on his way home at Sierra Leone, was not obtained. Slave vessels in unusual numbers were upon the coast enhancing greatly the demand and value of rice, and throwing every possible obstacle in the way of the traffic of the Agents of the Colony. Worse than all, several of the leading settlers were prepared to set at defiance the authority of the Agent, and openly avowed their purpose to aid in no survey of the lots,* or in any public improvements, and to leave uncleared and uncultivated the lands assigned them, until they should receive a reply to their remonstrance already sent home to the Board. It was at that time one of the regulations of the Society, that every adult male emigrant should, while receiving rations from the public store, contribute the labour of two days in a week, to some work of public utility.† Before the departure of Dr. Ayres, it had been announced, that on the 5th of June, 1834, all rations would cease except in case of special necessity, and that, unless those who had appealed to the Board on the subject of their lands, should, while their case was pending, cultivate some portion of land designated by the Agent, they should be expelled from the Colony. About twelve of the Colonists not only cast off the restraints of authority, but exerted themselves to seduce others from obedience. On the 13th of December, Mr. Ashmun published the following notice:

"There are in the Colony more than a dozen healthy per-
' sons, who will receive no more provisions out of the public
' store till they earn them." This notice proved inefficient, except as it gave occasion for the expression of more seditious sentiments and a bolder violation of the laws.

On the 19th, the Agent directed the rations of the offend-

---

* The lands were covered with a thick undergrowth, so that it was necessary to cut out every line before a survey could be made.

† This regulation was dispensed with, on condition that each individual should diligently cultivate his own lands.

ing individuals to be stopped. The next morning they assembled in a riotous manner at the Agency-House, endeavoured by angry denunciations, to drive the Agent from his purpose, which finding immoveable, they proceeded to the Store-House where the Commissary was at that moment issuing rations for the week, and seizing each a portion of the provisions, hastened to their respective homes.

Towards evening, the same day, Mr. Ashmun addressed a circular "to all the Colonists," setting forth the criminality of this mutinous proceeding; stating that a full representation thereof would be transmitted to America by the earliest opportunity; exhorting all to industry and energy in the construction of their houses and the cultivation of their lands during the dry season; and finally "warning them against disorder and rebellion, as they would avoid guilt, confusion, disgrace, shame, and ruin in this world," and in a future one the still more terrible judgments of God. They were reminded that their oaths were as binding as when first taken; that the prospect for themselves, their friends, and their children, depended upon their conduct; and that the Agent while disposed to use the language of friendship, would act as he had ever done, with the authority becoming the Representative of the American Colonization Society. This circular encouraged the well-disposed, confirmed in duty some of the wavering, and struck with awe the spirit of outrage. The leader of the sedition, almost immediately confessed and deplored his error.

On the 13th of February, arrived in the ship Cyrus, thirty-two days from the United States, one hundred and five emigrants, mostly from Petersburg, Virginia, inferior, as a company, to none of their class in intelligence, industry, and morality. Universal health had attended them during the voyage; all were safely landed; some had property; supplies of ordinary provisions had been sent out for all; the season was delightful for building and clearing their grounds, and a mutual affection seemed to bind them together as in one harmonious family. "God Almighty dispose us," exclaimed Mr. Ashmun, "to be grateful for all His past goodness, and not even in the ' depth of the furnace, to despair of the future."

These emigrants were immediately assembled, the views of the Society, the regulations of the Colony, and the circumstances and relations of their new situation, were fully explained, and while assured of every aid it was possible for the Agent to afford, they were encouraged to proceed diligently to build their houses, cultivate the soil, and resolutely to meet and subdue all the difficulties and obstacles standing in the way of their prosperity. "They conducted themselves on the occasion," says Mr. Ashmun, like sensible, inquisitive, efficient men."

Thirty houses had been partially constructed since the departure of Dr. Ayres, and a new magazine commenced, the apartment in the tower being found too damp to preserve the ammunition.

By the Cyrus, Mr. Ashmun transmitted to the Board a full and detailed account of the condition, wants, and prospects of the Colony. After alluding to the necessity for a new magazine, and to the great advantage of employing native laborers to construct it, instead of taxing the labour of settlers, whose constant and most vigorous efforts, at "that precious season," were required to prepare them to meet with safety, the approaching rains, he adds: "As your instructions on the sub-
' ject of contracting debts are, however, imperative, I shall
' forego the suggestions of my own judgment, while I remain,
' without an express credit, unless such a crisis of necessity
' should again recur, as to suspend some of the vital interests
' of the Colony, on the resumption of such a responsibility.
' Such a crisis, it is to be hoped, will not soon recur, since the
' Colony has obtained at length that establishment, with a
' view to which my former drafts were all hazarded. On this
' subject, as your letter alludes to it very pointedly, I beg leave

' to state, that I never thought myself authorized merely by
' my appointment to the Agency, to negotiate drafts on your
' funds—much less, to draw on Government funds without
' being authorized even to serve as their Agent. But in pur-
' chasing supplies for the Colony, in its extremities, I acted
' much as I should have done, had the Society and Govern-
' ment never heard my name. I declare in the face of Heav-
' en, that without some of those supplies, your Colony would
' have been destroyed by famine and the sword, if God had
' not performed a miracle to save it. Others were purchased
' to save the people from extreme suffering. A small amount
' might have been dispensed with, had I known (what I could
' not know) when the opportunity to purchase offered, that
' supplies were on the way from America. Now the neces-
' sity of assuming these responsibilities can never return again
' in the same degree. You never again will have twenty-
' five *men only*,* with a company of helpless women and
' children, five thousand miles distant from you, unsheltered
' in the midst of the rains, without fortifications, or even a
' slight paling between their habitations and a sanguinary
' and numerous enemy, in the bosom of a frowning forest,
' and one half of them wasted by sickness to a state of infant
' weakness. It was these circumstances—circumstances
' peculiar to the infancy of the establishment, which rendered
' extraordinary purchases, and unauthorized expenditures
' unavoidable."

The joy produced by the arrival of the Cyrus, was soon succeeded by dark events. All who came in this vessel were attacked by fever within four weeks. Not a pound of rice (an article most important to the sick) was in the public store, nor had the Agent either goods or credit, by which he could obtain a supply. Out of his own private stock† he advanced

* The ten others who took part, with Mr. Ashmun, in the war, were recaptured Africans, under the charge of Government.

† Doubtless, goods which he had purchased for the Government or Society, and for which the drafts given in payment had been returned protested.

to the value of about two hundred dollars, and despatched the Colonial schooner to Grand Bassa, which at the end of nine days, returned with but twenty bushels of rice, bought at double the usual price. The only individual who could act the part of a Physician, was the Rev. Lott Cary, whose skill resulted entirely from his good sense, observation, and experience.*

All these evils were light compared with those which the spirit of revolt and anarchy threatened to bring upon the Colony. Deficient in education, and ill informed on many of the important relations and duties of human society, dazzled by the light, and misled by false notions of freedom, disappointed in some of their expectations, and tried by affliction, a few individuals still continued utterly to disregard the authority of the Agent and sought to persuade others to imitate their example.

On the 19th of March, the rations were reduced one half; as it was found that so diminished, the supplies would last not more than five weeks. This act of prudence was counted by the malecontents an act of oppression; they violently reproached the Agent in his presence, and showed in the storm of their passions, that the assumption of the right of self-government had given them no mastery over themselves.

On the morning of the 22d of March, Mr. Ashmun assembled the people of the settlement, and made to them in substance, mainly, the following address:

"There is a mutual contract subsisting between the Ame-
' rican Colonization Society and every one of you. By this
' contract you are bound under the solemnity of an oath to

* *March* 11th.—"Astonishing," said Mr. Ashmun, "that in this atmosphere should exist causes so universal in their operation, as amongst all the varieties of age, sex, and habit, not to leave one in the whole number without disease, and that in less than four weeks: And stranger still, that the blast should be so tempered to the strength of the constitution of every individual, as only to have swept off three small children. Men may call these phenomena in human life, the effects of the laws of nature; I choose to call them singular proofs of the Providence of God over his creatures."

' certain duties to the Society—and the Society stands recip-
' rocally pledged, in certain engagements, to you. Your
' obligations are fully expressed in the articles of the Consti-
' tution—you have many privileges sacred to you in this same
' Constitution—you have far greater in reversion. You
' swore to the Society that you would obey their government
' and not attempt to overthrow it, but lend all your influence
' and all your aid to support it entire. And you acted wise-
' ly. Every blessing you have enjoyed in Africa, the security
' of your lives, property and families, is the consequence of
' this salutary arrangement by which an efficient government
' was constituted, and this security has always been in pro-
' portion to the constancy and fidelity with which you have
' obeyed and upheld it.

"Some of your greatest sufferings have resulted from your
' disrespect to the Agents, and your disobedience of the or-
' ders of the Society.

"In what I shall now say, I refer only to those who have
' been several months in Africa.

"Early in the present dry season, you were told that your
' supply of provisions and clothing from the Public Store,
' must cease on the 5th of June next. The term was seen
' and acknowledged to be liberal—you were surrounded by
' fertile lands—and had seven months of pleasant weather in
' which to put them in cultivation. The Agent has shown
' you every indulgence. Not one day in a month has been
' required of you for any public labour. Provisions, clothing
' and tools were furnished. The Agent has given you his
' best advice. He was animated with hope, and confidently
' imparted his own expectations to the Society at home.

"But all these expectations were to end in bitter disappoint-
' ment. Twelve of you refused to concur in the work.

"Your own consciences tell you with what earnestness
' and fidelity I laboured to prevent the folly and mischief of
' such perversity. I advised, explained, and even entreated,

'for I was your friend and willing by any means to persuade 'you to consult your true interest. You were unmoved, 'and retorted insolence to my condescension. I employed 'more rigorous measures. You seized the weapons of de-'struction, menaced me with death, and laid violent hands 'on stores, which your perjured conduct had made it unlaw-'ful for me to distribute among you. You have reproached, 'dissuaded and opposed to my certain knowledge the peacea-'ble and orderly settlers, and diverted them from their agri-'cultural pursuits.

"I told you that your neglect of duty would bring on your-'selves and families the severest sufferings before the termi-'nation of the approaching rainy season; and the warning 'is now beginning to be realized. Had you obeyed the Go-'vernment you have sworn to support, every man of you 'would see the comforts of life beginning to pour into his 'family.

"But you have nothing in possession. You have nothing 'growing in your fields. You have nothing—no not a week's 'supply of vegetables in prospect. You feel the pinching 'hand of want to-day. It will be worse to-morrow. Con-'tinue to neglect your duty, and it will either disperse you 'up and down the coast or destroy you by starvation.

"The evil remains. This very morning have I been told 'to my face, that you will not be governed—that instead of 'labouring, as you ought to raise food, you would obtain it 'by plunder.

"There sits the man who has used this language. You 'ask for provisions, but you know I cannot as an honest man, 'furnish provisions to support you in idleness, or wilful diso-'bedience.

"You know that as far as in me lies, I will never suffer 'another barrel of provisions to enter that Store-House if lia-'ble to be taken out by the hand of plunder and violence. 'No! the authority of the United States and of the American

'Colonization Society, must be reinstated in all their perfec-
'tion on this Cape, or you must be dispersed and perish. I
'ask you to take no new oaths, to assume no new obligations;
'but here, this hour, in the presence of that God who has re-
'corded your vows in Heaven, to recognize them and pledge
'yourselves to a future observance of them. I will act no longer
'the shadow of authority. It is egregious folly and wick-
'edness, and will ruin you all. Either sustain the authority
'of the Society and enable it to fulfil the ends of the Colony—
'or mark it well, the Society will not uphold you in a course
'which must conduct you to ruin, and themselves to certain
'disappointment and disgrace.

"I require every well-disposed man to give me the pledge
'I ask, and I will spare no pains to avert the impending cala-
'mity. I believe it possible, even now, to devise a plan of in-
'dustry, that will keep this people together through the ap-
'proaching rains. But all depends on your concurrence."

Most of the settlers tacitly assented to the truth and justice of this address, and Mr. Ashmun adopted every measure in his power to relieve and preserve the Colony. But the Colonists afforded him no vigorous support. The spirit of disorganization was at work, deranging all the movements of Government. Mr. Ashmun had some months before declared to the Board, that in his opinion, "the evil was incurable by any of the remedies which fall within their existing provisions." He now prepared and forwarded despatches* containing his best reflections on the state of the Colony, and the increasing elements of turbulence and danger threatening its speedy ruin.

Since the departure of Dr. Ayres, he had heard nothing from the Board of Managers. He perceived that his conduct in the Colony had been held up for censure in one of the public Journals of the United States. The stores of the settle-

* See Appendix No. 5.

ment were nearly exhausted; he saw that the least detention of the Packet beyond her time, must occasion severe suffering, and he had no means to prevent it. He attempted to make a small purchase from a transient vessel, but failed, having, to use his own words, "neither funds, produce, nor credit."

On the 15th of March, he addressed a letter to the Board, expressing a desire to be relieved from any farther duties to the Colony, which might require his residence in Africa. He declared, that just emerging from the period of youth, he was loaded with half the infirmities of drooping age.

"Next after the approbation of God and conscience," he adds, "I own that I have been ambitious, in the humble part
' which I have acted in your service, to deserve and receive
' that of the Board of Managers! and I have always felt con-
' fident, of the essential equity of their decision, when all the
' circumstances under which I acted could be known to them.
' I can say more: You would, Gentlemen, estimate my con-
' duct with more indulgence, than I dare to extend to myself.
' Without any canting professions of extraordinary modesty,
' which I know I never possessed, it is nevertheless true, that
' I am conscious of wanting several qualifications which an
' Agent of your Board ought to have; and have often been
' pained for your sake, and the Colony's, that I was not a wiser
' and a better man. In reviewing my services, I perceive
' many things, which I should on their recurrence the sec-
' ond time, manage differently; but no egregious blunders or
' gross neglects. These are, however, charged upon me, in
' a few rash assertions of a letter published in the National
' Intelligencer, of 1823; which I saw for the first time only
' two days ago. Never intending to publish to such accusa-
' tions a newspaper reply, (which commonly savours more of
' a desire of revenge, than an honest wish to explain to can-
' did men, misrepresented facts,) nor willing to labour in the
' opinions of the Board under the imputations referred to, I

'have taken the middle course of addressing, for your perusal, a letter to the author of those accusations. It is enclosed."

He now determined to proceed on a visit (by the way of Bissao, a Portuguese settlement, at the mouth of the Rio Grande,) to the Cape De Verd Islands. "Government," he observes, "without an armed force had become impossible." "I 'had expended all my strength in fruitless attempts to restore 'industry and order, and found myself wasting away under 'a complication of infirmities and complaints, which left ex-'istence a burden; and had long deprived me of appetite, 'sleep, and all bodily and mental vigor." A sea-voyage might restore his health; but should he remain at the Cape, he could hardly hope to survive the rainy season. Neither the state of his private affairs, nor his engagement to serve the Board until relieved, permitted him to think of abandoning the country. As circumstances were, he saw not that he could do more, than a provisional Government, for the Colony. Until the decision of the Board respecting the distribution of the lots was made known, he was unwilling to remain as Agent, without power to carry into effect a system of industry and other measures of vital importance. Whether he would ever return, appeared to him in view of the state of the Colony, and his own health, a matter of much uncertainty. All the property of the United States, the Colonization Society, and the Baltimore Trading Company, together with the books, records and papers of the establishment, were committed to Elijah Johnson as temporary Agent, with instructions as to his duties, and orders to account for all articles entrusted to him, to any properly authorized Agent who might arrive from the United States, to whom also he was to resign the power with which he was invested. While fatigued in making arrangements for his departure, "inventorying the property, writing letters, and disposing of some hundred applications," Mr. Ashmun unfortunately ruptured an artery, which had been injured in a bungling attempt to extract a decayed tooth, and a profuse bleeding commenced that nothing would stop. Advantage was taken of his helpless state, and on his way from the house to the vessel, he was robbed of a considerable part of the little stores put up for the voyage, and of other property to the value of one hundred and seventy-five dollars.\* He arrived on board the schooner Reporter, Captain Preble, from Portland, bound to Goree, at 4 o'clock on the 1st of April. The bleeding continued during the night and the next day; all applications and remedies were utterly useless. "I began," he says, "seriously to expect the termination of my poor services, vexations and life during the next night."— The following paper was left at the Cape, to be delivered to his successor in the Agency:

"J. Ashmun has cheerfully spent on this Cape, nearly two ' of the best years of his life. He is now about to leave it, ' probably forever. He has tried to do his duty—detected ' himself in occasional errors; and without asking or expect- ' ing any recompense from his fellow-men, wishes only to ' avoid the hard destiny of his predecessors in the Agency— ' the curses and false accusations of those whom it has been ' his constant aim to serve.

"His predecessors have been accused of transmitting false ' accounts of the Colony, to the Board. J. Ashmun here ' leaves it on record, that if any man after his absence ' brings this accusation against himself, that man is a slanderer ' and a liar.

"My predecessors have been accused of applying the stores ' and supplies sent for the people, to their own use. I further ' declare, that any man who accuses me, of using the public ' stores farther than my personal necessities, from day to day ' required, and whoever denies me to have defrayed a large

---

\* Settlers and recaptured Africans were mingled together on this occasion, so that it is not possible to say who had the chief agency in the business.

' part of my current expenses out of my own pocket, is a false
' accuser and a slanderer.

"My predecessors stand accused, in their absence, of having
' rioted and fattened on the Society's bounty; and consumed
' funds which were contributed for the comfort of the Colo-
' nists. Whoever says, after my absence, that for all my
' sacrifices, labours and sufferings, on this Cape, I have re-
' ceived one farthing of emolument, excepting only a valuable
' present of clothing, by the Oswego, asserts a falsehood which
' will one day cover him with shame.

"Most of my predecessors have been accused of pinching
' the people, to furnish their own tables and wardrobes with an
' unseemly and disproportionate abundance. My table, when
' alone, has consisted of one dish, and as great a variety of
' vegetables as I could procure. When favoured with compa-
' ny, I have given the best dinners I could conveniently pro-
' vide. They have been good enough for us; and never have
' made the dinner of a Colonist a cabbage-leaf the less.

"B. J. a man without principle, and as far as his wit lets
' him go, a mischievous calumniator, has accused Agents of
' selling the charitable contributions to the stores of the Socie-
' ty, for African produce, and converting the proceeds to their
' own gain. The fear of the pillory only restrained the fel-
' low's slander. Whoever shall connive, at the repetition of it
' in my absence, will discover a degree of malignity equal to
' his, and a degree of cowardice which J. never did; for he,
' Devil-like, dared to belch his scandal into my face.

"I have been blamed for trafficking with the natives. I have
' done so, and applied *more than the profits* of that very bar-
' ter to the feeding and clothing of the people. I have sunk
' stock, in supplying their necessities, and do not believe I
' shall ever be reimbursed by the Society, or from any other
' earthly quarter. Whoever names this barter, after my ab-
' sence, except to my advantage, is an *ingrate;* he thrusts
' his viper sting into the bosom which has nourished his ex-

'istence. To the galling scourge of conscious ingratitude, I
'consign him.

"My predecessors have been accused of carrying away with
'them, furniture, and a variety of little stores and moveables,
'which, being the Society's property, were intended for the
'use of the Colony, and their successors in the Agency. I
'shall carry away nearly all my private property, and if my
'health and convenience require them, any little articles of
'bedding, table furniture, &c. &c. that may chance to be on
'hand—always observing to take away considerably less than
'I originally brought into the Colony, of my own private
'supplies of these things.

"I do not wish to be remembered at all after I am gone.
'But if any of the Colonists do me that honour, as it is unso-
'licited and gratuitous, I require it of them, as they must an-
'swer for it hereafter, to remember with me, the command
'of the Most High, 'Thou shalt not bear false witness against
'thy neighbour.' And I respectfully request my successors
'in this arduous station, to preserve this paper; and if any
'individuals should take advantage of my absence, to accuse
'me in any of the foregoing premises, that he would have
'the justice to read to that individual, the paragraph which
'touches the case.

"I have too great a regard for the respectable members of
'this Colony, to be willing that my memory should suffer
'injuriously in their estimation.

"J. Ashmun."

## CHAPTER X.

Mr. ASHMUN had now sunk to the lowest point of his depression. Varying a little the Prophet's language, he might have cried, "All the bright lights of Heaven hast thou made dark over me, thou hast covered the sun with a cloud, and the moon doth not give her light." But his trust was in Divine Wisdom and Power. He knew that nothing could hide him from the eye, nothing remove him from the hand of the Almighty. He knew that it is when he can rely upon nothing else, that the Christian depends most upon God.— When he considered his remarkable experience of the Divine Mercy, how he had been shielded in the storm, the battle and the pestilence, how his soul had repeatedly escaped as a bird from the snare of the fowler, it was impossible for him to despair.

Reduced so low by the continued loss of blood for twenty-eight hours, that it was thought he could not survive for eight hours longer, the French frigate Hebe (whose officers had a month before enjoyed the hospitalities of the Colony,) providentially hove in sight, and her Surgeon in half an hour, by mechanical means, completely stopped the hemorrhage. For several days he could scarcely stand, but by the kindest attentions on the part of Captain Preble, and on his own part by strict and judicious rules of living, he gradually and slowly recovered his strength during the month occupied in his passage. We here insert, condensed somewhat, the information contained in his Journal, penned on his voyage at Bissao, and at the Cape De Verds.*

"Our passage was extremely slow, as the vessel after being
' twelve days out, was found to be in the latitude of Cape
' Mount. In running down the passage (one hundred and
' fifty miles) between the Bissagos Islands on the South-west,
' and the mainland on the North-east, our vessel struck on a
' hard sandy bottom, and was, with difficulty, set afloat again.

* The following statement from this Journal, may be useful to navigators on the African coast:

"The tendency of the great body of the waters of the ocean along the coast of western Africa, is naturally South-eastward. In the dry season, when only a daily alternation of gentle land and sea breezes fans their surface, and the sea breeze blows from a quarter commonly a little North of West, the flux of waters obeying this tendency, becomes a strong South-easterly current.— This current commences in December, and continues acquiring strength till the following June. Then the stiff and constant S. S. W. breeze which sets in at the beginning and prevails through the rains, gradually alters, and by the first of July has *reversed* the direction of the current. It sets to the North-westward, but with less strength, commonly, than it had, in the dry months, in the opposite direction. From Montserado to Cape Mount, this latter or dry season current, sets at the rate of three-quarters of a knot; at Cape Mount one and a half; at Galhinas a half; at Cape St. Ann one; off the South-west point of St. Ann shoals two knots; thence to the Northern point of the shoals, decreasing to three-quarters; thence to the commencement of Rio Grande shoals a half; around these shoals three-quarters; and on to the Northward as high as Goree half a knot. Such were the setting and drift of these currents, in the month of April; or within one month of the termination of the dry season, resulting from the comparison of the ship's reckoning with our observed latitudes."

'No one should attempt this passage without a Pilot. The
'mercy of Providence alone saved us.

"The approach to Bissao was to me delightfully animating.
'An expanse of beautiful country, cleared, and for more than
'seventy years under cultivation, scattered over with a count-
'less number of palm, cocoa, and other fruit trees, first sud-
'denly opens upon the view. Soon you perceive the whole
'region to be dotted over with some thousand conical ob-
'jects, which as you approach them, are discovered to be the
'huts of the Papels, the original inhabitants of the country.
'Four beautifully spreading pulloms* are now admired in
'the distance. The ramparts of the Fort soon after make
'their appearance, and last of all the town.

"Few houses are more than a single story high. This is a
'point rendered necessary by the prevalence of tornadoes at
'particular seasons of the year, and the vicinity of the walls
'of the Fort by which they are overlooked. There are not
'four white people, exclusive of the military, in Bissao. The
'negroes and mulattoes from the Cape De Verd Islands, are
'much superior in intelligence, and commonly in condition
'to the christianized natives of Bissao.

"The Christian town, as it is called, is situated on the land
'side of the Fort, and contains about fifteen hundred souls,
'descendants of the native Papels, all of whom are baptized
'and members of the Catholic Church. They build their
'houses of the same materials as the Papels, but of a larger
'size, and different form—those of the latter being circular,
'with a conical roof; those of the Christians, square or rec-
'tangular, and with a roof of inclined planes. The walls of
'both are of sun-hardened clay, cut into oblong cubes, and
'the roofs of thatch. A species of grass having a stem of
'three feet in length, is used for the purpose. The ceiling is
'a thick floor of clay, supported by rude joists, and effectually

* A large tree found all along the coast.

'secures the contents of the cabin from fire, to which the 'thatched roofs are particularly exposed.

"The Christian population are said to retain and blend 'with their worship many (if not all) the superstitions of Pa-'ganism. They have adopted something of the European 'dress, speak a corrupt dialect of Portuguese, but surpass 'their Pagan countrymen in every sort of unprincipled 'profligacy.

"The Fort covers more than two acres, has fifty guns, is 'surrounded by a fosse from thirty to fifty feet wide, and 'twelve deep, and is one of the finest on the coast. About 'three hundred men belong to the establishment, convicts 'from Lisbon and the Cape De Verds, one half of whom are 'detached to Cacheo and Geba, settlements in the vicinity. 'There are two buildings, without windows or floors, devoted 'to the sick. These are situated at a small distance without 'the Fort; and from the dirty, neglected and most wretched 'condition of the sick, (about thirty) may be regarded as the 'antechambers of the grave, rather than the nurseries of 'health. The astonishing indifference with which the loss 'of human life is here regarded, is the necessary effect of 'that depravity of morals which is so universal, undoubtedly; 'but it has its origin more directly in the practice which has 'so long been familiar to the inhabitants of trafficking in hu-'man flesh.

"The establishment is a century old, has derived all its im-'portance from the slave trade, and originated, no doubt, 'some of the most splendid fortunes of Lisbon and Rio 'Janeiro.

"Rice is cultivated in abundance, but chiefly on low lands, 'which require ditching and diking at intervals of six feet. 'The trenches are seldom without water even in the dry sea-'son. Both the straw and produce are enormous. Only 'the spade is used in tillage. If I am rightly informed, the 'returns amount to more than one hundred bushels to the 'acre!

"From the town may be seen at the distance of five or six
' leagues to the South-west, the Island of Bulama. Since
' the English sunk nearly one hundred and fifty thousand
' pounds in attempts to found a Colony on this Island, and
' failed, through mismanagement, and other disasters, the
' Island remains unappropriated. It is eighteen miles long,
' has no inhabitants, is fertile, well watered, and excellently
' timbered. The Portuguese are now cutting timber from
' it, for ships of war.

"We cast anchor at Bissao on the 4th of May, when I ad-
' dressed a letter to the Governor, stating the circumstances
' under which I had arrived, and desiring permission to land
' and take measures for the complete restoration of my health,
' without being subjected to any of the restrictions imposed
' on foreign traders arriving at the Port. This request was
' politely granted. Several airy apartments were provided
' for me, and I was hospitably entertained at the Governor's
' table during the whole time (six weeks) of my stay. The
' luxury of an open and delightful country to range in, my
' freedom from cares, good books, and a little intelligent so-
' ciety soon revived my depressed spirits, and perfected the
' re-establishment of my health after a painful confinement
' for a week with an inflamed foot and ankle, excited by too
' much exercise.

"I had the mortification to witness the despatch of two ves-
' sels, each carrying sixty slaves for St. Jago. The Governor
' owned himself interested in both, but attempted to excuse
' his conduct by lamely alleging the influence of a foreign
' power in the counsels of Portugal, and that measures re-
' strictive on the slave trade, were as odious at home, as in
' their tendency hostile to the prosperity of the Portuguese
' colonies.

"I took leave of the hospitable Governor on the 16th of
' June, embarking in a brig, in which he had politely offered
' me a passage to St. Jago. He had lost an estate worth

'eighty thousand dollars by a series of disastrous adventures
'in the slave trade, his supercargoes and consignees having
'taken advantage of the law, and pocketed the proceeds of his
'cargoes.

"On the 22d, we made the coast six leagues South of Go-
'ree. This is a dependency of Fort St. Louis, on the Sene-
'gal. The population is rated at thirty-five hundred—the
'port, free; duties moderate; and the station regarded as per-
'haps the healthiest and pleasantest in Western Africa. The
'natives in the neighbourhood of all the French settlements,
'are said to be more advanced towards civilization than any
'other. Head winds prevailed during the whole of our pas-
'sage, so that we did not make the Isle of May before the
'morning of the 4th of July, when a good Providence saved
'us from running upon the rocks, all hands being asleep
'until the roar of the surf became deafning.

"I was received by Mr. Hodges, the American Consul, and
'his amiable lady, with great politeness, and experienced
'from both, and from Mr. Clark the British resident, and his
'lady, those gratifying attentions which a stranger in Africa,
'is perhaps, of all others, best disposed to appreciate.

"The Cape De Verd Islands, nine in number, were dis-
'covered in the latter part of the fifteenth century, and soon
'settled by the Portuguese. The population is estimated at
'sixty thousand, mostly a mixed race, sprung from the union
'of the Portuguese and natives. The Government is lodged
'in the hands of a Governor General, and Judge, appointed
'by the Crown, and is perfectly despotic. These Islands
'serve the Portuguese Government as a place of exile, for
'State and other prisoners. They yield to the Crown a
'revenue of one hundred thousand pounds, by the monopoly
'of the Archilla, a dying vegetable, said to be the growth
'of no other country. It is the basis of a most beautiful
'scarlet. Porto Praya, the residence of the Governor,
'has about two hundred soldiers from Lisbon. Several of

' the active revolutionists are now reaping, on this burning
' spot, in poverty and exile, the harvest of their defeated hopes
' and disappointed ambition."

Here Mr. Ashmun anxiously awaited intelligence, both from the Colony and the United States. He recollected that, according to previous arrangements, the Baltimore Packet, Fidelity, was to have visited the Colony in April, and thought it probable she had conveyed thither some individual to succeed him in the Agency. On the 11th of July, he addressed a letter "To the Agent of the American Colonization Society at Cape Montserado;" in which, after expressing his extreme anxiety to hear from the settlement, and his purpose, if not previously relieved by the Board, to return thither in October, among other things, he adds: "At the present time I am
' pleasing myself with the supposition, that the Colonists are
' mostly on their own resources, and are diligently and suc-
' cessfully cultivating the soil. If the older settlers are still
' receiving rations from the Society, they are ruined, and the
' funds of the Society misapplied. Of the one and the other
' of these facts, I am certain—and fully believe that nothing
' is accomplished towards the establishment of the Colony,
' till the settlers are brought to subsist themselves, and very
' little, indeed, as long as a barrel of beef and flour continues
' to be imported, of *necessity*, from America.

"My heart, I can assure you, Sir, is much, much indeed
' with the Colony. I am fully resolved not to return to the
' United States, without first re-visiting the settlement. May
' I find the people orderly and industrious; the Agent beloved,
' active, enterprising, healthy, and happy. Expect, Sir, no
' reward in this life. It is a service replete with danger, suf-
' ferings, mortifications, and toil. But the object, Sir, is well
' worth any amount of individual sufferings; and these suffer-
' ings themselves find great alleviations in the present reflec-
' tions of an honest and devoted mind."

In the retiredness of his own sad thoughts, on this rude spot, (which nature convulsed, seems to have thrown up from her fiery depths,) we leave, for a few moments, the subject of our Memoir, to relate the course of events towards him in the United States.

The remonstrance sent home by some of the Colonists, and the communications of Mr. Ashmun, describing minutely the disorders and disturbances at the settlement, had convinced the Board that immediate and strong measures were required to prevent the subversion of the Colony, and the total extinction of their hopes. They could not remain insensible to the honest, lucid, and manly style in which their Agent had exposed the evils of indolence and disaffection; the boldness and firmness with which he had met them, or the candor shown in the acknowledgment, that to subdue them was beyond his power. Whatever might be his general merits, they felt that he was entitled to a recompense for his services; and that while invested with authority, on grounds of expediency, no less than right, he ought to be sustained.

On the 30th of March, (but a day or two before he left the Colony) they acceded to the proposition submitted in his letter by Dr. Ayres, and appropriated five hundred dollars for his benefit; and at the same time sanctioned a reply to the remonstrants, and an address to the Colonists generally, explaining the benevolent purposes of the Society, depicting vividly the ruin impending over any community that dared to violate, or even ceased to venerate the majesty of the law, the certain destruction to follow insubordination in a feeble and exposed settlement, and enforcing industry, order, and the strict performance of every duty, by warnings, appeals, motives of interest, and the solemn demands of religion. They declared that the Agents must be obeyed, or the Colony abandoned. They asserted their determination to punish offenders, while they assisted the obedient, and affectionately encouraged all the sober and virtuous to maintain the peace, and guard, as their very life, the authority of the laws.\*

Hardly had these documents been despatched, before letters were received from the Colony, charging Mr. Ashmun with oppression, the neglect of obvious duties, the desertion of his post, and the seizure and abduction of the public property. Currency was given to these charges by officers of the United States' Navy, who had touched at Montserado soon after his departure, and there listened to the rumors of the weak, and the calumnies of the wicked. Conjecture often feeds suspicion; nor can any clear-sightedness or honesty enable us to distinguish the true features of character, more than of the face, by twilight. Those who had doubted the integrity of Ashmun, now thought it certain that he had none; and those began to doubt who had never questioned it before. That very conduct which confers honour on the good, adds to the disgrace of the bad,—being regarded as a garment stolen, to cloak iniquity. Falsehood had thrown a cloud over the reputation of Ashmun, and within its shadow, truth seemed fiction, and fiction truth.

In this uncertain and alarming state of affairs, the Managers of the Society, represented strongly to the Executive of the United States, the importance of sending an armed vessel to the Colony, with some individual duly commissioned, both by the Government and Society, to examine the entire condition of the Agency; the people; and the property of the United States and Society; and empowered to make such temporary arrangements for the security of the public interests and the Government of the establishment, as upon proper consideration, circumstances might, in his judgment, require.

---

\* E. B. Caldwell, Esq. first Secretary of the Society, though in feeble health, shared largely in the preparation of these papers, which bear honourable testimony to his energy, zeal and piety. The effort was among the last he was permitted to make in a cause which had enlisted the best and strongest feelings of his heart.

The writer was deputed to perform this service, and late in June, 1824, he embarked at Norfolk in the United States' armed schooner Porpoise, Captain Skinner, for the coast of Africa. Habituated to suspect the soundness of opinions hastily formed; to regard, never, the popular voice as infallibly the voice of God; and where human character was concerned, to suspend judgment and exercise charity, until evidence compelled conviction, he proceeded on this mission, resolved, if possible, to discover the truth, and bring it forth from the darkness in which it was involved.

## CHAPTER XI.

On the evening of the 24th of July, Mr. Ashmun came on board the Porpoise, which had then just dropped anchor in the harbour of Porto Praya. There was that in his presence and aspect, which once seen, is never forgotten. The officers of the ship who were strangers to him, felt that he was an extraordinary man. In his whole appearance were blended dignity and humility. The serene light of reason, of goodness, of meekness, softened the stateliness of sorrow, and threw a charm on the grandeur of his storm-shaken, but self-sustained spirit. His soul seemed refreshed by tidings from his native land, and his social affections to gush forth, pure and simple, as those of childhood, from the deeply stirred fountains of his heart. His remarks on the Colony, showed an extensive and thorough knowledge of its interests, and the tone and manner in which they were delivered, left it hardly possible to doubt that they were among the most precious objects of his affection.* The feelings expressed in his countenance were particularly observable, varying, as less or more intense, the light and shade, so that his features, as was said of those of a great poet, like "a beautiful alabaster vase, were only seen to perfection, when lighted up from within."— Nothing was detected betraying a single motive or purpose which it was not honour to avow; and the recollection that Satan himself is sometimes transformed into an Angel of light, alone could guard the judgment against the instant admission of his integrity.

At our second interview, the proceedings of the Board and Government were developed, and the object of the special mission fully explained. He was told what representations of his conduct had been received from the Colony, and that confidence in his character and administration had given way before the corroding power of suspicion, and the multiplied insinuations and allegations directed against both. "I will ' accompany you to the Cape," said he; "my long and familiar ' acquaintance with the affairs of the Colony may enable me

---

* There is a passage in the writings of John Woolman, expressive of what I should have supposed from this interview, had been the experience of Ashmun:

"As I lived under the cross, and simply followed the openings of truth, my mind, from day to day, was more enlightened; my former acquaintance were left to judge of me as they would, for I found it safest for me to live in private, and keep these things sealed up in my own breast. While I silently ponder on that change wrought in me, I find no language equal to it, nor any means to convey to another a clear idea of it. I looked upon the works of God in this visible creation, and an awfulness covered me; my heart was tender and often contrite, and universal love to my fellow-creatures increased in me: this will be understood by such as have trodden in the same path. Some glances of real beauty may be seen in their faces, who dwell in true meekness.

"There is a harmony in the sound of that voice to which Divine love gives utterance, and some appearance of right order in their temper and conduct, whose passions are regulated; yet all these do not fully show forth that inward life to such who have not felt it; but this white stone and new name, is known rightly to such only who have it."

'to render you some aid in effecting the arduous duties of 'your mission;" and as he spoke, you marked the show of an unalterable purpose not to abandon a cause for which he had sacrificed every thing but life; you admired the elevation of his soul above all selfish considerations, towering like an eagle against the storm and the thunder-cloud, and already catching glimpses of the purity and brightness of the Heavens.

But his moral greatness was ordinarily sober and grave, as though it had felt unkindness, been touched by grief, and stood a solitary monument amid ruined hopes.

Accommodations offered by Captain Skinner in the Porpoise, were accepted by Mr. Ashmun, and this vessel after a visit of two days at Sierra Leone, came to anchor on the 13th of August, off Cape Montserado.*

During this voyage of three weeks, my mind was constantly and anxiously engaged in acquiring information concerning the Colony; the character of the settlers; the difficulties of their situation; the past measures of the Government; the causes of present evils and dissatisfaction; and especially in gathering from free and full conversations with Mr. Ashmun, materials, which with those to be acquired by subsequent investigations, might enable me to form an opinion of his qualifications for the Agency, and of the principles, upon which should be organized a new system of Government, adapted to the circumstances of the people; the advancement of their permanent prosperity, and to their preparation, in due time, for

---

* I can never forget the aspect and manner of Mr. Ashmun, when objection was made to receiving on board the vessel a few goods which appeared to constitute all his little property. I was requested to say to him, that the goods could not be taken. I found him standing in a small miserable hut, not far from the residence of the Consul, engaged in packing away in a chest, a few articles of crockery ware. His countenance was pale, tranquil, pensive, as of one chastened by affliction, yet unforsaken of God. His reply to my communication, was simply and without the least expression of dissatisfaction: "The articles can remain and be forwarded to me by some other vessel." If I mistake not, he was subsequently permitted to take them with him.

all the rights and privileges of self-government. I acknowledge that I felt an intense desire to do a lasting good, to aid in establishing over that community regarded as containing the elements of a free, a Christian, and a powerful state, a Government, beneficent, durable, and capable of an expansion to any extent required by the enlargement of its interests or the growth of its population.

My favourable impressions of Mr. Ashmun's character, received at our first interview, were deepened by each successive conversation, inquiry, and reflection on our passage; nor should I have hesitated to predict confidently, that not a shadow of evidence existed, to substantiate the charges that had been urged against him. The prediction would have been verified. There was no evidence. Not a man in the Colony dared to accuse him of an unwise or an unworthy action.— Every individual of the least standing, was examined, personally by me on the subject; and the result was, to my mind, moral demonstration, that no man could more faithfully, more disinterestedly, more resolutely, have fulfilled the duties of his station. The clouds that had darkened his reputation, arose from the low grounds of ignorance and the putrescent ingredients of malice, and the light of an investigation that revealed the sources of their origin, dispelled them forever.

During the absence of Mr. Ashmun, two events ad concurred to produce a decided change for the better, i the affairs of the Colony. The stores had been nearly or quite consumed, before the arrival of the Fidelity; and the pressure of want had proved an irresistible argument for exertion: while the despatches from the Society received by that vessel, had softened, if not subdued, the spirit of rebellion.

In the state of the Colony at that time, there were causes both for hope and fear. The general health and cheerfulness; the improvements and defences; the morality and religion; the quiet of the Sabbath; the Sunday Schools, one of which was composed of native children; and the warm gratitude expressed towards the Board, for a special mission in their favour, were encouraging: while the dissatisfaction with the decisions of the Board; the protracted debility of the emigrants by the Cyrus; the want of medicines and a Physician; of agricultural utensils, and a thousand other things that minister to comfort and aid industry; and above all, the feeble and relaxed condition of the Government, showed, that without some speedy and thorough change, there would remain serious grounds for apprehension.

The causes, to which most of the moral disorders of the Colony were to be attributed, as specified in the report made on my return to the Board, were:

First, and principally; the dissatisfaction of the earliest settlers with the decision of the principal Agent in regard to the distribution of the town-lots.

2d. An imbecility traceable to the former habits and condition of life, of many of the settlers.

3d. The turbulent and malicious temper of two or three individuals.

4th. Jealousy kindled by the proceedings of a commercial company established at Baltimore, for the prosecution of the African trade.

5th. The trials and hardships incidental to the founding of a Colony on a remote and uncivilized shore; and

6th. The deficiency of power in the Government to meet exigencies, to restrain the first tendencies towards insubordination, and enforce the authority of the laws.

To these should perhaps be added, a distrust of the disposition or ability of the Society to afford them adequate aid and protection. To their difficulties and privations, they could not be insensible; while few considered that of these, to an extent, they were themselves the authors, and that in some degree, they were inseparable from the nature of their enterprise. It was a ready argument, which even the ignorant could understand; "we suffer: if the Society have means

'and does not apply them to our relief, it is without bene-
'volence; if it have not means, it wants power, and in either
'case is unworthy of our confidence." The presence of an
individual who had been commissioned to visit them, examine their circumstances, hear their complaints, and assure them that every thing possible would be done to promote their interests, was an evidence of the care and benevolence of the Society which none were able wholly to resist.

The best endeavours of Mr. Ashmun and myself, during the eight days I remained on the Cape, were directed to relieve suffering, satisfy doubt, remedy discontent, and establish an efficient Government, founded in the approbation of the people, and adaptable not only to their present, but future political necessities. Not only was the day spent in labour, but a large portion of the night in watchful meditation how we might preserve unquenched those sacred fires beginning to sparkle in that hitherto dispairful darkness, and possessed, we knew, of a kindling power (if guarded for a brief space from extinction), to change to cheerfulness the mournfulness of nature, and light up that whole land with their constelled glory.

No subject was left unconsidered that required attention. Regulations were adopted for the benefit of widows, orphans, the infirm and the helpless. The requests of individuals, as well as the public wants, were noted, that they might be made known to the Managers of the Society. The Constitution of Government agreed on, while it took nothing from the power of the Society in cases of final resort, admitted of a full expression, on public measures, of the opinions of the settlers, and gave them a large share in the management of political affairs.*

* At first, Mr. Ashmun appeared to doubt the qualifications of the settlers for any share in the concerns of Government, and urged very strongly, that in case they were admitted to a share, the Agent should have the control of a small military guard. He could hardly hope for so great and beneficial a

All the decisions of the Agents, with the plan of Government they had resolved to recommend to the Society, were read and explained to the assembled Colonists, who expressed their approbation and fixed purpose to sustain both, (should they receive the sanction of the Board,) without a dissenting voice.* Beneath the thatched roof of the first rude house for Divine worship, ever erected in the Colony, stood the little company of one hundred coloured emigrants, who had adventured all things, to gain for themselves and children, a home and inheritance of liberty; and before God pledged themselves to maintain the Constitution of their choice, and prove faithful to the great trust committed to their hands.†

Mutual confidence was now restored between the people and the Agent; the people and the Society; and the hope was indulged, that a full and candid representation of the proceedings of Mr. Ashmun, would dispel from the minds of the Managers, every doubt of his integrity and ability. Shall I ever forget the joyous hour when standing by the side of this man of God, in whose features an almost Divine meekness and charity softened magnanimity into love, I saw the delight with which he beheld the desponding encouraged; the change as Providence now designed to accomplish. I thought the guard inexpedient, and that it would not be sustained. In deference to his judgment and experience, however, it was established; but in a short time was considered by himself unnecessary and disbanded. Mr. Ashmun lived to observe the excellence of authority "extending more over the wills of men than over their deeds and services;" and even then he approved all the measures adopted, whatever shades of difference existed between us in regard to their probable result. Governors and Lawgivers would do well to remember the observation of Bacon—"When Virgil putteth himself forth to attribute to Augustus Cæsar, the best of human honours, he doth it in these words:

———Victorque Volentes
Per populos dat jura, Viamque affectat Olympo."

* Many of the settlers who had been receiving rations, offered from that day, to support themselves; and a noble public spirit, appeared to animate nearly the whole community.

† Appendix No. 6.

weak resolute; order rising out of confusion, and the whole state of affairs assuming a new aspect of peace, industry, hope and obedience. Having empowered him to fulfil the duties of Agent, both of the Government and Society, until able to Report to them my proceedings, on the 22d of August, I grasped his hand, and bade him farewell, at the landing place of Monrovia, never more to see him, but on his death-bed, the scene of his last and greatest triumph.

## CHAPTER XII.

A reluctance to admit evidence proving error in our opinions, (especially if such error have gained strength by time and struck its roots deep into many minds,) is one of the infirmities of our nature. The mind, like the body, seems averse to sudden changes; it would escape the sense of its own weakness; and is ready, often, to prefer consistency to truth. We are so vain of our imagined independence, that in the company of Truth herself, we would lead, not follow, treating her as a handmaid, rather than a royal mistress, clad in the majestic robes of Heaven, to whom Kings may honourably bow, since over the Angels of God she holds rightful empire. Those who would promote her cause, must remember, that her throne is set up not more in the understanding than the affections; that she rules the conduct but as she sways the heart. The will bends less to authority than love; and would appear self-moved, rather than forced.* The judgment that resists, for a moment, any power of evidence or argument, may yield, as of its own accord, to their continued influence. The Divine economy in the spiritual, is like, in an important sense, to that in the natural world; since God himself encourages us to wait for the good seed of truth to ripen, "as the husbandman waiteth for the precious fruit of the earth, and hath long patience for it until he receive the early and the latter rain."

The proceedings, during the visit of the writer to the Colony, submitted, on his return from Africa, to the Managers of the Society, received, at first, in no one important particular, their approbation. The Committee to whom these proceedings were referred, arranged them in their Report, under six heads; upon each, they pronounced an unfavourable judgment; and this Report, adopted by the Board, was transmitted to Mr. Ashmun.†

Anxious as were the Managers to promote the best interests of the Colony, they were, as yet, unable to discern satisfactory reasons for entire confidence in Mr. Ashmun; and the doubts, which from this or other circumstances, had arisen in regard to the new measures approved by him, gained strength (in some measure, at least,) from the statements and opinions of his predecessor in the Agency. While, however, the Board gave no sanction to the new form of Government, yet, "such parts as could not well be dispensed with," as an "experiment of the Agent," they permitted to be tried.

Inquiries were now made for a person qualified to combine in himself, the offices of principal Agent and Surgeon to the

---

\* ———Now for me,
Right conduct has a value of its own;
The happiness my King might cause me plant,
I would myself produce ; and conscious joy,
And free selection, not the force of duty,
Should impel me. SCHILLER.

† Appendix No. 7.

Colony; and on the 12th of January, 1825, a respectable individual was appointed to the station.

But the time drew near when that Divine Providence which rules no less in human counsels, than in the operations of nature, was by events that none could gainsay or resist, to demonstrate to the Managers the policy required, establish order and good government in the Colony, and bring out into unclouded light, the character of Ashmun.

On the 16th of March, communications bearing date up to the 15th of December, were received by the Board, affording conclusive evidence of the zeal, industry, and ability of Mr. Ashmun, as well as of the extraordinary and most beneficial changes wrought within a very brief period in the whole condition and prospects of the Colony.

After expressing his regret, that for the unusually long period of five months, no conveyance had offered for a single letter to the Society, he remarks: "The communications
' enclosed, are necessarily voluminous; but not more so than
' the actual state of the Colony, and its most interesting his-
' tory for the last half year, seems to demand. After the se-
' vere struggles, reiterated disappointments, and nameless
' evils, which for so many years had filled the annals of the
' establishment—to see the whole course of things suddenly
' reversed—an horizon without a cloud, and unmingled, un-
' interrupted prosperity, such as perhaps never before marked
' the early progress of a similar settlement; our distinguished
' lot, may well excite in an individual situated as I am, and
' have been, feelings but little compatible with the coolness
' which ought to dictate an official despatch. I am sensible,
' too, that the most dispassionate statement of facts (for I have
' none to communicate, which will much shade the brightest
' colours of the piece,) cannot wholly escape the suspicion of
' a studied flattery of the picture. But He who knows all
' things, knows that I intend neither to overrate the actual
' measure of His distinguished mercies, nor to suppress any

'adverse circumstances with which He has chosen to temper
'them. My private sentiments are my own, the facts are due
'to the friends of the cause."

Having alluded to the ungovernable spirit which had continued to rage even after his departure from the Cape, he continues: "The communications of the Board, at this criti-
'cal moment, came to hand. The measures enjoined the
'Agent to take, and the searching language of the Society's
'address, by the blessing of God, wrought upon their minds
'with a force utterly resistless. They saw in their actual
'distress, some of the most appalling predictions of this paper,
'either fulfilling or actually fulfilled. The most contentious
'and clamorous covered their heads with self-conviction and
'shame—and astonishing as it may seem, their mouths have
'never since been opened on those topics. They were thus
'prepared to acquiesce in any measures the Board might
'prescribe, and to expect the return of their Agent or the ar-
'rival of any Agent with ungovernable impatience."

Having mentioned the good conduct of emigrants by the Cyrus, he proceeds: "The welcome given to Mr. Gurley
'and myself, I at first treated as insincere; but however ex-
'travagant in expression, I am now convinced that it was
'dictated by the heart.

"The official decisions communicated to them, along with
'the new modification of the Government, were received
'with an unanimity of acquiescence, which I confess, was
'painful to me. I feared either that they could not understand
'them, or thought opposition, *at that moment*, unseasonable.
'But the event has proved my fears unfounded; and I now
'consider myself authorized to state, that there is an enlight-
'ened and growing attachment rooted in the bosoms of the
'great body of the people to their laws, their officers, and
'the authority of the Society.

"The participation of the Magistrates and Council in the
'deliberations of the Agent, and the administration of justice,

'has tended chiefly to form the individual officers themselves,
'to a modesty of deportment and opinion, which they never
'manifested before; and to secure to the Government the
'united support of the people. Our laws and temporary
'regulations are multiplied with a most cautious regard to the
'exigencies to be provided for; but once established, they are
'conscientiously carried into complete effect. I witness, with
'the highest pleasure, an increasing sense of the sacredness of
'Law—and as far as I know, the feeling is universal. The
'system of Government has proved itself practicable. It dis-
'tributes to the requisite number of officers, without too
'much accumulating on a few, or giving occasion to inter-
'ference or confusion, the duties required by the public
'service. The Agent has adopted the rule never to inter-
'pose his authority, where that of the proper officer of the
'Government, however inferior, is adequate to the emergen-
'cy. Every officer thus finding his sphere of official duty
'left sacredly to himself, and knowing that he will be sup-
'ported in the vindication and exercise of his official pow-
'ers, comes deeply to feel his individual responsibility—
'spares no pains to qualify himself for his station, freely ap-
'plies for, and thankfully receives, advice and instruction;
'and pays the most conscientious regard to the province
'and rights of all the other officers of Government."

Near the close of the same letter, he speaks of a remarkable attention to religion, in the following terms: "But the
'richest blessing of all, remains to be acknowledged—a
'blessing, without which, I venture to say, the complexion of
'this paper would have been materially different.

"It has pleased the God and Father of our Lord Jesus
'Christ, in the sovereignty of His mercy, to visit the Colony
'with an abundant effusion of His Holy Spirit. This great
'event, an era in the history of the settlement, which has
'been marked in Heaven, and will long be celebrated by its
'witnesses and monuments on earth, occurred in all the month

'of September. About the middle of that month, were wit-
'nessed the first appearances, which gave evidence of the
'holy work. I feel that this is a theme to which a mortal
'pen ought to be approached with awful caution.

"But about thirty of our Colonists, of all ages and charac-
'ters, indiscriminately, have, as the fruits of the work, pub-
'licly professed their faith in the Redeemer. They have,
'*so far*, walked as the truly regenerate children of God. A
'change in their deportment and in their whole character,
'is as obvious, as would be their transformation to another
'order of being. From lovers of sin and the world, they
'have become the lovers of God and of His people. Bad
'husbands, wives, children, and subjects, are changed to af-
'fectionate relatives, industrious, sober, and useful citizens.
'As far as mortal instrumentality was concerned in this
'blessed work, it was exerted by silent, humble supplications
'to Almighty God, a holy deportment of Christian professors,
'and a plain, simple, and serious inculcation of the saving
'doctrines of Christ and His Apostles. I congratulate every
'Christian and devout friend of this establishment, on this
'signal answer to their prayers and crown of their precious
'hopes: Rejoice; your labour is not in vain:—put all these
'astonishing blessings together, and in the humble exulta-
'tion of your hearts, exclaim, the mighty God is our helper.
'You know how to appreciate and how to interpret spiritual
'blessings. By many this precious dispensation of Provi-
'dence, must be regarded as of little importance. But poor
'Africa will think otherwise; and to the days of eternity, a
'countless host of her children will look back and date from
'it, the first effectual dawning of that heavenly light, which
'shall at length have conducted them to the Fold and the
'City of God."

The same despatches informed the Board of the progress made in public improvements; that nearly every proprietor of land, single women not excepted, had a dwelling well advanced; that several roads had been cleared and opened; that a stone pier one hundred feet in length had been constructed in the river; that something important had been done for agriculture; that several schools, one for native children, were in operation; that two commodious houses for worship were building; and that the organization of the Colonial Militia (among which was a volunteer corps of young men in a neat uniform), had added to the strength and safety of the Colony.

The details of negotiations entered into, and happily concluded, by the Agent with the principal Chiefs in the vicinity, as far as Grand Bassa, securing a free trade with the natives of the coast and interior, were at the same time received. Between the Agent and these Chiefs in behalf of those respectively represented by them, it was agreed, that they should live in perpetual peace; that trade, without fraud or interruption, in any goods and productions to be disposed of in the Colony, should continue; that no impediments should be thrown in the way of any other people who might desire to trade with the settlement; that the Kings should surrender to the Agent any evil disposed person who sought to injure the Colony, to be punished by the Colonial Government; and that the Agent should give notice to the Chiefs of any unfriendly or malicious designs of which he might be informed, against them.

The abilities of Mr. Ashmun were seen less, perhaps, in what had been done since the reorganization of the Government, than in the papers submitted to the Board on a great variety of topics, relating to the future administration and interests of the Colony.* These papers showed that, while he

---

\* The following is a list of these papers:
Notes introductory to the Colonial Journal, 2 sheets.
Transcript of do do 7 "
Letter to the Executive Committee, 7 "
The Liberian farmer and letter accompanying, 13 "

could grasp large objects, he was not inattentive to minute; that he was not unfitted for ordinary business, because he had the talents of a Statesman.

The Committee of the Board to whom these despatches were referred, reported on the 28th of March—that in their opinion, Mr. Ashmun "had shown great attention to the important charge committed to him;" had conducted himself with "much prudence and propriety, generally;" and recommended an expression of the cordial approbation of the Managers of the Society. They also moved resolutions to diminish, by certain restrictions, (as suggested by Mr. Ashmun) the trade in ardent spirits, and for modifying, as he proposed, the plan of public labour; and their entire Report received the sanction of the Board.*

| | |
|---|---|
| Perspective view of the Cape, | 1 sheet. |
| Notes on the defence of the Colony, | 1 " |
| Copy of my account current to the Navy Department, | 3 " |
| Remarks on the Agent's domestic establishment, | 2 " |
| Draft of a store house built, | 1 " |
| Proposition relative to public labour, | 1 " |
| Do relative to the use of ardent spirits, | 1 " |
| Copy of Rev. Mr. Waring's tour to Bassa, | 2 " |
| Estimates of future supplies, and proposition relative to a freight of plank, | 1 " |
| Best method of subsisting the Colony, | 2 " |
| Notes on the extent of Territory, | 1 " |
| Inventory of goods, | 1 " |
| Rough map of the coast, | 1 " |

* In the earliest years of the Colony, emigrants, while receiving rations from the public store, were required to devote two days in the week to labour, on the public works. The labourers having no motive of reward, were inefficient; while they found their duty to the public an excuse for negligence in constructing their houses and cultivating their grounds. The following plan, proposed by Mr. Ashmun, has been productive of far better effects:

"1st. All invalids not twelve months in the Colony, and such others as must otherwise suffer, to receive rations if they have not resources of their own.

## LIFE OF ASHMUN.

Truth had begun to shake the fortresses of error which had risen against Ashmun, and no less against the Colony he had preserved; and an accurate observer of Providence, her constant and mighty ally, might have seen hung out, the prophetic signals of a speedy triumph. There was bright light in the clouds, though then, from most eyes concealed.*

Mr. Ashmun understood both the advantages and difficulties of his situation. He took a comprehensive view of his duties, saw clearly their mutual relations and the reciprocal influence which well discharged, they would exert upon the success of each other, and upon his general usefulness. If the irrevocable loss of reputation would injure himself only, it might be endured in silence. But he knew that he had not the right,—and more, that it would be highly criminal to permit this treasure to be sacrificed when power was granted to preserve it. It was the gift of Heaven; in the service of mankind he felt bound to use it; and thus offer it acceptably in tribute to the Divine Majesty.

Aware, however, that most men judge of merit only by success,—that wisdom in defeat is counted folly, and that he who blunders into prosperity gains the credit of wisdom, he trusted in the Most High, who often dashes to ruin the counsels of Ambition, and exalts Humility to distinction and power.

We may notice, briefly, his conduct and proceedings at this period; first, in respect to himself; second, to the Colony; and third, to the Board of Managers.

"2d. Emigrants not to be taxed with public labour, in consideration of any benefit or provision to be derived from the Society, in the first six months of their residence. But at the end of this term, they are to pay for all they receive.

"3d. Provisions, stuffs, shoes, clothing, and tobacco, to be held on sale; but only for the present consumption of the buyers; for which all sorts of labour will be taken—a preference always to be given to such labourers and mechanics as are less than eighteen months in the Colony."

* Job xxxvii, 21.

To himself, the motives and principles which governed him, we allude first, because these must be regarded as the sources and fountains of conduct—a knowledge whereof may explain what else were obscure, or interpret what were otherwise mysterious.

Of the spirit which animated him, we learn something from an extract taken from a letter addressed to the writer, under date of January 19, 1825:

"I have heard of your safe arrival in the West Indies, by a
' Pirate who is now near us, and four days ago boarded a
' craft of ours. The name is thought to be the General
' Winder, a Baltimore built schooner. Since you left me,
' has been one of the happiest periods of my life. Unnoticed
' and unremembered, humbly endeavouring to serve a world
' to which I do not feel myself much obliged, except for its
' Maker's and Redeemer's sake; the spectator of a blessed
' work of mercy, I have known nothing but contentment
' and desire to be thankful. You will, in perusing my des-
' patches, I think, see wonders of Divine goodness to admire,
' and no cause to regret your visit to us."

On the 24th of April, he wrote in his Journal:

"I have experienced some relief in my feelings from learn-
' ing that my pecuniary affairs in the United States are in a
' train of speedy settlement, on the footing of justice to my
' creditors; an event I have long desired most anxiously, and
' for which I bless God, through whose good Providence it
' has taken place. But I have information also from that
' country of a very trying nature."

He then expresses apprehension, that reports put in circulation against him in the United States, had made impressions unfavourable to his moral character which could never be effaced; his conviction that in many ways they had seriously injured him; that whether true or false, they were judged a sufficient reason for superseding him whenever another person of equal qualifications could be found to accept the

Agency; that the Government, not less than the Society, had withheld the evidence of entire confidence; he alluded to the facts, that few individuals in America had written to him, and that in the letters he received, there was a coldness and reserve destroying their value; that in reports concerning the Colony, his name was sedulously avoided, even in connexion with the very services he had rendered; and finally, that the information contained in his Journals and letters, had not obtained the full credit to which it was entitled.

"Why," he exclaimed, "have I not resigned a situation 'which I cannot hold without submitting to bear such a load 'of obloquy? Every month of my continuance in Africa, I 'do indeed sacrifice much of the proud sensibilities of my 'heart."

He felt justified in still occupying his station, by the following considerations:

1st. In so doing, he did nothing dishonourable in itself; and

2d. There were positive reasons which warranted and required the sacrifice.

To render his continuance dishonourable, he must be conscious either of the truth of the accusations urged against him, or of some other circumstance disqualifying him for his situation. But he was conscious of neither.

The reasons which required his stay, were—1st, the unfavourable impressions which might be drawn from his resignation. Might it not be regarded as a concession, that the reports which had injured him were founded in truth?

2d. He had at no time been able to retire from his station, without leaving the Colony destitute of an Agent, and thus exposed to great evils—perhaps to anarchy, famine, or war. Would it be right to put in jeopardy the interests of the Colony, for any reasons of a mere personal and private nature?

3d. The claims of his creditors demanded, that he should not voluntarily relinquish the prospect which his situation afforded of discharging them.

4th. Through the Divine Mercy, his health had been in a good measure preserved in Africa. "And why," he asks, " am I thus preserved, unless to perform some service in this ' country? And where can I express my gratitude so well, ' as on the very theatre of such signal mercies? I have ac- ' quired, from long residence, a better knowledge of the coun- ' try, and affairs of the Colony, than any other person living; ' and I am not willing to forego the opportunity put into my ' hands *alone*, to be extensively useful here. Besides, a ' change of Agents cannot rationally be expected to take ' place without the loss of one or more valuable lives."

In respect to the Colony, he saw every obstruction to the free and full exercise of his various talents removed. "We are," said he, "thanks to Divine Providence, prosperous be- ' yond any former period of the establishment. Health, union, ' content, and industry *within*,—peace, respectability, and ' confidence *without*, call for more gratitude than we possess ' here; and I hope that the hearts of our American friends ' may supply the deficiency."

Standing on the summit of the Cape, he extended his view over a magnificent scene, diversified by objects bright, beautiful, and sublime; the silver stream of the Montserado— Cape Mount fifty miles distant, jutting boldly into the sea—a wide-spread country, dense with an ever-green forest, "rising in successive ridges of verdure," far into the interior; the ocean, over which the eye glanced for more than one hundred and fifty miles of the horizon, in an instant catching each sail that ventured within this mighty compass of vision, and his admiration of the Great Author of Nature, but rendered him more compassionate towards those who amid these wonders of His hands, were blind to His glory. He felt how great was the work entrusted to him of founding a Christian State on the confines of a continent, where man had for ages been separated from Truth and Virtue,—where crime took license from authority, and vice was hardened by custom,—and where the light of intellect shone dim amid the sensual and selfish passions. But he knew that Humanity in its wildest and most degraded state, may be reclaimed; and hoped that beneath the extending wings of an empire, pervaded by the spirit of Liberty and Religion, would finally be gathered in peace the millions of Africa; or, should this hope be disappointed, he saw that a nobler race would occupy their places, adorning a land already abounding in the gifts of Providence, with the productions of knowledge, of genius, of taste, and of art.

The success of the Colony, he perceived, depended principally upon three things:—The stability and beneficence of its Government; its means of defence; and its means of subsistence; and these again must find their chief source in the union, morality, public spirit, and religion; or (to express all in a word), the *good character* of the people.

His first object then was, to animate the Colonists with a sense of their responsibility to God, themselves, and their race; his next, to instruct them how most effectually to show this spirit in the conduct of their affairs. Convinced that religion alone could qualify them, patiently, to endure their trials, and nobly to perform their work, he encouraged all sober measures designed to extend and increase its influence, and ceased not to solicit from the Board and other friends of Africa, the aid of enlightened and faithful Ministers of the Gospel. We have already seen with what delight he beheld the members of this little community, attending to their spiritual as to their greatest concerns; and how, from this, he derived assurance, that the Colony was an object of special favour and protection to the Almighty.

To secure the stable and beneficent operation of the Government, it was shown to the people, that its only firm basis was, their reason and affections. Mr. Ashmun explained to each officer the nature and extent of his duties; the proper mode of their execution; and then permitted neither himself nor others to interfere with a manly and independent discharge of them. The officers were respected, because they respected themselves. The people valued their Government, not simply because it afforded them protection, but because they saw their fellow-citizens, elected by themselves, filling offices of trust, and sharing largely in the administration of public affairs. The Government, they perceived, in a great degree, rested upon them, and therefore they felt it their honour, as well as duty, to sustain it.

For means of defence, the Agent looked not more to the organization and discipline of the Militia, and to the preservation of the arms and fortifications, in proper order and condition, than to that just and pacific policy towards the natives which should leave no reason or even plausible pretext for hostilities. If war should occur, he chose to have conscience an ally, even in the breast of the enemy. But he trusted not solely to measures of prevention. He gave orders for repairing the Fort, and for the erection of two new Batteries, one on the head of the Cape (to command the roadstead); and while he encouraged such exercises as were necessary to give confidence to the settlers, in their military powers, he taught them by precept and example, to fear none but God. What has been said of the ancient martyrs, may be said of Ashmun—"He could keep one eye steadily fixed upon his duty, and look death and danger out of countenance with the other."

In respect to means of subsistence, while he regarded agriculture as of primary importance, and demanding immediate, earnest, and general attention, he saw that the amount of labour required for clearing and cultivating the lands, (considering what must be applied to the construction of houses and other works within the limits of the town,) was too great to leave a hope that the Colony could at a very early day, derive subsistence from the products of its own soil.— Still he neglected no means in his power of encouraging and promoting this interest. He drew up many valuable directions to the Liberia Farmer, which it must be regretted were not then printed for the benefit of the Colonists.*

Supplies not to be derived from the present agriculture of the Colony, he perceived might be obtained in trade from the natives, and therefore sought to conciliate the neighbouring tribes, and to open with them, at various points on the coast, a mutually advantageous commerce. "There is no question," he remarks, "of the capability of this country to furnish ' the Colony with provisions. A little system and providence ' are all that is necessary to make the supply certain." He had proved, by actual experiment, that it was far more economical to subsist the Colony on African than American provisions.†

On the arrival of the brig Hunter, on the 13th of March, 1825, with sixty-six settlers, most of whom were farmers, Mr. Ashmun saw the necessity of extending, if possible, the limits of the Territory.

The following abstract from his own pen, contains a brief account of his negotiations to secure a tract of land on the river St. Paul's:

"The slow progress and ill success (he observes) of the first ' experiments in agriculture at Cape Montserado, directed the ' attention of the Agent, early in the year 1825, to an in- ' quiry into the causes of a circumstance so detrimental to ' the prospects of the settlement. In the course of this in- ' quiry, a number of obstacles to the prosperity of this leading ' branch of industry, occurred, which a length of time, and ' expensive improvements alone seemed likely to overcome. ' It was perceived, that the *quality of the lands belonging* ' *to the settlement of Monrovia, was unfavourable to cul-* ' *tivation.* The highlands of the settlement are rocky, and ' from having suffered the wash of the rains, are in many

---

\* Appendix No. 7.

† He thought the expense diminished nearly one half.

'places deprived of all their best soil; are liable to be sun
'burnt in the dry season, and swept of their crops by the
'sudden currents of the wet. The lowlands are too wet and
'low, for most of the purposes of farming; and can only be
'brought to their true and entire value, by cutting sluices,
'and forming dikes, at a great expense. The flat country
'bordering on the waters are alluvial; and extensive tracts
'consist of little more than the barren sands of the ocean,
'sprinkled rather than yet covered with a vegetable mould—
'the element of its future fertility. The distant *situation
'of the proprietors, living as they do in town, from their
'plantations*, presented a second obstacle, which, in regard
'to those settlers, it is believed, will never cease to keep back
'the business of agriculture. The people of Monrovia are, like-
'wise, and ever must be made up of a variety of trades, each
'of which, in addition to the little agricultural knowledge
'such a people can be supposed to possess, has its own pecu-
'liar views, both of the proper mode of agriculture, and of
'the expediency of engaging in it at all. Concert of action
'on this subject, has never been obtained, not even by the
'most positive public regulations:—without such concert,
'the interest at large, can never be much; and has hitherto
'hardly existed at all.

"The arrival of the brig 'Hunter,' March 13th, 1825, hav-
'ing on board sixty-six settlers, of whom nearly all had been
'bred farmers, and who, if fixed at Monrovia, must have
'been compelled either to relinquish, as the means of acquir-
'ing their livelihood, the only branch of business in which
'they were fitted to succeed; or pursue it under very serious
'disadvantages, determined the Agent to form a new agricul-
'tural settlement, in a situation more favourable to its suc-
'cess, than any offered in the immediate vicinity of the Cape.
'He accordingly explored, with a view to the discovery of
'such a situation, the Montserado river, as far as to the head
'of one of its sources, in the last week of April. But being

'entirely frustrated by the low and forbidding nature of all
' the lands examined in that quarter, he directed his attention
' to the St. Paul's. The tract of country stretching along the
' South bank of the St. Paul's, and bounded Westwardly by
' the Stockton, combined in it every desirable advantage for
' the proposed settlement, and fixed the Agent's choice im-
' mediately. The purchase of a right to occupy this land,
' which was the next object of solicitude, was cautiously
' opened to some of the most influential Chiefs of the St.
' Paul's without delay—and referred to the decision of a
' general council of the country authorities, which was con-
' voked at the Agent's instance, at Gourah, on Bushrod Island,
' May 2d. The Agent attended—but too many of the Chiefs
' being absent to admit of the accomplishment of the business,
' the Agent was obliged after waiting five days without see-
' ing more than two of the head men, to return on the 7th of
' the same month. But the matter was so vigorously pressed,
' that, after a variety of difficulties and delays, all of which
' were overruled by the favourable Providence of the most
' High, the cession of the whole Territory in question, was
' concluded; and a part of the purchase money paid on the
' 11th of the same month.

"Along this beautiful river were formerly scattered, in Af-
' rica's better days, innumerable native hamlets; and till with-
' in the last twenty years, nearly the whole river-board, for
' one to two miles back, was under that slight culture which
' obtains among the natives of this country. But the popu-
' lation has been wasted by the rage for trading in slaves;
' with which the constant presence of slaving vessels, and
' the introduction of foreign luxuries, have inspired them.—
' The South bank of this river and all the intervening coun-
' try between it and the Montserado, have been, from this
' cause, nearly desolated of inhabitants. A few detached
' and solitary plantations scattered at long intervals through-
' out the tract, but just serve to interrupt the silence, and re-

'lieve the gloom which reigns over the whole region. The
'labourers who carry on this cultivation, are generally
'slaves whose masters reside either on Bushrod Island, on the
'North bank of the river, or on the Island at the mouth of
'the Montserado. Those owners, finding the country unoc-
'cupied, select such tracts as are best adapted to their purpo-
'ses, and cultivate them as long as suits their convenience,
'without thinking about any property in the soil.

"The country to which I beg particularly to direct the at-
'tention of the Board, may be seen (best on the large plan) to
'commence Westwardly at the Stockton creek,—bounded
'North by the St. Paul's, South by the marshy mangrove
'country, skirting the Montserado river; and stretching East-
'wardly to an indefinite extent. Six miles above the Stock-
'ton, and on the St. Paul's, is a considerable town, (King
'Governor's;) four miles in the interior of this, is another,
'(Ba Konka's;) but with these exceptions, and perhaps one
'hundred acres of plantation-land attached to those two
'towns, the whole tract, comprehending a breadth of one to
'three leagues, lying along the whole navigable part of the
'St. Paul's, which I estimate at twenty miles, is nearly un-
'peopled and unoccupied. The jurisdiction is claimed by
'old King Peter, who resides on Bushrod Island; and *of this*
'*whole tract*, I have the satisfaction to inform the Board, *a*
'*purchase has been effected, and formal possession taken,*
'*for the American Colonization Society.* The deed I en-
'close.

"In regard to the sincerity with which this transaction has
'been conducted on the part of the natives, the Board may
'exercise the most unqualified confidence, of which a nego-
'tiation with native Africans, admits.     *     *     *

"In the late business, I told them, 'they knew I had never
'deceived, or injured them; or even treated their best inter-
'ests, with indifference. I knew they considered me as their
'friend, and my heart agreed with their opinion, in testifying

'that I was so. I had been long in their country—and for
' the same reasons which forbade me to be the enemy of my
' *own* countrymen, it was impossible for me to be *theirs*. They
' saw me spending my life in a strange country, in order to
' do black men good; and black people were all brothers. I
' felt much the same for all, and knew they would confide in
' me; as I certainly should in any deliberate act of theirs'.—
' It was at this moment that I became more fully convinced
' than ever before, of the happy effects which that course of
' exact justice, which I had so long endeavoured to pursue,
' could produce on savage minds. I felt that our policy had
' gained a moral conquest, and that was the moment of tri-
' umph. They reciprocated the confidence which I professed
' to repose in them; and as the Board will perceive from the
' Journal, yielded with little hesitation the important point
' sought of them. I am thus explicit in order to represent, as
' exactly as possible, the spirit in which this business was
' throughout conducted. The whole progress of the treaty
' will be seen in the narrative herewith forwarded. There
' remains an explanation to be given of the last article in the
' instrument of ratification, which provides for the appoint-
' ment, on the part of the Colony, of a man of distinction, ta-
' ken from the Kings of the country, to officiate as patron of
' the projected settlement.

"By the deed, the purchase includes generally all the lands '
' bounded North by the St. Paul's, and West by the Stock-
' ton; such expressly excepted, as are, or may be, at the time of
' forming and extending on it the Colonial settlement, occu-
' pied by, and necessary to the subsistence and comfort of,
' the natives of the country—it being no part of the intention
' of this purchase to deprive those people of a single real ad-
' vantage; but on the contrary, to improve them and advance
' their happiness, by carrying Christianity and civilization to
' the doors of their cabins.

"On the advantages likely to flow directly from this valu-

'able accession of territory, it would be easy, by loosening
'the reins of the imagination, to expatiate largely. But we
'are certainly authorized to expect from it the means of more
'effectually advancing the Colony to what it ought to be,
'than, from *any*, perhaps *all* other events, that have occurred
'since my connexion with the concern. Some of these ad-
'vantages have been already explained in this paper. Others
'may be inferred. And indulging me in the repetition of
'some of the former, the Board are at liberty to regard the
'following as among the most prominent and certain :

"1st. It entirely obviates in the case of all the farmers
'hereafter to settle in the country, the serious disadvantage,
'(next to ruinous,) of being several miles separated in their
'residence, from their plantations.

"2d. It gives them, instead of arduous bluffs, and a stub-
'born soil, which after severe labour would be fit only for
'coffee plantations, and one or two other purposes, a pli-
'able and fertile soil in a champaign country, easily cleared,
'and entirely adapted to every species of tropical culture.

"3d. It places such settlers in a situation to make pro-
'visions sufficient to subsist themselves and their families in
'from nine to twelve months after their arrival in the coun-
'try; whereas, without it, the experiment has proved, that
'two or three years are not sufficient to enable them to attain
'the same end.

"4th. It will enable the Society to dispose of ten thousand
'settlers in a compass of ten miles from town; but without it,
'two thousand could scarcely be situated within twenty miles.
'By an inspection of the map, it may be seen that the settle-
'ment is susceptible of an extension of twenty miles from
'Monrovia, without leaving the St. Paul's or big Eastern
'branch of the Montserado, distant more than three miles.—
'By these waters, the boat navigation is free and direct to
'town—thus affording to the settlements extended on this
'tract, advantages for communicating with the Cape, which

' none formed on the Mamba Tongue, or Montserado Terri-
' tory, could ever enjoy.

"5th. This acquisition of territory will secure to the Co-
' lony, in a very short time, the entire command of the St.
' Paul's; and with it, the trade of that river, which is already
' valuable, and may be rendered much more so; and will
' break up the slave-traffic which still continues to be carried
' on with foreigners,* by that channel.

"6th. The country on the St. Paul's being much more sa-
' lubrious than the Montserado, future emigrants will suffer
' less in their health. Even at the present time our invalids
' have a practice of repairing to some town on that river, and
' have never failed to derive benefit from the change.

"7th. As an inference from the foregoing view of the ad-
' vantages resulting from this extension of territory, the Board
' are authorized, finally, to expect the accomplishment of their
' hopes, in the future rapid advancement of the Colony.—
' Nothing but mismanagement on the part of your Agents in
' this country, can, *if their zeal is sustained by the Society
' at home*, be supposed capable of long deferring the period,
' when the surplus produce of the Colony will supply the con-
' sumption by new emigrants, during the unproductive period
' of their residence. The inviting quality of the soil, and
' charming situation of the country on the St. Paul's, will
' inevitably engage thousands in agriculture, who, if confined
' to the Cape, would depend, with some semblance of a pre-
' text, on the precarious profits of trade, till their habits
' would become incurably irregular, and their future pros-
' pects, ruined. Agriculture, I venture to predict, will, at
' no distant time, become as creditable and prosperous, as it is
' now neglected; and the St. Paul's, instead of the Montse-
' rado, the centre of population and wealth to the Colony of
' Liberia."

* At this moment, I observe from my window, three French and Spanish schooners lying off the mouth of the St. Paul's river, awaiting their cargoes.

"A few days after this transaction, a slight ferment was
' produced among the natives, by the violent remonstrance
' of some of the neighbouring Chiefs, against the sale of so
' large a tract of their country. But, the whole subsided
' without any serious consequences. Eleven families were
' soon after designated to lay the foundation of the new set-
' tlement; which thence forward took the name of *St. Pauls.*
' But their number was subsequently reduced to nine, by the
' death of Reuben Thompson, and Claibourne Davis. A
' large passage-boat, constructed to carry eighty persons with
' convenience, and of about ten tons burden, was immediately
' commenced for the purpose of plying between the *St.*
' *Paul's,* and Cape; and connecting the two settlements to-
' gether. This boat was launched on the 11th of the follow-
' ing November, when the new settlers had fully recovered
' from the sickness of which all severely suffered on their
' first arrival in the country. A provisionary form of civil
' and military organization and Government, had been drawn
' up for this settlement, on the 8th of November. The first
' draft of lands took place, both for building and plantation
' lots, on the 9th; and the appointment of the officers of the
' settlement, on the 12th.

"On the 13th of the same month, the annual rains very
' seasonably terminated—and on the 14th, the complete occu-
' pation of the lands, took place.

"The Agent, accompanied by A. Davis, his wife and
' daughter, Sally Taylor, John Williams, Cornelius Brown,
' Cary Kenny, Joshua Thompson, with seven labourers, and
' their boys, arrived at the head of the Stockton at one o'clock
' on that day, in the St. Paul's passage-boat, on her first trip
' up the Stockton. An hour was spent in making a landing-
' place near the West end of water-street. The grass was
' found too rank to admit of moving through it; and on the
' same evening a temporary landing-place was prepared on
' the St. Paul's, near a small town belonging to a native of

' the name of Jack Soldier—where the people, their small stock
' of stores and tools, were landed; and two small houses were
' hired for their accommodation, till they might provide a
' shelter for themselves. Such are the small beginnings of
' this settlement. The blessing of God Almighty, in whose
' name, and for whose praise, those beginnings have been
' made, and are humbly consecrated, alone, can raise its head
' to the elevation, which it is the prayer of the Agent, who
' makes this record, seated on a bamboo pallet, in a solitary
' native cabin, on the margin of the St. Paul's, that it may, at
' no great distance of time, attain." J. A.

In respect to the Board of Managers, neither his candor nor magnanimity, would permit his general confidence in them to be shaken, because error had weakened their confidence in him. He knew, also, that "confidence is a plant of slow growth," which, if it once begin to wither, requires the most delicate and watchful attention, and revives and flourishes again only under the mild light of truth and the genial dews of affection. Its roots strike not less into the heart, than the judgment. To attempt to force its growth, is to kill it. If doubt still rested upon any portion of his past, he resolved, if possible, to leave it in no man's power to question the integrity, wisdom, and energy of his present and future conduct. If industry, ever active and unwearied, zeal intense, fortitude unbending, resolution yielding only to Providence, and all the might of his intellectual power, applied to advance the interests of the Colony, could clear away the imagined stains on his reputation; he felt assured, that like gold he should come forth from the furnace, purer and brighter for the trial. His course towards the Board, was to be respectful, open, frank, and manly. His self-regard was ever to be held subordinate to affection for the interests of the Colony; and public duty, not private advantage, to be the ruling motive of his action.

By the Hunter, on the 13th of March, he received the decisions of the Board on the new form of Government, and the measures therewith adopted. By the return of this vessel, he explained fully his views in regard to these measures, and communicated such statements and suggestions as might enable the Board to judge correctly of the condition and wants of the Colony.

"In announcing," he observes, "the final decision of the
' Board on the allocation of the seven individuals settled with-
' out the original limits of the town, I confess I dreaded the
' possible effects of the chagrin which the order must pro-
' duce. It was, however, received with calmness; and while
' it discovered to them that the Board had been unhappily led
' to act, on very erroneous information, excited not a disres-
' peetful murmur."

Having stated in a very clear and conclusive manner why the grounds assumed in this decision were such as "could neither be felt nor understood by any person resident in the settlement," he adds: "I know that the decisions of the
' Board have been formed on what they considered the pre-
' ponderance of correct information. And this circumstance
' fills me with distress and alarm, at the possible consequences
' of this misplaced confidence, and for the preservation of the
' best interests of the settlement, from utter subversion. I ear-
' nestly, but with the utmost deference, entreat them to re-
' collect, that no other Agent but myself, has ever spent two
' weeks of the dry season, or set a compass three times, to my
' knowledge on this Cape; no white man able to judge, has
' ever, before the arrival of Mr. Gurley, to my knowledge,
' given himself the trouble to make, even correct ocular ob-
' servations, one hundred yards from my house, in more than
' one direction; that I have, on the contrary, repeatedly sur-
' veyed every inch of these grounds; that this spot is more
' familiar in all its features, than my native village; that I
' have arranged, and carried into effect, three different plans
' of defence, adapted to the different circumstances of the set-

'tlement on as many different occasions;—that of these plans,
' the two first have sustained the test of as powerful an as-
' sault, as the town can ever suffer from a native force; and
' that I have had occasion to employ the guns of the town
' upon objects at every point of our water-board. I am at
' this moment on the spot: my judgment in matters of specu-
' lation, I may distrust: but observations on the physical
' features of these grounds, conducted by the rules of mensu-
' ration, are incapable of error.

"I know not whose recollections reported to the Board,
' the foregoing statements oppose. My sole object is to im-
' part correct information, and if possible, to prevail on the
' Board to appoint Agents in whose statements they can con-
' fide, or to extend their confidence to such as are acting un-
' der their appointment.

"In a multitude of matters too numerous to detail, your re-
' sident Agent must always exercise a large discretion. It is
' not possible for the Board to direct—I will add, it is not pos-
' sible for the Board to review more than a small part of his
' measures. He can have neither the time nor means to com-
' municate—nor the Board to investigate them. I have al-
' ways transmitted voluminous details of my proceedings.—
' But how small a part of the whole do these comprehend!
' and on how few, even of these, has it been possible for the
' Board to act in season to control their effects! for most of
' them are of a nature to admit of no delay; and at the same
' time materially affect the best interests of the settlement.

"It is my most valued privilege to submit my administra-
' tion to the supervision of the Board; but it is a privilege of
' which I can avail myself only in regard to leading mea-
' sures. Of these I have ever aimed to state the facts, and
' give correct information; and afterwards, most implicitly to
' acquiesce in, and execute the decisions of the Board, found-
' ed on such information.         *        *        *

" These remarks are extorted by a perception of the dan-

'ger which seems to threaten more than one primary inter-
'est of this Colony. One of these is that entire confidence,
'which ought to subsist on the part of the settlers, in all the
'engagements, even implied and indirect engagements, of
'the Board."

Of the new form of Government, he remarks:

"The instructions of the Board in relation to the plan of
'Government submitted, after virtually doing away the of-
'fice of Vice-Agent, leaves its final fate to depend on the
'event of the experiment. I certainly had less confidence
'in its success at first, than now. And if the Board should
'appreciate its fruits as I do, they will long authorize the
'continuance of the 'experiment.'

"I am happy to express my entire accordance with the
'wishes of the Board, in regard to the Christian simplicity
'which ought to characterize the Government, policy, and
'institutions of the Colony. Compared with all other civil
'societies on this continent, it certainly does exhibit a repub-
'lican simplicity of structure, to foreigners scarcely credible."*

* In a letter to the Secretary of the Society, by the Hunter, he observes:
"I am sorry to find Mr. —— and myself, in so poor credit with the Board. Even if they differed from ourselves in their opinion of our *wisdom*, I still hoped they might confide in our veracity; and that if they saw fit to repeal our measures, they would not distrust the truth of our statements. As regards my own private interest in the good opinion of the Board, however mortifying to my feelings the inferences from some parts of the last letter of instructions, I regard it all of little moment compared with the effects I am apprehensive some of their decisions will have on the prosperity of the Colony. The Board are misled in many things—in some materially. But reflecting on my own circumstances, I have determined, that until I can enjoy a personal interview, it will be inexpedient, and may appear officious in me, to undertake to set them right. In this remark, I beg to explain, that I refer wholly to wrong information; and as the effect of such information, some wrong impressions respecting the actual state of things, both formerly and at the present time, in this Colony. I shall not undertake to contradict too roundly, what the Board seem to regard as good authority, till I am better assured that they will admit my own. In the mean time, as truth and sober reality commonly have a weight and consistency in themselves which fiction

By the same conveyance, Mr. Ashmun replied, fully, to a letter which had been addressed to him on the subject of the Repertory, and which contained sundry allegations against his conduct in connection with that work. We have alluded in a former chapter, to the unfortunate differences which arose between him and several of the gentlemen (who supervised the editorial department of the Repertory), in consequence of its pecuniary embarrassments. These differences had their origin, principally, if not entirely, in misapprehension. A public notice, however, had been sent forth on the cover of that work, after Mr. Ashmun's departure from the country, charging him, by implication at least, with a breach of trust. Though this publication was early and deeply regretted by some who lent it their sanction, others still retained the sentiments which dictated it, and to these sentiments as the main source must be traced, the suspicion and distrust of Ashmun which so long infected the mind of the Board and of the community in which they resided. A respectable individual had now frankly communicated the charges which existed against him, and he therefore felt required by duty to the cause in which he was engaged, as well as to himself, to meet and refute them. It would be useless to go into details on this subject, especially as the effect of this reply in connection with other circumstances, will presently be seen in the proceedings of the Board. The conclusion of this letter is inserted to show how deep were his feelings on this occasion, and how eloquently he could express them:

"However lightly the accusations in question may have
' been resolved on and published, the deed has drawn after it
' no trivial consequences. To have robbed an individual who
' is known to have the sensibilities of a man, of so great a
' share of his peace as I have suffered and must, would, if

and exaggeration never possess, and as I know my information to have substantially these qualities, I shall rest as easy as possible, and await the issue of things."

'truly weighed, be regarded as something; to shake, for a
'season, and perhaps till the grave shall hide them from me
'forever, the confidence of two venerable parents, on whose
'names calumny never before dared to affix a stain, and who
'would sooner follow their nine children to the grave-yard,
'than believe that one of them could disgrace it; to blast, for
'a season, at least, the fond hopes of one of the most respecta-
'ble and numerous families in the United States; to poison,
'with suspicion, the minds of a numerous connexion of be-
'loved and confiding friends, in half the States of the Union;
'to place me as an insulated being in the midst of the lower
'creation, bound to no part by the ties of a sincere respect;
'to injure the valued, and in some sense, sacred cause in
'which I have sacrificed much and hazarded more, by cur-
'tailing my usefulness and weakening the bonds of mutual
'confidence between my employers and myself—between
'me and the Colonists;—thus to tie up, for months, from effi-
'cient exertion, the hands of a young man, whose advanta-
'ges have been many, and whose obligations to be useful, are
'felt to be imperious; these are some of the actual fruits of
'that publication: the end of it, is yet to be awaited. The
'Board have seen on what grounds that tremendous respon-
'sibility has been incurred. As a dispensation of Heaven, I
'accept it with penitence for the punishment of my sins. As
'far as it has been the work of man, I protest against it with
'all the abhorrence and force which its character inspires.
'And I have done it in language which must have its weight;
'because it is the language of truth—of truth which, whoever
'lives, will see every opening circumstance in future to cor-
'roborate and establish.

"On leaving the United States, I formally assigned all the
'uncollected arrears of the Repertory to pay its debts. Avail-
'ing myself from conscientious motives, of no insolvent laws,
'I delivered up every dollar of disposable property I had, in
'proportionate shares, to my creditors. The compensation

' I received as Agent of your Board, was so applied; also a
' large edition of the Life of Bacon, which I have been mor-
' tified to learn, has not answered my expectations in the
' sales, and consequently left a larger unsettled balance, to be
' otherwise paid than I anticipated.

"I do not allow myself to cherish a bitter feeling towards
' any man living. * * I shall, I hope, never trouble your
' respectable body with a similar detail; and most probably,
' let the whole matter slumber in silence, till a higher power
' shall call it up for a final decision before an unerring tri-
' bunal."

By the same conveyance, he transmitted interesting papers
on many subjects,* particularly one relating to the moral and
social condition of the neighbouring tribes; the facilities for
Missionary efforts among them; and the best mode of conducting such efforts.† "In regard to public objects of atten-
' tion," he observes, "The most has been made of the scanty
' means at my disposal. Gladly would I expend on these
' objects thousands—and it could be done with vast advan-
' tage—where I have only a few dollars, and those raised by
' dint of management, which few besides myself, would ex-
' ercise."

The exhibition which he presented of the state of the Colony; the industry of the citizens; the progress of various

* The following is a list of his despatches received by the Hunter:
1. Official letter to the Board.
2. Two sheets containing surveys of the grounds on which the town stands.
3. Copy of a letter to Rev. Wm. McKenney.
4. Statement of account with the United States, to the 28th of February.
5. Plans and estimates of a Receptacle for emigrants.
6. Transcript of the Colonial Journal to this date.
7. A paper intended to correct erroneous accounts of this country.
8. A statement of certain facts required by ——— last letter, to be given
to the Board.
9. A memorial respecting a Missionary establishment near the settlement.
† Appendix No. 8.

improvements; the condition of the schools,* and especially the fact, that most of the salaries of the officers of the new Government had been paid; taken in connexion with numerous other evidences of the wisdom and energy of his proceedings, left it impossible for the spirit of distrust longer to obscure his character.

On the 25th of April, 1825, a motion was made in the Board, and adopted, to proceed on the 18th of the next month, to organize a permanent Government for the Colony; and on the day appointed, the following resolution, offered by Joseph Gales, Jr. Esq. was adopted :

"*Resolved*, That the Board of Managers, considering the
' satisfactory information afforded by recent accounts from
' the Colony, of the successful operation of the plan for the
' civil Government thereof, as established by the Agent in
' August last—and seeing therein reason to reconsider their
' instructions to the Agent, of the 29th of December, 1824,
' now approve of the principles of that form of Government,
' and give their sanction to the same."

On the 23d of May, the two following resolutions were *unanimously* adopted :

"*Resolved*, That so much of the resolution of January
' 12th, 1825, as constitutes Dr. Peaco Agent of the Society,
' be rescinded.

"*Resolved*, That Mr. Ashmun be appointed COLONIAL
' AGENT to the Society; and that Dr. Peaco, the Govern-
' ment Agent, be authorized and requested, on his arrival in
' the Colony, to assist Mr. Ashmun with his counsel; and
' fully authorized to take upon himself, all the duties of Colo-
' nial Agent, in case of the absence, inability, or death of Mr.
' Ashmun."

On the same day, Mr. Gales, from a Committee previously

---

* "One for heathen children, of whom we have forty-five between seven and fifteen."—ASHMUN.

appointed to consider the digest of laws, submitted by the Agents with the new form of Government, reported the same with two amendments, and it was directed that "two thou-
' sand copies of the Constitution, Government, and Laws of
' the Colony of Liberia, as established by the Board of Mana-
' gers of the Colonization Society at Washington, May 23d,
' 1825," should be printed.

On the 13th of June, an influential member of the Board, who was absent when the proceedings touching the appointment of Mr. Ashmun were adopted, moved that they be reconsidered on the 2d of July; and that in the mean time the grounds of certain charges supposed to exist against Mr. Ashmun, be examined by a Committee of the Board,* instructed to report the result of their investigation.

The Report presented by the chairman† of this Committee, on the 2d of July, gave it as the opinion of the Committee, that Mr. Ashmun "had done all in his power to afford
' to his creditors that satisfaction which they had a right to
' expect;" in regard to all other charges, adverted with pleasure, to the judgment of the Board, as expressed in their re-

---

* It ought to be stated to the honour of this gentleman, that he, not less than the other members of the Board, after the settled appointment of Mr. Ashmun to the Colonial Agency, gave to him a firm and constant support.— With a candor and magnanimity to have been expected from him, he submitted to the Twelfth Annual Meeting, a resolution instructing the Board of Managers to cause a suitable monument, with an appropriate inscription, to be erected over the grave of Ashmun; and in support of the resolution, said eloquently, that to him, the Society was "more indebted, than to all the labours of all its friends;" that from the time he had resolved to share the fate of the infant Colony, in the greatest peril when he arrived in Africa, "he had devoted all the powers of his mind and body, till he sacrificed health and life to the people he had saved." "It is well known," he adds, "how, in the varying circumstances of danger and difficulty, in which they were placed, every variety of quality and talent, that could be called for, military skill and courage, political sagacity and address, were most conspicuously exhibited in this remarkable man."

† Joseph Gales, Jr. Esq.

solution of the 28th of March; declared that whatever might have been the case formerly, he now enjoyed the confidence of the United States' Government; vindicated his reputation from all just reproach, and concluded in the following words:

"The Committee does refer with great satisfaction, to the
' long, the able, the devoted services of Mr. Ashmun, in the
' cause of the Society. However the Board here may have
' differed from him in their judgment, of his policy and mea-
' sures in detail—and however the Colonists themselves may
' have complained of the Agent, the ultimate fact obtains to
' the high satisfaction of the Board, that the Colony flourishes.
' To this fact the Agent—the Colonists—those who have
' visited Liberia concurrently testify—and of this fact the
' Government of the United States is satisfied. The Board
' will develope principles here, which must, by the Agent,
' be applied to circumstances on the spot—and however much
' of the present happy condition of Liberia is to be ascribed to
' the circumspect wisdom of the Board in devising, the Com-
' mittee must in sheer justice and in obedience to fact, as-
' cribe not less to the intelligence, fidelity, and firmness of
' Mr. Ashmun, in execution in Africa: And under this con-
' viction, recommends that Mr. Ashmun be continued the
' principal Agent of the Society at Liberia; and proposes the
' following resolution:

"*Resolved*, That the proceedings of the 23d of May, re-
' considered by the resolution of the 13th of last month, be,
' and they are hereby, confirmed."

The Report and Resolution were *unanimously* adopted.

Thus have we seen Ashmun treading alone, for years, his rugged and perilous way, bleeding at almost every step from the strokes of fortune; overcoming one obstacle to encounter others more formidable; in grief and sickness contending with danger and confronting death; the ghost of his departed reputation constantly haunting his ascent, while often, even the mountain-tops before him were hid in darkness.

But no bursting storm, no pealing thunder, though the forests bow around him and the rocks tremble, can shake the purpose of his soul. There were elements within him more powerful than the elements without. He now STANDS ON AN EMINENCE IN THE CLEAR DAY. The cliffs are becoming bright, and the mantling clouds below are touched with the colours of the morning. See! there is neither pride in his eye, nor triumph in his air; but silent, meek, he stands, in the attitude and act of devotion. He admires that Hand, which unseen had led him; his strength in weakness, his guide in perplexity, his defence in danger, and his shield in war; that Hand which corrected him, to teach him wisdom—that disciplined him for valour in adversity, and made him humble that he might be great. He realizes that it is good for him, that he has been afflicted. He feels that to be invincible, he must conquer himself; and that the victory overcoming the world, is FAITH. He sees in every past trial, a blessing—in every cross, an honour—in every chastisement, paternal love; that what seemed a judgment, was really a mercy; and that sorrow had gone before, but as the herald of joy. The book of Providence is now unsealed; he perceives that in the Divine counsels, not less benevolent in their secrecy, than revelation, his welfare and usefulness are indissolubly united. Sensible of the errors and sins of his life, he considers verified to him the promise—"If his children forsake my law, and walk not in my judgments—if they break my statutes and keep not my commandments: then will I visit their transgressions with the rod, and their iniquity with stripes: Nevertheless my loving kindness will I not utterly take from him, nor suffer my faithfulness to fail."

Not for myself alone, O God, might he exclaim, have I thus been chosen in the furnace of affliction. I stand here thy servant, rescued and preserved, as by miracle, on this profane and barbarous shore, to plant thy truth; to proclaim thy mercy, and publish thy laws to the perishing people of Africa. Here, where I weep to see superstition darkly and horribly enthroned amid the riches and grandeur of thy works, and man, formed in thine image, bought, and sold, and scorned, and chained like a vile brute; where avarice has plundered and crushed the weak, and blood, wantonly and cruelly shed, for ages cried to Thee from the ground for vengeance; here where the gloom of earth so dismal, is yet overhung by thy pure starred Heaven, less bright than thy mercy, would I found a CHRISTIAN COMMONWEALTH, to stand thy TEMPLE FOREVER.*

---

* How often are Christians made to feel the truth of the sentiments expressed in the following quaint, but eloquent passage, from Jeremy Taylor:—
"And therefore observe how it is that God's mercy prevails over all His works; it is even then, when nothing can be discerned but His judgments:— For as when a famine had been in Israel, in the days of Ahab, for three years and a half, when the angry Prophet Elijah met the King, and presently a great wind arose, and the dust blew into the eyes of them that walked abroad, and the face of the Heavens was black, and all a tempest; yet then the Prophet was the most gentle, and God began to forgive, and the Heavens were more beautiful than when the sun puts on the brightest ornaments of a bridegroom, going from his chambers of the East: so it is in the economy of the Divine Mercy; when God makes our faces black, and the winds blow so loud till the cordage cracks, and our gay fortunes split, and our houses are dressed with cypress and yew, and the mourners go about the streets, this is nothing but the *pompa misericordiæ;* this is the funeral of our sins, dressed, indeed, with emblems of mourning, and proclaimed with sad accents of death; but the sight is refreshing, as the beauties of a field which God hath blessed, and the sounds are healthful as the noise of a Physician."

## CHAPTER XIII.

Mr. ASHMUN stood among the Colonists like a father in the midst of his children. Affection tempered *his* authority, and respect dignified *their* obedience. His wisdom and firmness won their confidence, while his confidence in them increased as he beheld them inclined to instruction, and deriving profit from experience. The bond which so united him to this little community, was strengthened by the recollection of mutual cares, interests, labours, sufferings, sympathies, and dangers. He had infused much of his own spirit into the minds of the settlers; and while he saw intelligence, industry, fortitude, and enterprise springing up vigorously around him, he saw also testified in the gratitude beaming from many eyes, a conviction that, under Providence, these virtues had been reared and fostered by the discipline of his hand, and the energy of his example.

The anticipation of an early death, was with him, a powerful motive for exertion. "The candle of life," he observes, "burns fast in this region." "I wish to make the most of the inch that remains, and see the most work possible, accomplished in the least time." If there be truth in the maxim,

"Arcum intensio frangit, Animum remissio,"

his powers never suffered from relaxation. The execution of one work, incited him to attempt a greater; and like Paul, he forgot the things which were behind, in his onward course towards the mark of perfection. He extended his views and his plans. He chose to keep his armour polished by use; desiring as a faithful Christian soldier, that it might gleam bright to the eye of his great Captain, in the setting sun.

To build up a State in Africa, that might stand a model for future Colonies,—a State informed and cemented by the spirit of Christianity; to develope in due proportions its powers, and wisely to regulate its relations; to extend its Territory; to bind to it in amity, barbarous tribes, and if possible, gather them under the protection and benignity of its laws; to abolish extensively, the slave trade; to aid the cause of missions; open a way for the Christian Religion to the interior of Africa; and kindle into life and action, the spirit which must conduct it thither by just representations of the unbounded good to be thereby accomplished; to secure the adoption, by the Society, of a policy correspondent to his own, and to the necessities of the Colony; and finally, so to demonstrate and exhibit the utility and glory of the scheme of African Colonization, as to unite the American people in an application of the powers of the STATE AND NATIONAL GOVERNMENTS to consummate the work,—these were the objects to which he dedicated himself without hesitation, and without reserve. He was not satisfied with that moderate course of action which if it incur little censure, deserves less praise. He knew that an "innoxious and ineffectual character, that seems formed upon a plan of apology and disculpation, falls miserably short of the mark of public duty. That duty demands and requires, that what is right should not only be made known, but made prevalent; that what is evil, should not only be detected, but defeated. When the public man omits to put himself in a situation of doing his duty with effect, it is an omission that frustrates the purposes of his trust almost as much as if he had formally betrayed it. It is surely no very rational account of a man's life, that he has always acted right; but has taken special care, to act in such a manner that his endeavours could not possibly be productive of any consequence."* Penetrated by such sentiments, Mr. Ashmun considered less what was expected, than what might be achieved; not what others had done, but how he might do more. He knew that boldness was often as necessary as prudence; and to plan judiciously, hardly more important than to execute with despatch. He saw that as in nature, the planets were more sublime, because silent, swift, and constant in motion, so the mind was not more great and admirable by method and amplitude, than by facility, continuity, and rapidity of thought and action. He saw that to change the whole intellectual and moral condition of Africa, was a work for a nation and an age; but he knew it was practicable, and that the difficulty and greatness of it, were the best reasons in the world, why it should be begun without delay, and prosecuted in the most earnest and decided manner. His own zeal, his own energy, were of little value or effect, except as they served to kindle the zeal and awaken the energies of others. He perceived that it was easier to command the assent of the understandings, than the activity of the wills of men, and that measures of good failed less frequently to secure approbation, than performance. He knew that "in doing good, we are generally cold, languid, and sluggish; and of all things, afraid of being too much in the right. But that the works of malice and injustice, are quite in another style. They are finished with a bold and masterly

* Burke.

hand, touched as they are with the spirit of those vehement passions that call forth all our energies, whenever we oppress and persecute." To excite men to benevolent deeds, it is not enough to overcome inertness, we must conquer opposition. Mr. Ashmun felt that he was called to ACTION: not to action limited to specific and definable objects, but to action on the human mind, that glorious element of power which rightly moved, moves on in progressive majesty, imbosoming within itself all the essential fortunes and happiness of our race. It was but necessary that the American people should WILL Africa to be free, civilized, and Christian; and with the Divine blessing, the work must be accomplished.

In matters of business, he was not ignorant of the truth, so strikingly expressed by Lord Bacon:

"The ripeness or unripeness of the occasion, must ever be well weighed; and generally it is good to commit the beginning of all great actions to Argus with his hundred eyes, and the ends to Briareus with his hundred hands, first to watch, and then to speed. For the helmet of Pluto, which maketh the politic man go invisible, is secrecy in the counsel and celerity in the execution. For when things are once come to the execution, there is no secrecy comparable to celerity; like the motion of a bullet in the air which flies so swift as it outruns the sight.*" His system of operations was well arranged;

---

* Men err in nothing, perhaps, more frequently, than in their opinions and estimates of talents for business. Few men are qualified by original endowments, education, and a deep insight of the principles of human nature, (acquired only by extensive observation of men and much reflection,) for the higher kinds of business, such as depend for success upon the popular sentiment and will, or affect great public interests; and of course, the multitude are very liable to err in their judgment of the qualifications required for the conduct of such affairs. Men may be extremely skilful and accurate in the details of business, (very important in their place) who may be incapable of comprehending the principles and relations to be regarded in the management of extensive and complicated concerns. The three following remarks may, perhaps, deserve to be remembered:

1st. Men who understand the principles of important bnsiness, can never

his measures had been adopted with great deliberation, but to render these operations and measures successful, the Colonists must be made to feel their importance and to engage in them with resolution and alacrity. Their spirit and energy seen in the actual prosperity of their settlements, would create confidence in the scheme of Colonization in America, and stand an illustrious *fact*, showing its wisdom and benevolence, which sophisters and speculatists would be as impotent to darken, as confute. He saw that to inspire the Colonists with those just and noble sentiments becoming leaders, who in the cause of knowledge, liberty, and religion for their race, had stood forth in the midst of dangers, to found an asylum for their distressed brethren, a home for their posterity; who had commenced an enterprise designed to reclaim a continent from barbarism, and bring its millions within the domain of Christianity, demanded the immediate and zealous exercise of all his various and powerful talents. The ardour of his soul kindled in his eye, glowed through his features, and penetrated as with electrick rapidity and force the general mind of the Colony. At the head of this small community, formed principally of unlettered men, some of them degraded by their past condition, widely separated from the Christian world, exposed to the influences of heathenism, just ushered

(unless criminally negligent), find any difficulty with the details. If they are not familiar with the management of these details, they can make themselves so, or employ others who are.

2d. No error is more palpable than that of those who estimate more highly an acquaintance with the details, than a knowledge of the principles of business. It is like the mistake of the Pharisees, who tithed mint, annis, and cummin, and neglected justice, mercy, and truth. Those who commit this error, will probably succeed best in subordinate stations, and if wise, will not seek the control or direction of important affairs.

3d. There is, in a golden sentence of Lord Bacon, a volume of wisdom on the subject of despatch in business: "There be three parts of business—the Preparation, the Debate or Examination, and the Perfection; whereof, if you look for despatch, let the middle only be the work of many, the first and last, the work of few."

into circumstances adapted to prepare them for an independent political existence, it was his to create (we might almost say) their social and political character; to plant and cherish in their souls sentiments of honourable action; to excite industry, enterprise, and courage; to shape and polish the rough materials before him, and give to them order, strength, and beauty. Not only must he administer the laws, he must form the manners of the people.* Not only must he plan every public work, but superintend generally, its execution; give orders to the public servants, and then instruct them in the nature of their duties. He must provide permanent defences for the Colony. He must survey its Territory, and allot to each settler the farm he is to occupy and cultivate. Buildings are to be erected for the temporary accommodation of emigrants. Methods and means of economy are to be devised to supply the deficiency of the Society's resources, to provide subsistence for those dependant upon its bounty, and to command labour for the public works, without endangering the credit of the Agency. The system of Government is to be set and preserved in operation; courts of justice established, in which the Agent must preside; ordinances to be enacted in relation to subjects various and often new; schools founded; negotiations conducted with the natives; and full and detailed statements on all subjects of interest to the Colony, to be frequently prepared and transmitted to the Society. To all this complex machinery, dependant almost entirely upon the mind of the Agent, must be added the concern for the recaptured Africans, involving high responsibilities, and not to be conducted without a serious amount of care and labour.

---

* Manners are of more importance than laws. Upon them, in a great measure, the laws depend. The law touches us but here and there, and now and then. Manners are what vex or soothe, corrupt or purify, exalt or debase, barbarize or refine us, by a constant, steady, uniform, insensible operation like that of the air we breathe in "—BURKE.

There were other duties more private, but hardly less important and laborious. He must be the friend and guardian of the widow, the orphan, the destitute, the sick, the neglected; support the weak, encourage the timid, advise the inexperienced, rebuke the indolent and perverse, raise up the fallen, sympathize with the disconsolate, condescend to the humblest, and be patient towards all. And truly might he have adopted the language of the Apostle, "Who is weak and I am not weak? Who is offended and I burn not?"—so sensibly was he touched with compassion for the suffering, and so indignant when he beheld injustice oppressing the innocent.

During the first month after their arrival, nearly all the emigrants by the Hunter were attacked by the fever of the climate. A Physician who was to have accompanied these emigrants, had been detained in the United States, and Mr. Cary, the only person in the Colony, who had any medical skill and experience, was in consequence of a severe wound, unable to leave his house. The feelings of Mr. Ashmun, in these trying circumstances, are expressed in the following extract from his Journal:

"Sabbath, *May* 1st, 1825.

"I am pressed down under affliction. The hand of the
' Almighty is heavy upon us. Death with a drawn sword
' hovers over our little settlement. Several times weekly, his
' strokes are heard and the dead are multiplied among us.—
' Every hour we tremble with the apprehension of being sum-
' moned to pay our last duty to some new victim of the de-
' stroyer's power. Spare us, O Lord, spare thy people from
' the further progress of this sweeping mortality. How long,
' O Lord, shall we be consumed forever? Spare these thy
' sheep, O thou tender Shepherd, and destroy them not utter-
' ly. We acknowledge thy tremendous and resistless pow-
' er: our flesh trembleth exceedingly for fear of Thee, and we

'are afraid of thy judgments. Now Lord, let thy mercy
'visit us. O show us the tenderness of thy love and the
'riches of thy grace. Sanctify these, thy severe correc-
'tions, to our profitable advancement, in the fear and faith of
'Thee, and let the past, through thy effectual blessing, suf-
'fice. This favour, I supplicate, O most holy God, with en-
'tire submission to thy infinite and superior wisdom, and
'in the name alone of my heavenly Intercessor—who to save
'our souls and our bodies from eternal death, has died him-
'self for us. Glory be to the Father, and to the Son, and to
'the Holy Ghost, as it was in the beginning, is now, and ever
'shall be, world without end. Amen."

The disease proved less severe than was expected, and was confined in its fatal effects almost exclusively to children under seven years of age. On the 15th of June, 1825, he addressed a letter to the Board, stating the condition of the emigrants by the Hunter, and his opinion that a large amount of suffering might have been prevented by a Receptacle on the plan he had before recommended, "by a humane Physician and a Hospital under proper regulations." "The Board can-
'not," he adds, "I will venture to believe, omit to provide with
'the next shipment from home, these necessary means of pre-
'serving the health and lives of those confiding individuals,
'who, in so great a measure, commit their earthly prospects
'and happiness to its disposal."

In the month of April, he had accurately surveyed the Montserado Territory, and described it on a map for the use of the Society. He was occupied about a week on this object, and in consequence of his observations then made, was convinced that possession must be acquired of a more fertile Territory, or the Agriculture of the Colony could not prosper. Hence his anxiety to obtain a tract of land on the St. Paul's river, was great. "My heart," he observes, "is entirely set on
'the acquisition of this Territory, and I fear I should want
'grace to carry myself with Christian propriety in the event

' of a disappointment."* He resolved to urge negotiations with the Chiefs, in order to obtain it, with all possible vigour. For five days he remained at a native town waiting their tardy movements. The successful result of his zeal and enterprise, is told in our last chapter. His exertions and exposure affected his health; repeated attacks of fever,† warned him of his danger; and finding towards the close of May, his strength and constitution extremely impaired by his confinement and the climate, he resolved, as soon as his presence could be spared at the Colony, to return to the U. States. All personal considerations were, however, surpassed in his mind by a concern for the interests of the Colony, and although he might have embarked for America in June, he did not then feel at liberty to retire, even for a few months, from his post.

"A three years' residence (he observes in his letter to the
' Board) on this torrid coast, has produced a general lassitude
' and debility of the system from which nothing but a change
' of climate can restore me: and in consenting to forego the
' present opportunity to revisit the United States, I make a
' sacrifice of personal considerations to a sense of duty and
' regard to the welfare of the settlement, to which nothing
' but the consolation of a good conscience, could reconcile
' me. For, thank Heaven, through the justice of Govern-
' ment, I am now in a situation to discharge all my pecunia-
' ry obligations to my fellow-men, and which I trust will be

* He adds, "I desire with all humility and submission, to commit the issue of this undertaking to Him whose wisdom is infinite, and who may see in the desired success, the destruction of our Colony, for any thing I know, and whose favourable intentions in regard to it, may be hereafter demonstrated, in the frustration of my fondest hopes."

† Having mentioned the fever, he observes: "During my unpleasant stay in the country, about the first of this month, I began to be afflicted with an ulceration of the legs and ankles, very common both to the natives and strangers of this country. These eruptions are not very painful, but very difficult to cure."

'done in a few weeks; and restored to a state of indepen-
'dence, I can judge of the motives of my conduct, with less
'danger of error than before."

Mr. Ashmun knew that a grateful people will rejoice to celebrate those signal events of Providence by which they have been freed from fearful evils, or made to share in blessings of uncommon value. The Anniversary of American Independence; the 17th of May, the day on which land was first ceded to the American settlers, by the Chiefs of the country; and the 2d of December, memorable for the final repulse of the barbarians, when combined to destroy the Colony, are religiously observed by the citizens of Liberia.\* After a discourse in one of the churches, the officers of the Colony were accustomed on these occasions to dine together, and encouraged by the presence of Mr. Ashmun, who sought to throw an air of cheerfulness over even serious duties, and to plant a generous regard for the public good amidst the social affections.†

---

\* This name was, on motion of General Robert Goodloe Harper, given to the Territory of the Society in Africa, at its Seventh Annual Meeting. The principal town in the Colony, was, at the same time, called Monrovia, in honour of the late President Monroe, an early and efficient friend of the Society.

† "Toasts drank at the dinner given by the Monrovia Volunteers, July 4th, 1825:

"1st. *The present President of the United States:* The champion of the people's rights—he deserves the people's honours.

"2d. The day we commemorate—(prefaced with an explanatory address by the Agent.)

"3d. *The Colony of Liberia:* May the history of the nation which has founded it, become its own.

"4th. *Africa:* May it outstrip its oppressors in the race of liberty, intelligence, and piety.

5th. "*The Heroes and Statesmen of American Independence:* They fought and legislated for the human race; and struggled more to subvert the principles than the power of their oppressors. Even the people of England are freer and happier for their labours.

*The Monrovia Independent Volunteers:* Armed for the defence of rights which it is the trade of war to destroy: Never may they forget their character.

He thought that to consider, at stated periods, what the friends of God and man had achieved in other countries, might rouse the Colonists to emulate their deeds; that to meditate on the Providence which had so remarkably defended them in times past, might dispose them more confidently to trust for the future to its protection. He felt the importance of cherishing among the settlers the domestic and social virtues, assured that he who is an honour to his family, will be such to his country; and that mutual confidence between citizens, is the strong bond of the State.

At this period, the slave trade was carried on extensively within sight of Monrovia. From eight to ten, and even fifteen vessels were engaged at the same time in this odious traffic, almost under the guns of the settlement; and in July of this year, "contracts were existing for eight hundred slaves to be furnished in the short space of four months, within eight miles of the Cape. Four hundred of these were to be purchased for two American traders. During the same season, a boat belonging to a Frenchman, having on board twenty-six slaves, all in irons, was upset in the mouth of the St. Paul's, and twenty of their number perished". "This is one

"7th. *General Lafayette in America:* A veteran in the cause of civil and religious freedom. We join with our native country in honouring him—not because we are Americans, but because we are men.

("In politeness to our guest, Captain Ferbin:)
"8th. His Britannic Majesty—the Constitutional King of England.
"9th. Success to Agriculture.
("By Captain Ferbin, prefaced with a few appropriate remarks:)
"The health of the President of the United States, and prosperity to the Colony of Liberia."

"The day was observed as in the United States: at day-break a gun—at sunrise the United States' flag was hoisted, and a national salute fired with great precision. At ten a discourse was delivered by the Rev. Mr. Waring—and at three, P. M. a dinner, consisting chiefly of the productions of Africa, and provided by the Monrovia Volunteers, was served to more than fifty persons;—two cases of drunkenness occurred at night, of which the Justices took due cognizance the next morning."—*Ashmun's Journal.*

of the lesser scenes of tragedy," said Mr. Ashmun, "which are daily acting in this wretched country." We are not left to conjecture how keenly he felt the wrongs and outrage inflicted on humanity by this trade, nor how hardly he brooked the law inhibiting the American citizen from disturbing this abominable commerce as prosecuted under the flag, and by the citizens of a foreign power.

"The purchase money of two hundred slaves," he remarks, (July 18, 1825,) "has, during this week, been landed in our ' waters, to the incalculable detriment of the Colony, and dis- ' grace, shall I say, of our American Government, or of hu- ' man nature. The Colony only wants the right, it has the ' power, to expel this traffic to a distance, and force it at least ' to conceal some of its worst enormities." He at the same time expressed the deepest regret, that the influence of the Colony for the suppression of this trade, was nearly at an end, since those who were engaged in it on both sides, could, notwithstanding the protests of the Colonists against it, effect their atrocious designs with impunity.

In this state of things, he resolved to explore the whole line of coast from Cape Mount to Trade Town, and to bring, if possible, by treaties with the Chiefs, this entire extent of country under the jurisdiction of the Colony. He was confident the Colony would derive from such an extension of authority, important commercial and other advantages; and that it would be thereby enabled to banish the slave trade from that part of Africa.

The result of his inquiries and examinations was, that though on this tract some points might be more eligible for foreigners than others, yet nearly every portion was rich in soil, and other natural advantages, and "capable of sustaining a numerous and civilized population, beyond almost any country on earth." "Leaving the sea-board," he observes, " the traveller, every where at the distance of a very few ' miles, enters upon an uniform upland country of moderate

'elevation, intersected by innumerable rivulets, abounding in
'springs of unfailing water, and covered with a verdure which
'knows no other changes except those that refresh and renew
'its beauties. The country directly on the sea, although
'verdant and fruitful in a high degree, is found every where
'to yield in both respects to the interior. And what I con-
'sider remarkable, the average heat lessens in a very sensi-
'ble degree in the proportion of the distance from the sea
'coast. Its salubrity, depending in part on the same causes
'which moderate the heat, may (and I believe facts prove it
'does) improve in the same degree. The same difference
'in regard both to the healthiness and temperature, seems to
'distinguish the sea-boards and interior of this country,
'which is remarked in all the American States South of Ma-
'ryland, and probably will in time be traced to similar
'causes."

In the month of August, before any arrangements were finally concluded for enlarging the Colonial possessions, a flagrant piracy was perpetrated by the crew of a Spanish schooner, (the Clarida) employed in the slave trade, on an English brig lying at anchor off the town of Monrovia. Mr. Ashmun resolved, in discharge of duty to the interests and safety of the Colony, no less than in obedience to the principles of natural law, to inflict punishment on the offenders, and rescue from their rapacity such unfortunate Africans as were, or must soon be, within their merciless grasp. Ample testimony was taken at the Colony to prove the piracy. The English brig was placed under the direction of Mr. Ashmun. The Colonial Militia were ready to accompany him in an expedition against the Factory of the Spaniard. The Chiefs of the country were assured that the military movements they might witness, were not to be directed against themselves, but were intended to vindicate insulted justice, and the dishonoured rights of human nature. Mr. Ashmun embarked in the brig with twenty-two Volunteers, while Captain Barbour at the head of twenty-five men, proceeded with written instructions to the vicinity of the Factory at Digby, (a little to the North of the mouth of the St. Paul's,) and there awaited the orders of the Agent. The Spanish schooner was not to be found; the Factory with several Spaniards belonging to her, (but who it was proved were on shore when the piracy was committed,) a small amount of property, and a number of slaves, were captured without resistance. The Spaniards were dismissed; while the native Chiefs bound themselves to assist, in no way, in the collecting or transportation out of the country of any of the slaves bargained for by the commander of the Clarida.

"In this little expedition," said Mr. Ashmun in his letter to the Secretary of the Navy, "it gives me great pleasure to
' state, that not a musket was fired—not one untoward ac-
' cident occurred—not a single point of duty was neglected
' by the officers—not an instance of disorderly conduct was
' witnessed among the fifty-four men, who composed the
' force employed on the occasion. The order for respecting
' the persons and property of the natives, was so punctually
' obeyed, that by their own declaration and to their utter as-
' tonishment, not a fowl nor a plantain was taken—nor even
' a hut entered (except with consent) by the Colonists, even
' in Yellow Will's town, which was entirely deserted by the
' inhabitants—and in which the whole body encamped for
' forty-eight hours.

"I have, since my return, already received from several of
' the country Chiefs, deputations conveying their thanks for
' these substantial proofs of my friendly dispositions towards
' themselves, even when it became necessary to carry the
' arms of the settlement into the heart of their country. The
' policy which in the face of some sneers and opposition, I
' have uniformly pursued with the people of this country for
' the last four years, is that of justice, mildness, and firmness.
' And its success has been complete. I never menaced them

'with an empty or unnecessary threat, and they know I have
'never, in a single instance, forfeited my word. Nor do I
'believe that while a similar policy is persisted in, on the part
'of this establishment, any reasonable demand made by it
'upon the native inhabitants will be refused. The Hon. Sec-
'retary will perceive, that in these remarks, I have in view,
'the introduction of a measure on the part of the United
'States, for the entire abolition of the slave trade, with the
'concurrence of the native Chiefs, along a given line of coast
'contiguous to this Agency. But the particulars of this plan
'I beg leave to defer to a distinct communication. The ob-
'ject, if it can obtain the sanction of the United States' Go-
'vernment, is practicable, and all the means necessary to ef-
'fect it, are on the spot. Nor can I, in closing this communi-
'cation, suppress the mortifying fact, that whenever the Ame-
'rican flag is displayed at this Agency, it literally waves
'over, and I can almost add, *affords protection* to a slave
'factory, established in the immediate neighbourhood. In
'the short expedition just reported, it was with a sentiment
'of indignation and mortification equally idle and humiliating;
'that I was obliged to conduct the little force under my com-
'mand past two slave factories, of which the most distant is only
'five miles from the Cape. We heard the clanking of fetters
'as we marched along, and were annoyed with the groans of
'human beings who had lost their freedom without their
'fault; but as these tyrants, who regarded us with folded
'arms and a lear of barbarous exultation, had not commit-
'ted piracy, it was not in my power to interfere for the relief
'of the one, or the punishment of the other."*

A collusive plan entered into by the Captain of the Clarida, some of the native Chiefs and a French slave dealer on the St. Paul's, for violating the engagement by which the slaves originally destined for the Pirate, were to be delivered over

* Appendix No. 9.

to the Colony, induced Mr. Ashmun to break up two other slave factories, and to offer to the Chiefs concerned in transactions with the Clarida, a bounty of ten dollars for each slave, which in pursuance of their agreement, they should resign up to the Colonial Agent. The consequence of this was, that one hundred and sixteen slaves were soon received as freemen into the bosom of the Colony.*

At the close of the year 1825, Mr. Ashmun presented to the Managers a complete view of the condition, relations, character, and prospects of the Colony. He stated that health had been for some months restored; that adults resident for some time in Africa, preferred its climate to any other, and enjoyed as good health as in America: The Government had proved efficient and popular; the laws were venerated and obeyed; the sentiments of the people had been purified and elevated, and with some exceptions they could detect as readily and condemn as sincerely any deviation from the line of moral

* The conscientious regard to justice manifested by Mr. Ashmun in his conduct towards the natives, was clearly exhibited about this time, in the adjustment of a difference which had arisen between the Colony and certain Kroomen residing in a small town near the mouth of the St. Paul's. A daring robbery had been committed by one of these men upon public property of the Colony, which had been entrusted to one of the settlers. These Kroomen had previously been guilty of violating the rights of the settlement. A detachment of the Colonial Militia of the Colony, were directed to proceed to their town and demand redress—but to use no force unless the offer for a peaceful settlement of difficulties should be rejected. As this party entered the town, two or three of them fell in the rear of the others, and one of their number fired upon and fatally wounded a Krooman. He was indicted and tried by a jury for murder in the second degree. The trial continued for three days, and finally resulted in a conviction of manslaughter, (it being proved that the accused had acted from sudden impulse and a misapprehension of orders and not from malice,) and the guilty individual was sentenced to six months' imprisonment, or to a fine of one hundred bars, which sum was paid over to the friends of the deceased. The affair was settled to the satisfaction of the whole Kroo nation. "The blood that has flown," said Mr. Ashmun, on this occasion, "has been a cause of greater pain to me, than the torrents shed in our hostilities in 1822; because the former, differently from the latter, has left the appearance of a stain on the character of the Colony."

integrity and civil justice as any other body of people in the world: the fertile lands on the St. Paul's, already occupied by a small company of settlers, opened the best prospects for agriculture: the settlers generally lived in a style of neatness and comfort, approaching to elegance in many instances, unknown before their arrival in that country: not an interesting family twelve months in Africa, but had means of furnishing a comfortable table; not an individual, he believed, without an ample provision of decent apparel could be found: every family (and nearly every adult emigrant) was able to employ from one to four native labourers at an expense of from four to six dollars a month: the labour of mechanics was worth two dollars—that of common labourers from seventy-five cents to one dollar and twenty-five cents a day: trade was valuable, the Colony free from debt, and all the people successfully engaged in constructing their houses, clearing their plantations, adding to the means and developing the sources of private and public prosperity. He represented that several important public buildings had been commenced, and that some of them were nearly completed; that during the latter half of the year, two commodious and beautiful chapels, each sufficient to contain several hundred worshippers, had been erected and consecrated to the Christian's God; that a battery had been planned near the termination of the Cape, which finished, must effectually protect vessels in the harbour; that he had built and put upon the rice trade, between Cape Montserado and the Factories, to the leeward, a small schooner, adapted to the passage of the bars of the rivers on that part of the coast; that the Militia of the settlement was well organized, equipped, and disciplined; that in addition to the invaluable tract of country purchased on the St. Paul's, the right of occupancy and use had been obtained to lands at the Young Sesters and at Grand Bassa; that Factories had been established at both these places; that five Schools, exclusive of Sunday schools, were in operation, and the youth and children of the Colony discovered for their age unequivocal proofs of a good degree of mental accomplishment. He declared that the moral character of the Colonists was generally good; that there was a powerful preponderance of example and of influence on the side of moral virtue; that the Colony was in deed and reality a Christian community. He observes:

"The holy Author of our religion and salvation, has made
' the hearts of a large portion of these people, the temples of
' the Divine Spirit. The faith of the everlasting gospel, with
' an evidence and strength which nothing short of the power
' of the Almighty can produce or sustain, has become the
' animating spring of action, the daily rule of life, the source
' of immortal hope and ineffable enjoyment, to a large propor-
' tion of your Colonists. God is known in His true charac-
' ter—His worship is celebrated in its purity—the doctrines
' of salvation are received in their genuine simplicity, by very
' many. Occurrences of a favourable or depressing aspect
' are regarded as dispensations of the Almighty, and followed
' with correspondent feelings of gratitude or humiliation.—
' Tears of affectionate joy or sorrow are often seen to flow in
' the house of God, from hearts silently melting under the
' searching influence of His word. I have seen the proudest
' and profanest foreigners that ever visited the Colony, tremb-
' ling with amazement and conviction, almost literally in the
' descriptive phraseology of St. Paul, 'Find the secrets of
' their hearts made manifest, and falling down upon their
' faces, worship God, and report that God is in the midst' of
' this people 'of a truth.'

"These facts I have judged it my duty to state, to the praise
' of that God to whom we are entirely indebted for so precious
' a testimony of His favour,—and for the information of thou-
' sands in the United States, to whose prayers and pious at-
' tentions we may, under the Most High, refer it. I am not
' insensible of the delicacy and responsibility attending the

'publication of a statement of this nature; and of the great 'danger a more cautious pen than mine might incur, of com-'municating on it, either too little or too much. But as the 'grand secret of the improving circumstances of this Colony, '—of the respect it commands without, and of the happiness, 'order and industry which reign within it,—is wrapped up 'in the controlling influence of religion on the temper and 'habits of the people; I should greatly wrong the cause of 'truth, by suppressing, or too lightly passing by, a topic of 'such leading importance. The precious hopes of an immor-'tality of vigorous and beatific existence in the presence of 'God and the Redeemer, are no inefficient principles of ac-'tion and of happiness in the human mind, even in the midst 'of this mixed and tumultuous life: and they have attended 'and sustained a large number whom Providence has taken 'from us, till they passed rejoicing, the limits of mortality, 'and left us in tears. Many more are now waiting, full of 'the same 'glorious hopes,' for the final summons of their 'Heavenly Master. And shall it ever be, that a torrent of 'infidelity, heresy, or irreligion, shall, in judgment for our 'ingratitude, find its way from the dark caverns of hell to 'this consecrated retreat of the humble worshippers of God; 'and convert to a moral waste, a young plantation which He 'condescends himself to water and to keep!"

He testified to the good effects of the Colony on the neighbouring tribes. They had been treated as men and brethren of a common family; they had been taught that one of the ends proposed in founding civilized settlements on their shore, was to do them good; sixty of their children had been adopted as children of the Colony; they had learnt something of the great and interesting truths of the Christian Religion; that the friends of this Religion, in another and distant country, were deeply concerned to promote their happiness, and that the strangers (many of them at least), who had come from that country to reside with them, were men of justice and benevolence. "Our influence over them," said Mr. Ashmun, " is unbounded—it is increasing—it is more extensive than ' I dare at this early period, risk my character for veracity by ' asserting. On several occasions of alarm from the interior, ' the whole population of the country has been ready to ' throw itself into our arms for protection. No man of the ' least consideration in the country, will desist from his im- ' portunities, till at least one of his sons is fixed in some set- ' tler's family."

The Colony had checked in that part of Africa the prevalence of the slave trade; indeed it might be confidently said, had banished it from that district of the coast. Between Cape Mount and Trade Town, a line of one hundred and forty miles, not a slave trader dared to attempt his guilty traffic. A moral feeling was at work in the minds of the natives, derived from intercourse with the Colony, against this detestable commerce.

Nor did Mr. Ashmun fail, on this occasion, to appeal with all possible earnestness to the friends of Africa in behalf of education, inquiring whether minds as capable of moral and intellectual elevation, as those of any other people on earth, were to be doomed, "in perpetuity, to an involuntary detention on the very threshold of knowledge?" "Where," said he, "are the youthful philanthropists of my country? In ' what have those loud professions of zeal in the great cause ' of human happiness, of civilization and freedom, which I ' once heard from a thousand mouths, resulted—to say noth- ' ing of that Christian charity, which, when I left the United ' States, appeared to pour floods of tears over the moral abase- ' ment of the African race? Are we to expect in vain from ' the thousand seminaries and fountains of knowledge in that ' favoured country, a single young man or woman of suffi- ' cient enterprise and generosity to conduct the sacred stream ' to this Colony?"

"To the lasting honour," (he adds near the conclusion,)

"of the American Colonization Society, it has founded a new
'empire on this continent, of which the basis is christianity,
'intelligence, and rational liberty;—has conducted it happily
'through the perilous stages of its inception and early
'growth;—has seen its members in the full possession of the
'means of acquiring the comforts of life, and sustaining
'against any anticipated opposition, the stand to which they
'are advanced. The Society has demonstrated experimen-
'tally to the world, the soundness of the views with which
'they appeared before it in 1817–18, without funds, patron-
'age, or a precedent in the annals of the human race. And
'in having achieved so much, it has, in my opinion, compass-
'ed the special design of its institution; and must, from this
'period, resign up the great work of Colonization, considered
'as an object of national benefit, to the national patronage."*

Perhaps Mr. Ashmun underrated the good to be done by the single operations of the Society. But in the writer's opinion, he did not over-estimate the importance of endeavours to secure to the cause of African Colonization, the powers and resources of the nation. If such endeavours were important then, they are more important now. The policy of the Society cannot remain much longer unsettled on this subject, if indeed it be not settled by the very terms of its Constitution. The founders of the Society intended and expected that the plan they submitted, should become a national plan; they believed as patriotic, just and benevolent, it had merits which must unite in its support a Christian nation. Such a nation

* African Repository, Vol. 2d, pages 72–99.—Mr. Ashmun at the same time, after some calculations in regard to the expenses of the Colony and Society, and the probable income of the latter, (the income has exceeded the amount predicted by him,) says, "to me, the alternative appears inevitable, either that the United States, or a sufficient number of individual States, must immediately adopt and effectually patronize with its undivided influence, and its revenues, the Colony of Liberia, or that its progress is, from the present time, (considered as an instrument of national benefit to the United States, or of extensive advantage to the African race,) AT AN END."

owes high duties to itself and to mankind. It cannot consistently neglect means afforded by Providence for exalting its character, or for exhibiting to other nations the excellency of the principles which constitute its happiness, its strength, and its glory. The Divine Law by extending its authority over the universal conduct of individuals, becomes the moral bond of political society; and to say that Government among Christians, is or can be free from religious obligation, is a solecism. If to provide for and educate his children, be the duty of a parent, is it less clearly the duty of a Christian nation to provide for the happiness of any unfortunate class of its inhabitants, and should uncontrollable circumstances or the public safety forbid their incorporation with the political body where they reside, to assist them in removing to a land (if such can be found), in which they may enjoy the means of improvement without restraint in their use or limit to their advantage? And could the character of a civilized and Christian people be more ennobled than by the adoption of measures for the instruction and reformation of the uncivilized and unchristian? Such a people will select the best instruments to effect their worthy objects. With them, Government will not be a mere institution of selfishness or pride, but instinct with moral sentiment and of a sublime sanctity. They will venerate it as an ordinance of God for the good of men; nor will they depend upon private efforts to compass ends demanding the highest powers of the State.

The founders of the American Colonization Society viewed its plan as a *great leading* MEASURE, which our country was morally bound to adopt from respect to its own character and regard to those sacred and eternal principles which no one nation is at liberty to violate, since they are the common interest and good of all. The golden rule of our Saviour has been justly styled the perfection of the law of nature and nations. No relations or combinations of human society are exempt from its control, and for nations to disregard it while acknowledging that it should bind individuals, is as if suns, leaving to planets the regular courses of Heaven, should rush lawless through the Universe.*

The scheme of African Colonization originated in humanity and benevolence towards the coloured race. The good it would confer upon the free people of colour in this country, was the least of its expected benefits. It was designed to open the way to the voluntary, peaceful and entire abolition of slavery; and to civilize and christianize the barbarous millions of Africa. The friends of man at the South and at the North, saw that in this scheme they could unite. They believed that in respect to the great moral and political evil of slavery endangering the very existence of some of the States, and in respect to the slave trade, an evil at war with mankind, the scheme must prove remedial if fostered by the powers of the States and the Nation. It was clear that the National Constitution authorized Congress to provide for the common defence and promote the general welfare of the United States in the exercise of certain enumerated powers, among which is that of raising and appropriating revenue to an extent unlimited, except by the general sense and judgment of the American people.† The framers of that instrument were

---

*"But above all these, there is the supreme and indissoluble consanguinity, and society between men in general; of whom the heathen poet, whom the Apostle calls to witness, saith *we are all his generation.* But much more we Christians, unto whom it is revealed in particularity, that all men came from one lump of earth; and that two singular persons were the parents from whom all the generations of the world are descended; we, I say, ought to acknowledge, that no nations are wholly aliens and strangers the one to the other; and not to be less charitable than the person introduced by the comic poet:
*Homo sum, humani nihil a me alienum puto.*"—BACON.

† "But the power to appropriate and the power to execute, are two different things. The one may be used in aid of the interests, but never in violation of the rights, either of States or of individuals. The other, on the contrary, may, in promoting the general good, interfere with both the claims of individuals, and the jurisdiction of the States. The power to appropriate money for example, to roads and canals, is limited to the simple act of appropriation.

too wise not to know, that nothing could be more "fallacious than to infer the extent of any power proper to be lodged in the National Government from an estimate of its immediate necessities." They knew "that there ought to be a CAPACITY to provide for future contingencies, as they might happen; and as these are illimitable in their nature, so it is impossible safely to limit that capacity."* Blessed be God, our National Government has this CAPACITY. It was formed for great purposes, and by it such purposes are yet to be accomplished. It was never meant to be a petty mercenary corporation without character or dignity, but the right arm of a great Christian nation.

The right of Congress to adopt measures and appropriate money for the suppression of the slave trade, has been repeatedly exercised. Upon what principle except a just regard to the rights and interests of humanity? But though enough has been done for this object to redound to the eternal honour of our country, much more remains to be done; and the testimony of Ashmun confirms the conclusions of reason, that this trade can be most speedily and extensively abolished through the influence of Christian Colonies on the African coast.

The abolition of slavery depends, it is true, exclusively upon the will of the States in which it exists. But

But the power to make roads and canals, would authorize their location and protection, either with or without consent, on the property of any individual, and within the jurisdiction of any State. So too, an authority to create a fund, as proposed by Mr. King, "to aid in the emancipation and removal of such slaves as may by the laws of the several States be authorized to be emancipated and removed, could not in any possible mode, interfere with the rights either of the States or of individuals. But a power to emancipate and remove the slaves within the limits of a State, would be a most alarming power of interference with both. There is obviously, therefore, a very good reason why the active powers of the Government should be specified and defined, while the power of appropriation should be limited only by the general interests of the country."—*Essays by the late lamented Wm. H. Fitzhugh, of Virginia.*

\* Hamilton in the Federalist.

these States are members of the National Union, or rather they constitute that Union. Of this Union, it may be said, as of the Christian Church, though there are many members, there is but one body; so that if one member suffer, all suffer; and the prosperity of one, is the common good of all. The slaves are not merely property, they are men. Their condition is not merely evil to them; their removal, with the consent of their owners, would be the removal of an immense evil and danger from the State. Congress then is morally bound by regard to the general welfare, to aid such States as desire relief from slavery, and with timely foresight to provide a remedy to which others as 'they shall feel its importance, may resort. It is bound on general principles of benevolence, as the constitution and a due regard to all the great interests concerned will permit, to show how emancipation may be effected with advantage to the slave, and without danger to the public welfare. "If, said an early and able friend* of the Society, "a hostile army threatened to invade any portion of these United States, would it not afford a legitimate employment for the army or the fleet? Whether it were New Orleans or Eastport, that were threatened, would make no difference in the question. The object would be national, and the national force would be called forth to meet it. I ask, then, whether the existence of one or more of the States, is not a national object? And whether an evil threatening that existence, is not a national evil?" "Our object," said another distinguished gentleman,† "has been to point out the

\* General Harper in support of a resolution proposing an application to Congress.

† Mr. Clay in support of the following resolution moved by him at the Tenth Anniversary of the Society:

*Resolved,* That the Board of Managers be empowered and directed at such time or times as may seem to them expedient, to make respectful application to the Congress of the United States, and to the Legislatures of the different States, for such pecuniary aid, in furtherance of the object of this Society, as they may respectively be pleased to grant.

way, to show that Colonization is practicable, and to leave it to those States or individuals, who may be pleased to engage in the object to prosecute it. The problem which has so long and deeply interested the thoughts of good and patriotic men, is solved—a country and a home have been found, to which the African race may be sent, to the promotion of their happiness and our own."

That slavery cannot long continue in this country, I firmly believe. Its perpetuity is irreconcilable with the nature of our institutions, the spirit of the age, and the order of Providence. It stands in the temple of our freedom, like the image of death at the Egyptian festivities, to sadden our thoughts, cloud the light, and tune to melancholy, the instruments of joy.

The question how it shall be abolished, will soon be felt as the greatest and most interesting question that ever agitated the mind of this nation. On this question, public opinion is every thing. In portions of our country, this deep and mighty element is already sensibly moved on the subject, and daily accumulating power. It is too late to say the matter shall not be discussed; it were easier to stay the planets than prevent it. Nor ought it to be prevented.

What opinions on this subject shall predominate and govern the policy of the country?

On this question, I humbly conceive, may depend not the interests of millions only, but the peace and integrity of the Union.

The friends of African Colonization have thought, that the consent of the South was indispensable for the safe abolition of slavery; that the work should be done with caution and preparation; that circumstances and consequences should be regarded; that a separation of races so distinct as the coloured and white in complexion, habits and condition, is desirable for the happiness of both; that to plant communities of free persons of colour, with their consent, on the African coast, would most surely and speedily elevate their character, civilize Africa, and with reacting power on our country, stimulate and increase humanity towards their brethren; that it was a measure so free from exception, and pregnant with good, so comprehensive in its relations, and large of promise; that all the wise and patriotic in the nation, could sustain it unitedly, constantly, and with their might. It is among my deepest convictions, that the prosecution of this scheme by the *nation*, as the *main plan*, at present, of good for the African race, will retard no other rational plans for their benefit, but eminently conduce to their success. It will hasten emancipation on our own soil, more than all the abstract doctrines of human rights, which once promulgated amid scenes of cruelty and murder, at which humanity grew pale, by the Jacobins of the Old World, are now republished as divine oracles by their disciples in the New.

This scheme of Colonization is innoxious, it tends to unite public sentiment, to strengthen the Union, to increase confidence between the States, between the whites and the blacks, the master and the slave, while it invites a powerful nation of Christians to offer up minor differences and contrarieties of interest on the altar of an undivided patriotism and philanthropy. It invites such a nation, in the spirit of a prophetic sagacity, in the exercise of its constitutional powers, to guard itself from coming dangers; do homage to the great principles which have made it what it is; vindicate the purity of its honour; stand forth to suppress evils militating against the common welfare and breaking the common ligaments of human society; and in the silence of its passions and the majesty of its reason to build up an everlasting fame on the affections of mankind. It invites a nation, which in the ardour of its youth, has extended liberty, civilization and christianity over a continent late the abode of savage beasts, and more savage men; to endow another, a larger, a more miserable one, with the regenerating spirit of wisdom, and the incorruptible treasures of truth.

And what is that "armed doctrine" which comes forth under the snowy flag of peace, to overthrow first the Colonization Society, and next slavery? It is a doctrine that would enthrone the *abstract**  rights of the individual (a nonentity except in imagination), above those conservative principles upon which society depends not only for its value, but existence;—a doctrine which would settle questions of right between men, not on the principle of reciprocal benevolence, in view of their varied circumstances and relations; but by an independent standard, divorced from all the realities, and setting at naught all the wise forecast of life. It demands, in the sacred name of duty, of the supreme power of the State, to give instant liberty to all who have it not, even if certain to inflict thereby the greatest mischiefs upon those liberated,—to put in jeopardy the very life of the political body.

And in what temper, with what language is this doctrine enforced?

As the lightning fiercely glares athwart the sky from the dark folds of the cloud in the horizon, hiding all the sweet lights of Heaven, so from the minds of some of those who assume to be champions of this doctrine, flash forth the malignant passions, overpowering in their characters all the gentle attributes and virtues of humanity. To convert men to their opinions, they slander and vilify their characters; to promote what they consider truth, publish falsehoods; tyrannise men into their belief, out of zeal for liberty; and for peace sake, light up the elements of war with the torch of the furies. They dip out a strange mixture of truth, error, calumny and

---

* Man must be *in* society, to become entitled to any of the rights which belong to men in society. And can any man doubt that these rights are varied and modified by circumstances? In a ship at sea, with abundance of provisions, each passenger has the right to a full allowance; but has he this right when the general safety requires a reduction of the rations? Or suppose, in case of such reduction, some of the crew of stronger constitutions continue in health, while others, it is clear, must die, unless there be an increase of their allowance; does not the condition of the latter, give them a moral right to special consideration?

wrath, flaming hot from their alembic, and scatter it through the land, to destroy oppression and save the country. I speak only of the leaders* in the attempt to overthrow the Colonization Society†—of those who, disrobing themselves of the ordinary decencies and courtesies of life, are now incensing the North against the South, and the South against the North, infecting the minds of a large and suffering portion of our inhabitants with hatred towards their friends, and in their fury

---

\* I limit these remarks, touching the spirit and language of Anti-Colonizationists, to the conductors of two or three of their leading Journals. Their boldness and activity would be worthy of praise, were they governed by right reason.

† I do not question that the Anti-Slavery Society embraces many men of pure motives, intelligent, patriotic, and Christian. For such men I shall not permit a difference of opinion, however important, to diminish my respect or affection. While I shall continue to cherish towards them these sentiments, even should they not be reciprocated; and while I desire not to restrain them in the expression of their opinions, they will not expect me to be restrained in the expression of mine.

Some of the best men in the country; believe that the Colonization Society and the Anti-Slavery Society should both be sustained; that each should occupy its own field and controversy between them cease. But how stands the case? The leaders of the Anti-Slavery Society declare the extinction of the Colonization Society to be the first step towards the abolition of slavery, and the doctrine of immediate emancipation on our own soil, the grand means for the overthrow of slavery. Some of the members of that Society, doubtless, adopt the latter opinion, who reject the former.

Members there may be (and probably are) of the Anti-Slavery Society who desire not the overthrow of the Colonization Society, and members of the Colonization Society who find no difficulty in supporting what they regard as its views, and advocating at the same time the duty of immediate emancipation, to the fullest extent of the meaning of that phrase. Professor Fowler (a name which I cannot mention but with the greatest respect and affection), in his recent discourse before the Vermont Colonization Society, has expressed correctly, I doubt not, the views of these individuals in the following passage:—
"If the Anti-Slavery Society shall succeed in promoting the emancipation of the slaves, then it will assist the Colonization Society, by furnishing it with an opportunity for a better selection of emigrants for the building of the Colony. On the other hand, the greater the number the Colonization Society transports to Liberia, the more room there will be for future and progressive emancipation, without endangering the peace and safety of the country. In

seeking to extinguish some of the best hopes of this nation and mankind.

While I have felt it my duty thus to remark upon the conduct of a few rash men, who are, I trust, blind to the natural consequences of their actions, I would urge all the sober this way they can be helpers of each other as they ought to be, while they are efficiently promoting the several objects for which they were established.— Why then should these Societies, thus capable of benefitting each other, weaken their energies and waste their resources, in attacking each other, and in the consequently necessary self-defence? Why should these contests continue to produce among some of the partizans of each, a frenzied excitement, resulting in denunciation and outrages upon decorum and propriety; or in riots and outrages upon the laws of the land? Let us aid each of these associations as best we can. But let each confine itself to its legitimate object."

It should be recollected, that the leaders of the Anti-Slavery Society, unprovoked, commenced, with an exterminating spirit, their warfare upon the Colonization Society. Whether, had no such attack been made, those friends of the Colonization Society who are opposed to the doctrine of immediate emancipation, as enforced by these leaders, would have thought it necessary to avow their opinions on this point, it is for one only, that the writer can determine. But the Anti-Colonizationists have declared *that the Colonization Society must be destroyed; its scheme so far as regarded in its influence for the abolition of slavery, abandoned; and the doctrine of immediate emancipation be substituted therefor.*

Now, *what is the doctrine on this subject, which duty requires to become prevalent and practical in the minds of the American people*, is the great and momentous question submitted to their decision.

I have no fears of the effects of any *doctrine* founded in *truth*, and which is received by men in its *true* meaning. Some doctrines, *true* and *important*, it may be difficult to communicate to men in certain conditions and circumstances, so that they shall not be misapprehended, and in such cases, caution and explanation may be required in the inculcation of them.

The objections of the writer, to the doctrine of the Anti-Slavery Society, as expounded by its most zealous supporters, rest not upon his belief that the system of slavery as it now exists, is right; nor that what is therein wrong should not be immediately rectified; nor on the fact, that he is opposed to the early and entire abolition of slavery. They result from his conviction, that the doctrine as thus expounded, is *untrue*, and such, as should it prevail beyond a certain extent, must operate to retard the safe, peaceful and beneficial abolition of slavery—endanger the integrity of the Union—and put in jeopardy the best interests of all classes of the population of our Southern States.

friends of the people of colour and of Africa, to consider the vast work for both, to which our country is now summoned by every thing that touches either her interest or her honour. O that she would open her great heart to pity, to mercy, and

I have stated elsewhere my reasons, for concluding the doctrine of immediate emancipation untrue; and I shall here say only, that these reasons are derived from what I regard as the true meaning and intent of the Saviour's law: "Do unto others as ye would that others should do unto you." Here I am happy to quote from the able letter (just published) on this subject, of President Young, of Kentucky, the following sentences, containing sentiments strictly just:—"Again it is urged, that the maxim do unto others as ye would that they should do unto you, requires that all authority of the master should be at once relinquished. But were I such as a vast majority of slaves are, I would that I were, for a time retained under control, while vigorous means were brought to operate upon me, to fit me for the responsibility of self-government. I do not say that, if I *were* slave, such would be my desire, as *I would then possess all his ignorance and folly*. The rule does not require that I should do to another what if I were *stripped of my present capacity and judgment*, I would deem to be best for me—it simply requires me to *imagine myself in his condition;* and what I then think would be best for myself in such a *condition, that* to do for him.

"Any other exposition of this rule will strip it of all title to its well known appellation of the golden; and will make every man's desires the measure of his neighbour's duty. Were I a child, I presume that I would be disinclined to the rod, even when it was needed. *Now*, I would that were I a child, it should not be spared; and thus, when complying with the advice of the wise man, I do unto my children, as I would that they should do unto me."

I have confidence in truth. It has a mighty power over the conscience. It is never at war with what is, on the whole, for the interest of human society.—The worst tendencies of the doctrine of immediate abolition, result from its want of truth. It may excite the passions of the North, it cannot command the conscience of the South. It may excite the slave to demand instant freedom, it cannot make the masters generally feel it to be their duty instantly to grant it. It thus introduces and sets at work antagonist principles between the North and the South, the master and the slave. It is a doctrine which, if it prevail beyond a certain limit in this country, will do more than any which ever found respectable advocates in the land, to darken the glory of our prospects, and subvert the foundations of our Government. On the contrary, the doctrine that the slaves are men; that they ought to be treated as men; that they should be prepared, without unnecessary delay, for perfect freedom; and when prepared, should receive it in such way as may best promote their happiness, and consist with the general good, is one which must commend itself to the conscience of every humane and Christian man. Should it fail to be-to justice! That standing up from her guilty slumber, in giant strength, made stronger by her faith in God, she would hasten to strike the bonds from millions at her feet; to send them forth as the unfettered heralds of her power pledged to make the debased, the enslaved, the perishing of another continent, sharers in the hopes and the happiness of the people of this. So sublime a spectacle the world has never witnessed. Whatever ancient genius or power have effected, compared with such a work, loses its dignity,—the grandest monuments that look forth in solitariness, from the gloom of past ages, appear in the comparison, like toys cast by the way-side, in the sports of our childhood. This work can be done. And we are bound in duty to Him who is to be our final Judge, to do it. The Statesman of large and manly soul, informed by wisdom and inspired by eloquence, who fearlessly, in the councils of this nation, shall advocate this cause, on those eternal principles of truth and justice constituted by God the foundation and support of every Government which he hath promised to bless, will sooner or later find his name written on innumerable hearts; the spirit of his country will answer to his appeals; he shall know that there is in it an energy for good, which once excited, can rest no more, while there is a stain upon her honour or a just demand on her beneficence.

And shall we despair of witnessing a speedy union of the wise and good from every State in our Republic, cemented by a common opinion on this subject, and moved by one

come prevalent in this nation, it will not be the fault of the doctrine, but the sin of those who resist the power of its truth and the benignity of its influence.

Since most of this chapter was written, I have perused the able essays of my friend Gerrit Smith, Esqr. in the Journal of Freedom, and to differ on any points from him, a man who is an honour to his country, is painful. But while I admire the spirit of his essays, and feel the force of many important truths contained in them, I may not have the happiness to agree with him in some views, which I must regard as vastly important to the triumphant success of our common cause.

spirit, prepared to apply the treasure and the power of the nation to carry into effect, on a scale commensurate with the evils to be remedied, and the means entrusted to them by Providence, the scheme of African Colonization? Responsibilities, awful beyond expression, now rest upon the friends of the American Colonization Society. With the boldness of truth, and the meekness of wisdom, and the confidence of success, let them aim at nothing less than to gain for their enterprise the affection and support of the nation. "If ever there was a time that calls on us for no vulgar conception of things, and for exertions in no vulgar strain, it is the awful hour that Providence has now appointed to this nation.— Every little measure is a great error; and every great error will bring on no small ruin. Nothing can be directed above the mark that we must aim at; every thing below it is absolutely thrown away."*

And is it possible, there treads this soil sacred to freedom and Christianity, any man, who can look his countrymen in the face and pronounce domestic slavery an "indispensable element in an unmixed representative republic"†—a doctrine dishonourable alike to the benevolence of God and the nature of man? A doctrine declaring that the liberty of one portion of mankind must be perpetually dependant for existence upon the slavery of another! Let him who inculcates a dogma so abhorrent to the spirit which redeemed his country, and which if it survive here, must redeem the world, expect few disciples in this land, until the signatures which the Genius of Liberty has carved in our mountains, be forever erazed, and her glorious banner, now waving over us, be taken down, forever. Let him seek for proselytes among the Arabs of the desert, or the awe-struck minions of despotic power; but expect not his doctrine to prevail among a people, who have already taught wisdom to kings, and thundered forth the truth that makes the spirit of man free, in the ears of an astonished world.

\* Burke.
† Inaugural Address of the Governor of South Carolina, 1834.

## CHAPTER XIV.

The doctrine of a Divine Providence, ruling in human affairs, is clearly taught in the sacred Scriptures. The wisest of men uttered inspired language when he said, "man's goings are of the Lord; how then can he understand his own way?" Whatever darkness may rest upon the path of an individual, we are assured from the same source, "that the way of the Lord is strength to the upright;" that "the integrity of the upright shall guide them;" and that "to him that soweth, righteousness shall be a sure reward." How the Divine Agency is exerted in Providence, we may in few, if in any particular cases know, while the reality of such Agency is certain. How far, it is but the application of pre-established laws, or how far, the power of God suspending and controlling them, is perhaps as unimportant as impossible to determine. The field of Providential Agency lies within the secrecy of the Divine Counsel. The Holy Scriptures assure us of the fact of the existence of such Agency, and declare the great and benevolent ends to which it is directed.—

As the fulfilment of Prophecy is a proof of the Divine inspiration of the Prophet, so the correspondence seen by the good man, in the course of human events, and especially in his own experience, with the revelation of God's will and supreme Providential rule, verifies to him the testimony of Scripture on this subject.

The Providence of God infringes not upon the freedom of human actions, nor lessens human accountability. It cannot ordinarily be termed miraculous, because it neither suspends a general law, nor deviates from it, in a way *perceptible to sense*. It never interrupts, modifies, or changes those moral laws which extend their authority over us as free and responsible moral agents. It marks not men, to the eye of each other, either as the objects of the special love or displeasure of God. But it is a hand to lead, a shield to protect, an Almighty power to save the good man amid all the vicissitudes, darkness, and sufferings of life. That He exists, is as great a mystery to him, as that he lives, moves, and has his being in God. The evidence of a particular Providence, is discerned less, probably, by such a man, in the course and operations of nature, and the great movements and changes in the affairs of the world, than in the effects of the successive events in his own history on his own character. He sees himself to be the subject of a moral discipline, not of his choice,—opposed perhaps to all the devices of his own wisdom; yet exactly suited to eradicate his vices, to mature his virtues, and prepare him for a nobler life.* "How often,"

* The following sentences from the Edinburgh Review, (No. 100) contain the most plausible argument that the writer has seen against a particular Providence:

"Now, general laws, however for the most part yet undiscovered by us, govern alike the constitution of our nature, and the course of events. Upon the supposition that a general and continuing interference of Providence takes place (not for their maintenance, but) for their suspension and modification, it follows, in like manner, that all our attempts to trace a chain of cause and effect, and to found what would once have been considered a philo-

said Mr. Ashmun† before he embarked for Africa, "is the 'Providence of God employed for our highest good, without 'our co-operation! How often, even against our best con-'trived and most strenuous endeavours!" "To how slight 'a circumstance can every reflecting person refer the origin 'of some of the most momentous passages of his life!"

The disappointments, trials, and even errors of Mr. Ashmun, were made the means of elevating his character and ex-

sophical history, comprising, through their probable connexions, all the advantage that history can confer, ought to be abandoned as an inquiry after a thing which has no actual existence. If fresh trails can be thus interposed, the chase after human probabilities is one where the moral reasoner must lose the scent at every moment. To judge by the analogy, is there not every reason rather to presume that, if the general rules of the moral could be known but as accurately as those of the physical world, we should find the absence of special interference quite as great in one case as in the other?"

Not to remark upon the declaration concerning the nature of the laws which are acknowledged to be for the most part *undiscovered,* and upon the assumption of the very matter in question in the assertion, that general laws govern the constitution of our nature and the course of events; I observe, that the particular Providence of God is revealed in the Bible as one of the laws in His government of the world, and that all general laws are ever dependant upon His will, if indeed most, be not merely modes in which this will operates. The Divine Agency in particular Providence, is (except in the case of miracles) a secret Agency, and of course neither suspends nor disturbs, sensibly, the general laws of nature. That series of causes and effects which a philosophical history must comprise, is such as has arisen under the government of Him who in particular interpositions, acts not without rule or reason. but with constant and unalterable regard, to the nature, the freedom, and the interests of His intelligent creatures.

From experience of the past we determine probabilities for the future; not that all the causes of past events have been subject to our examination, (for even the Reviewer admits that most of them are undiscovered) but observing the circumstances in which those events have arisen, and their *apparent* antecedents, we learn to expect similar events under like conditions and circumstances. The admission of a particular Providence, alters in no way the facts in the history of mankind, which constitute the basis of all our conclusions concerning the probabilities of future events. But is it not a consolation to the devout man to know, that all things are under the *immediate* view and control of the great and benevolent Author of the Universe?

† Life of Bacon.

tending his usefulness. They became tributary to that high Providence which discerns the "end from the beginning," and leads forth its elect servants, not from the rosy bower of softness and repose, but from the rough ways of hard endurance, from the fierce and fiery conflict with temptations and afflictions, to great and honourable achievements. From the period of which we are writing, he might have expressed his feelings in the language of our first father to his Angel Teacher:

> "Henceforth I learn, that to obey is best,
> And love with fear the only God; to walk
> As in his presence; ever to observe
> His Providence; and on Him sole depend,
> Merciful over all His works, with good
> Still overcoming evil, and by small
> Accomplishing great things, by things deem'd weak
> Subverting worldly strong, and worldly wise
> By simply meek: that suffering for truth's sake
> Is fortitude to highest victory,
> And to the faithful, death the gate of life;
> Taught this by His example, whom I now
> Acknowledge my Redeemer ever blest."

His papers furnish evidences of astonishing activity and industry. Though his range of public duty embraced all the affairs of the Colony and even its remote relations to Africa and America, yet he found time to think and write upon various subjects, moral, scientific, political, and religious. He criticised the Philosophy of Paley, wrote Essays on the Tariff; the morality and political results of the Holy Alliance; on points of Law, Solitude, the Social Affections, Love and Marriage; Capital Punishments, the Prophecy of Malachi, the present state of the Argument in regard to the General Deluge as derived from geological phenomena; Providence, the Sabbath Devotion, and many other Theological topics, while he recorded many observations and reflections on the Geography, Climate, Natural History, and Moral and Political state of Africa.* He pursued, to some extent, the stu-

* Appendix No. 10.

dies of Botany and Ornithology. Most of his notes relating to his religious experience, and the ways of Providence towards him, are dated on Sunday, a day which he devoted to public worship, to a penitent acknowledgment of his sins, the study of the Scriptures, humble supplication for the Divine blessing, and a thankful remembrance of the works, goodness, and mercy of God. His religious sentiments and feelings at this period, (from autumn 1824 to the same 1825) are expressed in the following brief extracts from his private Journal:

"*October* 17th, 1824.

"A fever from about the 3d to the 9th of this month, con-
' fined me to my apartment. I found a softening of my feel-
' ings towards my enemies. I could forgive them all freely—
' was brought to expect and desire my happiness so entirely
' from God, as to be willing, if it were His pleasure, to give up
' all my other prospects and enjoyments for Him alone. I was
' willing to lose my friends, my heart's dearest idols; my re-
' putation, civilized and refined society, and spend my days
' in poverty, seclusion and sickness, if God would but be my
' God, and afford me the visits of His grace and the refreshing
' light of His presence. I mourned my former departures
' from Him, and feared more than death itself, to relapse into
' a life of blindness and disobedience."

The following passage, was written after a severe indisposition, on Bushrod Island, after having been exposed to fatigue for several days during the course of negotiations for Territory with the native Chiefs on the St. Paul's:

"SUNDAY, *April* 8th, 1825.

"It becomes me to record the goodness of God in my re-
' cent indisposition on Bushrod Island. When seized, I was
' in the humble employment of administering a little aid to
' a sick coloured man of our party. The cenery around—
' our own neglected persons—the half naked appearance of
' our attendants—our pedestrian mode of travelling by paths

'merely passable—all tended to deliver the mind from the
'imposing influence of human pride, and to cast it upon
'those resources which exist independently of the gifts of
'fortune, of health, or even of this precarious animal life it-
'self. Exhausted of strength and sensible of the rapid ac-
'cess of fever, I yielded myself entirely to the power of the
'instructive circumstances of my situation. My thoughts
'were directly occupied with the history of the blessed Re-
'deemer's humiliation, and of His solitary life, the labours
'and indigence which attended every stage of it, and the in-
'dignity and sufferings which marked its close. Thence
'reverting to my own actual situation, from which this train
'of reflection had taken its rise, I silently uttered in the fol-
'lowing language, a prayer which was entirely dictated by
'present feelings: 'O eternal Lord, thou hast reduced me to
'a state in which I am obliged to dismiss from my mind,
'every care and concern relating to this life—to turn for sup-
'port, away from every created object, and concentrate all
'my cares, all my thoughts, all my affections upon a single
'point, and that point, O glorious Jehovah, opens upon the
'ineffable perfections of thy nature in full display.' The
'sentiment which dictated this somewhat obscure phraseo-
'logy, may be illustrated by supposing the sight which had
'before been roving at large, at once confined to a single lu-
'minous point in the skies, and when once so intently fixed
'and confined, to have the power of prying through the em-
'pyreal concave and descanting upon a new and immense
'exhibition of celestial glories. Such was the imagery by
'which my soul was freed from the entanglements of sense,
'for the moment, and raised to the intent contemplation of the
'glories of the invisible God. The stimulus of the fever,
'without deranging the powers of the mind, quickened and
'assisted their operations. The Holy Spirit vouchsafed His
'instructions. Never had I a more impressive view of the
'extent and completeness of the ruin of human nature, and

'the infinite destruction incurred by the Apostacy. My
' imagination, for a moment, indulged the supposition, that
' God had not yet revealed to Angels a remedy for the deep
' damnation of the race. Never before did I so effectually
' feel the truth of the often-made representation, that on this
' supposition, Angels would say such a remedy is impossible.
' * * * Now was my mind prepared for the annunciation
' which I supposed to follow, of God's purpose of giving His
' son a ransom for the sins of the world. At this moment a
' new and enlarged conception of the infinitude of the Divine
' nature, of the glory of the co-equal Son in Heaven, took
' place in my mind. O how entirely, how convincingly did
' the thoughts of the sacrifice of the Son of God in this view
' of His mighty power and ineffable dignity and glory, do
' away the painful sentiment which a perception of the pre-
' ceding difficulty had introduced. The intelligence was
' too great for faith itself to receive without staggering. But
' the proofs were complete. * * Jesus Christ has been
' revealed from Heaven in the execution of this magnificent
' labour of grace—has been evidently set forth crucified
' among us. Doubt was excluded, and at the end of this
' edifying reverie, I found myself refreshed, confirmed, and
' excepting some remaining uncertainty, as to my personal
' interest in the Redeemer, easy and satisfied in my Father's
' hands, and willing to abide the event of my present illness,
' whether it were to end in death or health."

"*April* 26th.

"This evening I called to see Mrs. Benson, who has for
' several months been in a declining state of health. She
' was very low indeed, but full of Faith and the Holy Ghost.
' She told me, with every appearance of sincerity, that she
' had been much afraid of self-deception—had strove and
' prayed for many years against it—and had at last arrived
' to an entire certainty, that she was not deceived. She la-
' mented the levity and inconsistency of many professing

'Christianity in the settlement. Formerly, when expecting
'to leave the world, she had some doubts and fears; but
'now God has removed several of her children, whom He
'has thus undertaken to make provision for himself—she
'rejoiced that the 'Master' had taken them, and was entirely
'resigned to His will. She had been greatly afflicted—very
'greatly; but it was all the 'Master's' work, and she could
'not object a word. The goodness of Christ!—it ought to
'win all hearts—and could they but know that He had power
'to forgive sin, and give the evidence of it which she felt,
'they would embrace Him. She spoke of the death of her
'father, who had been buried the same evening, with perfect
'composure, and with praises to God, who had so ripened
'him for Heaven. She told me, that she has not, amidst all
'her afflictions, one gloomy hour, and was confident when
'called to go, the 'Master' would give her a pleasant passage."

"*May* 1st, 1825.

"Finished, in the intervals of worship, the reading of Mrs.
'Judson's 'Mission to Burmah.' Thanks to God for the con-
'firmation which the history of that Mission adds to my
'faith in the truth and promises of the Christian Revelation.

"I commenced the little volume with a sort of prejudice, I
'scarcely knew or inquired why, both against the persons and
'ministry of these pious missionaries, who were permitted to
'introduce the gospel into that empire. This was caused, per-
'haps, by their forsaking the communion of those religious
'societies which sent them out to India. But whatever was
'the cause, and as long as the uncharitable sentiment had
'dwelt in my heart, the perusal of this book has destroyed
'it. I can embrace them with a fraternal affection, and bid
'them God speed in their work. They deserve for their
'zeal, faith, and constancy, amidst numerous difficulties and
'tedious delays, the encouragement and gratitude of every
'one who has made the interest of the Redeemer his own.
'They have mine. The blessing of the Holy Spirit be on
'them and their work, to the end!"

"*Myself.*—The old Platonic maxim, Γνωθι σεαυτον, what is
'its tendency but to make a world of egotists? Is egotism
'then an evil? The philosopher saw the source of whatever
'there is of vice and folly in the character, to be a superficial
'acquaintance with ourselves: and saw, farther, that it could
'be only cured or prevented by that profound and universal
'self-knowledge which should render the faults and weak-
'nesses of our nature as obvious to ourselves, as our better
'qualities.

"A man must study himself very injudiciously, and very
'unsuccessfully, indeed, who does not discover more of the
'former than of the latter, in every view which he can take
'of his subject: and if his estimation of himself is graduated
'by his observations, he cannot fail to divest himself of much
'of that blind and arrogant conceit which forms a part of the
'character of most young men. But for all practical and
'useful ends, he will acquire in its stead, a far more valuable
'and rational confidence in himself. A man who can clearly
'perceive, and is willing to confess to himself his faults, has
'a secret consciousness of a power of reforming them. The
'fact that he does see the blemishes of his character, is proof
'that he is not deceived in the opinion which his judgment
'has formed of his better features. He knows of what he is
'capable; and, limiting his attempts to his powers, succeeds.
'Every success inspires fresh confidence. Every attempt
'adds to his experience. He rises in the scale of existence,
'and rises on strong supports. No giddiness attends the ele-
'vation—for the daily proofs of infirmity and folly which
'occur, serve as an antidote to that danger.

"Now to practise on my own theory:

"*I perceive that I am no zealot, and every day less likely*
'*to become one.* Where others are confident, I hesitate—
'where others deal in absolute and universal assertions, I
'speak hypothetically; and even if I assent, it is on the possi-
'bility that I am drawn to a false conclusion by surveying

'only a part of the evidence. Where others devote their souls
'to a particular system, as if all truth were condensed within
'its maxims, I embrace a part of several, and reject much of
'all—and still regard my knowledge of the subject as too im-
'perfect to form any system for myself. Where others de-
'vour a few favourite dogmas, and satiate the appetite of
'their minds at a meal, I am constantly tasting, laying aside
'and carping, and even finding exceptions to the most re-
'ceived maxims.

"If an object of extensive utility to the human race is pre-
'sented, I approve and patronize—but cannot surrender my-
'self entirely to it; and compared with the zeal of many of
'its advocates, my approbation is frozen into a species of in-
'difference.

"I smile at the zeal which I every day see so many lavish-
'ing on objects of such subordinate importance, that I am
'sure they will one day blush at the review of their own con-
'duct. When young I could cramp the whole of experi-
'mental and practical religion into the compass of a few pro-
'positions. I could create out of an equally small number of
'Calvinistic principles, a perfect standard of orthodoxy. But
'I have since perceived that I then saw, but very imperfectly,
'only one, out of the infinitude of aspects, of which the sys-
'tem of celestial doctrines is susceptible. Every variation
'of my own station, would, on the principle then assumed,
'have given me a new theory of practice, and new standards
'of orthodoxy."

"Should I live a few years, it may be useful for me to know,
'in what way my thoughts are employed, and my hopes and
'fears exercised, at this period, relative to the great interests
'of my salvation.   *   *   *

"In the first place, I state with gratitude to God, that my
'solicitude about my future wellbeing is habitually too great
'to permit me to rest without some definite preparation for
'death and judgment. I dare not embrace the world, and

' content myself with the prospect of faring at last as the peo-
' ple of the world must. I have too penetrating and habitual
' a belief of the truth and justice of God, to indulge in my-
' self for an hour, an allowed contempt of His revelation.

"I have often this train of thought in my mind: Mahome-
' danism is certainly a falsehood—Pagan systems are too
' ridiculously absurd to deserve a moment's inquiry into their
' origin—Atheists, Infidels, Jews, and Roman Catholics, are
' flattering themselves with speculations and errors, as vain
' and false as their effects on moral character are blinding,
' corrupting, and hardening. Away with them all: My
' heart and judgment equally reject their sophisms, and their
' dependence. None of their speculations, rites, and rules,
' can reform the life or purify the heart. They have all,
' their foundation in the lusts of the depraved heart. I know
' too well the tendency of my own to doubt it. The gospel
' of Jesus Christ then, as contained in the Testaments, is the
' last and only piece of 'terra firma' which shows itself on
' this broad and fluctuating ocean of doubt on which I am
' tossing. In this I find all the characters of truth which my
' reason asks for. Why then do I not embrace it with my
' whole heart? Ah! here's the difficulty: My understand-
' ing resolves this problem, too, by recollecting that the gos-
' pel is too holy to engage the entire confidence and love of
' a heart that retains its relish for sin. Not an objection of-
' fers, but I am able to answer it to the satisfaction of reason.
' But still I do not entirely and effectually believe. I do not
' embrace with my entire soul, "unto righteousness," this
' glorious gospel. I do not make its precepts my *only law*—
' nor its hopes my *only portion*. Why not? Sloth—divided
' views between it and the world—strong and unsubdued
' corruptions, passions, appetites, all tend to *blind, harden,*
' and defeat the resolutions of the better part of my nature.
' *My last resort then is*, give up myself to the belief of the
' gospel, and perplex my mind with doubts, no more. If it

' is not true, nothing within the reach of the human mind is
' so. If I live and die in the full faith of the gospel of Christ,
' I live and die with the best prospects a mortal can have on
' this side of the grave. My wish is to establish the resolu-
' tion with myself, to live and die in this faith—and never let
' my thoughts perplex me more, with objections, or doubts.
' They are useless and pernicious. I wish to believe every
' truth of the Testaments—and aim to become a perfect Chris-
' tian—sensible that God will accept me, and all will be well
' for ever.

"I thank God that the foregoing minutes delineate some-
' thing more than cool and fruitless speculations. As far as
' the sketch goes, it represents the actual struggles and la-
' bours—in other words, the experimental exercises of my
' mind, which have a correspondent influence on my practice.

"I live daily under a more impressive view of the certainty
' and nearness, and solemn consequences of my dissolution—
' the termination of my probationary state, and the surren-
' der of my accounts to God. Dreadful event! Alas! who
' can abide it? How, indeed, shall I? \* \* \*

"Another fact I cannot suppress. Examining the structure
' of a flower, and explaining to Mr. Waring the uses of its
' several parts, about the same time—I preached myself into
' a transport of rapturous astonishment at the wisdom and
' other adorable attributes of the Almighty, displayed in that
' little piece of His workmanship. A new view of His uni-
' versal Providence, from that moment, took place, and has
' continued to instruct and affect me to the present hour.

"A week ago, I was thinking on the tender love of Jesus
' Christ to His disciples while with them in person, and on
' *their* love to Him. My bosom caught the passion. I was
' melted into tears: The love of Jesus affected me as it never
' had before—and as I want language to convey any idea of to
' others, or even to revive it in my own mind, if I ever forget
' the sensations of that and the two following days. Now

'these things are encouraging. And my base heart wants encouragement. They are tokens for good—'the day of small things;' and to me who have lived such a fruitless and
' guilty life, they are precious intimations of the returning
' kindness of my faithful Redeemer. I make my boast of
' them—and thank God that His grace has not suffered them
' to be entirely lost upon me."*

"Sabbath, 11th *September.*

"I am in great doubts respecting my true spiritual state.—
' Generally fears—fears lulled only by insensibility prevail.
' But to-day, the exercises of my mind, formed an exception.
' I enjoyed a confidence of hope in my Lord Jesus Christ al-
' together unusual.

"In the morning the depression of animal spirits and gene-
' ral dulness under which I laboured, almost discouraged me
' from seeking the divine blessing; but God gave me, I cannot
' tell how, grace to rise above the temptation, and to shake
' off my sloth. I engaged in fervent secret prayer, and con-
' tinued long in it, from the sweetness of pouring out my con-
' fessions and desires into the bosom of my Heavenly Father.
' Devotion gave to my mind a tone which grace enabled it
' to support through the day. I was enabled *for* Christ, and
' *through* Him, to surmount several temptations: and got an
' impulse towards God which sent me a little heavenward,
' against the winds and tides of this world.

"I found out a number of long hidden secrets this day, and
' the evening following; as, the charm which engages pious
' people in the reading of the missionary and other pious la-

---

\* I have been reminded by this passage, of an old Latin epigram remarkable for antithesis, as well as for force and beauty of sentiment:

"Pro servis dominus moritur, pro sontibus insons
Pro ægroto medicus, pro grege pastor obit.
Pro populo rex mactatur, pro milite ductor
Proque opere ipse opifex, proque homine ipse Deus
Quid servus, sons, ægrotus, quid grex populusque
Quid miles, quid opus, quidve homo solvat? Amet.

'bours of such as are spreading the gospel: the reason and
'source of that fervid eloquence which the advocates of
'those blessed charities, and of truth generally, in these days,
'so often discover, to my former perplexity."     *     *

"SABBATH NIGHT, *September 25th.*

"Doubtful—yet hoping. Can unassisted nature, stirring
'in my breast, produce such a love of the Bible? such a con-
'quest over my revengeful tempers? such pleasure in the se-
'cret worship of God? such respect to future retributions?
'such a reverence of God's providential care? such a percep-
'tion of the divine excellence of the Gospel of Jesus Christ?
'I know that all these things are to be found in me but in a
'most imperfect degree. But would they exist in this corrupt
'breast at all, if not inspired by the Holy Spirit? If not, then
'may I not with deep humility, and taking my station
'amongst the less than least of all saints, plead a covenant
'interest in the promise of God, and appropriate some of the
'precious hopes and confidence which belong to his adopted
'children? Lord God, instruct and confirm me in thy fear,
'faith and love, yet more and more to the end."

"SABBATH, *October 2d,* 1825.

"Alas! how the world runs away with my fluctuating affec-
'tions! I thank God that I am not utterly given up to delu-
'sions, nor abandoned of hope.     *     *

"I have some remaining sense of eternity—some just ap-
'prehensions of the vanity of this world with all its wealth—
'some desires after communion with God—some reverence
'of his authority—as much hope as so poor a professor of the
'gospel ought to have in its promises—some desires to live a
'life of humility, meekness, labour, cross-bearing, penitence,
'and obedience, before God.     *     *     *

" I thank God, that His spirit has taught and enabled me
'the week past, in some degree to get the better of my vindic-
'tive feelings towards certain individuals who have very se-

'riously injured me. The means were somewhat remarkable. I had seen the impropriety of indulging in the bitterness of resentment against any of my fellow-men—especially against some, who being professors of Christianity, might yet have repentance and grace given them, and be enthroned in the divine glory in Heaven. But whenever I recollected the extent of the injury I had experienced at their hands—the greatest perhaps that they could do me, short of murdering me in my sins—and that I must continue to suffer in consequence, to my dying day—perhaps my memory and my children after me—I had never been able entirely to suppress the stirrings of a revengeful and bitter spirit in my breast. To this infirmity one thing contributed: I was not certain that the precepts of Christ required me to forgive and pass over the offence, till I had evidence that the persons committing the injury, had repented, and undertaken to prevent the effects of their injurious conduct. To settle this point of duty, I determined to consult every precept relating to the duty of forgiveness in the New Testament; which I undertook accordingly, assisted by Scott's notes and references.

"I was already satisfied that I ought to pray for them, and indulge nothing like malice and revenge. But the question was, 'Am I to treat them with the politeness and tenderness, and kindness, *in all respects*, due to others who had not offended me—or who having offended, had offered me satisfaction?' 'Do good to them,' &c. was plain I knew; but was I required to speak to them, salute them, and treat them with kindness, if they ever chanced to fall in my way? This was the question to be resolved. The first passage I consulted was in the 5th of St. Matthew—'If ye salute your brethren, only, what do ye more than others? Do not even the publicans the same?' I closed the blessed book, astonished, convinced, and satisfied—with an involuntary exclamation of assent, and praise to God. Since that time, al-

'though many bad and sensual passions have been active in
'my breast, yet God has given me grace to forgive, and re-
'gard the formerly so obnoxious individuals, with sincere
'kindness. It is a great victory which the power of Christ
'has in this matter gained over the strong and inveterate malice
'of a very hard and revengeful heart. To Him be praise.

"I have also another instance of the great goodness of my
'God. Owing to the failure of an expected remittance from
'America, I was almost in despair—and in great anxiety and
'trouble on account of an acceptance to a considerable
'amount, considering my circumstances—and the payment
'was to be made in specie;—of which there was next to none
'not pledged, in the Colony. In my extremity I betook my-
'self to my Father in Heaven. The burthen was soon after
'in a good measure removed, and that in a way most unex-
'pected."

"*November 4th*, 1825.

"Mrs. Tabum is said to be in her last agonies. To Thee,
'Father of Spirits, Father of Heaven, and Father of Mercies,
'I commend her soul. Suffer her not to fall from thy grace,
'in this the season of her extremity. Make thou, God, her
'deliverance from the fear and sting of death, thy care. She
'has professed the name of Christ, before many witnesses.—
'May she be now received into thy glory—and through the
'merits of the Redeemer, be owned of Him, whom I trust
'she has not denied. O! Lord God, hear this my last prayer
'for her—give her assured and victorious faith, and may she
'if called this day or this hour, to her eternal estate—this day
'or this hour, be with Christ her Lord, in Paradise. O!
'Jesus, thy rich mercy and grace is all my hope—and it is a
'sure ground of hope for this thy servant. To Thee and
'thine eternal love, be all the honour and praise of her eternal
'salvation. Glory be to the Father, and to the Son, and to
'the Holy Ghost; as it was in the beginning, is now, and ever
'shall be, world without end. Amen.

"Sabbath, *November 27th,* 1825.

"*My Mercies.*—1st. The great dispensation of mercy
'through my Lord Jesus Christ, under which, in common
'with my fellow-men of this age, I live; and in virtue of
'which the good things of the life that now is, and the prom-
'ise of the life to come, are enjoyed.

"Praise God from whom all blessings flow,
Praise him all creatures here below—
Praise Him above, ye heavenly host,
Praise Father, Son, and Holy Ghost."

"2d. The Revelation of the great mercy of God through
'His Son, which I was early made acquainted with, and never
'suffered entirely and openly to discard.

"3d. The firm faith given me from on high, by the renew-
'ing influences of the Holy Spirit—even 'when I was dead
'in trespasses and sins'—and the conservation of this prin-
'ciple in my soul, although neglected, despised, and ungrate-
'fully forgotten by myself, in repeated and grievous back-
'slidings, and under the provocation of innumerable presump-
'tuous sins.

"4th. My preservation from an untimely death, in repeat-
'ed instances, when others have fallen in multitudes around
'me; and when it seemed to myself and others nearly in-
'evitable.

"5th. My deliverance, so far as I have been, perhaps, able
'to bear it, from a state of wounding ignominy—rendering,
'during its continuance, life itself an intolerable burthen; and
'naturally urging me to despair, and utter abandonment.

" 'Out of the depths, hast thou delivered me.'

"6th. Removing me from the snares of Satan in America,
'and fixing me in a situation here, suited to wean me from
'those sins which must otherwise have proved my destruc-
'tion in that country.

"7th. Giving me success in my administration.

"8th. Providentially aiding me, in my deliberations, and
'active labours for the government and welfare of this people.

"9th. Giving me, in this country, a number of attached 'and steady friends.

"10th. Providentially aiding me in the discharge of my 'pecuniary and other obligations—in many instances—espe- 'cially in this one (Ferbin—Specie, &c.)

"11th. The growth of certain moral qualities in my mind, 'which I cannot name, I fear, without danger of self-flattery; 'but which I gratefully and humbly attribute to the great 'goodness of my Heavenly Father—and without which I 'know I can never see His face. 'Blessed are the pure in 'heart, for they shall see God.' Lord, I pray for this purity."

He who knows not the natural effect of humility, may wonder that a man of high religious attainments should discern in his heart and life, so much cause for regret and so little for self-complacency. But to see distinctly, the eye must be clear and the object in the light. He whose intellectual vision is undimmed by sense, who looks upon his character in the light of the Divine Law, will need no one to interpret to him the language of Job, commended of God for his integrity—"I have heard of Thee by the hearing of the ear, but now my eye seeth Thee; wherefore I abhor myself, and repent in dust and ashes;" or the penitent confession of Paul, chief among Apostles, and exalted to revelations unutterable, of heavenly glory, that he was "less than the least of all saints." The kingdom of God cometh not with observation: in the retirement of his own mind, the Christian detects his foes, fights his battles, and achieves his victories. At every avenue of temptation he sets a watch, fortifies himself when weak, rouses his slumbering conscience, restrains his vagrant imagination, chains his wrathful passions, confirms his reason, summons fortitude to endurance, and resolution to expel from his soul the enemies of his peace, and establish therein the eternal empire of truth and righteousness. The world knows him not.

Such a man will not measure himself by human opinion,

but by a perfect standard of duty. The brightest parts of *his* character will appear to him darkness in contrast with the *Divine*, and those actions which mankind admire, be deemed unworthy of the approbation of God. Others may observe in him dispositions which he notes as deficient, and fail to discern those which it is his great object to repress. The faults to which others may think him least liable, it may have cost him the most pains to correct; and the virtues which were most alien to his nature, have become, by culture, the ornaments of his person.

It is a striking fact, that in the judgment of his friends, Mr. Ashmun was distinguished for the virtues opposite to the faults, set down in his private Journal, as those, which he was most inclined and accustomed to commit. He speaks of himself as "fickle and ever varying in his temperament;" as "deficient in independent fortitude;" as "precipitate" in action; as addicted to "censoriousness;" whereas, the writer can testify from an intimate acquaintance with him, during, perhaps, the most trying period of his life, that fortitude and meekness, humility and charity, pervaded with their blended influences his entire character, and elevated him tranquilly and triumphantly above all the discomposing vicissitudes of life.

> "As some tall cliff that lifts its awful form,
> Swells from the vale, and midway leaves the storm,
> Though round its breast the rolling clouds are spread,
> Eternal sun-shine settles on its head."

## CHAPTER XV.

Few men give stronger proofs of disinterestedness, than the managers of our large charitable Institutions. Their office is without emolument; the reputation they may acquire, wants the individuality that tempts ambition; and the time and thought devoted by them to their object, is seldom known and more rarely appreciated by the public.

The Managers of the American Colonization Society, engaged in a work difficult, remote, to which hindrances and discouragements were incident in its early stages, and the greatest benefits of which, will be seen only by posterity.— They have devoted to it a liberal share of time and attention. They have made to it large sacrifices of convenience and interest. They have prosecuted it, earnestly, perseveringly, resolutely, and with success. The effects of their labours shall survive them—a nation will be their monument.

The commencement of the year 1826, found Mr. Ashmun at the head of a prosperous Colony, which the Managers of the Society, encouraged by his statements, were prepared, vigorously to sustain and enlarge. This Colony, and he who was its defender and guide, had become, extensively, objects of interest and affection, to the people of the U. States.

On the 23d of January, 1826, Mr. Ashmun wrote to the Board—"Our town begins to assume the appearance of a 'beautiful little commercial West India seaport; and certain-'ly has one of the most delightful situations on the face of 'the globe. In beauty, and grandeur of prospect, no station 'can be taken on the Potomac half so charming, or half so 'commanding. It would, I am confident, prove to the mem-'bers of your Board, an ample remuneration for much of 'their disinterested labours for Africa—to make a single visit 'to their Colony, and see a well-organized, improving, and 'Christian society, founded by their hands, deservedly 'taking rank among the most virtuous and happy commu-'nities."*

* Having expressed his purpose soon to return to the United States, he adds:—"Am I wrong in my expectations that the friends of the Colony will make one strenuous and united effort to obtain this winter for it, (the Colony) the patronage of Congress? The Board have done well; they have, I think, redeemed every pledge and fulfilled every hope held out by the Society to the world. But they can do little or nothing more in this country. The concern is becoming too extensive for the funds of any private Society to sustain. You have, as will be seen from the letter; a line of one hundred miles to protect—establishments forming on every part of it to maintain and cherish—harbours to fortify—a coasting and inland trade to regulate—military expeditions to provide for—schools, hospitals, and benevolent institutions of various descriptions to endow, and in one word, you have from this time, a little empire to create and advance to maturity. To throw emigrants into the Colony, *while the very frame of it is left without support*, is a thing easily done—but it will subvert it. A shelter must first be provided, and well sustained. This work is first in order, the introduction of Colonists is next. That provision *neglected*—I say it with great assurance, the coloured people of the U. States are better in that country."

The Colonization Society sustained, as several of our charitable institutions are, may do much; and in the writer's opinion, the Colony, without aid from Government, will grow and prosper. Still he believes with Mr. Ashmun, that immediate, earnest, and persevering applications for assistance, to the States and to Congress, are required on grounds of humanity, policy, and duty.

In the same letter, he stated that during the preceding year, he had expended in the purchase of lands, and in founding of settlements at a distance from the Cape, about eight hundred dollars; and had learned with pleasure, that it was the intention of the Board, to send out a large company of emigrants. He expressed his regret, that the interests of the Society and Colony should suffer, for want of a regular correspondence; and his hope that arrangements would soon be made with some commercial house in the United States, by which two or three vessels should be constantly employed as packets to ply between this country and Liberia. He suggested that a wealthy merchant of New England, who had already commenced trade with Liberia, might agree on terms advantageous, and at regular intervals, to convey emigrants and supplies to the Colony. He stated that this individual had been given to understand, that the Colonists would regard themselves as under no obligations to favour his commercial views, unless *lumber** should be found a prominent article imported in each of his vessels.

The Managers were reminded in the same letter, of the necessity of adding to the School books and stationary of the Colony.

On two points of importance, in his view, to the success of the Agency, Mr. Ashmun at this time, modestly, but very decidedly, expressed his opinions. The *first*, related to the appointment, by the Board, of assistant Agents; and the *second*, to a provision in the early Constitution,† established by the Society for the Government of its African settlement, by which authority was vested in a Board of Agents, who

* This fact shows with what industry the settlers were employed, in constructing houses and public buildings.

† This provision was evidently abrogated by the form of Government established in 1824, but Mr. Ashmun seems to have been doubtful whether the Board so understood the matter—or what is more probable, might not, when this letter was penned, have received intelligence of the confirmation of the new form of Government by the Board.

were to discuss and settle by their united counsels, the public affairs.

On the subject of Assistants, he declared that *none* was infinitely preferable to persons of ordinary qualifications.— Though he had performed, for years, the duties of several active men, "he would sooner continue to sustain the burthen, 'than be troubled with young men not of *very superior* qual-'ifications." "My ideas," he adds, "of the point of perfection 'to which every department of duties devolving on the pub-'lic servants, ought to be brought, are such, as entirely to ex-'clude, from our little system, all half formed instruments. 'I would rather see all such, in use at home, where their ex-'ample is to have less effect on the community they live in. 'The truth is, Sir, we have men of superior sense and dis-'cernment amongst us—some are not wholly destitute of 'good taste—and Monrovia is the constant resort of foreign-'ers: The youth of the Colony require improving exam-'ples, and it is probable that a person not highly respected 'and useful in the United States, would be less so here."

In regard to a Board of Agents, he believed that it was certain to be attended with most injurious effects. He referred to the total failure in the operations of the Government, in every instance, in which authority had been divided among the members of such a Board. He declared that to a Colony circumstanced as that was, the advantages of one directing head, were incalculable; and that much of the strife and anarchy of former years would return, should the powers of the Managers, in the Colony, be confided to a Board of Agents.

Before the arrival of this communication, it had been determined to despatch two expeditions to the Colony.

The brig Vine, with thirty-four emigrants,\* a Missionary,

---

\* These emigrants were mostly from Newport, Rhode Island. Eighteen of their number were just before their departure, at their own request, organized into a church, and the impressive exercises of the occasion, upon which thousands attended, deepened the concern for the prosperity of the expedition.

(the Rev. Calvin Holton) and a Printer, accompanied by the Rev. Horace Sessions, an Agent of the Society, who proposed to return in the same vessel, sailed from Boston, on the 4th of January, and arrived at Liberia on the seventh of February. A press, with its necessary appendages, many valuable books and other important articles, were sent out in this vessel, by the generous citizens of Boston, who assumed the entire expense of the printing establishment for the first year.

The Indian Chief left Norfolk with one hundred and fifty-four persons, mostly from the State of North Carolina, on the 15th of February, and completed her passage on the 22d of March. In this vessel, went as passenger, Dr. John W. Peaco, Agent of Government for the recaptured Africans, who was empowered, also, to act as an assistant Agent, and Physician for the Colony.

By the return of the Vine, Mr. Ashmun informed the Board, that the greatest benefits were to be expected from the press and from the efforts of Mr. Holton, who had been employed by the Society to establish and superintend, under the direction of the Agent, a system of Colonial education. He expressed his intention of sending, in future, at regular periods, and in a printed form, all important public documents, and a copious compend of the public Journal. He stated that Mr. Holton (of whose excellent qualifications for this work, and entire devotion to duty, he felt assured) would organize a system of instruction, to embrace *all* learners—of all the four classes: 1st. The children of the Colonists; 2d. Native children living in the settlement. 3d. Recaptured Africans (of whom there were one hundred and twenty); and 4th. A class of young men and women, either actually engaged as teachers, or preparing to become such. It had been determined to adopt the Lancasterian method of instruction among the lower classes, while the higher would enjoy the lectures and personal tuition of the Principal.

We have seen how strong was the affection of Mr. Ashmun

for the cause of Missions. The Baptist Board of Missions in the United States, had instructed the Rev. Mr. Holton, to act as their Missionary in Africa; and to animate the efforts of this Institution, Mr. Ashmun made to it a grant (subject to the decision of the Board) of a tract of ground adjoining to Monrovia, on the condition that a School-house should be forthwith erected upon it, and devoted forever to Missionary purposes.

Sounds of joy were still heard in the settlement on account of the arrival of the Vine, and Mr. Ashmun had found time only to consider how he should best direct this new accession of numbers and means to the good of the Colony, when the entire company were attacked by the worst form of African fever, and about half their number, which was subsequently increased, including Messrs. Sessions, Holton, and Force (the Printer), fell victims to its power. "It was the will of God," said Mr. Ashmun, "which often humbles the pride of human theories, ' disappoints human hopes, and covers with the wreck of its ' plans, so large a space of human life."*

The Rev. Horace Sessions had but just entered upon the duties of his sacred office, when he accepted an Agency for the Society, and did much to kindle the zeal and arouse the exertions of New England in behalf of Africa. He superintended the embarkation of the emigrants by the Vine, accompanied them to Liberia, to acquire information which might render more efficient his future exertions for the Colony, and on his passage home, was summoned from the labours and trials of this world, to the endless happiness of a better.

* With one exception, these emigrants were either natives of the Northern States, or had long resided there. They left Boston in the depth of winter, and arrived in Liberia during the hottest season of the African year. "The disadvantage of the rains," says Mr. Ashmun, "has long since proved itself to consist chiefly in want of shelters, and not in any particular malignity of the atmosphere in that season:—an inconvenience now no longer felt, and which at worst, is more than counterbalanced by the advantage of leaving America in summer."

His remains sleep with those of the beloved Mills in the depths of the ocean; but they rest secure under the protection of Him "who is the resurrection and the life," and who will finally bring the dispersed bodies of His saints from every land and every sea, into reunion with their souls in glory everlasting.

The Rev. Calvin Holton had visited Africa under the influence of that divine charity which is now animating his brethren in India and in Burmah, to win immortal honours, not by the weapons or the machinations of a wordly policy, but by the powers of truth and goodness, urged to victory, over the worst vices that debase and ruin our nature. For some time after his first attack of fever, he was thought to be convalescent. In July he gradually declined, until on the 23d of that month, he gently expired. "He laboured," said Mr. Ashmun, "at no period of his illness, under the appre-
' hension of death; and often in the most dangerous crises of
' his disorder, was as little concerned about the issue, as in
' the most flattering convalescence. His spirits were uniform-
' ly sustained by a steadfast faith in the promises of Christ;
' to whom, in an early stage of his sickness, he had resigned
' himself, without reserve, and appeared never after to admit,
' for a moment, any distressing anxiety as to the termination
' of his affliction." The power of his religion, was seen not more in his life, than in his death; he had so detached his affections from this world, that he could leave it without regret; and he died as a Christian should die, anticipating the gracious rewards of fidelity, and the glories of the Divine presence.

In cheering contrast with the melancholy fate of the emigrants by the Vine, were the circumstances of the larger company by the Indian Chief, who free from all alarming disease, experienced little suffering,* while some of their num-

† But three of this company, (one hundred and fifty-four) one adult, and two small children, died in the course of the season, and these from other causes than climate.

ber who left Virginia in bad health, derived, ultimately, benefit from the change of climate.

A survey was almost immediately made, under the direction of Mr. Ashmun, of lands on the St. Paul's river and Stockton creek (a small stream uniting that river to the Montserado); and in the month of June, no less than thirty-three plantations on the creek, (at the distance of half-way between Monrovia and Caldwell, the settlement on the St. Paul's) and seventy-seven at Caldwell, were occupied by settlers, most of whom had arrived by the Vine and Indian Chief. "Having," said Mr. Ashmun, "disposed so soon of these emigrants,
' most of whom will be on their own lands, and in their own
' houses, in four weeks from the present time (June 21st), I
' trust you will not think it unreasonable in us, to ask for more.
' Let them come, as soon as they can be despatched, provided
' lumber and six or eight months' stores come with them. If
' they come from the South, they cannot come very unseason-
' ably in any part of the year. * *  More funds, more ac-
' tivity, more emigrants, and I am satisfied. Has the hope
' of liberal appropriation, by the State Legislatures, been
' given up? A slaveholding State must take the lead, and
' give an example in the exercise of this noblest of public
' charities. Others will then follow."

On the 16th of April, during the absence of Mr. Ashmun and four other members of his family, at the Anniversary Meeting of the Liberia Missionary Society, at Monrovia, the Agency-House which he had occupied for several weeks, at Caldwell, was struck and much injured by lightning, and the only person in it, the Housekeeper, instantly killed. The event is mentioned with much sensibility, and an acknowledgment of God's providential care, by Mr. Ashmun, who adds—"The impression was deeper, more lasting, and more
' effectual than any which had been made on my heart for a
' long time before."

An expedition, assisted by the Captains and crews of two

Colombian armed vessels, was conducted, during this month, by Mr. Ashmun, against Trade Town, a notorious slave mart, one hundred miles south of Cape Montserado, which terminated in the capture of three vessels, engaged in the slave trade, the liberation of fifty-three slaves, and the entire destruction of the establishment.

A Spanish schooner, (the Minerva,) while waiting for the collection of her cargo, of three hundred slaves, at Trade Town, had committed piracy on American and other vessels, and obtained possession of several recaptured Africans belonging to the United States' Agency in Liberia. Mr. Ashmun, as Agent of the United States, demanded of the Spanish Factor and native authorities of that place, the restoration of these Africans, and threatened in case of refusal, to destroy, as soon as Providence should grant him power, entirely and forever, that nest of iniquity. The demand was treated with contempt. Intelligence of the character of the Spanish schooner was communicated by Mr. Ashmun to the commander of a French brig of war, who soon captured her, though her establishment on shore, at which two hundred and seventy-six slaves were ready to be shipped to America, remained unmolested.

Early in January, were landed at Trade Town, from a French schooner, (the Perle,) goods sufficient for the purchase of two hundred and forty slaves, though in April, she had obtained but one hundred and twenty-six.

A Brigantine, (the Teresa,) from Havanna, armed with seven large carriage guns, and manned with forty-two men, with goods for the purchase of three hundred slaves, arrived in March, landed about one-third of her cargo, and had commenced her odious trade.

Three slave factories were in full operation in Trade Town, guarded by two vessels, mounting between them, eleven carriage guns, and having a complement of sixty men and twenty more on shore, all well armed; when on the 9th of April, arrived at Monrovia, the Colombian armed schooner Jacinta, Captain Chase, who in accordance with the instructions of his Government, offered to co-operate with Dr. Peaco (then Principal Agent of the United States for the recaptured Africans,) and Mr. Ashmun, in any plan they might adopt for the punishment of these offenders against justice, and the laws of nearly the whole civilized world. The offer of Captain Chase, was accepted; and on the 10th of April, Mr. Ashmun, accompanied by Captain Cochran of the Indian Chief, who generously offered to become his aid, and thirty-two volunteers of the Colonial Militia, embarked in the Jacinta; and on the 11th, arrived off Trade Town, and had the happiness to find anchored there, the Colombian brig of war El Vincidor, Captain Cottrell, mounting twelve guns, which had the same afternoon captured, after a short action, the Brigantine Teresa. Captain Cottrell agreed to unite his forces with those of the Colony and Jacinta, in an attack on the place. It was resolved to attempt a landing on the morning of the 12th, over the bar of the river in front of the town, where the passage is only eight yards wide, lined on both sides with rocks, and across which, at that time, the surf broke so furiously as to endanger even light boats, and leave scarce a hope of the safety of barges filled with armed men.

The Spaniards were seen drawn up on the beach within half musket range of the bar, resolved to take advantage of any accident which might occur to the boats, and defeat, if possible, the attempt of those on board, to reach the shore. The brig and schooner were ordered to open a fire on the town, but owing to their distance, their shot produced no effect, except to disperse the unarmed natives who had assembled as spectators of the scene.

The two boats in advance, commanded by Captains Chase and Cottrell, were exposed to a rapid fire from the enemy, and were filled by the surf, before they reached the shore. Their crews, though few of them landed with dry arms, forced the

Spaniards back into the town. The flag boat, in which were Mr. Ashmun, Captain Cochran, and twenty-four men, was upset, and dashed upon the rocks; several of the men (among whom was Mr. Ashmun) injured; and some of the arms, with all the ammunition, lost. Captain Barbour observing the dangers of those who preceded him, ran his boat on the beach, a little to the left of the river's mouth, and thus landed in safety.

Immediate possession was taken of the town, and a messenger despatched to King West, (the principal native chief) demanding the delivery of all the slaves belonging to the Factories. He was told, that if there were deception, or unnecessary delay in the matter, not a vestige of Trade Town should exist two days longer. On the same day, the Kroomen of King West, brought in thirty-eight slaves; and on the next morning, fifteen more; the latter a wretched company, evidently the refuse of all that had been collected at the station. The natives assembled and united their forces to those of the Spaniards, and continued from the rear of their towns, to pour in, at frequent intervals, their shot upon their invaders. Captain Woodside, Surgeon of the Jacinta, was severely wounded, and several of the Colonial Militia, slightly.— Every man under the command of the Colonial Agent, lay on his arms during the night of the 12th; and until noon, on the 13th, every disposition was evinced by Mr. Ashmun, to settle, peacefully, the questions which had excited hostilities. But in vain. At twelve on that day, the boats were prepared just outside the breakers, to receive on board the rescued slaves; and at two, the canoes began to carry off the marines; and at half past three, all were embarked, the officers leaving the shore last, and having set fire to the principal buildings of the town. "The flames," says Mr. Ashmun, " communicated with the utmost rapidity to every roof; and ' the town exhibited a single immense mass of flame, before ' the canoes could get off from the beach. In one minute af-

'ter, the explosion of some single casks of powder commenced:
'and the moment the canoes reached the boats, a scene of ter-
'rific grandeur was displayed, which rivals the powers of de-
'scription. It was the effect of the ignition, at the same mo-
'ment, of two hundred and fifty casks of gun-powder. The
'concussion shook the earth, and for a few moments, appear-
'ed to hold the very swell of the ocean motionless. Every
'vestige of what was once Trade Town, was swept from the
'ground on which it stood. The surrounding country and
'neighbouring water, were strewed with ignited thatch, and
'house palings descending from a height of more than one
'hundred feet, to which they had been raised by the explosion.
'A quantity of these ruins fell among the boats, and some
'heavier objects were observed to be carried beyond the an-
'chorage, which was more than a mile from the shore. At
'half past four, the officers, troops and slaves, were all safely
'on board, and on their way with a light breeze for Cape
'Montserado."*

The destruction of Trade Town, contributed in Mr. Ashmun's judgment, more towards the suppression of the slave trade, on the western coast of Africa, north of the Bight of Benin, than any one single event, except only the enactments

* Alluding to the aid which he had received from the Commanders of the Colombian vessels, Mr. Ashmun observes:—"Were it not for the power of prejudice, aided by misrepresentation, it would be little necessary or decorous for me to observe, that the dignity of the Colombian banner, newly displayed on this ocean in defence and vindication of the sacred rights of human nature, has never here been tarnished by an act upon which malevolence itself could reflect the shadow of dishonour. And while it shall float over the quarter decks of such commanders as a Chase and a Cottrell, it will be hailed, whenever it appears, not only as the signal of victory, but as the best guaranty of a rising empire's moral greatness." Of Captain Cochran, he says: "His services voluntarily devoted in the Trade Town expedition—and which were of the most laborious and perilous, as well as useful kind, deserve something more than my individual acknowledgments. I owe my own life, in one instance, at least, to the promptness with which he interposed his own person between me and the danger which threatened it."

of the English and American Legislatures. It made every slave trader along the coast, feel the insecurity of his commerce; and the natives of a great extent of country, sensible that a powerful and resolute enemy to their crimes, had gained establishment on their shore. "We have thought proper," wrote Mr. Ashmun on the 10th of May, "to interdict 'this trade on the whole line of coast, comprehended between 'Cape Mount and Trade Town, both inclusive. The ground 'assumed, is that of a qualified jurisdiction actually held by 'the Colony over the whole district. It is believed that no 'slaver coming from Europe or the West Indies, will proceed 'to land his cargo (and without landing it he cannot get 'slaves), in the face of such an interdict, formally notified to 'him; which we can easily do in all cases. But, in case his 'audacity prevails and goods are landed, we have only to an-'nounce to the native Chiefs of the place, that according to 'the laws of the Colony, those goods are forfeit, and an instant 'seizure of the whole, in nine out of ten cases, is certain to 'follow. The public boats now on the stocks, cannot fail to 'render us the most important service in this business—and 'our hopes are high, that the world is to hear little or noth-'ing more of the ravages of this detestable and outlawed 'traffic, from this part of the coast."*

* The writer doubts not that these hopes would have been realized, had it pleased Providence to prolong, but for a few years, the life of Mr. Ashmun. From the opinion expressed by Mr. Ashmun, in a former chapter, it is evident that his hopes of the utter extinction of the trade, had been disappointed. On the 20th of April, he wrote : "Since the 10th of October last, God has honoured me and the forces of the Colony, as the instruments of liberation of one hundred and seventy-eight Africans, who have been received at the U. States' Agency. In the same letter, he suggests to the Board the propriety of putting in a claim for "the bounty allowed by law for recaptured and liberated slaves, *delivered over into the custody* of the Marshalls or Agents of the U. States, authorized to receive them." "It will have," he adds, "at least the effect of a recognition on the part of the Government of the freedom of the people—and the whole amount will go more or less to the advancement of the Colony."

It is, perhaps, worthy of remark, as an evidence of the facility with which Mr. Ashmun turned his thoughts from one object to another, that his able letter, addressed to Dr. Blumhardt, on the subject of Missions, (see Appendix No. 3,) is dated April 23d, 1826, a few days only after his return from Trade Town.

From May to October, Mr. Ashmun was confined to his room, in consequence of the effects of an injury, which he received in landing at Trade Town. On the 10th of May, he wrote—"The contusion was a little troublesome at first, but
' I soon, as was supposed, got the better of it, and felt little in-
' convenience until the 2d of May, when it took on every cha-
' racter of an ulcerous affection, and made it necessary to
' submit to a course of medical treatment, which I fear must
' be continued for weeks. But my confinement to my office
' is little or no impediment to the business I have to do; and
' I have the satisfaction to add, that the public work, in all its
' parts, never went forward more regularly, or more success-
' fully."

It would be difficult, without extending our work beyond the limits prescribed, for it, even briefly, to allude to the great variety of objects to which the thoughts of Mr. Ashmun were directed, during this period of confinement, and upon which many valuable observations are introduced into his Journal and communications to the Board. But he rested not in speculations—he sought to carry into speedy effect, whatever plan he adopted.

Dr. Peaco was absent from the Colony, at Sierra Leone, from the 21st of June, to the last of July, to settle certain claims held there, against the United States' Agency in Liberia.

As the Government of Sierra Leone had put the line of coast from that place, to the Gallinas, under blockade for the prevention of the slave trade, and as complaints had been made to Mr. Ashmun, that this blockade was violated with impunity by the merchants of Freetown, Dr. Peaco was requested to ascertain to what extent and under what colour such violations had been permitted, and to state explicitly, "That the members of the Colony of Liberia would be required to submit to no restraints on their trade with the blockaded coast, which were not actually and universally enforced upon the subjects of Sierra Leone."

The exclusion of the ordinary commerce, from this part of the coast, induced the Chiefs of Cape Mount to open a regular trade with the Colony, and the supply of rice and other African provisions in the colonial settlement, became unusually cheap and abundant.

During the absence of Dr. Peaco, Mr. Ashmun adopted several important measures for improving the condition and extending the influence and Territory of the Colony. To encourage agriculture, he granted leases of the public grounds in the vicinity of Monrovia, for three years, rent free, on condition that the lessees should proceed immediately to clear, enclose, and improve them.

He imposed a tax of two dollars a head on all landholders, for the purpose of raising funds for the construction of a town school-house, although the act occasioned expressions of the wildest and absurdest notions on the subject of taxation and republican liberty. "The measure," he observes, "was una-' voidable."

In July, the hope cherished by Mr. Ashmun, that the destruction of Trade Town would put an end to the slave trade in that vicinity, was for a short season suspended by an active combination between several piratical vessels and native Chiefs, to restore this town to its former nefarious distinction.

The brig John, Captain Clough, from Portland, and the schooner Bona, from Baltimore, were plundered on the 27th of July, when lying at anchor off the town of Monrovia, by a piratical brig, mounting twelve guns, and manned chiefly by Spaniards—the former, of two thousand five hundred dollars, and the latter, of two thousand eight hundred and sixty-two.*

Intelligence reached the Colony, nearly at the same time, that eight vessels engaged in the slave trade, had resolved to maintain Trade Town as a station for their traffic; that they had commenced a battery on shore, and were determined to defend themselves against any force which might be brought against them. "The slave trade," he observes, "is the pretext
'under which expensive armaments are fitted out every
' week from Havannah, and desperadoes enlisted for enter-
' prises to this country; in which, on their arrival, the trade
' is either forgotten entirely, or attended to as a mere secon-
' dary object, well suited to conceal from cruisers they may
' fall in with, their real object. Scarcely an American trad-
' ing vessel has for the last twelve months been on this coast,
' as low as six deg. north, without suffering either insult or
' plunder, from these Spaniards."

In this state of things, Mr. Ashmun directed that a strong battery should be immediately erected near the termination

<small>Owing to the little resistance made by the Americans, or violence offered by the pirates, the robbery was not perceived from the town. The cabins of both vessels were entirely stripped of their little furniture—and officers and crew robbed of all their clothing and private property. This brig was said to have been fitted out at St. Thomas', and to be commanded by an American. Mr. Ashmun stated, that after this piracy, she proceeded to Gallinas, purchased and sailed from the coast with six hundred slaves. The Journal of Mr. Ashmun about this time, contains an affecting account of the murder of Capt. Ferbin, (a former visiter to the Colony) and his crew at St. Andrews' bay.— "Captain Ferbin had unfortunately, on a former voyage, given to a Frenchman, information which led to the seizure and transportation out of the country, of several of the St. Andrews' people, and the nation determined to have its revenge, and Capt. Ferbin had been repeatedly warned not to put himself in its power. The Captain was ill when his vessel was attacked, and though his crew defended themselves with all their might, they were soon overpowered, the Captain himself taken on shore and shockingly murdered, while not one of his men was left to tell the horrors of the scene. The St. Andrews' people are among the most treacherous and cruel of the whole coast."</small>

of the Cape, for the protection of ships at anchor in the roadstead,* while he represented to the Hon. Secretary of the Navy, the absolute necessity of the presence of a sloop of war for the defence of American commerce on that coast.

* The Friends of Peace deserve great praise for their efforts to abolish, utterly, the odious custom of war. Whether war in any case is justifiable, is questioned by some eminently enlightened and Christian men. We have never seen the arguments for and against defensive war, so clearly and briefly stated, as in the following extract from an Address by the Rev. C. S. Henry, of Hartford, Connecticut, a gentleman whose writings do honour alike to his scholarship, piety, and genius:

"On the one hand, it is common to observe, that taking life is not in itself absolutely wrong;—that the man may kill his aggressor without hatred or revenge, but with sorrow and regret;—that the preservation of life is, within certain limits, a clear duty;—and, moreover, that the *instinct* of self-preservation, though not an absolute moral guide, since duty may sometimes require us to risk and to sacrifice our lives,—is yet *in favor* of the right of self-defence, and therefore must modify those passages of the New Testament from which the duty of non-resistance is deduced;—and finally, that to construe those passages with literal strictness would not only forbid the taking of life in the case supposed, but would prohibit any resistance, such as the attempt to overpower and disarm the assassin.

"On the other hand, it is equally obvious to remark, that duty, whatever it be, is worth more than life. It is better for the man to do his duty, than to save his life. If the precepts and the spirit of Christianity forbid the taking of life in self-defence,—then neither the fact that they run counter to the instinctive love of life, nor any regard to the *consequences* of obedience, are to outweigh them. Whatever is our duty is on the whole best for us. Obedience is wisest and safest, in the large view of our welfare. On our part will then remain only an implicit reliance on Providence for protection, in all cases where we should do wrong in defending ourselves. And if life be the sacrifice to duty, it is well sacrificed, no less in this case, than in the numerous other supposable cases. That Christianity does require the sacrifice in the case supposed, is argued from the fact, that the peaceful precepts of the New Testament, are directed precisely against the principle of self-defence. They do not merely forbid *aggression*, but *resistance*. It is precisely when we are assailed by violence or injury, that these precepts come in, commanding endurance, forbearance, peace. These precepts are universal in their form, making no exception in favor of cases where life is assailed. Add to this, the unquestionable fact, that those precepts were thus understood in the earliest times of Christianity,—that the Gospel was, in the first ages, universally and practically construed as a doctrine of non-resistance. To test this construc-

His influence and authority with the native chiefs, however, contributed more than any other means to prevent the destruction of the Colonial factories and the threatened subversion of the Colony.

In his letter to the Board of the 3d of August, he writes:—

"I have judged it advisable to send for preservation in the
' Society's office, rough, but accurate plans of the surveys from
' time to time accomplished,—of the public buildings, &c.—
' the former taken from the authentic records of the Colony.
' Accompanying, I send

"I. A complete survey of the St. Paul's—Caldwell settle-
' ment—with the surrounding country.

"II. A survey of the Stockton, including the *Half-way*
' *farms*, and showing the position of these farms relatively
' to Caldwell.

"III. The town and settlement of Monrovia—completed
' from the last surveys.

"IV. Front side-view of the market-house of Monrovia—
' building.

"V. End and side-views of the Lancasterian school and
' town house of Monrovia; now nearly completed.

"I also send the final receipt and discharge of the St. Paul's
' kings, for the purchase money of the territory on that river.

tion, it may be said, it is supposable, that the true Christian spirit—the spirit of forbearance and love, if in its highest and purest exercise, might prompt the individual, in the case given, to sacrifice his life rather than destroy the assassin;—and that we should pronounce it a noble disposition. And the question would then come up, whether the highest and purest exercise of Christian love, is not the *duty* of all;—whether all ought not to be actuated by a disposition, which we cannot but pronounce admirable?"

One idea of some importance, seems to the writer, to have been omitted by Mr. Henry, viz.—that in case the question be not decided expressly by the language of the New Testament, the right of self-defence may be exercised not from any excessive self-love, but from regard to the general good. Even the Christian might say, in destroying the life of an assassin, if my enemy and myself, were the only human beings on earth, I might yield up without resistance, my own life; but as things are, I am bound to consider the effect of such an act on the general interests of society.

"The purchase of *Factory Island*, was definitely concluded
' early in July.

"The boats sent out by the Government, promise to be of
' inestimable utility to the Colony.  Our establishment at the
' Sesters, although within five miles of Trade Town, is still
' sustained—cultivation, building and trade, are carrying on
' there on a small scale; but for want of rainy-season-craft,
' little has been done to advance it since the month of May.
' Bassa factory is a source of very valuable supplies to the
' Colony.  We keep up at this inclement season, an inter-
' course with this place along the beach—but the transporta-
' tion of goods or produce by this route is expensive and labo-
' rious—and there is a considerable amount of property re-
' maining there, which we leave to the dry season.

"I cannot well express to the Board, the general gratifica-
' tion felt here in the establishment, at length, of a line of
' packets between the U. States and this Colony, on which it
' is believed dependence can be safely placed.  The entire
' cargo of the brig John, (the first of the line) which arrived
' July 22d from Portland, the 9th of April, was instantly
' purchased, and another vessel is expected early in October.\*

"The Board will recollect the mention of the arrangement
' with Mr. C., merchant of Portland, in a former letter, by
' which he engaged to place two or more brigs on this line, in
' order that four arrivals may be depended upon in the year.
' I stated to him (Mr. C.) explicitly, that he must engross the
' trade of the Colony only by means of a fair competition, and
' this he might do for the present, by

"1st.  Making the supplies certain.

"2d.  Laying in all such goods and stores, and such only, as
' should be ordered.

"3d.  Always bringing a deck-load of lumber.

---

\* This arrangement continued but for a short time,—the success of the owner of the vessels not equalling his expectations.

"4th. Holding his merchandise, &c. at the following prices:

"Tobacco,          100 per cent. on the American Invoice.
"Rum,              75    do.           do.
"Salted provisions, 45  do.           do.
"Flour,            75    do.           do.
"Butter, Lard,     75    do.           do.
"Lumber,           100   do. and all other goods and merchandise, at 50 per cent.

"The experiment has completely justified the anticipation on which it was founded. Our port regulations prohibiting on penalty of the forfeiture of the amount, any goods introduced into the Colony, from being sold on credit—when I say that the cargo of the John has been wholly disposed of in ten days, the Board will understand me to say that it has all been also *paid for*. The amount, after deducting the part carried off by the pirates on the 28th, is about eleven thousand dollars.    *    *    *    *

"The Board is respectfully solicited to direct their early attention to the deplorable want of Schools under which the Colony now labours. All our former arrangements are confounded, and our hopes blasted on this interesting subject, by the lamented death of the Rev. Mr. Holton. A gentleman from the southern part of the country, especially the alluvial country of the southern states, need be under no apprehension of suffering severely or permanently in his health in consequence of removing to Africa. A female of superior accomplishments for training our numerous girls and young women, is scarcely less needed than the first. And as our hopes have been so highly excited by the provision made for carrying on the printing establishment, a severe mortification and several sore inconveniences must be the consequence of a disappointment in regard to it. The patronage that will be afforded to a paper by the settlers, will diminish the burthen of supporting a printer."

On the 18th of August, Dr. Peaco, whose health was much

reduced by repeated attacks of fever, embarked in the brig John for the United States, expecting an early recovery in his native land, and prepared to explain and enforce at the Navy Department, the statements of Mr. Ashmun in regard to the exposed condition of American vessels on the coast of Africa. At the moment of his departure, Mr. Hodges, a boat builder, from Norfolk, and the only white man remaining with Mr. Ashmun at the Colony, was leaving the world.— "He sustained," says Mr. Ashmun, "a blameless character, 'the crowning excellence of which was a deep, humbling, 'practical and inward piety, which the living may remember 'with advantage to themselves and which must excite sin-'cere and lasting regret for the departed."

The next day, he entered the following sentence upon his Journal: "It is a most remarkable and affecting circum-'stance, that the present Colonial Agent is this morning, by 'the death and departure of his associates and assistants, 'left for the seventh time, the only white person in the Co-'lony."*

The firmness of Mr. Ashmun was exhibited during this year, at the annual election of public officers. A few individuals belonging to the Independent Volunteer company, (composed, said Mr. Ashmun, of high spirited young men, all excellent soldiers, but bad politicians,) took offence at certain restrictive regulations, and particularly at the summary method, which on the failure of all others, had been

* 1st. September 16th, 1822: by the death of his wife.

2d. October 1822: by the death of Jones, an assistant Surgeon.

3d. February 1823: by the death of Mr. Gordon and eight of his crew and the withdrawing of the three survivers.

4th. December 6th, 1823: by return to the United States of Dr. Ayres.

5th. August 1824: by return of Mr. Gurley.

6th. May 1825: by the death of Mr. Dicksley, a young Englishman employed as an Assistant.

7th. August 19th, 1826: by the deaths of Messrs. Force, Holton and Hodges, and the return of Dr. Peaco.

adopted to raise money for most necessary improvements in the town. By zeal and activity, they soon formed a party, went forward in a body to the polls, and while the more sober part of the community were little aware of any political danger, elected their own candidate for the Vice-Agency. The Colonial Agent refused to confirm the chosen candidate in office, and stated his reasons, which were entirely of a political nature.

In the afternoon, a circular was issued to this effect: "That the right of election conferred by the Board of Managers on the people of the Colony, as it never had been, so it never should be interfered with by the Agent; consequently appointments to offices of trust in the Colony, once legally made by the concurrence of the popular choice, with his own approbation, should never be rescinded by any arbitrary act on his part; and that the actual incumbents must remain in their offices till removed in the only way prescribed by the provisions of Government; that is, by a vote of a majority of the electors of the Colony."

The disappointed, perceiving that the present officers would, without a new election, be continued, hastened to the polls, and gave their votes for a ticket the most unsuitable, that could well be proposed, in the judgment of the Agent.— On that day they were a large majority. But as the voters from Caldwell had mostly retired to their homes at the close of the first election, it was necessary to keep open the polls during the next day, when the body of the settlers alarmed at the probable consequences of their remissness, rallied with zeal and perfect union, and elected new candidates well qualified for the offices assigned them, and whose appointment was immediately confirmed by the Colonial Agent. "The Agent," remarks Mr. Ashmun, "has the high satisfaction of ' finding himself sustained by a body of assistants, in whose ' good dispositions and capacity he has great confidence."

On the 3d of September, an extraordinary panic seized

many of the settlers, and we here insert, somewhat abbreviated, the notice taken of it in the Colonial Journal:

"There is an unaccountable propensity in human nature
' to fabricate, diffuse, and at length believe whatever can ex-
' cite anxiety or apprehension, however unfounded and im-
' possible. It is only by referring to this principle, that the
' Agent can explain the agitation which possesses the mind
' of a large proportion of the recent emigrants, some of whom
' have abandoned their houses, carrying with them their
' goods, they know not whither. Ask them the cause and
' not one of them can make any answer. It is only seen
' that their imaginations are so possessed with the idea of
' war and midnight attacks, conflagration, butchery and de-
' struction, as to exclude all sober reflection, and wholly to
' take from them the power of judging rationally of their situa-
' tion. Never were the native tribes more friendly. Never were
' they so little capable of bringing war upon our settlements
' or causing any disturbance. A rupture with the Colony
' would cut them off from supplies which they regard as
' among the necessaries of life, and they dread it as the great-
' est of calamities. They are ready to explain any circum-
' stance in their intercourse with us which may be construed
' to their disadvantage. By steadily resisting the importu-
' nities of these frightened individuals, for arms and ammuni-
' tion, and other means of defence, the Agent in a few days
' succeeded in laying them under the necessity of imagining
' themselves secure again, and it is the imagination alone that
' can be addressed in so high a fever of excitement as has
' prevailed among this people."

With what promptitude and decision Mr. Ashmun defended not the rights of the Colonists only, but those of the native tribes who were entitled to his protection, is manifest from the following record in the Colonial Journal:

"On the 5th of September, a flagrant robbery was commit-
' ted by the people of Little Bassa, upon a company of Young

'Sesters people, on their way from the Lower Factory to the
'Cape, with rice, oil, stock and ivory. A messenger was
'despatched to Little Bassa at an early day thereafter, to de-
'mand redress for the insult and violence offered to these tra-
'ders. Those who committed the outrage lived at some dis-
'tance inland, and were under the jurisdiction of King Tom,
'now at war with the Condoes, whose frequent incursions
'upon his territories near the sea coast, have for several
'months kept a part of his people in constant alarm and dis-
'order. Many of them are under arms, and the bands of
'Government very much relaxed. The Sesters' traders were
'plundered of about half of their property by a straggling
'company of these warriors. King Tom at once acknow-
'ledged the justice of our claims and engaged to make full
'and immediate restitution."

In the Colonial Journal for October, after enumerating many public works then in progress, he observes: "The
'Agent was closely confined to his chamber, and a great part
'of the whole time to his bed until the first week in October,
'when he ventured cautiously abroad, in order to superin-
'tend the launch of the small schooner. It has been built on
'the summit of the hill, three hundred yards distant from
'the river, and on an elevation of about ninety feet from its
'level. The launch was accomplished without accident, and
'occurring on the anniversary of the Agent's marriage eight
'years before, he gave the little vessel the name of his depart-
'ed wife, whose ashes rest at no great distance from the
'place, and have hitherto remained without any visible me-
'morial. Her rigging was set up by a French rigger, whom
'accident had thrown into the Colony at the time when his
'services were much needed. She carries a brass six poun-
'der, pivot mounted, twelve stands of muskets, twenty-four
'boarding pistols, twelve cutlasses, and a plentiful supply of
'ammunition. A crew of ten men have been shipped and
'organized in the best manner the Colony will admit of, and

' her first trip was made to Cape Mount to convey two com-
' missioners sent to treat with the country authorities, for cer-
' tain rights and privileges which a part of the chiefs had al-
' ready taken upon them to engage to the Agent for a small
' compensation."

The intelligent natives near Cape Mount and the river Gallinas, had expressed a desire to open an advantageous trade with the Colony; and in November and December, Mr. Ashmun visited them in the schooner Catherine, and acquired much information concerning their country, character and religion. He found them distinguished from their southern neighbours by superior intellectual endowments, urbanity of manners, profound dissimulation; by their profession of the Mohammedan faith;* by their sobriety, perseverance, activity and avarice; by their extreme jealousy of the interference of strangers either in their trade, their territorial jurisdiction or their civil affairs. Negotiations were commenced for obtaining territory in the vicinity of Cape Mount, and a brief report comprising valuable facts and reflections, transmitted to the Board.†

At the close of the year 1826, the Colony was blest with

---

* The Fey or Vey nation inhabit this region. Their country, says Mr. Ashmun, limits the progress of Mohammedan proselytism towards the south-east. Few or none of the Deys, and none to the leeward, either profess this faith or entertain its teachers. It is a singular circumstance, that our Colony occupies the point of separation between Mohammedan and Pagan Africa, on the western coast.

† Between the 1st of January and the 15th of July, 1826, no less than fifteen vessels touched at Monrovia, and purchased the produce of the country, to the amount, according to the best probable estimate, of forty-three thousand nine hundred and thirty dollars, African value. The exporters of this produce, realized on the sale of the goods, given in barter for it, a profit of twenty-one thousand nine hundred and ninety dollars, and on the freight, of eight thousand seven hundred and ninety-six dollars, making a total profit of thirty-thousand seven hundred and eighty-six dollars. A merchant of New England, who landed his cargo in Liberia, to the value of eight thousand dollars, received payment therefor, in the course of ten days.

health, peace and prosperity. Much progress had been made during the year, in the construction of public buildings and works of defence. Two handsome churches adorned the village of Monrovia. Fort Stockton had been rebuilt, and a powerful battery far advanced towards completion, on the extremity of the Cape. A large building capable of accommodating one hundred and fifty emigrants, had been finished. The new Agency house, Market-house, Lancasterian school house, and Town house in Monrovia, were far advanced, and the last strokes about to be given to the Government house at Caldwell. "There are," said Mr. Ashmun on the 6th of December, "more than twelve public buildings, including three new fortifications, going forward,—of which a particular account may be expected by the next opportunity of writing the Board." A room had been set apart in the wing of the old Agency house, for the Colonial Library, consisting of one thousand two hundred volumes, covered accurately, labelled, and systematically arranged in glazed cases with appropriate hangings. Files of American newspapers were here also preserved, and it was intended to render this apartment, both a reading room and a museum, for African curiosities.

The commerce of the Colony had increased with almost unexampled rapidity. New settlements had been founded on a soil inviting cultivation, from the hand of industry, and promising to labour an ample reward.

FIVE of the most important STATIONS on the line of coast from Cape Mount to Trade Town, (one hundred and fifty miles) had been acquired either by actual purchase or by deeds of a perpetual lease, and negotiations concluded, by which all Europeans were excluded from any possessions within these limits.

The territory on the St. Paul's has been already described.

The tract granted to the Society at the Young Sesters river, situated in the midst of a productive rice country, abounding in palm oil, camwood and ivory, includes all the land on each side, to the distance of half a league, and extending longitudinally from the river's mouth to its source.

On the south side of St. John's river, north, nine miles from Young Sesters, the right of use and occupancy had been obtained of a region of country, a Factory established upon it, and arrangements made for the cultivation of rice, the chief of the country agreeing to furnish the labour.

Deeply impressed by the upright conduct of the superintendent appointed by Mr. Ashmun to this station, with the superiority of civilized and Christian men, and the importance of their settlement in the country, an offer made by the Colonial Agent for the purchase of Factory Island, (in the river St. John's, four miles from its mouth, from five to six in length, and one-third of a mile in breadth, and among the most beautiful spots in Africa,) was accepted by its proprietor, and preparations immediately made to found thereon a settlement, "which cannot fail," remarks Mr. Ashmun, " in a few years to be second to no other in the Colony, except Monrovia."

A perpetual grant, rent free, had been secured of an indefinite tract of country, lying between the two Junk rivers, from thirty to forty miles south of Cape Montserado. Mr. Ashmun regarded this as a very important acquisition, and believed that eventually whole districts would become, on easy terms, the property of the Society.

A hope was expressed by the Agent, that negotiations already undertaken, might soon give to the Colony the whole trade with Cape Mount, estimated at an annual value of fifty thousand dollars, and ultimately result in its annexation to the territories of Liberia.

The following sentences, are from the last letters addressed by Mr. Ashmun, to the Board in 1826:

"The country people begin, as a customary thing, to hon-
' our me with the title of 'Head-man for all their country,'

'and 'Father of we all;' and whenever a proposition is sub-
'mitted to them, they are in the habit of replying, 'you know
'best what is good for us;' and in case they shall ever be
'straitened in consequence of yielding to my requests, they
'are careful to let me know that the Colony will ultimately
'be obliged to provide them with the means of subsisting
'themselves.

"All this region of Africa opens its bosom for the reception
'of her returning children. I rejoice in the testimonials
'furnished in different ways, of a growing and enlightened
'interest in the objects of your Board, among the American
'people. It is one of those great and benevolent designs on
'which the merciful Father of all mankind loves to smile,
'which the American Colonization Society has undertaken.
'Its root is deep, and its growth, however gradual, I entirely
'believe, will be sure. But the greatest difficulties—for diffi-
'culties the cause has always struggled with, I never supposed
'to lie on this side of the ocean. To obviate prejudices, and
'unite the exertions, and rouse the enterprise of the whole
'American people; this is the great labour, and to such as most
'successfully engage in, and prosecute it, will be chiefly due
'the acknowledgments of posterity."

## CHAPTER XVI.

Mr. ASHMUN had now entered upon the last entire year of his labours. Its first sun beheld him in his wakefulness of duty, as though premonished that the night drew near in which he could no more work. Whatever his hand found to do, he did with his might. The shorter his time, the greater was his activity. The fire of his spirit grew more intense as he approached the source of its animation and power.

Reputation had become the attendant of his virtues: He enjoyed the affection of the Colonists, the respect of the native inhabitants of the country, and the unlimited confidence of the friends of African Colonization in America. He saw the seeds of truth which he had planted in an unkindly soil, beginning to germinate; nor doubted that men of another age would gather in their rich and abundant fruits. Divinely assisted, he had laid, immovably, on that heathen shore, the foundations of a Christian empire; but he knew that it rested for other hands to build it sublimely up—a sanctuary inviting the oppressed to find refuge within its gates, and kindle their hopes from the inextinguishable flame upon its altars.

"One thing is certain," observes a philosophical and eloquent writer,* "that the greatest of all obstacles to the improvement of the world, is that prevailing belief of its improbability, which damps the exertions of so many individuals; and that in proportion as the contrary opinion becomes general, it realizes the event which it leads us to anticipate. Surely if any thing can have a tendency to call forth in the public service the exertions of individuals, it must be an idea of the magnitude of that work in which they are conspiring, and a belief of the permanence of those benefits which they confer on mankind, by every attempt to inform and enlighten them. As in ancient Rome, therefore, it was regarded as the mark of a good citizen, never to despair of the fortunes of the republic; so the good citizen of the world, whatever may be the political aspect of his own times, will never despair of the fortunes of the human race; but will act upon the conviction, that prejudice, slavery and corruption, must gradually give way to truth, liberty and virtue; and that in the moral world, as well as in the material, the farther our observations extend, and the longer they are continued, the more we shall perceive of order and benevolent design in the universe."

The success of the Colony of Liberia, under the administration of Mr. Ashmun, had confirmed a large body of reflecting and benevolent men in this country, in the opinion, that the scheme of African Colonization was entirely practicable, and that in all its relations, it promised vast and enduring good to mankind. The American Colonization Society had enforced its principles, extended its influence, and augmented its resources. Able pens, and eloquent voices, and strong

* Dugald Stuart.

hands, were engaged in its support. The pulpit and the press had become its advocates. The church had acknowledged its claims in her ecclesiastical councils, and nearly half the States in their legislative capacity, pronounced its object to be of signal interest to the nation, and entitled to the consideration and aid of the National Government.

The cause of the Society had grown from weakness to strength, and probabilities existed, that it might soon be planted in the affections and made prosperous and triumphant by a "happy conjunction, with the great consent of hearts" of the whole American people. Auspicious omens cheered the eyes of the Managers, and they were excited to enlarge their plans, and increase their means and energy of action.

The repeated acts of piracy in the vicinity of the Colony, and the necessities of the U. States' Agency within its limits, induced the Secretary of the Navy to despatch to that place, the United States' schooner Shark, under the command of Lieutenant Norris, with a supply of arms and ammunition; and this vessel arrived at Monrovia on the 12th of January. The presence and services of Lieutenant Norris, contributed to aid the influence of the Colonial Government for the suppression of the slave trade, and to strengthen sentiments of good will towards the settlement among the neighbouring tribes. "I have visited," observes Mr. Ashmun, "our leeward 'establishments twice on board of this vessel, and been ena- 'bled to advance our interests, and extend our influence ma- 'terially, by her means, in that direction." Lieutenant Norris reported on his return, that from all he could learn, while on the coast, the slave trade was nearly extinct between Cape Mount and Trade Town, and that the Colony was in a flourishing condition.

On the 11th of April, arrived at the Colony, (after a passage of forty-five days) the brig Doris, Captain Mathews, with ninety-three emigrants, most of them from North Carolina. These people suffered but slightly from the effects of the climate, and at an early day, took up their residence at Caldwell, on the St. Paul's.*

The ship Norfolk sailed from Savannah on the 10th of July, with one hundred and forty-two recaptured Africans, and arrived at Liberia on the 27th of August. Of the whole number, Mr. Ashmun wrote, "it may be interesting to the
' Board, as a proof of the extensive business and resources of
' their Colony, to observe, that not more than twenty remain,
' even at this early date, (only seven days arrived) a charge
' to the United States. Two-thirds of the whole number
' have situations in the families of the older settlers, for terms
' of from one to three years. The remainder are at service,
' on wages, to be paid them at the year's end—when it is my
' intention to treat them, in all respects as settlers, the na-
' tives of the United States, (unless the Board shall, in the
' interim, order differently) and assign them their lands as to
' other emigrants. I have, however, engaged to all who em-
' ploy these people, whether as apprentices or on service for
' wages, materials for one suit of clothing, and one month's
' provisions, or its equivalent in tobacco, for as many as they
' take. And this trifling gratuity forms the last object of ex-
' pense to the United States, which it is expected will ever
' arise on this account. And for this early relief, they are
' wholly indebted to appropriations made, however cautious-
' ly and sparingly, towards the Colony; the members of
' which, to repay the benefits received from the United States,
' thus take the burthens which would without them, still
' continue to press heavily, and fulfil the benevolent inten-

* "Two small children, one very young, have been carried off. * *
The most protracted case of illness in the whole number, has not lasted longer than five days. Three days is perhaps the average time of the indoors confinement of such as could be pronounced sick; about one-third part have not been closely confined at all."—Mr. Ashmun.

Of Caldwell, he observes: "Taking its past history for a criterion, a healthier settlement of equal extent, is not, I presume, to be found in all the salubrious regions of the extensive west of our own country."

'tions of Government towards the recaptured Africans in
'their most extensive sense."

In relating the proceedings of Mr. Ashmun during this year, we shall regard rather a methodical arrangement of the subjects to which they relate, than an exact order of the time in which they severally occurred.

Early in March, he resolved to visit the United States, and engaged his passage in a vessel which was then expected to leave the Colony on the first of April. He was disappointed by the sudden departure of that vessel at an earlier day, and before the public affairs could be so adjusted as to admit even of his temporary absence. He purposed, however, to seek an early opportunity for his return, and hoped to be in Washington in the month of May.

In his letter to the Board, by this vessel, he observes: "I
'have a negotiation pending with Mama, for the purchase of
'the northern part of Bushrod Island—three different pieces
'of fortifications to complete—the frame of a receptacle for
'emigrants one hundred feet in length to finish and roof—two
'large buildings erecting for the United States' Agency, to
'shut in—besides countless arrangements in regard to smaller
'matters to make, before I can possibly leave the Colony. I
'have more than forty workmen employed on these different
'works, and hope to see them in a state to leave, in three
'weeks."

Having stated that preparations were made for the reception, before the next rains, of at least one hundred emigrants and two hundred recaptured Africans, the first of whom were to remain at Monrovia and the last to be settled in a town on Stockton creek, about two miles from Caldwell, he adds:—
"At this point, formed by the junction of the St. Paul's and
'Stockton, where I reside, I have now a most commodious
'house completely finished with kitchen and out-houses sepa-
'rate. There is also a public store-house—an extensive
'fortification—a block house—Jail—and now erecting, a re-

'ceptacle for emigrants, one hundred feet in length, over-
'looking both rivers. At the Cape, I have just completed a
'new and extensive warehouse, of which the second story
'is fitted up for a printing office. Besides this building, the
'three settlements contain no less than six public stores and
'warehouses, altogether sufficiently capacious to store com-
'modiously more public property than will soon find its way
'into the Colony. I have been enabled to collect an ample
'supply of rice, and hope to leave a sufficient supply of pro-
'visions and other necessaries for all the dependants of the
'Agency—should other sources by accident be closed against
'them, during my absence."

After alluding to the expense which he had felt it his duty to incur in the expectation of retiring for several months from his station, he assured the Board, that for the same objects no considerable expense needs soon to be incurred again. "I 'have the prospect," he remarks, "of leaving the Colony in a 'safe and generally in a prosperous state. The last year 'has, however, brought with it trials and disappointments— 'but through the mercy of Heaven they are not of a nature 'to affect, materially, the welfare of the Colony—and do 'not even touch on the great questions of its feasibility; which 'I hope every candid mind will admit to be favourably de-'cided."

Having mentioned the loss of a small amount of property at the St. John's Factory; the temporary suspension of the Sesters Factory; the failure to secure all which he proposed in his negotiations with the chiefs of Cape Mount, he adds:—
" Among my trials, none affect me more painfully, than the
'want of public spirit, and ingratitude for favours received,
'shown by the Colonists—particularly the people of the
'Cape settlement. But there are noble exceptions, and
'those who form them, it may be necessary and an act of
'justice, hereafter particularly to name.

"It is and long has been my opinion, that too much has

'been done for these people, for their own advantage. A
' habit of indolent dependance on the hand of another to feed
' them, and a restiveness approaching to mutinous, under the
' slightest burthens imposed for purposes most nearly connect-
' ed with their own safety, respectability and social welfare,
' are the unhappy consequences of the Society's generosity
' towards this people—at least as *respects a majority of them.*
' I have seen the error, and in the case of the Caldwell set-
' tlers, have avoided it so far. The good effects of throwing
' them at an early period on their own resources, already ap-
' pear; and in despatching emigrants to the Colony, I think
' it cannot be too early or plainly inculcated upon them, that
' they have in this country no resources except their own
' diligent exertions—and that they can never rise much above
' the level of the native Africans, without a generous and un-
' tiring devotion to the common welfare of the new commu-
' nity they come to form. Some among us are only impressed
' by these motives, animated with this spirit—and they are
' worth to the Colony *all the rest.*"

On the 22d of April, soon after the arrival of the Doris,
Mr. Ashmun wrote to the Board:—"I am at length reluctant-
' ly compelled by a sense of duty to the Colony, to relinquish
' my intention, so long indulged, and so fondly cherished,
' of visiting the United States the present season. The ar-
' rival of so large a company, at so late a period of the dry
' season—the absence of my colleague—the multiplicity of
' delicate and arduous duties devolving on an Agent in con-
' sequence of the recent extension of our settlements—the
' very expensive improvements commenced, and *nearly,* but
' not *quite* completed, are motives for remaining, to which I
' dare not oppose private inclination, or any probable good
' which might grow out of my return to the United States.

"Mr. Hawley has intimated to me his opinion of the im-
' propriety of the step at the present time—and I confess that
' the report just received of the untiring and laborious strug-

'gle in which all the active friends of the cause in America, are the present year engaged in its behalf, has affected me with no slight feeling of self-reproach, for having so lightly determined myself to quit, even for a season, the important post of duty assigned to me. My friends, I fear, will do little justice to these motives; but I shall apologise to them in the best way I can—and put up with the accusation I know they will allege of having trifled with their feelings by exciting expectations which my present determination is obliged bitterly to disappoint."*

In the month of May, the schooner Catherine in attempting to cross the bar of the river, was thrown on shore and seriously injured; an event much regretted by Mr. Ashmun, who was compelled, in consequence, to buy provisions from trading vessels, and thus incur expense which would have been saved, could he have found means of conveying produce from the Factories to Monrovia.

Having exposed himself, for four hours to a heavy rain, in directing efforts to save the schooner, Mr. Ashmun was soon after seized with a rheumatic fever, which came near depriving him of life, and which produced, during the three weeks of its continuance, more acute suffering than he re-

* The question of Mr. Ashmun's return had become a political consideration of interest among the chiefs (near Cape Mount) of the Fcy or Vey tribes. They somewhat cautiously convoked a number of the "prognosticating fraternity," to decide by their auguries "whether the white Devil of Cape Mount would leave the American place or not this year." They decided that the chiefs must be cautious in adopting any measures founded on the presumption of his absence. Mr. Ashmun did not believe that his departure would expose the Colony to danger, but that attempts might in consequence be made to obtain from the Colony, either in the terms of trade or otherwise, what might prove to its disadvantage. "I am unfortunate enough," he adds, "to hold in the estimation of African friends, that bad eminence, to which military success is apt to raise my betters in the civilized world." * * * "But from the bottom of my heart, I disclaim the vanity and reproach of supposing that my presence or absence—life or death—is to affect the existence or any material interest of the Colony. An Omniscient and Almighty Providence conducts its progress and guards its safety."

membered ever before to have endured in as many months. " The prescriptions," he remarks, "of our excellent and experienced assistant Physician, the Rev. L. Cary, under the blessing of Divine Providence, so far succeeded as to afford complete relief; only leaving me in a very emaciated and enfeebled state, about the end of the first week in July."

In this state, on the 12th of July, he was carried on board of the schooner Eclipse, from Philadelphia, then lying at anchor near the Cape, that he might enjoy the benefit of the sea air. The Captain of the vessel determined, on the next day, to visit Sierra Leone and the Rio Pongas, in which voyage, Mr. Ashmun, incapable as he was of attending to his ordinary duties, resolved to accompany him. An abridgment of the material parts of his Journal, we here insert.

SIERRA LEONE, *July* 17*th*.

"About twenty vessels of different descriptions are lying in this port; which, in common with the ports of the West Indies and other British colonial possessions, is closely shut against American vessels.

"Several most expensive and spacious public and private buildings have been erected at this place, since my former visit in 1824. The public buildings alone of Sierra Leone, exclusive of churches, and schools, and superintendents' houses in the remote settlements, cannot have cost less than four hundred thousand pounds (one million seven hundred and seventy-six thousand dollars). (What have the public buildings of Liberia cost?) Early in the morning, an Aid of Sir Neil Campbell, the Governor, came on board with a very polite invitation to make his Excellency's house my home during my stay at Sierra Leone. My feeble health compelled me to decline this invitation, which, had I been permitted to accept, might have afforded opportunities of free and full conversation and saved the labour of a correspondence, in which I had determined to engage with the Government of that Colony, in order, if possible, to obtain its consent to

'a free commercial intercourse and barter, of the products
'and imports of the two Colonies.

"At Sir Neil Campbell's house, I met three young English
'ladies; but a single month in the Colony! I could only re-
'gard them as victims destined to the altar. Their already
'fading bloom seemed mournfully prophetic of the mortal
'ravages already commenced on their health by a climate
'which few or no white females can withstand. Sir N. seem-
'ed entirely sensible of the evils and defects which had, from
'different sources crept into the civil and social state of Sierra
'Leone—and equally desirous to find out and apply their
'proper remedies. The spirit of his Government, like him-
'self, are too military to be popular with a community formed
'under the lax and indulgent administration of Governor
'M'Carthy—nor does he ever condescend to those explana-
'tions which could, at so easy a rate, do away much of the
'odium of his most unpopular acts. But, of his assiduity,
'and upright intentions, I believe all bear the most honoura-
'ble testimony.

"The department of recaptured Africans has lately been
'separated wholly from the Colonial Government, with a
'view to lessen the burthens of the latter; and placed under
'the management of Major Denham, the resident Superin-
'tendent General, who reports directly to the Government
'at home. Major Denham receives a compensation of three
'thousand pounds sterling per annum (thirteen thousand
'three hundred and twenty dollars!)

"After remaining forty-eight hours at Sierra Leone, we
'sailed for the Rio Pongas. The Isles de Loss, which we
'passed at day-light, on the 29th, are a dependancy of Sierra
'Leone, seventy-five miles distant. On the second largest,
'(Crawford's Island) four miles from the mainland, are two
'merchants and several small traders, who conduct a valua-
'ble barter with the natives for their wax, rice, gum, oil and
'ivory. We found the British armed Colonial steamboat,

' lying off the mouth of the Pongas, and the North Star sloop
' of war, guarding the entrance of the Nunez. In attempt-
' ing to cross the bar of the Pongas, our schooner struck the
' ground, unshipped her rudder, and was seriously endan-
' gered.

"The Pongas is little more than four large inlets, running
' from the sea nearly parallel with each other, and at right
' angles with the coast. Two of these inlets, only, admit of
' being entered by vessels of burthen. They are distinguish-
' ed by the 'mud' and 'sand'-bars. By the former, distant
' eighteen miles to the north-west of the sand-bar, our schoon-
' er entered the river. These inlets are all joined together
' by navigable bayous, or arms, a few miles from the ocean.

"Like all the rivers of western Africa, the navigable mouths
' of the Pongas are obstructed with extensive shoals; of which
' the shoalest part of each takes the name of bar. The bar
' of the 'mud channel,' extends in a semicircular line, four
' miles in front of the river's mouth, quite around from shore to
' shore. The deepest water over it, does not, at ebb tide, ex-
' ceed two and a half fathoms. To find it, open the mouth
' of the river, and bring the centre of the river's mouth in a
' line with the central point between two prominences of a
' mountain called the Paps, and which are too conspicuous
' not to be distinguished—and steer directly in. The course
' will be almost due north-east, by the compass. Keep the
' middle of the river, up.

"For twelve miles the river is, on an average, three-quar-
' ters of a mile wide—and winds its sluggish way through
' a low mangrove, unhealthy, and uninhabited country, which
' is wholly divided by branches of the river into Islands of
' various sizes.

"Twenty miles from this mouth, you open that, distinguish-
' ed by the name of the sand-bar; and, five miles higher up,
' come to the first upland, admitting of being inhabited. This
' spot, which presents fine elevated banks and an extensive

'ridge of gravelly upland, is called Domingo—but was de-
'populated in 1824, and burnt in a war between Wilkinson
'and John Ormond. The extensive ruins of the old town,
'discover it to have been a place of consequence.

"The banks of the river above Domingo, are more thinly
'skirted with mangroves; and in many parts are composed
'of the highland ridges, which extend quite down to the
'water-side.

"Three miles above Domingo, the river divides into two
'navigable branches, each about one-third of a mile broad.
'That which takes a north-eastern direction, is called Ban-
'gerlang—and reaches but eight or twelve miles above the
'forks, when it degenerates into an insignificant stream of
'fresh water. The south-eastern arm of the river is called
'Bashea, and can be ascended in boats thirty-five miles. At
'this point, the tide-water terminates, and the river dwindles
'into a small fresh-water stream, as the other. At the forks
'a most beautiful and somewhat romantic country, of long,
'level and moderately elevated ridges, and intervening val-
'lies, begins; and, I am informed, continues gradually assum-
'ing a more mountainous aspect, quite into the interior of the
'country.

"The Pongas admits of a safe navigation for vessels draw-
'ing fifteen feet water, to the forks, thirty miles from the
'mud-bar—eighteen from the sand-bar; which may be carried,
'by a good pilot, about four miles higher up, on either branch.
'But the Bashea is in one part so much obstructed by rocks,
'a few miles above the forks, as not to admit of the passage
'even of a row-boat, except at high water.

"The rise of the ordinary tides, in this river, is ten feet.

"The sand-bar is said to have never less than three and a
'half fathoms of water; but from the hardness of the bottom,
'and the narrowness of the channel, is less used than the
'other.

"The country in its general characteristics, has been al-

'ready described. For several miles from the ocean, it is
'low and marshy. Thence, inland, it is dry and elevated.—
'Its prominent features are long ridges of gentle declivity—
'no great height—destitute of rocks, admitting of, and even
'inviting cultivation, quite over their smooth and rounded
'tops—which, on being ascended, are commonly found to
'consist of extensive tracts of table-land. Occasionally the
'intervening valleys sink too low, and become marshy—but
'they are all extremely narrow,—some barely wide enough
'at bottom for the channel of a fresh-water brook, which few
'of them are without.

"The soil of the uplands is of two varieties. The most
'prevalent is hard and gravelly—and deeply tinged with the
'oxyde of iron; of which metal, the ore is said to exist in
'many places, in a very perfect state, and in the greatest
'abundance.

"The other variety of soil, is a light, warm, sandy loam, of
'a light reddish colour—and for rainy-season crops, very
'productive. This soil, from its early tillage, as well as pro-
'ductiveness, is that generally chosen by the natives and re-
'sident foreigners for cultivation. Most of the uplands of
'the Pongas have been divested long since, of their primary
'growth of trees, and reduced to that slovenly culture which
'is practised by all the native tribes of maritime Africa. The
'features of this country certainly seem to warrant a pre-
'sumption highly favourable to its general salubrity.

"The people of this region are a mixed race, descended
'from the former conquerors of the country, from the interior
and the native inhabitants. Those dwelling between the
'Dembia river and the Pongas, and who claim jurisdiction
'of its southern bank, are called Naloes; those inhabiting
'its northern bank, Bagoes. They speak different langua-
'ges and appear to be of a different origin. The Naloes are
'at present independent and happy, under the Government
'of Fernandez, a coloured chief of considerable intelligence,

'and of a prudent and pacific character. The Bagoes, un-
'der the shadow of a Government directly administered by
'a great number of petty and jealous chiefs, are wholly at
'the mercy of a powerful Foulah chief, by the name of
'Mahmud, who, with a numerous division of that enterpris-
'ing and intelligent people, is settled at the distance of two
'days' journey to the north-east of the sources of the Pon-
'gas. The Naloes and Bagoes are mild and unwarlike.—
'The neighbouring Foulahs are neither.

"Rice, and the ordinary vegetables of the coast, are culti-
'vated, by the natives, for their own subsistence. A small
'surplus of the former, remains for exportation. Goats,
'sheep, poultry and swine, are also reared in sufficient quan-
'tities for domestic consumption, and to supply the few trad-
'ing vessels which visit the river. The country is indiffer-
'ently stocked with a fine breed of red cattle, which are all
'brought down by the Foulah traders from the interior.—
'Three kinds of rice are cultivated—but all on the uplands,
'and grown only in the rainy season.

"The trade of the country has respect both to the interior
'and to the foreign vessels by which the river is visited. Salt,
'manufactured from the water of the ocean, by boiling, togeth-
'er with European and American merchandise, are the arti-
'cles bartered for the productions of the interior—and wax,
'oil, a few hides, and a still smaller amount of turtle shell,
'are the only products furnished by these tribes from their
'own territory, for exportation.

"But the trade from the interior, which is wholly in the
'hands of itinerant companies of Foulahs and Mandingoes—
'and brought from the distance of one hundred to fifteen
'hundred miles, is vastly more important and valuable.—
'These industrious people arrive monthly, at the different
'trading stations on the river, with gold, ivory, coffee, bul-
'locks' hides, and bullocks, in companies of from forty to
'four hundred persons; of whom, far the greater part are do-

'mestic slaves, who serve as pack-horses for the merchants
'who own, or hire them. Their barter at the Factories is
'regulated by the *bar* method of computation—and is said
'to be managed with prodigious keenness and craft, on the
'part of the Foulah merchants. The practice of making
'presents has prevailed to a most ruinous extent, in this
'trade; but, on the south bank of the river, is now nearly
'discontinued. The articles of foreign merchandise, and
'coast produce, most in demand, consist of tobacco, gums,
'powder, scarlet cloth, cotton stuffs, rum, salt, and the cocoa
'nut—produced abundantly on this part of the coast. The
'gold is said to be the least profitable commodity compre-
'hended in the Foulah trade. Hides are one of the most
'advantageous to the purchasers.

"Formerly, both banks of the river were occupied by a
'large number of slave Factories. But the trade has gradu-
'ally fallen into decay under the vigilant and persevering
'opposition of the English—and has been superseded by a
'brisk trade in the products of the country, carried on chief-
'ly by foreign resident factors, with Sierra Leone. Most of
'these factors being the owners of small vessels, of which,
'some, of very good size and workmanship, have been con-
'structed in the river, are their own carriers.

"Of the factors, two are American, three or four French,
'and nearly half a dozen Spanish and Mulattoes, of whom
'several of the latter have a good English education. The
'most considerable traders on the north side of the river,
'have been driven by the Foulahs to seek the protection of
'Fernandez, on the southern (or Bashea) branch.

"All these individuals have allied themselves, by something,
'which in Africa, passes for marriage, with the most pow-
'erful native families, and are the proprietors of slaves. One
'factor has upwards of seven hundred people, each of the
'Americans about one half of that number. For misconduct,
'these domestics are liable to be sold to the Foulahs of the

'interior, and bring, the men, on an average, five bullocks,
'and the women always something more. Slavery exists
'here in a more revolting form, than on any other part of the
'coast which I have visited.

"The seasons do not materially differ from those of Libe-
'ria; except in the prevalence and effects of the harmattan
'wind, which is never a cause of inconvenience to the south
'of north latitude eight degrees. This breeze, at Montserado,
'always of gentle force, and generally grateful and salu-
'brious, assumes at the Pongas the harmattan character;
'blows with the violence of a gale; and descending from the
'mountains of the interior, diffuses a chilliness, little short
'sometimes of freezing, throughout the atmosphere, and is of-
'ten the cause of pulmonary complaints, and sometimes of
'great mortality.

"The rains here seldom fully set in before the early part
'of July, (six weeks later than at Montserado) become copi-
'ous with strong blowing weather throughout the month of
'August, from which they gradually decrease until their
'termination, about the first of November. The upland
'country commencing at Domingo, twenty-five miles from
'the sea, is in my opinion, as healthy as any part of the coast."

Mr. Ashmun then states, that his chief object in exploring
and transmitting this cursory description of the Pongas was,
to enable the Board to form a correct judgment in regard to
the expediency of undertaking to found a settlement on its
banks. The following comprise, in a brief view, his reasons
for and against the measure:

"1st. The Society's settlements in Africa, require a port,
'which vessels of all sizes may safely enter for trade, but es-
'pecially for repairs, at all seasons of the year. There is no
'such harbour at Monrovia. But a settlement on any of the
'navigable parts of the Pongas, would possess, in an eminent
'degree, all the advantages of a safe and commodious harbour.

"2d. The site of a settlement, whether for trade or agri-

'culture, can, at present, be obtained with little difficulty or
'expense. I was urged by persons of the first influence, to
'select the site of a settlement—and promised their interest
'with the chiefs who hold the country by hereditary right.—
'The present factors would gladly yield up a part of their
'present feeble independence, in order to enjoy the protec-
'tion of an organized Government. It was farther stated,
'that the American factors, in conjunction with other influ-
'ential residents and chiefs, drew up a memorial, addressed
'to the Colonization Society, so early as 1820, setting forth
'the advantages of the river, for an American settlement,
'and offering to use their interest in the country in favour
'of such an establishment. Their memorial either miscar-
'ried, or was for other reasons, passed over, unanswered.—
'Their views and wishes continue the same.

"3d. The advantages to be derived to the Colony at large
'from the trade of this river, are great—and to render them
'still more valuable, the river supplies the very articles of
'African produce, which Liberia, at present, wants.

"4th. The occupation of a place on the Pongas would se-
'cure to the Colonization Society a territory for future uses,
'on a central and important part of the windward coast of
'Africa.

"5th. Another inviting circumstance belonging to the
'lands of this river, is found in the large proportion of them,
'already reduced by the natives to cultivation. The present
'settlers at Montserado, who never had it, can best appreciate
'the value of such an advantage.

"On the contrary, I remark, 1st, that the policy of extend-
'ing the territorial limits and multiplying the individual set-
'tlements of the Colony, by dividing and consequently weak-
'ening its strength, may admit of a question. To perfect
'the organization, business, and institutions of the Colony, it
'is necessary to concentrate its population.

"2d. Perhaps the jealousies, which so grasping an act as

'that of comprehending the Pongas within the Colony, must directly arouse, in the foreign Governments having African colonies, and in those colonies themselves, would subject the future operations of the Society, to a troublesome scrutiny, (which it has hitherto escaped) and to frequent embarrassments. * * Would it not be best to leave off contention before it be meddled with?

"3d. The inquiry must naturally arise, *In what way is the growth of a Colonial settlement likely to be affected by the vigorous system of slavery, and of the slave trade, carried on from the sea coast to the interior, as they now exist on the Pongas?*

"It were safer, and, in my opinion, easier, to found, and *carry on for five years*, a settlement of the Colony, on a part of the African coast unfrequented, certainly not inhabited, by European and American traders, than to receive the aid of such at first, and run the great risk of their hostility afterwards—easier and safer to colonize St. John's, than Pongas.

"A fort, it must be admitted, is essential to the future prosperity of Liberia. But, with such a river as Montserado, and such a promontory as our Cape in direct contact—the one of a sufficient depth of water to float the heaviest ships, and the other of sufficient height and projection to shelter them, it is impossible, the Colony, peopled by the natives of the United States, should long be without a commodious harbour. A little more experience and skill to project, and *much more* money than we yet have, to execute the necessary works, is all that the Colony requires to furnish it with one of the safest and most accessible harbours in Africa."

In the correspondence to which we have already alluded between Mr. Ashmun and Sir Neil Campbell, Governor of Sierra Leone and its dependencies, the former, after expressing the friendly sentiments cherished by the Board of Direction in America and by the people of Liberia, (which he declared had been inspired in part by favours conferred on the American settlement in its early stages, by the Government of Sierra Leone) suggested, that the proximity of the two colonies and the diversity of the imports into each from their respective parent countries, pointed out the mutual advantages, to be expected from a more cherished and intimate commercial intercourse than had yet been cultivated. English products and manufactures brought either from Great Britain or her African and West Indian colonies, had thus far been introduced without restriction or duties into Liberia, and it was thought but reasonable, to expect that this liberality would be reciprocated by the Government of Sierra Leone, and become the basis of a permanent commercial intercourse between the colonies.

In reply to Mr. Ashmun's first letter, the Governor of Sierra Leone, after expressing his best thanks for the sentiments contained in it, on the part of the writer, the direction, and people of the American Colony of Liberia, towards the Colony of Sierra Leone, adds: "Be assured, Sir, that corresponding feelings are sincerely and cordially cherished in this Colony towards Liberia by myself and every inhabitant, and therefore I trust you will not ascribe an adherence to the instructions of the British Government, and acts of the Parliament of Great Britain, to the slightest diminution of those feelings. By a reference to the last document upon the subject of your letter, which is the order in council, dated 27th of July, 1826, (and which I have the honour to send herewith) you will see that I have it not in my power to exercise any discretion with regard to the reciprocal accommodation, which you have been pleased to suggest in such friendly terms; as goods, the produce of the United States of America, can only be imported into British possessions on the coast of Africa, in British ships registered and navigated according to law."

In his second note, Mr. Ashmun observes: "It affords me

'the highest possible satisfaction to be apprised of the preva-
'lence of those very friendly sentiments towards the Colony
'of Liberia, which dictated several passages of your Excel-
'lency's letter, and while I regret the existence of causes,
'which, operating in distant hemispheres, have proved the
'occasion of restraining the natural correspondence of those
'remote and neighbouring settlements, I console myself with
'the hope, that the restraint is not to last always; and will
'not, during its continuance, be productive of that alienation
'of feeling, which often sunders in all their moral sympathies,
'communities locally united."

In a third letter to Sir Neil Campbell, Mr. Ashmun expresses the hope that the object of an unrestricted trade, may be viewed as of such interest, not to Liberia only, but to Sierra Leone, as to authorize a particular representation to his Britannic Majesty's Government. He informed his Excellency, that Liberia could not be viewed as a Colony of the United States; that it had sprung up under the protecting care of a Benevolent Society; "that individuals could be nam-
'ed, to whose counsels and influence the settlements of Libe-
'ria, in part owe their origin, whose splendid talents, moral
'worth, and high official rank, make them conspicuous
'amongst the brightest ornaments of Great Britain and con-
'tinental Europe;" that the Constitution of this Colony was designed to prepare the people for all the rights and privileges of self-government; "and the ultimate and permanent
'object of the establishment, the improvement and benefit of
'the African race;" and in conclusion, observes:

"This explanation of the character and intention of the
'establishment of Liberia, will, I flatter myself, clear the
'*main* proposition which I have the honour to submit in
'these papers, from all objections arising out of the supposed
'political relation of Liberia to the United States of America;
'and present it to your Excellency, and the Executive of
'England, as an infant community, appealing in the weak-

'ness of its separate and solitary existence, to the magna-
'nimity, not to say, the justice of the British Government,
'for an exception from certain commercial disadvantages,
'under which the U. States, by acts in which the Colony
'could not participate, has placed itself.

"It must readily occur to your Excellency, that, from the
'nature of the African trade, the demand in the Colony of
'Sierra Leone for the merchandise of Liberia, (of which a
'most important part consists of certain articles, not the pro-
'duce of Great Britain, or any of her colonies) will ever be
'urgent:—and on the other hand, that a similar demand for
'English manufactures must ever exist, and continually in-
'crease with the extension of trade, in Liberia. Permit a
'free trade, and both colonies enjoy an important accommo-
'dation and invaluable advantage. Prohibit such an inter-
'change, and a most important vent for the staples of trade
'in which the colonies will respectively abound, is recipro-
'cally closed up. For restriction on one side, must, by a
'natural course, be followed by answerable restrictions and
'prohibitions on the other. But from the proximity of the
'colonies, which their growth and extension must every year
 increase, another evil of a fearful character, must, I appre-
'hend, unavoidably grow out of the restrictions, *on one hand*,
'and the temptation to great pecuniary advantages, on the
'other:—I allude to that most pernicious of the perversions
'of commercial enterprise—smuggling. And in this uncom-
'fortable anticipation, I deceive myself, if I have not the re-
'sult of every experiment made on human nature, under si-
'milar inducements, for my authority.

"In conclusion, your Excellency will pardon a zeal which
'in its efforts to secure an important benefit to Liberia, should
'advert to the advantages of the proposed measures of accom-
'modation, to the Colony of Sierra Leone. It probably will
'not be questioned, that the proposed free intercourse be-
'tween the sister colonies, will prove much **more** conducive

'of the prosperity of Sierra Leone, *separately considered,*
'than the actual restrictive system. And has not the Colony
'of Sierra Leone some peculiar claims on the indulgence of
'its paternal government? Does she not derive such claims
'from the truly liberal, and even charitable nature of the
'work—the work of colonizing Africa, and restoring her ex-
'iled children to their home and country,—which led to the
'establishment of the Colony? Has Sierra Leone no claims
'to special indulgence on account of the great sacrifices,
'struggles, and even sufferings of its people to preserve and
'carry on their Colony, from the period of its origin nearly
'down to the present time? And has not the justice of the
'British Government always generously recognized these
'claims? But which of these considerations will not, with
'the enlightened philanthropy of the age, amount to an ar-
'gument of easy and obvious application to the congenial
'Colony of Liberia?

Early in the year, a treaty of peace was concluded between the Colonial Agent and the principal chief at Trade Town, by which the two parties were bound, mutually to maintain and encourage between them friendly intercourse and an equitable trade, and to regard as sacred and inviolable the persons and property of each other.

Almost simultaneously the Colonial Factory at Young Sesters was suspended, in consequence of depredations committed upon it by the surrounding people, and especially, on account of a fierce war beginning to rage between the chiefs of that country and Trade Town. Mr. Ashmun visited both of these places, and for three days, was engaged in unavailing efforts to reconcile the contending parties. Both agreed to respect the Colonial property, and both offered to give to the Colonial Agent, the whole country of their enemy, provided he would assist them to subdue it.— Freeman (the chief of the Young Sesters country) and his allies, engaged to enrol themselves with all their people and country, as vassals and fiefs of the Colony, on condition that they were assisted by the Agent and his forces against their foe of Trade Town; "but from the first," says Mr. Ashmun, " all were given expressly to understand, that our whole ' force was sacred to the purpose of self-defence alone, against ' the injustice and violence of the unprincipled; that while ' we were ready to benefit *all* our neighbours, we could in-' jure *none;* and that if we could not prevent or settle the ' wars of the country, we should never take part in them."

This war terminated amicably, and for the advantage of the Sesters, at an earlier period than was expected; the Colonial property confided to King Freeman, had been scrupulously preserved amid all the disorder and alarm of hostilities, and the Factory was re-established in strength and prosperity. The chief would, he said, relinquish one half of all his territories, rather than see the Colonial settlement, in the midst of his people, abandoned.

Mr. Ashmun founded, during this season, an Infirmary for invalids, on a plan which, while it secured to the sick, infirm, and aged, the means of a comfortable subsistence, good attendance, and medical aid, enabled such of them as were not incapable of exertion, to contribute by their labour to the support of themselves and families.* It was not designed to admit emigrants during their sickness caused by change of

---

* The ends to be accomplished by this Infirmary, are represented by Mr. Ashmun to be,

1st. To secure the comfort of the diseased and sick.

2d. To furnish them with constant and regular medical attention.

3d. To oblige them to such diet, exercise or rest, and to the use of such remedies, as shall effect, in most cases, a speedy cure.

4th. To put even the invalids of the Colony in a situation to support, in part, or whole, themselves and their families.

5th. To provide an asylum for the poor and otherwise helpless of the Colony.

6th. To teach industry and skill, particularly in the little arts of domestic life, to many of the ignorant, slovenly, and slothful of both sexes.

7th. To render it a Seminary of manufactures.

climate, into this Institution; but to reserve its benefits for friendless, aged, and distressed persons, whose circumstances or condition would not permit them to resort elsewhere for relief. In the month of November, Mr. Ashmun stated that the Infirmary answered its design fully; that patients almost hopelessly afflicted, had there rapidly recovered; that about half of those then under its care, were in perfect health; and that the expense of the establishment was less than the original estimate.

The whole system of schools which had been suspended in its efficient operations, by the death of the Rev. Mr. Holton, was re-organized early in this year, on the Lancasterian plan, and placed under the general superintendence of the Rev. G. M'Gill, an intelligent and experienced coloured Teacher, from Baltimore. The schools were sufficiently numerous and ample to afford instruction to every child (including those of the natives) in the Colony, and all were obliged to attend them.* The expenses of these schools were defrayed in part out of surplus funds in the Colonial Treasury, and in part by an annual subscription by the Colonists of one thousand four hundred dollars, including the sum of three hundred dollars subscribed by the Colonial Agent to be paid out of such means as might be placed at his disposal. The native school under the direction of Messrs. Cary and Lewis, derived partial support from the Baptist Missionary Society of Richmond, "and 'the hopes of the African tribes," said Mr. Ashmun, "from 'Gallinas to Trade Town, are at present suspended upon it. 'Most of the boys who attend it, are sons of the principal in-

* The following is a list of the schools, with the number of scholars attached to each:

| | |
|---|---|
| Rev. Mr. Cary's school for native children, | 45 |
| Rev. Mr. M'Gill's classes, | 16 |
| Mr. Stewart's school, | 44 |
| Miss Jackson's do. | 40 |
| Mrs. Williams' do. | 30 |
| Mr. Prout's do. | 52 |

' dividuals of the country; and more than half can now read
' the New Testament intelligibly, and understand the English
' language nearly as well as the settlers of the same age.—
' The number of these interesting learners may be indefinite-
' ly increased, if means are supplied; and with the prospect
' of vast advantage, both to the native population of the coun-
' try and the Colony itself."

The method by which emigrants just arrived in Africa, could be most economically subsisted, and most beneficially aided in the commencement of their labours, had been to Mr. Ashmun long a subject of deep reflection. He now expressed distinctly his views upon it, to the Managers. In regard to subsistence, he reiterated the opinion, that to purchase African provisions with trade goods, (an assortment of which should always be in possession of the Colonial Agent) was incomparably the most economical course that could be adopted, and that the expense of such provisions adequate to the support of a company of settlers for six months after their arrival, might be fairly estimated, by the cost of their supplies, during their passage across the ocean. He was convinced that this mode of subsistence would be far more promotive of the health of the emigrants, than any other. In respect to further aid, he advised that all emigrants should be encouraged to bring with them mechanical tools and agricultural* implements, with cooking and domestic utensils; that such as had not these articles, should receive them from the Society; that all should be provided gratuitously, for a reasonable term, with comfortable houses; that every man should have assigned to him at once, his building lot and farm; and that the frugal and industrious should

---

* "When tools, &c. are bought for emigrants, they ought, if for mechanics, to be of course, those of their trades—otherwise, to consist almost wholly of *axes,* broad and narrow, a large supply;—*hoes,* tilling and grubbing;—picks, spades; saws, whip, crosscut, and hand; *files, trowels, drawing-knives,* and jack-fore-planes."—*Ashmun.*

derive such additional assistance, as might comport with the means of the Society and their own respective merits. Few, under these circumstances, it was believed, would long delay to fix themselves on their own premises, and be occupied with their own improvements. Those not settled on their lands, it was suggested, should, if mechanics, labour at their trades—if farmers, cultivate a public farm, and receive a reasonable compensation in provisions and clothing from the public store.

Individuals, while on the sick list, were to be subsisted and furnished with medical attendance at the public expense; but only, until so far recovered as to be able to contribute to their own support.

It was reported by Mr. Ashmun, as a fact well attested by experience in the Colony, that the aged were peculiarly liable to fall victims to the African climate. Under circumstances the most favourable, they could gain but little by removal to Africa; while the probability was great, that even should they survive the earliest impressions of the climate, the natural decay of age would be hastened rapidly to death.

Mr. Ashmun neglected no means of animating the Colonists with zeal and enterprise in the adoption and prosecution of plans of public utility. A company was formed this year, for the purpose of improving the navigation of Montserado river, stock subscribed to the amount of about one thousand dollars, and pledges given to raise the sum to four thousand, if necessary to effect the object.

The recaptured Africans had proved orderly, industrious, and useful. Familiarly acquainted with the ordinary modes of African agriculture, and comparatively insensible to the injurious influences of the climate, they had commenced their settlements with the fairest prospects of success.

Alluding to the probability that the U. States' Agency in the Colony, might be discontinued, or its importance extremely reduced, Mr. Ashmun expressed the hope, that as Cape

Montserado must become a sort of depot for American commerce in that quarter of the world, and a rendezvous for that portion of the U. States' Navy, which must in future (more than in time past) be employed along that coast, the Government might be persuaded to construct a strong fortress on the height of Thompson Town, (near the extremity of the Cape) or at least sustain and extend the battery already there erected. He declared his belief that an arrangement between the Government and the Society, by which the latter should agree, for a stipulated annual consideration, to accomplish the humane objects proposed by the former, in the establishment of an Agency in Liberia, would prove of great mutual advantage to the parties; that the money appropriated by the former, would be better applied, its work more economically executed, while all collision of different interests would be prevented, and the Colony derive strength from the entire unity of its members in their political responsibilities and character. The property of the United States, consisting principally of fortifications and public buildings, should, he thought, in case the Government should recall its Agent, be relinquished to the Colony. These buildings, he observes, were indeed constructed with the U. States' money. "But 'who furnished workmen and mechanics? Who the ground 'on which they stand? Who has protected and preserved 'them? Certainly the property of the United States in those 'erections is qualified, to say the least, by these and other 'considerations, and will be so admitted, I believe, by the 'Executive."

In the month of December, touched at the Colony, the United States ship of war Ontario, Captain Nicolson, on her return from the Mediterranean to the United States, and the friendly interest evinced in the affairs of the settlement by her commander, as well as a valuable donation of seeds, which he had taken special care to obtain in the Archipelago, Asia Minor, and at Tunis, are gratefully acknowledged by the

Colonial Agent. On his arrival in America, Captain Nicolson bore testimony to the general contentment and industry of the Colonists—the rapid progress made by them in public and private improvements, and to their salutary and growing influence over the native tribes.

On the same day, Mr. Ashmun welcomed to the Colony, the first of several Swiss Missionaries, who in consequence of his communication to the venerable Dr. Blumhardt, had consented, under instructions from the Basle Missionary Society, to devote their lives to the propagation of Christianity among the Africans.

The system of Government adopted in 1824, had continued without any material alterations, to fulfil the great purposes for which it was established. The annual election resulted in the re-appointment of most of the officers of the preceding year. The political year was commenced with every prospect of the vigorous and harmonious operation of the Government. "The principles of social order," said Mr. Ashmun, "of a good, equitable and efficient Government, are ' deeply and plentifully implanted in the minds of the *influ-* ' *ential* part, if not of a *majority*, of the Colonists; and ' promise the certain arrival—I do not think it will be early, ' however—when the Board can safely withdraw their ' Agents, and leave the people to govern themselves."

In his last communication to the Managers, during this year, Mr. Ashmun presented a comprehensive view of the state, progress, and prospects of the Colony. Dividing the settlers into four classes, he described the *first*, embracing nearly one-half of the whole population as settled in circumstances of independence, in comfortable dwellings on their own cultivated premises, and industriously occupied with mechanical or commercial pursuits: The *second*, as just placing themselves in their new, but in some cases, unfinished houses—clearing their lands, and though contending with difficulties in their efforts to sustain themselves and families, and occasionally desponding on account of the embarrassments and hardships of their condition; yet, with a prospect of attaining in the course of a few months, to an easy and respectable establishment: The *third*, as constituted of those less than a year in Africa, mostly in the public receptacles or rented houses, imperfectly inured to the climate, partially dependant upon the Society, beginning moderately to labour on wages for the older settlers, or in constructing their houses and preparing their lands for cultivation; and the *fourth*, as including all the idle and improvident, not entirely useless to the Colony, but securing no valuable interests for themselves.

The Colony was sustained in its growth, almost wholly by its own industry. It was a subject for regret, that the life of this industry was rather in its trade and commerce, than its agriculture. The country fertile, the products thereof various, rich and abundant, the prosperity induced by trade, obviously more fluctuating and precarious than that arising from agriculture, yet situated as were the Colonists, on the central part of an extensive coast, with a vast field of commercial enterprise opening before them—tempted to seek immediate gains, rather than remote, though surer and more important advantages, Mr. Ashmun expressed his belief, that for some time, at least, agriculture was destined to follow in the train of trade, and not to lead it. The former interest had been fostered and encouraged, in every possible way, by the Colonial Government. The premiums proposed by the Board to such as should engage most successfully in this employment, had proved, to some extent, beneficial. The farmers at Caldwell, had associated themselves into an Agricultural Society, at the weekly meetings of which, the members reported, individually, their progress on their plantations, discussed freely one or more practical questions, on which a vote was finally taken, and each question unanimously determined, recorded as a maxim in the practical agriculture of the settlement. The members were pledged to re-

duce these maxims to practice. Mr. Ashmun attended the meetings of this Society, and testified to its utility. "Many," he observes, "of the settlers at Caldwell, are actively employ-
' ed on their farms, this season; and there remains not a doubt,
' that the products of the Colony, the ensuing year, will equal
' its consumption, in every article except rice. I have led
' the way in a farm of eight acres—which, considering the
' richness of the soil—the perennial growth of every plant
' and crop—and the most prolific nature of vegetation in this
' country, is no contemptible piece of tillage."*

Four military cmopanies had been voluntarily organized and equipped by the Colonists, of whom, only about half a dozen were not enrolled to bear arms for the public defence.

Nearly the whole expense of the Colonial Government and the United States' Agency, had been defrayed by the profits realized in the trade of the Factories established by the Agent. A small schooner was constantly employed in conveying to these Factories articles for the barter traffic, and in bringing in return supplies of rice and other products of the coast. The nett profits amounted, during the year, to little short of five thousand dollars.

* The following list of animals and products then rearing in the Colony, and which Mr. Ashmun remarked, could not in future be wanting, unless through the inexcusable negligence or indolence of the settlers, may be of some interest to our readers:

Of *Animals*, Horses, Cattle in *abundance*, Sheep, Goats in *abundance*, *Asses* are lately introduced, Fowls, Ducks, Geese, Guinea Fowls, Swine *numerous*—Fish nowhere found in greater quantities. *Fruits* are *Plantains, Bananas*, in endless abundance, *Limes, Lemons, Tamarinds, Oranges, Sousop, Cashew, Mangoe*, 20 varieties of the *Prune, Guava, Papaw, Pine Apple, Grape*, tropical *Peach and Cherry.*—Vegetables are *Sweet Potatoe, Cassada, Yams, Cocoa, Ground-nuts, Arrow-root, Egg-plant, Ocre, every variety of Beans*, and *most sorts of Peas, Cucumbers and Pumpkins*. Grains are *Rice*, the staple—*Indian Corn*, Coffee excellent and abundant—Pepper of three varieties, of which each is equal to Cayenne—Millet and Guinea Corn—Cotton, staple good, but not yet cultivated. To these may be added Indigo, which, it is thought, may be raised to advantage, and the Sugar-Cane, which may, and doubtless will, ultimately receive attention.

Important accessions had been made, during the year, to the Colonial Territory.

The chiefs of Cape Mount (with whom negotiations had been commenced the preceding year) had stipulated to construct a large and commodious Factory for the Colonial Government; to guaranty the safety of all persons and property belonging to the Factory; to exact no tribute from those who might resort to it; to encourage trade between it and the interior; and forever to exclude foreigners from similar privileges, and from any right of occupancy or possession in their country.

The right bank of Bushrod Island, extending the whole length of Stockton Creek, (which unites the Montserado and St. Paul's) had been ceded to the Society. This Island contains twenty thousand acres of fertile, level land, promising greatly to enrich the agricultural interest of the Colony.

An invaluable tract of land, of indefinite extent, on the north side of the river St. John's, contiguous to Factory Island, had also been added to the possessions of the Society. Factories had been erected on the Island, and on both branches of the river, "and they form," said Mr. Ashmun, "new links 'of union between the tribes along the St. John's and your 'Colony." "The interests of both and all," he continues, " are, I trust, at no great distance of time, to become perfect-'ly identical, and one numerous and Christian nation, using 'our language and enjoying our institutions, to cover the 'whole western coast of Africa."

At no less than EIGHT STATIONS, on the line of coast from Cape Mount to Trade Town, had the Colonial Government obtained the right of founding settlements; and over this entire line of coast, extended the influence and partial jurisdiction of the Colony.

It was a part of the plan of Mr. Ashmun, (a plan thus far carried into effect) to cultivate a farm or farms, at each of the Colonial Factories, in the belief, that it would prove mutually advantageous to the Colonists and the people of the country. He expressed a deep sense of the importance of founding schools for the native youth and children of the respective tribes in which the Colonial establishments were situated. "Whether," he remarks, "we regard such schools 'as a cheap means of extending the power of the Colony—'as the most effectual instruments of civilizing the continent '—as a noble exercise of Christian philanthropy, or the best 'expression of Christian piety, (and the object, I think, is sus-'ceptible of each of these views) no work connected with the 'rearing of the Colony, is, in my opinion, more desirable. I 'think it nearly capable of moral demonstration, that the *African tribes may be civilized without expulsion from their chosen settlements and villages, and without that fearful diminution of their population, which has, from causes that do not exist here, as in regard to the Indians of America, accompanied the march of civilization in that hemisphere.*"

A citizen of the Colony, during this year, penetrated into the interior to the distance of one hundred and forty miles, where he discovered a numerous population, industrious and intelligent, possessed of a written language, with some knowledge of the useful arts, of a productive agriculture, and sharing largely in the comforts and social enjoyments of life. To open and maintain a friendly intercourse with these people, was an object of much solicitude to the Colonial Agent.

That the chiefs between Cape Mount and Trade Town, had bound themselves to exclude all others, except the people of Liberia, from a settlement in their country; that they were anxiously seeking an education for their sons in the Colony; that they were universally at peace with its inhabitants; and that when a robbery had been committed by a few lawless individuals on a company of the Bassa people under the protection of the Agent, more than one thousand native men were marched under arms, to place themselves, at his command, were facts, demonstrative of the powerful influence acquired over rude minds by a policy, in which truth was blended with meekness, and justice with humanity.*

To what, under Providence, above all things else, is the extraordinary success of the infant Colony of Liberia to be attributed? What, that principle, animating a feeble company of illiterate and hitherto obscure, if not oppressed men, on the borders of a remote and savage land, in sickness, and want, and peril, to manifest a degree of patience, and fortitude, and valour, not unworthy of the educated and the honoured of the most enlightened age and nation? What, that power, which enabled such men to rise above all the misfortunes of life, and all the terrors of death, that they might bequeath to their posterity and their race, certainly, a worthy example, possibly, the unmeasurable blessings of freedom and Christianity? It was the spirit, the power of true Religion. They lived under the influence of the world to come. Their faith and hope were alike in God. More concerned to secure the rewards of another life, than to escape the afflictions of

---

* In December, Mr. Ashmun spent several days in attendance on a Council of the Dey chiefs. They complained much of the influence of the Colony in diminishing the slave trade, and resolved to raise the price of their wood and rice, about one hundred per cent., making many insinuations against the Colonists. These were promptly met by a statement of facts, on the part of the Agent, which left the sensible among them, nothing to say; as well as by an immediate regulation on the part of the Colony, inflicting a heavy fine on any member thereof, who should pay them more than the usual prices for their produce. On the 15th of this month, eight of these Chiefs and about fifty of their people, dined with the Colonial Agent, who ordered a bullock dressed for the occasion. "Very little rum," says Mr. Ashmun, "was used, which I gave them particularly to understand, was withheld by design; that a regard for their own good and that of their countrymen and subjects, had determined the Fathers of the Colony very sparingly indeed to dispense to them this secret poison—a precaution which their own good sense must tell them, deserved their gratitude, and must prove to them how different were the characters of those gentlemen, from that of the mercenary foreigners, who to serve their own selfish ends, never hesitated to drown the reason of half the country, with puncheons of rum, and take advantage of their intoxication to carry off their people by hundreds."

this, they found a remedy for the one, in the anticipations of the other.

At the time of which we write, few, if any villages, in our own country, exhibited less to offend, or more to gratify, the eye of a Christian, than the village of Monrovia. The general order and sobriety, the universal respect for the Sabbath, and the various Institutions and duties of Christianity, struck the natives with surprise, and excited the admiration of foreigners.*

* The following sentences are extracted from a valuable article in the Amulet for 1832, ascribed to a distinguished British Officer, who had been three years on the African coast:

"Nothing has tended more to suppress the slave trade in this quarter, than the constant intercourse and communication of the natives with these industrious colonists. The American Agent, Mr. Ashmun, took every opportunity and means in his power, to extinguish a traffic so injurious in every way to the fair trader; and at Cape Montserado good and correct information was always to be obtained of any slave vessels on the coast within the communication or influence of the Colony. This active, respectable, and intelligent man, is since dead, but his spirit still actuates all his people. They have several large boats and small decked vessels belonging to their community, and others in progress of building. These are actively employed in trading along the coast, and in keeping up the intercourse with Caldwell and the interior.

"The character of these industrious colonists is exceedingly correct and moral, their minds strongly impressed with religious feelings, their manners serious and decorous, and their domestic habits remarkably neat and comfortable. * * Their houses are well built, ornamented with gardens and other pleasing decorations, and in the inside are remarkably clean—the walls well white-washed, and the rooms neatly furnished. They are very hospitable to strangers, and many English naval officers on the station have been invited to dine with them, and joined in their meals, which were wholesome and good. The man of the house regularly said grace, both before and after meat, with much solemnity, in which he was joined by the rest of his family with great seeming sincerity. They all speak good English, as their native language, and without any defect of pronunciation. They are well supplied with books, particularly Bibles and liturgies. They have pastors of their own colour, and meeting-houses in which divine service is well and regularly performed every Sunday, and they have four schools at Montserado, and three at Caldwell.— By one ship alone they received five hundred volumes, presented by Dartmouth College, and several boxes and packets of school-books, sent by friends at Boston.

"How it is," remarks Mr. Ashmun, "in other parts of the world, I have only heard and read. But in this Colony I 'have seen the direct and inseparable connection of Christi-'anity, taking in its doctrines, its worship, and its practical 'fruits—with all that is mentally and morally improving, 'all that is exalting to human nature—in a word, with all 'that is good and excellent among us.

"There is no room for speculation on this point, no room 'for reasoning. Premises and conclusion are both embodied 'in one and the same obvious fact. There is a pious family— 'and there stands a firm pillar of the Colony. Industry, in-'telligence, order, competency, and peace, are its character-'istics. There is a family without religion; I have only to 'reverse the characteristics of the first, and that family is 'described."

An address, transmitted by the citizens of Monrovia, in the summer of this year, to the coloured people of the U. States, was happily adapted by its facts, argument, and eloquence, to create strong confidence in the wisdom of the enterprise in which they had engaged. They declared that in removing to Africa, they had sought for civil and religious liberty, and that their expectations and hopes in this respect had been realized. The great mortality which had occurred in the earliest years of the Colony, they attributed principally to the dangers, irregularities, privations, discouragements, and want of medical experience, which are almost necessarily attendant on the plantation of new

"The complete success of this colony is a proof that negroes are by proper care and attention, as susceptible of the habits of industry and improvements of social life as any other race of human beings; and that the melioration of the condition of the black people on the coast of Africa, by means of such colonies, is not chimerical. Wherever the influence of this colony extends, the slave trade has been abandoned by the natives, and the peaceful pursuits of legitimate commerce established in its place. * * A few colonies of this kind, scattered along the coast, would be of infinite value in improving the natives."

settlements in a distant, uncleared and barbarous country. After a few months' residence in Africa, they enjoyed health as uniformly and in as perfect a degree as in their native country. They believed that a more fertile soil than that of Liberia, and a more productive country, so far as it is cultivated, did not exist on the face of the earth. The virtuous and industrious were nearly sure to attain there, in a few years, to a style of comfortable living, which they might in vain hope for, in the United States. "Truly we" (it is their own language) "have a goodly heritage; and if there is any thing lacking in the character or condition of the people of this Colony, it never can be charged to the account of the country: it must be the fruit of our own mismanagement or slothfulness, or vices. But from these evils we confide in Him, to whom we are indebted for all our blessings, to preserve us. It is the topic of our weekly and daily thanksgiving to Almighty God, both in public and in private, and he knows with what sincerity,—that we were ever conducted by his Providence to this shore. Such great favours in so short a time, and mixed with so few trials, are to be ascribed to nothing but his special blessing. This we acknowledge. We only want the gratitude which such signal favours call for. Nor are we willing to close this paper without adding a heartfelt testimonial of the deep obligations we owe to our American patrons—and best earthly benefactors; whose wisdom pointed us to this home of our nation; and whose active and persevering benevolence enabled us to reach it.—Judge, then, of the feelings with which we hear the motives and the doings of the Colonization Society traduced—and that, too, by men too ignorant to know what that Society has accomplished; too weak to look through its plans and intentions; or too dishonest to acknowledge either. But, without pretending to any prophetic sagacity, we can certainly predict to that Society, the ultimate triumph of their hopes and labours; and disappointment and defeat to all who oppose them. Men may theorize, and speculate about their plans in America, but there can be no speculation here. The cheerful abodes of civilization and happiness which are scattered over this verdant mountain—the flourishing settlements which are spreading around it—the sound of Christian instruction, and scenes of Christian worship, which are heard and seen in this land of brooding pagan darkness—a thourand contented freemen united in founding a new Christian empire, happy themselves, and the instruments of happiness to others: every object, every individual, is an argument, is demonstration, of the wisdom and the goodness of the plan of Colonization.

"Where is the argument that shall refute facts like these?—And where is the man hardy enough to deny them?"

Mr. Ashmun was accustomed to write upon those practical subjects which claimed his attention. He has left a great variety of papers containing his reflections on the affairs and interests of the Colony. There is one, penned near the close of this year, specifying some of the objects to be promoted during his contemplated visit to the United States, and the rules for his own conduct in his endeavours to accomplish them. These objects related both to the Colony and to his own personal duties and improvement.

To obtain the establishment of a packet to run, at least thrice a year, from the Chesapeake to Liberia—a Superintendent of schools—a female Teacher—(if possible from the south) and a Printer, were among the objects deemed principal in importance. Of the rules adopted for his own conduct in matters of business, we copy the following:

"Attempt to carry no point not worthy of my utmost zeal
' and exertion.

"Never press a measure till those with whom I would car-
' ry it, are sufficiently enlightened as to its nature and neces-
' sity.

"Let the grounds of every measure be perfectly ascertained
' to my own mind.

"Have never more than one, at most two measures, on
' the carpet at one time, unless there is such a connexion
' between them, that they shall mutually support each other.

"My time is short. Waste not a moment. Let my zeal
' glow in every feature. It will open a speedy way for me
' through every other man's engagements, indolence and dis-
' affection.

"Do thoroughly every thing I undertake.

"Avoid every thing personal, especially all such personali-
' ties as have the most distant relation to myself.

"Mix none of the trifles of the day, with serious business.

"Cultivate, as the best means of succeeding in business, an
' unaffected, but exact politeness.

"Too great punctuality with myself or others, cannot be
' observed.

"Too great modesty of deportment or language, cannot be
' shown.

"In doing business, the great key to success, is to aim only
' at effects—the effects produced are the only measure of
' success."

Under a calm and meek aspect and demeanor, there was in Ashmun an ever burning desire for intellectual and moral improvement; a restless spirit of activity not to be satisfied, but with the boundless and the Eternal. It is true he had moments of peace, but only as he communed with hope, and felt conscious of sympathies and affections uniting him to the invisible world. That melancholy thoughts sometimes darkened the light of his soul, is certain. These might be traced to his constitutional temperament—to the extinction of his earliest and most precious hopes of worldly happiness, and to a deep sense of deficiency in those religious attainments which both reason and faith had taught him to seek as the paramount and imperishable good of his nature.

Minds capable of high excitement, are generally subject to occasional depression; that sensibility, which is productive of great happiness, becomes not unfrequently, an inlet to misery.

Nor can we doubt, that the deep fountains of the heart were mingled with private sorrow; that those gentle affections which once had gathered in homage around an object now lost to him forever, were cast in bitter grief upon her image in memory enshrined, like withered flowers upon the lifeless form of beauty and of worth.

Those who have witnessed the funeral of their own hopes, can best appreciate the fortitude which gains strength by suffering; and the resolution that enables its possessor to triumph over his own weakness, while by public virtues he wins public honours, and builds up, even amid the mouldering ruins of his own expectations, the fortunes of mankind.

He, who, as he has less reason to live for himself, lives the more for others, finds a compensation for all his losses in his benevolence, and turns his private evils to the public good.

> "By those that deepest feel, is ill exprest
> The indistinctness of the suffering breast,
> Where thousand thoughts begin, to end in one
> Which seeks from all, the refuge found in none."

Yet the melancholy thoughts of Ashmun *did* find a refuge in that which has been called the "Sabbath and the port of all man's labours and peregrinations." Religion opened before him scenes of peace and felicity, more sweet and charming than the fabled regions, to which Æneas was conducted through the land of shades and of death, the

> ————————locos laetos et amoena vireta
> Fortunatorum nemorum, sedesque beatas
> Largior hic campos æther et lumine vestit
> Purpureo: Solemque suum sua sidera norunt.

"His ardent spirit could not satisfy itself with things seen, though gilded with all the glories of intellect and imagination; it soared away in search of other lands, looking with unutterable desire for some surer and brighter home beyond the horizon of this world."*

As he approached his eternal home, not dimly, nor doubtfully revealed, his love for its objects became more intense; but as his faith acquired vigour, and his hopes rose, he descended in humility.

This last virtue shone forth from amidst the others which adorned him, like a retiring beauty, the more observed as she would escape observation; admired, because unconscious of any claim to praise. How, in the judgment of Ashmun, did all human excellence sink, in comparison of that surpassing moral beauty, once only seen among men, in the person of their Redeemer; that in despair of themselves, they might trust in the Divine mercy, and aspire through His power and grace to a victory over death, and to a sinless immortality in that new heaven and new earth, wherein dwelleth righteousness.

It will be seen by the following extracts from Mr. Ashmun's private Journal, that he entertained a very humble opinion even at this period, of his advancement in the religious life:

"I pray for more strength—more light—more grace—more
' of the spirit of holiness. When I look at my life, my heart,
' I despair; when to the greatness of God the Father's mer-
' cy, and the infinite merits of His Son's atonement, I hope:
' and occasionally Christ appears a greater Redeemer than I
' a sinner. But if I know my own heart, there is not, on earth,
' there never was a child of God in the comparison of my-
' self with whom, I do not feel ashamed. But I still have
' hope: and look forward to that God, whose gift if I have
' grace, that grace is to perfect his own work, and glorify
' himself in and by me.

"Wednesday 4th—Thursday 5th—Friday 6th—Saturday
' 7th—Sunday 8th—Monday 9th—Tuesday 10th July, were
' days of distressing and dangerous illness. Perhaps my bodily

* Schiller's Life.

'sufferings were never greater. But my mind was commonly
'kept in peace—some murmers, and more impatience; but
'God be praised for the measure of grace He did give me.—
'I resolved (and I believe His spirit moved, and will enable
'me to accomplish the resolution,) to live more to the glory of
'God—to bear my cross—and sell all my earthly wealth for
'the pearl of heavenly value. My feelings were not rapture
'—they were not triumph—but they were deep, peaceful,
'confiding and penitent; blessed be God the Holy Ghost.—
'I often wandered, through the force of my most painful dis-
'order—but found my spirit in every lucid interval, still
'trembling back to its celestial polar star. I have ventured
'to set down so much—too much, were nothing but my poor
'self concerned in these imperfect exercises of a renovated
'mind. Let the record, then, remind me, as often as I read
'it, of the infinite grace of God, which chose such a mean
'and venomous worm to operate in such sort, upon:—and
'it will never inflate my pride, but shame it.

"Sunday, August 12.

"God is pleased to cause His face to shine upon me, and
'be gracious. I read His Word with some pleasure and pro-
'fit—am strengthened, and assisted in, and moved to, my
'duties. Crosses are light—and His grace (for to Him I as-
'cribe all) disposes me to embrace them, and to deny myself.
'But there is always at hand a dark reverse of all that is right,
'dutiful and holy, in the inbred corruptions, and practical de-
'fects which I feel, and mourn, and detest in myself. When
'I refer to the work of God's grace, in and for me, no lan-
'guage can celebrate it sufficiently, or express my wonder
'and joy: When I advert to myself, no language can equal
'the sense I have of my guilt, and of the worthlessness of my
'character. I even suffer in comparison with the worst of
'my fellow-men. Captain C. in a scurrilous letter he sent
'me in the Pongas, called me a 'liar.' I was less indignant
'at him, than smitten with the justice of the reproach; and
'applied to myself—'if when ye do evil, and suffer for it, ye

' take it patiently, what thanks have ye?' But, liar, my own
' conscience testifies, I do not wish, or intend to be. O Lord,
' for humility to cover and be worn by me, like a garment, all
' the days of my life! *Cure me, holy God, of my propen-*
' *sity to backbite and slander thy creatures, whose judg-*
' *ment is with Thee.* 'Tis my fault—and a besetting one.

"Overrule and conquer my habit of 'idle speaking.'—I
' adopt the language (with greater reason) of my dear depart-
' ed Brother F.—'Not one in ten thousand of my words has
' been right.'

"I read Owen with great pleasure, and find him evangeli-
' cal and spiritual, far beyond expectation. One trait of his
' writings is particularly pleasing—the fullness with which
' he constantly insists on the necessity of the illuminating and
' sanctifying inspirations of the Divine Spirit to understand
' and relish the doctrine of Christ—and the believer's privi-
' lege to enjoy direct communion with the great God, through
' His Son Jesus Christ. I know not how I came by the pre-
' judice, but it has long kept me from entering on the peru-
' sal of his works, that Owen was rather a verbal critic, and
' polemic, than an evangelical, discriminating, practical
' Divine, of too sound and sanctified a judgment, to trifle
' with the word of God, by descending to tedious and unpro-
' fitable refinements. But thanks be to God, for so rich a
' treasure of scriptural instruction as I find in these writings."

The following letter was addressed to his friend, the Rev.
William Hawley, of Washington City:

"CALDWELL, *March* 11, 1827.

"*Rev. and Dear Sir:*—It is Sunday—and one of the
' last I expect, for some months at least, to spend on this
' coast—but lately making a part of the region of the sha-
' dow of death—and even now an extreme outskirt of the
' Christian world. I have a direct conveyance for a letter home
' —and both the occasion and my feelings urge me to write.
' I have, during my long residence in this country, had few
' correspondents of a truly Christian character, and even

' with them, have not cultivated what deserves to be named
' a Christian correspondence. And I have been a great suf-
' ferer by it, in that interest which I, in common with my
' friends, have in the great salvation of the Son of
' God. Silence and concealment, I grant, may expose a
' Christian less to the danger of a feeling of self-important
' vanity, and that odious egotism which is the attendant and
' mark of the worst sort of hypocrisy, than the ostentation
' of zeal and a forward profession. But they may be carried
' too far and proceeding at first from unaffected modesty,
' come at last to arise from a real want of zeal and devotion
' in the cause of God. And there are times in which, and
' persons to whom, every decided Christian may and ought
' to signify the inward and true state of his mind, in regard
' to the great warfare carrying on between Christ and his ene-
' mies. Is it enough that a believer enrol his name once in
' his life in the books of some Christian congregation—and
' so he spends a tolerably correct and moral life, and attend
' in common with the throng of Christian professors to the
' external offices of religion, imagine that he has answered
' to God and his church, and to his own soul, the great ends
' of his high vocation? I cannot so satisfy my conscience,
' however my life may have disagreed with its dictates. And
' in unbosoming myself with some degree of freedom, to one
' whom I know not to be disposed to judge uncharitably of
' the motives of others, I have my own advantage chiefly in
' view—and some slight desires to honour the God of all my
' mercies. Yes, my Dear Sir, as the ancient saints superadd-
' ed to the name of their adorable Jehovah certain titles sug-
' gested by His providential dispensations towards themselves,
' I would thankfully and devoutly record His name as the
' *God of all my mercies.* It was a dispensation of His mer-
' cy which sent me to Africa. Of this I am more sensible
' than any other can be. And all computation fails, creduli-
' ty and faith itself are confounded in tracing out the good-
' ness and mercy which have followed me through all the ma-

'zes of sufferings, labours, perils, sins, follies, and infirmities
'in which my course has subsequently laid. The greatest of
'all is, that I am not abandoned to utter insensibility and im-
'penitence—that I am not without an honest wish to spend
every moment of every future day of my life, in His service
'and obedience—that I do detest my former sins, and present
'sinfulness, as far as I can discover them—and pray for still
'more extensive and more humbling discoveries of my cor-
'ruptions. If you knew, my Dear Sir, how much I have
'lived under the influence of sinful and inordinate passions,
'and how deeply drunk into the spirit of this world, since I
'came to Africa, you would think the strain, a bold one for
'me to use. Perhaps it is imprudently so. Indeed, I should
'be unwilling to say as much to the members of my own fam-
'ily, here. But God is my witness that I am sincere in what
'I write you. I have these feelings, and pray and labour,
'that they may remain, and increase, and overcome all the
'workings of sin in my heart. But I am a mere child, and
'an exceedingly dull, perverse, and unhopeful one, in all
'that concerns practical godliness. My weakness and igno-
'rance, in all that concerns the work of my salvation, and
'desperate hardihood in the contempt of Christ's com-
'mands, when for a little left to myself, no created being
'knows. But I have not a thought to retire from the great
'conflict, 'till the Spirit of God and the power of Christ, have
'given me the victory over all. It is my unspeakable conso-
'lation, that there is no besetment—be it pride, or lust, or sloth,
'or envy, or fear of man, or spiritual cowardice,—which the
'grace of God, sought by prayer in Christ's name, cannot de-
'liver the soul from. This has been the theme of my medi-
'tation, and a source of great encouragement to me this
'morning. Where sin abounds, O that desponding believ-
'ers might all see that grace much more abounds, and that
'God, when He devised a salvation for sinners, adapted it to
'the whole extent of their spiritual maladies and dangers. I

'hope to make it a chief part of my errand home to derive a
'little strength from God's blessing on the intercourse of my
'Christian friends. I shall come like a famished wanderer,
'as I am in more senses than one, from the fold of Christ.—
'Pray that it may be with a teachable and humble spirit: For
'God resists the proud, and *gives grace* only to the humble.
'If any have injured me, I forgive and forget it, recollecting
'how much I am myself obliged to be forgiven by our com-
'mon Master. If I have injured others, it is equally my prayer
'that God and they may forgive me. My Dear Sir, to live
'for eternity, and for Christ, we shall soon find to be our true
'wisdom, and I trust are both old enough to know it to be the
'only life worth the troubles and labours of mortality. That
'we may so live, and mutually aid each other by our exam-
'ple and our prayers, to the glory of our common Lord, and
'the eternal advantage of the numerous immortals under our
'influence, is the sincere prayer of your friend and servant,.

"J. ASHMUN."

## CHAPTER XVII.

"They shall never perish," were the memorable words of the Son of God speaking of the final destiny of His faithful disciples. The subject of our Memoir, is soon to prove the value of this promise, for he has passed the threshold of that year in which he must die.

On the 15th of January, 1828, arrived at Liberia, the brig Doris, after a passage of sixty-one days from Baltimore, with one hundred and seven emigrants, principally from Maryland, sixty-two of them liberated slaves; on the 17th of the same month, the schooner Randolph from South Carolina, with twenty-six Africans, manumitted by a single individual; and on the 19th of February, fifty-four days from Hampton Roads, the brig Nautilus, with one hundred and sixty-four emigrants, mostly from the lower counties of North Carolina.

Early in January, Mr. Ashmun made a fatiguing visit of inspection, to the Factories south of Monrovia, and returning on the 17th, found the commanders of several vessels waiting to settle concerns of business, and hasten their departure.—

The Doris came to anchor the same evening. This was the sixth vessel—the affairs of which demanded consideration. "Such an accumulation of labour," he observes, "I never felt 'pressing on me before. Days and nights were too short.— 'But I despatched previous to the 25th, *three* of the vessels, 'when another arrived from Sierra Leone, with special 'claims on my attention." A piratical and strongly armed Spanish vessel now menaced the settlement with an attack at night, and until a late hour, Mr. Ashmun exposed himself in arduous efforts for its defence. Immediately after, on the receipt of a proposal from the Dey chiefs on the St. Paul's, for opening a way for trade into the interior, on condition of the establishment of a settlement at the head of navigation, on that river, he visited all the intermediate kings on both sides of the river, and was occupied for three days and nights in negotiations, terminating in the conclusion that a number of the Colonists should occupy, without delay, the beautiful tract of country now bearing the honoured names of Mills and Burgess. For the four next successive days he was engaged in a difficult judicial investigation. The duty of assigning, to the company of emigrants just arrived, their lands was then discharged, followed immediately by a laborious session of the Court, for two days. Even after he felt his strength sinking, his exertions were unremitted, until seized by a raging fever on the 5th of February, under the power of which, up to the 21st of that month, he was (to use his own words) "tossing on the brink of eternity." The daily intervals of reason with which, subsequently, he was favoured, were employed in giving instructions to those who were entrusted, during his illness, with the general management of affairs.

To add to his distress, the emigrants by the Doris were heavily afflicted; the season was unhealthy, their passage had been nearly twice the usual length, and in the case of twenty-four from Maryland, the disease baffled all the medical skill existing in the Colony.*

On the 25th of February, he was able to write to the Board and state the circumstances of the new-comers and his own situation. "For the last four days," he remarks, " my strength has returned almost as rapidly as it went. But 'I hope the event will advertise the Board, that the constitu- ' tion of their Agent, here, is not to be depended on—and ' that a most probable item of intelligence may very shortly ' be, that he too, is numbered with the departed. May pro- ' vision be made accordingly. For myself, alone, the event ' has no appalling features—but to leave the Colony—to quit ' a field of labour forever, in which so little is yet done and so ' much ought to be done—here, I fear, will be the distressing ' pang of dying. But the Colony depends, I am persuaded, ' on the life of no one or ten individuals; and it is a vanity, ' I do not indulge, that it has any such dependence on my ' own. But it is a field of labour, in which, if better work- ' men are not employed, I wish to be myself, so long as, with ' the Divine blessing, I can do any good."

Though his weakness would have exempted him, in the opinion of all except himself, from the obligations of official duty, he failed not to express to the Managers, his thoughts on one or two points of essential concern to the Colony. He insisted that for at least two years to come, a more discriminating selection of settlers must be made, than ever had been, even in the earliest expeditions, or the prosperity of the Colony must inevitably and rapidly decline.†

* The emigrants by the Randolph and Nautilus, suffered slightly. Of the one hundred and seven by the Doris, twenty-four died, all from the north of the Potomac. "Draw a line due east and west," said Mr. Ashmun, "across Elk Ridge, Maryland, and not a death has invaded the people from the south of it."

† He was of opinion that, at the end of that time, (to use his own words) "a healthy proportion of working and idle people, would be found there," and that the coloured population *taken up just as they are*, might be introduced, and, under good management, *not be found to be a burthen.*

On the 25th of March, having received a written opinion from his Physician, that his return to the United States offered the only hope of his recovery, escorted by the military, and accompanied by a large majority of the inhabitants of Monrovia in tears, to whom he spoke affectionately, but briefly, he went on board the brig Doris, and with the feelings which seek despairingly for expression, through the eyes of the dying, in their last, fixed look upon an object which the heart holds fast to its last moment, left Africa forever.*

During a passage of forty-seven days to St. Bartholemews, in the West Indies, his sufferings were nearly indescribable, and for two weeks he indulged but a faint hope, of ever again seeing land.

Again he observes: "if rice grew spontaneously, and covered the country, yet it is possible by sending few or none able to reap and clean it, to starve ten thousand helpless children and infirm old people in the midst of so much plenty. Rice does not grow spontaneously, however; nor can any thing necessary for the subsistence of the human species, be procured here without the sweat of the brow. Clothing, tools, and building materials, are much dearer here than in America. But send out your emigrants, laborious men and their families only—or laborious men and their families, accompanied with only their natural proportion of inefficients; and with the ordinary blessing of God, you may depend on their causing you a light expense in Liberia, and fixing themselves speedily and easily in comfortable and independent circumstances. I further think I may safely say, that in no new country in the world, would they be likely to meet with so many advantages, and find it so easy to get in a way of comfortable living, by their own moderate industry."

"I know that nothing is effectually done, in colonizing this country, till the Colony's own resources can sustain its own and a considerable annual increase of population. To this point, it has been my great anxiety to bring it; and adopting and persisting in the course I have recommended, I am certain the Board will see it soon reach this point."

* "Never, I suppose, were greater tokens of respect shown by any community on taking leave of their head. Nearly the whole (at least two-thirds) of the inhabitants of Monrovia, men, women and children, were out on this occasion, and nearly all parted from him in tears, and, in my opinion, the hope of his return in a few months, alone enabled them to give him up. He is indeed dear to this people, and it will be a joyful day when we are permitted again to see him. He has left a written address containing valuable admonitions to officers, civil, military and religious."—L. CARY.

On the 10th of May, the day after his arrival at that Island, he wrote to the Board: "I am now in the hands 'of a Physician of the Island, who has the reputation of being 'skilful—and with whom it will be necessary for me to remain—I hope not many days—but God knows, and I am 'submissive. I was enabled to arrange the concerns of the 'Colony with Mr. Cary, even to the minutest particulars; and 'I have the greatest confidence that his administration will 'prove satisfactory, in a high degree, to the Board and advantageous to the Colony."*

It was soon decided, that to proceed home in the Doris, would, in all probability, either hasten his complicated maladies to a fatal termination, or render them incurable.

He saw the Doris sail without him, and with quiet resignation to the Divine will, awaited the consequences of a mild and gradual course (the only one his system could endure) of medical treatment.

For a few days, his spirits revived; he wrote to the Society, and to the Secretary of the Navy, on matters of business, and derived pleasure from intercourse with a few intelligent individuals kindly solicitous to relieve his sufferings, as well as from the refreshing and delightful scenery of

* Mr. Ashmun's instructions to Mr. Cary are very full and interesting.—"The first grand object," he remarks, "for the next six months, doubtless is, to see every man and every working family now in charge, placed on their lands, and supported no longer, even in part, at the public expense.

"To effect this object, they must be furnished with a few simple tools—to pay for them if they can—if not, to receive them gratuitously. Their allowance must be withheld if they neglect or negligently follow the improvement of their lands, and the building of their houses. Much may be done, by visiting the people separately, getting at their intentions and circumstances, and spurring, advising, or reproving as they may require. I am persuaded it will be useful, and in most instances possible to get, at least all the men out of the public receptacles, and on their lands, before the rains set in." He then gives very particular instructions in regard to the *buildings belonging to the U. States —buildings belonging to the Colony—the arms and armament, water craft, farm and public garden; printing establishment, forts, public servants, Millsburg settlement, finances, &c. &c.*

the Island. From this place, on the 12th of May, he addressed the following letter to his parents:—

"*My Dear Parents:*—I am so far on my return towards
' the United States—and fifty days—a very long passage from
' Liberia. I left there March 25th, compelled, I am sorry to
' say, by bad health—having suffered from a severe fever in
' February such a loss of strength, and derangement of the
' system, as my Physician said could not be repaired without
' a change of climate. I am yet quite low—but in the hands
' of a good Physician, and at the house of a kind and affec-
' tionate American lady—who more than most women, re-
' minds me of my own mother. I have, too, my own boy
' Cecil along, and assure you, I could no where be better at-
' tended or nursed. I am, besides, attended, I gratefully trust,
' by the great Comforter, whose presence is health and life to
' the soul, let the body sicken, suffer, and even die. Pray for
' me, but give yourselves no needless anxiety. I *may* recov-
' er and be in Champlain before the end of July. My Doctor
' says my case must yield to his medicines. True, it is more
' than he knows, but I cannot contradict, and partially be-
' lieve him. I cannot walk much. But I keep up most of
' my time, and since I came on shore, have suffered little pain.
' Remember me to the family and my former acquaintances,
' and the blessed Redeemer remember us all.
    Your dutiful Son,
          "J. ASHMUN."

He commenced a Journal of his observations, which comprises many facts in regard to the Government, commerce, productions and agriculture of this portion of the W. Indies.

He soon proceeded from St. Bartholemews to Basseterre in the Island of St. Christophers, but suffered from the fatigue and exposure of the passage, which though of less than twenty-four hours, was accomplished partly by land and in the night.

For a day or two he was extremely low; but on the 6th of

June, he was able to write to a lady (herself an invalid) in St. Bartholemews, in whose family he had received the kindest attention: "I have enjoyed," he remarks, "a most pleasant 'season in this delightful Island, and am pleased to state that 'my health seems to be very constantly but very slowly im- 'proving. I have often thought that if Mrs. Doyle were with 'me, in some of my morning and evening rides, it might, 'with God's blessing, be the same with her.

"I am delighted to find the people of this Island, kind and 'attentive; but nothing can exceed the kindness and attention 'I have received in your family—to which I shall always 'attribute, in a great measure, the recovery of my health, 'should it please God to restore it."

He gives in a few notes, on St. Christophers, a general view of its population, commerce, agriculture and religion. The condition of the slaves was investigated, and he accounts for the decrease of their numbers by their being overworked, scantily fed and badly lodged. "Slaves," he observes, "are 'treated well here, comparatively. But scarcely any where 'on earth, do they fare as well as free labourers; and there 'is something so unnatural in compulsory labour, that even 'a light daily task imposed by force, weighs down the strength 'and spirits more, and is truly a greater hardship, than four 'times the same task voluntarily performed."

On the 9th of June, he informed the Society of his increased illness, and that but for the attention of kind friends, raised up by the goodness of Providence for his relief, he should probably before that time, have sunk under their weight. He adds:

"Resigning my individual self and interest to the disposal 'of the same Divine goodness, I earnestly beg that the Go- 'vernment of the Colony may immediately, and permanent- 'ly, be provided for. In the choice of a successor, it is im- 'possible for me to express my anxiety, that wisdom from on 'high, may inspire and direct the counsels of the Board.—

' Accept, my Dear Sir, for yourself, and convey to all the
' members of the Board, this fresh, and sincerest assurance
' of the highest personal esteem and affection, and of the en-
' tire satisfaction, with which, I at this moment contemplate
' the best part of an active life spent in their service."

He found among strangers the kindness of friends, and by their attentions and good medical advice, he was so far strengthened as to take passage for New Haven on the 16th of July, at which port he arrived, after a long passage, on the 10th of August. The following prayer, found in his pocket-book, was probably composed about this time. It is marked number one, and was designed, doubtless, to be the first of a series of humble confessions and supplications to the great Father of life and mercies, to whom only, he now felt that he could look for help, and in whom alone, in the extremity of nature, find refuge for his soul:

### Prayer against hardness of Heart and Unbelief.

"O heart-searching and rein-trying God, who requirest
' truth in the inward parts, a broken heart, and spiritual wor-
' ship of all who seek to please and serve thee; mercifully
' behold me lying in this wretched condition of alienation
' from thee, and from all the tokens of thy love and favour,
' through spiritual death, and the prevalence of unbelief.—
Known unto thee is the extent of my backsliding, and the darkness, insensibility and strong hostility of my heart, in
' regard to all thy spiritual and holy precepts. Vain is the
' attempt to soften so hard a nature, and to convert affections
' so estranged, and so nearly extinct, by any resolutions and
' endeavours of my own. Vain are all the preparatory means
' and helps, to which my indolence seeks recourse, either to
' abate the force of the mortal disease, or even heartily to dis-
' pose me to return, and seek help of thee. Thou know-
' est, my God, that notwithstanding my former public profes-
' sion of thy faith, and exercise of the Christian ministry,

'that my present hope is little or nothing better than a bold
' presumption; and that little else remains, except a fearful
' looking for of judgment, and fiery indignation at thy hands.
' I am in terrifying doubt, that my unbelief and hardness of
' heart, have even now the seal of thy judicial dereliction.—
' But, merciful God, I have heard much, and tasted often and
' sweetly of thy divine compassion and goodness. No sin-
' ner is delivered from the curse of thy law, for his own in-
' nocence, or good works, good endeavours, or good resolu-
' tions—but through thy sovereign grace and mercy abound-
' ing in Jesus Christ thy Son. I have in vain made trial of
' my own powers, in every way which the wisdom of the car-
' nal mind suggests, and confess my utter impotency. My
' heart becomes daily harder—my affections daily more em-
' bittered against the holiness of thy nature, and the purity
' of thy law. Even my complaints are insincere—and the
' language of my confessions stronger than the feeling of
' my miserable and dangerous malady. And in this extremi-
' ty—thus lamely and indolently—thus insincerely and irre-
' solutely, I essay to apply to Thee, the free, and abundant,
' and only source of spiritual influences, and Author, and
' finisher of faith. May thy word and spirit break and sub
' due effectually, my hard, unbelieving heart. And may the
' same power which breaks and melts, be evermore present
' to preserve my soul in a broken and contrite frame. O
' keep my heart like fresh-tilled soil, forever, that it may
' drink freely the gentlest dews of heaven; receive kindly
' and deeply, every good seed of thy word, and bring forth a
' speedy and abundant return of mature and precious fruits.
' May the benefit be mine, and my fellow-creatures': but the
' glory all redound to thy free salvation, as established, com
' municated and perfectly wrought by the glorions and un
' divided God, Father, Son and Holy Spirit—to whom be
' praise, dominion and glory, now and forever. Amen."

The sweet prospect of his native land, the anticipated joy

of an interview with his friends, the anxious kindness of the citizens of New Haven, the efforts of skilful Physicians intent on saving a life dear to humanity and religion, and which had been willingly hazarded amid a thousand dangers in their cause, inspired him with transient energy, and lighted up, for a day or two, a trembling hope of his recovery.

In a letter to a friend at Washington, dated on the 12th of August, after stating "that without speedy relief, the little ' remaining strength he had, must give way, and death be ' the consequence," he adds: "You will naturally inquire, ' with what feelings, I contemplate the prospect before me? ' I can only reply in general, that my mind has so far been ' preserved under the nearest and most solemn views of ' death it has yet taken, from all distressing agitation and ' alarm; my confidence in the great Christian foundation is ' steadfast and unshaken—but am I building on this founda- ' tion? This inquiry forms the theme of my most anxious ' solicitude and fervent prayers; and I am thankful to the ' Author of all grace, that the evidence of my personal inter- ' est in the Redeemer, occasionally shines forth with consid- ' erable clearness; so that hope, more precious than the ' treasures of the world, commonly prevails against my fears, ' my doubts and my sins. If I had no more to repent of than ' most people, I should have more confidence in the sincerity ' of my repentance; but ranking, as I do, among the chief of ' sinners, I have only to trust the more to the Saviour's mer- ' its, and I can find occasionally, even hope and consolation ' in this act of faith and confidence."

But the time of his departure was at hand. To a friend who called on him soon after his arrival, he said, "I have come here to die."

He then expressed a deep sense of his guilt as a sinner, and a want of those spiritual consolations he desired. A day or two afterwards, to the same friend, he said, "I have been praying for light, and a little light has come, cheering and refreshing beyond expression." Requesting the prayers of the congregation, he said, "I have a desire to recover, but I do 'not wish that to be the burthen of the prayer. Let it be that 'I may acquiesce entirely in the will of God and have com-'munion with God. I wish the Colony to be remembered;" and as he spoke these words, he wept. "Excuse my weakness," said he, "there are many good people there, and they 'are so dear, that when I think of seeing them no more, my 'feelings are too strong." From this time, he declined rapidly, but gently; peace was in his soul, and on his aspect some rays of light from the world he was so soon to enter.— It was the writer's privilege to watch beside him during the last twenty-four hours of his life.

At this season, when the soul looks forth in helplessness from its falling tabernacle which it must quit forever, for an existence untried and the scenes invisible of eternity, the subject of this Memoir was unappalled. It was not forgetfulness, nor self-confidence, nor insensibility which made his spirit calm as the clear waters, that in some hour of nature's deep repose, reflect untremulously the beauty and magnificence of Heaven. He had cast himself upon the greatness of His strength who is mighty to save. Persuaded "that it was a faithful saying and worthy of all acceptation, that Christ Jesus came into the world to save sinners, and that whosoever believeth in Him, shall not perish, but have everlasting life," he penitently and joyfully trusted in these Divine words, while he saw the hand of death ready to lift the mysterious curtain, and conduct him to the presence of his final Judge.

The softest expressions of human praise, or even of approbation, fell like discords on his ear; and one who alluded to his services in the African cause, was checked by the remark, "I am a dying man, and desire that alone which is suited to my situation—I know of no such thing as self-righteousness—I can rely only upon the righteousness of Christ." Resignation, devotion, humility, and charity, so long the growing habits of his life, shone forth almost in perfection, near its close.

In weakness, in pain, he often forgot himself, but *duty* NEVER. His last day was spent not in complaints —not in anxious efforts to prolong life—not in vain wishes to see once again, if but for an hour, the faces of his parents—to catch, were it but a word, from lips often pressed to his, in affection; but in active duty, as a faithful servant watches with trimmed and burning lamp, the coming of his Lord. He dictated a letter on business, and signed it with his own hand. He expressed, earnestly, his thoughts and desires concerning the Colony. Observing an attendant, moved by his sufferings, in the spirit of Him who, on his way to the cross, said to the sympathizing daughters of Jerusalem, weep not for me, but weep for yourselves, he exhorted him to consider, and prepare for his own death.— Assisted to sit up, that he might thus better endure one of those paroxysms in which life seemed contending unequally with death, his little African boy standing in tears by his side, he offered his last prayer; that his faith might not fail under the weight of his affliction; that those whose kindness he was experiencing, and that his relatives and friends might never come into condemnation; and that the poor people among whom he had laboured, might ever enjoy the blessing of that Almighty Being, to whom, in this awful crisis of his existence, he was confiding the everlasting interests of his soul.

He arranged, minutely, his worldly affairs,—bequeathing of his small property, a large share to the cause of Missions in Africa. A sum of money in his hands was counted and delivered to a friend by himself.

It is evening—the sun has already gone down that shall rise for him no more.

A few individuals gather in sorrow around his bed.— But sorrow cannot stay there. It is not for them to give but to receive consolation. Their tears are those only of admiration and love. Cheerful words are on the lips of the dying, his eye kindles with the spirit, his countenance beams with the smile of immortality. The faithful, the toil-worn, the victorious soldier, is going from the field of his conflict, and his fame, to his long repose. He is not alone. The conqueror of death conducts him to the eternal honours of his kingdom.

"Pretiosa mors sanctorum, pretiosa plane tanquam finis laborum, tanquam victoriæ consummatio, tanquam vitæ Januae, et perfectæ securitatis ingressus."*

He expired gently, and in a moment, on the evening of the 25th of August, 1828, in the thirty-fifth year of his age.

On the next day, a large concourse of the citizens of New Haven, and of the neighbouring towns, united in a solemn tribute of respect to his memory, and attended his remains to the grave. The assembly had already filled the Central Church, to which the body of the deceased was conveyed, and the Minister of Christ just concluded his humble supplications to the God of all mercy and consolation, when a venerable, solitary female, entered the congregation, and with a look which told what her tongue might in vain have essayed to speak, approached the corpse. It was the mother of Ashmun! Every heart in that vast assembly beat fainter, as they beheld this aged matron, who had travelled for several days and nights from a remote part of the country, in the hope of embracing her living son, pressing her lips and her heart upon the coffin which concealed all that remained of that son in death, forever from her sight.†

---

\* "Precious is the death of saints—precious as the end of their labours, the consummation of their victory, the gate of life and entrance into perfect security."

† The warmth of the season rendered it imprudent to open the coffin—a circumstance painful at the time—but which left uneffaced in the memory of the venerable parent of Ashmun, those pleasing ideas of her son, which his early manly beauty had impressed upon it.

The Discourse of the Rev. Leonard Bacon, on this occasion, (which has been given to the public) was a just and eloquent defence of the spirit, that animates the martyrs to a great and good cause, and under the power of which, Ashmun had sacrificed his life in the service of Africa. "His example (said the preacher) shall speak."

"There have been men whose names are way-marks; whose examples, through successive ages, stir the spirits of their fellow-men with noble emulation. What has been done for God, and for the souls of men, and for the cause of wretched human nature, by the luster which gathers around the name of DAVID BRAINERD. How many lofty spirits has the simple history of his toils and sorrows kindled and roused to kindred enterprise. Other names there are, which beam from age to age with the same glory. HOWARD, CLARKSON, SWARTZ, MILLS,—what meaning is there in such names as these. Our departed friend will add another to that brilliant catalogue. He takes his place

> " Amid th' august and never dying light
> Of constellated spirits who have gained
> A name in heaven by power of heavenly deeds."

"Let us praise God for the light of his example, which shall never be extinguished, and which, as it beams on us, shall also beam on our children, and our children's children, moving them to deeds of godlike benevolence."

> " Praise! for yet one more name with power endowed,
> To cheer and guide us, onward as we press;
> Yet one more image, on the heart bestowed,
> To dwell there, beautiful in holiness."

We have come to his grave. A simple, but beautiful monument erected by the Managers of the American Colonization Society, in the church-yard of New Haven, (a spot which nature has made lovely, and which affection and piety have planted with trees and flowers, as if anxious to throw a charm and fragrance around the resting-places of the dead,) bears the name of Ashmun. This monument may perish, but that name never. It is engraven on the heart of Africa.

In his person, Mr. Ashmun was tall—his hair and eyes light—his features regular and cast in the finest mould—his manners mild, yet dignified—and in his countenance an expression of the gentlest affections softened the lineaments of a lofty, firm, and fearless mind.

He early saw the truth and felt the power of the Christian Religion. Its principles were ever living and active in his soul. The passions of youth might war against them—in the conflict with temptation, they might seem, for a moment, giving way; but they were indestructible—of the seed of God that liveth and abideth forever.

In grief, and temptation, and reproach—in want, and danger, and pain—when so cast down by affliction, that his soul became weary of life, he acknowledged himself under the discipline of the Almighty; he praised the name of God with a song, and magnified it with thanksgiving.— While, with David, he remembered the works of God and his wonders of old, his troubled thoughts were soothed, and he exclaimed, "Why art thou cast down, O my soul? Why art thou disquieted within me? Hope thou in God; for I shall yet praise Him, who is the health of my countenance and my God." Strengthened by the consolations of God, his spirit rose towards the innumerable company of just men made perfect, who once in tribulation like his, now stand inaccessible to misery or to danger, on the "mountains of glory," and seem to bend upon him looks of tenderness and love.

"Such is the power of dispensing blessings which Providence has attached to the truly great and good, that they cannot even die without advantage to their fellow-creatures; for death consecrates their example; and the wisdom which might have been slighted at the council table, becomes oracular at the shrine. Those rare excellencies, which make our grief poignant, make it likewise profitable; and the tears which wise men shed for the departure of the wise, are among those that are preserved in Heaven."*

Spirit of Ashmun! dost thou not look down upon me, while to that cause, to which thou gavest thy all, thy life, I dedicate this humble offering to thy worth. I cast it on thy grave—for there, a potent and unslumbering spirit dwells, which will not leave it voiceless. Thou hast not lived—thou hast not died in vain. I hear responded from ten thousand tongues, thou hast not lived—thou hast not died in vain.— The light thou hast kindled in Africa shall never go out; the principles thou hast exemplified, are true and everlasting. Thy country shall yet—shall soon do justice; and when in all her borders no fetter shall be worn by the guiltless— when upon Africa now just awakening to a sense of her miseries, and stretching out her hands for help, she shall have conferred, in the free spirit of the Great Master of Christians, her language, her liberty, and her religion; rewarded with the gratitude of millions, and the honours of all nations clustering thick upon her—Africa—America—the World shall know, thou hast not lived—thou hast not died in vain.

"Thou hast left behind,
Powers that will work for thee! air, earth, and skies;
There's not a breathing of the common wind
That will forget thee! thou hast great allies!
Thy friends are exultations, agonies,
And love, and man's unconquerable mind."

* Coleridge.

# APPENDIX.

# APPENDIX.

## No. 1.

*Extracts from the early Diary of Ashmun.*

THESE extracts comprise but a small portion of the Journal of Mr. Ashmun, while preparing for college, and during his college life. They will serve to show, however, much of his early character, the depth and sincerity of his piety, the burning ardor of his zeal, and his aspiring resolution in the cause of Religion.

*November* 27, 1810.—Having at this time a term of leisure, and for want of suitable opportunity having heretofore neglected it, I shall attempt an imperfect detail of the dealings of God with me the summer past; as such an account, although somewhat circumscribed, may be of use in assisting my memory at some future period.

*June* 24, 1810.—I attended Church as usual; but having been from home most of the past winter, residing chiefly with such as made no profession of religion, and being warmly engaged in pursuits after some earthly good, religion was seldom thought of seriously. The cares of a school, the prospect of realizing, at some future time, all my foolish, thoughtless imaginations, and my consequent exertions, but above all, my wicked heart, operating all to the same purpose, hardened me more, I believe, against

## APPENDIX.

God, than two years' impenitence had done before! And as might be expected, the preaching of the Word had very little effect, but to harden. And I recollect with pain, that on hearing a discourse of the most alarming kind, on the horrors of damnation, instead of receiving the intended warning, I, calm, stupid, and composed, endeavored to criticise the language in which the solemn ideas were clothed. This sermon, by the gracious application of God's spirit, was made the means of awakening (and I trust, to the renewal of the heart) one of my companions, elder than myself. I secretly despised his meekness when I first understood his fears; and though I intended, at some time future, to make religion my business, yet the thoughts of devoting my best days to God, or the sight of such a purpose in others, excited in my depraved nature, emotions of disgust. And Oh! may I ever remember with humility, that this was my condition, when only in my seventeenth year. My associate, who about a week before had been gloriously relieved from his burdened conscience, afterwards made some remarks, which I very little regarded, until he observed, " I think, if I know my own heart, I have enjoyed more this day, than in all my former life. " On this I reflected; happiness I had ever been in quest of; had tried various diversions and gratifications within my reach, but never could obtain the desired end. I reflected that at some future period I must begin to be religious; and now having seen one who had ventured before me, who above all, brought such joyful tidings from the land of Canaan, I determined, with headstrong resolution, to seek until I found Religion. I proceeded homeward ; endeavored to notice as few surrounding objects as possible, and to increase conviction ; and not suspecting the secret workings of the finger of God, I thought I had the good success of increasing my anxiety. Meeting with one of my youthful companions, I, without calling at home, persuaded him to accompany me into the house of Mr. ———, and wait his return from church. I conversed, and endeavored to think of nothing but religious and eternal matters ; and by the time Mr. P. arrived, which was about an hour after conference, God had, as I trust, increased my anxiety to such a degree, that my whole frame became sensibly affected. I cannot say that I felt any great degree of horror. I saw a wicked, hardened heart; *total* alienation of affections from God and all holiness; but I think my greatest concern was, lest I should be suffered to lose my seriousness, and relapse into sevenfold stupidity. I expected that when Mr. P. came, he would immediately explain the scriptural way for a sinner to take, and I intended to become immediately a Christian. But he stated the truth just as he had many times before, "Repent and be converted." He told me that repentance and a new heart were what was first of all required in the Word of God: and that whatever a sinner would perform, previous to a change of heart, was sinful, and consequently must be displeasing to God: that God had been at infinite expense to provide salvation for mankind, and should they only be heartily willing, never could a sinner miss salvation. This was not the advice I expected, but I felt it to be the truth; I think I felt myself completely in a lost condition, but no particular sins appeared to my view which were of prominent appearance. My whole past life appeared like an ocean of darkness, and guilt and sin. My thoughts were brought to see the necessity of an atonement, and to see in some small degree its superlative worth. Oh, I could exclaim, Oh, the riches of that redemption, which delivers mankind from this state of ruin. I tried to love the Saviour; but alas! for want of faith I could not see him. My reason told me that God was present and superintended all his works, but I could not realize the truth. I strove to pray, but was sensible that I only mocked the God I pretended to address. I almost feared to retire to rest, lest I should lose my impressions before morning; for I thought that even if I must go to hell at last, this world was so transitory, that it mattered not whether I spent it in reflecting on my future misery, or in carnal mirth; yea, rather I chose the former.

*Monday morning.*—When I awoke, I thought my serious impressions had all left me. I was alarmed, immediately began to pray for their return. I found myself quite weakened in body; but after a few minutes, I recognised the same feelings as the night before; and when I prayed for relief, my desires appeared to break, as it were, through a cloud, and rose away towards God, which feelings I considered immediately to be conversion. I took the Bible, tried to love it; I read it, and persuaded myself it appeared new. I mentioned my feelings to Mr. P., he warned me to be cautious lest I settled my hope on a false foundation. The caution I considered as almost needless. But I did not ask myself, whence springs thy joy? Nor whether my views were such as the Bible would justify? But because I considered myself renewed, I rejoiced and felt a kind of selfish love to the God to whom I owed this mercy, "but the hope of the hypocrite shall perish." And blessed be the Lord, in two hours' time, all my joyful sensations left me; but I however flattered myself that I was renewed, and should be revisited ere long. I went to visit my religious friend; stated my exercises to him, and left him something dissatisfied that he did not believe me converted; but I found by his conversation, that I knew nothing of the God and Saviour that he described. On my way home, I called at a Masonic meeting, heard the eloquence of the preacher, but was far from receiving the least comfort; and I think I may say also, instruction. O, may false teachers be confounded or changed! The remainder of the day I spent very unhappily, and what was worst of all, I felt and thought that I was fast sinking back into stupidity; still my selfishness prevailed, I wished to be saved for the sake merely of my own salvation; but praise to the Lord, that he has prepared no such heaven as I was anxious for! Tuesday—my feelings were much the same as in the morning; I gave over all business except reading. About noon, finding that my works of devotion did me no good, I retired and endeavored to seek assistance from God alone. I felt that I could pour out my soul, as I never could before. My own salvation appeared to be of so little consequence, in comparison with the great design of Jehovah and other things, that I was perfectly passive about myself. I opened a small book, and found an observation respecting the future glory of the Church—the reinstatement of the Jews; and God's determination, ever to have a church on earth, and that millions were yet, in all probability, to be brought from this earth to eternal glory; and that the accomplishment of these glorious events was not left to man, but that God had engaged to perform it. Who can describe the joy that arose in my soul, on reading this. I could heartily exclaim, glorify thyself, O God. Without ecstacy, I was completely happy. I thought Christ appeared almost exhibited to the view of my natural eyes. I knew I could embrace him, and wished for nothing else, except the salvation of my fellow mortals. These soul satisfying views continued and increased till night, when my religious friend came to see me. And O, what an evening of bliss almost divine! Heaven almost appeared to have descended; my friend as happy as myself, and every object excepting impenitents, appeared to sing my Saviour's praise. I imagined myself able to persuade all to come, but found many a bitter disappointment, and I am now persuaded that the power of conversion is alone from God. The next day these high joys left my sinful breast. I began to doubt the reality of the change. Thursday, they again returned with sweetly conquering power, and I believe subdued my rising pride. From that to this time, I think I have enjoyed much of the presence of Jesus.

*November 27th*, 1810.—But frequent darkness fills me often with doubts and fears. But, blessed Saviour! thou canst, and wilt, I trust, lead me through. O increase my faith—I expect shortly to walk the golden streets of bliss, beyond the stars, to join the church triumphant, in shouting praises to the Lamb, eternally. O may I give away all hopes of my own righteousness availing me, where all are clothed in robes washed in the blood of Jesus! Having resumed my studies, Mr. P. advised me to prosecute them with an intention of preparing to publish abroad the news of salvation. I hesitated, but on subsequent reflection, considering the station and opportunity Divine Providence has offered me, I have thought it my duty to study with that intention; and should no direction of Providence operate to prevent, I hope I feel willing to devote the remainder of my forfeited life to the immediate service of God, and my fellow mortals. But in one thing I am doubtful respecting my duty; in relation to entering College and spending four years enthronged about by temptations, perhaps the most engaging to my disposition of any in the world. And although I am sensible of the absolute necessity of a proper education; yet I am not confident, that it ought not to be obtained in some other way, than by passing through all the forms of a College, where pretensions to the religion of Jesus, are most strictly observed, yet the student, involved in literary mazes, is liable to the hurtful influence of sentiments of rivalship. A man may become qualified for the business of the world, but the simplicity and purity of the religion of Jesus, is certainly liable to exceeding great corruption, and the student to spiritual loss; disadvantages have resulted to the world, which might be remedied by studies more private.

# APPENDIX.

*Tuesday afternoon, August 27th.*—I was taken unwell; before this I suffered myself to be off my guard; was enabled, as I trusted, to put my trust in my merciful Creator. I think that I had some sense of the situation of a person on the borders of death, though very imperfect indeed. Wednesday and Thursday, grew better, the latter of which days, I began again to study; but Friday, my indisposition returned to a considerable degree, and I may, before the end of the month, which commences to-morrow, be in eternity! O may my heavenly Father afford me every needed grace, whether to live or die, for one is as solemn as the other, and perhaps not more so.

I am at present engaged in studying, which is so agreeable, that I am in danger of being so engaged, as to neglect my duty to my God, but his grace is sufficient for me.

*February 15th—Bristol,* 1813.—Religion is life's great work. As it is the business of preparation for eternity, it certainly is most important; as it is wrought in, and towards God, is most solemn and interesting; and as it is the chief end of mortals, its process on the soul, and the process of our advancement in it, ought most seriously and carefully to be known, and noticed in ourselves. Our worldly engagements are commonly the subject of our most accurate and scrutinous investigation. The men of the world are not only acquainted with the present state of their affairs, in all the circumstances and varieties attending them, but can usually review and recount with ease, the whole train of transactions which have preceded, and tended to bring them to their present posture, but the Christian, (shame to his careless indifference, and criminal stupidity,) is frequently unapprised of his present state, and seldom able to retrace his footsteps with precision, or describe the devious path that has conducted him through former scenes and dangers. The workings of his own heart are thus unattended to, and he remains ignorant of himself. The operations of the Spirit are not carefully and seriously noted, and he thus remains ignorant of God, and the more liable to easy imposition from the spirit of Anti-Christ, and the influence of spurious affection. By the neglect of attention to all the vicissitudes of christian experience, we remain lamentably, and most unhappily ignorant of the great art, of applying scripture to all the variations of state and feeling, to which the wisdom of their Divine Author has surprisingly adapted their use. Growth in grace consists in the knowledge of God, and a saving understanding of divine things, gained through faith. It is always evinced by fruits of holiness. These fruits are inseparable from progressive sanctification, and are such as mark the distinction between the saint and sinner. To Christians the fruits of righteousness observable in each other, are almost conclusive evidence of their glorious state; but still there is a great liability to deception, not only in regard to others, but even in regard to ourselves, if we found our judgments on externals alone. The heart is the seat of operation of all grace, here the springs of action must originate, and from their peculiar nature must Christians judge of the nature of all their conduct. The heart is deceitful above all things, and desperately wicked. And its depths and subtilties can only be fathomed and unravelled by the Word of God, which is quick and powerful, and sharper than any two edged sword, piercing even to the dividing asunder of soul and spirit, and accompanied by the energy of divine grace, will enable the understanding to make all needful discrimination, and find out our real situation relative to divine things. May the Spirit of divine grace from on high, be my aid in the all-important work of self-investigation, and direct me in the description of all my views, in the subsequent pages. May they be filled with the sweet narration of many seasons of most endearing consolations, and most heavenly refreshments, in the course of that part of my earthly pilgrimage, which they shall embrace. For more than a year past, I have neglected to keep a religious diary, and not inconsiderably, I have thought, to my disadvantage. By perusing a written experience, we are led to review our past life, which most necessary work is otherwise neglected. Even the time devoted to the noting down of our religious exercises and spiritual state, may be spent in a manner highly edifying, while it leads to a survey of our heart in all its actions. Last summer for several months together, was the most barren part of my whole life; the world had almost entirely overcome me. I was filled with its pride, fully engaged in its pursuits, possessed of its spirit, and participating in its employments and pleasures. Political conversation, and newspaper investigation, had taken the place of religious exhortation and fervor, and the study of the scriptures. The great object to which I had formerly aimed, and my exertions in the literary path were almost forgotten.

If I have ever known, or ever shall be restored to the smiling aspect of an approving Saviour, what a wonder of grace; Lord, to thy name be all the glory. Conscience often in the course of the summer, awoke in all its array of terror, and reduced my mind to all the acuteness of guilty misery. When brought partially to realize and deplore my back-slidden condition, my resolution was not so strong, nor my zeal so vigorous, as I think they formerly were, when in the enjoyment of God's presence.

Early in September, I entered College at Middlebury; on my passage thither, as indeed before my departure from home, I indulged, almost unbridled, my corruptions; and, O my God, canst thou forgive it, I most presumingly trampled under foot the sacred sabbath institution, without the shadow of an occasion.

After several weeks however, God in a manner revealed the riches of his grace, in granting a hopeful remission: and through the fall months I enjoyed some sweet hours of refreshment from the presence of the Lord. And I believe the faithfulness and pious example of my religious fellow students was used as a powerful instrument, of rousing the torper of my soul.

*Bristol, Monday, February* 23, 1815.—This morning, with some little sense of divine things, I went nine miles into Starksborough, to attend the funeral solemnities of old Mr. Marshall, who for forty years, I think, has been a champion in the service of the cross. He died turned of eighty, an example of piety and most ardent devotion to the work of God; a pillar in the Churches; most prevalent and powerful in his prayers to God; and perhaps in his conversation, the most edifying of any Christian in all this northern world. After the funeral ceremonies were closed, I learnt that two of my sisters in Champlain, had recently died; the one elder than myself, the other younger. I left them all in perfect health. The shock was great, but I enjoyed, I think, divine support. God appeared for my comfort. I had a remarkable season of nearness to God in prayer by the way; on my return, His glory appeared so far to transcend all earthly considerations, that while entertained with the marvelous and blessed theme, I almost forgot the wound that had transfixed my heart.— In contemplating the distraction, sinfulness, and tremendous judgments of God, prevalent on the earth, at the present day, the world stood revealed in all its deformity and emptiness. Nothing stood forth in the whole gloomy scenery, on which the anxious eye could bear to rest, or my sickening heart endure, except the church and cause of God, which shone in all its splendor to meet my gaze. Here, here, my soul could move with delight, find a charm that softened all the rigor of a horrid world.

This evening by special request of a dying woman, in company with Mr. B. paid her a visit. She was alarmingly sensible of her unprepared state for death. I felt much confidence in prayer for and with her. Endeavored in conversation to exhibit to her view, her own heart and life, in all their corruption and sins; to lead her to despair of all help from man, or earth, or heaven, but by, and from and through the Saviour, (who must effect the whole) to seek the renovation of her heart.

*Wednesday, February* 20*th*, 1813.—In consequence of the information received on Monday, I considered it my duty to return to Champlain. About 10 A. M. left town in a comfortable state of mind; thought I felt a degree of submission to God, and to praise him for his own perfection. Enjoyed great serenity of mind all day; felt a degree of resoluteness, and support in making religion the theme of conversation with those with whom I met. And finally, for me, weak, and sinful, and unfaithful as I am, the enjoyments and continued solemnity of this day, equal those of my most favoured seasons of intercourse with my God. In the evening, however, at the tavern, my faith was weakened, unwarily conversing with some irreligious people on worldly topics. My natural sins of vanity and pride, and a desire of worldly esteem, made their appearance, and insensibly led my heart aside from its fixed attitude.

O Lord of all-supplying grace, assist me ever in the discharge of duty, both as respects the season, matter and manner of it. Teach me in all my reproofs, warnings and exhortations, to go entirely to the bottom of the ground that I may attempt to explore and improve; and make thou me as thorough as the great day of the Lord, in all the scrutiny of its discerning Judge, may require. And rather than in any way, cry a false peace, or daub with untempered mortar, may I feel happy to subject myself to all the opposition and contemptuous or angry retorts of a blind world.

My business and feeling concurring to prevent it, I unseasonably neglected to advocate and inculcate, even when suitable occasions offered, the duties of religion. O my unfaithfulness, O my sin! Lord of love, I have frequently of late exclaimed, can it be, that I ever loved thee? Have not all my supposed experiences of religious joy and grace in the heart, been delusory and vain? Can it be, that one of thine adopted should ever be so weak, so timid, and so little engaged, and so very inconstant in thy service?

But usually I feel a support that will not let me sink, and having obtained help of the Lord, I still maintain a lively hope of an interest secured by the incomprehensible love of God, my everlasting Saviour. I have lately been led to view in a more accurate manner than usual, the superlative wisdom and goodness of God in the dispensations of his providence towards me. And even my own past wickedness I sometimes view as contributing an essential part towards my preparation for some station, to which God intends me.

*Saturday, 13th March.*—To day on my way to school, I overtook brother Fisk, from Middlebury, on a Gospel errand. His solemnity, zeal, and humility, as usual. On contrasting my daily deportment with his upright walk, I became in some measure affected with my uniform deficiency in christian holiness and watchfulness. We set out together for Starksboro, and after much edifying conversation on his part, staid at Mr. P's. I this afternoon had a comfortable reliance, and support.

*Sabbath* 14.—In prayer this morning had a season of sensible nearness.—Some little sensation of prevailing faith. Much elevated in petitioning for a foreign spread of the gospel of grace. Could I ever enjoy such mornings of earnest wrestling, and such filial assurance, I think that I should sink some in humility; and rise in my views of God, and the strength of my attachment to him. Spent the day in a very reviving and precious frame. Spoke and conversed much. My prayers easy. Consideration of my own and others' responsibility in dealing out the treasures of Gospel truth, weighed powerfully on my mind this afternoon.

My thoughts are of late much engaged on the subject of missions. My greatest happiness arises in finding a pious brother whose soul flames with love to the souls of the poor heathen. I have lately been much enraptured with the idea of a martyr's death, after a life of laborious faithfulness in heathen lands; and I consider, that all the honors and glories of this world enjoyed for ages, are by no means to be compared with it. O my God, fit me for the overtures of thy providence, and if consistent, make me a zealous, faithful, humble, and very successful minister of the Saviour's grace to heathen and destitute nations, and raise up to the blessed work many, from all christian countries, illustrious for real piety and ardent for the honors of thy name. O Lord, shall apostolic resolution, shall primitive devotedness and attachment to the Saviour, no more characterise thy dear children; no more add lustre and energy to thy ministers of salvation in this world? with Thee is the residue of the spirit, and the interests of Zion are thine own.

Alas! how sadly do I fail of that circumspection of conduct which the gospel enjoins, relative to those without. How can the Christian walk, except his God brace every footstep!

When we go to the Throne of Grace, the darkest side of our condition should always be first and most humbly exhibited before God.

*Rules to be observed:*

To peruse the subsequent articles weekly.

I. To retire for secret prayer three times, daily.
1. As soon in the morning as returned from recitation.
2. As soon at noon as returned from recitation.
3. At evening as soon as returned from prayers.

II. To read the scriptures after social prayer in the morning: and always a portion of the Greek Testament immediately before a dedicatory prayer, which is next to precede my retiring every evening.

III. To attend exclusively to my classics, from the time of the conclusion of the morning exercises, till eleven.
2. From short exercises after dinner to attend to my classics until half past 3 or 4 o'clock.
3. From that time till prayers, to attend to useful reading.
4. From my return from prayers till dark, on Monday, Wednesday, and Tuesday evenings, to attend to speaking or writing.
5. During the same interval on Tuesday, Friday, and Saturday evenings, to prepare a subject for the evening meeting.

IV. To spend the whole of Monday, Wednesday, and Thursday evenings, in useful reading.
2. To employ the remnant of Tuesday and Friday evenings, after meeting, in writing my diary, letters, or pieces, for Societies.
3. Saturday evening in reading the Bible.
4. Sabbath evenings in reading the Bible and Greek Testament, and in writing and reading my diary.

V. Wednesday and Saturday afternoons, from after speaking till prayers, either in reading, writing, conversing, or transacting necessary business. Saturday afternoon, all possible preparation to be made for the Sabbath—and if possible, my Greek lesson to be read. Saturday P. M. also, may be spent most commonly, in religious visiting.
2. Sabbath to be sanctified as the Lord directs.

VI. From these articles on needful occasions, my conduct may often vary; but let the strictest attention be ever given them, when circumstances permit.

*May 1st*, 1813.—The latter part of the week much entertained with the reflections excited by a passage in xi. Hebrews. "They wandered about in sheep-skins and goat-skins, being destitute, afflicted, tormented, of whom the world was not worthy. They wandered in deserts and mountains, and in dens and caves of the earth." My part, I reflect, is yet to be acted among the multitudes of the race that have past, and are passing, through this probationary world. Now is my glorious opportunity to choose, whether in the pursuit of wordly distinctions, led on by wordly hopes, and captivated by wordly attractions, I pass into eternity; or whether, trusting in the Lord, only anxious for the honors of his name, I live by faith, equally separated from the rudiments, and destitute of the spirit of this world, with the holy prophets, patriarchs and apostles of old, (if not equally deprived of the conveniences and common blessings of life) looking every day and labouring every hour for a better inheritance in the upper world, seeking for gracious acceptance with my God, and a blessed part in the first resurrection. I have daily temptations of the most persuasive kind, when the darkness of this world draws its obscurity over my mind, to conform myself to the respectable, the sensible, (in the language of the suggestion) and the wise ; of maintaining a certain dignity of character, of choosing and forsaking certain associates, and in effect, of quitting the humble walks of a disciple of Jesus, for a certain course, which my Bible tells me leads directly away from God, away from Heaven, and finally, leads honorably down, by insensible declivities, to the gates of Hell! Great God, give me of thine abundant mercy, faith in the Lord Jesus, and a firm reliance; suitable views of divine things, of this world and the world to come. While in the most hearty language of my soul's sincerity, I make a solemn engagement, recalling to mind all I have formerly vowed, and feeling the weight of thy commands that bind me to it, to forsake the honors and pleasures and vanities of the world, be for Christ, and him alone, make his cause my cause, his honor mine, his cross my glory, shame for his name my greatest rejoicing, and the light of his spirit, the vital principle of my existence.

*May* 16, 1813.—My constant, ruling propensity for prayer, I found in the first stages of the decline, began to relax into a kind of indifference ; soon the duty became not agreeable, and lastly, a real burden. Thus, in the first symptoms of backsliding, if the care of the soul be not regarded with a trembling solicitude, and penitence immediately exercised, we may depend on a wicked downfall.

When the Christian has given him, through God's self-dictating goodness, timely notice of apostacy from the divine life, to cold impenitence, and yet deliberately stops his ears, tarries negligently without pressing onward for shelter from the clouds that already begin to blacken over him ; when this transcendent love and care on the one hand, is violated by sinful senselessness on the other ; God might justly, as respects the desert of the offender, make him an eternal monument of his righteous indignation, and of his regard for the honor of his own authority. For

1. At such seasons, God calls on the creature most expressly, for his prayers; and this he understands.

2. Disobedience to an injunction intuitively enforced by the voice of heav-

## APPENDIX.

en, must be, of all the most conceivable sins, one of the most heinous. To lose ground once by the grace of God obtained, the enlightened mind of the Christian knows an actual and important sin.

3. The backslider in such circumstances, sins with the criminal presumption, that God will, when himself pleases to desire it, recall his vagrant desires, forgive his sins, and light up a flame of love in his soul.

4. The professing Christian, in a special manner, breaks deliberately his consecrating vows; and turns against every precept in the Word of God, which binds him to the Lord, and to no other, consecrated in heart and affection, as well as in speech and action: and

5. Because he knows, that once darkened, his heart may heedlessly be led to the exercise of every unhallowed feeling; and he have, in a measure, lost the power of withstanding.

The long-suffering patience of God, thus abused, only because its very nature is divine, has not left me.

*May 22nd.*—Arrived towards night at Mr. H——d's in Brandon: was welcomed with uncommon cordiality, and found in his neighbourhood great encouragement for faithful prayer and unremitting exertion in the cause of our Master. Some praying souls in the neighbourhood stood waiting for better times; but as a body, the church lay a dead weight against the progress of a work of reformation. What an awful responsibility rests on opposing professors! They are set as lights of the world, yet darkening all around them! They stand as watchmen on the walls of Zion, yet sleep while the enemy triumphs over the rifled treasury of their King.

Found to-day, one Christian, whose heart appeared right; who acknowledged substantially the truth of the doctrines of entire submission, dependence on sovereign grace, and total depravity; but owing to a constitutional weakness of intellect, and want of information on the subject, could not admit at once, the whole system of doctrines connected with those truths which the Bible exhibits. Let charity in such cases be exercised; and destroy not with your strong meat, him for whom Christ died.

*May 26th.*—Spent this evening in conversation with Mr. H—— on the distressing circumstances of Zion in the vicinity, and of our land in general. He had that afternoon returned from an association of ministers which met at Benson; had learnt the most melancholy tidings from the churches in every direction. No reformations; no increasing love; no encouragement, apparently, for ministerial labors; no life in Christians; no concern in sinners. Heresies were fast multiplying, and gaining advocates. Political distractions rent in pieces even the professed unity of the house of God. A spirit of persecution was fast ripening, and the enemy concentrating his forces to the highest point of desperate resistance. The circumstances of most of the ministers, as regards their maintenance, were becoming more and more embarrassed. The pestilence had raged through all their parishes, and carried off many who stood as pillars to their churches; and the bloody scenes of war, together with the prospect of a distressing scarcity of provisions, seemed to complete the grand universality of human woe, and heavenly judgment on a guilty land. Since the first of January, upwards of ten thousand had gone to the bar of God from the State, and still the epidemic prevailed in some places, but not with its former violence and mortality. Conversing on fanatical sentiments and practices, this evening, I am convinced that the affections may be heated to a great degree of fervor from religious considerations, which originate and are limited wholly in self. These may actually assume the exact counterfeit of holy breathings of a devotional soul; and a specious kind of love be produced, and continued together with sensations of high delight, even for years, and the wretched object of the deception all the time dead in trespasses and sins.

*Sabbath, October* 31st, 1813.—Have resolved—

1. To retire thrice daily for secret prayer.
2. To read daily at least three chapters in the Bible.
3. Not to pass a day without religious conversation, with some person—nor three days, with an impenitent.
4. To study for God.
5. Not to utter a sinful, an unseasonable, or an unnecessary word.
6. To endeavor to maintain kindness, humility, and an equal temper.
7. To watch over myself, and endeavor to repress the first risings of pride, and every other inordinate passion.
8. To read over these resolves carefully and with prayer, thrice weekly, to wit; Monday, Wednesday, and Sabbath morning, after my return from prayers.

*Monday, Tuesday, and Wednesday.*—Had most convincing views of the infinite imperfection of saints, and all their services; that every ray of light and beam of grace which shines in upon them, only serves to discover more darkness, and to reveal the fathomless depths of iniquity into which they have sunken.

*Sabbath, November* 21, 1813.—Close and metaphysical speculations into the abstract nature of virtue and vice, &c., I am as much disinclined as disqualified to indulge. I had rather experience one humbling sensation of a broken and bleeding heart, than get all the speculative, fancied knowledge of moral philosophy ever known, for practical purposes.

*November* 22.—I have lately been firmly persuaded that duty required me to make previous preparation for conferences, and other religious interviews, wherever it would be proper for me to speak. I was made so sensible of my presumptuous and most inexcusable negligence in this particular, that I was almost overwhelmed with an apprehension of the injury I may have thus occasioned to the cause of Christ; and may God enable me hereafter to study His word with all diligence; "to find out acceptable words;" to connect my thoughts in a judicious manner; to deliver with solemnity, sensibility, composure, order and force.

*Tuesday, November* 23, 1813.—Attended a blessed, and most impressive meeting last evening. Had, previous to the meeting, a spirit of earnest supplication. Felt an assurance of support and assistance. In the assembly all was solemn; God was evidently in the midst of us. All, without apparent exception, seemed affected; a number under deep concern.

*Wednesday, November 24.*—For two or three days past, God has discovered to me myself in such a manner as never before. Former experiences of joy and peace, and measures of grace formerly in a degree satisfactory, could give me little or no comfort or rest; for I knew that a depth of iniquity was still unfathomed within me. Was led to earnest supplication for the work of grace to be deepened. I know I am the most superficial of Christians, from the want of humility and solemnity in my ordinary deportment. My greatest anxiety, if I am capable of judging of my own desires, is to be so richly stored, from the treasures of grace, with all the gifts of the Spirit, as to be instrumental of saving sinners; comforting, edifying, and promoting the sanctification of saints.

*Wednesday, Dec.* 1, 1813.—Suffered not inconsiderably from spiritual pride. It has, on some occasions lately, made its entrance awfully into my breast. Helpless, ruined wretch that I am, were I any thing than a mass of depravity, I should be humbled.

*Tuesday, May 2nd,* 1814.—According to an agreement entered upon in our P. D. Society, nearly all the pious students in College met in prayer, for the heathens and for missionaries, labouring among them, and missionary exertions making, or about to be made, in their favour.

In our P. D. Society, a resolution has been adopted appointing, semi-annually, a Committee of Enquiry to report monthly in the Society, on the subject of Missions. I have lately taken some measures to establish a contributory Foreign Society, to increase the funds of the Mass. F. M. Society. A missionary spirit evidently pervades, to an uncommon degree, the churches of Christ in this vicinity.

In the Spring of 1814, Mr. Ashmun made a journey into several parts of Vermont and Connecticut, in very feeble health.

The purposed journey before me, has tended to steal away my heart from the pursuit of God's glory, and a regard for the good of souls. During my absence from this place, blessed Saviour, do Thou qualify me to act in future, a humble, a laborious, a wise, and by Thy strength and grace alone, a most successful part in Thy church. O may this short journey be to Thy glory—may I view it as the Lord's errand, and myself, as his weak and unworthy messenger.

My affection for my missionary brother S—— increases. I indulge the welcome anticipation that God will make us field labourers together,—but to Him, I would gladly resign the disposal of this, and every other attendant circumstance and event of life. Will the Lord vouchsafe to me the smiles of my Saviour, and the fellowship of the Holy Ghost!

*Weybridge, May* 17*th,* 1814.—I spent the evening past in conversing on the missions in the East. Saw that the change which has occurred in the sentiments of Messrs. Rice and Judson, had been already instrumental in exciting among the Baptists a general interest in the cause of missions in the East, and throughout the world. From the instability, and apparently unhappy defection, of those men, from the truths into which they had been indoctrinated, have arisen motives to the American Baptists, to support a foreign mission, which no event that we could choose, could, perhaps, afford them. They have seen these men change their opinions, with every motive except truth and conscience, to dissuade them from it; and with nothing to move them to it, but those obligations which bind the most disinterested and devotional souls to their God, and attach them to the faith and purity of the Gospel. Such is the view my Baptist brethren and fathers throughout the United States, have taken of this important occurrence. While they derive from it new confidence in the truth of their distinguishing sentiments, they are led to interest themselves deeply in that cause to which their champions are attached. They feel their exertions in support of it, loudly demanded, and their obligations, greatly increased. They cannot hesitate to support and encourage by their prayers, their contributions, and their friendly assurances, those men, who have withdrawn from the support of the Mass. Miss. Society, and now rely on them for support. Mr. Rice's exertions, since his return to the United States, have effected among the churches what, perhaps, no other individual in America could so well have done. I think we may finally venture to trust, that God has kind designs toward the mission cause, in exciting among the Baptists in the United States, so general and so operative a spirit, as the past year has given us the pleasure of witnessing.

How strongly do the senses, when delightfully employed, tend to deaden down devotion, and prevent that exclusive, holy rising of the soul to God through Jesus Christ. They may, nevertheless, be sanctified. All may become the avenues of impressions the most spiritual, and the medium of praise, the most pure and exalted. Lord, work this temper into the very texture of my soul. The exactions of custom must command our attention. These it is always the part of a wise man to diminish, as far as his influence and ability render it safe to attempt it; but it is equally the part of a prudent man, not to attempt their total abolition. When the church becomes pure from her dross, we shall behold in this, as in other things, a glorious alteration.

The pernicious use of ardent spirits, pervades every rank and character of men throughout New England. This habit is becoming inveterate. Unless soon broken, and the practice of treating friends, &c. with the polite poison is discontinued, the consequences to the next generation must be sad beyond expression.

*Saturday morning* rode to Williamstown before breakfast. The recent donations made this College, are to be appropriated to the support of professorships. A new and valuable philosophical apparatus, has lately been added to the endowments of the institution.

## APPENDIX.

*Tuesday,* I visited the Shakers in Hancock. Hancock village is inhabited only by the Shakers—it consists of farm houses, and other buildings, extending on a street nearly three-fourths of a mile. Perfect neatness shines throughout the whole settlement. All is activity—a bee-like industry. I drove leisurely along their village, almost unnoticed, and repaired to their office, at which their produce is contracted for, and all their commercial affairs transacted. Was very kindly received by an elderly lady very neatly attired, with the sun-shine of serenity beaming in her countenance, and a degree of delicacy in her carriage and features, which bespoke her exemption from the ordinary drudgery of her sisterhood. She conversed with a most pleasing frankness, and with a degree of intelligence which highly entertained and surprised me. She soon withdrew and sent in their Elder and some of the lay brethren. I spent two or three hours in close conversation with them. They were as communicative as I could possibly desire, and treated me with all the kindness and respect of my very best friends. My conversation with them gave me a pretty full view of their distinguishing errors, and the grounds on which they rest. Regeneration is a progressive change—progressive before grace—progressive in grace—and progressive after grace has purified from all sin. When the Holy Ghost is conferred, actual sin is no longer committed. Its force is broken; and though it may, on some occasions break forth slightly, still it is not wilful, and owing more to the infirmity of our natures, for which we are not culpable, than to a depraved disposition. In proof that regeneration is progressive, they speak of "following Christ in the Regeneration"—of "the light which shineth more and more unto the perfect day."

"The immediate disciples of our Lord," say they, "walked in sin and imperfections, while their Master was on earth, after they had received grace. They frequently erred. Peter sinned grievously. But after the effusion of the Holy Ghost on the day of Pentecost," said my instructer, "I challenge you or any other person to show me, in their whole lives, a single instance of sin." I repeated to him the exclamation of the Apostle, Romans vii, 26; and referred him to the whole chapter 1 John i, 7 and last; and especially to the assertion of St. Paul, Galatians ii, 10 and 11—"And when Peter was come to Antioch, I withstood him to the face, because *he was to be blamed.*" The old Shaker twisted himself half round, appeared a little discomposed, and by some trivial equivocation, evaded the force of Scripture which he could not confront.

In support of sinless perfection, he felt himself on the whole well strengthened by other passages, which he thought direct to the point; such as "He that is born of God doth not commit sin; neither can he sin, because his seed remaineth"—"If we say we have fellowship with Him, and walk in darkness, we deceive ourselves," &c.—"Be ye holy, for I am holy; perfect as your Father which is in Heaven is perfect." And is God so unreasonable as to lay on his creatures an injunction with which it is absolutely impossible to comply?—

They firmly adhere to the opinion of justification by works. This they repeatedly asserted, and with peculiar emphasis. Grace fits for working; works justify, sanctify, and gain the reward in glory. In proof of the truth of this most dangerous heresy, they added some detached passages, which I have frequently heard from the mouths of moralists; especially one from the Epistle of James. They delight to boast of their own purity and good deeds; recounted over to me what crosses they had borne; what attachment to God they continued to evince; what darkness they had been delivered from, and what supplies of grace and heavenly illumination they have received. All this they did without a remote symptom of the least humiliating sense of the depth and malignity of human depravity, and without exhibiting evidence of ever having known the true character of God. They most arrogantly and unequivocally assumed to themselves the certain knowledge of their own exclusive rectitude and understanding. The Scriptures they hold in considerable estimation. Some parts of them are truth—some parts error. Some parts are the sayings of men—some of good men, others of bad—and some parts are the word of God. Of these last, some parts have become antiquated—others have lost their importance by the non-existence of the occasions and circumstances for which they were expressly written. The Old Testament is, I believe, wholly exploded; the words of the Apostles less divine than of the Saviour, and even His, were not so unerring and circumstantial a guide as the Spirit which influences believers. This is necessary to direct in all things; is equal in all cases to the authority of Scripture; and sometimes authorizes a violation of Scripture. Whatever be its impulses, it is infallible.

They employ the Scripture to sanction the guidance of this spirit, and follow the motions of the spirit to violate Scripture. The following passage they adduce—" But when the comforter is come, &c. he shall lead you into all truth."

The day of judgment is now progressing! As a specimen of their abuse of Scripture, I will note their observations on this awful topic. The passage is 2d Thes. i. 7, 8, 9, 10; which was quoted by me in refutation of their dangerous sentiments last alluded to. Christ has come once—engaged to come again—of this last coming, the seventh verse is an intimation; and with the 8th, expresses the manner. He is to be *revealed*; not actually and visibly to appear from Heaven. The expression "with his mighty Angels" is equivalent to the figurative phrase " in the clouds of Heaven"—that is, with, or by means of a *cloud* of witnesses—these are in short terms the Shakers. The flaming fire, verse 8th, is refining truth—Mat. ii. 2, &c.—"When (v. 10) he shall come to be glorified *in* his Saints and to be admired *in* all them that believe." Here note, it is not said shall be glorified amongst, or *by*, or *in* view of all them that believe—but *in* them—that is, in their hearts, in their souls, during the third new and last dispensation, which is Christ's second coming, and now already commenced. His Saints, without any explanation, are the Shakers. They spiritualise away the glorious doctrine of the resurrection,

## APPENDIX. 17

by degrading to nonsense, all those plain and express Scriptures, which substantiate it in the most undoubted, unequivocal language. The world is to stand, if I rightly apprehended his communication, the eternal residence of the Shakers. The Scriptures which predict its destruction, are easily wrested from their plain import, and *for world* is to be understood the sinful *inhabitants of it*. Their abandonment of society and communion of property, they justify by the example of the Church at Jerusalem. This alone, of all the primitive churches, was perfect; and a fit model for the organization of the churches of the new dispensation.

All literature, even a sufficient acquaintance with letters to spell out a chapter of the Testament, is denied their youth and children, on the ground of the Saviour's example, and his omission to positively enjoin it in his precepts. Such an acquisition would expose their youth to the contamination of the world, by admitting them to all its profane publications; and all that is necessary to be known of the Bible, may be gained from the expositions of their elders.

Celibacy is justified from the example of Christ—from that of many of his disciples—from his own declaration—" The children of this world, marry and are given in marriage—but they that shall be accounted worthy of *that world* and of the *resurrection from the dead*, (i. e. of Shakerism) neither marry nor are given in marriage, but are like unto the angels of God;" from the Apostle's explicit prohibition, and finally from the very nature of the thing; for it is evident, say they, that all intercourse of the sexes, not for the express and sole purpose of the propagation of the species, is an indulgence in our vilest and most unruly propensities. Never was, and never can a connection of the sexes be formed, for the above purely benevolent purpose, and consequently the very nature of the union, should condemn it forever. It was permitted, as were many other sinful practices, under the old legal dispensation. This permission was then necessary, in order to perpetuate our race to the present day, and afford the materials for a Royal Priesthood, a holy generation. These are to become co-workers with God in the destruction of the world; that is, of the profane; and the pure people of God, in their perfect state, to which the Shakers will arrive about this period, will become immortal.

Their sacrilegious rite of dancing, &c. on God's holy day, is styled *labor*. This they do to subdue the sins of their members; and for the practice, they find Scriptural injunctions in the exhortations "to labor," "strive," "agonise," "work out your salvation," &c. &c. These were the subjects of my inquiry and of their explanation, in a conversation of two hours. They comprise most of their distinctive peculiarities.

In their intercourse with their neighbors, they have ever sustained the character of the most punctilious fidelity; are proverbially industrious, modest, unassuming—though to this, there are many exceptions. The human mind is evidently depressed a few degrees below the ordinary standard, in such as have, from their infancy, been among them. They are penuriously economical, and much attached to their wealth. They all assemble, at a stated hour, on the Sabbath, in a spacious Hall, furnished with seats, around the walls within. To males and females, different parts of the floor are appropriated. Their exercises, after an introductory silence, are prayer, singing, exposition of Scripture by an elder, singing and dancing, in concert. The dance is plain, consisting of an uniform, moderate, and most exactly measured step—alternately, in advance and retrograde, across the chapel floor. They move over a space of ten or twelve feet. Their fraternity's government, is entrusted to a selection of elders—male and female. These rule with diligence and lenity, and usually receive from the others, a very cheerful subjection.

*Castleton, May* 18*th.*—Yesterday commenced our journey—had a comfortable conversation with brother S——; derived sensible advantages from it. What an invaluable blessing is a true brother in Christ, as I have every reason to believe brother S. to be. The whole world is vacant as the wind, of every charm, and of all its boasted value, when viewed separate from my Saviour's glories. When connected with his kingdom, I see it created by His hand, and upheld by His power, to fulfil His great designs. When thus viewed, every object smiles His praise. I love to gaze on the Sun, the Clouds, the Stars, and Sky. I love to send my eyes roving over the broad face of nature, on which was once acted the great scene of His sufferings, His afflictions, his labors, his temptations, persecutions and death. I love to look at the mountains which will flee; at the rivers and lakes which will be dried up at His appearance. Come, Lord Jesus, from Thy Throne in glory, quickly come, and grant deliverance to all Thy servants—come and perfect in them Thy glory.

Unless the Lord interpose His grace, my most serious and frequent resolutions cannot regulate even my external conduct. I believe my constitutional frailties are more numerous than those of most others. Alienation of heart from God, I perceive, however, is the prime reason of all my misdemeanors. Literary emulation has lately glowed with too much ardour in my mind.

*May* 27th, 1814.—My mind not uniformly prayerful—omitted several opportunities of saying something for Jesus; how long shall I be obliged either to disregard truth, or note in my diary a long succession of departures from God! What, O my Jesus, shall I do? Can I think to renounce my profession?—that would be to pierce through in the most murderous manner the heart of my dear Redeemer. Can I resolve to devote myself anew to His service!—though I have failed in my resolutions repeatedly, I still will renew my trust. O Saviour, confirm thou it, or I cannot again resolve.

I have often abstained from doing good merely on account of unpreparedness in my own soul; but am convinced, that instead of thus confirming my unbelief, by shrinking into voluntary darkness, it is then, in a peculiar sense, my duty to rise from the dead and "come forth." I always have as much strength and ability to rouse myself, as dead Lazarus had. And blessed be God, He is ever ready to exert His resurrection power.

## APPENDIX. 19

*June* 11.—I went last week a circuit of three days' duration, through the neighbouring towns. Rev. Mr. Perry, of Richmond, gave me some encouragement of accompanying me, but his health was so poor that he judged it unsafe to set out. A member of his family, however, went with me, and I think I have reason to bless God that the journey was not altogether unprofitable to me.

Two things exist at the present day, which never did before, and, which afford us good ground to expect unexampled enlargement of the Church. The one is a spirit for missions to promote the extension of divine truth throughout the earth, and the unheard of, and almost miraculous exertions which this spirit has actuated. The other is the almost universal coalition, lately formed of all the regular and orthodox churches in Christendom. The union of the Congregational and Presbyterian Churches in America, is so complete as to produce unity in exertions—unity in sentiment and practice, and unity in several cases, in the promotion of some general and important designs. One of these objects which, at the general convention of Presbyterian and Congregational ministers in the United States, lately met in Philadelphia, received the sanction, and will doubtless still continue to have the support of the Clergy of America, is the correction of the violations of the Sabbath, practised by public patronage. The particular abuses referred to, in the petition of this numerous and influential body to Congress, are the transportation and opening of mails on the Lord's day.—Ministers I verily believe, always have sufficient influence to support conferences, where the attachment of their people is sufficient to support them.

Travelled a few miles this morning in company with a student of Theology, from Princeton, and brother to Mr. Swift, of Stockbridge. He informed me that a work of reformation had very recently taken place in the vicinity of the institution—begun, under the private, faithful labors, of some of the members of the Seminary—that the students are twenty-two—that Dr. A——— is one of the eminently distinguished christians of the age—he excels in humility, ardent feeling, faithful laboring, and in uniformly exhibiting a lamb-like, shining, christian deportment.

Called to-day in a very debilitated state in Granby—a good meeting house; no preacher—no preaching—the people, I learnt, had dismissed their Minister six years before. The present state of religion must be deplorable. O! how I longed to be fitted to preach! if it might be to the glory of God—if I might be qualified with talents, knowledge, grace, humility, trust in God, and a soul swallowed up in devotion. Without these, I think, I do not wish to live.

Arrived in a feeble state, towards night, at E. Hartford—called at the Rev. Mr. Yates' house, but found him absent on the happy business of visiting his people, and meeting a portion of them in a religious conference. Brother Humphrey was likewise gone to attend a religious conference, in another direction—he soon returned, and gave me very encouraging information of the reformation in Weathersfield and Oxford, especially in the latter place.

Thursday—towards night, I went in company with brother H., to deacon Stillman's—found his house filled with a company of serious and enquiring females, some rejoicing in God their hope of glory, others trembling with the hope of salvation. How terrible, my soul exclaimed, is this place; it is none other than the house of God, and the gate of Heaven.

Thursday evening, brother H. and I, attended in the conference-house. No one was present with us, who had been accustomed to conduct a part of the exercises in public, except dear S——.

Brother H. and myself spoke with great freedom: the people were very solemn and much affected. The next day I tarried in the place; visited a few families, and though in a very low state of health, could not forbear spending a principal part of the time in conversation. I found the season refreshing. Of one hundred who exhibited satisfactory evidence of a change of heart, only forty have yet joined the Church.

*Saturday, June 18th.* Early this afternoon I returned to Hartford, and called upon Dr. Strong. He is a man of very deep penetration—eminent talents—a mind abundantly furnished and cultivated—and always prepared to act with decision. Religious meetings are still well attended in Hartford—one hundred, mostly young, have joined Dr. Strong's church. Thirty or forty more, exhibit hopeful evidences of regeneration.

This afternoon I rode into Oxford—I was led to reflect on my way to this place, in what manner the Lord had dealt with me, in my whole previous course. In afflictions and disappointments, I saw a Father's tenderness and wisdom. In prosperity and mercies, I felt cause for thankfulness, that they had not been followed by a curse.

I soon found out the place of Mr. C.'s residence—Deep devotion, heavenly mindedness, and spiritual anxiety were strongly marked on his visage—his age is twenty-seven—has preached about one year and a half. His ministerial talents are good—his acquaintance with scripture extensive—his memory retentive—his manners affectionate—his address familiar and easy—his conversation well adapted to his solemn employment—his language plain—his preaching pungent, evangelical, and attended by the spirit of God, it falls with irresistible force and authority.

*Tuesday, 21st.* To-day Mr. C. went on a ministerial visit to the people of Weathersfield; I spent the morning at his house, and in the afternoon held a meeting with the youths and children: about seventy—all under fifteen years of age. On no occasion did I ever before feel more solemnity, and a greater sense of responsibility, than when entering among this little host.

Mr. Ely, Minister at Lebanon, I found at my residence on my return.—Visited with him, one family much to my satisfaction—the wife was awakened last Sabbath evening, and appeared to be truly convicted of sin, and ruin. She is aged about twenty-five. Her husband is pious—lately moved into the place. He had heard of the glorious work now progressing, and moved into the place, induced by the hope, that the dear wife of his bosom, might be made an heir of grace. Mr. Ely preached in the forenoon from the passage, used last Sabbath by Mr. C. "all things are now ready, come unto the marriage." The object of his discourse was to point out the sinner's need, and the competent and most abundant provision of the gospel. The discourse was truly evangelical—delivered in the spirit of the gospel, and of the reformation, and I trust was not without effect upon the souls of those who heard it.

*October* 24th—Just risen from my bed after several days very alarming illness; after examining my preparations for death, I find them not only incomplete, but not effectually begun. Some resolutions were the consequence of this discovery—1st: to live more prayerfully; 2d: to guard my conversation more effectually; 3d: to be active in the extent to which the duties of my present employment render it expedient, for the salvation of souls.

*Wednesday, October* 24th, 1814.—Much out of health—I am necessitated totally to suspend study; and have not the desirable comforts of grace. How just, how suitable, and if duly improved by me, how merciful is this interruption of my unsanctified progress! An excursion into the neighbouring towns on horseback, would, with the Divine blessing, contribute much to the restoration of my health. I may make one; I desire above all, to acquiesce in the wise Providence of God.

*October* 29th.—I have this day determined, to take a dismission from College; the language of God's Providence calls me to the act. My health appears essentially impaired. It may be the purpose of God to call me soon into eternity. I have so long had my expectations of recovery delayed, that I am inclined to believe, I shall never be restored. I feel a sensible support from on high; I have derived to-day, great satisfaction from renewing the dedication of myself to God. I could appropriate to myself the language of Watts:

> Firm as a rock His promise stands,
> And He can well secure
> What I've committed to His hands,
> 'Till the decisive hour.

Am now from a conference. Was affected with the consideration, that the opportunity of this evening is the last of a religious nature that I shall probably enjoy with many—perhaps with most present. I pray my God to send them the frequent visits of His grace. I addressed my brethren and fellow students on the propriety, and enforced the duty of aiming at the glory of God in all things; the appearance of the students was solemn.

Unless my present constitutional habit is very speedily and thoroughly corrected, I think I cannot hope to see the termination of another year. I have attempted to submit all my state to the disposal of my Heavenly Father; still I discover an increasing anxiety to be spared to preach the Gospel, if the will of God be so. If grace qualifies me for any active office in the Vineyard, I am inclined to believe, it will be rather to break down the hedge and root out the tares, than watch over, water, cultivate and rear to maturity, the springing fruit.

*December* 1814.—The faint palpitations of spiritual life continued to-day. I am ready sometimes to give up to some desperate opinion of myself on account of the faintness of my best desires—the uniformity, and feeble languid exercises of my mind. O that I might despair of my own capacity to recover myself—be brought to a deep and sickening loathing of my best doings—be made to see the imperfection, sloth, unfaithfulness and sin, which has ever attended and characterised my best performances. I have raised up myself to a most unseemly height, on my past humility, attainments in grace, commendable exploits, &c. which I verily believe Satan has dressed in the garb they have lately appeared in to my imagination. My temper is naturally ardent and headlong. When I professedly engage in the work of the Lord, the genius of my natural mind, especially when stimulated by a conscious communion with the Holy Ghost, dictates such labours and occasions such a flow of zeal, as I believe have both raised the admiration of others and pampered my own pride. My talents, slender as they are, are almost altogether of the popular kind. I almost always carry too much sail for my ballast—hence I never sail long even in a moderate gale, without being thrown keel upwards. Prayer sometimes recovers me. But when the immediate occasion which gave exercise to my zeal, and the humbling trial of the strength of my graces may have withdrawn, even prayer frequently becomes formal, ineffectual and seldom. I can say on the very best grounds of sincerity, that if I am chosen of Christ, I am indeed less than the least. My sensibility was lately arrested, and a new, not unprofitable train of ideas inspired by reading in my Greek Testament, the 20th and 21st verses of the 3d chapter of Ephesians.— Precious Scripture! calculated to humble any soul but mine. What endless treasures of knowledge, glory and love, are comprehended in Christ Jesus!— And O, the nothingness of all my attainments hitherto! They bear no comparison with what they might be, were they not the shameful testimonials of time misspent, opportunities neglected, and blessings misused.

I am daily much employed in examining, and attempting to ascertain, the strength, comparative excellence, and nature, of my mental powers—in labouring to discover the kind of improvement, and the sphere of labour in the Ministry to which my disposition is best suited, and may best be accommodated. I discover my natural manner of speaking to be flowing and ardent— my perception to be rapid and naturally superficial; or when intensely exercised it is liable to escape control, entwine among the thoughts, a thousand minute and eccentric particulars, foreign from the subject to which I would hold it. My imagination is wild and too easily instigated to interfere officiously when judgment and discretion only are needed. In speaking, it often begins to blaze, puts out the eye of reason, and by embarrassing memory, and interrupting the associate chain of my ideas, and inviting the mind to follow it in some new track, it often has led me out of the sight of my first arrangement of thought, and either proves too unsteady or weak, to help me out—or runs me into some unprofitable speculation.

These, and many other discoveries, have resulted in the adoption of two or three practical rules and conclusions—1st: to study well, and examine faithfully in every light, whatever I propose to execute; 2d: having once resolved on any course of action, to prosecute it with the most prompt and persevering energy; 3d: never to scruple the expediency of attempting any innovation in established principles or practices, when once assured from the teachings of the Word and Spirit of God, that His cause requires them; 4th: never, from irresolution or indolence, to break off a work half executed; 5th: in all things to be humble—but to consult God and judgment, rather than man and present inclinations, and never to "daub with untempered mortar," a building erected for eternity.

*Sabbath, March* 5, 1815.—The love of God has lately so reigned in my soul that I cannot discover a sinful gratification which I have not resolved to forego, a necessary cross which I am not resolved to assume, nor a required effort which, *pro tempore,* I did not resolve to make. A sweet, astonishing, melting, humbling sensation of forgiveness for my past crimes, the heinousness of which is enhanced on every repetition, was divinely impressed on my soul. Oh! I cannot doubt the infinitude of my dear Redeemer's love and grace. I now have clearer and more extensive views of the gracious nature of the gospel.

I am reading Baxter's Saint's Rest. 'Tis refreshing; 'tis edifying. Why are the searching, conscience-arresting volumes of a Baxter, a Flavel, a Russel, or a Whitfield, left unread on the shelves of some aged Christians?

*Thursday morning, March* 23, 1815.—Yesterday read a part of Mrs. Newall's Journal, after her embarkation for India; and a part of Buchanan's Researches. I feel myself shamed in contemplating the character of that lovely female as a Missionary, in contrast with my own, and was much affected, even to weeping, in reading that part of Buchanan's diary which described the condition of the dear lambs at Tanjore, who have but a few rays of light, to show them their way to Zion, though their eyes are opened and anxiously waiting for more; who have a relish for the waters of life—yet almost destitute of any knowledge of their source—who are hungry for the blessed Bible. O how I wish they were near, that I might give them one of the three, which lie on my table before me—and yet whole churches are destitute!

The Christian in every situation must keep up the line of distinction between himself and the world, he must most sensibly *feel* it, others must *see* it. I still intend to associate as frequently as possible with pious company. The danger which I receive in the company of the ungodly, is not so formidable as that which offers amongst respectable worldly professors of religion. I feel less restraint, am less vigilant, and either forget or neglect too often, the peculiar obligation resting upon me, to watch over, and reprove any misdemeanor in them, as I would correct any impropriety of my own. I find myself this morning, spiritually in the hands of the blessed and loving Father of all. Oh! that I may always rest here. Lord, give me not over to Satan or myself.—Glory, and honor, and dominion, eternally be to the Father, the Son, and Holy Ghost. Amen.

*April 8*, 1815.—Wrote a letter to Mr. S—— dictated in a style of gospel plainness. I have recently adopted the practice, invariably to pray over my letters while writing them; and often when sealed, kneel down and present them to the Lord, praying Him to employ their contents in promoting the glory and peace of Zion; to fill the soul of the person to whom they are addressed, with holiness and comfort; and to blot out, by some dispensation of his providence, any error of thought or manner, which may inadvertently have found a place in them.

*Wednesday, June 22*, 1815.—Resolved to adopt a resolution of President Edwards, to study the sacred Scriptures, so as to make a very perceptible weekly progress in the knowledge of them.

*Thursday, 23d.*—Find on perusing President Edwards' Life, and parts of his diary, that I can transcribe many portions of the last into my own Journal, and adopt some part of the first as answering to my own. When I bestow most time and care upon the Scriptures, I always live in the exercise of the most faith.

*Resolved*—Always in the most trifling and apparently indifferent thing, both in speaking, thinking and writing, most strictly to adhere to truth, as I would be judged at last by "the God of truth."

*Wednesday, June 28th.* I am sensibly embarrassed in my progress in this, and every other labor, undertaken for God, by my ignorance of the Scriptures.

*Monday morning, July 3d*, 1815. God has visited me this morning in my closet—O! how sweet His presence! how awfully sweet—How large His grace; how refreshing! But O, how holy! how sin-condemning.—I often think of the appellation of Jesus, addressed to his Father—"Holy." What a word was that on the lips of Immanuel. What a check ought the example of our Redeemer in addressing the Infinite Majesty, be to all his followers—who like myself, have been accustomed to rush like a heedless horse into the midst of the mighty and mortal contest!—O, my God—may I always feel myself in the immediate presence of the Holy, holy, holy—God.

*July 4th.* Read with some profit a part of Fuller's, "The gospel its own witness." Some letters and sermons by the same. He seems grounded in the truth, as it is in Jesus—to have known in his heart the power of grace—but, I should judge, not to have been the man of prayer that Whitfield, Edwards, and Milner were. The reasonings are good, but his writings want solemnity, want a little of the unction which sweetens; and gives that more than earthly savor to all that is written under the Spirit's glow, and teaching:—the proportion of truly evangelical publications among the "Ocean Tide" of *religious books*, which are monthly flowing into being, is smaller now, I believe, than fifty years ago. Modern writings are more perspicuous—the style of them, better finished; and in the orthodox part of them, the doctrines of Christianity are stated with more precision and accuracy.—There is in our recent publications more of the frame, but less of the finish and beauty of the gospel, than in those which preceded them—they are rather addressed to the understanding, than to the heart and conscience. The reader must supply from his own bosom this deficiency of *spirit*, or expect rather to find his head crowded with ideas, than his soul edified *with the word of truth.*

*Friday, July* 21*st*, 1815. Have had my faith tried with respect to temporal provision for several days past. Before I have been fully aware of my error and my folly, I have several times found myself indulging, in a criminal, unbelieving, and *treacherous* anxiety on this account; notwithstanding my God had *always* appeared for my relief when straitened, and notwithstanding my resolutions and promises, so often renewed, to distrust his watchful providence, again to sin herein, appears doubly criminal. I find this morning that all the apparent difficulties are seasonably and wholely removed. With my grateful thanksgivings to my Redeemer and my Portion, how ought I to be reproved! O Lord, Jehovah, may I never doubt again.

*Resolve.*—When my prospects for temporal provision are most clouded, ever to be extremely cautious, *then*, to seek more exclusively, and pursue more eagerly after the things of the kingdom of God.

## No. 2

The following resolutions of the Trustees of the Maine Charity School show that they still retained their entire confidence in Mr. Ashmun's integrity and piety.

At a meeting of the Trustees of Maine Charity School, Hampden, March 26, 1819,

Mr. Professor Ashmun having resigned his office of Professor of Classical Literature in this Institution,

*Voted*, That we accept his resignation.

*Voted*, That we cordially reciprocate those kind feelings expressed in the note accompanying the resignation. That we present him our sincere thanks for his faithful and efficient exertions while in our employment; and that we commend him to the blessing of God, and the friendship and communion of good men; assuring him that he will ever be remembered by us with sentiments of affectionate esteem, and that we shall never cease to feel a lively interest in his welfare.  HARVEY LOOMIS, *Secretary*.

A true copy.

Attest: HARVEY LOOMIS, *Secretary*.

*Dear Sir:*—It is hoped you will continue in the agency of the Board, and make such exertions as your convenience will permit, to obtain money and books for the Seminary.  HARVEY LOOMIS.

## No. 3.

The following papers, (one written in 1825, the other in 1827,) exhibit strongly the views of Mr. Ashmun in regard to the importance of Missionary efforts among the native Africans, as well as of judicious and systematic Religious Instruction for the Colony.

MONROVIA, WESTERN AFRICA,
*Sabbath Day, March 20th, 1825.*

*To the Board of Managers of the Am. Col. Society:*

GENTLEMEN,—While I recollect distinctly the sole object of your very respectable Association, is the establishment of a Colony in this country, I cannot forget that several of the gentlemen who compose the Board of Direction, are practical believers in the Evangelical Revelation of Jesus Christ. In this character you will pardon the liberty I take of addressing you on a subject to which as individuals you cannot be insensible; and which, from the distinguished influence conferred by situation and talents, you have it in your power, probably more than many others, to rouse the public mind to action. I mean the establishment of a devout and able Christian Missionary, with the requisite assistants, in the vicinity of this Colony.

I have thought that the intervals of public worship on this holy day, cannot be more usefully or acceptably employed, than in submitting the result of observations made in relation to this object, during a residence of nearly three years on the very theatre of the idolatry, superstition, cruelty and ignorance, which the establishment in question, by the appointment of God, and in the judgment of man, offers the only means of curing.

Following the train of my own reflections, I shall submit a few considerations:

1st. On the moral, religious and social condition of our neighbors, which call for the christian effort proposed.

2d. On the facilities which seem to invite to it.

3d. On the most proper manner of commmencing, founding and conducting the mission.

And Lastly, Its effects.

I. The general condition of the people of Western Africa has been the theme of too many reports and treatises, to remain at this period a matter of inquiry to persons of reading or general intelligence in any country. Towards the North, the intolerant system of Mahometanism prevails to the exclusion even of the less offensive delusion of Paganism. From the Gambia, to the Sierra Leone, a discordant mixture of Moorish austerities and Pagan licentiousness, in regard to religious things, divides the professions of the miserable people, and distinguishes them into two distinct classes. From Sierra Leone to the South-eastward, far below Mesurado, the ever-varying absurdities of the human fancy, goaded to action by an inward consciousness of guilt and fear, and wholly uninstructed by divine revelation, enslave the minds of the inhabitants, and sink them perhaps to the lowest state of debasement, to which human nature can descend.

Those who inhabit the coast have heard of one Supreme God; and because they have no belief of their own, have adopted that great truth: but they pay him no homage, and are wholly at a loss what sort of character to attribute to him. Some pretend to admit him to have a general care of his creatures; but finding a difficulty in accounting for the difference in their situation, they generally solve it by concluding, that if God created he does not govern men; for they choose rather to believe that God has nothing to do in the world, than that he acts with so much of what their blindness calls partiality. They have no forms of worship, nor do they commonly appear in the least to act from the belief that the Supreme God will so far notice as to reward any sacrifices of present convenience they may make to the cause of truth, to temperance, or moral virtue. But, accustomed only to the grossest conceptions, their minds can hardly frame the idea of so sublime and recondite an object as the invisible Spirit of the universe; and if raised to so unwonted a height, by the inquiries of others, they tend by their own stupid weight down to their ordinary level of sensuality. They, like all other human beings, have consciences to which "their thoughts" in the language of inspiration, "are continually accusing or else excusing one another." But having no knowledge of future retributions, their inward fears wholly confine themselves to the apprehension of temporal punishments. From this constant dread, many drag along a most wretched existence, and all endeavor to deliver themselves by a multitude of charms carried about their persons, and by others, erected upon or suspended from their houses, and set up in their towns, at their fisheries, and on their most frequented roads. These, which go by the common name of *fetishes*, are thought to derive little or no value from the materials of which

## APPENDIX.

they are formed, but wholly from the skill employed in compounding them, and the reputation of the fabricators and venders of them. A distinct order of men, held in high repute, acquire all the comforts of rude and savage life, by trading in these articles, on the credulity of the people. The most enlightened among them are commonly the most superstitious—as even their *wise men*, are but sufficiently enlightened to see their need of something adapted to religious beings; of which the body of all the people are too brutish and grovelling in their mental character, to be able to form, it would seem, any comprehension at all.

Children, 'till arrived nearly to an age to act for themselves, receive as far as I have learnt, no instruction whatever; nor even then, from their parents. But the boys are led into a deep and solitary forest, where persons of age and reputed sagacity, and commonly with injunctions of perpetual secrecy, enforced by the severest penalties, impart to them, together with many useless, perhaps, pernicious mysteries, instructions relating to the superstitions, the laws and the policy of the country, and, it is said, of the trade and more ordinary business of manhood. They remain under this tuition, commonly about half the season; and some have the privilege of several times separating themselves in the course of their lives to receive these instructions.

The girls undergo a similar rustication at the proper time of life, and are taught what it is supposed concerns them most to understand in the narrow sphere of duty to which custom restricts them in life.

Children very seldom receive parental correction, and are seldom restrained in any course to which their passions and propensions incline them. Lying, petty thefts, and the entire catalogue of childish vices and follies when seen in children, only excite merriment, as long as the consequences are not seriously injurious to themselves or others. The adult is commonly devoid of moral principle altogether. The strongest minds among them, I observe, see farthest the inconvenience of dishonesty, intemperance and other vices, and endeavor in a few instances to avoid, and in all, to conceal them. The least intelligent, are uniformly the most openly and the most absolutely vicious and unprincipled.

Polygamy and domestic slavery, it is well known, are as universal as the scanty means of the people will permit. And a licentiousness of practice which none—not the worst part of any civilized community on earth can parallel, gives a hellish consummation to the frightful deformity imparted by sin to the moral aspect of these tribes. There is not a feature of their social character, but proves them abandoned to that depravity, the common inheritance of apostate man, which knows no remedy but the Gospel of the Grace of God. They are degraded to the condition nearly of the better sort of brutes in human form; discovering at the same time, the gleamings of that intelligent soul which never dies. They are still the objects of the redeeming love, and daily care of the Christian's Saviour. They are the materials of which faith assures the children of God, that the temple of Jehovah in which his glory will blaze for ever, is destined to be built—Where sin has abounded, grace is much more to abound. This is an axiom in the economy of the Divine Mercy; and therefore, the Christian World may hope yet for Africa. But to raise these people by any other means than the renovating power of the Spirit of God administered as himself has limited the holy influence, through the preaching and reception of the doctrines of the Divine Saviour, is an absurdity, which all experience exposes, and which their own accumulating suffering for many thousand years confirms; and to expect it is to consign them deliberately against the express law of providence to certain destruction.

II. But let us enquire whether there are any circumstances suited to invite the attention of Missionary Societies, and direct their efforts to these people, rather than to any other particular portion of the Pagan World? There is in my opinion a concurrence of these propitious circumstances, which I cannot help regarding as the signal of a favoring providence held out to the Christian World, particularly to the American Churches, to announce the grand and glorious crisis.

Such is to be regarded the firm and peaceful establishment of a civilized and christian community, in the very bosom and centre of all this barbarism. There are hundreds whose prayers and whose influence will gladly be extended to the holy Missionary: he and his assistants may derive from the vicinity of what the native African considers as a powerful settlement, all the security and protection which he can desire from this arm of mortals. His necessary intercourse with the Colony will blunt, if not exclude the sense of exile from home, country and civilized life. In case of abandonment or opposition from the poor objects of his benevolent labors, he may obtain temporary aid from hence, and find an asylum in extremities. But it is perfectly easy for the Government of the Colony to obtain of all the Kings in the neighborhood a friendly stipulation in favor of the Mission, and exact a strict adherence to such stipulation.

A second circumstance highly favorable to the undertaking, is the profound peace which prevails at this time between all the tribes and the colony, and between the respective tribes. Our settlement was established in blood. The struggle on our part, the effort on that of the natives, was severe and violent; but the issue was such as to terminate their hostile machinations, it is believed totally, and for ever. We were more than two years since, regarded as invincible by any native force: and the single policy now becoming general among our neighbors, is to cultivate the most amicable relations with the Colony. The temple of Janus is closed, and who shall say that the Augustan period of this part of Africa has not arrived; and who will withhold from it its long predicted Saviour?

*The natives have universally a most affecting persuasion of the superiority of white men.* They see the superior perfection of our fabrics, our arts, our jurisprudence, our mental culture, and I can now say it, thanks to the power of religion on the minds of many of our colonists, of our moral character. Our worship is serious and impressive, beyond any thing they ever witness among themselves, and they acknowledge generally the superiority of our religion, and almost wish themselves white (or civilized) men, that they might adopt it, for they all retain the absurd idea, that however excellent or true our religion and institutions, they are doomed to understand and be benefitted by none except their own.

A fourth facility which few pagan tribes offer to the American Missionary, is to be found in the circumstance, that every head man around us, and hundreds of their people speak, and can be made to understand our language without an interpreter. He may, immediately on arriving in the country begin his work, and while acquiring the language, render himself nearly as useful as afterwards.

I might mention the cheapness of living, and the small expense of maintaining a plain industrious missionary family, in this country—the tractable and mild natural dispositions of the poor Africans—the absence of every thing resembling intolerance in the systems of superstition by which they are enslaved—the distance of this country from that of the persecuting Moors, and the animating successes which have attended the simple preaching of the gospel, and the other related means of religious instruction, at Sierra Leone, and in the colony of the Cape of Good Hope; and these circumstances and facts, must have their weight with all who wish well enough to the cause, to engage themselves, or others in it. But I cannot enlarge.

III. *I will make a few suggestions on the most proper manner of commencing, founding, and conducting the mission.*

I cannot hesitate to say, that the Missionary, or Principal of the proposed establishment, ought of preference to be a white man. Some of the reasons for this opinion have been given. Others will readily occur. He ought to be an honest, holy, and eminently disinterested person, neither old, nor too young. To acquire the entire confidence of the natives, and do justice to the responsible undertaking, he ought to engage for life, and make his tomb in Africa. He must love the employment, and appear to love it, and have no pleasure so great, as that of doing good to the souls and bodies of men. Science, prudence, humility, and a good constitution are all useful auxiliaries, and he should not be without them. Let him repair to the colony—spend half the first year, with whatever assistants and family he has, in the settlement. The airy and salubrious settlement of Thompson-Town, forming on the summit of our mountain, would serve better than probably any other situation in Western Africa to form his habit to the climate.

Here he might be extensively useful, and fully employed among the re-captured Africans, in acquiring the language, obtaining an accurate knowledge of the country, and manners, &c., of the inhabitants, and in arranging the plan of his future operations, collecting the materials, and otherwise actually forwarding the building of the missionary houses.

The centre of a numerous population is to be found on the banks of the

River St. Paul's, from five to ten miles above its mouth.  Here, a sufficient quantity of land can be obtained.  The country is dry—the situation airy and delightful, and the inhabitants less engaged in the slave trade, and more independent of its gains for a subsistence, than nearer the sea-board.

The King, Peter Bromley, has actually consented to give the land, and afford protection to any good white man, recommended by the Governor of the Colony, who shall come to spend his life in teaching his people.  There would be no difficulty in procuring the most eligible situation.

Let the Missionary collect around him a numerous family, entirely separate and a little remote, from any native town.  Here let him introduce the worship of God—establish, or rather render the whole establishment, a school, in which the word of God shall be taught and be read to all, but especially to children, in the English language.  The members of the family must all be taught and required daily to labor at stated periods, and made as soon as possible to support themselves in a simple plain style ; not deviating too much at first, from that, to which all are accustomed.—The buildings may also be of the country construction, gradually introducing in future erections, a more expensive and permanent style.  The Agricultural and other improvements, should proceed from the present simple methods, to those which are more artificial.  Once founded, and conducted judiciously for a few years, the mission would prove a generating point of other similar establishments, till, with the blessing of Almighty God, whose work alone it is, the knowledge and profession of Christianity, shall become as general, as the abominable and vile rites of Paganism at the present time.

Such is the ultimate and grand effect to be expected, and to be prayed for—But in closing this paper, I will enumerate—

IV. Lastly, some other fruits of such an establishment of a most gratifying nature, and of a more immediate occurrence.

The first will be to preserve our neighbours from adopting the vices, without the virtues of civilization.  For this colony, I am sorry to say, already has, and ever must have, strong samples of both.  Vice can be propagated without instruction.  But who ever heard of the moral and social virtues being taken up by uninstructed Pagans, merely from the example of a few good men?  Every month's experience proves to me that our neighbours are corrupted by the influence of bad example, and derive no benefit from the good, that are set them in the colony.  The Mission will in part, cure this evil.  It will afford no vicious examples, and will fortify the good with religious and moral instruction.

Another effect will be in some measure, to prevent the vicious examples of the natives from re-acting upon the colony, and corrupting the morals, and debasing the views, especially of our young people.

A faithful Missionary must soon possess himself of the confidence of the tribes.  Through his mediation, differences between them and the colony, may, in most cases, be composed, or prevented altogether.  Such an establishment

I consider as forming the best security and pledge of peace and friendship, between the natives and this colony.—These advantages, let it be in conclusion recollected, are only secondary to the great end of saving a multitude of immortal beings from the power of sin, and the wrath of God: and the rescue of new territories from the power of Satan, for the Son of God to rule by his grace to the end of time. This is the grand argument on which this humble appeal for the African tribes near us, chiefly relies for success. It is respectfully submitted to all who can feel its force—and may the blessing of God attend it. J. A.

CALDWELL, MAY 20, 1827.

DEAR SIR:—While we recollect with gratitude the signal success with which Divine Providence has crowned the arduous undertaking of the American Colonization Society, I pray it may not be forgotten that that success is only partial; and that there are to be moral effects wrought on the great body of the settlers after their establishment in this country, without which, all that has been—all that can be accomplished, even *with the national patronage*, must still leave the work incomplete, and short of our early hopes.

The enemies of the whole scheme say, and say truly *(fas est etiam ab hoste doceri)*, that "Such is the supineness of the moral and intellectual character of nine-tenths of the subjects of colonization, that without vast improvement, they cannot become the materials of a civil society, blest with free institutions and the right of self-government."

And here, my dear Sir, is the weak point of our cause; here, the arguments of our adversaries, which, on most subjects connected with colonization, are palpably inconclusive, become seriously weighty and pertinent.

I flatter myself that I see causes already at work, which must, in time, effectuate so much of the grand enterprise as consists in the removal of the annual increase, at least, of all the free colored population of the United States, and their permanent settlement in this country. But, fixed here, what is their situation, on the supposition which you will permit me, by way of illustration, to adopt—That NO effectual means for their moral improvement are employed?

In the proportion of 6 out of 10, the emigrants may be expected to be ILLITERATE. And, when we consider that most of the actual means of moral and intellectual improvement, the strongest motives which affect the conscience, and stir the soul to action; and those impressions, which, more than any others, are the germs and fostering soil of virtuous principles in the human character: when we consider that all these ennobling influences are, in this age, derived to such as feel them, more through the medium of letters—from tracts, periodicals, religious books, and the Bible, than from all other sources; think, my dear sir, under what a deplorable disadvantage and calamity, that rational creature in human form labors, who never drew from this store-house, directly, one motive to moral action—one countercheck to his appetites and depravity—who cannot read a precept of his Bible—a law of the community he lives in—a page of all those excellent little manuals which are in such wide circulation, and which bring home to every man's bosom and fireside, particularly of the poor, the principles, the duties, examples and enjoyments of Christianity! What must be the moral state of a society composed, in proportion of three and four to one, of such individuals? And such, my dear sir, is the picture; it begins to develope itself already, of a society springing into existence in the settlement of this Colony.

Your emigrants, I must also assume to be generally, *immoral*.

I do not give this character to the actual settlers. There are reasons of a particular nature, and which cannot apply to the great body of future emigrants, why the *first* should not deserve it. Nor do I believe that the immorality, however deplorable, of the free blacks of America, considered as a race of men, is of that matured and positive character which the strong and absolute language sometimes employed on this topic, would ascribe to them. Their vices are certainly of a low order, often extremely troublesome, and always disgusting. But their depravity, both in respect to its *degree*, and its form, may be accounted for, (the corruption of our common nature always considered,) from their circumstances. The faults of their character are nearly all of a negative kind, and may be more properly denominated moral defects, than vices.

Take a colored man from the mass of that population in America—suppose him to commit a fault, it may be an act of personal violence. Inquire into the circumstances. It was an act of revenge or passion. I allow it; and that it was *vicious* in its own nature, and a punishable offence, by the laws of God and man. But, more nearly investigate the circumstance, and analyse the motives of the act; and you will ascertain it in nine cases out of ten, to possess little or nothing of that sturdy aforethought character, which belongs to the higher order of crime. It was the offspring of a blind malice, acting rather *without*, than *in violation of*, perceptible moral restraints. No felt principle of moral conduct was sacrificed to the vindictive impulse, which produced the act; because no such principle had ever been implanted and cherished in his bosom. It is astonishing, how vague, general, and unfelt, are the ideas of right and wrong, which have a faint and floating existence in the minds of a majority of this uncultivated race of men. And even for the best of them, large allowances must, in the estimate of their moral conduct, be placed to the account of this want of the early and effectual inculcation of moral and religious principles.

After this explanation, I must renew the painful inference, that *the emigrants to this country will bring with them no established moral habits.*

Imagine, then, a large community, and this community laid at the foundation of a future empire, without upright moral habits, and without operative moral principles. The mutual want of confidence among the members, must, in a short time, dissolve so far the social tie, as to draw around the several families a line of demarcation, separating them from each other, and establishing in each a separate interest, independent of, and in most instances adverse to, the common interest. Domestic discord, and intestine strife succeed. Property, liberty, life, are without security—are violated—and their violation goes unpunished, and unredressed.

I have here traced the consequences of immorality to the ruin of this Colony, from the single property there is in vice to destroy all social confidence. It must operate to the same end by a thousand other ways, all equally direct, and equally certain. And is the inevitable curse of Heaven on such a people nothing to be regarded? Rather will it not prove a brazen bar in the road of their prosperity, which the wisdom of mortals cannot evade—nor the united strength of a world remove?

These emigrants, from the hour of their arrival in Africa, are also acted upon by the vitiating example of the natives of this country. The amount and effects of this influence I fear, are generally and egregiously underrated. It is not known to every one how little difference can be perceived in the measure of intellect possessed by an illiterate rustic from the United States, and a sprightly native of the coast. It may not be easily credited; but the fact certainly is, that the advantage is, oftenest, clearly on the side of the latter. The sameness of color, and the corresponding characteristics to be expected in different portions of the same race, give to the example of the natives a power and influence over the colonists as extensive as it is corrupting. For, it must not be suppressed, however the fact may be at variance with the first impressions from which most African Journalists have allowed themselves to sketch the character of the natives, *That it is vicious and contaminating in the last degree.* I have often expressed my doubt, whether the simple idea of *moral justice*, as we conceive it from the early dawn of reason, has a place in the thoughts of a pagan African. As a practical principle of morality, I am sure that no such sentiment obtains in the breasts of five Africans within my acquaintance. A selfishness which prostrates every consideration of another's good; a habit of dishonest dealing, of which nothing short of unremitting, untiring vigilance, can avert the consequences; an unlimited indulgence of the appetites; and the labored excitement and unbounded gratification of lust the most unbridled and beastly—these are the ingredients of the African character. And, however revolting, however, on occasion, concealed, by an assumed decency of demeanor, such is the common character of all; and it operates with all the power of an ever-present example on the Colonists, (and with many it is not without its facinations,*) from the mo-

---

* It is very true of the grosser and shocking vices, what Pope erroneously affirms of wickedness in general, that

" Vice is a monster of so frightful mien,
" As, to be hated, needs but be seen;
" But grown too oft familiar with her face,
" We first endure, then pity, then embrace."

ment of their arrival in Africa. It must produce its effects. It *has* produced them. And without a powerful counteracting agency, it must, at no great distance of time, as surely leaven the whole mass, as human nature shall continue what it is.

I will only add one more instance of the change, which the condition of emigrants is obliged to undergo, in consequence of their removal to this country, tending greatly to confirm and assist their moral degeneracy. In the United States, they are surrounded with examples of piety and moral excellence, in persons whom their relative rank and condition in life, engages them to respect, and even to imitate. Such examples not only allure by their excellence; but control by their authority; and the whole effect is of the best and happiest kind. But, in Africa, few or no such examples are present— no such influence is felt or obeyed. Colonists thus suffer a double disadvantage—are subjected to all that is contaminating in the practices of the natives; at the same time that they have passed beyond the reach of the corrective example of enlightened Christians. This I admit to be theory. But is it not theory based on acknowledged facts? God grant it may never become history—the history of this Colony.

Permit me here to offer a slight but faithful sketch of the actual moral state of one of the settlements of the Colony.

The new settlement of Caldwell offers more and truer examples than Monrovia, of the manner in which the great body of the emigrants are likely to be morally affected by their new situation—the settlers here agreeing more nearly in character with the great body of colored people in the United States, than their more select predecessors. And it is here that the evils of which my fears are prophetic, are already beginning the most plainly to discover themselves.

The settlement reaches along both rivers, a distance about two miles. A single individual, whose age and sincere piety certainly render him in many respects useful, assisted by some two or three *utterly illiterate* exhorters, whose moral influence from causes different from simple ignorance, is a cypher; is their only instructer, in all that pertains to the improvement of their mind, to the correction and regulation of their moral practice, the sanctification of their hearts, and the salvation of their souls. Read, they cannot—nor are they capable of intent and steady thinking. No stirring changes, or variety of arousing incidents—but the even tenor of a secluded, rustic life, and the daily vicissitude of rough labor, and sound sleep, weave the simple web of weekly, monthly, and annual history. It is no absurd definition of human nature which I once heard no ordinary adept in it use with great sincerity and emphasis, *that man*, enumerating his other distinctive qualities, *is an indolent animal*—never to be aroused from the most lifeless torpor, but by the force of some sort of necessity. Now, of these people, the physical necessities are quite within the reach of a little hard work, which can be, and is, accomplished without mental effort. And, really, they have not mind and thought enough, to set mind and thought to work. In better language, their minds are quite too uncultivated, their faculties quite too imperfectly developed, to supply moral motives for the exertion of either. It must be an influence from without, motives applied and *forced* upon them by the benevolent care and labors of others, which is to arouse and engage them in the great and principal work of life—the cultivation of their rational and immortal natures. The precepts and doctrines of Jesus Christ, from Alpha to Omega, must be inculcated with Apostolical earnestness and perseverance, and I may add, with *pedagogical precision*, too, before they can become Christians. Example, precept—all that can be urged and displayed of both, by enlightened and indefatigable instructers, is necessary to supply motives of moral virtue, undo inveterate habits of moral indolence—enlighten and awaken the slumbering conscience to a quick sense of moral justice, and moral obligation; and engage the soul in the active discharge of moral duties.

But, not one in five of these people, habitually attend, even on Sundays, such religious instruction as they possess. And when they do occasionally place themselves under the sound of their preacher's voice—alas! how can it profit them? Their minds have not soil enough, I repeat, for the seeds even of religious knowledge to grow in. They sit like so many inanimate stocks, or if acted upon at all, and the religious part of them often are, it is chiefly in the way of the excitement of their animal spirits—at best of their religious *feelings*. Mere sermon-hearing on Sundays, so confirmed is their mental apathy, so unable to command and wield their faculties, so fixed their habit of inattention,—in a word, so incapable of reflection, almost of *thinking*, are they, that mere sermon-hearing on Sundays, bring the whole population to attend, and let the sermons be ever so sound, the language ever so intelligible and precise, and the sentiment ever so rich, cannot regenerate their mental habit, and make them either intelligent Christians, or enlightened Citizens. But what do these sermons, abstracting the pathos, and, *generally*, the good intentions, and good feelings of the preacher—what does all the rest of these performances amount to? "Vox et ———" absolutely *nothing*, my dear sir, that can instruct the understanding—nothing that can implant in the mind any solid or abiding motive of exertion or piety—nothing that shall become the radical spring of a regenerated and consistent moral or Christian character. Consequently, such means form—rather, God employs them to form—*no such characters*. People of this class whom we call, and hope to be, pious, do not possess such characters. There is nothing in this settlement to originate them—nothing to foster them—perhaps, not a heart that can *desire*, or a mind that can *imagine* them. But, as I have before said, and must be indulged in repeating, however defective and unprofitable the means of moral improvement enjoyed by these people, even these are treated with general neglect and inattention.

And what is to arouse them from this torpor? I can only conceive of one of two causes which is able to do it: a direct miracle of the Almighty's power—which I do not expect, and am not authorized to pray for; or His Divine blessing on such faithfully applied human means as the wisdom of God, and the moral history of mankind, unite to prescribe. And, the Christian Ministry supplies these means. Considered in their own nature, and separately from their sanctifying efficacy, and the promised co-operation of the Divine Spirit, if the doctrines of the Saviour, and the Ministry of Christian Teachers, can be so considered, these are, of all the means of arousing human nature, and setting the heart and understanding—body and soul—in action, beyond comparison the most certain and the most effectual.

How it is in other parts of the world, I have only heard and read. But in this Colony, I have *seen* the direct and inseparable connexion of Christianity, taking in its doctrines, its worship, and its practical fruits—with all that is stable, all that is patriotic, all that is mentally and morally improving, all that is exalting to human nature—in a word, all that is good and excellent among us.

There is no room for speculation on this point—no room for reasoning. Premises and conclusion are both embodied in one and the same obvious fact. *There* is a pious family, and there stands a firm pillar of the Colony. Industry, intelligence, order, competency and peace, are its characteristics. *There* is a family without religion. I have only to reverse the characteristics of the first, and that family is described.

We have tried the effects of schools. These are by no means so well conducted as they should be. Still their influence is salutary. But these effects are partial and inadequate, operating only on the child, while the parents are left unprofited. And common schools have never been known to exert a moral power over children sufficient to counteract and do away the demoralizing influence of corrupt examples assailing them at home. Children carry abroad their home-acquired qualities. But in few instances, indeed, do they borrow from abroad any good qualities to carry home to their parents. No such inversion of the ordinary laws of domestic and social life has, at least, been witnessed here. None is expected. Our schools may enlighten the children of the Colony: but they, alone, cannot be expected much to mend its morals; or effectually to check the common tide of degeneracy, which acting first on parents, and next upon their children, seems likely to sweep both before it, and drown all together, in perdition. In short it appears to me egregious trifling, to suggest any other remedy for this great and threatening evil, than that which the wisdom of God has appointed in the labors of the pious, enlightened, and self-denying Christian Ministry.

Such as worthily sustain this office come with an authority which none dare wholly despise. They come with motives which all who must die—all who know what a guilty conscience is, all who believe they have a God to account to and a soul to save, are obliged to feel.

Let then, the Colony be a parish. Let the Minister visit, instruct, and labor from house to house. Let him have no other engagements in the Colony— no other work on earth, to divert his attention from his spiritual charge. Above sectarian prejudices and feelings, let him be equally at home among christians of every name. A man of discrimination, education, and humility; let him employ the whole various compass of means, submitted to his selection in the Book, whence he derives his commission, to obviate the prejudices, obtain the confidence, conciliate the affections, instruct the ignorance, correct the errors, amend the morals, and save the souls, of all. Such a man might indeed, meet with trials and discouragements; might realize a success at first, by no means commensurate with his wishes and his labors. But he would sow seed which must grow. He would receive some aid. A few would, to the utmost, strengthen his hands and encourage his heart. Even our teachers if humble and pious, as several are, would gladly sit at his feet and receive instruction: if conceited and self-willed, they would, of all others, most require it.

I, therefore, beg respectfully, but most pressingly to recommend, as in my opinion, the only means of rendering this Colony, what it is intended to be made, the truly christian and civilized asylum of an outcast race of men, the immediate engagement of at least one laborious Christian Minister, of the most ardent piety, and untiring zeal.

If it be doubted for a moment, whether such an appointment be consistent with the simple and declared object of the Colonization Society; the only question to be determined is, whether it be not absolutely necessary, as a means of accomplishing that object?—Is the simple and unique object of the Society accomplished by only landing emigrants on the African coast, without regarding their future situation?—Should the freight of her transports hereafter be beached in lat. twenty-five degrees North, where all must famish and die on the sands of the desert, what less would await the Society, than the execrations of the world? And, can a Christian Institution feel less reluctance in abandoning a whole community—a community, which promises to become immensely populous, and extensive—a community derived from the bosom of a christian nation, to a moral desert, equally desolate—to a moral famine, equally certain?

I have trespassed, my dear sir, farther than I fear I should, in the length of these remarks—but I have done it under a feeling of most sacred obligation to report what I sincerely believe to be the most urgent of all the actual necessities of the colony, where they ought to be known, and whence, if from any quarter, those necessities are to be supplied.—None of us who are now active in this work, can act or labor long. And to do seasonably and effectually what little Divine Providence permits us to attempt, is no doubt, the way to accomplish the most in the end. It is in these views that this paper is submitted, and I cannot more appropriately bring it to a close, than by humbly supplicating the Almighty—in his infinite wisdom and goodness, to supply the means of accomplishing a work so agreeable to the great ends of his moral government; which his word assures us, is to build up an universal empire of holiness, of which the foundations are to be laid in the hearts of all mankind.

Respectfully and truly, dear sir, your obedient servant,

J. ASHMUN.

APPENDIX. 39

## No. 4.

The following Notes on Trade appear to have been written in 1822; the first paper about the time of Mr. Ashmun's departure or, the second soon after his arrival in, Africa.

The objects of my visit to the African coast, are,

I. To obtain and transmit home, such information relative to the country, and our settlement, as shall be perfectly accurate, minute, full, and in all points satisfactory to the American Colonization Society, and to the public.

II. To make the Agents fully acquainted with the views of the Managers at home, on every subject connected with the interests of the colony.

III. To assist by my advice, and otherwise, in planning, and executing measures of utility to the settlement.

IV. To open and superintend a regular, honorable and permanent trade in the productions of the country, between Cape Montserado, and the vicinity, and the United States.

This trade must be made,

*First*, advantageous to the interests of the Society.

*Second*, Advantageous to the natives.

*Third*, Advantageous to the American Merchant, and

*Fourth*, Advantageous to myself.

I. The interests of the Society, will be essentially promoted by establishing a regular intercourse between the United States and Montserado. If four voyages annually, were to be made, without any obligation on the part of the merchant, to advance otherwise the interests of the Society, the latter would, nevertheless, derive from the opening of the communication, the following immediate advantages.

*First*, It would never again be obliged to charter vessels to carry out colonists, and stores.

*Second*, It would always be able, seasonably, to communicate with the colony.

*Third*, Vessels proceeding to Montserado for objects of trade, could afford to transport emigrants, and stores, at half the expense, attending the charter of ships for the purpose.

But if, besides opening a profitable trade to the American Merchant, the Society can bring him under a pecuniary obligation, the advantages resulting to their interests from a commercial intercourse, would be enhanced in proportion to the extent of the obligation.

The question then is, how can the Society make the most of this trade?

*Ans.* Not by turning merchants themselves. Such an appendage would prove most unpopular at home, and would probably absorb in the expenses of its own support, all the profits. But,

APPENDIX.

*First*, By prohibiting all foreign ships from trading to the settlement, *absolutely*.

*Secondly*, By laying a duty, amounting to a prohibition, on all exports, and imports, not in vessels in the interest of the Society.

*Thirdly*, By restricting the license of trading to Montserado to a single house in America.

*Fourthly*, By permitting this house to have an agent, resident in Africa—but subject to the general regulations of the Society, and liable to be recalled, whenever they judge that he has violated his instructions.

Vessels licensed to trade with these immunities and privileges, ought to carry out the Society's passengers for a sum not exceeding 10 dollars an individual, perhaps for still less—they finding their own provisions.

2. Such a trade would prove advantageous to the natives.

*First*, It would divert them from the slave trade.

*Secondly*, It would supply their wants. They must, without the substitution of a regular trade in the fabrics of civilized countries, in lieu of that, which the suppression of the slave trade has broken off, suffer great inconvenience.

*Thirdly*, By conducting this trade on principles of strict justice, their habits, and some of their principles, will come to be meliorated.

*Fourthly*, It would compel them to the exercise of honorable industry, in procuring, and transporting the articles of trade to the coast.

*Fifthly*, It would induce them to visit, and by degrees to imitate the industry and manners of living, among our settlers.

3. Trade to this country will be profitable to the American Merchant, if he can be assured of a full cargo always in readiness for shipment at the Cape, on the arrival of his ship, and sufficiently so, if he can make on his outward shipment, one hundred per cent. and on his return cargo two hundred.

4. The agency will be advantageous to myself, provided I can receive a dividend of thirty-three and a third per cent. on the gross amount of the sales of the cargo in America.

---

The following is a concise exposition of the reasons, which led to the mission of J. Ashmun, to the Coast of Africa, and of the views according to which the committee expect it to be conducted:

The exertions hitherto made for colonizing Africa, have been directed to objects which may be regarded as preliminary to the main design. The practicability of the undertaking was to be demonstrated by acquiring lands, and securing a sufficient number of American Emigrants, in the peaceful possession of them; by attesting experimentally, the productiveness of the soil to support, and the salubrity of the climate to admit of the general health of the colonists; by ascertaining the willingness of the black people of the United States to remove thither, and finally to settle, by actual trial, the much disputed question, whether the happiness of the African race, would be essentially increased by the change, and the United States, reap an important advantage from encouraging and promoting their general emigration.

These are the preliminary objects to be accomplished by the Society, before the principal ends of their institution can be completely gained. They have been partially accomplished, but not fully. Much indeed, remains to be done before the *experiment*, as the business must yet be regarded, will be considered as fully and successfully completed. The number of settlers must be greatly augmented; considerable progress made in the cultivation of the soil; churches, shops, school-houses and a large number of comfortable and permanent dwellings for the people, erected; a regular intercourse between the United States, and the colony, must be kept open; and a general and eager desire to emigrate, must be made to manifest itself, in the black people of the United States. When the exertions of the Society shall have received this degree of success, the facilities for carrying on their ulterior designs will be abundantly multiplied, and, *until* that desirable period, they will be obliged to labor under great embarrassments from a deficiency of means.

Public sentiment in all the northern States, has, by a variety of untoward events, unhappily determined itself against the whole plan of African colonization. Thousands are to be met with in every part of the Union, equally unfriendly to the cause. The obvious consequences of this hostility are, 1*st*, *A determined refusal on the part of a numerous, and influential part of the community to aid the work, either by their contributions or their encouragement; and* 2*dly, the refusal of Congress, and the State Legislatures, to afford any pecuniary aid, or directly espouse the cause, by any public act whatever*. Legislation in the United States, is but the expression of the public and popular sentiment. Effect in the latter, a change in favor of colonization, and you secure at once the patronage of Congress, and the State Legislatures.

Now, what do the objections offered by the opposers of colonization, amount to? They may be all resolved into these two: 1*st, Its impracticability*. 2*nd, The vanity of hoping to improve by such means, the condition of the American free people of color.*

But, if the experiment now carrying on by the Society, ever reaches the point of success so fondly anticipated, and to which their labors are so assiduously directed, both these objects will be radically obviated, and what will be the direct consequence? Opposition must cease. The popular sentiment, where it now opposes, must be reversed. The zeal of its friends must be inflamed. The influence of the northern States, the most efficient in the Union, will be secured to the cause. The amount of individual contributions must be increased on a fifty fold ratio. Congress will patronise the design. The States, certainly all the slave-holding States, will vote subsidies—the latter, with a liberality, proportioned to the burdens under which they labor, from the excess of black population.

In the interim, ample funds are required by the Society, to prosecute the work they have in hand; gradually augmenting the sphere of their operations

F

in order to reach that consummation, which is to produce the expected revolution in the popular mind.

These funds must be derived from individual munificence. Government will very soon have so far fulfilled the purposes of the African agency, as to satisfy itself with a very limited annual appropriation for the purpose of keeping up that slight establishment on the coast, which alone was contemplated by the Act under which it was founded. It is indeed doubtful, whether the President will feel himself authorized to pay the expense of transporting more than one or two hundred additional settlers. The heavy expense of freighting ships for the purpose, will then fall upon the Society—an expense which they have never yet been obliged to sustain, and which has been anticipated with more serious apprehensions, than any other attending, or likely to attend the prosecution of their work.

After the present year, it is desirable that four large ships should annually arrive in the colony with settlers from the United States. The charter and expense of these ships, alone would cost 24,000 dollars.

A conditional agreement has been entered into with a commercial house in Baltimore, by which two or more ships of the first order, are to be fitted out, to run constantly between the United States and the coast; *provided a sufficient inducement can be presented in the trade of that part of Africa, over which the Society may be expected to have some control.*

It is believed that, in consequence of the cessation of the slave trade, at Cape Montserado, the mouth of the river will naturally become a depot for many valuable productions of the country, and may be made the mart of an honorable trade with the natives, which in a short time will admit of extension to a degree rendering it an object of very considerable importance. The native tribes bordering on the banks of that river, for hundreds of miles in the interior, must shortly be able, with encouragement, to procure, and furnish at its mouth, an abundance of Camwood, and other dye woods, bees-wax, Palm-oil, and a smaller quantity of hides, elephants' teeth, and gold-dust. They have been from time immemorial, accustomed to the use of European and Indian fabrics, obtained in barter for slaves. Of this means of supplying their wants they are now, it is hoped, forever, and effectually deprived. Their industry must be aroused, and directed to other pursuits. They will be, very soon, both able and willing to furnish many articles of value in the American market, and over the whole of this trade, the Society ought to exercise the most entire control, and if possible, turn it to the advantage of the natives, and of their own designs.

It is believed that a treaty of commerce may be established by the Society, with some of these tribes, *immediately*—and with all, *eventually.*

Let it be to this effect, *The Society agree to furnish the natives, at the mouth of the river, with every article which they shall require, and to the amount for which they can furnish camwood, &c. to pay, and at a fair price. No frauds shall be practised on either hand. The trade is to be carried on wholly, through an Agent* residing, with the consent and concurrence of the Society, at Cape Montserado. The natives to sell their produce to no foreigner, and to trade with no vessels not recognized as in the interest of the Society.

Similar arrangements it is believed may be entered into with the natives inhabiting Cape Mount, and the interior. Another depot may be established both there, and at the mouth of the St. Paul's, under the same Agency. It is very desirable, likewise, to engross all the trade of the coast, extending and connecting it as far as possible, interior, and to the southward as far as Cape Palmas; where another mart may be established; and if practicable, even to Cape Coast. This trade, if not monopolized by the Society, will be occupied by others, probably by foreigners. The Society will not only thus lose the pecuniary advantages which it might derive from it; but, what is a still greater evil, will inevitably see the natives alienated by degrees from their interests, and possibly excited at no very distant period, to a state of hostility to the Colony.

It is, therefore, a dictate, not of mercantile cupidity, but of the soundest policy, and of benevolence to the natives themselves, to endeavor if practicable, at the earliest period, to convert into one honorable and profitable channel, the whole trade of the coast for several degrees, both to the north and south of Montserado.

Except in their own territory, the Society have not, perhaps, the right or the power of enforcing any regulation of the trade. But here, it certainly has the right; it ought to possess the *power*, and *must*, as a measure of self-preservation, make the attempt. What right have the English to control the trade of all that part of the coast, extending from the Sound of Sherbro, to the Rio Grande? But they assume it. This fact, though it proves nothing about the *right*, yet will silence all objections which *they* may urge against an imitation of their example, by the Society, in the neighborhood of their settlement. The right itself is to be founded on a fair and honorable treaty of commerce concluded with the natives.

To avoid the odium of a *monopoly*, it is purposed by the regulations of the Society, adopted at the Cape, in addition to the absolute prohibition of the trade of the Cape to *all foreign vessels and subjects whatever*, to lay a duty on American vessels,* which by absorbing the profits, will amount to a prohibition.

Thus leaving the trade open to a single house in America, the whole advantage of it, will be secured to the Society. That already alluded to, stipulates, on these conditions, to furnish a sufficient quantity and variety of goods most in esteem with the natives, to pay for all the produce they bring to the coast; and, after deducting a reasonable profit, to devote the proceeds to the advancement of the Colony. Their agent on the coast, is to be nominated by the Society, who is to furnish the latter with a statement of all the

* Not proceeding under commission of the Society.

shipments and other operations connected with the trade, in order that the most accurate knowledge may be ever possessed by the Institution of its actual profits.

The advantages of such an arrangement, have been already presented. It will aid and relieve the funds of the Society. It will secure the attachment of the natives. It will wean them from the slave trade and reconcile them to its abandonment. It will give an impulse to their laudable industry; and supply their wants. It will accustom them to an observance of the principles of honesty and justice in their commercial transactions; and by all these efforts, help, in an important degree, to civilize, and prepare them for the reception of the richer blessings of Christianity. It will establish a regular intercourse and communication betwen the United States and the Colony. The Society will be exactly and regularly informed of the state of the settlement, and can, at any time, send such supplies as the latter may require. It will enable black people possessing property, to emigrate at option. Masters of slaves, desirous to liberate and transport them to the Colony, can do it at a trifling expense. It will furnish, in the productions of Africa thus brought regularly to the United States, ocular testimony of the fertility of the African soil, and the resources of that country. This circumstance will do more towards silencing one class of objectors, and rousing some of the friends of the cause to redoubled zeal and activity, than a volume of arguments derived from less equivocal sources. Finally, it will accelerate the desirable period when all parties are to be united in the advancement of this great national object, and Congress take it under its efficient patronage.

## No. 5.

Mr. Ashmun considered too little, we believe, at this crisis, the particular causes productive of insubordination. He regarded the spirit of revolt, as a development of general character brought out by new circumstances, rather than the result, principally, of misapprehension, and that irritability which trials and afflictions in minds not thoroughly disciplined, too frequently excite. Some of those who were ungovernable at this period, became afterwards, firm supporters of the Government, and enjoyed the unqualified confidence of the Colonial Agent.

## No. 6.

These heads were,

1st. The extension of the Town beyond the original limits.

2d. The claim of some of the old emigrants under the drawing for lots which took place at Fourah Bay, in 1821.

3d. The plan of Government proposed.

4th. The digest of the Laws.

5th. The salaries and rations of the proposed officers.

6th. The prices of articles to be sold.

All these subects had been deliberately considered by the Agents, and on all, had our decisions (subject to the judgment of the Board,) been announced to the Colonists, who with an unexpected unanimity expressed their approbation of them. The Managers, who, for their long and arduous and uncompensated labors in the African cause, deserve respect and thanks from all men, acted on these subjects, with desire to know and do their duty, yet the result proved how slowly good men admit evidence going to overthrow their long established opinions. We here insert a few pages extracted from the Colonial Journal, to serve as a specimen of the record made by him of events, and to show the state of things immediately after the reorganization of the Government: also his remarks on the most economical mode of subsisting the Colony. Also a paper on the subject of ardent spirits.

Monrovia, August 22d, 1824.

The new civil organization went into effect. The prices of labor accepted in compensation for provisions, are fixed at the following rates:

Common Laborers in general, - - - 50 cts. or 2-3 Bar.

Lime-Burners, Coal Makers, and others requiring some skill, &c., - - - - - - - 75 cts. or 1 Bar.

Proper Mechanics, - - - - - 100 cts. or 1 1-3 Bar.

The United States' Agent, the Rev. Mr. Gurley, sailed in the United States' Schooner Porpoise, for America, by way of the West Indies. The weather, till to-day, had been remarkably fine, since the arrival of the Porpoise, on the 17th inst.: but owing to the thickness of the rain for 24 hours past, the Schooner has, with difficulty, been able to communicate with the shore in that time.

Our people are divided into two religious sects—the Methodist and Baptist, each of which has its separate Preachers, and places of worship. The Methodists are also divided into the Wesleyans, and the followers of Bishop Allen. The Preachers of the latter, act under his license, and ordination. Each has its separate discipline, but occupy alternately the same place of worship. [Since the date of the foregoing, the two parties in the Methodist Church have divided from each other entirely, and established separate places of worship.]

*Monday, August* 24. The Council was convened by the Agent.

*Resolved,* 1. That the town-lots and plantations remaining to be assigned, be surveyed and appropriated immediately.

2. That a road, ten feet wide, be immediately opened and formed, along the centre of the Main Avenue, to the summit of the Mountain; and that the labour of the captured Africans and Colonists, be directed to that object.

3. That the Colonists interested in the plantation-survey, proceed to open paths along the lines of the plantations; and while so occupied, be exempt from any other public labor.

4. That all public tools be charged to the receivers; and if not produced when required, be paid for, and the amount collected by the proper officer.

David White appeared, and offered to support himself. Twenty-seven Bill Hooks, and seventeen Axes, were distributed to the settlers and Superintendent Captured Africans, and charged to the receivers. Every proprietor of lands is required to set two substantial land-marks, and replace them when decayed, at the two diagonal angles of his lot. N. Butler is engaged to labor constantly on the new Agency-house.

The conductor of ordnance is directed to place the arms, ammunition, and military stores, in a state of order and security, or report to the Agent the necessary repairs requiring the aid of some other workman.

W. W. Barbour is engaged to open a Town School for *Boys* on Tuesday the 25th of August, and promised a compensation of 9 Bars and his rations per month. This school is to be held in the Methodist Meeting-House.

The rations are fixed for an adult at 4 pounds pork, 3 pounds flour, 1 pound bread, 1-2 pint molasses, and 1 gill of vinegar—val. 95 per week.

It is to-day decided, that the legal value of the Bar, compared with the dollar, shall, in all transactions originating after this date, be 75-100ths, or three quarters of a dollar.

*August* 25. The object of the accommodation offered to settlers by supplying them with provisions, on sale, being to encourage a spirit of industry and independence, and the prices being regulated with a view only to supply the place of provisions thus taken from the store, it is *decided* that when provisions are taken agreeably to the foregoing regulation, by the barrel, &c., and the payment made in cash, or other produce not liable to a diminution of value; the retail price be abated 12 1-2 per centum.

This day, Wm. Steward commenced his school; also, John S. Mill en-

## APPENDIX.

tered upon his duties as Colonial Secretary pro tempore.* A. D. Williams also assumed the superintendence of the captured Africans. The laborers have been occupied, when the rains did not forbid, in forming a road to the summit of the Cape.

*August* 29. The appointment of F. Devaney as Captain of the Liberia Guard, with the rank of Lieutenant, was confirmed: his commission to date from this day. He is ordered to superintend the fitting up of a temporary rendezvous, and to enlist soldiers, promising a bounty of five Bars. The S. C. A. Reports, that the persons under his charge have labored the past week with great spirit. Contracts have been formed for getting out the timber for two houses on the summit of the Cape: each of which is to be an L, 27 feet long—the perpendicular, 18,—and the width, 9. These are to face each other. The shortest wing of one is for the Superintendent; and the corresponding part of the other is to serve as a school-room. The military lands about the Fort have been laid out in a convenient and ornamental style.

The two guard houses are to be each 26 by 9 feet, 20 feet to two rooms, each to accommodate a mess of 3 privates—6 feet for a room in each, to lodge a non-commissioned officer.

The Court of Sessions dismissed two vexatious suits which had been sent up by appeal from the Justices Court, and sentenced one Krooman, of some distinction, to two dozen stripes, and two weeks' confinement at hard labor, for stealing. The Brig "Union," from Bristol, England, left for the leeward.

*Monday* 31*st*. It is decided to pay for good plank, 25 dollars the thousand—and square timber of small size, at the same rate per the running foot. It is also decided to lay off to each of the settlers, entitled at this time to draw plantation-lots, two acres, situated at the south-westward of the Town; and the remainder due, to the south-eastward; because

1. It will ensure the early cultivation and improvement of the first-mentioned Tract.

2. The measure will give to each of the settlers a small plantation near their town-residence; and tend to advance agriculture more generally than to send one-half these persons to the distance of two miles from their plantations.

*September* 1st, 1834. The Monthly Report of the Agricultural Committee returns,

| | | |
|---|---|---|
| Whole No. of Town Lots assigned, | - - - | 80 |
| Do. do. do. cleared, | - - - | 24 |

---

* It may here be inserted by way of anticipation, in transcribing, that Mr. Mill continued 'till the 30th of September, to fulfil his duties with great fidelity and ability. The records were most correctly and beautifully copied—and the books reduced to order, and many collateral services rendered. From that time he has returned, as if tired of the restraints of civilized life, to his former habits. I seldom see him.

## APPENDIX.

| | | |
|---|---|---|
| Whole No. of Town Lots partly cleared, | | 29 |
| Do. do. do. inclosed, | | 27 |
| Do. do. do. on which buildings are erecting, | | 14 |
| Do. do. do. which are gardens, | | 15 |
| Plantation Lots, assigned, | | 34 |
| Do. do. on which improvements are begun, | | 2 |

Report of the Health Committee returns,

| | |
|---|---|
| Invalids in toto, | 19 |
| Of which are adults, | 15 |
| Ulcers, | 14 |
| Debility, | 4 |
| Chronic | 1 |

Of the preceding, there are 3 bad cases; and 16 slowly convalescent. This Report is here given as a tolerably correct exhibit of the general state of health of the Colony since the beginning of the rains.

The name by which it is decided to distinguish the Town, about to be founded for captured Africans, is Thompson Town, after the late Honorable Secretary of the Navy, under whose superintendence the present measures for training these persons to Civilization and Christianity went into operation. If the wishes of a few nearly forgotten individuals are gratified, the name will be retained by the Board. Sailed for Sierra Leone, a small Trading Sloop, last from the leeward.

The Agent, some months ago, having addressed several inquiries to the Government of Sierra Leone, relative to the existing regulations of the port, expressing at the same time a wish that the intercourse between that Colony and our own, might be impeded by no needless restrictions, has received from the Governor and Council, a communication enclosing in reply, an ordinance of their Board, that "Vessels owned in, and bona-fide attached to the American Colony of Montserado, be admitted to the Port of Free Town, to trade in any of the productions of the country, without being liable to any Custom House, or port charges, whatever."

*September 4th.* A large Brig, said to be French, and strongly armed, passed down, which the Agent is informed is bound to Whydah, having —— dollars aboard, and intended for 600 slaves—same day, a French Schooner, some weeks on the coast, anchored in reach of the guns of the Fort, where she continued, occasionally weighing and standing off a few hours, five days. The rains return uniformly every morning; and subside towards evening.

*September 6th.* Clothing, to the amount of thirty-six ready made garments, and six hundred yards of cotton stuffs, were to-day issued to the people, and captured Africans. A considerable amount of the best clothes, were also sold for shingles, plank, squared timber, and scantling for building the public houses projected.—The street leading directly down to the river from the Agent's house, has also been opened, and partly formed.

## APPENDIX.

*September 7th.* J. Dickson, and Thomas A. Harris, cease to receive public rations, by their own desire.

The Kings of all the neighboring tribes to the Northward, in April last, forbade their *people to trade with* the Colony in Ivory and wood, before more satisfactory prices should be obtained. This prohibition naturally affected the supplies of Rice, vegetables, and other productions, not expressly included in the interdict. But the effect has been, to distress themselves, without compelling the Colony to offer higher prices. Of this they seem at length convinced, and about a week ago, called a meeting to deliberate on the question, of removing the restriction; or of entering into stipulations, respecting the prices, with the Colony. They immediately after heard the rumor, that the Condoes, Boatswain's tribe, intended another attack upon the remnant of the Queahs,[*] to revenge an old quarrel. Bromley directly despatched a messenger with a present of sixty Rolls[†] of salt, to King Boatswain, begging him to prevent any dependant chief of his, from carrying the war against his neighbors. A few days afterwards, a great number of Queahs arrived on the coast, to implore an asylum among the Dey people. The assembly of head men at Bromley's dispersed in order to protect their own towns from a possible irruption of the Condoe Chief, without having decided on any one question, which brought them together.—To-day, a messenger was sent from the Island, to report to the Agent, that the Condoes have made an expedition down to the Queahs and secured and marched off eighty-six prisoners. The fact is presumed to be so.

*September 11th.* A free and open path, twenty feet wide, has been formed from the settlement to the summit of the mountainous part of the Cape—the ground chosen for the site of the Captured Africans' Town. This labor has been accomplished almost entirely by the labor of the Africans themselves. The Superintendent reports them to have labored with great cheerfulness and alacrity, and to have demeaned themselves in a very orderly manner. I am informed there are four slaving vessels at the Gallinas, and three at Cape Mount, and Chubris—three leagues beyond.

The Colonists are excited by recent changes in the Government, by the chagrin of past irregularities, and the dread of a recurrence of the distress and confusion of the last half-year, to an effort of strenuous activity, never before witnessed in the settlement. Heaven send them perseverance. The most cheering hopes of the beneficial influence of the new government, are with good reason, entertained.—The reform caused in the police system by the formation of a Guard, independent of the Colonists, although not yet completed, has put an *entire end* to the little depredations so frequent before. Sleeping on

---

[*] This tribe inhabits the upper waters, near the source of the river Montserado, about forty-five miles from the settlement.

[†] So named from the shape of the hamper in which it is enclosed, being 5 inches in diameter, and 35 or 40 long.

post, subjects the delinquent, if a citizen, to three days' imprisonment. The penalty has been twice exacted. Several respectable natives came and secretly assured the Agent, that the hostilities, which the Dey people would persuade us are directed against the Queahs, have our settlement for their object. Reports of this nature having been circulated previously, and many of our native laborers having left us in consequence, it was deemed necessary to take precautionary measures, accordingly. The whole military force was paraded at sun-set, and after hearing such an explanation as the occasion called for, were marched off under their proper Officers, to the different batteries, and lay on their arms through the night.—A very strong guard was posted at the different stations, every night, for five days, till we were authentically informed that any combination which may have been thought of, or begun, against us, was broken up, and the movers returned to their respective towns.

*September 20th.* William Draper, (per Cyrus,) Charles Butler, and Jacob Warner, (per Oswego,) withdrew their names from the ration-list.

*21st.* Joseph Blake, Charles Branden, and Benjamin Vaughan, also withdrew their names to-day. Several messengers have for a week past come in to assure us, that the rumor which had caused our recent apprehensions, was groundless, and the authors of it, instigated by malicious motives, and that the arrival of the fugitive Queahs had excited all the commotion—which had been represented to us, as much greater than it was. Kings George and Gray, paid a visit to the settlement, to renew their assurances of friendship, and offered to enter into a contract to supply it with Rice.

The rains are abundant, and have prevailed for a succession of days and nights incessantly. Public works consequently, get on slowly.

Died, Samuel Weeks, from Baltimore, per Fidelity, July 1823, aged about sixty-five. He sickened about four months after his arrival; his convalescence was attended with disordered bowels, and dropsical swellings, from which resulted a decline, that has at length carried him off. He has no family in the Colony.—King Peter Bromley sent the Agent a letter, in which he renews his professions of friendship, and promises to send into the Colony for sale, a large quantity of Rice. He engages to use his influence with his brother kings, to have old difficulties settled speedily, and to pay to the colony a visit as soon as they shall be ready with definite propositions relative to the trade.—The Agent procured three hundred Orange scions, which are to-day set.* Average of Thermometer seventy-four and a half degrees by day, and seventy-six by night. The Dey people keep up the prohibition of the trade of their country with the Colony—in Camwood, and Ivory only; and with manifest advantage to the industry of the Colony.

---

* I regret to say, that at this date, Dec. 4th., not a dozen of these settings are alive. They all struck root, and flourished while the rains lasted, but have withered since. The proper time to transplant, &c. is at the beginning of the rains.

# APPENDIX.

*September 22d.* By appointment on the part of the Agents, met at Monrovia, Kings Gray\* and George† and Ba Caia of the Island; all of whom have been often accused of interfering to stop our Rice-trade on its way to the Colony.—The Bassa branch of this trade, alone, which has been cut off, ought to produce the settlement five hundred bushels annually. Caia, it is believed, had only blocked up the road unintentionally, and as the consequence of a long unsettled quarrel with Kings, Prince Will, of the Junk, and Tom, of Little Bassa. Gray and George have acted on the monopolizing policy, which all the coast-people have in a greater or less degree adopted in relation to the trade of the interior, and from distant tribes. By intercepting it in its afflux to the settlement, they make their profit without any industry, and at the expense both of us, and the growers of the produce.

After stating our grievance, and hearing the best apology which the Kings could invent, the Agent proposed a definite and effectual settlement of the matter, by adopting such a course as must terminate all past suspicion and prevent it in future. They acceded with little hesitation to the proposals, and the following agreement was executed on the spot.

J. Ashmun, Agent in behalf of the Colonization Society, and people of Monrovia,—Chief Caia, in behalf of himself and people—Kings George and Gray, of themselves and people, *agree*,

I. To live in perpetual peace.

II. To trade without fraud, or interruption in any goods and productions we may have to dispose of.

III. Never to hinder the trade and intercourse of any other people whatever.

IV. The Kings agree to send any evil disposed person, who shall undertake to injure the settlement by lying, stealing, or spreading false reports, to Monrovia to be punished.

V. The Agent agrees to notify the Kings, of any of their people undertaking maliciously to injure their good name, or stir up in their mind a suspicion of their hostile intentions against the American people.

VI. The Agent and Kings particularly *agree*, to send each a messenger immediately, to the Junk people—to the Pequenino and Grand Bassa people, to declare in their names to those people, that their trade with the Americans, is and shall be free; that the path is entirely open, and that neither the Kings, nor their people shall in any way hinder or molest the free trade of any other people with the American town."

In witness, &c.

J. ASHMUN.
KING GRAY, his ✕ mark.
KING GEORGE, his ✕ mark.

---

\* Gray lives on the sea-coast, two leagues distant from the Cape, South.

† George has his town on the Junk, four leagues from Montserado, in the same direction, and formerly resided at, and controlled the watering-place of the Cape.

## APPENDIX.

In pursuance of the last article of the foregoing agreement, the Rev. C. M. Waring was selected to visit, in conjunction with the messengers of the Kings, all the tribes, as far as Grand Bassa inclusive, in order to execute the object of the foregoing agreement. He was instructed,

"To proceed in company of the Messengers of Caia, George, Gray, Prince Will, and Tom Bassa, none of whom was he to pass without bringing them to accede to the agreement foregoing, if they had not before. He was to be careful in explaining, strenuous and precise in exacting their adoption of the paper; and to give them every assurance that the road would ever after, be kept open. In these declarations and assurances, the three first Messengers, particularly, were to be required to unite in the names of their principals. At Grand Bassa, it was especially desired and expected that he would assemble the Regent and other Head Men, and publish the information and assurance as effectually, and as largely as possible, and endeavor to induce them and all others having rice for sale, to take advantage of the re-opening of the road, as early as possible." He was supplied with goods for small presents; took his departure on the 23d of September, and returned after having very satisfactorily executed the Mission, on the 2d of October. A copy of his account of the journey is forwarded for the Board.

*September 25th.* George Mason from this date, supports himself. At the Court of Monthly Sessions holden to-day, Mrs. T―――― was arraigned on a charge of threatening, abusing and attempting to hinder Lieutenant Daveny in the execution of his duty. Verdict, not guilty of the charge; but deserving, for her boisterous, and scurrilous language, the admonition of the Court; which was accordingly administered. Last night, a very impudent robbery was committed. At 7 o'clock this morning, the Guard took into custody all the straggling and suspicious natives about the settlement—on the testimony of some of these, it appeared that the thief was a Bassa man, who had gone off with his plunder early in the morning. A reward of fifty bars was offered for his apprehension, and the detained persons discharged.

Charles Francis, who has been an invalid 20 years, and long lingering in the settlement from complicated chronical infirmities, is now evidently near his end. The prescriptions of the Surgeon of the Porpoise, procured him some temporary relief; but nothing could remove his disease.

For ten days past, there has been a religious excitement among all classes of people, of a most extraordinary character. It first discovered itself in the more zealous and frequent application of the communicants of the different religious persuasions, to social prayer. Others became affected; and commonly cried out as if in the deepest mental horror and distress during the earlier stages. Some of the religious assemblies certainly exhibited a scene of confusion, which I am sorry to say the conducting individuals seemed too willing to encourage; and in a few instances, the decorum of the house of prayer was departed from. But with these abatements, it is most evident, that all classes of people, and perhaps every individual of adult age, on the Cape, has been very wonderfully, and deeply affected with the great Truths of the Gospel. The preachers and most influential members of the different religious bodies were cautioned, and repeatedly advised to conduct their assemblies with Christian decency and order. Some of them profited from this counsel; and after a few days, a deep and deliberate seriousness, the manifest result of a cause entirely supernatural, pervaded the very souls of the people. The most hardened and irreligious were subdued. Some of our most turbulent subjects have assumed an entirely altered character; which I am persuaded, nothing but the renovating power of the Word and Spirit of God can account for. Their conduct has become strictly exemplary. They have, to my knowledge, in a great variety of instances, offered every satisfaction in their power for any former acts tending to the injury of others. Upwards of twenty persons, all professing the faith of Christ for the first time, have been added to the Methodist Society—and about half that number to the Baptist. I am at this date of (December 6th,) transcribing the Journal, and add with great pleasure and gratitude to God, that the revival and extension of religion among us, is proving itself to have been the genuine work of the Divine Spirit, as far as its holy fruits have yet had time to declare themselves. It has done more to render our people industrious, obedient, humble, just, provident, attentive and affectionate in the discharge of relative duties, than all the human instruction and discipline, which they could ever receive. To the Board, and the friends of Colonization, the event may justly inspire a gratifying confidence in the improved character of their Colonists; and the Christian, whose views range in a more extensive and a sublimer sphere, will derive from it a gratification peculiarly his own.

Our roads have not been one week clear of Spanish and French Slaving Vessels, since the sailing of the Porpoise. There are now present two—one under each flag.

*Monday, September 27th.* Died at an early hour this morning, Charles Francis, from Virginia, per the Elizabeth, aged about 50.

It is necessary even to interrupt other laborers in order to prepare a rice granary. It is to be constructed of good materials, and be two stories high. See the draft and description, inclosed. The number of invalids on the sick list has not diminished since the last entry. There are a few occasional cases of ague and fever, but all slight and transient. Every scratch or puncture becomes an ulcer; and months are often required to dry it up. We have two cases of the kind, 18 months old.

Lot No. 119 is assigned to the Methodist Society, for building a house of worship on. They have already prepared a part of the timber.

About 11 o'clock, P. M., the two Slaving Vessels in the roads, commenced an irregular firing, which continued for several hours. Cause unknown.

*Tuesday 28th.* Dark and rainy. Day light discovered both the Slavers fast ashore among breakers, about 1 1-2 miles to the northward of the Town. The Frenchman being the smallest, had gone highest on. The Spaniard stranded exactly in her track, and at pistol shot distance. Both are totally lost. At half-past 7, the Agent despatched a boat with a letter in French, offering the crews the protection of their lives. The boat met the Spaniard's jolly-boat, ashore, with the Captain and other Officers, who threw themselves upon the mercy of the Colonial Government. They reported, that at ten o'clock, the night preceding, finding themselves adrift, they threw out an anchor, which refused to bring the Schooner up; and that having only a kedge and hawser more, aboard, they were obliged to go ashore. This is the account of the pilot (or first mate.). The Captain states, that the Mate, whose watch it was on deck, finding the Schooner had parted, and supposing the Frenchman standing away from the land, blindly followed him ashore, without consulting his compass. The wind and weather was much as it had been since both vessels came to an anchor; and the accident is involved in great mystery. The Captain reports himself, the Biscayenne, Captain de Mina, six weeks from Havanna, with a valuable cargo, and crew of 28 persons in all; in quest of ———; but he was instantly given to understand that no attempt at deception would be allowed, and desisted. He begged the Agent to receive himself, his officers and men under his protection; and to direct such measures to be taken as would prove most effectual in saving his wreck and cargo. The vessel had no water when he left her—and if the crew and natives could be restrained from plunder, it was judged that a considerable amount of property could be saved from her.

In reply, it was stated that both the laws and sentiments of the American Nation, were utterly hostile to the object of their voyage—which the Agent would not promote, even indirectly; but that they might depend on the protection of their persons; and every aid in securing the property on board the wreck, from destruction, which the laws of humanity dictated in such cases. They resigned themselves and their vessel up, on these terms. The ship's papers were stated to have been lost, and only a defective Invoice preserved. Arrangements being made, the Agent immediately employed the crew and such of the settlers as chose to assist, in discharging and saving the cargo. The Specie, and about 12 cases of dry goods were soon landed—when the vessel bilged, keeled and filled. Most of her provisions and other property aboard, were spoilt; and the difficulty of getting the heavy cargo out of the hold, became insuperable. Several accidents occurred from the violence of the surf, by which half a dozen boat loads of property were lost. The seamen, who were chiefly employed aboard in breaking out, in their anxiety to get at the most valuable articles, threw overboard, and otherwise destroyed a large amount of provisions and goods. During the whole time employed about the wreck, the rains were incessant and violent. After the first night, the state of the wreck rendered it dangerous for any one to attempt remaining on board after sun-set. To restrain the depredations of the natives in the absence of the people, the brass field piece was sent down to the nearest projection of the beach from the American side; and about a dozen rounds of grape

## APPENDIX. 55

fired into the wreck through the night. But even this precaution did not deter the natives, many thousands of whom had assembled on the beach, from stealing aboard and plundering to a large amount. In the meantime, the Frenchman, having declined all communication with the settlements, was almost wholly abandoned to the Kroo and other country people—not a 20th part of her cargo having been saved to the owners. The crew did not wholly give her up 'till she became worthless, and ready to go to pieces. Having raised the American flag on the Spaniard, and informed the natives that she belonged to the Agent; that he had the right of insisting on the delivery of the property, taken from aboard of her, into the public store-house, Caia of the Island, having encouraged his people to secrete a few casks of spirits which they had brought away, and refusing to restore them, made it necessary for a volley of musketry to be discharged on the people employed in conveying it away. On their persisting, two or three shots from an 18 pounder were directed upon them, which compelled them to relinquish their stolen property to the claimants. No material injury was done by the fire of the fort. It was matter of mortification that the powder used on this occasion was so damaged by the climate, (having been in the country two years,) as not to project a round shot, more than two-thirds of the distance from the fort to the wreck. Even the insolence of Kroo Town might defy the effects of our heaviest guns.

It was soon perceived that the temptation to theft, was too great, to render it proper to permit the captured Africans to assist in transporting the goods brought ashore—three of them having been sent to prison the first hour they were employed, for petty depredations. It was indeed difficult to procure the faithful discharge of the trust reposed in them, from *some of the settlers*, and measures of some energy became necessary, to prevent embezzlements to a considerable amount. Having recovered about fifty twenty-gallon casks of spirits, fifteen barrels of provisions, one hogshead of tobacco, twenty casks of powder, fifty stand of arms, two great guns, one of which is a double-fortified, long revolving nine, about a thousand pieces of cloth, with four masts, two anchors, spars, rigging, copper, and a variety of other property, to the amount in all, of about seven thousand dollars, the wreck was abandoned to the settlers in five days, as not worth the farther attention of the Government of the Colony, and on the 19th or 20th day, went entirely to pieces.

Nace Butler, a very respectable settler, was unfortunately drowned by the upsetting of a canoe, on the 8th of October, returning from the wreck. About five of the natives also perished—chiefly by overloading themselves with plunder and attempting to swim ashore.

The Agent used every effort of persuasion and authority, to induce the people employed about the wreck to save the provisions. But they were neglected till too late to save only a very small part.

On the evening of the 2nd of October, the Agent, from care and fatigue, (having for near a week been loaded with additional labors, from the absence of Mr. Mill, the Secretary,) was taken sick of ague and fever; and for a week confined to his bed, under a course of medicine. The Rev. C. M. Waring having returned to the settlement from his journey to the leeward, submitted a very satisfactory report of the success of his mission. It is inclosed for the perusal of the Board. It will be seen from this paper, that coffee is a common production of this part of the coast. It is to be found indeed, in every place near the sea, and how far back unknown; from the Montserado river, to Grand Bassa. Since Mr. Waring's return a slight search, has discovered hundreds of the trees, and perhaps, thousands of the plants, growing in the mountains, and scattered through every part of our forests. The trees attain an almost unheard of size. Often rising thirty feet, and having a girth of fifteen inches about the stem. The natives have agreed to bring us hundreds of bushels of the berry, as soon as they ripen; which will be in December. But it remains to be determined wholly by the event, what quantities can be collected. We *may* be able to export the article in six months. We *may not* obtain enough for our own consumption. But the discovery is certainly to be considered as one of the most important, yet made in Liberia.

The Agent having become no longer able to fulfil the duties of his station, the Administration passed to-day, into the hands of the Rev. C. M. Waring, Vice-Agent, by whom it was for about ten days conducted with judgment and propriety. The rains are nearly incessant. Their violence surpasses any former example since the Agent has resided in the country.

*October 6th.* The Agent remains closely confined, but slowly recovering. On Sunday last, four persons were baptized by immersion. The rains are so incessant as to spread a gloom over all surrounding nature, and keep every thing, bedding, clothing, books, and stationary constantly wet. Labor has for some time been nearly at a stand, in the settlement. The bones of Nace Butler's body, have been recovered, without an ounce of flesh upon them. The river abounds with ravenous fish of all sizes. The natives are in much greater fear of one, weighing about twelve pounds, but which seizes his prey with amazing energy, than of the Shark.

*October 8th.* There are ten slaving vessels, including the two wrecks ashore, between Gallinas and Trade-town. Three weeks ago, a Spaniard having a badly assorted cargo ashore at Grand Bassa, fired into, and instantly seized upon a Frenchman having two hundred slaves aboard, and quite ready for sea. There had been no previous provocation. Having transferred *all* the slaves to his own vessel, and compelled the Frenchman to accept in lieu thereof an order for his cargo ashore, he took his leave, and made sail for the colonies. The Frenchman a few days after, lost his mate by accident, and has since died himself, of vexation and grief. The vessel is still at Bassa.

# APPENDIX.

*Remarks on the most economical mode of subsisting the Colony, in its infant state.*

To the Executive Committee of the Board of
    Managers of the American Colonization Society :

It is the true point of policy, to draw from all the resources of the neighboring countries, without depending ultimately on any but our own. Experience proves, that for large quantities of provisions, for clothing, and very many of the conveniences and comforts of life, the Colony must for many years, look beyond its own limits.

The inquiry is, can these supplies be obtained most economically, and certainly, from beyond sea, or in this country? and previously, it ought to be ascertained, whether the country is able to afford the Colony these supplies at all. To this I shall reply, by stating the resources of this part of Africa.

From Cape Palmas, three days' sail to the leeward, to the river Sesters, which is distant from the Cape one hundred miles in the same direction, the country abounds in cattle. The Dutch and English purchase them in great numbers for their establishments on Cape-Coast. The price paid for them is from five to eight bars, and I am informed that a very few days are sufficient to make up a cargo. The only reason why the experiment of obtaining from this quarter the meat provisions of the Colony has not been made, is, the want of a vessel of sufficient burthen to bring a cargo of live stock. In the dry season, a vessel of the Fidelity's tonnage, could easily carry eighty small bullocks. The trip might be made in from ten to fourteen days.

That extensive district of the interior, known by the general name of the Gurrah and Condoe countries, commencing about one day's walk to the northeastward, and reaching as far inland, as our geographical information extends, rears a fine breed of cattle. Owing to the desolating effects of the slave trade, they are presumed to be far less abundant than in the vicinity of Cape Palmas. The price is consequently higher, and the number that could be bought, not so great. But the breed is finer, and the expense attending their purchase, and conveyance to the settlement, less by one-half. The Colony has already procured a number of very excellent bullocks from this quarter; and a measure is in progress for obtaining on the best terms, as large and additional supply as our limited means will purchase.

Goats and fowls ought never to be sought for hereafter, out of the limits of the settlement. But every part of the surrounding country abounds with both, and in order to obtain any number of either, you have only to purchase.

The two slaving stations of Cape Mount and Cape Montserado, have for several ages desolated of every thing valuable, the intervening very fertile and beautiful tract of country. The forests have remained untouched—all moral virtue been extinguished in the people, and their industry annihilated, by this one

H

ruinous cause. They are often embarrassed for the necessaries of existence, and never acquire a surplus of provisions. The Colony can derive nothing from these people, a little wood excepted—worth the pursuit.

As long as the Colony remains at peace with the neighboring tribes, cattle may be had from the interior, without difficulty. But not longer. For it is easily in the power of the weakest tribe in the country effectually to cut off all intercourse, by way-laying the path. But having once stocked the settlement, we should at no distant period, be so well supplied, as to be able to meet any temporary interruption, without inconvenience. Provided the Colony could be accommodated with the use of a vessel, two or three times a year, to bring as many cargoes from the leeward coast; the certainty of the supply would be much greater.

There are two more articles of provisions, even more important than beef. These are Rice, and Oil. The latter, until six months old, answers every purpose of Olive-oil, as used for culinary purposes in the south of Europe. Butter and lard, have all their uses fulfilled, and perhaps with advantage to the health of the people, by the Palm-oil. After the first six months, it becomes necessary to subject it to a very simple, refining process, which leaves the oil nearly tasteless—rectifying entirely any previous tendency to rancidity. Very little of this article is ever to be procured to the northward of the river Junk.

Below, it may in the proper season—which is throughout the dry months—be purchased in any quantity. The first cost, is half a bar the gallon—which in cookery, is equal to six pounds of butter.

Rice is produced every where, except in the very vicinity of slave trading stations; where there is never sufficient industry to produce *any* thing. The country lining the sea-coast from the Junk, thirty miles below, to Cape Mount fifty miles above the settlement, limits its annual growth of rice to the consumption of the inhabitants. Farther above, the surplus is bought up for Sierra Leone. Below, it remains open to us.

Rice is most abundant from October to February. A few hundred bushels are annually in this season, brought by the country people to the settlement—but never enough to supply even its present demand. More, will perhaps never be brought in without attention bestowed on our part, to its purchase, while the coast continues to be as much frequented by slaving vessels, as at the present time. Every cargo that leaves the coast requires a large supply of rice, and often the master pays enormously for it. The native growers of rice, are disposed to reserve it for these occasions. Hence it is necessary to establish a temporary factory either at the Junk, at Grand Bassa, or at Grand Battou, during all the former part of the dry season, in order to make sure of a supply for the Colony.

With this precaution, there would be no uncertainty in securing as much as will meet the annual consumption of the settlement. But the whole expense must be reckoned about two and a half bars the heaped bushel, or about five American pecks.

## APPENDIX. 59

I am at the date of these remarks, about to carry a young man of the settlement, with goods, to purchase six or eight hundred bushels of rice, at the mouth of the Junk. He will there establish himself, and remain till recalled. The distance may be walked by a native, in twelve hours.

There is no question then, of the capability of this country to furnish the Colony with provisions. A little system and providence, is all that is necessary to make the supply certain. The only inquiry remaining relates to the comparative expense of provisioning the new-comers, and invalids of the Colony from America, and from this country.

My own sentiments on this subject, I believe, are well known to the Board already.—So much more economical have I found the purchase of African, than the use of American provisions, that I have often had the latter sold, to purchase the former. The experiment has proved the saving to be nearly one half.—Take the following estimate in illustration:—

One barrel of beef costs the Society, on arriving in Africa, $13 50 cents at least. This sum, in bars, of 40 cents, (which is more than the first-cost average of the bar in Africa,) is within a fraction of thirty-four bars, and on the most disadvantageous terms, will pay for two prime bullocks. The average weight of the Condoe bullocks is three hundred pounds. Two bullocks at this rate make three barrels of beef. Three barrels of African beef, is certainly equal to two from America:—or, six hundred pounds of fresh beef, will go further for subsistence than two barrels of salted beef.—The saving is at least one hundred per centum.

For bread-stuffs—one barrel of flour on arriving in the Colony, on the most favorable terms, must have cost $ 9 50 cents—or (the bar at forty,) about 24 bars. This amount of goods will pay for forty-eight pecks, or four barrels of rice, delivered at the Colony. The saving to the funds, is the difference, for the purposes of subsistence, between one barrel of flour, and four barrels of rice. The flour weighs one hundred and ninety-six pounds.—The rice, seven hundred and fifty.

I therefore beg to propose, that the Society will authorize, and furnish the resident Agent with the means to provision the settlement chiefly from the country in which it is situated.

The goods required, and their proportionate quantity, (or value in America,) are,

| | |
|---|---|
| Tobacco, | 5 parts. |
| Whiskey, | 2 " |
| Blue* and White India or English Imitation Bafts, | 2 " |
| Printed Calicoes, | 1 " |
| Printed Cotton Handkerchiefs, | 1 " |
| Black and Flag Silk do. | 1-2 " |

* Blue, Red, Striped, and Check Domestic Cotton Stuffs, will answer the trade as well (not better) per yard, as the India Bafts.

# APPENDIX.

| Gun Powder, | | | | | | 1 part. |
|---|---|---|---|---|---|---|
| Cheap large calibre Guns | | | | | | 1 " |
| Small (pound) Beads of various colors, | | | | | | 2 " |
| Mugs, Bowls, Pitchers, white or colored, | | | | | | 2 " |
| Clasp Knives, | - | - | - | - | - | 1-4 " |
| Tobacco Pipes, | - | - | - | - | - | 2 " |
| Ready made Shirts and Trowsers, | | | - | - | - | 1-4 " |

Dividing the whole sum into 20 "

A larger supply of Salt, than heretofore, will be necessary in case the foregoing arrangement takes place.

In order to ensure the requisite supply of Rice and Oil, a boat of burthen, adapted at the same time for sailing, is absolutely necessary. It is my opinion that a boat of 7 or 8 tons burthen, and answering to a description which follows on the next page, would be more useful, and the risk attending the navigation of it much less than a vessel of a larger denomination. It cannot be concealed, that we have not skill and energy enough to navigate a vessel of burthen. We have no port to shelter one; and I will add that we have neither the resources for employing and paying for, nor a sufficient public object to answer by such a vessel. Your Agent cannot be your Merchant; and without a Merchant to manage a vessel of 40 to 60 tons, it will inevitably prove a losing concern. If you will send out an American crew—and an experienced factor, such a vessel may be useful, but not otherwise.

Permit me, therefore, with deference, to recommend, earnestly, that by the next conveyance, be sent out *two boat frames*, on precisely the same model—the one to be housed—the other to be put up by the Carpenters of the Colony, for the use of the Agent. Keel 30 feet, and Beam 7 1-2, uniting both burthen and good sailing qualities; to be half decked, and Schooner rigged and coppered. The Timbers ready to put together, Spars ditto, Sails made, Cordage in the coil, Plank in the rough, Copper in sheets, with Nails, with fastenings, Rudder ready, with half a dozen barrels of Pitch and Tar, for repairing our water craft generally, and four sweeps to each boat. I could put such a boat up, and fit her for use in a very few weeks. She could pass out and in, over the bar—could make trips between Sierra Leone and Palmas for six months of the year with perfect safety—could carry 250 bushels of Rice, or 4 tons of Wood with ease; and could be navigated by two men and four Kroomen. We could command all the trade which an Agent ought to make, and save to the friends of the Colony, thousands, annually. The second frame, in case it should be furnished, &c. would be saved, for use in case of accident to the first.

I hope the Board will do me the justice to believe that these suggestions are the result of all my past experience in conducting their concerns, as well as the most accurate calculation in my power to make. It may look greater to have a large vessel; but the expense will utterly exceed the utility of such a craft over the boats described; and with the boats, all the Rice necessary for the consumption of four times the present number of Colonists, may be procured; and as much Wood and Ivory brought as can be readily bought, while in the pursuit of provisions.

I would farther suggest, that the packet or chartered vessels arriving in future, be subject to be sent, if the Agent should require the service, to Cape Palmas, for a load of Bullocks. The Agent ought to exercise a discretion of this nature, only in the dry season, unless the exigencies of the Colony should very pressingly demand it.

I have drawn out this paper to a length not intended. But the Board will excuse me for being minute on a subject which so nearly relates to the prosperity of the settlement. I have farther to request that it be made the matter of a separate and particular investigation, and arrangement by the Executive Committee; of whom, I have the honor to remain,

The devoted servant,
J. ASHMUN.

*Monrovia, December,* 1824.

*To the Executive Committee of the Board of*
*Managers of the American Colonization Society:*

There is a standing prohibition of the sale and use of ardent Spirits in the Colony, enrolled among the earliest special arrangements of the Board of Managers. But the paper, containing the only registry of those arrangements, having been withdrawn from the Colony by my predecessors; I never saw or knew of its existence 'till sent out in May, 1823. But by the same vessel, also arrived 19 barrels of Spirits, *all* of which was either *sold* or *used* in the Colony. Such a commentary on the prohibition, was certainly not calculated to place the meaning of the Board in a very clear light; and I now write to, desire instruction.

Although the sin of drunkenness cannot be said to be a prevailing vice among us, yet there is a tendency to an excessive use of rum nd whiskey, very apparent in a number of individuals; and a habit of the daily use of it, threatens to become in a short time, quite too general. No man is so poor as not occasionally, either by his labor, or petty barter, to buy a gallon of ardent Spirits; and twenty persons in the Colony keep the article on hand for sale. The pretext is, to make out a good assortment of trade goods for the natives. But whoever pays for, obtains what he pleases. I shall immediately apply some restraint on the abuse of the article. But the Committee are doubtless well apprised of the extreme difficulty of *regulating* a thing of this nature, which is directly calculated to work the utter ruin of the Colony. I am fully of opinion that the use of Spirits cannot be wholly, and at once, abolished, as long as a trading vessel is permitted to touch within 50 miles of the Cape. In that case, it would be secretly introduced—secretly distributed—and secretly used by all who have a taste for it. But I beg to assure the Committee that something *must be done* in the matter. Leave the thing wholly to the discretion of the settlers, and in six months we have tippling shops, tipplers, and drunkards, forming in every part of the settlement.

I have the honor, &c.<br>J. ASHMUN.

*January 18th, 1825.*

---

## No. 7.

CAPE MONTSERADO,<br>NOVEMBER 23, 1824.

SIR:—

The Rev. Mr. Gurley on his late visit to this Colony very naturally witnessed with great regret the small progress yet made among us, of Agricultural industry and improvements; and concurred in opinion with myself that the general neglect was in part owing to the embarrassment necessarily felt by the settlers from the great change of the climate, and the consequent necessity of adopting new modes of tillage, and new crops, to which none had been previously accustomed. He desired me to draw up the outlines of an Agricultural Manual, from the best sources at my command, and send it home to receive such a revision, as the friends of the design might afford it in America; and thence, if the Board of Managers should concur, be sent back in a printed form, to be placed in the hands of the settlers. You will receive with this the most useful observations which I have been able, in the multitude of other duties, to throw together in manuscript. It will show perhaps little more than my willingness to aid in the advancement of the Agriculture of the Colony. But I hope that Mr. Gurley's inquiries on the subjects of which it treats, while in the West Indies, on his return passage, will have obtained something, and that the recollections and science of Dr. Thornton, and other gentlemen in Washington, will supply other materials, which I should be glad to see incorporated in the work, with such corrections and retrenchments as the utility of the little compend calls for.

I have aimed to simplify the style and language, in accommodation to the ideas and conceptions of the illiterate; and in the introductory parts, to impress a few economical maxims by a direct reference to local facts and circumstances. The necessity of those remarks has been but too long and anxiously felt by myself; and I presume by Dr. Ayres, during and since his residence at the Cape. Should it be printed, I beg that it may be given in charge to the Rev. Mr. Gurley to read the proof-sheets, and that the type may be large.

Respectfully, sir, your obedient servant,

*To the Secretary of the Am. Col. Society.* J. ASHMUN.

# THE LIBERIA FARMER;

OR,

## COLONIST'S GUIDE

TO

## INDEPENDENCE AND DOMESTIC COMFORT.

INSCRIBED TO ALL THE INDUSTRIOUS SETTLERS OF LIBERIA,

BY THEIR FRIEND AND AGENT,

J. ASHMUN.

1825.

## INTRODUCTION.

You have come together from different and distant States in America. The climates, soils, productions and mode of Agriculture, to which you were there accustomed, are very various; but all are widely different from those of Africa. Some of you were mechanics in your native country, but you are all farmers here; and have every thing belonging to the business, to learn anew. American crops, and the American modes of tillage, must nearly all be given up; and a new system of farming adopted. Of this, I can easily convince you.

Look at our African seasons, and compare them with the seasons in America. Here, you can find neither Winter, Spring, Summer nor Autumn. These interesting changes have disappeared from the African year. Now, the whole system of cropping in America depended on the seasons. Some grains and fruits in that country, you recollect, required even the frosts and snows of its terrible winters. Before other seeds could be planted, it was necessary the warm Spring months should be considerably advanced. Three or four Summer months, then made up nearly the only season of the year, in which vegetables and grains would grow and ripen. The last months of Summer and all the Autumnal months, varying with the nature of the crop, were the harvest season.

But not having any of these seasons in Africa, you must learn an entirely different way of farming, and turn your attention to new productions, agreeing

## APPENDIX.

better with your new climate and seasons. It is the intention of this little treatise, to assist you to acquire this necessary information, in the shortest time, and use it in the best possible way. It does not profess to teach a perfect system of African farming. That can only be discovered by the light of a great number of experiments and facts, which depend on your own future industry and observation. But it is all-important, you should begin your farming operations in possession of all the correct information that can be obtained; and lay aside all your prejudices in favor of American modes, which will not answer in this country. This is the only way to turn your labor and time to any good account; and support your families with credit and comfort, by the proceeds of your own industry.

On this last point, suffer me to put down two or three remarks, of the truth and importance of which you cannot be too sensible. The first is, *That the cultivation of your rich lands, is the only way you will ever find out to independence, comfort and wealth.*

It is hard for some of you to understand, or to believe this maxim. But it is, nevertheless, most true, and capable of being clearly proved.

I will suppose you to be a mechanic, and that your trade is worth one dollar a day—you have, then, 300 dollars a year to support yourself on. But if agriculture is neglected here generally, you must send to America for every article of provisions and clothing; or buy of trading vessels, which will make you pay 100 per cent. profit, besides expenses. What will a dollar laid out in this way, buy you? Not more than thirty or forty cents' worth in America. If you are single, you may in this way feed and clothe yourself poorly. But, if you have a family, you must all suffer for want of the necessaries of life, if you rely on your mechanical labors alone.

But, perhaps you hope to buy rice, fowls and plantains, of the natives; and 40 cents a day will go, you imagine, a great way with them.

Suppose, however, the natives should do what they often have done already, prohibit all trade and intercourse with you? Rely on it, the moment they find you depending on them, they will do so; or else, make you pay four or five prices for every thing they sell you. But, if there is no agriculture, there will be nothing in the Colony to pay mechanics with; and consequently, no employment for them. The natives, likewise, are often too poor to feed themselves. And had they cassada to sell you, and you tobacco to buy it; are you so lost to all sense of shame, as to be willing to depend on a half naked Savage to feed you?

But there is another bewitching spell, which I fear will keep some of you in poverty, debt, and wretchedness, as long as you live. I mean, *That most deceptive hope of supporting yourselves by trade.*

You could not succeed in the attempt, if you had all been bred merchants; and for this good reason, the Colony has not trade enough to support twenty families. The natives bring you nothing but Camwood, and small Ivory. No Camwood grows on your own land, and all the natives cut between this and Cape Mount, does not amount to 300 tons. Trading Vessels will always take one-half of this, for they can always undersell you. No man in Africa can make more than 20 dollars clear profit, on a ton; so that 3,000 dollars is the most you all can ever make on this article: and this sum in Africa will support ten families. Now, suppose 100 families depend on this trade? They may make 30 dollars each. And 30 dollars will buy one barrel of Pork, and one of Flour, and nothing more. They must starve.

The Ivory part is not worth a fourth part as much as the Camwood. The clear profits it would afford, are not worth five dollars to a family: and yet, some of you hope to *support* your families, and grow rich by trading!—Twenty poles of Lima Beans, will be a much surer dependence, and actually go farther towards supporting a family, than the whole trade in Camwood and Ivory, if it was equally shared among you all. You can make the calculation for yourselves. Some of you have already gone too deep in trade. And you feel the bad effects of it. Show me a man without a good house, without improvements on his lands, who is deep in debt, and pinched and harrassed in all his circumstances; and I will show you a man who has foolishly depended on trading with the country people for a support. Look around, and tell me how many exceptions there are to this remark. Trade and day-labor as a mechanic, may then be reckoned as your worst dependence. If you have no other you must content yourself to keep as poor as a native, while you live.

"Have we then been sent to Africa to starve?" No. You may if you please, and God gives you health, become as independent, comfortable and happy, as you ought to be in this world. The upland of the Cape, is not the best. The Creator has formed it for a town, and not for plantations. But the flat lands around you, and particularly your farms, have as good a soil as can be met with in any country. They will produce two crops of corn, sweet potatoes and several other vegetables in a year. They will yield a larger crop than the best soils in America. And they will produce a number of very valuable articles, for which in the United States, millions of money are every year paid away to foreigners. One acre of rich land, well tilled, will produce you three hundred dollars' worth of Indigo. Half an acre may be made to grow half a ton of arrow root. Four acres laid out in Coffee-plants, will, after the third year, produce you a *clear income* of two or three hundred dollars. Half an acre of cotton-trees will clothe your whole family; and, except a little hoeing, your wife and children can perform the whole labor of cropping and manufacturing it. One acre of canes will make you independent of all the world, for the sugar you use in your family. One acre set with fruit trees, and well attended, will furnish you the year round, with more Plantains, Bananas, Oranges, Limes, Guavas, Papaws, and Pine-apples, than you will ever gather. Nine months of the year, you may grow fresh vegetables every month, and some of you who have low-land plantations, may do so throughout the year. Soon, all the vessels visiting the coast, will touch here for refreshments. You never will want a ready market for your fruits and vegetables. Your other crops being articles of export, will always command the cash, or something better. With these resources, (and nothing but industry and perseverance is necessary to realize them,) you cannot fail to have the means of living as comfortably, independently and happily as any people on earth. If you forfeit such prospects through indolence or folly, thank yourselves for it. No one else, I promise you, will condole with you.

This little treatise is intended only for the industrious, and for such as are willing to become so. And in order to assist your industry to produce its full effects, I shall throw together the brief notices which I have to offer, into several short chapters, each one relating to some subject in agriculture, which you may directly reduce to practice.

## CHAPTER I.
### THE CLIMATE OF AFRICA,

Is uniformly sultry and moist. But the heat is not excessive. You who keep thermometers, will perceive the mercury to stand in the wet season, at about 77 degrees, and in the dry, after sunrise, at about 82 degrees. Now the heat of a summer's day in Baltimore, and Richmond, is from 84 to 90 degrees. So that the heat of Liberia is never insupportable; and commonly, very comfortably moderate. But, the difference of heat at night and by day, seldom exceeds three or four degrees of the scale. In America it often sinks and rises in the twenty-four hours, more than ten or twelve degrees. This uniform heat has a most favorable effect on the growth of plants and vegetables. It sustains the vegetable life in a constant and unabated state of activity. The cold nights and cold storms of America, never are felt here. Consequently, as long as your plantations and gardens have moisture sufficient, you may expect every blade of rice, every stork of corn, every fruit-tree and vegetable, to flourish with the utmost luxuriance. The papaws and plantain trees are a good example of the power of an uniformly heated climate, to accelerate vegetation. You may see in the gardens many of the former, not more than fifteen months from the seed, already fifteen inches round the stem, and fifteen feet high, with several pecks of ripening fruit. Clear your lands; plant your crops; keep the weeds down; and the most favorable climate in the world, alone, under the direction of a bountiful Providence, will do more for you than all your toil and care could accomplish in America.

## CHAPTER II.
### THE AFRICAN SEASONS,

Are very properly divided into the wet and dry. The wet season begins at Montserado, about the 10th or 15th of May; after three or four weeks of frequent thunder-showers, and very short and sudden tempests of wind from the land.

The latter part of May, and the whole of June, comprise perhaps, the most rainy period in the year. It is vastly important that your new grounds should be cleared, well burnt, planted and fenced, before these rains come on. It is not possible to do either, well, afterwards. The natives who have no almanacs, and who are accused of great indolence, are never behindhand in their rice-plantations. In the months of March and April, their plantation fires send up columns of smoke in all directions; and the month of June witnesses a most verdant display of springing rice in the neighborhood of all their towns.

July and August are, commonly, almost as dry as the same months in America. The weather is delightfully cool; and seems to have been appointed for the convenience of dressing gardens and plantations. You have now an opportunity to weed and grub up the sprouts and bushes on your crop lands, to make fences, and set out fruit, cotton, and coffee trees. After having performed all that your plantations and gardens require, you may find a few weeks of this cool and pleasant season to provide timber and materials for building out-houses, or enlarging your dwellings. Should birds or insects have destroyed any part of the young crop of rice, or vegetables, you can now fill it in with new seed, before the September rains come on. But never expect a crop planted in July and August, will succeed as well as that which enjoys the benefit of the June rains.

On the last of August, the second, and much the longest course of rains, usually sets in. They prevail without much intermission, throughout September and October. In November, the thunder-gusts return, and the rains gradually subside. Your rice crop is now fit for the scykle; and you must stand by every fair day to secure it, as soon as possible. The corn-crop, if planted seasonably, will come in, early in September. The second planting, sometime in November. That part of the Indigo, and Coffee crops, which comes to maturity in these months, must be carefully gathered as it ripens, and cured under cover. But, after all these labors, many days of this dripping season will remain, and they can be best employed by mechanics at their trades, and by all others in dressing and mortising fence-posts, and making gates, refitting their implements, and performing all the rough work required about their houses and plantations, which can be done under shelter. Fruit, cotton and coffee-trees, may also be transplanted.

The month of November puts an end to the redundant rains of the year. The season for clearing lands, now begins. No industrious man will neglect commencing this work beyond the first day of December, while an acre remains to be cleared on his plantation. Occasional showers may be expected till the first week in January.

January, February and March are the driest—March and April, the hottest months in the year. These are the months in which one day's work in clearing and burning brush-wood, killing weeds and sprouts on your plantations, grubbing up roots and stubs, will effect more than a whole week in any other season. December and January, are the months for cutting down the timber, vines, and brush-wood. February and March, for burning and clearing your plantations. April and May, for fencing and planting them. You can have no crop without thoroughly burning over your new plantations, and you never can burn well, after the tornadoes set in, towards the last of March.

## CHAPTER III.

### THE SOIL OF LIBERIA,

Depends for its quality much on the situation of the lands. The upland of the Cape and Coast, has two varieties of soil. The first is, that strong and deep mould which is always found, where the hard, brown granite rocks are most numerous. This soil is certainly very capable of being turned to a very profitable account. Observe every where in the beds of those rocks, the thrifty and sturdy growth of timber. The largest trees are commonly found in such situations. This is however, a wet-season soil; and must not be expected to give you a crop in the dry months. I shall call this, *The Strong Upland Soil.*

The other species of upland soil, is of a much inferior quality. It consists of a reddish, clayey earth, every where more or less mixed with soft, rust-colored rocks, stones and gravel. The red color of the soil and rocks is caused by the rust of the iron particles intermingled with it. Manure may, in time, render it productive. But the best mode yet discovered to fertilize this soil, is to burn over the surface in clearing the land; and to spread small quantities of ashes or lime over it, after the first crop. I shall distinguish this as *The Weak Upland Soil.*

There are three sorts of lowland soil. The first and richest is that formed on the sides of rivers, and from the wash of the uplands. It is always wet during the rains, consists of a loose, deep, black mould, and is entirely free from rocks and gravel. This soil will produce any crop which you choose to plant; but is especially adapted to early rice, and to all those vegetables which thrive in the dry season. I shall call this *The Rich Lowland Soil.*

The second variety of soil in the bottom land, I shall name, *The Stiff Clayey Soil.* It consists of a lightish colored clay, sometimes a little tempered with coarse sand. It is subject to the extremes of wet and drought; but produces good crops, and can be much improved by manuring.

The sandy soil is the third variety found in the level country. It is most prevalent wherever the land has, in course of time, gained upon the ocean, or channels of rivers. It is a light, warm soil; and will yield only slender crops without manure. Sweet potatoes, beans, cassada, and succulent fruit trees, will succeed best in it.

APPENDIX. 69

## CHAPTER IV.

## METHOD OF CLEARING LANDS.

Before you can have plantations, your industry must conquer them from an almost impenetrable forest. In this laborious business, your success wholly depends upon your going properly to work in the right season. The time to clear lands is from December to March. Enter your forest in December and January, provided with an axe, and bill-hook. The axe is to be used with all the large trees and saplings, the hook to clear away the vines and brush-wood. Let every thing be cut near the ground. The saplings should be taken off even with the surface. After bringing a hanging mass of vines and trees to the ground, never quit it till you have trimmed every branch from the trunks of the trees, divided them into proper lengths, cut up every bush and twig by the ground, and piled the branches and brush-wood into two or three snug heaps for burning. This is the only neat and cleanly style of cleaning your lands. Let the whole lie till, not only the leaves, but the very wood itself is perfectly dried and combustible. Fire it then, on the windward side, at one o'clock in the day. The whole surface will be burnt black; and every thing except the trunks of the trees, consumed. Now lay these together in snug piles, saving out such pieces as will answer for timber and fencing, and burn them.

The advantages of this method are, to save immense labor—to kill at once, all the shrubbery and small roots—and to prepare the surface of your lands, in the best possible way, to receive a crop. A plantation managed in this way, never requires ploughing or digging, for the first crop.

If you depart from these directions, either in the time of clearing, or the manner of heaping and burning your brush, you may depend on being obliged to fight against a forest of sprouts and weeds, all the year; and not get half a crop in harvest.

## CHAPTER V.

## METHOD OF MAKING AND USING MANURE.

In cropping your lands, the first time, the seed is thrown upon the surface of the ground, and covered in. For the second crop, the soil requires ploughing or digging, with a grubbing hoe; and all the soils except the *strong uplands* and the *rich lowlands,* require manure. Every particle of this substance should accordingly be saved, and the greatest possible quantity produced for enriching your lands. You must carefully collect all the impurities and rubbish about your plantations and town lots, into a heap, at a proper distance from your dwelling. Old mats, straw, bones, ashes, sweepings, the weedings of your gardens, every rejected thing, in short, of a vegetable and animal nature, should be collected into this heap, and the whole left to ferment and mellow, till fit to be carried out and bestowed upon your plantations.

Manure should be given to your lands immediately before or after planting your crop. For rice, the best way of applying it, is to spread it equally over the surface. For cassada, corn, sweet potatoes, indigo, canes, arrow-root, ginger, cotton and coffee, the proper method is to give it in shovels-full to the hills, or to lay it in a line along the upper side of the row. After once or twice cropping your new lands, their produce may be doubled by the use of manure.

## CHAPTER VI.

### FENCING.

Next after sheltering your families with a good house, you ought to enclose your lots and plantations with a substantial fence.

Your town lot ought to be surrounded by a picket board fence at least six feet high. The upright pieces ought to be planed and pointed, and not exceed five inches in width. A stone wall ought, as soon as possible, to take the place of this fence.

On your plantations, you have the choice of a horizontal, or upright board fence, or one of posts and rails. The latter is cheapest at first, but must never have fewer than five or six rails. Less will turn neither goats nor bullocks. For want of the last rail, you will often lose your whole crop. Plantations ought not to be fenced into larger fields than of two acres; and those of smaller size, into fields of a single acre, in order to admit of a due rotation and change of crops, together with tillage, fruit and coffee plantations; into which every man should distribute his lands.

## CHAPTER VII.

### AFRICAN PRODUCTIONS—KITCHEN GARDEN.

The climate of Africa is adapted to a much greater variety of productions than those of America and Europe. But your attention must be given to the cultivation of such alone as serve directly to supply your wants, promote your comfort, and lead to independence and wealth. Of these, RICE and CORN must always be leading articles. Without these grains, you have no bread.

## APPENDIX.

The demand for them will always be great; and the produce of the Colony can never exceed the demand. Cassada and yams are doubtless the best vegetable substitutes for the grains. They may be made the source of comfort, and in time, of wealth, from the abundance, cheapness, and usefulness of the crop. Every plantation should grow sweet-potatoes the year round. Light soils answer well—but manure improves them. The pumpkin is a natural product of Liberia; and should never be forgotten. The flavor is superior to that of the American pumpkin. Twenty plantain and banana trees, well manured, will afford you the greatest abundance of those valuable fruits. Your residence should be surrounded with them. Oranges attain the greatest perfection, and require no more care than the commonest apple tree of America. Limes and guavas may be propagated from roots or offsets; both of which are to be procured with a little pains, in any quantities. The thick rind or lemon species of the former, ought to be preferred. A walk of pine-apple plants ought to ornament every plantation. Half an acre of cotton trees will clothe yourself and family; and, except a little hoeing, all the labor of rearing and manufacturing the article can be performed by your wife and children. The same quantity of land devoted to the culture of the sugar cane, will render you independent of all the world, for the sugar necessary for your family. Coffee, whether considered as a staple of trade, or a valuable article of domestic comfort, demands a large share of your attention. Two acres in every five, is not too great a proportion of your lands to devote to the crop. The trees produce double the quantity here, that they do in the West Indies; and the article is of a superior quality. No man should be in Liberia twelve months, without, at least, two acres set with coffee plants. They afford a certain income at small expense. Indigo, when successful, is a still more profitable production. It will admit of being cropped eight times in the year, at least. A quarter of an acre, well managed, will give you ten pounds at a cropping. Lose no time. Ginger, aloes, arrow-root, and pepper, are all valuable articles of export, and will abundantly repay your pains in cultivating them. The following chapters will point out the mode of their culture.

It is an important inquiry, how ought town lots to be occupied? I can, as a general direction, tell you, that every town lot ought to contain a subtantial dwelling house, placed twenty-five feet in rear of the street; a kitchen in the rear of the house; a store house and granary under the same roof; and a kitchen garden. This last should occupy at least one-half of the lot. It should be manured as highly as industry and skill can reach; and never exhibit a neglected plant, or an useless weed. The hoe should pass over it every week—cabbages, onions, charots, radishes, lettuce, tomatoes, cucumbers, simblins, and every sweet-scented and aromatic herb of American kitchen gardens, will flourish if planted, and produce you more domestic comforts than half your income would buy you without a garden. The man who neglects a kitchen garden, I set down for a very lazy, or a miserably inprovident fellow. Remember, a garden will not support your family without a plantation; neither will a plantation render them comfortable without a kitchen garden.

## CHAPTER VIII.

### THE CULTURE OF RICE.

The natives of the coast never neglect this crop, without expecting a famine for their folly. Trade, pleasure, their natural indolence—all give way, on the return of the year, to the necessity of preparing a rice plantation.—Imitate them.

Three species of rice are cultivated on the coast: the round grained—the large white or Carolina rice; and the red African rice. They all succeed well but I am told that the American is considered the best. This alone succeeds well in a foreign market.

Rice answers in all soils; but the best soils are to be chosen, and the mode of culture is to be regulated by the nature of the lands.

For an upland crop, clear your plantation in the midst of the dry season; and burn and prepare it for planting in March and April, as directed in chapter IV. After the tornado rains become frequent, and the surface of the ground a little softened, put in your crop. Sow about two bushels of seed to the acre, and cover it with a hoe, or harrow on the same day. It is now necessary to see that the birds do not filch away the grain, and to continue to watch it until the blade is several inches out of the ground. Five or six weeks after planting a newly-cleared field, you must carefully destroy with a hook, all the springing sprouts, and pull the weeds, and if necessary, this operation must be gone over again before the crop ears.

The rice will be fit for the sickle early in September, and it ought to be dried and threshed or beaten, as early as convenient, afterwards. The grain is easily preserved in the chaff, or husk, if kept dry. and it can be hulled and cleared at your leisure.

The lowland crop, is sown in September, October, or November, on wet, marshy lands, which have been prepared during the rains. These lands should be so situated as to retain a large share of moisture 'till the crop is fully half grown, and the weeds and sprouts kept down in the upland crop. The grain will be fit for the harvest in March and April. The natives prefer the summer [upland] crop, and it is presumed to be the most productive.

But the upland culture, it should be recollected, answers in bottom lands, except the most marshy, quite as well as in upland soils, and I think ought to take the place of the other altogether.

A second crop cannot follow the first, on new lands, without plowing up the soil to a good depth. The same directions must then be observed which have just been given for cropping new lands.

APPENDIX. 73

Lands once ploughed will not produce two successive crops, without fresh ploughing, always, and manuring, unless the soil is very rich and marshy; when manure is not necessary.

Rich lowland soils under the best culture, produce from forty to fifty bushels to the acre; but the upland crop is a good one if it yields you thirty.

---

CHAPTER IX.

## CULTURE OF INDIAN CORN AND CASSADA.

The culture of corn, observing the proper time of planting, does not vary from the method pursued in America. As the crop grows during the rains, the upland soils are preferable to the marshy.

The preparation of the lands should be the same as for rice, and the best season for planting, is in all the month of May. The crop ripens early in September. A good return is often made from seed planted in July, which matures in November and December. But the June rains, it should never be forgotten, are of more service to all African crops than any other, and ought never, through neglect or sloth, to be lost.

CASSADA may be raised from the seed, or propagated from the root, or the stem. The latter method is the least troublesome, and most commonly practised. All soils will answer for this valuable vegetable; but the dry and sandy are preferable to the marshy, even when the latter is much the richest. Cassada ought to be made to fill up all those lands which would otherwise remain vacant and neglected on account of their poverty. A succession of crops may follow each other on the same ground; the decayed stalks and leaves of the former crops, serving to keep the land in heart. It may be planted in any month of the year.

After preparing the ground, line it four feet asunder, and form on the lines, trenches three or four inches deep. Cut the stem into pieces containing each, two joints, and drop them horizontally into the trenches, two feet apart. Cover on three or four inches. Keep the weeds down, and hoe the crop once in two months. In six months, the young Cassada will be fit for use, at half growth. The crop can be dug as your own domestic uses require; and will last from 15 to 18 months. Pigs, cattle, and goats, may be fattened on this root, with very little trouble and expense; and Tapioca, a valuable article of sale, manufactured from it by a very cheap and simple process. Its produce is greater than that of any other known vegetable.

K

## CHAPTER X.

### YAMS, SWEET POTATOES, PLANTAINS, BANANAS, AND THE ORANGE.

The Yam grows spontaneously in some situations on the coast, and can be easily cultivated in all. The root improves in quality under proper management, and degenerates by neglect to a bitter, heavy and very inferior vegetable. It is propagated from the root.

Divide the upper half of a yam of good size, into two or three parts. Plant these, from twelve to twenty inches asunder, in trenches prepared as for Cassada, which ought to have four feet intervals between them. This crop requires manure, if the land is not newly cleared. See chapter V.

The most proper time for planting, is at the commencement of the rains, in May. But the vegetable will succeed at any time, except two or three months of the dry season, and even then, if the land is moist. Wet soils produce yams of an inferior quality.

They should be carefully hoed, at least three times; and at the end of the first month, they must be furnished with two poles, set along the row, at the distance of two and a half feet, for the vines to dispose themselves upon. Two crops may be made in the year.

SWEET POTATOES are another invaluable vegetable, which may be cultivated on nearly every variety of soils, and at any season of the year. They may be reared from the seeds, the root, or the vines. To preserve the species from degeneracy, plant the roots, and even the seeds, occasionally. But the crop is much more conveniently and speedily reared from the vines.

*Method.*—In the month of May or June, (of preference,) dig your land into loose ridges about three feet asunder. Manure these ridges plentifully, and mix the compost well with the earth. Insert, by hand, along these ridges, and not more than fifteen inches apart, some of the thriftiest vines taken from the preceding crop. Keep the weeds from springing, by repeated hoeings; at the same time loosening the earth about the roots of the vine. In two months, the young potatoe will make its appearance, and about the end of the fourth, will have come to maturity.

PUMPKINS, are reared from the seed. They are a succulent vegetable, and will scarcely succeed if planted in the dry months. But vines which have obtained a thrifty growth during the rains, will flourish and bear fruit throughout the season.

Plant every variety. Manure the hills well, and a single vine will not find room in a square pole of ground to expand itself in. This vegetable acquires a much harder and thicker rind in this country, than it has in America.

PLANTAINS AND BANANAS are propagated from the suckers which spring out of the root of the parent tree. They may be separated from the old stock and transplanted at any period, but most successfully, in the early rainy months.

Let the earth be dug into a loose bed for the roots to spread in, and the ground be enriched by several shovelsfull of manure, during the year. The plants should be set at six feet distant, and commonly, in rows parallel to your garden fence, and not more than three feet from it. The first crop will come, in about a twelve month. Whenever the old stock begins to decline, cut it off near the ground, and remove it along with the fallen leaves, to your manure heap, and carefully cherish as many of the new shoots as are necessary to supply the place of the old. These are permanent fruits, which ripen and renew themselves throughout the year.

THE ORANGE TREE is of slower growth; but one of the most verdant, thrifty and beautiful trees of the woody species, in nature. Every man should keep a well tended nursery of these trees, which he can obtain from the seed in six months. Transplant them to your garden, and plantation, when three feet high, during the prevalence of the rains. The trees, in an orange orchard, or walk, ought to be set eight feet apart, and at the end of four or five years, every second tree cut away or transplanted. Let the earth about the roots be frequently stirred, and well mellowed with manure. The two first years, you may continue to crop the ground with corn or vegetables, as before. Liberia will afford ripe oranges every month in the year.

The orange tree is also propagated by scions taken from the branches of the full grown tree, and set in the earth, like the offsets of the currant tree in America.

## CHAPTER XI.

### THE LIME TREE

Is of a more hardy nature than the orange; and will thrive in a poorer soil. It is managed in the same way.

### THE PAPAW

May be raised from the seed to the height of two feet, or a suitable state for transplanting, in six weeks—set them eight feet asunder, and three plants together; manure and weed the ground. In six months, the flower will appear, and distinguish the sex of the tree. Cut up all the males, excepting one to every ten females; and reduce the females to one tree at each station. In ten months, the fruit will begin to ripen, and afford you a weekly supply for as many years as the tree lives.

### THE GUAVA

May be managed in the same way as the orange; and will commence bearing the third year. It may also be propagated by setting the scions.

## THE PINE APPLE

Requires a rich, moist soil, and is propagated by planting the bud and corn of leaves growing at the head of the ripe fruit, in hills two feet apart. The suckers cut from the base of the ripe fruit, answer the same purpose; and so do the young shoots springing from the root. Insert and transplant your suckers in the rains. Hoe and weed the plant with especial care; and the crop will come forward with the return of the season.

## CHAPTER XII.

### THE COTTON CROP.

It is believed that none of the varieties of the American cotton shrub answers in all respects, to the indigenous African tree. The cotton of this country is, on all hands, allowed to be of a good quality; and the mode of growing, curing, and manufacturing the article pursued in America, may be adopted here, making due allowance for the much greater size and duration of the African tree. It is raised from the seed, and ought to be reared to the height of three feet, in a nursery, and transplanted into the field in rows, six feet distant from each other. This process should take place in the rainy season. The same tree bears a succession of crops for a great number of years.

The trees should be pruned into shape, and the plantation kept clean with a hoe.

The driest upland situations should be chosen for this crop; and weak upland soils will answer. It comes to maturity early in the dry season; and ought to be gathered as soon as the wool appears through the seams of the pod. Dry and separate the wool from the pod and base, to which it adheres. Gin it, and afterwards hand-pick it carefully, to separate broken seeds and damaged cotton from the good.

N. B. Cotton growers should carefully note every fact attending the culture of the article, till the most profitable culture is much better understood.

## CHAPTER XIII.

### THE SUGAR-CANE

Is of biennial growth. Its culture in the Colony, ought at present, to be limited to your own domestic supplies. To make sugar for exportation would require more capital and more skill than any of you at present, possess. For a family of seven persons, half an acre of canes will furnish an ample supply of sugar and vinegar.—To cultivate them,

Mellow the land to a good depth with the plough or pick. Trench it in lines four feet apart—cover in four inches of earth on the stems of the cane, cut into pieces containing two or three joints. Manure on the upper side of these trenches—hoe it repeatedly. In fifteen months, the crop matures—cut it with a sickle at the ground—top and leaf the stalks, and send them in bundles to the mill. The juice must be boiled on the same day in which it is expressed, or your sugar will not grain. Copper boilers are preferable to iron. The skimmings are to be reserved for vinegar.

To make good sugar, requires great skill, which can be acquired only by experience. You would often fail in attempting it. Syrup, or cane juice, boiled to a consistence of thin molasses, and carefully refined, will answer every purpose of refined sugar, and is better suited to the dampness and heat of this climate.

The rich lowland soil will produce the best canes. The season for planting is the three last rainy months.

Having cropped your cane field, either plough or dig the ground between the old rows, adding a new supply of manure. The old stocks will send up an abundance of suckers, which are to be thinned out, and managed precisely as the planted crop. This operation may be several times repeated; and it is considered a better method of renewing the plants than by planting the stems.

## CHAPTER XIV.

### COFFEE.

Every proprietor of lands, should keep a flourishing nursery of young coffee plants. No country will bring the product to higher perfection than Africa. Whether it is a native of the country, or was introduced at an early period, by the Portuguese and Spaniards, cannot now be certainly known. It is enough for you to know, that it has propagated itself on your hills, and along a great extent of the African coast, without culture, for many ages. South of your river, it grows every where; and the tree and berry attain a size unknown elsewhere.

Transplant the young trees at an early period of the rains. Few dry soils are unfavorable to their growth. And they are found in a state of nature in many situations where moisture predominates a great part of the year. The dry upland gives the small grained and fine flavored kernel; rich lowland for the greatest crop.

Line your plantation into squares of six feet; and mellow the beds which are to receive the plants. Let the young tree, at the time of transplanting it, be two feet high; crop it ten inches from the ground; and save only the most thrifty young shoot which springs from the root.

For the first two years after setting your plantation, cultivate on it corn or some vegetable which requires the frequent use of the hoe. Superfluous branches must be carefully pruned off; and only about thirty or forty left to the tree. These will begin to bear, the third year. The tree should be topped at a convenient height and prevented from shooting higher ever afterwards.

The berries when ripe, have a darkish red appearance; and should be then gathered and cured. It is customary to gather the crop at three different periods, and stages of ripeness.

To CURE THE COFFEE, pass it through a simple hand mill, immediately after gathering it, in order to grind off the pulp, or outside envelope. When quite dry, either beat the kernel in a large mortar, or pass it through a hulling mill, of a construction different from the first, in order to separate from the kernel the parchment hull, in which it is closely wrapped. This process may also be performed by the pestle. The chaff may then be carried off by a common fan. The flavor of the coffee improves by keeping.

To REMOVE THE TREES in your plantation, (which must be done once in ten years,) cut away every alternate tree by the ground; and raise one of the suckers from the old stock or root.

No crop is surer; and African coffee frequently produces four pounds to the tree in a season.

## CHAPTER XV.

### INDIGO.

This crop affords a very quick return; and when successful, is the most profitable one that can be produced by the same labor in tropical climates.

It is annually raised from the seed—One peck of seed serves for more than an acre.

Prepare the land as for corn or potatoes. Trench it slightly in lines two feet asunder. Scatter the seed in the trenches, and cover on the earth. Use the hoe freely, while the crop continues.

The seed should be planted in April, and the crop will be fit for the first cutting in August. Six or eight successive cuttings may be had of the same crop, at intervals of six or seven weeks between. The ground should be changed, and a new crop sown every year.

To MANUFACTURE THE INDIGO.—Cut the plant three inches above the ground. Place it in layers in a steeping vat, and cover it over with water. Let the mass ferment 'till the liquor becomes nearly transparent. Then draw it into the battery, or churn-vat. Churn it 'till the Indigo begins to appear on the surface. Add lime-water. Let the Indigo subside. Draw off the water; and hang up the Indigo, in small canvass bags, to drain and dry. It is then shifted into small boxes, to harden and mature for use.

## CHAPTER XVI.
### GINGER

Is as easily cultivated as the potatoe. The richer the soil the more abundant the produce.

Plant it eighteen inches distant, immediately after the rains set in. Hoe and nurse it as the potatoe, and when the tops begin to turn, as they will, in the following dry season, gather and wash it.

*To cure it.*—Gradually immerse the root in hot water, and dry it by a fire, or in the sun, and you have the Black Ginger.

The Yellow, is obtained by scraping off the outside of the root; and exposing it with frequent turning, to the hot sun, 'till thoroughly dry.

### ARROW ROOT

Is cultivated as the ginger: and like Tapioca, is prepared by rasping, or grinding the root fine, and then steeping the pulp; as is practised in the preparation of Starch.

### BIRD PEPPER

Should be planted in May, June or July, in continuous rows, two feet from each other—the ground manured highly, and the crop often hoed. The pepper gradually ripens towards Christmas, and is a valuable article, both for exportation, and domestic use.

### ALOES

Are indigenous in Liberia, and possess valuable medicinal qualities. They are propagated from suckers, in the same way as the Pine-Apple; and the same mode of culture is applicable.

To prepare the article for market, pull up the plant with the roots. Wash it. Cut the whole into small pieces, and inclose them in hampers. These are to be thrown into an iron cauldron, and boiled 'till the liquor becomes highly colored, and even black. Strain it into a vat, or cask having a cock three inches from the bottom. Let the sediment subside below the cock. Draw off the liquor in six or eight hours; and boil it down to the consistence of honey. If burnt in this process, the whole is lost. Put it into gourds, or earthen pots, for sale. It hardens by age.

## APPENDIX.

### No. 8.

We have inserted, under number three, two letters from Mr. Ashmun, on the character of the native Africans, and the importance of introducing Christianity among them. His able letter subsequently addressed to the Rev. Dr. Blumhardt, on the same subject, is too important to be omitted.

MONROVIA, APRIL 23, 1826.

*To the Rev. Dr. Blumhardt, Principal of the*
*Missionary College at Basle, Switzerland:*

REV. AND DEAR SIR: Your much valued favor of the 18th of October, 1825, arrived in Africa, by way of the United States, nearly two months ago; but a very unusual press of other duties has hitherto deprived me of the power of answering it satisfactorily, and must render, I fear, the present reply much less perfect and detailed than the importance of your communication authorizes you to expect.

While I tender you my sincere thanks for the information your letter affords of the object, origin, and operations of the two allied Institutions in which your own labors, have borne so distinguished a part, you will do me and many thousands of my countrymen only an act of justice by assuring yourself, that both had already shared deeply in our sympathies, our hopes, and our prayers. Our civil institutions and ancestral relations, perhaps, direct our natural affections towards a different district of Europe; but as heirs of the pure faith and blessed hopes of the Gospel, American Christians have still stronger sympathies to bestow on the land of Luther and the glorious company of his associate reformers. The rekindlings of the holy light of the sixteenth century, in Geneva, Basle, Frankfort, Dresden, and many other places in Switzerland, Germany, Holland, and Prussia, are reflected to the Western World, where it mingles with a kindred radiance, proceeding, we trust, with increasing brightness from the American churches. Gladly, I am persuaded, would those churches, or the individuals who compose them, reunite their labors with those of their brethren of Continental Europe, as they have their affections, in the cultivation of the common African field, hitherto too much neglected by both. A copy of your letter to the Board of Direction of this Colony, has been put into my hands; from whom, I doubt not, you will receive assurances of their most cordial co-operation so far as the paramount and single object of their labors, "the Colonization of American Blacks in Africa," to which they stand pledged to the world to appropriate their funds, shall authorize them to act. The answer which you may expect to that communication will, I trust, prove sufficiently full and explicit to satisfy your inquiries on all the points stated in your letters, except those of local information; and on these inquiries

## APPENDIX. 81

I shall now endeavor to afford you all the information which a residence of nearly four years in Africa, and a very large intercourse with the natives of the country, have enabled me to communicate.

Before proceeding to take up the questions of your letter, in their order, you will permit me to premise, that the district of Western Africa more immediately within the actual or prospective sphere of this Colony's influence commences towards the north from the river Gallinas, (Spanish Gallinas,) 100 English miles to the northwestward of Cape Montserado, and terminates, towards the southeast, at Settra Kroo, (the country of the Kroomen,) 180 miles distant from the Cape; thus comprehending a line of 280 English miles of seacoast, but reaching less than one-sixth part of the same distance towards the interior. We have very little connection with, or even knowledge of, any of the nations comprehended in this extent of country, excepting the tribes of the seacoast. The Fey or Vey tribe occupies the line of coast between the Gallinas river and Grand Cape Mount, comprehending a district of fifty miles, and may have extended their settlements twenty-five to thirty miles inland. The character of these people is active, warlike, proud, and, with that of all their neighbors, deceitful. The slave traffic has furnished them with their principal employment, and proved the chief source of their wealth, to the present year, when it is believed to have been broken up entirely and forever. Their intercourse with the whites has been very great; and few of the men are unable to speak indifferent English. Three-fourths of the population are domestic slaves, now engaged in a civil strife with their masters for an extension of their privileges. The whole population of this tribe, I state at twelve to fifteen thousand.

Occupying the coast between Cape Mount and Montserado, fifty miles in extent, is the Dey tribe; reaching only half the distance of the Veys inland, and containing about half their population. They are indolent, pacific, and inoffensive in their character: but equally treacherous, profligate, and cruel, when their passions are stirred, with the Veys. The different subdivisions of the Bassa tribe are disposed along the remaining line of coast towards the southeast, over which the influence of the Colony is beginning to be felt. No writer on Africa, within my knowledge, has comprehended the inhabitants of this last division of the coast under the general designation of the *Bassas*. But the propriety of the designation is seen in the facts, that the language of all is radically one and the same, and that their manners, pursuits, characters, and the productions of their country, present a striking uniformity. These countries, taken in their order and reckoned by their distinct governments, are from Cape Montserado 15 miles, *Mamba*—thence 20 miles, *Junk*—thence 15 miles, *Little Bassa*—thence 20 miles, *Grand Bassa*—thence 12 miles, *Young Sesters*—thence 15 miles, *Trade Town*—thence 12 miles, *Little Colo*—thence 13 miles, *Grand Colo*; after which occurs *Teembo* (Sp. Timbo), *Mana, Rock Sesters, Sinou, Little Botton, Grand Botton*, *Settra Kroo* and *Kroo Settra*. This maritime country may reach on an average twenty miles inland. It is de-

L

cidedly the most populous of any seaboard district of equal extent in Western Africa. In rice, oil, cattle, and the productions of the soil, it rivals, I will not say any part of the African coast, but any part of the savage world. An immense surplus of these articles, after abundantly supplying the wants of the inhabitants, is every year transported to other countries. The people are domestic and industrious, many of them even laborious in their habits. Their number may be estimated at 125,000. Their stationary and even manner of life, the infrequency of wars among them, and their own importunity to be furnished with the means of improvement, seem to declare their readiness to receive among them the instruments of civilization, and the heralds of divine revelation.

I have already said that we yet know but little of the natives of our interior. The vague accounts received from ignorant slaves, and by a few other channels of information, agree that they are much more extensive and powerful, and less broken into tribes, than those of the coast. All the people of the seaboard have a character made up, as their language is, of parts borrowed from their intercourse with Europeans. But both the one and the other, remote from the seaboard, are of necessity, unmixed and peculiar. Very recent accounts received from an expedition of Englishmen into these very regions, represent the populousness and even civilization of these countries in a very imposing light; accounts not without their corroborating proofs in many circumstances, well known upon the coast.

Between the settlements of the coast and those in the interior, it ought to be stated, is in most places, a forest of from half a day, to two days' journey, left by both as a barrier of separation, and which is seldom passed except by erratic traders, who are in many parts of this country very numerous.

The Dey and Vey languages have an evident affinity between themselves, but I have not been able to trace it to any other dialect of Africa. It is very imperfect in its structure, wants precision, has no numerals above 100, and abounds in sounds absolutely inarticulate. I think it not worth the labor of reducing it to a grammatical or graphical form, as the English can be used for all the purposes of education, with equal facility, and incalculably greater advantages, and as otherwise several thousand new terms must be introduced, before the language of the country can be made the medium of exact theological and philosophical instruction. The Bassa dialects may be readily reduced to one and the same written language. But no attempt of the kind has yet been made. It is more copious and artificial than the former, but an European of education can scarcely credit the fact, that a jargon so rude in its structure and pronunciation, should exist as the medium of communication among rational beings. The people of these countries universally inhabit villages of from forty to one and two thousand souls. Every town or village has its head, and several subordinate chiefs, and exhibits the harmony, and much of the economy of one great family. The chiefs have over the people of their respective towns, unlimited authority, which is seldom resisted on the part of their subjects, or abused by themselves. Polygamy and domestic slavery are universal. The women and female children are to the males in most of their towns as three to two; the inequality being sustained by frequent purchases of female slaves from the interior. The men perform no servile labor, (a few of the newly acquired domestic slaves excepted,) and pass their entire year in indolence, except the months of February, March and April, when all are industriously occupied in preparing their rice and cassada plantations. The women are incessantly busy either in the plantations or in domestic duties.

The people have no taste, and very little capacity for abstract thinking. Except their games of hazard, they have nothing in the shape of science among them. In their habits they are temperate and abstemious, and capable of incredible fatigue, when impelled to it by war, or stimulated by the hope of reward.

Such, Sir, is a general description of the materials to be operated upon by missionary establishments in this part of Africa. It may serve in part to answer or prepare the way to a more intelligible answer, than could be given well without it, to your inquiries. The first demands "by what kind of Missionaries the first attempt should be made? By such as more exclusively fitted for teaching, or by such as have also a competent knowledge of mechanical trades or agriculture; or whether trades or agriculture could be most advantageously introduced, or both continued from the very beginning?"

These people have their own little trades, arts and implements, and a system of agriculture which produces them, in sufficient plenty, the necessaries of animal life. An air of comfort pervades most of their towns and dwellings. Even an European Missionary, if accustomed to self-denial, might soon come to content himself in an African dwelling and the use of African food, taken nearly as he finds them. Their miseries are of a moral nature. The eyes of their understandings are put out: they even want to be told that they are superior in their nature and destiny to the brutes that perish. They need to be taught the first, and, thence in order, the higher principles of religious truth. It must be line upon line, precept upon precept, &c., and by a labor of years perhaps, before effectual impressions can be made upon minds unaccustomed to receive and nearly incapable of comprehending the plainest instructions. Your teachers must first teach them to think, to reflect, to inquire, before they can hope to see their doctrine take root in their hearts or even in their memories. I see no necessity to defer for a single month the work of teaching—the more advanced, in their own towns and dwellings; the children, in schools and missionary families, or villages formed for the purpose. This I conceive to be the great work for which they ought especially to be fitted, and on which they ought chiefly to depend for all the success they expect. Trades and agriculture will, and ought to come along of course: but if cultivated too much in the beginning, will be apt to preoccupy the attention of the people, and entirely preclude the effect of what religious instruction may be given. Owing to the very state and circumstances of the country, something like the actual modes of agriculture must be practised for many years by a settlement of European Missionaries.

I do not think that a missionary establishment in Africa, either requires or ought to comprehend any agriculturists or mechanics who are not also well qualified teachers. It seems unnecessary. Those arts will advance as fast as christianity advances among the people; and is any missionary purpose answered by substituting them in its place? From the Colony and our Factories both will be acquired. Both are beginning to be introduced among them ; but, alas ! the Colony cannot, as such, do the peculiar work of missionary laborers and instructers. Let the Missionaries be accomplished teachers, and let them come furnished with tools and a few agricultural implements, such as may be used in this country; and know something of the use of both, so as to be able to build their own houses, make their own plain furniture, and cultivate their own plantations and gardens: and I am decidedly of opinion that they have every requisite qualification for success in their appropriate work.

*Question 2d.*

" Are there any, and what preparatory labor accomplished, for facilitating the teaching Department?"

Absolutely none, if we except the circumstance already stated, that very many in all the maritime tribes, speak a corruption of the English language ; and have incorporated into their own language many English and Portuguese terms, which they apply to objects of European manufacture and origin. There has never yet been collected even a vocabulary of the Vey or Bassa language: consequently, no attempt to reduce either to rules, can have been made. One fact may, however, be mentioned, as having some relation to this inquiry. There are now in a course of education in the Colony, about fifty boys, belonging to the different tribes of the neighborhood. These boys will all be taught to speak, read and write, the English language readily, and are receiving instruction in Religion. One object ever kept in view in their tuition, is the fitting them to act as interpreters to American and European Missionaries, and should the Divine Spirit renew their hearts, to become able religious teachers themselves. Of those youths, your Missionaries might serve themselves materially, in any labors relating to the acquisition or systematizing the languages of the country, and they shall be at their service. The Bassa language is, in my opinion, well deserving of this labor. I should propose to have its orthography provided for, by means of a new alphabet, in which the letters should have generally the powers they possess in the Italian alphabet, and no letter in any possible combination, more than one sound. A few Missionaries of respectable philological acquirements and talents, ought accordingly to be sent to accomplish this work. The printing press of the Colony shall be, as far as we can give it up, at their command, in the preparation of small elementary books and tracts. A printer,* with a small stock of materials, might then be advantageously sent out from the commencement of the establishment.

*Question 3d.*

"In what way might a friendly intercourse, between the Missionary settlement and the Colony of Liberia, be kept up, and the protection of the latter be secured to the former?" 1st. The Government of the Colony, is willing to stipulate with the authorities of the country, for a grant of land sufficient for the actual use of the missionary settlement or settlements, and hold them responsible for their safety. This measure may not in all cases secure the Missionaries from the treachery and occasional violence of the natives; but, in my opinion, it will go a long way towards assuring their safety. 2d. As the Colony has factories at different stations along the coast, and in the interior, the missionary settlements, by being situated near them, may share the protection, which we are obliged to afford to these factories. 3d. An arrangement can be effected, by which the Missionaries shall enjoy the advantage of medical attendance and prescriptions at the Colony. Supplies of the American and European fabrics, groceries, &c., can be at any time had through the Colony. Drafts may here be negotiated, orders and letters forwarded hence to any part of the world—tools, and so forth, here fabricated for their use and comfort—and what a Missionary ought to prize, they will enjoy the friendship, sympathies, prayers and support, of a large and intelligent body of Christian Colonists; indeed, this indirect aid and support to be expected from the American settlement, will, in my opinion, prove incalculably more valuable, than any which the government of the Colony will be able to bestow: and this latter you will clearly perceive, must depend greatly on the private views, and sentiments relative to missionary objects, which the individuals in the administration of the government of the Colony may happen to entertain. A large proportion of our settlers, are by profession, the devoted servants of the Redeemer. We have no fewer than four religious communions, and a deep, lively, and I hope, sincere and lasting interest is felt by many, for the salvation of their pagan African brethren. The arrival of your Missionaries would be hailed with joy; and, so far as they ought to lean on an arm of flesh, I think they may confide in the cordial support of the numerous friends of God in this Colony.

*Question 4th.*

"What communication is there between Cape Montserado, and America, and Europe?"

* A Missionary having some knowledge of printing.

Once in three or four months, we shall have regular packets, from the middle states of North America, besides the visits of about twelve trading ships from the United States, which touch at Montserado, either out or home.

A few Dutch Traders, bound to the Gold Coast every year, touch at Monrovia, as do a large number of English and French; but at present, the Colony has no mercantile correspondence with any part of Europe, except England.

Messrs. King and Sons, Merchants, Bristol, (England,)—a very respectable house, having three vessels in the African trade, some of which are monthly at Montserado, might afford you any facilities for direct communication with the Colony, by the way of England, which you shall ask. We have no port charges nor duties to exact, either of foreign vessels visiting, or on foreign articles introduced into the Colony.

It might, I think, be easy to open and keep up, a frequent correspondence with the Colony, through some Dutch House in Amsterdam; who might direct their vessels to touch at the Cape without subjecting them to more than twelve hours' detention on their way to D'Elmina, on the Gold Coast.

### Question 5th.

"What part of the outward wants of the missionary establishment might be supplied on the spot; what would be required to be procured from a distance; and what country would supply it best and most expeditiously?"

For building, may be had in the Colony, lumber, carpenter and smiths' work, and masons' services; for subsistence before the settlement shall be able to cultivate its own rice, vegetables, &c., may be obtained directly from the natives, grain, fish, fowls, goats, and vegetables, on the most moderate terms; a few small stores only, in the article of provisions, need be procured from abroad, and I hesitate not to say, that these stores can best be obtained from the United States, by American vessels.

Remittances made to your Missionaries, from Europe to the Colony, could be transferred to some house in America, without loss on the exchange, and shipments made on the same at a moderate freight.

Indeed the supply for the Colony is so economically carried on with the United States, as to admit of any little addition for a missionary settlement near the Colony, with perfect facility, and I believe on the most advantageous terms possible.

### Question 6th.

"Can you form any idea of the possible expense of the first establishment of a Mission on a small scale, and its continuance?"

It has been found by a course of experiments, now repeated for six years, that *all* Europeans and Americans coming to reside in Africa, are more or less affected by the great change of climate attending the transition. It is fair to calculate, that Missionaries from Switzerland would, during the first half year, be incapacitated from much actual labor, and for at least one-third part of that period, require medical and hospital attendance. They must, during this period, find a home at one of the settlements of the Colony; and will require many little comforts, and some medicines, all of which they ought to bring out with them from Europe. Besides this provision, they ought to have a credit either on England or America, or money in hand, to meet contingencies during this period, of one hundred dollars per person. This will be sufficient for their wants, preparatory to their entrance upon the regular labors of the Missions.

Suppose the mission family to consist of males and females: the latter ought to be married, and as many of the former as do not possess the power of uncommon command over their passions. After six months spent in the Colony, they remove to a situation previously chosen, having an easy water communication with our principal settlements. They would require a large well-built boat, which they ought to bring out with them. Six houses must then be built for their residence, place of worship, store-house, and for the accommodation of a number of native laborers and children, all of whom ought to receive daily instruction in religion, letters, &c. These buildings completed in the best native style, will not cost more than twenty-five dollars each: and, so built, will need no repairs; but must be replaced with new buildings at the end of four or five years.

Meantime let the Missionaries employ their own leisure, and the services of the native members of their family, in constructing permanent houses in the European style. Mechanical labor, and building materials, may be had from the Colony: but only at prices which would be thought high even in Europe. If you have funds to spare, your Missionaries may avail themselves of aid from this quarter. But it is by no means absolutely necessary, either to their comfort and health, or to the establishment and success of this Mission, and thousands would be saved to the same fund on which it will be still necessary to draw for purposes of less questionable necessity.

You ask, "what will be the possible expense of founding and sustaining the settlement?" *The necessary expense* of the first eighteen months, will be moderate. But if the Missionaries preserve the European style of living—particularly an European table, the expense will be great.

Were I at the head of this family, the six months seasoning over, and a comfortable outfit of apparel, and little domestic utensils and furniture on hand:— I should accuse myself of want of economy, if for the next succeeding twelve months, including the six buildings, the preparation of a little farm and garden, and the subsistence of twelve to twenty native laborers and pupils, and the support of the five persons constituting the Missionary family, I should expend more than $1500. I hesitate not to say, that comfort and economy of expenditure may be more easily combined in this country, than in any other part of the heathen world, if we except the Islands of the Pacific. After the first year, the expenses will diminish, in proportion to the age of the settlement, admitting the number of its members to be stationary. But these will, of course, be multiplied monthly. I cannot, however, yet suppose it would be expedient to suffer any one settlement to incur an annual expense of more than three or four thousand dollars; but to send off from it, periodically, the instruments and means of founding new ones, either along the coast, or farther in the interior.

You will excuse the liberty I take to state the project of a Missionary establishment by your Society in this country. The family consists of two young married men and their wives, and two single men: all well educated—having some knowledge of gardening, and the useful mechanic arts. Their health shall be good—their manners plain, and all inured to great industry, and capable of enduring fatigue, and submitting to great privations cheerfully. They proceed to Amsterdam or Bristol, England; lay in a good supply of useful books, clothing, stationery, tools, and domestic utensils, and small furniture, with groceries,* and sick-stores—and money, or letters of credit on America, to the amount of two thousand dollars, after paying the passage out to Montserado. If they sail from Amsterdam, they take passage in a Dutch ship, bound to D'Elmina, which is to touch and put them ashore at this place: if from Bristol, the vessel will naturally make this Cape as her first land. They pass their first half year in the Colony, during which period they form acquaintance among the colonists—become familiarized to the African character—explore the surrounding country—visit the different tribes—enter into arrangements with the country authorities, for the founding, accommodation, and protection of their future settlement—settle a definite plan of future operations—do some good to our own people, and above all, acquire a habit of body conformed to the sultry influences of a tropical African climate. They then remove to the site of their intended establishment—avail themselves of the labor of as many natives, as they may require to erect the first houses—form a regular family of about twenty persons—begin from the first, the great work of teaching the natives—study their language: if the Bassa, collect in a vocabulary, all its words, construct an alphabet and a grammar, print a few elementary tracts, translate select portions of the scriptures, and teach the young negroes to read and write them in their own language. If the language is Dey or Vey, substitute as the written language, the English; but preach and teach in the native dialect, the older classes. Meantime the agriculture and mechanical business of the settlements is carried on with a view to supply the wants of itself. The example thus given, will have its effect: first, on such as embrace the religion of the establishment, who will naturally come to settle themselves in or near to it, and afterwards on the people of the tribe generally.

In the foregoing project, perhaps unnecessarily minute, you will perceive no allowance made for deaths, protracted illness, wars, the opposition of the natives,

---

* Meaning with us, tea, sugar, wine, butter, cheese, and other articles of the kind.

# APPENDIX.

discontent and perversity on the part of the Missionaries, and nameless other casualties which may occur, and are at the disposal of the Almighty.—The door is an open one to human appearance, but God may close it suddenly and entirely, by means which human foresight would never have discovered. But on the other hand, I do not, Sir, write from theory; God has made me one of his humble instruments for building up, amidst unnumbered difficulties and discouragements, from the humblest beginnings, a flourishing and hopeful Colony. I have descended in the preceding *project*, by your kind permission, to a plain matter of fact detail, which with the blessing of Providence, I know can be carried into full execution. I see no reason for delay.

There are situations offering, which I should account it a very great privilege, to be able to provide with Missionary families immediately. The populous country of Grand Bassa, is one of these. The Chiefs of the country are importunate in their demand, for good white men to come and reside with them, and teach them the Book of God, and the good customs of their country. They offer to provide with houses, lands, rice, and whatever their country affords, such as shall come recommended from the Colony. Little reliance can be placed on these promises, I admit, but they at least prove the commencement of a missionary settlement in that country, to be easily practicable.

This letter will be accompanied by another from the Directors of the Colony in Washington; and if both together shall authorize an establishment by your Society, in connection with this Colony, none will experience a sincerer gratification, and more cheerfully aid in the undertaking, according to his ability, and prior obligations; than,

Rev. and Dear Sir, your devoted,
And very humble Servant,
J. ASHMUN,
*Agent for the American Colonization Society,
and Principal of the Colony of Liberia.*

P. S. In the *project* of a Mission to this country, I propose that the Mission Family have an outfit of two thousand dollars: should half this sum be laid out in trade goods in Europe, the advantage would be great; and this purchase ought to have been particularly insisted upon, in the body of the letter. Of this merchandise the chief articles are Leaf-Tobacco, large smoking pipes, common, printed Cottons, India Cottons, Cotton and Silk Handkerchiefs, Pocket Looking-Glasses, common Beads, Cutlery, cheap Hats, Iron Pots and Cast Ware, Iron Bars, Earthen, and Glass Ware. The four first enumerated of these articles, are the most important.

J. A.

## APPENDIX.

### No. 9.

Mr. Ashmun was censured by individuals in the United States for his bold and successful attacks on these and other Slave Factories on the Coast. The following paper contains his own vindication of his proceedings against these enemies of the human race.

MONROVIA, FEBRUARY 10, 1827.

SIR: In regard to the demolition of the piratical slaving establishments in the neighborhood of our settlements, and on *our own Territory*, which your letter as the organ of the Board and of the public opinion in the United States disapproves, it is not my wish to add any thing to the narrative of those transactions already in the possession of the Board. One or two points, however, explaining the leading motive from which I acted, I desire to place in the clearest light, and submit myself to the wisdom and candor of the Managers, Society and Public.

1. *These establishments were not demolished on the ground, merely of their being Slaving Establishments.* The slave trade as carried on by foreigners with the independent tribes of the country, is an evil, which, however deplorable, I have always been sensible that I have not the shadow of a right to attack and subdue by force—nor simply *as such* have I attempted it. Nor

2. *Did I derive any authority from my appointment and instructions from the Government of the United States, to demolish slave factories in this country.* I consider myself to have been authorized, as United States' Agent for recaptured Africans, to rescue the individuals belonging to the Agency from the factories of St. Paul's and Trade Town; and after a simple demand had proved ineffectual, to do it by force. But not destroy those or any other slaving establishments *in virtue of any authority I possessed as the Government Agent.* But

3. *On the principle of self-preservation, I possessed the right as the head of the little community which your Society has planted in this country, to pursue a pirate,—* HOSTIS GENERIS HUMANI, *by sea and land—and deprive him by means of any force at my disposal, of the power which he had previously employed for the indiscriminate destruction and plunder of human life and property.* I followed him to his haunt at Digby by permission, and demolished his factory, with the assistance of the independent authorities of the country. The expedition in its essential motives and causes, had no relation to the slaving business. That in breaking up the establishment of the pirate, a few negroes fell into my hands, I never regarded in any other light than an accidental circumstance: as also, the effect which the destruction of the piratical factory, has happily had in curtailing the slave trade. I rejoice in this effect—but self-defence against a set of marauding outlaws, was the motive of the expedition.

4. The French establishment at Mammas was destroyed. 1st. *As being situated within our purchased territory and jurisdiction :* and consequently prohibited by the constitution, institutions and spirit of all the laws of the Colony. My permission had never been obtained or asked for the continuance of this factory, after the purchase which placed it within our limits. And 2dly. *As an establishment at war with all the principles of law, justice and society—and which had, by kidnapping, or purchasing, and attempting to detain in slavery the free people from the Colony, openly declared, and made itself thus hostile, and injurious with all that part of the civilized world with which it came in contact.*— The injury they attempted to inflict upon us was deep and vital ; and the attempt was openly avowed, and carried to the extreme extent of their power. These were the causes assigned in a written exposition of my motives, delivered to *Millot and Poussin,* in the morning of, and immediately before breaking up their establishment.

5. The Spanish establishment at Trade Town, was notoriously piratical. The vessel which upheld it, was at my request, seized by the French Brig of War, *the Dragon,* and condemned at Goree, on a charge of piracy, sustained by five distinct specifications. The connexion of this vessel with the business ashore, was such as to implicate the whole in the guilt of its piratical acts. This is my first reason, as Colonial Agent for breaking up the Spanish establishment at this place. 2dly. In buying eight of our people, refusing to surrender them to my demand ; and employing force and arms to sustain their refusal, the Spaniards of Trade Town, had virtually made war on the Colony, and justified the employment of force for our preservation and safety. 3dly. The employment of force was the only means of rescuing eight of the people belonging to Montserado from the power of the piratical and belligerent establishment.

King West made himself and people, a party in the contest, on the second day, by making the cause of the Spaniard, his own—justifying and imitating this injurious act—and actually attacking the force under my command.

The preceding review of the transactions of last season, presents, not only their main features, divested of circumstances necessary to be stated in the original report, but of no use in determining how far my agency in them is justifiable. I do not controvert the opinion of the Board, that *the course pursued by me was impolitic;* as I am sensible they can best judge of the nature and effects on the prosperity of our cause, of the impressions which those transactions will produce on the American public. But of the *justice* and *necessity* of that course, in a moral point of view, it is not in my power after the most deliberate review of it, to raise a doubt in my own mind. Nor do I perceive that, on this last point, the opinion conveyed by your letter is much at variance with my own. It would probably be less so, if it were perfectly known with what religious circumspection, I abstained from any act, which malevolence itself could justly denominate *offensive.* On landing, I issued an order, forbidding my people on the severest penalty to appropriate to themselves the most trivial article, or amount of the property of the factory. And this order was most rigorously enforced. I paid the troops on their return a per diem allowance fixed before they had volunteered their services for the expedition. We acted, sir, on the defensive, strictly—and I trust, acted with all that deliberate and cautious respect to justice, and that sense of responsibility to God and man, which ought to characterize a resort to force by a christian people. The *motive*, I know, does not always vindicate the *act*. But I wish to remove wrong impressions, as to the manner in which our expeditions were conducted. I may and often do err in judgment. But my errors are not those of precipitancy, which excludes reflection : and our military expeditions, if conducted with decision, were not blindly engaged in, nor submitted to the guidance of passion or circumstances. And if God has made them instrumental of the abolition of the slave trade near us, the increase of our trade, the emancipation of nearly 200 slaves, the extension of our influence, and increase of our territory, thanks to his own infinite wisdom and goodness. Those were not the objects for which I undertook them, nor the effects from which I infer their justification.

It may not be beneath a moment's attention to remark here on that part of Captain C——'s libel, which says "*that*, owing to the quantity of plunder we brought from Trade Town, Bafts were selling at $1 the piece, at Montserado, and other goods in proportion." I repeat it, neither I nor my people brought a fragment of Merchandise or any other property from Trade Town. But two Colombian armed vessels, the Jacenta and El Vencedore, then on a cruize against the enemies of that Republic, were permitted to sell by auction in Town, such part of their prize goods as they could not convey to Laguayra: and these goods sold greatly below their real value.

El Vencedore, I believe to sustain, as a private armed vessel, a highly respectable character. I never heard to the contrary intimated either of the vessel or her Commander. It is not true that the vessel ever molested or attempted to molest British commerce on this coast, or was ever chased by an English Man-of-war.

It *is* true that a Spanish Pirate at Trade Town, detained, after being thrice demanded, from five to eight of our people—five were identified and admitted by the Spaniard, and by West, the native king, to belong to us—and still detained. It *is not* true that one musket was fired by us on the natives, for more than 24 hours after being in quiet possession of the Town; nor then, till we had received volleys from them, which I forbade to be returned, at the imminent hazard of my own and people's lives, in hopes, even then, to conciliate them by forbearance.

APPENDIX. 93

## No. 10.

We here insert letters expressive of the views of Ex-President Madison and Chief Justice Marshall, on the subject of African Colonization.

MONTPELIER, DECEMBER 29, 1831.

DEAR SIR: I received, in due time, your letter of the 21st ult., and with due sensibility to the subject of it. Such, however, has been the effect of a painful rheumatism on my general condition, as well as in disqualifying my fingers for the use of the pen, that I could not do justice " to the principles and measures of the Colonization Society in all the great and various relations they sustain to our own country and to Africa," if my views of them could have the value which your partiality supposes. I may observe, in brief, that the Society had always my good wishes, though with hopes of its success less sanguine than were entertained by others found to have been the better judges; and, that I feel the greatest pleasure at the progress already made by the Society, and the encouragement to encounter remaining difficulties afforded by the earlier and greater ones already overcome. Many circumstances at the present moment seem to concur in brightening the prospects of the Society, and cherishing the hope that the time will come, when the dreadful calamity which has so long afflicted our country and filled so many with despair, will be gradually removed and by means consistent with justice, peace and the general satisfaction: thus giving to our country the full enjoyment of the blessings of liberty, and to the world the full benefit of its great example. I never considered the main difficulty of the great work as lying in the deficiency of emancipations, but in an inadequacy of asylums for such a growing mass of population, and in the great expense of removing it to its new home. The spirit of private manumission as the laws may permit and the exiles may consent, is increasing and will increase; and there are sufficient indications that the public authorities in slave-holding States are looking forward to interpositions in different forms that must have a powerful effect. With respect to the new abode for the emigrants, all agree that the choice made by the Society is rendered peculiarly appropriate by considerations which need not be repeated, and if other situations should not be found eligible receptacles for a portion of them, the prospects in Africa seem to be expanding in a highly encouraging degree.

In contemplating the pecuniary resources needed for the removal of such a number to so great a distance, my thoughts and hopes have been long turned to the rich fund presented in the western lands of the Nation, which will soon entirely cease to be under a pledge for another object. The great one in question is truly of a national character, and it is known that distinguished patriots not dwelling in slave-holding States have viewed the object in that light, and would be willing to let the national domain be a resource in effecting it.

Should it be remarked that the States, though all may be interested in relieving our country from the colored population, they are not equally so; it is but fair to recollect, that the sections most to be benefitted, are those whose cessions created the fund to be disposed of.

I am aware of the constitutional obstacle which has presented itself; but if the general will be reconciled to an application of the territorial fund to the removal of the colored population, a grant to Congress of the necessary authority could be carried, with little delay, through the forms of the Constitution.

Sincerely wishing an increasing success to the labors of the Society, I pray you to be assured of my esteem, and to accept my friendly salutation.

JAMES MADISON.

RICHMOND, DECEMBER 14, 1831.

DEAR SIR: I received your letter of the 7th, in the course of the mail, but it was not accompanied by the documents you mention.

I undoubtedly feel a deep interest in the success of the Society, but, if I had not long since formed a resolution against appearing in print on any occasion, I should be now unable to comply with your request. In addition to various occupations which press on me very seriously, the present state of my family is such as to prevent my attempting to prepare any thing for publication.

The great object of the Society, I presume, is to obtain pecuniary aids. Application will undoubtedly be made, I hope successfully, to the several State Legislatures by the societies formed within them respectively. It is extremely desirable that they should pass permanent laws on the subject, and the excitement produced by the late insurrection makes this a favorable moment for the friends of the Colony to press for such acts. It would be also desirable, if such a direction could be given to State Legislation as might have some tendency to incline the people of color to migrate. This, however, is a subject of much delicacy. Whatever may be the success of our endeavors to obtain acts for permanent aids, I have no doubt that our applications for immediate contributions will receive attention. It is possible, though not probable, that more people of color may be disposed to migrate than can be provided for with the funds the Society may be enabled to command. Under this impression I suggested, some years past, to one or two of the Board of Managers, to allow a small additional bounty in lands to those who would pay their own passage in whole or in part. The suggestion, however, was not approved.

It is undoubtedly of great importance to retain the countenance and protection of the General Government. Some of our cruisers stationed on the coast of Africa would, at the same time, interrupt the slave trade—a horrid traffic detested by all good men, and would protect the vessels and commerce of the Colony from pirates who infect those seas. The power of the government to afford this aid is not, I believe, contested. I regret that its power to grant pecuniary aid is not equally free from question. On this subject, I have always thought, and still think, that the proposition made by Mr. King, in the Senate, is the most unexceptionable, and the most effective that can be devised.

The fund would probably operate as rapidly as would be desirable, when we take into view the other resources which might come in aid of it, and its application would be, perhaps, less exposed to those constitutional objections which are made in the South than the application of money drawn from the Treasury and raised by taxes. The lands are the property of the United States, and have heretofore been disposed of by the government under the idea of absolute ownership. The cessions of the several States convey them to the General Government for the common benefit, without prescribing any limits to the judgment of Congress, or any rule by which that judgment shall be exercised. The cession of Virginia indeed seems to look to an apportionment of the fund among the States, "according to their several respective proportions in the general charge and expenditure." But this cession was made at a time when the lands were believed to be the only available fund for paying the debts of the United States and supporting their Government. This condition has probably been supposed to be controlled by the existing Constitution, which gives Congress "power to dispose of, and make all needful rules and regulations respecting the territories or the property belonging to the United States." It is certain that the donations made for roads and colleges are not in proportion to the part borne by each State of the general expenditure. The removal of our colored population is, I think, a common object, by no means confined to the slave States, although they are more immediately interested in it. The whole Union would be strengthened by it, and relieved from a danger, whose extent can scarcely be estimated. It lessens very much in my estimation, the objection in a political view to the application of this ample fund, that our lands are becoming an object for which the States are to scramble, and which threatens to sow the seeds of discord among us, instead of being what they might be—a source of national wealth.

I am, dear, sir, with great and respectful esteem,

Your obedient servant,

J. MARSHALL.

---

RESOLUTION, submitted to the Senate of the United States, by the Hon. Rufus King, of New-York, February 18th, 1825.

*Resolved,* That as soon as the portion of the existing funded debt of the United States, for the payment of which the Public Land of the United States is pledged, shall have been paid off, then and thenceforth, the whole of the Public Land of the United States with the nett proceeds of all future sales thereof, shall constitute or form a fund, which is hereby appropriated, and the

Faith of the United States is pledged, that the said fund shall be inviolably applied to aid the emancipation of such slaves, within any of the United States, and aid the removal of such slaves, and the removal of such free people of color in any of the said States, *as by the laws of the States* respectively, may be allowed to be emancipated, or removed to any territory or country without the limits of the United States of America.

The following resolution was moved by Mr. Tucker, of Virginia, in Congress, March 2d, 1825:

*Resolved*, That the Secretary of War be required, to ascertain the probable expense of extinguishing the Indian Title to a portion of the country lying west of the Rocky Mountains, that may be suitable for colonizing the free people of color; the best routes across the Mountains, and the probable cost of a road and military post, necessary to a safe communication with such Colony, and to report the same to this House, at the next Session of Congress.

It is well known that the Land Bill introduced by the Hon. Henry Clay, and which passed the Senate on the 25th of January, 1832, provided for the distribution of the proceeds of the sales of the Public Lands, among the twenty-four States of the Union, according to their respective federal representative population, "to be applied by the Legislatures of the said States, to such objects of education, internal improvement, colonization of free persons of color, or reimbursement of any existing debt, contracted for internal improvement, as the said Legislatures may severally designate and authorize."

## No. 10.

### *Miscellaneous Papers of Mr. Ashmun.*

#### No. 1.—1819.

Question. *What rules are to be observed in order to improve the gift of prayer?*
The gift of prayer principally respects the manner in which the overt part of the duty is performed; and it is valuable, considered as conducing to the improvement of the hearers, rather than to the person who performs the duty. But we seldom contribute to the improvement of others, without benefiting ourselves. The gift of prayer is therefore valuable, as respects the possessor; and as it consists in the ability to pray with external propriety and effect, it must greatly depend on possessing a *spirit* of prayer. From this consideration, I

deduce the first rule to assist us in acquiring the gift of prayer. *Cultivate a praying spirit.*

The Spirit of God, which is necessary to produce and preserve the spirit of acceptable prayer, not only assists the possessor to perform christian duties to the acceptance of God, but for the edification of men. By this sacred influence reigning in the breast, the objects with which we converse in prayer, become familiarized to the mind; and in regard to familiar objects, we ever express ourselves with more promptitude, and pertinency, than of others. The Spirit of God likewise makes us acquainted with his glorious perfections, and the sublime things of his kingdom in their proper nature. We all know that it is essential to eloquence to be able to seize on the most striking points of a subject, and present it in the most affecting attitude. In order to this we must be so fully and exactly acquainted with our subject, as to be able to see, and select, its most appropriate and impressive features. The same remark is good with a little qualification in regard to the acquirement of a talent to pray with due effect. Hence the importance of the aids of the Divine Spirit, by "which we may know the things of God."

The next rule that I shall prescribe for acquiring this gift, is *to obtain a just and intimate acquaintance with the language, and sentiments of the Scriptures.*

A great part of the effect of prayer on the minds of the hearers, is owing to an appropriate introduction of the transcendently sublime and impressive conceptions of the inspired writers. Those conceptions are always just—they carry with them the influence of truth—and as they concern the most affecting of *all* truths, and are conformable to them, they cannot fail to affect themselves. The figures of Scripture do, to a certain extent constitute a species of language for which the plain historic style could never be substituted without the sacrifice of sentiment.

The figures of Scripture, when employed by the inspired writers to illustrate or enforce what might be expressed in a plain style, never fail of their end; and add greatly to the life and energy of prayer, when judiciously used.

The language and style of the sacred writings, after all due abatements are made for the antiquity of our translation, and for Greek and Hebrew idioms, must be regarded as the most simple, concise, energetic, and copious vehicle of thought that has ever been employed in our world. Were our object the perfection of eloquence, no composition would be more worthy to be studied with care than the sacred writings.

For a third rule, *I enjoin frequency in the exercise of prayer.*

Facility in the accurate performance of any act, which involves an exercise of the judgment, is acquired, only, by the frequent, and careful repetition of that act. In virtue of an established law of Divine operation in the moral world, even the *spirit of prayer* is cultivated by the frequent practice of the duty. How much more, then, may we suppose the gift of prayer, which it is not improper to say is in a high degree artificial, to depend on practice?

God, by his special blessing, makes proficients of those who habitually wait on him, in the sincere discharge of any religious duty.

My last rule, in reply to the question, shall be *to study to improve in the manner of performing this duty, in all our addresses to God, private as well as public.*

The principal attention ought to be ever bestowed on the heart,—and to offer acceptable desires to God, ever sought as an object immensely preferable to that of commending ourselves to the acceptance of our fellow-men. But there is a species of remissness of spirit, which often produces negligence in the choice of words, and a confused and languid manner of expression, against which, as well as those faults that result from it, we ought ever to be guarded. The mind should, in this duty, be awake. God should be felt and feared, as present. The mind will then naturally apply itself to every part of the duty, with the utmost care. Away with every thing like affectation, from the responsible and awful work of addressing the God of our salvation. Affected solemnity,—affected elegance of expression and eloquence in the style, gesture, or voice, are alike criminal, and degrading to the sacred dignity of the performance. There is a becoming attention to arrangement and language in prayer, that is not at all inconsistent with devotion; nay, which contributes to *promote* devotion—and this is the case which the rule prescribes, and enjoins.—Any sensible effort of the mind, which may be requisite at first, to correct a habit of negligence, even should it check the ardor of feeling, will imperceptibly be gotten over, and abundantly compensated by the increase of our usefulness in the church, and the eventual promotion of our own progress in enlightened piety.

## *The advantages of Devotion.*

### No. 2.—1825.

1. It calls the slumbering faculties of the mind into a state of temperate, rational and cheerful action; which, besides the pleasure attending the consciousness of intellectual vigour and life, fits us better than any other stimulus, to perceive, judge, reason and resolve, with distinctness, truth and promptness, in all the business and concerns of life.

2. It delivers the mind from the perturbation of the passions, and so extends the empire of reason in the breast.

3. It silences the remonstrances, and quiets the alarms of conscience.

4. It secures the concurrence of Divine Providence in our endeavors to do our duty. If God should, notwithstanding, send disappointments and adversity, it renders even these salutary, and satisfies the mind that they are so.

5. It inspires us with patience, resolution, and a spirit of faithfulness, and perseverance, in all the difficult duties of life.

These are some of the blessed fruits of devotion, which I know not, that I have ever failed to reap, whenever it has been sincerely and faithfully practised: and they are advantages which I do not know that I ever enjoy in the neglect

## APPENDIX. 99

of it.—But they are only the concomitant circumstances of a devout practice. The essential and direct blessings which devotion brings, are,

1. An humbling and abiding conviction of the blindness, weakness, and wickedness of our poor natures—accompanied with a corresponding sense and persuasion of the sufficiency of our Lord and Father in Heaven.

2. A sublime and heart-expanding sentiment of the ineffable perfections, glory, and majesty of Jehovah. It is only by intimate and long continued intercourse with God through the Spirit, that his true nature can be learnt; and O! how unspeakably holy, lovely, and adorable do the glimpses of his glory, which sometimes dart into the devout soul, show him! They carry with themselves an evidence springing from the eternal source of truth and light, which satisfies the mind that God is the true God, that Christ is indeed the Son of God, and that the gospel is the true testimony of the grace of God. I never fully believed 'till the Holy Ghost thus convinced me. I doubt and disbelieve still, except as my faith is enlivened by this inward illumination of God's Spirit.

3. Devotion teaches us the offices and glory of the Redeemer. It shows us our insufficiency in ourselves. We look beyond ourselves for help. We have a strong feeling of our need of some aid, which no earthly hand can afford us. We cannot come to God for it directly. We want arguments to plead with him why he should show us mercy. Then comes to our view the Saviour, Jesus Christ—the very desire of our souls. He satisfies all our expectations, and supplies all the deficiencies and inabilities, under which our souls were desponding. We contemplate this wonderful Redeemer in a nearer and still nearer view as devotion warms, and faith gains strength in the mind. He is all, and more, and better, than we ever felt our wretched case require. We rejoice in him as those who unexpectedly acquire immense riches. The soul is all delight, astonishment, humility, adoration, and thankfulness. That he is God, we learn by a sort of intuitive and experimental feeling of his grace and power. That he is man, is a truth, which I think depends more on the testimony of the Scriptures, than his Divinity. But this inward illumination directs us to, illustrates, enforces, and applies the doctrines of his written word. And the word enables us to judge of the inward light which irradiates the mind, that it is of God.—Both agree. We find the same holy unction which pervades the mind running through all the doctrines and mysteries of the written word. The word is nothing without this Spirit. The influence of the Spirit, was never designed to be perfect and complete in itself without the word. But together, their testimony is demonstrative, their guidance is infallible—They lead the soul, by a path that never deceives, to God its portion and its salvation.

Devotion is the proper business of the human mind. In every other employment, it serves below its nature. Here it walks at large in its native dignity; and basking in the sun-shine of the Deity, rejoices in its own element. Existence runs to waste, when through indolence, or the hurry of business, I omit my daily retirement and intercourse with God. Would that I never may omit it more. For I cannot preserve a devout frame of spirit, without, if I may so term it, the labor of devotion. God my teacher, Holy Spirit, inspirer of every good thought, Author of every acceptable work, make me a diligent waiter evermore at the posts of thy doors, an earnest seeker of thy face, and the rejoicing object of thy favor, through Christ Jesus, my Lord   Amen.

## Divine Providence.

### No. 3.—1825.

One would suppose that the contemplation of the minute mechanism of the vegetable and animal kingdoms of nature—contrived in every individual after the same specific model—complicated beyond the power of human sagacity to comprehend—and exact and perfect in its operation, beyond the simplest productions of art—not a moment inactive—renewed without its own agency, at stated periods, and all conspiring to some common end, of which, many are obvious to human reason, and many others are explained by Divine Revelation; one would suppose that a survey of this wonderful system of organization and action, discovering in things without mind, proofs so undeniable, of the constant presence and exercise of the sublimest intelligence and wisdom, would establish on the firmest basis of reason, the conviction of a particular Providence, as universal and as constant as the great scene of busy activity, which it superintends. But all passes nearly unnoticed by the mass of vulgar observers; and is often studied with exactness by the philosopher, with no other effect than to remove God at a greater distance from his works, in his apprehension than before. There is but one rational account to be given of this fact, and that the Holy Scriptures give, when they teach us, that man has become altogether brutish in his imaginations, and does not like to retain God in his thoughts. To gratify this innate disgust of the mind of apostate men, with God's holiness, most will violate the first dictates of reason, and contradict the most express testimony of those very Scriptures, which they boast of believing. But let me pray for grace so far to yield to the principal dictates of my rational nature, and to fall in with the plainest doctrines of Divine Revelation, as to believe from the heart, that "He who made, governs the world," "working all things, after the counsel of his own will." But it is not my object here to satisfy my own, or othe 'doubts as to the extensiveness of God's dominion in the natural world; but to contemplate some useful lessons of his Providence in the moral, or the laws by which it operates in their relation to the moral conduct of men.

I am, in the first place, far from supposing the measure of justice to be filled, or that God intends to teach any such lesson, in the rewards and punishments which fall to the lot of the human race in this world. But rather judge the laws of God's moral Providence chiefly adapted to the conservation of society, of human life, of moral virtue, and pure religion; the establishment and universal extension of the Redeemer's church—and all these objects considered in relation to the present, rather than a future life.

1. It appears to be one of the laws of Providence, that certain apparent virtues, or practices and duties which commend themselves to that sense of moral propriety, which God has implanted in the breasts of men, should secure to the possessor certain temporal blessings—for the most part related to the virtue which procures them.

*Examples.* 1. Filial piety, to use a Roman phrase, is thus connected with length of days, and domestic peace. 2. Moral justice in the commerce of society, has an established connexion with the durability and permanent usefulness of the gains acquired in the rigid exercise of this virtue. "I leave you but little," observes Chief Justice Hale, in his letter of paternal counsel to his children, "but it will wear like iron." 3. The exemplary devotion of persons high in authority, leaving the question of their personal piety undetermined, is productive of national blessings. 4. Blood, murderously shed, by the indolence or false compassion of those charged with the execution of the laws, unavenged, will sooner or later find out, and send a curse after all by whose connivance the murderer went unpunished. 5. Murder, and perhaps a few other crimes, are destined to meet a characteristic retaliation in this world. God himself becomes the accuser, often, and commissions the most unexpected providences to expose the dark and almost forgotten deed.—The fact is proverbial: David's adultery met a kindred and severe rebuke and penalty in the incest of Absalom.

These examples will serve to illustrate the principle; of which, I have only to remark further, that God binds himself no more to an exact and unvarying uniformity in the laws of his moral Providence, than in those of the natural world. The tendency of human conduct is meant, in this part of the Divine economy, to be strongly and unequivocally indicated. But there are many exceptions to be admitted—lest men should presume it unnecessary and improbable that God should arraign them at a future tribunal, and there adjust his rewards, to the scale of their deserts, without reference to their sufferings, or enjoyments in this world.

2. I have long been of opinion that the power of habit, education, honor, friendship, and many other passions and motives, is much stronger, and more effectual in regulating the lives of men of the world, than the same principles are in governing the conduct of the disciples of Jesus Christ.

The final end of this law, is doubtless, the conservation of human society. Most men having no other than mere natural motives to govern them, require that these should be sufficient to restrain those excesses of passion and vice, which would sweep away the pillars of human Society. God has accordingly so arranged it in his Providence. But for the other part of the axiom, that these motives operate less effectually in the disciples of Christ, the fact appears undeniable from their being under the guidance and promptings of an infinitely higher and more efficatious influence, the grace of God. This carries them to lengths of purity, to which no inferior motive can ever reach. It does not oppose, but renders almost useless in a few favored cases, the power of habit, education, and the constitutional virtues, by carrying the subjects of them entirely past the remotest goal which they ever sought, and bears them along to a higher prize than nature and constitutional pride ever aspired after. The moon is of admirable utility at night; but when the sun arises, her beams are no longer perceived, because no longer necessary. Now, out of the use of these superior guides and helps of a virtuous and holy life, naturally grows the disuse of those inferior kinds, which are in the disciple of Christ so nearly superseded. The mind is divided between the two, and loses the strong hold which it had of the first. The mere worldling here has the advantage of bending the undivided force of his nature to his rules and principles. The man of God is sometimes nearly suspended between the two, and can avail himself of the entire virtue of neither. And a rule occasionally disused, cannot long preserve the force of a sufficient safeguard and directory.

This axiom teaches us a truth, which I think is verified by observation. Let the child of God but cease to receive succour from on high, and be exposed to temptation, (if habit formed on christian principles, and by a long continued christian practice, has not yet regained its empire in his constitution,) he falls an easier, and more powerless victim to vice, than the mere man of the world, having the advantage of a correct education, and upright habits.

## The Prophecy of Malachi.

### No. 4.—1824.

I have perused this book with new convictions of its Divine authenticity:

There is an argument for the truth of these Scriptures, which as often as I read them, obliges me to feel and admit its force. Seldom has it presented itself with more force than in looking over this prophecy aided by Scott's Commentary.

If it be not the word of God, this prophecy is the production of an unprincipled imposter. But it reproves, with a severity, demonstration, and authority, which none but the best of men are able to employ, and nothing but a sort of Divine perception and love of truth could sustain, all sin—those minute and specious ones, especially, which pride, interest, and human blindness, would never have discovered. There is a double impossibility—1st. A wicked man becomes the devout advocate of Divine Holiness, and acts without a motive in a way opposed directly to every motive that can operate on his conduct. This is a moral paradox, which carries on its face the proof of its absurdity and impossibility. 2d. The same man, besides acting against all the propensions of his nature, discovers that deep and universal science in the things of God, which every impartial reader of this book must admit can never be acquired without an ardent love of truth and holiness, and long discipline of the heart in piety; or the direct and effectual inspiration of the Holy Spirit.

In this Scripture, I find the stamp of its authenticity further impressed by
1st. Its prophecies—
Of the utter annihilation of the Edomites, while the Jews were promised Divine protection—
Of the termination of the prophetical succession under the Old Testament—
Of the speedy establishment of the Christian Dispensation—
Of the annunciation of this event by the Precursor of Christ, and—
Of the nature of the Saviour's mission and work.

2d. By the agreement of its sublime doctrines of purity, sincerity and piety, with the most enlightened, unbiassed, and serious duties of conscience—such decisions as conscience makes on the same subjects, in the dying hour. Nothing short of perfect and entire sincerity, purity, and devotion to God is tolerated. The most specious substitutes for this unexceptionable virtue which human genius ever invented, or human interest, passion or fears ever adopted, are here utterly exploded, reproved and condemned.

3d. By the most strikingly exact portraiture it affords of human nature, under the circumstances in which the Jews were at that period. Here I must advert to the incomparable superiority of the Sacred Scriptures, to all other writings, in the truth and minuteness of its pictures of the human character. Other writings universally skim over the surface of this most interesting theme of investigation, and give us human nature, seldom with accuracy, and never with a precision which lays open the hidden springs of action, and delineates the nicer shades of the soul. Reverse this assertion, and apply it to the sacred writings. Then, tell me how to reconcile the fact with any other position than that of their Divine origin.

I do judge this single trait of the sacred writings to reprove sin—all sin—simply, plainly, authoritatively—as demonstrative evidence, independent of any other, of their divinity. Other writings reprove some vices, but not *all sin*. They seldom reach the thing in its proper and specific nature, at all. Other writings reprove the faults of human nature, but admit palliating circumstances, in extenuation, which sin never can deserve. They reprove faults, but on wrong and insufficient grounds; either as degrading to the dignity of men, injurious to their happiness, or to human society. They reprove, but not authoritatively. Their reproofs operate, or are intended to operate on pride, self-love, interest, or ambition; the reproofs of the Scriptures, directly on the conscience. THE SACRED VOLUME MUST BE TRUE!

## The Social Affections.

### No. 5.—1825.

There is an important difference, which I think is not sufficiently observed, between man considered as a solitary, and man as a social being. It was strongly suggested to my thoughts this evening, by the remarks which Dr.

Reed, in his essay on the "obligation of contracts," has, on that class of moral virtues which have their foundation in the social properties of human nature. How few of the moral virtues are in the power of a solitary human being! His vices it is admitted would find an ampler range; of which his very solitude, if voluntary, would probably be none of the least. I never have read Zimmerman's wordy volumes on this subject; and know not the view which he has taken of it; but cannot conceive how a rational man, taking an accurate survey of human nature, should, if not strangely biassed by interest, misanthropy, or superstition, become the advocate of an entirely secluded life. Zimmerman, no doubt, confines his commendations, (for I remember he deals largely in the praises of solitude,) to temporary seclusion, for the noblest of all purposes, commmunion with God, the study of his works, and the study of ourselves. And these, I confess, are all objects, attainable no where else. But there are certain moral virtues, and a numerous class of tender, ennobling affections, capable of being called into exercise, and reared to maturity by no other means, except the well regulated intercourse of society. The last will form the subject of the following thoughts; and I shall attempt not simply to enumerate, but briefly to sketch and describe them. 1st. The earliest, and perhaps the last to be eradicated by vice or disuse, is the filial sentiment. It grows out of a sense of weakness, want, and dependence on our part, accompanied with a persuasion of the kindness, munificence, superiority and power of the parent. Such it is, in its origin. It is a singularly pure and ennobling affection—not wanting in tenderness, but tempered with veneration, esteem, and a conviction of superiority. If parental partiality blinds the mind to the perception of the imperfections of a child, sure I am that the illusion is mutual. A virtuous child, even if he suspects his parent to have weaknesses, or faults, dares not lift the mantle which filial affection has thrown over him, and minutely scrutinize them. On the other hand, it is the property of this same affection, to magnify any real or imagined excellence of a parent—not only in the immature period of childhood, but down to the end of life. Even if it should suspect itself to err in this estimate of a parent's character, filial piety would hardly submit to the correction of an error so ungrateful. The filial sentiment commonly admits of a slight modification, as the father or the mother is its object. Towards the former, there is a greater prevalence of profound esteem—towards the latter it carries in it more of ineffable tenderness. A pious son feels for his father, a composed, steady, and exalted affection, in which gratitude and respect are paid from principle, and which is attended with the sanction of the judgment: but for the mother, the sentiment rises to a lively passion, does not consult the judgment nor care for any measure or rule in its overflowings. It is altogether a matter of sensation here: she is my mother! my dear mother! cries the bounding heart, no longer master of its own emotions, and dissolves in a flood of tenderness, gratitude and love.

If I were to hazard an opinion as to the comparative strength of these different varieties of the same social affection, I should say that the affection felt for a mother, would prompt to the greatest sacrifices, in a moment of trial; while that for the father, exerts the steadiest and of course the most important influence on the tenor of one's life and character.

My affection for my mother would prompt me soonest, and probably without reflection, to offer my last shilling to supply her necessities. My regard for my father would most effectually restrain me from a dishonorable action.

2. The fraternal affection is not without its tenderness, and a mixture of blending esteem and partiality; but it has in it less of each than the love towards parents. It is less profound—less operative—and more easily disgusted and alienated. Towards my senior brother, I however, have a sentiment of consideration and of esteem, resembling in its measure, my affection for my father: towards my junior, in the same relation I have a sort of parental tenderness; but towards them all a tender and steady friendship. I certainly would sacrifice my own comfort in life, to secure that of my parents, if the price was required.

3. I have already alluded to that variety of the social affection which is not necessarily founded on the relation of consanguinity; but which forms the so much celebrated tie of *friendship*. Its first effect is to cement an union of interest and happiness, reducing both, if not quite to an identity, yet almost to a common stock.

---

### Punishment of Murder by Death.

#### No. 6.—1823.

Reasons in favor of the practice:

1. Nothing less is judged by natural reason and conscience, an adequate punishment for the crime.

2. God commanded this punishment of the crime, to Noah. This command is certainly among those which our Saviour says, are in force now, *because* they were so "from the beginning;" i. e., in the ages prior to Moses. These commands "cannot be disannulled by the law, which came" many "years afterwards."

3. The same command was renewed in the establishment of the judicial code of the Jews. Now, the judicial precepts of the law of Moses, were few of them typical. Many are applicable, and some even necessary to all social communities. Now to prove them no longer in force, it must be shown that they were wholly typical, and that their prototype was presented at the Christian era; or that they were manifestly unfit for any other people except the Jews. Neither of these positions can be demonstrated. The law is then in force.

4. Civil Government, as distinct from Ecclesiastical, is recognized in the New Testament. Consequently the laws, as the objects of each, must be dis-

tinct from those of the other. The command to punish murder with death, was one addressed to Civil Governors. It has never, as addressed to them, been revoked.

Civil Government, armed with extensive and formidable power, was established by command of God himself, among the Jews. St. Paul also asserts it, as existing among the heathen nations, an ordinance of God,' appointed for the promotion of moral virtue and the punishment of crimes; and commands Christians to reverence it as such. Now all Civil Governments in that age, punished murder with death.

The objections are :

1st. That the command to Noah was temporary—*No proof of it.*

2d. That witnessing capital punishments, hardens the heart and thus multiplies capital crimes.

*Answer.* The distinction between the physical and moral effect, or the effect on the nerves, and the principles of the heart, of witnessing, &c., is not regarded in this argument. That a man accustomed to the spectacle of public executions, witnesses them with less nervous agitation than one less accustomed, is not doubted; but that the awful solemnities of such a scene necessarily corrupt the principles of the heart, and impair the vigor of the conscience, has never been proved. Nor can it be. As well may it be said that the Surgeon, who from long practice, can use the knife with a steady hand, must necessarily have contracted such a malignity of disposition, as to be inclined to maim and mutilate every man he meets.

It is objected,

3dly. That the universal forgiveness, and the non-resistance of evil inculcated by our Saviour, are fully opposed to the infliction of death on capital offenders. But this argument lies equally against the slightest punishment, and every possible restraint put on offenders. It proves too much, and is good for nothing to the argument. Further, let all the ministers of public justice and all others, govern their feelings by the spirit of this command. Let all individuals, acting as individuals, regulate their practice by it likewise. But further than this, neither Church nor State—Ecclesiastical or Civil Government, can go, without violating an express mandate of the Almighty. God has given to Civil Governments the sword, not to gratify the passions of the individuals, into whose hands it is given ; but to minister justice among *his own creatures* according to a measure ascertained by himself. Let them look to it how they execute their solemn trust.

The great error of most who employ argument against capital punishments, drawn from the New Testament, is to confound under the general head of the "Christian Dispensation," the obvious distinction which is throughout that Holy Volume, every where, either expressly or tacitly intimated to exist between Civil and Evangelical communities. The church is nowhere said to supersede civil society—nor the precepts of the one to apply literally to all the purposes of government in the others. Civil Government is intended only for the regulation of the conduct of communities of the good and bad, in the present life. The Gospel, to govern the tempers of the heart, and the spiritual society of believers, with a principal reference to the life to come.

When, therefore, passages from the New Testament are adduced as in the foregoing argument, let the previous questions be stated; does the text apply literally at all? If so, is it addressed to the officers of Civil Government, acting *only* in their official capacity? Or does it concern the individual, *acting as an individual?* Or lastly, does it apply to the Evangelical community, in other words, to the Church of Christ in its Ecclesiastical quality?

Observing this rule, we should less frequently misapply and pervert the language of Divine Revelation.

---

*Religious Principles which I most sincerely and firmly hold, as the Doctrines of Divine Revelation, and of right Reason.*

No. 7.—1824.—[Imperfect.]

### FAITH,

In its highest and primary Scriptural sense, is that qualification of the mind effected by the mysterious operation of the Divine Spirit, by which it has power to see the substance, beauty and worth of Divine Truth—to receive it with reverence, affection and love, so that it shall effectually control the temper, purposes and conduct.

Faith, although distinguishable from the doctrines of religion, revealed and natural, just as taste is distinguishable from food, yet cannot be conceived capable of any exercise whatever, except *by the medium* of Divine Truth.— Faith, if it ever exists in the soul without the presence of Divine Truth, must be identified with that state of the mind in which simple regeneration leaves it before it has had opportunity of exerting its renovated affections. I do not here say either, that faith or the regenerated affections ever do remain in a dormant state. But the supposition is made for the sake of distinguishing and more clearly setting forth the true nature of the former.

*Remark* 1. Faith, being the fruit of a Divine operation on the mind, may, if God please, dwell in persons, who have no knowledge of any Divine Truths, but such as are derived from natural sources : but

*Remark* 2. As there is such an intimate connexion between true faith and Divine Truth of the holiest and sublimest nature, we must naturally conclude, with the direct testimony of Scripture, and observation, that very few who have not the Gospel, possess faith; and that fewer still of this part of mankind, bring much of its fruits to maturity.

*Remark* 3. As infants cannot exercise faith in distinct and visible acts, there is no great impropriety in saying *they are not capable of faith;* and still, as it is a quality of their moral as well as intellectual nature, they may have all that is essential to the grace, and consequently be qualified, on Scripture grounds.

*Remark* 4. If it be inquired, how faith differs from that conviction and belief of the truths of Christinity, which a merely studious and virtuous man comes to acquire, after attentively and fairly weighing its evidences, and tracing its consistency and harmony, considered as a system of doctrines? I answer, much in the same way, that renovated affections differ from discoveries in science: i. e., as to the *nature* of the two things. The one is merely a natural, the other a spiritual operation of the mind. The first is related to the latter just as thinking is related to the study of philosophy—or as breathing to a healthy state of the body. The study of philosophy always includes thinking; but thinking by no means necessarily includes the study of philosophy. A healthy body always breathes, but breathing does not always prove the body to be in health. Faith in its proper exercise, always includes a belief of the truth; but a belief of the truth by no means necessarily amounts to true faith. To particularize:

This conviction may take place in the mind, where there is no mysterious and supernatural operation of Divine power; faith cannot.

Religious truth can be most implicitly believed, where there is no perception of its true Divine beauty and excellency: faith always carries with it, when in exercise, this perception.

Divine truth may be most freely assented to, with only that cold approbation of the mind, incident to the discovery and reception of the truths of history and science: faith carries with it a reverence, affection and love for the Divine doctrines which it embraces. Finally,

Faith effectually controls the temper and conduct; or rather, where this grace exists, such is the impression of truth on the mind, as to produce this fruit, and consequence. But the simple belief of Christianity and its doctrines, sometimes has no perceptible effect to meliorate the internal dispositions of the mind, or to regulate the external conduct. And where it *seems* to answer these ends, it does not effect them thoroughly, but superficially and imperfectly.

## THE CONSTITUTION OF MAN,

Theologically considered, presents him to our view, as a moral and a physical being. These constituent parts of his nature, are not actually separable, but easily capable of being separately conceived of. Man's *natural* endowments are, 1st. His animal frame, and all the appetites and affections which are properly and exclusively inherent in it; and 2dly. The understanding or mind, considered so far forth as its operations are limited to the acts of perceiving, judging, reasoning, remembering, and willing—or when the objects of these intellectual exertions are wholly of a natural kind.

The moral nature of man is that part of his constitution, which is limited in its exercises to some exhibition, either direct or indirect, of God himself. Now God can be exhibited to mortals, only by his attributes, authority, providences, and works. The moral part of man's nature is that which is excited to affection or disgust, by every distinct exhibition of God, through any or all of these media. It is wholly intellectual, but clearly discriminable from the mere natural powers and actings of the mind. It is true that the mind may exert itself both *naturally* and morally on the same objects, and as far as I know, at the same time, and in one and the same act. For there are few natural objects, and few truths of natural science, which are not in some way very closely connected with some exhibition of the character or authority of God. For illustration, present to the mind, the historical fact of the delivery of the ten commandments to the Jews. While this fact is contemplated only in its circumstances, of time, place and mode; and the political consequences of the reception of this code by the Jews ; we suppose its operations merely natural. But when the mind comes to survey this law as a transcript of God's character, the reception of it as an act of obedience to the authority of God, and its flagrant violations, so often repeated by the Jewish nation; so that a feeling, affection or sentiment arises thereupon in the breast, it has put forth a moral act. I will not say that there is no exercise of our moral nature where the affection or feeling is not distinctly perceived by ourselves. God perceives many an exercise and emotion of our spirits, which are neither remembered, nor noticed by ourselves. And in every exhibition of himself, whether by a declaration or an instance of his holiness, or of his authority over us, in his word—or by his works and providences—he sees a sentiment of approbation, and love, or of aversion and disgust arise in our minds ; and we are often conscious of the same, ourselves. God has interwoven throughout all his works, the tokens of his presence and attributes. So that the moral powers of man are doubtless as often excited to action as his natural.

Whatever truths are divine, sui generis, or, of their own nature relate to the holiness, and the rights of God, are those which, however they may engage the natural faculties of our minds, are the peculiar objects of the moral part of our constitution.

There are many virtues, and pleasing qualities, in common language termed moral, possessed by man—which I conceive to be strictly *social*, and natural; as a disposition to do justice ; to pity and relieve the miserable ; to exercise kindness and tenderness to relations. These qualities may have place, where "God is not in all the thoughts." In order to render them moral, theologically, they must be made to be the fruits of submission to Divine authority, and of Divine love.

## MAN'S APOSTACY, AND ITS EFFECTS.

The latter extends to his whole nature, but so as to reach the physical, through the moral part of his constitution. The effect of the apostacy on his moral nature, is, wholly to deprave and pervert it. Every exhibition of the holiness of God is painful to apostate man, in proportion to its clearness, and evidence. Every exertion of Divine authority over him raises in his heart a sentiment of rebellion. Every moral virtue which he is called upon to cherish, is viewed with an invincible and spontaneous disgust. An apostate man, may cultivate freely, and with pleasure, the social virtues—because they do not necessarily involve the consideration of God, or require a holy temper. But he cannot but feel either direct enmity, or a secret dissatisfaction, springing in his breast, in every view of all that is peculiar and universal in the character of all true believers—of all that is peculiar to the acceptable worship of God—of all that is peculiar in the example of Christ, and the morality of the Gospel, and of all that is peculiar in the doctrines and conditions of salvation. This is as clear a definition of what I understand, when I employ the phrase of "Total depravity," in relation to man's apostate character as I can make out. It is the utter aversion of his moral nature from God.

The effects of the apostacy on the understanding, must, by filling the breast with a war of lusts and passions, directing it to unworthy studies, and by virtue of the Divine curse, have been extensively debilitating and debasing to the understanding. But this deterioration of the human intellect admits not of a more particular or exact account. The fact is certain; the degree conjectural.

The mortality of the animal frame followed the apostacy, as a collateral consequence, so far as it sprung from the Divine curse: and more directly, as it is gradually induced by vicious passions and practices, and by a mind ill at ease with itself; or, as it is caused by the violence of others.

## MAN'S WILL,

Has been the subject of many fruitless speculations. But it appears notwithstanding the perplexity in which it has been involved by tedious discussions, to be closely connected with some of the very highest of our practical interests. Nor can I perceive that it is more difficult to arrive at a just knowledge of the moral power of the will, than of most other practical subjects.

Most of our serious and digested confessions of faith, concur with Scripture, and experience, in declaring man, in his fallen and unrenewed state, to be utterly without the power of repenting and turning to God, through a defect and perversion of the will. This account of the matter I most firmly believe. Fallen man, however sensible of his guilt, or of his folly, or of his danger, as an enemy of God, does not see the beauty of holiness—indeed he has a very slight perception of holiness at all. Why, then, should he choose it?—Whatever perception of religious things he does possess, excites only disgust and opposition in his mind. How then can he choose those very things which he only loathes and rejects?

To remove these two impediments to faith and conversion, the want of spiritual perception, and a holy taste, the Presbyterian catechism most appositely refers to that operation of the Divine Spirit, whereby "enlightening our minds into the knowledge of Christ, and renewing our wills, He doth persuade and enable us to embrace Christ, freely offered to us in the gospel." This quotation I believe expresses the only way by which men come to repent effectually, and turn to God. If so, the will, unrenewed by the Divine Spirit, has not the power of effectually submitting itself to the law of Christ. And here our inquiries on this subject might cease, and leave it precisely where the Scriptures do, but for an objection often raised even by serious and pious men.

"If," say they, "our wills want moral power, our actions must want moral blame."

Without undertaking a philosophical refutation of the sophistry of this objection, it is here sufficient to remark, that its fallacy consists, generally, in attributing to the sinful perversion of the will, the same moral effects, as to an absolute *constraint laid upon the understanding, or the bodily powers.— Thus stands the whole argument on which the objection is founded: an action which my will freely resists, but which I am compelled to perform by force, is not blamable: therefore, bad actions which I perform, (or culpable omissions which I allow) with the *full consent* of my will, are not blamable, because my will is too perverse to choose any other than bad actions. I answer; in the first instance, you acted unwillingly; in the last, from choice. And no sinful perversion or impotency of the will, excludes choice; none consequently, can justify the breach, or neglect, of God's commandments.

In proof of some of these last positions, no man was ever conscious of acting in religious matters directly against his wishes; but every man who has accurately examined the phenomena of his own actions, knows the reverse to be true. Every person whose conscience is properly enlightened, and animated with a due degree of sensibility, feels in his own heart, a conviction of guilt for all that he ever did against God's law, even under the most enslaving circumstances of his depravity. If he suffers punishment for his sins, his conscience consents to its justice. Men thus carry the refutation of the foregoing objection in their own bosoms, would their pride, their passions, their ignorance of themselves, or their speculative errors, but let it speak.

But the grand confuting argument, is the universal strain of crimination and reproof in which God's word addresses itself to transgressors of every grade of obduracy. It asserts in one breath, the enslaved condition of the sinner's will; and in the next, commands him to repentance, and denounces the guilt and penalty of despising the command.

## RELIGIOUS EDUCATION,

By which is meant the education of a native-born Christian in the bosom of a pure Church, is, by the Apostle represented to be an invaluable advantage; where he states the possession of the oracles of God by the Jews, to be the chief of their privileges.

Religious education, when effectual to salvation, does not, however, lead to the attainment of this blessing, in the same way in which instruction and discipline conducts to the acquisition of any given art or science; because in the latter case, no constitutional obstacle is to be overcome by means which the education and discipline do not themselves supply. In the former, the depraved constitution of the will and affections must be renovated by a power which does not reside necessarily even in the Divine word and ordinances.— And this power is bound in its operations by no invariable law of Divine Providence. They are dispensed according to the sovereign counsels of the incomprehensible Deity. The great advantages of religious education, are nevertheless sufficiently apparent in the following particulars:

1. God has in his word, established religious discipline and instruction, as the ordinary channel of his grace. This is too apparent a truth to have escaped the observation of any attentive reader of the sacred volume. It is an ordinance of his own; and even if no natural connexion between the means and the benefit could be seen by us; we might with safety and certainty confide in the pledged faithfulness of the Almighty, to honor his own inst' tion.

2. But this natural connexion is visible. Suppose the change and renovation of corrupt human nature were the effect of moral suasion, and carried on by the force of virtuous habits. Now, however, Divine influence operates in this great work, certain it is, that it proceeds by these auxiliary means. Divine Agency reigns over the holy change, but all the means which christain discipline and doctrine supply, are the instrument which Divine p ver operates by. Salvation is the result of faith and obedience. But faith can only subsist through the knowledge of the truth; and obedience follow an acquaintance with the command. But the communication of Divine knowledge is the chief part of a Christian education.

---

## THE MOST HOLY TRINITY,

Is a mode of the Divine existence, on the truth of which the whole structure and tenor of the Holy Scriptures seem to depend; and which, by being interwoven with every view of the Divine nature there afforded, with every duty inculcated, and every hope and expectation of the obedient soul there presented, is taught in the most effectual manner. Its Divine and mysterous dignity is not abated by any one single, minute and detached disquisition of it in any of

## APPENDIX.

the sacred writings. I believe it, therefore, as far as I can reverence and receive any part of the testimony of God. That I cannot comprehend it, recommends its truth and glory the more to my reason—I believe it, because the Gospel is a "sounding brass and tinkling cymbal without it." Take from this Divine remedy for sin and the eternal curse, a Divine Sacrifice, a Divine Helper, a Divine Advocate, a Divine Judge, a Divine Sanctifier, Instructer, and Comforter; and alas! where is its efficacy? Since I saw the exceeding sinfulness of sin, its giant dominion in my heart, the weight of the Divine curse, and the infinite Holiness of the Divine nature, I never have doubted but my salvation could only be the mighty work of a Divine Redeemer, Sanctifier and Judge. But I do not believe the Gospel to be a cunningly devised fable. I believe it can and will prove the power of God unto salvation, to all who embrace it. I therefore believe in the doctrine of the most holy and undivided Trinity, as it is commonly set forth in our creeds and confessions of faith; persuaded that as I grow in grace, and in the knowledge and fear of God, I shall have a still juster and more extensive insight into this deepest of all mysteries. As regards the Athanasian Creed, it may have carried its definitions no farther than the Holy Scriptures warrant. But I dare not say that I am able to comprehend, or to adopt them all. They go to define this mystery with more precision than seems to me to appertain to human weakness and ignorance. The creed may not be destitute of its uses: and my own blindness and dulness may be a greater cause of any objection I may have to it, than any thing presumptuous or obsure in the formulary itself.

---

## A GOOD CONSCIENCE

Depends principally on our justification and acceptance before God, in Jesus Christ. This is the foundation on which it must rest.

But it cannot be preserved without the faithful concurrence of our own exertions with this grace. The more a person's sphere and knowledge of duty is extended, the more labor, self-denial, and pains it will cost him, to preserve a good conscience. A *habit* of self-mortification, and submission to God's will, does much, however, for the advanced Christian. He has experienced the pleasure of obeying; and finds, perhaps, less real difficulty in rendering that high degree of obedience necessary, to preserve in himself a good conscience, than from the ignorance and weakness and inexperience of the youngest Christian, may be necessary to fulfil in him the lower demands of a conscience void of offence! Blessing of blessings! how my soul envies to the most abject, outcast slave, the possession of thee! Could I purchase thee with all I have, thou shouldst be the companion of my pillow this night. Could I earn thee by the most servile daily drudgery, could I find thee among the sweepings of the streets, could I rake thee from the very sewers, thou shouldst

P

be mine. But no, thou art the gift only of the Father of mercies. Thou art deposited among the Heavenly treasuries of his grace. Of his free bounty, I must expect it. Deny it not to thy servant, O God, for what good will my wretched existence do me without it?

---

## THE SACRAMENTS.

The commonly received orthodox expositions of Baptism and the Lord's Supper, appear to me, to set them forth in a scriptural light.

Baptism is the ordinance which initiates into the visible church and kingdom of God; and accompanied with the inward and spiritual grace, of which it is the sign and vehicle, it seals to the soul, its title to the promises and privileges of the gospel. This grace ought always to accompany the visible sign; but what means of grace have not the unbelief, indolence, and impenitence of men rendered, as respects themselves, nugatory and useless?

The Lord's Supper is a powerful and affecting remembrancer of the sufferings and death of our blessed Lord.—By renewing to the believer's heart, this mysterious theme of grief and sorrow—the grand consummation of our redemption—it softens the soul to a state of penitential tenderness, and prepares it for the reception of every spiritual grace. This may be said to be the preliminary and natural design and effect of this sacrament, growing out of the mode and occasion of its original institution, and the expressive character of the symbols employed in it.

But the Scriptures authorize a still more important estimate of the essential nature of the Lord's Supper. The Lord's death is not only "represented," but "its benefits are hereby sealed and applied to believers." Far from adopting the gross and idolatrous heresy of transubstantiation, I can best utter my real meaning, by saying, that the heavenly manna, the grace of sanctification, the spirit of Christ, (synonymous, but all inadequate expressions,) are blended and received with the elements, to the abundant comfort and edification of the believer.

An important use of the sacraments, is to engage the senses on the side of religion; that, by directly subserving the work of inward purification, and spiritual comfort, they may the more easily be brought into entire conformity to the gospel; and instead of inlets to worldly seductions, prove the avenues to salutary and holy impressions.

---

## EARLY REMINISCENCE.

I cannot remember, ever to have disbelieved, or anxiously doubted the doctrine of the Triune nature of the Great God. I first received it as most children having a religious education do, from authority—or rather authority supported by the Scripture proofs, which were early taught me. When fifteen years of age, I had my belief confirmed by a powerful influence of the Divine Spirit illustrating and impressing, beyond all human power, the Divine declarations of Holy Scripture respecting this doctrine, on my mind.

## THE SABBATH.

Why keep the Sabbath? 1st. Because God commands its observance. 2d. Because, having fatigued myself through the week, not only with the labors and cares of life, but even the vain pursuits of worldly enjoyment, I find in the devout worship of God, refreshing rest, and positive pleasure. What should I do to solace me amidst all the trials and burthens of life, without the holy Sabbath? 3d. Because I have future labors and cares in expectation, which nothing will enable me to encounter with decent fortitude, and despatch with dignity, but an inwrought habit of depending on the Lord, and the succors of his powerful Spirit—neither of which can be acquired without a faithful application to him at the times and in the ways appointed by himself. If I remember God's Sabbaths to sanctify them, He will remember, to assist and bless me in the hour of my necessity. 4th. Because I should bring upon my conscience a distressing load of guilt, by neglecting to keep the Sabbath. 5th. Because I am persuaded that a most conscientious and exclusive devotion to the duties of the Sabbath, is commonly followed by the particular blessing of God on the secular labors of the week; as on the other hand, a neglect of Sabbath duties, or the profanation of the day, often draws down a curse on our worldly affairs. 6th. Because I have a soul to save, and a holy heaven to press on to, by acquiring a love for, and learning to delight in the holiest exercises of which men are capable in the body; or to be forever and inexpressibly miserable.

These are my chief reasons for engaging in the work of God to-day, and dismissing, as far as his grace shall enable me, all worldly thoughts, imaginations, affections, and cares, from my mind.—I would read none but books conducing to spiritual edification—engage in no conversations not having the same tendency—endeavor to habituate the mind to an intent application to God, and the things of his kingdom, and deal honestly with him and my soul. I would let conscience, moved by the Divine authority, govern me—and in the language of the holy prophet, "seek not my own pleasure or profit, think not my own thoughts, nor speak my own words, but call the Sabbath a delight, and the holy of the Lord, honorable." This is my part—The blessing, whatever, and how great, or small soever it may be, I leave with the Lord.

"I will sing with the spirit, and I will sing with the understanding also."

"God is a Spirit, and those that worship him, must worship him in spirit and in truth."

"Man is compounded of body and spirit," most intimately, and to the human imagination, perhaps inseparably united. We may conceive, because we have seen, bodies destitute of a soul—but it is beyond the power of the imagination to conceive, of a soul existing and operating without a body; because, however firmly we may believe in its separate existence, it has never been presented to our senses in this state. It is the duty, and we are most certainly convinced, the noblest exertion of the faculties of man, existing in the body of man, consisting of body and soul, and in every effort of the one, in some degree exerting some faculty or power of the other, to worship God. He is a Spirit, and requires spiritual worship. But spiritual offerings, if made in the flesh, must be accompanied with animal oblations also. They seek, and must have for their vehicle, some of the functions of the corporeal nature. They can find expression in no other way, but by engaging some of the inferior faculties of the human constitution, to aid their utterance. Nor is it the engaging of any bodily functions to concur with the understanding, in the worship of God, that debases the offering, but the substitution of mere animal exertions and affections, in their place. If the offering consists wholly of these, there is no worship. If there is a disproportionate share of anxiety, or pains bestowed upon these, and they are suffered, instead of assisting, to burthen, and overbear the more rational part of the service, they debase it. But let the sacred spark which first lights the altar descend from heaven,—let it, fed with such oblations as God, as a Spirit, can accept, and as his word requires, till a flame is raised, and then increase, by subjecting to it every thing which God has not declared absolutely unclean. Speech and music; speech in nearly all its modifications, and music in all the variety and richness of its powers, may come in to aid the holy sacrifice. Eyes, feet, hands; every thing pertaining to the body—wealth, possessions, office, youth, beauty and learning, may unite to honor the Holy King Eternal, "Mighty Maker of Heaven and earth."—We praise Him, we worship Him, in the secret recesses of the soul. From this radiating point the flame begins; but it flashes forth, and seizes upon all surrounding objects. It is insatiable. Were it otherwise, could it content itself with a limited indulgence?

## DREAMS.

I think, in regard to our sleeping reveries, that a mean ought to be observed between superstition, and scepticism. The latter mode of treating this portion of our intellectual operations, which not being wholly under the guidance of our will, must be controlled by some higher power, is commonly either the attendant on, or the cause of a certain hardness and incredulity of the mind unfriendly to virtuous impressions. Impressions are certainly made on the mind in sleep, which lead to the most happy results. "A scene was once represented to mine in that state, with remarkable distinctness, which actually occurred two days afterwards, in its most minute circumstances. The best of people have often declared that they have (in this way) received premonitory notices of some remarkable trials or changes, which awaited them. I have little to say from experience, of any such intimations; but have thousands of sleeping reveries from which it is my own fault, if I do not deduce some valuable lessons of self-knowledge. A man can hardly even in sleep, assent to and take pleasure in a criminal or dishonest action, who has a sufficient abhorrence of similar things when awake. Nor do I believe it customary for irreligious persons to enjoy, even in a dream, the society and exercises of serious christians, into whose company his roving thoughts may happen to transport him. I had two nights ago a somewhat remarkable, because very impressive representation in my sleep of the dying scene, of which I was myself an actor in person. The awful solemnity of the impression still remains on my faculties; and I think has been the happy means of engaging me much more heartily than before, in the great preparatory work for so important a change.

## HISTORY OF ONE'S SELF.

Who would write a true history of his own life?—Not I. It were easy for

\* \* \* \* \* \* \*
\* \* and many of their brethren of the auto-biographic line, to say many things about themselves, and following the order of time, arrange those relations in a connected history very much resembling an honest and complete biography. But let me ask the judgment of a sensible man, whose long experience of human nature at large, and close observation of its operation in himself, entitle him to reply to the question, Has *any one* of those biographical sketches the merit of exact truth? Do they not all carry a coloring too flattering to the subject of those respective delineations?

Do they not all omit the true motives of many actions which they record? or the basis of some entire trait of character, or line of conduct, which they put to their credit, whereas, but for such omissions, they would stand to the disgrace of the authors? Has not every scribbling mother's son of them, while penning his relation, recollected meannesses, which as truly belong to his life and character, as any fact or trait delineated, and which, if truly related, would have materially altered the complexion of both; but which (and how is such conduct honest in the biographer who virtually engages to write the truth, as far as the essential characteristics of his subject are concerned?) he has been unprincipled enough to pass over altogether.

The first and most natural art of distorting an auto-biographical sketch, is by suppressing facts. No author pledges himself to his readers, to exhaust his subject. No reader would be willing to encounter an author who should undertake to write up to such an intention. But every biographical author tacitly engages to omit no class of facts which are absolutely needful to a just exhibition of the character he delineates. But so inveterate is the duplicity of the human heart, that we have no biographical portraits, without this fault. Every writer has some idea of what the public taste requires, and no one dares blend in his sketches such strokes, (and in every human character how many such there are!) as will utterly disgust it. Every writer too has his ideal standard, and exemplar of excellence:—and in writing his own life, none yet has had the resolution to state such facts as would leave no portion of this excellence to his share. He may, from the force of principle, be constrained to introduce into the picture some of the darker shades of the original; but never all. And even these blemishes are either varnished, or placed as a fril to what he imagines entitled to commendation. Many foibles, or vices, (it matters not which,) are introduced into the earlier chapters of the treatise, which wholly disappear in its progress. They soon get reformed; and it is well they are so. But had the writer set himself about his impartial task at that period of his life, when those faults made a part of it, before reformation had ensued—and tell me which chapter of his book would have contained the relation of them? And does he now expect to impose on the credulous world the belief that even the sound reformation of his early vices and errors, has not left others at least as gross, and quite as degrading? I put the point in question, to the single test of every honest man's consciousness and experience. Who ever saw delineated by writers of this class, such a character as his own? I do not now refer to any of those traits which may have been the production of his peculiar circumstances. But such, as judging from the place they hold in his own character, must be deemed common to human nature. He has seen others act and feel, as far as he can judge, much like himself. And what in himself are the sources of those very actions and sentiments in which he discovers this strong and near resemblance of those of others? They are what no author in describing himself, ever wrote; because they admit of no redeeming counter-qualities—and would expose the pride of the author to the smart of a wound which could not be healed.

AFRICA.—*Qualifications of an Agent at Liberia.*

Judging from the universal economy of nature, we must concede that every man is constitutionally fitted for some one sphere of action, rather than for any other; and that Providence has ordained no post of duty, without having qualified some person to fill it. This abstract truism applied to this Colony, which we suppose of course to be a lawful establishment, leads directly to the conclusion that there exists somewhere, and within the Society's means of engaging his services, an individual in all essential points qualified to become their Agent in Africa.

## APPENDIX. 119

As most of the candidates who may offer ought, indubitably, to be set aside, I shall first enumerate, negatively, in relation to the general inquiry, the *disqualifications* which amount to good grounds of rejection:

1. Want of sufficient age. The idea of youth is hardly compatible with that of much experience. But there is no room here for experiments; nor for the mistakes of inexperience. Either must be of pernicious consequence to the advancement and good government of the Colony. Add to this objection to a very young man, the want of the respect and confidence, which is naturally conceded to age, both by the old and young. His measures would be received with distrust; the factious and conceited would be forward to seek after and take exceptions; and the whole social machine, would betray by its retarded and irregular movements, the very extensive influence of this single disqualification in the person of the prime mover. A young man, reposing great confidence in himself, would do unbounded mischief by his rashness; and if prudent and conscientious, would too much distrust his own judgment to govern with the necessary decision and vigor.

2. Effeminacy—in other words, that refinement of delicacy, whether relating to the taste, the sensibility, personal habits, or the choice of society, which would render disgusting and intolerable, even the roughest scenes of privation and affliction, or the rudest forms of human nature, is clearly an absolute disqualification for this Agency.

3. A thirst for science, or a habit of devotion to literary pursuits, ought to render suspected a candidate's fitness for the post. The evil to be feared is, lest he should alienate too much of his time from the appropriate duties of his charge. The temptations with which such a mind, in order to avoid this failure, must struggle, are known only to those whose misfortune it has been to learn them from experience. His mental faculties, in order to maintain their natural tone and elevation, would constantly call for the accustomed excitement of study, and gratified curiosity. His sober, every-day duties, would soon want the interest necessary to convert upon them with undivided force, the current of his thoughts. His attention to them would be coerced and involuntary. The attraction of his favorite pursuits, would keep up in his mind, a constant impatience of all others. The consciousness of habit would never cease to accuse him secretly of a waste of the time not spent in improving the mind, and pressing on to new discoveries and acquisitions in the regions of literature and knowledge. The dominion of appetite itself could hardly amount to a more absolute disqualification.

4. A man of suspected integrity will prove a source of perpetual anxiety to the Society, in a matter about which, of all others, their minds should be at rest. An air of mystery will mingle in all his doings; and the Board will seldom have the satisfaction to read in his communications, the simple expressions of nature and truth—the first suggestions of an ingenuous heart. Nor

5. Must he be a man without points, and strong ones too, in his character. There is a sort of negative character, to which no positive faults can be ob-

jected, because, among other reasons, those who possess it have not sufficient energy of character to commit them. They show a consistent deportment, because they have no ruling passion to need the curb, or betray them into irregularities. These people will do little mischief in the world, perhaps, and still less to restrain and prevent the mischievous doings of others. If not deficient in talents to *project*, such a man would utterly fail in the zeal and resoution to carry into prompt effect, the often difficult and unpleasant measures of his government. The true candidate's character is certainly drawn in high relief. It may want the exact symmetry of a perfect one; but it does not want prominence: and among these positive qualifications will be found,

1. A mind capable of grasping, and a heart of feeling the magnitude and importance of the object. It is no objection that the imagination should even be tinctured with a dash of enthusiasm, and hope incline to be a little visionary on this subject. In a mind well regulated in other respects, this warmth of feeling will act as a salutary and useful stimulus. And his situation and duties will often be so trying and difficult as to put his fortitude and zeal to the severest test, and require even adventitious aids. Besides, a mind capable of enlisting its sensibilities in behalf of such a cause, will not soon be disgusted with monotony and the plain practical nature of an Agent's duties, nor tired of the solitude of his situation. His mind, like the appetite of a temperate man, is satisfied with plain fare, and seeks after no high-flavored gratifications. He should be

2. A practical man. This qualification implies experience; and of course, a sufficiently advanced age to have afforded opportunities for experience. It comprehends also that tact, as much perhaps the gift of nature, as the result of education, which some men possess, of taking a thrifty, business-view of every subject which falls under their notice. I have known many individuals to excel in a knowledge and capacity of this useful pragmatical kind, who were still ignorant and simple, even to puerility, on subjects removed but a single step beyond the limits of their immediate sphere of action. They inquire no farther than they have occasion to project, and project with less pleasure and avidity, than they execute. The character in hand is, that of a person, in fine, who chooses rather to be busy than to speculate; and who mingles by a sort of natural aptitude in all the busy scenes with which his duties or situation connect him. But,

3. As long as the track of an Agent's duties continues unbeaten, and actual circumstances are to be weighed for his direction, in the balances of judgment, it follows that the Agent must possess a mind capable of the most accurate observations, and very nice discrimination. It should be able to gather from books the very important aids which they offer in almost every exigency of his duty; and in order to this, it should have been previously formed to a habit of extracting, arranging, and digesting the useful without confounding it with the trash of his authors. And a facility of doing this, requires something like a scholastic turn of mind, and very close application of thought. Nor

APPENDIX. 121

4. Is it unnecessary for him to be well grounded in the rudiments of most of the useful sciences? Without this qualification, it is absurd to expect him to proceed with either regularity or success, in his inquiries into the various branches of natural history, which his duties require him to cultivate, or to communicate intelligibly, the result of those inquiries; and nearly allied to this knowledge, in point of utility, is a general acquaintance with the principles and their application, of law, medicine, divinity, navigation, trade, agriculture, politics, and manufactures. Not a month will elapse, perhaps, in the year, in which his duties will not exact—and often largely—on his practical acquaintance with each of these branches.

5. He should possess an easy and affable, but not too familiar address: the first to render him popular, the last to make him respected.

6. Nor are great firmness and self-command, dispensable ingredients in the character in question. The two are joined in one view, because they can hardly exist apart. A person liable to paroxysms of anger, and sudden transports of passion, commonly in his cooler moments, repents the purpose which he conceived, and perhaps rashly expressed, in a moment of irritation. A man, in order to govern others, must be firm; but firmness without self-government, is firmness without reason—the very definition of sullenness and obstinacy.

7. But the conduct of an Agent should evince a high degree of flexibility, without a vicious imbecility of character. Look at the direct offspring of Divine Wisdom—the economy of the universe. See what calm, unruffled uniformity of system co-exists with an endless variety in the details! Let principle, then, sit enthroned in iron, in your Agent's breast, while the inventive faculty sends forth its forces in every necessary direction, and under every useful form. This definition of a flexible character, is nearly identical with a genius fertile of resources, freely availing itself on proper occasions of them all. I might

8. Enlarge on the necessity of a very uncommon measure of what is expressively called, in the language of Theology, "deadness to the world," were it not included under the next concluding head of *piety*. For what can a man do in this humble, difficult, and forlorn situation, whose heart is cankering with avarice, or burning with ambition, to shine in civilized society? Neglect, impatience, and indifference, will accompany all his sluggish movements. The chilling influence of his example, will extinguish the vital warmth of other minds; and the whole concern tend rapidly to crumble and drop asunder, for want of a common point of attraction and support.

9. To state all the reasons why the Society's Agent should be a man of religion and piety, would be not only to repeat nearly all the foregoing qualifications, which have their only sure foundation in a devout heart; but to enumerate also nearly all the fruits of genuine godliness. For what Christian excellence would not, by its direct exercise, or by way of example, materially

Q

conduce to the great ends not only of government, but of the establishment itself? And what assurance can be afforded without it, of the stability and competency of any plausible set of qualifications whatever?

---

## NOTES ON AFRICA.—1824.

Thermometer at this hour, 7h. 30 m. past 6 P. M. 86 degrees, cloudy, accompanied with thunder and lightning. None are greater deceivers than those who confine the course of the seasons, in any part of the world, to the limits of any exact description. The economy of nature will nowhere, in her meteorological operations endure such a degree of constraint, nor submit to too measured a pace. Writers on this, as on all other subjects, love to reduce their descriptions to the quality and precision of a system. Hence we read, in so many African voyagers, of a regular period of incessant rains; commencing according to some, in March; to others in April; and others still, in May, or June, continuing 'till September, October or November; and then terminating in a season of uninterrupted dry weather, of four, five, six or seven months continuance. Others subdivide the long season, into the foggy, and the clear, the limits of each of which they assign with the same exactness. These subdivisions of the seasons are still further multiplied by nearly every author of a true description of this coast, by an account of the prevalence of the parching harmattan, or dry N. E., wind from the interior. Now there is no reason to doubt that different seasons have conformed to all these descriptions, and verified in particular instances, most of their details. Nor can it be doubted that accurate observers, after a long residence, or frequent visits to the coast, may come much nearer a true general theory of the seasons, than I can pretend to do. But the truth requires that such a theory, in order to be generally applicable, must allow nature great latitude of variation; much greater perhaps, than may suit the views, or perhaps the *scientific reputation* of a precise and systematic writer.

In 1822, the rains began in March; became copious and nearly incessant in May; and were entirely suspended, from early in July, 'till past the middle of August. This interval of dry weather, was a season of vigorous vegetation. The atmosphere was more or less clouded; the sea-wind incessant; and the thermometer not more than two, or three degrees above its range in the rainy months. The rains having again set in, the latter part of August, continued with few remissions, 'till the early part of November. Thence until the first of March, the serenity and uniformity of the dry season, were interrupted as often as once or twice weekly, by heavy showers of rain, commonly at night, and attended with thunder and lightning.—From March 1st, to the early part of May, the sun was little obscured; his rays insupportably powerful to any except native constitutions—little or no rain fell; vegetation faded, and nature

## APPENDIX. 123

seemed to droop. About the 10th of May, the periodical rains returned, and continued, with frequent remissions and not much violence, till early in July. Two months succeeding this period, afforded less rain than the uses of vegetation required. September, October, and November were again showery, but did not send us the rain in torrents, as in the preceding year. Early in December, the dry weather became settled; and has so continued till the present week. It is the week of the full moon, and has been distinguished by frequent showers at night, rainy appearances during the days, and considerable thunder and lightning.

In 1822, the electrical appearances of the atmosphere, which return on the approach of the dry season, were not visible till the 20th of October. In 1823 they commenced on the 18th, perhaps the 15th, of September.

In 1822, judging from a general recollection of the continuance and violence of the rains, much more must have fallen between March and November, than in the year 1823.

I have experienced nothing which answers to the current description of the harmattan winds; hence they are not an uniform incident of the season. Sometime during the dry season, (I think in the early part,) of 1822-3, the colonists were almost universally afflicted with sore throat; which in most cases kept them sick for a week. The weather at this time was cooler than usual, but none of the effects of increased dryness of the atmosphere, are recollected.

1. Between the two periods of May 10th, and October 10th, 1823, the mercury in Fahrenheit's thermometer, ranged between the 74th and 79th degrees—the average about 76 1-2 degrees. When the degree of heat was so low as 74, which it very seldom was, except at night, our invalids (myself among the number) uniformly suffered such an acerbation of any remaining aguish tendencies of the system, as to cause a paroxysm of fever.

2. A large tree situated on the river bank, directly opposite our front windows, was observed in the latter part of September, (1823,) gradually to lose the verdure of its very ample foliage, for a pale yellow. This color gradually degenerated into a pallid red; and this last was rapidly succeeded by an intenser green, than the tree had previously, for a length of time, exhibited—amidst these phenomena, I could not perceive that the tree parted with a single tuft of its leaves.

3. Ligneous plants of the palm species, abound in the country. Such are the bamboo, the plantain, and banana trees—the papaw, the cassada, sugar-cane, Indian corn, and a variety of useless shrubbery, of which *most* have a rapid growth, and several are distinguished by a canopied top. The formation of this last peculiarity is thus accounted for: after the stem has risen a moderate distance above the ground, it is encased by hard, and often a silicious rind. The pith, or whole of the succulent substance enclosed, may be viewed as a bed, or substratum of vegetable soil, from which shoots would issue with great vigor, if not mechanically restrained by the hard cortex. Towards the top of the stem, the rind not having outgrown the pulpy stage, admits the

shoots to protrude; and the vegetative energies of the whole trunk thus acquiring a scope, send out these germinations with wonderful vigor and rapidity, in the form of horizontal branches. Each of these branches may be considered as another miniature stem; and on the principle just explained, carries its foliage in a tuft at its very extremity.

As the general trunk shoots upwards—that part of it which served for the ground of the crop of branches just described, acquires the indurated rind in its turn: and by thus withholding from them the requisite nourishment, causes them to shrivel and drop off; and while this process is going on, another tuft of branches are sending out of the superior part of the stem. The effect is, that the tree always presents a tuft of foliage at top, such as has been described, with a straight, often a slender stem, of nearly uniform size, and entirely destitute of branches.

4. Most of the fruits of Africa, hang from stems of only sufficient length to contain them, which put out directly from the main stem of the tree. Of these, some spring from that part of the trunk which serves as the substratum of the branches, and make a part of the tuft. But many species put out the fruit stems all along the trunk from near the ground to within a short distance of the top, but never so high as the branches. Two trees of this sort I discovered, but have nowhere seen described. The first had a fruit of the size, and much resembling the form, of the plum, excepting a pulpy instead of the petreous kernel in the centre. The taste is insipid, but not disagreeable. The other is one of the finest fruits of Africa. It resembles in appearance the red cherry, but is one size less, and has a pulpy kernel. The taste is similar to that of the American cranberry; but the taste is of a milder character, and tempered with an aroma not entirely dissimilar to that of the black cherry.

5. All the trees of this coast are evergreens. I believe, they commonly deposite their leaves annually, but never entirely dismiss a former growth, till the new has in a great measure taken its place. Hence, and probably from the different seasons in which the various species renew their foliage, the forests never exhibit a leafless or even unverdant appearance.

A pullom of eighteen inches diameter, which was left to grow in front of the government house, cast its entire investment of leaves in April. Before the 10th of May, it was beautifully re-arrayed. A flight of rice birds took possession of the upper half of the top, and filled it with their nests, at least three hundred, in June. Before the 1st of August, they had cut off every leaf from the part of the tree in their occupancy, in order to procure themselves free access and egress to and from their nests. About the middle of October, these leafless boughs began to repair the damage they had suffered, which they would have effected, but for the mischievous industry of their little depredators. The tree is, at this time, (October 24, 1823,) nearly as bare at the top as ever. The lower branches have not been visited by the birds, and have now a thrifty and verdant covering remaining of the June crop of leaves.

# APPENDIX. 125

6. Radishes sown in the latter part of June, and lettuce, in the month of July, are now in the fresh pod. The red snap bean planted with the radishes, ripened on the 1st of October; and the Chili (pole) bean of the same planting, began to show a few brown pods about the middle.

7. Cucumbers planted early in August, grew flourishingly 'till the middle of August, and then put out abundance of blossoms; but the vines directly afterwards began to decay, and were thrown out of the garden in a week afterwards. But possibly, some accident destroyed them, as they grew in a dangerous vicinity to the kitchen.

8. Sweet potatoes set the latter part of June, and yams planted the 1st of August, are now in a very flourishing way.

1. The carcase of a Serpent, (said to measure thirty feet, and to be of the Boa Constrictor species,) was discovered on a height of rocks, quite at the extremity of the Cape. It was recently dead.

2. The Cape was travelled round near the beach, the first of October, 1823. Many springs and small streams of water were discovered, issuing out of the superior parts of the promontory, and often rushing down its sides, in abrupt cascades. Many of these, there is reason to believe, are perennial; and some of them produced by the prevailing rains, and which will not survive them.

As far as I can learn, the water is perfectly sweet.

3. Paper, after having been a few months in the Colony, so far loses one of its most important qualities, as to spread the ink, laid upon it with the most delicate hand, into an almost continuous blot. Notice, an example! On paper of a particular texture, the lines, without spreading into a blot, in a few weeks strike through the paper; probably by the corrosive property of the ink acting upon the dissolved and unresisting texture of the paper. Writing done in wet weather spreads the worst.

4. Ananas ripen three times a year.—The first growth matures in June, and continues till August. The second in November, and continues till late in December. The third ripens about February, and remains through a part of the month of March.

5. Lunar influence is very conspicuous in this country. When the dry season is actually begun, a full moon often brings heavy rains for several days; and always increases their violence during the wet season. Commonly the highest, or spring tides, have occurred two days after the full; and at this time the worst surf prevails.

6. *Dress, proper for Americans in Africa.*—It certainly ought to be light. But owing to the copious perspiration, produced by the solar heat in the dry season, and the heavy and clammy sweats of the wet, caused by the saturated atmosphere; I think that cotton ought to be worn next the skin, on account of its absorbent quality. Flannel, I have found inconvenient, for two reasons. The one is, that it increases the heat of the body, by retaining the transient caloric. The other, that once thoroughly wet, it hardly becomes entirely dry, until thrown off.—My present dress, which I find perfectly convenient, is a calico

shirt, and cotton drawers and stockings, a thin coat, jacket, or gown, a cloth waistcoat, thin pantaloons, a black silk cravat, and unlined straw-hat, with a broad brim.

In the dry season, except early in the morning, or late in the evening, no change in this dress, except of the thick, for a thin waistcoat, will be requisite. When the thermometer falls as low as seventy-four degrees, I find it always necessary to add a thick coat, or run the risk of getting an ague.

7. For the week past, I have been affected with a dysenteric affection of the bowels.

The weather has been humid, rather than dry. Fahrenheit at about seventy-eight degrees. Land and sea-breezes alternately prevalent. My habits sedentary, and my food less vegetable than I could desire. It is not yet more than a month that I have acted on the resolution, to eat meat but once a day. An indifference, approaching to a loathing of animal food, had taken place; and my appetite and strength reduced by confinement, constant study, and the change of regimen.

*July 7th, 1825.*

To-day commenced the excavation of the bank, directly above the new pier, for the new road from the water-side. Most of the sick, decidedly convalescent—four have been employed the day past in this work.

I have, during the present week, attended, for the first time, to the general definitions belonging to the beautiful science of ornithology; and from the facility of mastering the elements of the study, I am surprised and chagrined that my inquiries have never been directed that way before. Alas! what irrevocable losses is he sure to suffer whose education has been cramped by the want of money, books, instructers, or literary associates! This misfortune has been mine.

I am at present engaged in reviewing my Botany, with a view to the practical application of it, in the examination of the vegetables of this country.

Would it not be a most agreeable thing to form a little herbary, of the rarest and most interesting trees and plants of the Colony, in my garden. Let me set about it immediately.

NOTE. Lott Carey reports the discovery of a bank of sand, just this side of little Cape-Mount, containing a visible mixture of gold particles.

---

Among the most striking proofs of the perpetuity and universal obligation of the Sabbath, I account the weekly divisions of time marked in celestial characters, by the four periods of the Moon's increase and deliquation. I do not recollect ever to have known an argument in proof of that important point, drawn from this fact.

# APPENDIX.

## NOTES TAKEN ON MY FIRST VISIT TO PETER BROMLEY'S.
### 1825.

Bromley's jurisdiction extends from the ocean West, as far North as the second Salt Town above the St. Paul's; and thence up that river, comprehending all the country on its right bank as high as the Dey settlements reach on that side. King Willy, King Jimmy, (living nearly opposite the mouth of Stockton,) and an old man by the name of K. Peter, living high up, are some of Bromley's head men.

Bromley's town resembles most others in its plan, and the style of its houses. Near the centre is an open palaver house, having the earth raised for the floor, to the height of a rail, two and a half feet above the common level. This house is twenty-five feet long. Adjoining, or in the same central part of the town, is a circular building kept for the reception and entertainment of such strangers as are considered respectable. The building in the Northern parts of Africa, and in Asia, would be termed the Caravansera. Its roof is conical, and the apex pointed with a sort of spire, which is commonly ornamented, and tufted or capped in a fantastical manner.

These two buildings are common to the native towns. Another appendage is commonly the tomb of some Patriarch, or former King of the place, whose memory is cherished with particular veneration. The tomb is commonly covered with a thatch roof house, plentifully loaded with gregrees of every description. Bromley's father's bones are entombed in his palaver house.

A fourth appendage of most towns, is the palaver tree, near which the palaver house is built; but the latter sometimes answers the purpose of the former.

In forming a town, the ground is first cleared, then levelled beautifully in the manner of a parade. The rubbish is deposited in a circular bank just without the level area; and with whatever litter afterwards accumulates forms a rich bed, which is thickly planted with banana and plantain, and sometimes other fruit trees. The houses are disposed in no regular order, except that the more important are the most centrally situated: cooks' houses, and womens' and servants' apartments occupy the skirts. The houses after being plastered, are washed commonly with clay, which is sometimes colored red or brown. The area is always neatly sanded. The houses are commonly of a circular or oblong form, and the latter covered with thatch roofs of the form called hipped. There are two kinds of leaves used in this part of Africa for thatching—the bamboo, and another resembling oak leaves, but of a larger size, which, however dry, are said to be nearly incapable of being burnt without the addition of other fuel.

Kroomen often build without the shelter of trees, on the bleak and barren rocks or sand of the beach. But the other tribes, (their "Salt" and "Half Towns" excepted,) never; but choose, where choice can be had, a lofty and nearly impervious forest, in the bosom of which they open a spot of one to three acres, corresponding to the projected size of their town. No plantations are ever suffered to be made directly contiguous to the site of the town,

APPENDIX.

and often are formed at the distance of one to three miles from it. When, for the convenience of the people employed on these plantations, it becomes necessary to build a dozen houses near them, they take the name of "Half Town." The ground is not levelled for these towns, nor have they either palaver house or ordinary.

"Salt Towns" stand on some salt water, commonly the sea shore, and are for the accommodation of a few superannuated domestics and children, whose business is to boil salt, for the traffic in the interior.

Banana and plantain stocks grow, produce fruit, decay, and renew themselves throughout the year. Each stock springing from an old root, matures a single racemus of fruit, if in the rainy season, in three months—a longer time is requisite in the dry.

I observe that the country near Bromley's, is cleft into a species of islets, channels of ten to twenty feet wide, and four to six or eight deep, which are dry one half the year, and filled with water during the summer and autumnal months, and which finally communicate with the river St. Paul's, intersecting it in all directions. The timber is lofty, and I think of a greater age than that which covers the country on the opposite bank of the river.

## COLONIAL NOTICES.
### 1826.

AGRICULTURAL.—The progress of agriculture in the Colony, has been already stated, to be extremely slow. The causes which have retarded it, are sufficiently obvious; have been more than once enumerated in my communications to the Board of Directors; and unhappily, still continue, though with diminished force, to operate. They are however, of such a nature as to appear, from a simple recitation, by no means invincible. Some are merely accidental; several will be obviated by a little more experience of the peculiarities of the Country: and time, the growth of our settlements, and the spirited exertions of the Patrons of the Colony, will remove the rest. I have no fear that so delicious and prolific a climate and soil as those of Liberia, capable of maturing the most desirable and the richest productions of the earth, in an abundance which in all other countries, similarly blessed, affords the tropical cultivator a source of wealth, should be suffered by a population in character, and origin American, for any considerable length of time, to remain idle and unproductive.

The languid efforts of the Colony, in this branch of improvement, are to be imputed,

1st. To the insecure and disturbed state of the settlement, during the two or three years immediately following its commencement.

2d. To the very unpropitious situation and quality of the lands contiguous to the first settlement. The uplands are rocky, and liable to the worst effects of that extreme drought which prevails throughout one half of the year. The lowlands of the Cape are either sandy and unproductive, or alluvial and marshy;

APPENDIX. 129

subject to inundation during the rainy season; or incapable of repaying the labor of tilling them. The Cape lands having moreover, from time immemorial, been consecrated by the superstition of the natives of the country, are every where loaded with a thick and lofty forest, of an ancient growth; and consequently, to be cleared only by a slow and laborious process. The agriculture of the Colony has been further retarded,

3d. In consequence of a majority of all the Colonists declining the acceptance of the lands assigned them, to so late a period as the latter part of the year 1824.

4th. In consequence of the general poverty of the settlers; the subsistence of their families; the building of their houses, and the necessary improvement of their building-lots, wholly engrossing the means at their disposal during the two or three earliest years of their residence in the Colony. The

5th cause which has operated prejudicially to the farming interest, is to be found in the facilities, and inducement presented the settlers to engage in a small barter-trade with the natives of the country. This trade, which is open alike to all who choose to engage in it, and requiring them to bring to it only moderate funds, and as little skill, offers the powerful temptation of an immediate, and certain profit. Thinking less of the future and general welfare of themselves and the Colony, than of present and apparent advantages; and stimulated with the pressure of their immediate wants, all, or nearly all the settlers, have in different degrees, given in to this pursuit, to the neglect of the more laborious occupation of husbandry. A single fact will show the very seducing nature of this traffic. The demand for mechanical labor, particularly that of carpenters, joiners, and masons, has always exceeded by more than double, the supply. The wages of these mechanics has consequently risen to a rate, seldom heard of in the United States. A most indifferent mechanic has been known to reject a job which promised him, not less than two and a half to three dollars per diem. And, without a single exception, the mechanics of the Colony, even the most skilful, have repeatedly sacrificed the profits of their proper business to the precarious gains of this country traffic.

6th. The frequent disappointments experienced in regard to our expected supplies of seeds from America, has tended greatly to discourage the agricultural spirit of the people. Ample preparations for planting, at the proper season of the year, have been twice made, in anticipation of seeds promised to be sent us from abroad, and as often defeated either by the failure of those supplies, or the badness of the seeds on their arrival. By the Indian Chief, we received not less than three tierce of well assorted seeds—but all failed.

7th. A large majority of the settlers arriving in this country previous to the present year, are from the large towns of the United States, of whom few understand the business of agriculture, and fewer still from their previous habits are disposed to engage in it.

8th. To these unfriendly circumstances of our population and situation, if we add that which arises from the great natural dissimilarity of this country

R

in every thing relative to its agriculture, to every part of the United States, from which settlers have emigrated, we shall feel no surprise in view of the little that has yet been done in this line of improvement; nor, I trust, will a just survey of the past tend to produce any discouragement of our hopes respecting the agriculture of the Colony, in future. The present year has indeed presented some cheering indications of a growing attention to this subject, authorizing the hope that it will soon come to be regarded, with an interest more commensurate with its importance.

About sixty families of country farmers, from the lowlands of North-Carolina, have within that period been placed on the excellent level lands of the *St. Paul's*, and between thirty and forty families in Monrovia, have received a part of their allotment on the equally fertile tract of the *Half-way Farms*. These settlers, particularly the former, have given already a good proof of the rapid progress they are expected to make in the reduction and culture of their lands. These are of a very inviting quality—and the habits of their owners fit them well for all the rough, laborious, an d dirty work, required about new plantations. They have never suffered from the restraint of a town life; and begin already in idea to lay off their fields and their acres, while their less rustic neighbors think it enough to calculate the more familiar dimensions of a town building-lot, or the width of an alley.

There is, in my opinion, more merit than appears, on a superficial view, in the first experiments in agriculture of a people, situated like the colonists of Liberia. They are too poor to lose without serious inconvenience, the labor of an entire year. And less time is insufficient to attest the success of any method of tillage, which they may employ. They have no example to stimulate them. But groping in the dark, a path untrod before; unacquainted with the means of obviating its difficulties, and uncertain as to the results to which it may conduct them—the few that *have* persisted, amidst so many discouragements, to the attainment even of a partial measure of success in their agricultural prospects, cannot be thought wholly undeserving of commendation. The merit will hereafter certainly be less, even when the success is greater, as fewer difficulties and discouragements will exist to be struggled with.

HARRIS CLARKE,—a farmer, from the vicinity of Petersburg, Virginia, was the first to lead the way, in the culture of garden vegetables, on a scale sufficiently extensive to deserve particular notice. His first experiments were made in 1824, the same year of his arrival in Africa, and when suffering from its climate, on a patch of the Cape lowlands; where, although the property of another person, he went to the expense and labor of clearing for the purpose. On this spot he reared the first vegetables of *colonial growth*, ever brought into our market; and, though his little plantation suffered considerably from insects at one season of the year, and from being overflowed at another; yet it was gratifying to learn that its little proceeds, nearly, or quite repaid him for all the labor and pains which it cost him.

The same individual, by renting an unoccupied town-lot, contiguous to his own, has since been enabled to enlarge the sphere of his labor, by throwing both into one—and has in the two last years made a very profitable use of the experience acquired in the first. He now enjoys the praise of furnishing earlier, better, and a greater abundance of American vegetables, than any other settler. It is still more to his credit that he had sense enough from the first, to see the fallacy of those expectations, by which too many are misled to form temporary trading connexions with the natives, to the neglect of the more permanent and certain interests of themselves, their families, and the Colony. Mr. Clarke has a place now for the third successive year, at the Agricultural Board of the Colony.

The Rev. C. M. Waring was the first to adventure a large and valuable amount of labor and funds, in a then novel experiment of an untried crop, in African lands. In the latter part of 1824, before he had completed his dwelling-house, he brought nearly the whole of a plantation of ten acres under cultivation, at a very great expense. Nothing was omitted which was judged necessary to ensure a plentiful return in the harvest of the following year. And a beautiful young crop of Rice, Cassada, and other vegetables, seemed in the early part of the season, to promise the accomplishment of the hopes, which had been excited. But the first mentioned of these crops failed entirely, from an error in the proper season for planting lands of the peculiar quality on which the experiment was made, and from the myriads of ants which invaded and destroyed it, down to the ground, in the ear. The Cassada underwent a similar fate from the vermin swarming upon it, a few months afterwards, from the surrounding wilds. The whole plantation miscarried. As great advantages were anticipated from so generous an experiment, in case it had been crowned with success; so the failure of it, could not help increasing the general diffidence previously entertained of the American system of husbandry. Several persons about to follow so bold an example of farming, curtailed at once the extent of their preparations; and others deferred them for the present, altogether.

Lewis Crook, is next in the order of early adventurers in the culture of the staple grain of the country—rice; and unfortunately for the farming interest among us, met with no better success, except that the scale of his operations was much narrower than Mr. Waring's. The lands which he cultivated, were different from his; elevated, and rocky. But possessing a deep and strong soil, they produced a heavy crop of excellent grain—which was invaded by no destroyer, until the first cutting had nearly matured. But the rice birds, and monkeys, seemed now bent on a full indemnity for the respite with which they had, till this period, indulged the growing crop. Nor without several vigilant sentinels posted by day and night, in different parts of the field, was it possible to preserve it. The industrious proprietor was unable to save enough rice to replace his seed. This happened in 1825.

On the same kind of land, and in the same year, the Rev. Lott Cary lost a promising crop of rice under similar circumstances. The principal experiments of this year, seemed thus by their failure to augur but indifferently for the future prospects of at least, the *Monrovia* farmer; and the effect was such as was naturally to be expected. The conclusion generally inferred from trials conducted in several different ways, and all terminating in the same ill success, was either *that the wretched modes of tillage followed by the natives must be adopted;* or that *nothing valuable in the way of farming, could be accomplished till the country should be generally and extensively cleared of its woods, and the plough with the whole system of an improved agriculture be introduced.*— It was unfortunate, that several individuals had exhausted in these fruitless experiments, all their little resources, and were under a necessity of engaging for the subsistence of their families in such pursuits as promised a surer return to much smaller disbursements.

But there was one exception. Mr. Cary determined to try the effect of cropping the same piece of ground, the following season, after breaking it more thoroughly than had ever before been practised either by his neighbors or the country people. It is the custom of these last, after clearing the ground imperfectly, to dig in their rice with a small hoe or mattock, which is worked with one hand, and scarcely disturbs the surface of the soil. Mr. Cary, after enlarging his plantation of the former season, and clearing it of all its brush wood and shades, had the whole turned up with picks and hoes, to the depth of several inches, early in June last. The rice was then sown, in the proportion of two and a half to three bushels (rough) to the acre; and covered in to the depth of two or three inches. The rains had already commenced. A crop of Cassada, after the custom of the country, was inserted in the same soil, about the same time, to follow on slowly after the rice crop, and come to maturity the succeeding season—both were prosperous. The rice proved a very abundant upland crop, and matured its first cutting about the 20th of October; the last ripened in the first week of September. The produce is estimated at about 50 kroos\* the acre. It is singular, that on the very ground where, the preceding year, the porcupines and monkeys had destroyed an entire crop, no damage was suffered from either, in the present; and that even the rice birds desisted from their customary depredations on a field of grain, in the destruction of which, their very name is indicative of their mischievous activity.

These successful results of a very laudable perseverance have already been productive of the best effects, in correcting the too hasty and erroneous conclusions which had been drawn from the ill success of the farms the last year. They have proved either that the vermin of the Cape have diminished in an almost incredible degree, within the last twelve months, or what will have on the practice of the farmer nearly the same effect, that they are not at all seasons equally or even seriously destructive. They prove that the more the lands are wrought, the better is the prospect of a good crop—and have obviated a still more unfortunate prejudice, derived from the practice of the country, that the same piece of upland will not yield two successive crops of

\* Kroo, an African measure varying from 3 to 5 Winchester gallons.

this grain, and that the only way to restore its heart after a single crop of rice has been followed with one or two of cassada, is to abandon it until again overrun with a young forest.

The culture of arrow root on a small scale, and its preparation for use, have more than two years ago, been brought to perfection. It has since become a common article of food with persons of delicate habits or imperfect health. I have some specimens on hand to be forwarded to the United States by the first convenient conveyance. The wives of L. Crook and A. Edmondson, have been among the most active in the culture and manipulation of this useful article.

INDIGO.—This article has been cultivated, and the extract of the dye prepared, just to a sufficient extent, to prove that if undertaken on a large scale by experienced operators, the raising and manufacture of it might be made a most lucrative business. For all the experiments in this article, the Colony is indebted to the attention given to it by the Rev. Richmond Sampson. He is about laying down an extensive plantation of this valuable shrub; and if sufficient skill can be brought to the difficult process of expressing and concocting the dye, I doubt not, that a few months will ascertain to us the interesting fact, that the soil and climate of the Indies are in no respect more congenial to this valuable product than those of Liberia.

SARAH DRAPER, a single (widow) woman from Philadelphia, who arrived in June, 1823, without property, friends, or a lucrative trade, deserves an honorable mention among such of the Colonists as have distinguished themselves by their well directed industry. She has at the present date, a well cultivated, enclosed, and otherwise improved building lot in town, on which she has completed a commodious dwelling of good materials, to which she has gone far towards completing a still more valuable addition. She provides respectably for two African children, whom she has undertaken to educate for the United States' Agency; and who are daily enjoying the advantages of the Free School of Monrovia.

But the activity of this deserving female has not been confined to her little domestic improvements. In 1824, (September,) she, with many other females of the Colony received the common allotment of two acres of plantation lands. Unfortunately, hers fell on one of those rough and rugged spurs of Montserado, whose rocky surface and sturdy forest growth seemed to defy the efforts of industry itself to subdue and tame it down to an arable state. But Sarah Draper has accomplished this task. The whole lot is under cultivation; and I this day had at my dinner three different species of vegetables, the growth of this plantation! *She is the first female in whose name Title Deeds for lands in Liberia have been executed;* and to increase the merit of this distinction, she has acquired the right to this valuable freehold, by her own unassisted exertions. And what she has accomplished, any female similarly circumstanced, who is capable of exercising the same degree of resolution, activity and perseverance, may achieve in the same time.

J. ASHMUN

## SKETCHES OF CHARACTER.

### Stephen Kiah.

It is due to the memory of this worthy man, to transmit, at least, a simple notice of his excellent character, to his descendants in this Colony, and to all who may inherit after him the blessing of a civil and religious community, which his example, his influence, and above all, his prayers have largely contributed towards establishing in this country.

He was a native, and for upwards of the first 70 years of his life, an inhabitant of the Eastern Shore of Maryland. It was his lot to be born a slave; but long before the middle of life, by his industry and good conduct, he obtained his freedom, and became the father of a numerous and highly respectable family—the condition of whose birth spared them all from the reproach (however unjust) of having ever been in a state of servitude.

His age it was impossible exactly to ascertain; but he has told me, that at the time of Braddock's defeat, which he perfectly recollects, he must have been well grown. As that event occurred in the year 1759, Stephen Kiah could not have been under 76 years of age, at the time of his embarkation for Africa, in 1822; and, as rarely as such a circumstance occurs, he at this time retained, under so great a weight of years, and even to the last hour of his life, much of that soundness of judgment, promptness of recollection, and strength of memory, which had distinguished him in an unusual degree through life. The traits of his character were happily blended, and formed together an assemblage of very striking excellences, to which none who knew him could long remain insensible. Cheerfulness without levity; kindness tempered with discriminating severity; firmness joined with the most amiable docility, were among the most conspicuous. The manly firmness of inflexible principle, united with the lamb-like meekness of a dependent and submissive child,—were qualities, which, however opposite in appearance! were most harmoniously interwoven in the texture of his moral habits.

His constitution had been robust, his habits laborious, and as a consequence, his circumstances, at the period of his emigration, were easy. His motive for this step at so advanced an age, he explained by observing to me, that the remnant of his own life was of too little importance to oppose any obstacle to the promotion of an enterprise, which he was anxious to aid by his example, for the sake of his descendants, and the colored people in America. He could not but make a sacrifice of some few of the comforts of old age, by the removal; but he saw in the Colony an asylum prepared by the Providence of God, for the people of color, on which he was firmly persuaded, that the dew of his Heavenly Blessing would copiously descend to the latest period. In this confidence, he cheerfully accompanied his numerous family to this distant coast, which, like Moses, he most earnestly desired, at least, to be permitted to behold; and like Jacob, to have his bones deposited there. And his desires were fulfilled.

But he was not exempted from those severe afflictions, which his faith so eminently fitted him to meet with composure, and sustain with the most exemplary patience. His aged partner, who had made three-fourths of the journey of life with him, was among the first of the expedition, who fell victims to the change of climate. But the separation was rendered easy by the mutual confidence of a speedy re-union in the Kingdom of Heaven, which animated the bosoms of this aged couple. A pious widowed sister, who was even his senior in age, soon followed, in the same assured hope of passing to the immediate fruition of a holier and immortal life. To witness this scene of—what shall I call it? it certainly was any thing but mortality—it was any thing but affliction—it was the accomplishment of long cherished hopes! it was putting off of mortality, and the putting on of immortality—it was the triumph of faith and hope, and of the peace of God, which passeth all understanding. To witness but one such scene in one's life, must leave a lasting conviction of the power and excellence of the Holy Religion which brightened it, in the most sceptical mind.

But a few days after parting with his friend, he was called to furnish, in a new furnace of trials, another proof of his Christian fortitude and confidence. In the attack of the natives upon the settlement, on the morning of the 11th of November, two of his grand children fell almost before his eyes—one of them having been killed by a musket shot, and the other, a female, assassinated under circumstances of the most appalling barbarity. In the same hour, a very worthy son-in-law, his boast and principal earthly dependence under the infirmities of age, was disabled for life, by a most severe wound in the shoulder, and five small grand children carried into captivity! To discover no marks of affliction under such wounding dispensations of Heaven, would be to manifest an insensibility of heart, which, to say the least, is no part of Christianity. Mr. Kiah felt the chastisement in all its severity. His heart bled, and his eyes overflowed, but in all this, he sinned not, by repining against the ordinance of Heaven, by despairing of the Divine mercy, or charging God foolishly. It was the severest trial of his life, and the more so from being sudden and unexpected: but he soon evinced the power of faith, still superior, and discovered, that though wounded and pierced, his spirit was not broken; and a faithful Saviour, not only sustained him under his sorrows, but delivered him from them by repairing, as far as was possible, his multiplied bereavements.\*

He continued, although nearly worn out by the infirmities of age, to employ himself in such labors as his strength would permit,—was the advocate and promoter of every thing laudable; a powerful reprover of all deceit, slothfulness, vice and irreligion; a most devout and humble worshipper of

\* His captive grand children were restored to him.

God, both in public, in social meetings, and in his closet, a peaceable and exemplary member of the civil community, and a most earnest, active and faithful friend to the souls of his fellow men, till his peaceful removal to a better world, in April, 1825.

L—— C——,

A black man, has been a member of this Colony since the beginning of the year 1820. He had made a profession of religion in America: but never since I knew him, either discharged its duties, or evinced much of its spirit, till within the last ten months. He was a man of good natural sense, but wretched in the extreme; and the cause of equal wretchedness to his young family. His wife, naturally of a mild and placid temper, failed in almost every thing to please him, or prevent the constant outbreakings of his morose and peevish humor. He was her tyrant—and so instinct with malevolence, the vain conceit of superiority, jealousy, and obstinate pride, as to resemble more an Arab of the desert, or a person destitute of natural affection, than a person by education and in name, a Christian. As a neighbor, his feelings were so soured and narrow, as to render him disobliging, suspicious, and equally an object of general dislike and neglect. His heart was a moral desert—no kind affection seemed to stir within it; and the bitter streams which it discharged had spread a moral desolation around him, and left him the solitary victim of his own corroding temper.

Such an ascendant had these evil qualities over the other faculties of his mind, as in a great measure to dim the light of reason, and render him as a subject of the colonial government, no less perverse and untractable, than he was debased and wretched, as a man.

Several times have the laws, which guard the peace of our little community, been called in, to check the excesses of his turbulent passions, by supplying the weakness of more ingenuous motives. Still this person discovered, in the midst of this wreck of moral excellence, a few remaining qualities, on which charity might fix the hope of his recovery to virtue, usefulness and happiness. But these were few, and mostly of a negative kind. He was not addicted to profane discourse. He allowed himself in no intemperate indulgences. He observed towards sacred institutions a cold, but still an habitual respect. And, strange as the fact may seem, he was laborious in his avocations, even to severe drudgery, and equally a stranger to avarice, and a passion for vain ostentation. Whether these relieving traits of his character were the effects of habit, produced by the influence of former piety; or whether they were the result of constitutional temperament, or of education, is not for me to decide. But such was L. C., until the autumn of 1824; when not only a reform, but an absolute reversal, of every perverse disposition and habit in the revolting catalogue of his character took place. A more obliging and affectionate husband I am convinced is not to be found on this Cape, few in the world! And there is no appearance of constraint, or affectation in this display of tenderness. It is uniform, untiring, cordial, and increasing, as far as it is permitted to any one, except the Searcher of hearts, to judge. In all his intercourse with his family, and neighbors, he carries with him, an inimitable air of sweet and profound humility. You would pronounce it to be the meekness of the heart springing from some deepfelt sentiment of the interior of the mind. But so far from abasing the possessor, in the estimation of others, this very trait commands their respect, and their love. It gives to him a value, which he never appeared to possess before. Ten months have I now had daily opportunities to observe this altered man in a great variety of circumstances, and some of them, it must be confessed, sufficiently trying. In one instance, I have had to regret, and censure the appearance of that perversity, which made an important part of his former character. But happily this fit of turbulence was of short duration; and some months have passed since, without witnessing a repetition of the infirmity. Were I this evening asked to name the man in the Colony, who would most carefully guard against offending, or causing even a momentary pain to any of his fellow-men, I should not hesitate to say that in my judgment, the man is L. C. On this point I insist, because it was precisely in his revolting and unfeeling churlishness, that his greatest and most incurable infirmity seemed to consist. I hardly need add, were silence not liable to misconstruction, that the duties and ordinances of religion are matters of his most devout and diligent observance. How often have I been awaked at the dawn of Sabbath, by his devout strains of prayer and praise, sent up from the midst of a little company of praying people, who at that hour assemble for religious exercises in a vacant building near my residence. How sure am I to find him reverently seated in his place, among the earliest who assemble in the house of God. What an active promoter of every commendable and pious design, is sure to be found in him.

Every laudable habit, which had survived the general extinction of all practical virtue, seems to have acquired additional confirmation: and from the operation of higher principles, seems to follow of course, and derive the best guaranty of its continuance. I might go on to particularize; but it would only be to fill up the outline already sketched, and which, whether relating to his former, or his present character, however imperfect, is strictly true. Ask of him the cause of so obvious and surprising a change, and he humbly, but unhesitatingly ascribes it wholly to the power of the Divine Spirit, operating, he cannot tell how, but evidently by means of the word and ordinances of God, upon his whole mind. Such was the origin of this great moral renovation, and such are the agency and means by which its effects are sustained, and under the operation of which they are beginning to combine into a habit of holiness. He rejoices in the hope of its duration to the end of life, solely he would say from the confidence he has in the immutable love and faithfulness of the Holy Being, who has wrought so great a work in him. And let philosophers cavil and doubt, if they must; but this man's example is a refutation in fact of a thousand of their sceptical theories. He is a new man, and the change was effected chiefly before discipline, or example, had time to work it. He is an honest man, and soberly asserts that to his certain knowledge he did not perform the work himself. But where is the example to be found of *such* and *so great* a change, wrought by mortal means? The history of the human race is challenged to produce it. To God then who created man, to Christ who redeemed him, and to the Holy Ghost who sanctifies him, be ascribed without abatement, or reserve, the power and the grace displayed in this and every similar instance of the conversion of a blind, and hardened and wretched sinner.

---

MONROVIA, WESTERN AFRICA, AUGUST 7, 1826.

*To the Reverend Pastor, (if any,) the Deacons and Brethren of the Congregational Church of Christ, in Champlain :*

RESPECTED AND BELOVED FATHERS AND BRETHREN:

A review of the sixteen years of my connexion with your body, in the holy ties of a common faith, and a common hope, while it overwhelms my mind with the number, and infinite value of the blessings derived to me from that connexion, produces, also, a painful conviction of having failed in many of the duties which it imposes. The delinquencies of which I have to accuse myself, are chiefly to be traced up to the neglect of that direct and frequent correspondence with your Pastor and yourselves, which it was equally my privilege and my duty to have cultivated. But, separated from you for so many years, and often, as at present, by a distance of some thousands of miles, I fear, I have almost ceased to be regarded by you as one of your number—and that I retain only a small interest in your affections and your prayers, which I desire might be the greater, as my privilege of being watched over, counselled, and encouraged by you, is the less.

It is my earnest wish and resolution, however, the grace of God assisting, to repair hereafter, by every means in my power, those neglects, and retrieve the many lost advantages which I have to regret as the consequence of them. And here I cannot repress the affecting recollection, that so many of our beloved and esteemed members—some of whom we all accounted fathers and mothers in our little Israel, when I last met you at the Sacramental Supper of the Redeemer, are now withdrawn forever, from our communion on earth, and can assist us no more, except by the example which they have left us, and the seed sown by their prayers and watered by their tears, now exchanged for the joys and the praises of Heaven. But, I trust, your thinned ranks have been, from time to time, replenished by accessions from the world; and that the engagement of the Almighty Saviour to his general Church, that "the gates of Hell shall not prevail against it," has been fulfilled, in respect to your particular communion. But my want of exact information, in regard to your

APPENDIX. 139

present state, is both an evidence and reproof of that neglect of my covenant engagements for which I blame myself: and desire forgiveness both from God and yourselves.

The books of the church will show that I became an unworthy member, in the summer of 1810; and from that period till September, 1816, while pursuing my studies at the school of a neighboring state, was permitted by my situation, occasionally to unite with you in worship, and the ordinances of the church.

From 1816 to 1819, without withdrawing or desiring to withdraw from my relation to your church, I enjoyed in Maine, the benefits of a very endeared connexion with another, which God had been pleased to gather out of the world, partly by my own instrumentality. The temporary nature of my engagements and residence in Maine, did not, I think, allow of my applying to you for a dimissory letter ; but I think, I then erred, in not asking, and using, if granted, a certificate of my standing, accompanied with your recommendation to the communion of sister churches.

A similar neglect was indulged during a residence of three years ensuing, in the City of Washington; and, to add to my present regrets, I believe I did not in that whole time, inform you of the circumstances in which I was placed in that city. I had received in Maine, a license limited to three years, to preach the gospel, but without ordination. At the expiration of that term, having engaged myself in the publication of a Religious Monthly Magazine, which occupied much of my time ; I deferred, and at length relinquished for the present, the intention of applying for a renewal of my ministerial credentials. One reason for this course was the occurrence of some doubts as to the expediency of such an application ; believing, and I think perceiving myself to a certain extent, useful in another line of duty. The circumstance of there being no Congregational Churches and Ministry of the orthodox faith in that part of the United States, also had an influence, I fear, *too much* influence, to dissuade me from resuming the Ministry, to which I had in a manner consecrated myself. I have often since lamented that I did not, at that time, freely correspond with my brethren in Champlain, on those subjects. God might have blessed their counsel ; and it was equally my privilege and duty, to have recourse to it for direction. I wandered in much darkness throughout this period, and suffered in the strife of conscience, on the one hand, and of uncertainty as to the path of duty on the other, many distressing conflicts.

My lot had been providentially cast with the second Episcopal Church in the City of Washington, which I found blest with an Evangelical Ministry, a pure faith, and a pious congregation. I addicted myself to the worship and communion of this particular congregation ; and *generally*, to the service of the Episcopal Church of the middle States, until May, 1822, when having accepted of a joint appointment of the Government of the United States, and of the American Colonization Society, to this country, I left the United States, and have since been an inhabitant of this country.

My duties here have been, and continue to be various; and my sphere of influence as a Christian as well as a man, every month extending itself. I am not left to an entire insensibility of my dread responsibility to God and this generation; and of the folly of expecting to make one right step without a special Divine guidance. I cry to God for his all-sufficient grace, and have often been heard. And blessed be his name, my very heart ascribes to Him all the glory. In my present protracted affliction, while confined to my chamber, and for the most part, to my bed—his promises and his comforts quiet my impatience and sustain my spirits. It is not for my sake, He has given me well to understand, my brethren—it is not for my sake, but for His own great name, that he has afforded me so many tokens of His favor, and so signally approved of some of the works of my hands, in this dry and solitary land, where the waters of his sanctuary have never till lately, flowed.

The same faith which God enabled me to profess in Champlain, in 1810, has been the steadfast anchor of my soul, in the floods of heresy, the tempests of affliction, and the more dangerous, because more seductive sunshine of worldly prosperity, by which it has been successively assailed. I do not say that my views of the glorious doctrines of the Saviour, have not, from reading the Scriptures, and other means of improvement, been somewhat extended since that period—on a very few points they have undergone a change. But the grand system of Evangelical Doctrines held by our Church, and set forth in its "confession of faith" and approved formularies, I am fully satisfied is according to the only revelation which Jehovah has made of his will and his truth, to man. They are essentially, those alone by which the mind can be awakened, and Divinely illuminated—the heart changed—the soul sanctified—the true God seen in his own character—Christ exalted—the principalities and powers of this world and of Hell subdued—and our anxious hopes and desires crowned in the end with eternal life. These are their blessed fruits wherever God owns them in all the world; and he *does* own them as his peculiar doctrines, wherever they are published. The poor children of Africa have, in this country, had their hearts opened to receive them; and they have "converted their souls." The reception of this holy faith produces on the most ignorant and savage, equally as upon the enlightened and polished, the peculiar characters of self-abasement, penitence and conformity to the Divine image. And this faith is found to be the *only faith* which *can* accomplish such effects. Wherever it is neglected, the life of holiness in such as are called Christians, disappears. Wherever it is decried, vice, and sin are seen to erect themselves, triumphantly, in a thousand forms.

Let us then, my brethren, hold fast the profession of so excellent a faith without wavering; and O, may we look well to it, that we hold it not in unrighteousness. We have a glorious, but a most righteous Master; He has given us all, and I do not think it humility to deny it, many talents—and will be as speedy as we know him strict, in calling us to account for them. You are in the bosom of a Christian community; and He there, my brethren, has laid you out abundance of work, without which, your own souls and the souls of many others, cannot be saved. To me is appointed, with perhaps equal obligations and fewer privileges, in this land of darkness, the great labor of planting his Church, and making provision for the sheep and lambs of his flock. Much depends on my fidelity—strengthen my weakness by your prayers, my brethren. And may the Author of the great salvation we are hoping and laboring after, multiply to us abundantly, the graces of his Spirit— perfect in us that which is lacking—and bring us safely to his eternal glory, through Jesus Christ, our Lord.

JEHUDI ASHMUN.

MONROVIA, SABBATH MORNING, MAY 27, 1827.

*To my Three Youngest Brothers.*

DEAR BOYS :—It is my lot to have been wholly separated from you, almost from your infancy. I have a faint recollection of your features, in early childhood; but no knowledge whatever, of your present dispositions or even of your persons. And, as little as I know you, I am probably more a stranger to *you*, than *you* to *me*.—But there is still a strong and mysterious tie of endearment which unites us, and renders your interest and welfare most precious to my heart. I cannot feel towards any one of you as towards a stranger. You are my brothers; partners of the very blood which warms my bosom—it would afford me the most sensible pleasure, if the climate of this country were not too dangerous, to have one or more of you with me in Liberia; I have almost thought of sending for you—but am not willing to run so great a risk of sacrificing your health and life, merely to gratify my private feelings. Were you with me, it would be my delight, to be of some service in training you to future usefulness, respectability, and happiness. Nor is this desire less, because you are separated from me by a wide Ocean. But how shall I do you good ?—If I had money to send, which should enrich you, would this do it ? So far from riches being of use to you in the *end*, they *might* not—probably *would* not, render you one particle the happier, even in the present world—and would certainly endanger your salvation in the world to come.

Could I raise you to posts of distinction and honor, as you advance in life, the elevation might only increase your power of injuring yourselves and others. It might only be to lift you from the ground, in order to give you a heavier and more ruinous fall. Temporary and vain distinctions in this poor life, are often, even while life lasts, the occasion of deep disgrace—and I am afraid too commonly prepare the soul for endless disgrace and mortification, after life is at an end.—Had I the power to command with a word, all the pleasures and delights of this earth, and at a word, to make them all your own, my dear brothers, I should not, dare not, confer on you so cruel and fatal a gift. "Wherefore? Because I love you not? God knoweth." No—but, because he who made the world, has told us, that all these things are only snares and temptations to such as are living in it; has warned us, as we regard his authority, and our own safety, to forsake and dread them, as the enemies of both.—I am afraid that all this *shocks* you. "What," you ask, "deprive us of the hope of 'wealth, distinction, and pleasure, in life; and what do you leave us?—Would 'you consign us, young as we are, to gloom and indolence? Take away the 'prospect of these things, and what motive have we to study?—to improve our— 'selves?—to industry, and action?—What can our hopes take hold of, to keep 'us from dejection and misery?" I know well, what a hard task I have, to answer these inquiries to your satisfaction. I am afraid after all, that I cannot satisfy you. Take away those things from three-fourths of the world, and I know well that they have nothing left; that they are as wretched as sin and a world of troubles, can render them. But, my brothers, I must remind you, at first, of two great delusions, belonging to those objects of worldly attraction, which I have warned you against. The *first* is, *That the riches and honors, and pleasures of this life, are no such matters at all, as your imaginations represent them.* It is but a little of any of them, that I have tried—but that little has proved to me, that, *one and all*, are "vanity and vexation of spirit." There is no substance, nor reality, in them all. They are shadows, which, seen at a distance, appear to be substances. The whole world, almost, are gone away after them. The Devil makes them reflect a dazzling brightness into the minds, especially of the young. The example of so many thousands, many of them men of sense and learning, has, also, a surprisingly imposing effect, and most are deceived, and will not own their deception, till it is too late to escape its consequences. *There are no such things then, in this world, or any other, as your young hearts represent to you, the riches, pleasures and distinctions of the world, to be.* This is the *first* delusion I spoke of. The other is, *that these things, have an influence on the mind, which no one knows, till he has suffered from it.* They place God at a distance—they harden and brutalize the heart, and feelings; they make repentance ten thousand times more difficult; they give a certain stoutness of feeling to the worst and most God-provoking dispositions of our nature. They bring error and unbelief, in torrents and floods, into the mind. Understand me. These are the certain effects of wealth, fame, and worldly enjoyment, when not sanctified with God's blessing. And these effects will stay with the soul, as long as the soul exists, no matter in what worlds, or what local position. When this world shall have been turned into a heap of ashes, then, my dear brothers, such as sought their portion in it, shall be lamenting its effects upon their immortal natures. But your young hearts have, perhaps, never imagined such a sting to exist in these desirable objects—nor such a curse to follow after the unsanctified enjoyment of them. Here then is the second delusion the world is endeavoring to put upon you. Fair as her portion is in the prospect—'tis foul and deformed as hell itself, to which it leads, after you have

## APPENDIX. 143

embraced it—And O, remember, the deadly sting it is certain to leave behind it. "It will bite as a serpent, and sting as an adder." And lest the pleasures of sin should be too kind to you, the Lord Omnipotent will take the matter in hand himself and punish all who drink of them, for the offence *they commit against him*, in doing so. For, he has told us all, to let them alone. "But all this does not," you may say, "answer our question"—"If you take from us these things, what have we left?" It does not. But I will now reply to it. You will have left you, if you resign the world for the Lord's sake, and because his word requires it; you will still possess, *a God as your friend*—his Son, your Redeemer—his Spirit, the companion and associate of your spirits. God will then give you, in place of what you give up for him, a conscience forever at rest—hopes full of immortality and joy—a heart full of love, and charity, affection, and peace—a mind enlightened with heavenly wisdom—the esteem, and respect, and confidence, and love, of all the good and excellent of the earth—so much of the good things of the world as you can bear; and "his blessing, which maketh rich, and addeth no sorrow with it." He will "write your names in heaven;" revoke the curse which his law has uttered against you as sinners; and will show you the heights and depths, of his love, and grace, in Christ; revealing mysteries which angels never, till lately, knew; and teaching you the things which it never entered into the heart of the natural man to conceive. All this you get in exchange for this mean world. And may the Spirit of God assist you, now in the days of your youth, to make the wise exchange immediately.
J. ASHMUN.

SKETCH OF THE LIFE

OF THE

REV. LOTT CARY.

# SKETCH OF THE LIFE

OF THE

# REV. LOTT CARY.

---

THE Rev. LOTT CARY was born a slave, near Richmond, Virginia, and was early hired out as a common laborer in that city, where, for some years, he remained, entirely regardless of religion, and much addicted to profane and vicious habits. But God was pleased to convince him of the misery of a sinful state, and in 1807, he publicly professed his faith in the Saviour, and became a member of the Baptist Church.

It is remarked by one who was intimately acquainted with his situation and character previous to his embarkation for Africa, "that his Father was a pious and much respected member of the Baptist Church—and his Mother, though she made no public profession of religion, died, giving evidence that she had relied for salvation upon the Son of God. He was their only child, and though he had no early instruction from books, the admonitions and prayers of his illiterate parents may have laid the foundations for his future usefulness."

A strong desire to be able to read, was excited in his mind, by a sermon to which he attended soon after his conversion, and which related to our Lord's interview with Nicodemus; and having obtained a Testament, he commenced learning his letters, by trying to read the chapter in which this interview is recorded. He received some instruction, though he never attended a regular school. Such, however, were his diligence and perseverance, that he overcame all obstacles and acquired not only the art of reading, but of writing also. Shortly after the death of his first wife in 1813, he ransomed himself and two children for $850, a sum which he had obtained by his singular ability and fidelity in managing the concerns of the tobacco warehouse. Of the real value of his services there, it has been remarked, "no one but a dealer in tobacco can form an idea. Notwithstanding the hundreds of hogsheads that were committed to his charge, he could produce any one the instant it was called for; and the shipments were made with a promptness and correctness, such as no person, white or black, has equalled in the same situation."*

As early as the year 1815, he began to feel a special interest in the cause of African Missions, and contributed probably more than any other person, in giving origin and character to the African Missionary Society established during that year in Richmond, and which has, for many years, collected and appropriated annually, to the cause of Christianity in Africa, from one hundred, to one hundred and fifty dollars. His benevolence was practical; and whenever and wherever good objects were to be effected, he was ready to lend his aid. He became a preacher several years before he left this country, and generally engaged in this service every Sabbath, among the colored people on plantations a few miles from Richmond.

A correspondent, from whom we have already quoted, observes, "In preaching, notwithstanding his grammatical inaccuracies, he was often truly eloquent. He had derived almost nothing from the schools, and his manner was of course unpolished, but his ideas would sometimes burst upon you in their native solemnity, and awaken deeper feelings than the most polished, but less original and inartificial discourse." A distinguished Minister of the Presbyterian Church, said to the writer, " A sermon which I heard from Mr. Cary, shortly before he sailed for Africa, was the best extemporaneous sermon I ever heard. It contained more original and impressive thoughts, some of which are distinct in my memory, and never can be forgotten."

Mr. Cary was among the earliest emigrants to Africa. For some time before his departure he had sustained the office of Pastor of a Baptist Church of colored persons in Richmond, embracing nearly eight hundred members, received from it a liberal support, and enjoyed its confidence and affection.— When an intelligent Minister of the same Church inquired, why he could determine to quit a station of so much comfort and usefulness, to encounter the dangers of an African climate, and hazard every thing to plant a Colony on a distant heathen shore? His reply was to this effect, " I am an African, and in this country, however meritorious my conduct, and respectable my character, I cannot receive the credit due to either. I wish to go to a country where I shall be estimated by my merits, not by my complexion; and I feel bound to labor for my suffering race." He seemed to have imbibed the sentiment of Paul, and to have great heaviness and continual sorrow in his heart, for his brethren, his kinsmen according to the flesh.

* It is said, that while employed at the warehouse, he often devoted his leisure time to reading, and that a gentleman, on one occasion, taking up a book which he had left for a few moments, found it to be " Smith's Wealth of Nations."

## APPENDIX. 149

At the close of his farewell sermon in the First Baptist Meeting House in Richmond, he remarked in substance, as follows: "I am about to leave you and expect to see your faces no more. I long to preach to the poor Africans the way of life and salvation. I don't know what may befal me, whether I may find a grave in the ocean, or among the savage men, or more savage wild beasts on the Coast of Africa; nor am I anxious what may become of me. I feel it my duty to go; and I very much fear that many of those who preach the Gospel in this country, will blush when the Saviour calls them to give an account of their labors in His cause, and tells them, 'I commanded you to go into all the world, and preach the Gospel to every creature;' (and with the most forcible emphasis he exclaimed,) the Saviour may ask where have you been? what have you been doing? have you endeavored to the utmost of your ability to fulfil the commands I gave you, or have you sought your own gratification, and your own ease, regardless of my commands?"

On his arrival in Africa he saw before him a wide and interesting field, demanding various and energetic talents, and the most devoted piety. His intellectual ability, firmness of purpose, unbending integrity, correct judgment, and disinterested benevolence, soon placed him in a conspicuous station, and gave him wide and commanding influence. Though naturally diffident and retiring, his worth was too evident, to allow of his continuance in obscurity. It is well known, that great difficulties were encountered in founding a settlement at Cape Montserado. So appalling were the circumstances of the first settlers, that soon after they had taken possession of the Cape, it was proposed that they should remove to Sierra Leone. The resolution of Mr. Cary was not to be shaken: he determined to stay, and his decision had great effect in persuading others to imitate his example. During the war with the native tribes, in November and December 1822, he proved to be one of the bravest of men, and lent his well directed and vigorous support to the measures of Mr. Ashmun during that memorable defence of the Colony. It was to him, that Mr. Ashmun was principally indebted for assistance in rallying the broken forces of the Colony, at a moment when fifteen hundred of the exasperated natives were rushing on to exterminate the settlement. In one of his letters, he compares the little exposed company on Cape Montserado at that time, to the Jews, who in rebuilding their City, "grasped a weapon in one hand, while they labored with the other:" but adds emphatically, "there never has been an hour or a minute, no, not even when the balls were flying around my head, when I could wish myself again in America."

At this early period of the Colony, the emigrants were peculiarly exposed; the want of adequate medical attentions, and the scantiness of their supplies, subjected them to severe and complicated sufferings. To relieve, if possible, these sufferings, Mr. Cary availed himself of all information in his power, concerning the diseases of the climate, made liberal sacrifices of his property to assist the poor and distressed, and devoted his time, almost exclusively, to the destitute, the sick and the afflicted.

In December, 1823, Mr. Cary was unfortunately engaged in a transaction, which inflicted a deep wound upon his conscience, and which but for his speedy and sincere repentance, might have left a lasting stain upon his reputation. He was one of those who appeared at that time to have lost confidence in the Society, and who ventured to throw off those restraints of authority, which though severe, were deemed absolutely necessary for the general safety of the settlers. In the ninth chapter of the Memoir of Mr. Ashmun, we have given some account of the origin and progress of that spirit of insubordination, which finally resulted in an abduction by a few individuals, of a portion of the public stores, in open violation of the laws. Mr. Cary had no small influence and share in this seditious proceeding. But there is reason to believe, that in this conduct, prejudice and passion were permitted to usurp the place of reason, rather than, that he deliberately sacrificed his integrity. In communicating the account of this disturbance to the Board, Mr. Ashmun remarks, " The services rendered by Lott Cary in the Colony, who has with very few, (and those recent exceptions,) done honor to the selection of the Baptist Missionary Society, under whose auspices he was sent out to Africa, entitle his agency in this affair, to the most indulgent construction which it will bear. The hand which records the lawless transaction, would long since have been cold in the grave, had it not been for the unwearied and painful attentions of this individual—rendered at all hours—of every description—and continued for several months."

No sooner had Mr. Ashmun issued a circular address, exhibiting the nature of the offence in its true light, than Mr. Cary " came forward and deplored the part he had taken; he felt that he had inflicted on his character, usefulness, and peace, a wound that could not in this world be healed, and betrayed the great confidence reposed in him by his pious employers and patrons at home. He acknowledged frankly, that his influence had seduced others, and seemed to view the evil in all its extent. He told the Agent it was his wish hereafter to receive no more supplies from the Colonization Society, and live less enthralled with secular connexions; but professed his willingness to be useful in the way the Agent thought fit to propose. The latter then suggested to him the care of the liberated Africans. To this proposition he very promptly acceded, and it is believed, he will discharge the trust with fidelity and ability."*

In the summer of 1824, the writer visited the Colony, and enjoyed, during the few days he remained there, frequent interviews with Mr. Cary. He appeared to welcome the return of Mr. Ashmun at that time. He entered most cordially into the views of the Agents in regard to the establishment of a new form of Government. He readily comprehended the principles upon which it was organized, and entirely approved them. Seldom has the writer met with an individual of a more active or reflecting mind. He appeared to re-

* Mr. Ashmun.

alize the greatness of the work in which he had engaged, and to be animated by a noble spirit of zeal and resolution in the cause of his afflicted and perishing brethren. His services as physician were invaluable, and were then and for a long time afterwards, rendered without hope of reward.

The Managers of the American Colonization Society, in the autumn of 1825, invited Mr. Cary to visit the United States, in expectation that his intelligent and candid statements concerning the condition and prospects of the Colony, and the moral wants of Africa, would exert a beneficial influence on the opinions of the people of color, as well as recommend the cause of the Society to the public regard. In the month of April, 1826, he made arrangements to embark for the United States, in the ship Indian Chief, and received from Mr. Ashmun testimonials of his worth and services. The following is extracted from a letter addressed by Mr. Ashmun, to the Managers of the Colonization Society:

"The Rev. Lott Cary, returning by the 'Indian Chief,' has, in my opinion, some claims on the justice of the Society or Government of the United States, or both, which merit consideration. These claims arise out of a long and faithful course of medical services rendered to this Colony, (the only such services deserving much consideration, if we except those of Dr. Ayres and Dr. Peaco, since the commencement of the settlement, in 1820.)

"Mr. Cary, it is well known, came to this country in the capacity of a Missionary, from a Society in Richmond; and has ever since, I believe, been in the receipt of a considerable salary from the Society, appropriated for the express and sole intention of putting him in a situation to devote his time and labors to the work of the Sacred Ministry.

"It is perhaps known to the Board, that Mr. Cary has declined serving in any civil office, incompatible with a faithful discharge of his sacred functions; and it may be added, that although one of the most diligent and active of men, he has never had the command of leisure or strength to engage in any Missionary duties, besides the weekly and occasional services of the congregation. More than one-half of his time has been given up to the care of our sick, from the day I landed in Africa, to the very moment of stating the fact. He has personally aided in every way, that fidelity and benevolence could dictate, in all the attentions which all our sick have in so long a period received. His want of science acquired by the regular study of Medicine, he has gone a long way towards supplying by an unwearied diligence which few regular physicians think it necessary—fewer superficial practitioners, have the motives for exercising.

"Several times have these disinterested labors reduced him to the verge of the grave. The presence of other physicians has, instead of affording relief, only redoubled the intensity of his labors, by charging the ordinary routine of his attentions to the sick with the exhibition of their own prescriptions.

"Mr. Cary has hitherto received no compensation, either from the Society or the Government, for these services. I need not add, that it has not been in his power to support himself and family by any use he could make of the remnants of his time left him, after discharging the amount of duty already described. The Missionary Board of Richmond have fed, clothed and supplied the other wants of himself and family, while devoting his strength and time to your sick colonists, and Agents in this country. Justice seems to demand that he should be placed in a situation as an honest man, to refund the whole or a part of the fund thus engrossed, not to say *misapplied*, to the Missionary Board.

"I beg leave also to state, that on the 15th of February, 1826, I came into an agreement with Mr. Cary, to allow him a reasonable compensation for his medical services, devoted to the then sickening company of Boston emigrants. His time has from the date of that agreement, to the present hour, been incessantly occupied in attending upon the sick."

Until near the time of the Indian Chief's departure from the Colony, Mr. Cary cherished the hope of embarking in her for America. But as there was no other physician in the Colony, it was finally thought best for him to postpone his departure to another opportunity. By the return of that vessel he addressed the following letter to the Secretary of the Society:

"*Monrovia, April 24th,* 1826.

"REV. AND DEAR SIR: I received your letter sent to me by the order of the Board of Managers of the American Colonization Society; and I expected until a few days ago that the return of the Indian Chief, would have enabled me in all respects to have realized their wishes—But on a more minute examination of the subject, Mr. Ashmun and myself both were apprehensive that my leaving the Colony at present, would endanger the lives of a number of the inhabitants; Mr. Ashmun, however, has made a full statement to the Board, which I have no doubt will be satisfactory to them. I think that through the blessing of the Almighty, I shall be able to get the last expedition through the fever with very little loss: we have lost only three, the Rev. Mr. Trueman, from Baltimore, and two children belonging to the Paxton family. But the emigrants who came out in the Vine, have suffered very much; we lost twelve of them. The action of the disease was more powerful with them than is common—they unfortunately arrived here in the most sickly month in the year, February. I am strongly of the opinion, sir, that if the people of New England leave there in the winter, that the transition is so great, that you may count upon a loss of half at least. They may, in my estimation, with safety, leave in the months from April to November, and arrive here in good time; I think it to be a matter of great importance; therefore I hope, that you will regard it as such.

"I am respectfully yours,
"LOTT CARY."

Although it was the purpose of Mr. Cary to devote himself to Missionary efforts in Africa, yet the necessity for his services in the Colony was so great, that he felt it his duty to deny himself much of the happiness which he anticipated from endeavors to bring the Native Africans, to the knowledge and worship of the Living and True God. He was elected in September, 1826, to the Vice Agency of the Colony, and discharged the duties of that important office until his death. In his good sense, moral worth, public spirit, courage, resolution, and decision, the Colonial Agent had perfect confidence. He knew, that in times of difficulty or danger, reliance might be placed upon the energy and efficiency of Mr. Cary.

The following letter addressed to the writer by Mr. Cary in 1827, is in his own hand writing, and is marked by that simple, strong good sense, for which he was distinguished. We give it without the alteration, even of a letter.

"JUNE 16th, 1827.

" *To the Rev. R. R. Gurley.*

"REV. AND DEAR SIR, I transmit to you a few lines, which I trust may find you well. The last emigrants that you sent out, has fared remarkably well, as it respects the disease; we have only lost two children. We have several cases of bad ulcers; and from seeing advertised in the Compiler of Richmond, a medicine called Swaim's Panacea, said to be a sure cure for ulcers; please try if possible to procure some, and send out, for we should have a very healthy inhabitants and present, but for the prevalence of that uncontrolable disease. We are also in want of Salts, Castor-oil, Cream of Tartar, mignesea, and Mustard, as much as you can send well put up. I am greatly in hopes to be over the next spring, and try to wake up my colored friends in Virginia. We have a plan in contemplation which if accomplished will, I think insure my making one vissit to America, that is, to purchase, or aid in the purchase of a vessel to run constantly from this, to America, to bring out our own supplies, emigrants, &c. I hope sir, when such an attempt is made you will facilitate it all that you can.

"I think that you would be pleased with the improvements that we have made since you left if you were to make another vissit to this country—both our civil and religious state I think has improved very much. No more but wishing that the blessing of the Lord may attend you, both in your public and private life, and the Board of Managers, in all their administrations.

"Yours, &c.     "LOTT CARY."

When compelled in the early part of 1828 to leave the Colony, Mr. Ashmun committed the administration of the Colonial affairs into the hands of the Vice Agent, in the full belief, that no interests would be betrayed, but that his efforts would be constantly and anxiously directed to the promotion of the public good. The following extracts are from the Journal of Mr. Cary, after the departure of Mr. Ashmun:

"The Colonial Agent, J. Ashmun, Esq., went on board the brig Doris, March 26th, 1828, escorted by three companies of the military, and when taking leave he delivered a short address, which was truly affecting; never, I suppose, were greater tokens of respect shown by any community on taking leave of their head. Nearly the whole (at least two-thirds) of the inhabitants of Monrovia, men, women, and children, were out on this occasion, and nearly all parted from him with tears, and in my opinion, the hope of his return in a few months, alone enabled them to give him up. He is indeed dear to this people, and it will be a joyful day when we are again permitted to see him. He has left a written address, which contains valuable admonitions to Officers, Civil, Military, and Religious. The Brig sailed on the 27th. May she have a prosperous voyage.

"THURSDAY, MARCH 27.

"Feeling very sensibly my incompetency to enter upon the duties of my office, without first making all the Officers of the Colony well acquainted with the principal objects which should engage our attention, I invited them to meet at the Agency House on the 27th, at 9 o'clock, which was punctually attended to; and I then read all the instructions left by Mr. Ashmun without reserve, and requested their co-operation. I stated that it would be our first object to put the Jail in complete order, secondly to have our guns and armaments in a proper state, and thirdly to get the new settlers located on their lands; as this was a very important item in my instructions. This explanation will, I think, have a good effect; as by it the effective part of the Colony is put in possession of the most important objects of our present pursuit; and I trust through the blessing of the great Ruler of events, we shall be able to realize all the expectations of Mr. Ashmun, and render entire satisfaction to the Board of Managers, if they can reconcile themselves to the necessary expenses.

"MARCH 29.

"From a note received from Mr. James, dated Millsburg, I learn that he visited King Boatswain, and that the new road from Boatswain's to Millsburg will shortly be commenced.—The Headmen expect, however, to be paid for opening the road. Messrs. James and Cook, who came down this evening, state, that the Millsburg Factory will be ready in a few days for the reception of goods, and wished consignments might be made early. But as I had been on the 27th paying off the kings towards the Millsburg lands, and found that one hundred and twenty bars came so far short of satisfying them, I thought best to see them together before I should attempt to make any consignments to that place.

[The following is a copy of a deed between Lott Cary, acting in behalf of the American Colonization Society, on the one part; and the after mentioned Kings, of the other part.]

"KNOW all men by these presents: That we, Old King Peter, and King Governor, King James, and King Long Peter, do on this fourth day of April, in the year of our Lord one thousand eight hundred and twenty-eight, grant unto Lott Cary, acting Agent of the Colony of Liberia, in behalf of the American Colonization Society, to wit:

"All that tract of Land on the north side of St. Paul's river, beginning at

# APPENDIX.   155

King James' line below the establishment called Millsburg Settlement, and we the Kings as aforesaid do bargain, sell, and grant, unto the said Lott Cary, acting in behalf of the American Colonization Society, all the aforesaid tract of Land, situated and bounded as follows: by the St. Paul's river on the South, and thence running an East Northeast direction up the St. Paul's river, as far as he, the said Lott Cary, or his successor in the Agency, or Civil Authority of the Colony of Liberia, shall think proper to take up and occupy; and bounded on the West by King Jimmey's, and running thence a North direction as far as our power and influence extend. We do on this day and date, grant as aforesaid for the consideration [here follow the articles to be given in payment]; and will forever defend the same against all claims whatsoever.

"In witness whereof we set our hands and names:
OLD ⋈ KING PETER,<br>LONG ⋈ KING PETER,<br>KING ⋈ GOVERNOR,<br>KING ⋈ JAMES.

"Signed in the presence of,
ELIJAH JOHNSON,
FREDERICK JAMES,
DANIEL GEORGE."

"JUNE 18, 1828.

"I found it necessary, in order to preserve the frame of the second floors of the Government House, to have the frame and ceiling painted, which is now doing. I have also been obliged to employ another workman to make the blinds, or else leave the house exposed the present season, as —— refused to do it under the former contract. On the 13th I visited Millsburg,* to ascertain the prospects of that settlement; and can say with propriety, that according to the quantity of land which the settlers have put under cultivation, they will reap a good and plentiful crop. The Company's crop of rice and cassada is especially promising. The new settlers at that place have done well; having all, with two or three exceptions, built houses, so as to render their families comfortable during the season. They have also each of them a small farm, which I think after a few months will be sufficient to subsist them. But I find from a particular examination, that we shall be obliged to allow them to draw rations longer than I expected, owing to the great scarcity of country produce, the cassada being so nearly exhausted, that it is, and will be, impossible to obtain, until new crops come in, much to aid our provisions, unless by going some distance into the country. Therefore I think it indispensably necessary, in order to keep the settlers to their farming improvements, to continue their rations longer than I at first intended; as I consider the present too important a crisis to leave them to neglect their improvements, although it may add something to our present expenses.

"The people at Caldwell are getting on better with their farms than with

*Mills & Burgess.

their houses. I think some of them are very slow, notwithstanding I have assisted them in building. The Gun House at Caldwell is done, and at present preparations are making for the fourth of July. I think that settlement generally, is rapidly advancing in farming, building, and I hope, in industry. Our gun carriages are done; the completion of the iron work alone prevents us from mounting them all immediately. We have four mounted, and I think we shall put them all in complete order by the end of the present week.

"Captain Russel will be able to give something like a fair account of the state of our improvements, as he went with me to visit the settlements on the 13th and 14th, and seemed pleased with the prospect at Millsburg, Caldwell and the Half-way Farms.

"Mr. Warner, who has been engaged nearly the whole of the last twelve months on business of negotiating with the native tribes to the leeward, is at present down at Tippicanoe, the place which I mentioned in my former communications, as being a very important section of country, since it would connect our Sesters and Bassa districts together. He is not however, now engaged in business of negotiation, but only in business of trade."

In his letter to the lamented Mr. Ashmun, Mr. Cary states—

"Things are nearly as you left them; most of the work that you directed to be done, is nearly accomplished. The plasterers are now at work on the Government House, and with what lime I am having brought down the river, and what shells I am getting, I think we shall succeed.

"The Gun House in Monrovia and the Jail have been done for some weeks; the mounting of the guns will be done this week, if the weather permits.

"The Houses at the Half-way Farms are done; the Gun House at Caldwell would have been done at this time, had not the rain prevented, but I think it will be finished in three or four days. The public farm is doing pretty well. The Millsburg farms are doing very well. I think it would do you good to see that place at this time.

"The Missionaries, although they have been sick, are now, I am happy to inform you, recovered; and at present are able to attend to their business, and I regard them as entirely out of danger.

"I hope we shall be able to remove all the furniture into the new house in two or three weeks."

June 25th, Mr. Cary writes—

"About three o'clock to-day, there appeared three vessels—two brigs and a schooner. The schooner stood into the Roads, and one of the brigs near in, but showed no colours until a shot was fired by Captain Thompson; when she hoisted Spanish colours, and the schooner the same. All their movements appeared so suspicious, that we turned out all our forces to-night.—About eight this evening it was reported that they were standing out of our Roads; and at sunset, that the schooner had come to anchor very near the "All Chance," from Boston; and that the brig which had passed the Cape, had put about and was standing up, trying to double the Cape; and that the third vessel (a brig) was standing down for the Roads. The first mentioned brig showed nine ports a ride. From all these circumstances I thought best to have Fort Norris Battery manned, which was immediately done by Captain Johnson. I also ordered out the two volunteer companies to make discoveries around the town, and the Artillery to support the guns, and protect the beach; which orders were promptly executed, and we stood in readiness during the night. At daylight the schooner lay at anchor and appeared to be making no preparations to communicate with us; I then ordered a shot to be fired at a little distance from her, when she sent a boat ashore with her Captain, Supercargo, and Interpreter. She reported herself the Joseph, from Havana, had been three months on the coast trading, but *not for slaves*, had one gun, and twenty-three men. Also, that the brig was a patriotic brig in chase of her, and that through fear she had taken shelter under our guns. The Captain wished a supply of wood and water; but I told him I knew him to be engaged in the slave trade, and that, though we did not pretend to attempt suppressing this trade, we would not aid it, and that I allowed him one hour, and one only, to get out of the reach of our guns. He was very punctual, and I believe before his hour."

Speaking of the celebration of the Fourth of July in the Colony, under date of the 15th July, Mr. Cary remarks—

"The companies observed strictly the orders of the day, which I think were so arranged as to entitle the officers who drew them up to credit. Upon the whole, I am obliged to say, that I have never seen the American Independence celebrated with so much spirit and propriety since the existence of the Colony; the guns being all mounted and painted, and previously arranged for the purpose, added very much to the grand salute. Two dinners were given, one by the Independent Volunteer Company, and one by Captain Devany."

To the Secretary of the Society, July 19th, Mr. Cary writes—

"I have the honour to acknowledge the receipt of your letter, forwarded by Captain Chase of Providence, also your Report and Repository, directed to Mr. Ashmun, but owing to his absence, they have fallen into my hands; and permit me to say, that these communications are read with pleasure, and that nothing affords more joy to the Colony, than to hear of the prosperity of the Colonization Society, and that you have some hopes of aid from the General Government, which makes us more desirous to enlarge our habitation and extend the borders of the Colony.

"I must say, from the flattering prospects of your Society, I feel myself very much at a loss how to proceed, in the absence of Mr. Ashmun, with regard to making provisions for the reception of a large number of emigrants, which appears to be indispensably necessary. Therefore, after receiving your communication, we conceived the following to be the most safe and prudent course. *First*, to make arrangements to have erected at Millsburg, houses to answer as receptacles sufficient to shelter from one hundred and fifty to two hundred persons. I have therefore extended the duties of Mr. Benson so as to embrace that object. I was led to this course from the following considerations. *First*, from the productiveness of the Millsburg lands and the fewness of their inhabitants. I know if Mr. Ashmun were present, it would be a principal object with him to push that settlement forward with all possible speed, and that for this purpose, he would send the emigrants by the first two or three expeditions to that place. I think that those from the fresh water rivers, if carried directly after their arrival here, up to Millsburg, would suffer very little from change of climate. *Second*, the fertility of the land is such a temptation to the farmer, that unless he possesses laziness in its extreme degree, he cannot resist it; he must and will go to work. *Thirdly*, it is important to strengthen that settlement against any possible attack ; and though we apprehend no hostilities from the natives, yet we would have each settlement strong enough to repel them.

"I am happy to say, that the health, peace and prosperity of the Colony, I think, is still advancing, and I hope that the Board of Managers may have their wishes and expectations realized to their fullest extent, with regard to the present and future prosperity of the Colony."

*July* 17.—" If I could be allowed one suggestion to the Board of Managers, I would mention the importance of having here for the use of the Colony, a vessel large enough to run down as low as Cape Palmas. It would, I think, be found to save a very great expense to the Society. She might occasionally run up also to Sierra Leone.

" Until we can raise crops sufficient to supply a considerable number of new comers every year, such an arrangement as will enable us to proceed farther to the leward than we have ever done, in order to procure supplies, will be indispensably necessary ; as there we can procure Indian Corn, Palm Oil, and live stock. For these, neither the slave traders nor others, give themselves much. Corn can be bought there for from fifteen to twenty cents per bushel. Fifteen or twenty bushels which I bought of Captain Woodbury, I have been using instead of rice for the last two months. Besides, it can be ground into meal, and would be better than any that can be sent. Upon the supposed inquiry, will not the lands of the Colony produce Corn? they will produce it in abundance ; but with the quantity of lands appropriated at present, and the means to cultivate them, each land-holder will, I think, be able to raise but little more than may be required by his own family, and consequently will have little to dispose of to new comers.\*

" Permit me to inform the Board, that proposals have been made by a number of very respectable citizens in Monrovia, to commence a settlement near the head of the Montserado River, which would be a kind of farming esrablishment; which, should it be the pleasure of the Board to approve, would be followed up with great spirit, and found to contribute largely towards increasing our crops, for the soil is very promising."

But amid his multiplied cares and efforts for the Colony, he never forgot or

---

\* It has been resolved by the Board of Managers to increase the quantity of land allotted to each settler.

neglected to promote the objects of the African Missionary Society, for which he had long cherished the strongest attachment. His great object in emigrating to Africa, was to extend the power and blessings of the Christian Religion. Before his departure from Richmond, a little Church of about half a dozen members was formed by himself, and those who were to accompany him. He became the Pastor of this Church in Africa, and saw its numbers greatly increased. Most earnestly did he seek access to the Native Tribes, and endeavor to instruct them in the doctrines and duties of that religion, which in his own case, had proved so powerful to purify, exalt and save. In one or two instances of hopeful conversion from heathenism, he greatly rejoiced; and many of his latest and most anxious thoughts were directed to the establishment of native schools in the interior. One such school, distant seventy miles from Monrovia, and of great promise, was established through his Agency, about a year before his death, and patronized and superintended by him until that mournful event. On this subject, by his many valuable communications to the Missionary Board, " he being dead yet speaketh" in language which must affect the heart of every true Christian disciple.

Mr. Cary was thrice married; about the year 1813, his first wife died, and soon afterwards he bought himself and two little children for $850.* He lost his second wife shortly after his arrival in Africa, at Fourah Bay, near Sierra Leone. Of her triumphant death, he gives a touching account in his journal. His third wife died before him at Cape Montserado.

For six months after the first departure of Mr. Ashmun, from the Colony, Mr. Cary stood at its head, and conducted himself with such energy and wisdom as to do honor to his previous reputation, and fix the seal upon his enviable fame.

On his death bed, Mr. Ashmun urged that Mr. Cary should be permanently appointed to conduct the affairs of the Colony, expressing perfect confidence in his integrity and ability for that great work. But, alas! he was suddenly and unexpectedly, and in a distressing manner, forced from life in all its vigor, into the presence of his final Judge.

* The manner in which he obtained this sum of money to purchase himself and children, reflects much credit on his character. It will be seen from the salary he received after he was free, and which he relinquished for the sake of doing good in Africa, that his services at the warehouse were highly estimated, but of their real value no one except a dealer in tobacco can form an idea. Notwithstanding the hundreds of hogsheads that were committed to his charge, he could produce any one the instant it was called for; and the shipments were made with a promptness, and correctness, such as no person, white or black, has equalled in the same situation. For this correctness and fidelity, he was highly esteemed, and frequently rewarded by the merchant with a five dollar note. He was allowed also to sell for his own benefit, many small parcels of waste tobacco. It was by saving the little sums obtained in this way, with the aid of a subscription by the merchants to whose interests he had been attentive, that he procured this $850, which he paid for the freedom of himself and children. When the Colonists were fitted out for Africa, he defrayed a considerable part of his own expense.

The circumstances of this melancholy event were these. The Factory belonging to the Colony at Digby, (a few miles North of Monrovia,) had been robbed by the natives; and satisfaction being demanded, was refused. A slave trader was allowed to land his goods in the very house where the goods of the Colony had been deposited, and a letter of remonstrance and warning directed to the slave dealer, by Mr. Cary, was actually intercepted and destroyed by the natives. In this state of affairs, Mr. Cary considered himself solemnly bound to assert the rights and defend the property of the Colony. He therefore called out instantly, the military of the settlements, and commenced making arrangements to compel the natives to desist from their injurious and unprovoked infringements upon the territory and rights of the Colony. On the evening of the 8th of November, while Mr. Cary and several others were engaged in making cartridges in the old Agency house, a candle appears to have been accidentally upset, which caught some loose powder and almost instantaneously reached the entire ammunition, producing an explosion, which resulted in the death of eight persons. Six of the unfortunate sufferers survived until the 9th, and Mr. Cary and one other, until the 10th. The house, (which was, however, of little value,) was entirely destroyed.

The tidings of Mr. Ashmun's death had not reached the Colony until after the decease of Mr. Cary. How unexpected, how interesting, how affecting the meeting of these two individuals, (so long united in Christian fellowship, in benevolent and arduous labors,) in the world of glory and immortality!

It has been well said of Mr. Cary, that "he was one of nature's noblemen;" had he possessed the advantages of education, few men of his age would have excelled him in knowledge or genius.

The features and complexion of Mr. Cary were altogether African. He was diffident, and showed no disposition to push himself into notice. His words were few, simple, direct, and appropriate. His conversation indicated rapidity and clearness of thought, and an ability to comprehend the great and variously-related principles of Religion and Government.

To found a Christian Colony which might prove a blessed asylum to his degraded brethren in America, and enlighten and regenerate Africa, was, in his view, an object with which no temporal good, not even life could be compared. The strongest sympathies of his nature were excited in behalf of his unfortunate people, and the Divine promise cheered and encouraged him in his labors for their improvement and salvation. A main pillar in the Society and Church of Liberia has fallen! But we will not despond. The memorial of his worth shall never perish. It shall stand in clearer light, when every chain is broken, and Christianity shall have assumed her sway over the millions of Africa.

THE END.